Globe Law
and Business

Oil and Gas Sale and Purchase Agreements

SPAs for International Oil and Gas Acquisitions and Divestitures
Second Edition

Consulting Editors **John C LaMaster** and **Caroline-Lucy Moran**

Consulting editors
John C LaMaster
Caroline-Lucy Moran

Managing director
Sian O'Neill

Oil and Gas Sale and Purchase Agreements: SPAs for International Oil and Gas Acquisitions and Divestitures, Second Edition
is published by

Globe Law and Business Ltd
3 Mylor Close
Horsell
Woking
Surrey GU21 4DD
United Kingdom
Tel: +44 20 3745 4770
www.globelawandbusiness.com

Oil and Gas Sale and Purchase Agreements: SPAs for International Oil and Gas Acquisitions and Divestitures, Second Edition

ISBN 9781787423985
EPUB ISBN 9781787423992
Adobe PDF ISBN 9781787424012
Mobi ISBN 9781787424005

Table of contents

Foreword ______ 5
J Scott Porter
Shell

Introduction ______ 9
John C LaMaster
Caroline-Lucy Moran
Akin Gump Strauss Hauer & Feld LLP

Preliminary agreements ______ 11
Afzaal Abidi
Christopher Strong
Suzana Vukasinovic
Vinson & Elkins RLLP

Sale structure ______ 25
Joanna Kay
BW Offshore
Peter Roberts
Cross Keys Energy Limited

Consideration in oil and gas sale and purchase agreements ______ 45
Olivier Chambord
Allison Soilihi
Morgan, Lewis & Bockius UK LLP

Conditions precedent and deferred completions ______ 65
John C LaMaster
Akin Gump Strauss Hauer & Feld LLP

Covenants in upstream acquisitions and divestitures ______ 99
Kevin Atkins
Matthew Daffurn
Locke Lord LLP

Oil and gas warranties ______ 131
Caroline-Lucy Moran
Akin Gump Strauss Hauer & Feld LLP

Disclosure letters ______ 165
Alexander Msimang
Suzana Vukasinovic
Freddie Wright
Vinson & Elkins RLLP

Warranty and indemnity insurance ______ 179
Matthew Foster
Sophie O'Connor
Norton Rose Fulbright LLP

Liabilities and indemnities: allocation and limitations on liability, and the use of indemnities ______ 195
Hussain Kubba
Holly Stebbing
Kimberley Wood
Norton Rose Fulbright LLP

Environmental provisions in oil and gas transactions 217
Julie Vaughan
Herbert Smith Freehills LLP

Decommissioning 231
Nicholas Antonas
Akin Gump Strauss Hauer & Feld LLP
Marc Hammerson
Stephenson Harwood LLP

Competition law provisions in sale and purchase agreements 253
Peter Crowther
Lisa Hatfield
Winston & Strawn LLP

Anti-corruption 275
Paige Berges
Amanda Raad
Sean Seelinger
Ropes & Gray (London)

Tax aspects of oil and gas mergers and acquisitions 309
Paul White
Druces LLP

Material adverse change clauses 327
John C LaMaster
Akin Gump Strauss Hauer & Feld LLP

Private equity considerations 349
Simon Tysoe
Latham & Watkins LLP

Governing law and jurisdiction clauses 375
Richard Ellison
Solicitor
David Waldron
Morgan, Lewis & Bockius UK LLP

Oil and gas boilerplate provisions 401
John C LaMaster
Akin Gump Strauss Hauer & Feld LLP

About the authors 415

Index 425

About Globe Law and Business 443

Foreword

J Scott Porter
Shell

The world of energy mergers and acquisitions was turned upside down in 2020 with the advent of the global COVID-19 pandemic. As a result, we have seen highly volatile oil prices, a sharp fall in demand and potentially long-lasting, shifting demand patterns tied to a potential acceleration of the timing of the transition from fossil fuels to renewables.

The activity level in the acquisition market for the second quarter of 2020 is one of the lowest on record. Despite a single day of unprecedented negative oil prices for West Texas Intermediate, there is a growing perception that prices are likely to stabilise in the $40 to $60 range. If one looks back on the past 20 years, real oil prices have averaged close to $60. Stable prices tend to increase M&A activity and build confidence in business forecasts that both buyers and sellers can agree on. A key trigger for this will be a successful vaccine announcement. This will begin to allow firmer forecasts of irreversible economic re-openings and drive a recovering demand/supply outlook, resulting in a more normal level of global oil inventory levels.

However, once the necessary condition of a more stable macro-environment matures, the industry will continue to face the fact that oil and gas companies now represent less than 3% of the S&P 500, down from 15% just a decade ago. After seeing limited cash returned over the past few years, private equity investors are sending a clear message to smaller independents that they want current cash-flow distributions, thus limiting the independents' ability to reinvest. This is generally expected to lead to far more consolidation – especially in the onshore shale industry in the United States, where there are too many players, too much overhead, too much operating inefficiency and a lack of scale.

As the energy industry scrambles to react and price volatility recedes, many opportunities will arise. What will be some of the key elements for deals in a post-COVID-19 world?

- The majors are more likely to be patient, perhaps jumping back into the M&A market in late 2021 or 2022. They are not immune to the financial strain that low prices have created and are subject to increasing pressure from environmental, social and governance (ESG)-focused investors.

With balance-sheet leverage exceeding targets, their short-term focus is on cost cutting, capex high grading and improved operations. With the energy transition playing in the background, some may buy more aggressively to extend drilling inventory; while others may divert more of their capital budgets to the renewables sector.

- The boards of directors of smaller players with limited access to capital may be forced to consider the benefits of mergers of equals. This would allow for overhead cuts, bigger operating scale and greater cash flow at a given oil price. However, investors are demanding no or low premium deals to achieve shareholder approvals. If no such deal is available – potentially a bigger challenge in some international markets – then the higher-quality assets within these portfolios could come to the market via asset sales.
- In the asset sales market, buyers and sellers need to reconcile conflicting views of price, market demand and asset performance. A lack of capital here can also drive differentiated deal structures. Contingent payments based on price or asset performance are most common, but one must always be aware of the risk of later litigation if the parties differ on how the calculation methodology was implemented. Often, parties may pay part in cash and part in shares (if the buyer is public), while the seller may allow for deferred payments if there are few buyers for a particular asset. Other ways to bridge value include granting an override (a share of revenue) which can minimise disputes over costs and operational efficiency.
- Virtual data rooms are being conducted successfully in the current pandemic environment. Just as working from home is becoming a more accepted norm, so too will completely virtual data rooms, potentially easing more global players back into the US M&A market and vice versa.

The following types of M&A deals will likely characterise the industry in the near term:

- Exploration farmins: This is still one of the primary growth vehicles in the deep-water Gulf of Mexico. There is more limited corporate and large asset M&A offshore; it is largely an organic-led industry segment, where companies make exploration discoveries and then move to develop. That process often uses farmins to bring in partners for risk sharing. A farmin agreement is a simpler form of sale and purchase agreement (SPA) where there is no production flowing yet, so from the effective date to closing, there is little for which to adjust in terms of cash flow and working capital. Therefore, if you can master the more complex SPAs as described in this book, you should be quite comfortable operating with farmin agreements.
- Traditional corporate acquisitions: The Chevron/Noble deal is an

obvious example. As described above, the majors may take some time to get their financial houses in order, but they are likely to participate in M&A as drilling inventory wanes and scale needs to be maintained. Some of the larger public independents could make the first move in this arena by buying small to medium-sized targets.

- Mergers of equals: The smaller independents do not have the scale to be of interest to majors and often their overall portfolios of assets do not fit the strategic objectives of majors. This will likely result in 'mergers of equals' between smaller independents. One likely side effect of a rash of 'mergers of equals' is an upturn in asset sales coming to market as the newly combined companies upgrade their portfolios.
- Asset sales: This is the bread and butter of the industry, as companies generally look to create efficiencies and upgrade their portfolios. For onshore, this can often take the form of a swap – although asset sales are equally common to raise cash for those under financial pressure or that want to focus operations.
- Bankruptcies and distressed assets: Bankruptcies are on the rise in the US energy industry. Equally important is the fact that there is a real lack of available capital:
  - Banks are increasingly withdrawing from oil and gas lending, due to ESG concerns;
  - Private equity firms have been unable to recycle their capital and are therefore reluctant to invest more; and
  - Public markets are virtually closed to this industry.

  Given these dynamics, where will bankrupt firms raise capital to reorganise under Chapter 11 and emerge with cleaner balance sheets? Many will not, which could likely result in a surge of Chapter 7 bankruptcies and liquidation. Savvy investors will always be ready to buy such assets – at a price. This may be one of the true growth areas for asset sales in the next few years.

Good SPAs are a critical enabler to facilitate assets changing hands. Anyone active in the purchase and sale of oil and gas assets will benefit from this book and the roadmap it provides to understanding how SPAs can be used to enable a defined and understood risk transfer between buyer and seller. For instance, the risk of asset performance and operations should change at the effective date; but certain risks, such as unknown liabilities, may be shared in the future for a limited time period, giving buyers confidence in the integrity of the purchased asset and providing time to confirm there are no 'skeletons in the closet'. Buying from a bankrupt estate should allow for a court-endorsed cleaner transfer, but will still require an intelligent SPA to ensure that such risk allocation is clear.

The SPA is a document that can be quite flexible, and ideas on how to use this to one's advantage to solve negotiating hurdles and structure an acceptable deal will be invaluable for anyone active in the industry in the coming years. Most of all, understanding the detail in these contracts is key to avoiding future post-closing surprises. Although rare, invoking a material adverse change clause can be a game-changer, and there is a wide variety of ways to limit this (as a seller) or to widen the scope (as a buyer). Conditions precedent should be carefully evaluated and drafted, as they can become a primary vehicle for preventing closing after the SPA contract is signed. Environmental and decommissioning risks are other lingering elements in most deals. Therefore, you will want to understand methods to limit your exposure in value and time as a buyer or how to ensure a fuller risk transfer as a seller.

Thanks to the editors and authors of this second edition of *Oil and Gas Sale and Purchase Agreements* for making their insights available and for helping to build the educational foundation for quality negotiations in this field.

Introduction

John C LaMaster
Caroline-Lucy Moran
Akin Gump Strauss Hauer & Feld LLP

Sale and purchase agreements (SPAs) for oil and gas assets or for shares in a company that owns oil and gas assets are highly specialised agreements, due to the unique nature and characteristics of the oil and gas industry. In this regard, the phrase 'sale and purchase agreements' includes farmout agreements, which are essentially a specialised form of asset SPA. This book is intended to provide a practical review of the provisions typically included in an SPA, including analysis of sample provisions.

This second edition of the book includes updates of the chapters in the first edition, as well as new chapters on preliminary agreements (memoranda of understanding, letters of intent); disclosure letters; private equity; warranty and indemnity insurance; and material adverse changes.

This book refers primarily to English law, because English law is the governing law used most commonly in cross-border acquisitions and divestitures in the oil and gas industry. The chapters, however, focus more on practical issues than on issues of black-letter law.

Written by experienced and well-known oil and gas industry practitioners, this second edition is intended to benefit lawyers and commercial negotiators working in the oil and gas industry who handle sale and purchase transactions, and who want to become more conversant in the usual and customary terms and conditions involved in such transactions; as well as law professors and law students looking for a teaching aid based on practical, real-world experience.

Most of the chapters in this second edition include sample provisions for SPAs. These sample provisions have been obtained from various sources. Some are from standard oil and gas industry forms, such as those promulgated by professional organisations Oil & Gas UK and the Association of International Petroleum Negotiators (AIPN). Since the first edition of this book, the AIPN updated its Model Form International Farmout Agreement in 2019 and issued a new Model Form International Asset Sale and Purchase Agreement in 2020, and these new model forms are referenced and discussed in several chapters. Other sample provisions are from the authors' own files and transaction bibles. Some of these sample provisions may be model forms, whereas others may have been heavily negotiated.

The chapter entitled "Governing law and jurisdiction clauses" includes sample arbitration provisions from the International Chamber of Commerce, the London Court of International Arbitration, the Singapore International Arbitration Centre and the United Nations Commission on International Trade Law. The model arbitration provisions are published on the respective organisations' websites. Please note that the model arbitration clauses are updated and revised from time to time. Anyone wanting to use these model arbitration clauses should check the relevant website for the latest, up-to-date version.

In each case, the sample provisions included here are for illustrative, informational and educational purposes only, and should not be considered as the rendering of legal advice for specific oil and gas transactions. Readers are responsible for obtaining such advice from their own legal counsel.

On behalf of the authors who have contributed chapters, we would like to thank you for reading, and we hope that this book will be helpful to your next oil and gas acquisition or divestiture.

Preliminary agreements

Afzaal Abidi
Christopher Strong
Suzana Vukasinovic
Vinson & Elkins RLLP

---

1. Introduction

Preliminary agreements (variously known as memoranda of understanding, heads of agreement (sometimes called heads of terms), letters of intent or term sheets) are short-form documents that outline the key terms of a proposed transaction and that contemplate the negotiation and execution of a further definitive agreement. In complex oil and gas transactions, the preparation of sale and purchase agreements (SPAs) can be an expensive and drawn-out process, often requiring input from numerous stakeholders across different stages of negotiations. In this context, preliminary agreements can be extremely valuable tools; they bring focus to the negotiations, outline the agreed key terms of the underlying transaction, enshrine the commitment of the parties to the transaction and establish a timeframe for the negotiations.

The use of preliminary agreements, however, is not without risk. In some instances, documents that are clearly labelled 'preliminary' will state that certain terms contained therein are binding, even though the document does not contain all terms necessary to constitute a binding contract; whereas other documents that contain the terms necessary to form a binding contract will state that they are subject to a further definitive agreement. The term 'preliminary agreement' itself has been described as a contradiction in terms. If the commercial and legal terms recorded in preliminary agreements are not intended to be binding and do not represent a fully fledged deal to the mutual satisfaction of the parties, is it fair to call them 'agreements' at all?

For some, preliminary agreements can be extremely beneficial; for others, the lack of certainty over their binding effect can be devastating. This chapter will consider the merits of preliminary agreements and whether they are necessary; whether and if so to what extent preliminary agreements should be considered binding; and some of the provisions they should typically include.

2. Are preliminary agreements necessary?

In some circumstances, the time and resources spent discussing and drafting preliminary agreements may be better spent towards settling the terms of the definitive SPA. In others, preliminary agreements can aid in establishing whether there is sufficient common ground to proceed with lengthy negotiations, may prevent later misunderstandings and may provide a helpful roadmap of the steps needed before a formal agreement is executed. The utility of preliminary agreements therefore turns on the nature and context of the transaction at hand. Set out below are some of the potential advantages parties may wish to consider when deciding whether to enter into a preliminary agreement:

- Preliminary agreements allow parties to examine the key issues early on, bringing to light any potential misunderstandings. Streamlining the process in this way can save the parties additional time and expense in the subsequent negotiations. If there is a fundamental issue that cannot be resolved and that prevents the transaction moving forward, the parties can reduce the risk of incurring abortive time and expense by identifying such 'deal breakers' early on.
- Preliminary agreements can confirm a moral commitment from the parties. From a psychological standpoint, it may be more difficult for a party to renege on earlier commitments if they are recorded in a formal document (albeit non-binding), or to walk away for fear of reputational damage. Furthermore, the time spent discussing preliminary agreements provides the negotiating teams with the opportunity to develop trust in each other and the negotiation process.
- In the early stages of a proposed sale or purchase, the parties may need to explain and 'sell' the key terms of a deal to internal stakeholders and third parties, whether to the board of directors of a parent company where negotiations are being handled by a subsidiary or to lenders where an acquisition requires external financing. Preliminary agreements offer an efficient way of doing so, providing a useful statement of the key terms of a proposed transaction. Furthermore, having something in writing can be attractive; for internal purposes, evidence of a signed document may help in showing the progress made when seeking to justify a transaction.
- Some parties may wish to introduce certain binding commitments during the early stages of negotiations. This is usually relevant where the parties need to start working together pending execution of the definitive agreement; for example, the parties may enter into an interim agreement for the provision of 'transitioning-in' services where these are needed. The parties may also wish to contemplate the treatment of costs in the event that negotiations break down, as well as any confidentiality, exclusivity or lock-out undertakings. These commitments can be of vital importance during the parties' negotiations, even if no formal agreement has been reached on the key commercial deal points.
- Draft preliminary agreements can provide a useful roadmap when it

comes to instructing the parties' advisers; if a preliminary agreement contains the key agreed terms, it can serve as a solid foundation for the lawyers when it comes to drafting the definitive agreement, expediting the process of drafting and potentially saving legal fees.

- Transactions in the oil and gas space are often subject to a host of governmental or regulatory approvals or consents, and competition clearances may need to be obtained before a transaction can complete. In some cases, a preliminary agreement may be sufficient to commence the regulatory review process, thereby allowing the regulatory process to proceed in parallel with the negotiation of definitive agreements.
- Certain jurisdictions may require public announcements to be made in the context of a share purchase. In England and Wales, for example, the City Code on Takeover and Mergers requires companies to make an announcement before a bidder has fully formed an intention to make an offer. Preliminary agreements can form the basis of any such public announcement.

In some situations, preliminary agreements may not be appropriate. Set out below are some of the potential disadvantages that parties should consider before entering into a preliminary agreement:

- Preliminary agreements may create legally binding commitments, even if this is not the intention of the parties. If the parties do not wish a preliminary agreement to be binding, this should be expressly stated; otherwise, it could have the undesired effect of being binding and enforceable, provided that the other elements of contract formation have been satisfied. Furthermore – and of special relevance given the often cross-border nature of oil and gas transactions – the courts of the United States and those of certain European jurisdictions may imply a duty of good faith into preliminary agreements. Such a duty may give rise to liability if one of the parties withdraws from the negotiations; this is discussed in more detail in section 3 below.
- Preliminary agreements can also limit the flexibility of the parties in subsequent negotiations. For example, where party A has agreed certain terms in the early stages of negotiations that are then reflected in a preliminary agreement, and that ultimately prove unfavourable, party B may insist that the preliminary agreement established the parameters of the negotiations notwithstanding that the preliminary agreement is not binding. This would have the effect of limiting party A's flexibility during the subsequent negotiations.
- As has been discussed, the time and money spent in negotiating a preliminary agreement may well outweigh the benefit. When deciding whether to enter into a preliminary agreement, the parties should

consider whether they have sufficient time and resources to prepare such a document, as well as the nature of the parties' relationship. In some cases, the parties may have a strong enough track record to forgo the need to establish ground rules or to enshrine their commitment in documentary form.

For some, preliminary agreements can be a useful tool: they enshrine the commitment of the parties; provide contractual cover where it is needed; act as a roadmap for the negotiations; and shine light on any potential 'deal breakers' early on. For those with a strong history of working together or a desire to retain some flexibility in the negotiations, it may be preferable to dedicate their time and resources to negotiating and drafting the definitive agreements. There is no hard-and-fast rule here; it will depend entirely on the context and nature of the transaction at hand.

3. Are preliminary agreements binding?

3.1 Preliminary agreements governed by the laws of England and Wales

When entering into preliminary agreements governed by the laws of England and Wales, parties should ensure that:

- they are clear on what their intentions are – specifically, whether they intend to create legal relations;
- the preliminary agreement is drafted clearly, and the terms contained therein are certain and not vague or ambiguous; and
- their subsequent conduct reflects their intention, as well as the drafting of any preliminary agreement entered into.

As will be seen, this last point is crucial. Even where a preliminary agreement clearly states that its terms are "subject to contract", or that "the terms [t]herein are not binding", the court may find that a contract has formed based on the parties' intention to create legal relations and their subsequent conduct.

3.2 Clear intention to create legal relations

The test for whether there is a mutual intention to create legal relations is an objective test.[1] Generally, in the context of commercial agreements, there is a rebuttable presumption of an intention to create legal relations. The difficulty in establishing a clear intention arises where:

1 See *Barbudev v Eurocom Cable Management Bulgaria Eood* [2012] EWCA Civ 548. In *Barbudev*, the Court of Appeal found that a side letter demonstrated an intention to create legal relations on the basis that it:
- contained language consistent with the intention to create legal relations (eg, "in consideration of…");
- contained a jurisdiction clause and referred to the Contracts (Rights of Third Parties) Act 1999;
- was drafted by legal advisers from a reputable law firm; and
- contained a legally binding confidentiality clause.

- the intentions of the parties are unclear – preliminary agreements are composed in the early stages of a transaction and the precise intentions of the parties may not yet be known; or
- the preliminary agreement is not clearly drafted – in the early stages of discussions, if the parties' intentions are not yet clear, it may be difficult for them to put in writing the basis on which they are entering into the agreement. If this results in vague or unclear drafting, the courts may conclude that the preliminary agreement in question is not binding.

3.3 Clear drafting that is not vague or ambiguous

If the terms of a preliminary agreement appear vague or incomplete (ie, the preliminary agreement lacks the essential terms required to create a binding contract), a court may struggle to enforce it notwithstanding the fact that the parties intended to create legal relations. If the parties to a transaction wish a preliminary agreement to be binding, they must ensure that the document contains no uncertain or ambiguous terms. The parties can minimise the risk of a dispute as to whether an agreement is binding by inserting an express clause stating that the preliminary agreement imposes no legally binding obligations. For example:

Notwithstanding the foregoing, this preliminary agreement does not describe all applicable terms of the relevant transaction and does not constitute a commitment to enter into a transaction or otherwise create any legally binding obligation. Any such commitment would be evidenced only by one or more separate agreements being executed by the authorised representatives of each party.

If any individual clauses are intended to be binding – for example, a confidentiality provision or an exclusivity provision – an express clause describing the non-binding nature of the document, paired with a carve-out explicitly referring to any binding provisions, may be employed. For example:

Paragraphs [•] and [•] of this preliminary agreement are legally binding on the parties. No other provision of this preliminary agreement is legally binding on any of the parties, or creates any legally enforceable rights or obligations between the parties.

If the parties do not wish a preliminary agreement to be binding, they can also introduce certain conditions to the preliminary agreement – for example, that the preliminary agreement is conditional on satisfactory due diligence taking place or on the execution of a further definitive agreement. This may support the view that it is clear and unambiguous that the preliminary agreement was never intended to create legal relations.

3.4 Parties' conduct reflects intention and drafting of any preliminary agreement entered into

However, if a court finds that the parties intended to create legal relations, and that the parties' conduct matches such intention, a preliminary agreement may bind the parties irrespective of any wording to the contrary. This has been made apparent in a number of cases, as discussed below.

RTS v Muller[2] demonstrates "the perils of beginning work without agreeing the precise bases upon which it is to be done. The moral story is to agree first and to start work later".[3] In *RTS*, the respondent successfully tendered for a project to supply the appellant with new equipment for its yoghurt packaging. The parties entered into a four-week letter of intent, stated as being "subject to contract", to enable the work to begin pending negotiation of a definitive agreement. A draft contract was drawn up, but was never finalised. The Supreme Court found that, in commencing the work contemplated by the letter of intent, the parties had by their conduct waived the "subject to contract" provision contained in the preliminary agreement. The Supreme Court also held that where a contract was being negotiated subject to contract and work began before the formal contract was executed, it could not be concluded that there would necessarily be a definitive agreement on the terms that were stated to be subject to contract. As noted by Lord Clarke:

> *Whether there is a binding contract between the parties, and if so, upon what terms depends upon what they have agreed. It depends not upon their subjective state of mind, but upon consideration of what was communicated between them by words or conduct, and whether that leads objectively to a conclusion that they intended to create legal relations and had agreed upon all the terms which they regarded or the law requires as essential for the formation of legally binding relations. Even if certain terms of economic or other significance to the parties have not been finalised, an objective appraisal of their words and conduct may lead to the conclusion that they did not intend agreement of such terms to be a pre-condition to a concluded and legally binding agreement.*[4]

In *Jirehouse Capital v Beller*[5] the High Court confirmed the principle that a "subject to contract" qualification will cease to apply:

- where the parties expressly agree that it should be waived; or
- by necessary implication.[6]

The case concerned email correspondence in which the defendant proposed, and the claimant approved, terms upon which they were prepared to settle the claim. The correspondence in question was stated as being "subject to contract". The court, having regard to the circumstances of the negotiation, held that the "subject to contract" restriction was expunged. The court based its decision on the fact that:

---

2 *RTS Flexible Systems Ltd v Molkerei Alois Muller GmbH & Co KG* [2010] UKSC 14
3 *Ibid*, para 1.
4 *RTS Flexible Systems Ltd v Molkerei Alois Muller GmbH & Co KG* [2010] UKSC 14 para. 45
5 *Jirehouse Capital v Beller* [2009] EWHC 2538 (Ch)
6 *Cohen v Nessdale Ltd* [1982] 2 All ER 97.

- the claimant's solicitor was not alive to any subject to contract restriction during the negotiations and had been authorised by the claimant to negotiate a final compromise;
- both parties' solicitors believed they had reached a final decision; and
- the parties' conduct implied they believed a final settlement had been reached, and the claimant's solicitor accepted instructions that would have prevented him from appearing at trial.

The case again affirms the principle that the use of clear language stating that a preliminary agreement is not binding may be disregarded by the courts if the conduct of the parties was consistent with the view that the agreement was binding.

The parties should thus take great care to:

- decide whether and, if so, to what extent they want a preliminary agreement to be binding (whether fully, partially or non-binding); and
- reflect such intention clearly and accurately in the wording of the preliminary agreement, and make sure the nature and function of the preliminary agreement, as well as their conduct, match the 'label' given to the document.

3.5 The position in other jurisdictions

The position in the United Kingdom[7] differs somewhat from that in certain civil law jurisdictions, in which the courts will imply a duty to negotiate preliminary agreements in good faith. The duty of good faith applies to all commercial relationships and will usually commence when the parties begin their negotiations. Although the scope varies from jurisdiction to jurisdiction, generally speaking, a duty of good faith requires the parties to:

- act with reasonable diligence;
- take into account each other's legitimate interests and expectations; and
- where the other party may reasonably anticipate entering into a binding agreement, not terminate negotiations without reasonable cause.

Parties entering into agreements governed by the laws of civil law jurisdictions should therefore take particular care; preliminary agreements may provide an aggrieved party with a platform from which to bring an action for breach of a duty to negotiate in good faith, even where they are not intended to be legally binding. If a party enters into negotiations with a third party or decides against a transaction without providing reasonable cause, the innocent

7 See *Walford v Miles* [1992] 1 All ER 453. In *Walford*, it was held that the duty to negotiate in good faith could not be enforced for lack of certainty. Furthermore, it was held that such a duty was "inherently repugnant to the adversarial position of the parties".

party may be entitled to damages to restore it to the position it would have been in had negotiations not taken place. Depending on the jurisdiction, this may occur even if the relevant document has been stated to be "subject to contract"; the signing of a preliminary agreement may serve as evidence that the parties had reached an agreement in principle.

The position again differs where the parties are entering into preliminary agreements governed by the laws of the United States.[8] New York law classifies preliminary agreements as one of two types:[9]

- Type I preliminary agreements occur "when the parties have reached complete agreement (including the agreement to be bound) on all the issues perceived to require negotiation. Such an agreement is preliminary only in form – only in the sense that the parties desire a more elaborate formalization of the agreement".[10] Courts applying New York law will interpret Type I preliminary agreements as binding in spite of the fact that a further formal document is contemplated, and regardless of whether such further document is in fact entered into. To work around this, the parties may make the execution of the anticipated formal document a condition precedent to the formation of any binding agreement.
- Type II preliminary agreements are those that "express mutual commitment to a contract on agreed major terms, while recognizing the existence of open terms that remain to be negotiated".[11] Although Type II agreements do not bind the parties, they do oblige the parties to negotiate any open terms in good faith and refrain from actions that contravene the negotiations (ie, the terms of the preliminary agreement).[12] Any failure to enter into a definitive agreement does not create liability, provided that the parties have used good-faith efforts.[13]

Parties entering into agreements governed by the laws of the United States should consider the following when entering into preliminary agreements:

- The parties should ensure that any preliminary agreements clearly state their intentions. If a preliminary agreement is intended to be non-

---

8 State law on this subject in the United States varies from state to state. As a result, legal advice specific to the state whose laws govern the preliminary agreement is critical.

9 See *Teachers Insurance & Annuity Assoc v Tribune Co* 670 F Supp 491 (SDNY 1987), in which District Court Judge Pierre Leval recognised two types of binding preliminary agreements. This view was reiterated by the Second Circuit in *Vacold LLC v Cerami*, 545 F 3d 114, 124 n 2 (2d Cir 2008), in which the two types of agreement were categorised as 'Type I' and 'Type II'. See also *Arcadian Phosphates, Inc v Arcadian Corp*, 884 F 2d 69, 72 (2d Cir 1989), and *Adjustrite Systems, Inc v GAB Business Services, Inc*, 145 F 3d 543, 548 (2d Cir 1998).

10 *Teachers Insurance & Annuity Assoc v Tribune Co* 670 F Supp. 491 (SDNY 1987), paragraph 9.

11 *Ibid.*

12 *Brown v Cara*, 420 F 3d 148 (2d Cir 2005), quoting *Adjustrite Systems, Inc v GAB Business Services, Inc*, 145 F 3d 543, 548 (2d Cir 1998) (applying New York law).

13 *Frazier Indus, LLC v Gen Fasteners Co*, 137 F App'x 723, 734–35 (6th Cir 2005).

binding, that fact should be clearly stated. The parties should also consider whether the obligation to negotiate in good faith should expressly be debarred.

- The parties may wish to limit their damages to prevent a court from awarding expectation damages for any failure to negotiate in good faith. To do this, the parties may specify that only certain types of damages will be available for any breach of the preliminary agreement.
- Finally, the parties may wish to introduce conditions to any definitive documents – for example, that the documents are conditional on satisfactory due diligence taking place or on obtaining the requisite internal approvals. Such factors may support the view that a preliminary agreement was never intended to be binding and would preclude the court from finding that a deal would have been concluded but for the bad-faith negotiations.

The path taken by parties entering into preliminary agreements may be fraught with peril. If the parties are not yet clear on their intentions, they should take special care to avoid accidentally contracting based on an objective manifestation of their intent, which may not match their subjective state of mind when entering into the agreement. Accordingly, the parties should

- be clear on what their intentions are;
- make sure their intentions are clearly drafted into any preliminary agreements; and
- ensure that any subsequent conduct manifests such intention and language.

4. What form should a preliminary agreement take?

While there are no hard and fast rules as to what form a preliminary agreement should take, preliminary agreements are generally short documents, often in the form of letter agreements. There are, of course, exceptions to this and the parties should always consider what is appropriate based on the transaction at hand. Where each party is confident that the other is committed to getting the transaction over the line and will be cooperative in negotiations with a view to reaching a mutually beneficial agreement, some of the advantages associated with preliminary agreements may be less pertinent. In such cases, a shorter agreement may be more appropriate. On the other hand, if the parties do not have a history of working together or if, for whatever reason, there is perceived to be a need to reach agreement on certain key points before committing time and resources to detailed negotiations, they may elect to draft a more detailed preliminary agreement to identify 'deal breakers' and enshrine the parties' commitment.

Set out below are some of the provisions most commonly featured in preliminary agreements. As ever, the challenge is to outline the agreed principles without getting unduly involved in detail more appropriately dealt with in the subsequent definitive agreements.

4.1 Parties

The details of the parties should be included, together with those of any parent company guarantors, as applicable. Where a party anticipates forming a special purpose vehicle for the purposes of a transaction, the preliminary agreement will often state that the party to any definitive agreement will be an "affiliate of" the relevant special purpose vehicle.

4.2 Description of the transaction

Preliminary agreements generally contain an outline of the proposed transaction, describing whether the buyer is acquiring an asset or part or all of the issued share capital of a target company. The parties may also specify their anticipated ownership interest in the target asset or company; and where parties are jointly bidding for shares or an asset as part of a consortium, they may stipulate their respective shareholding in any BidCo being incorporated for the purpose of submitting the bid and acquiring shares in the target company. Transactions relating to oil and gas assets may also entail the transfer of additional rights, such as operatorship rights where the buyer is acquiring oil and gas exploration and production assets. This can also be reflected in any preliminary agreement.

4.3 Price

Along with the anticipated contract price, the methodology used to calculate the contract price is often included in preliminary agreements, as well as details as to how and when the price will be payable, including any price adjustments or contingent payments. Any assumptions upon which the price is based should also be included; this can be useful for the buyer, which may be entitled to revise the contract price in the event that an assumption turns out to be false. Assumptions may relate to, for example:

- the date as of which the price is calculated (which typically precedes the closing date);
- the target's profit and net assets;
- any liabilities of the target; or
- whether the target will be acquired on a cash-free or debt-free basis.

In share sales, price provisions typically clarify that the contract price will be paid as consideration for the transfer of the shares forming the subject of the transaction.

4.4 Definitive documents

Preliminary agreements often detail the definitive agreements that the parties anticipate entering into.

In the context of an asset sale, along with the negotiation and execution of an SPA, the parties may anticipate entering into joint operating agreements or production sharing contracts where a purchaser will hold and/or operate an asset jointly with the seller or a third party, or certifications or other documents deemed customary and appropriate for transactions similar to the transaction contemplated by the parties.

In the context of a share sale, the parties may wish to make clear which documents will need to be executed or issued in order to complete the transaction. This may include:

- drafting a written transfer instrument to effect the transfer of the shares forming the subject of the transaction;
- issuing a share certificate to the buyer with respect to the shares; and
- updating any company books to reflect the transfer of the sale shares and, where applicable, the resignation of any company directors or officers.

Notwithstanding the above, where discussions are in their early stages and it is not yet clear what sort of documentation may be required, the parties may elect instead to incorporate a general statement that, following the date of the preliminary agreement, the parties shall negotiate with a view to entering into a definitive and legally binding transfer and settlement agreement. Good-faith language can be included here; but, as has been discussed, it is unlikely to bind the parties unless there is a clear intention to create legal relations and the parties' subsequent conduct manifests such intention.

4.5 Conditions

As has been discussed, transactions in the oil and gas industry are subject to a host of governmental and regulatory approvals. These may be required under the terms of any project documents awarded by the host state or the governing laws of the country where the target assets are located. Requirements such as these are typically structured as conditions precedent in the relevant SPA. The parties may wish to introduce such conditions precedent into the discussions early on and reflect them in any preliminary agreements entered into. Along with ensuring that any governmental, regulatory or competition clearances have been obtained, conditions precedent may relate to the obtaining of any third-party consents and any internal approvals needed to effect a transaction, the incorporation of any SPVs or the securing of any requisite financing.

4.6 Warranties and indemnities

Buyers and sellers generally require certain protections to be included in SPAs in the form of warranties and indemnities. While warranties and indemnities are typically addressed in the definitive documents once any due diligence process has been completed, it is common for parties to include a general statement anticipating such protections in any preliminary agreement:

The SPA will include customary representation, warranties and covenants that are typically given by the [Buyer/Seller] in transactions of this type.

Parties may list customary, typically non-contentious, fundamental warranties to be given by each party. For example, the parties may warrant that they:

- are validly existing and duly incorporated;
- have the legal right and authority to enter into the definitive agreements; and
- have taken all corporate action required to enter into the transaction.

4.7 Limitations of liability

Setting limits on post-closing liability is often a key issue for the seller, and buyers are also very interested that these limits be set at an appropriate level. As a result, preliminary agreements will often spell out any limitations to the seller's liability under its warranties and indemnities.

4.8 Confidentiality

As has been discussed, the seller may want to introduce binding confidentiality provisions early on to prevent sensitive information being leaked into the market. In practice, parties may prefer to enter into a separate confidentiality agreement, but a confidentiality provision may be included in the preliminary agreement for extra protection. If a confidentiality agreement has been entered into before any preliminary agreement is prepared, the preliminary agreement may contain a provision incorporating the terms of such confidentiality agreement.

4.9 Exclusivity

A binding exclusivity provision may be desirable from the buyer's perspective, as it prevents the seller from playing off potential buyers against one another and can allow the buyer time to make any necessary arrangements (eg, financing) before the transaction completes. Again, in practice, exclusivity terms are often set out in a separate exclusivity letter, but the buyer may want an exclusivity provision to be included in any preliminary agreement for extra protection. An exclusivity provision may state, for example:

Seller hereby unconditionally and irrevocably undertakes that it will not, directly or indirectly, for a period of [•] months after this preliminary agreement is signed, (i) solicit, initiate, encourage or accept any proposal or offer from any person or entity other than Buyer relating to the subject matter of this preliminary agreement, including without limitation the acquisition of any share capital or material assets of the Seller or (ii) participate in or facilitate any discussions or other communications regarding any of the foregoing. The Seller shall immediately cease and cause to be terminated all existing discussions, negotiations and other communications with all parties conducted heretofore with respect to any of the foregoing.

4.10 Legally binding

As has been discussed, the parties may wish to include a provision expressly stating that the provisions contained in a preliminary agreement will not bind the parties:

Notwithstanding the foregoing, this preliminary agreement does not describe all applicable terms of the relevant transaction and does not constitute a commitment to enter into a transaction or otherwise create any legally binding obligation. Any such commitment would be evidenced only by one or more separate agreements being executed by the authorised representatives of each party.

If the parties wish certain provisions to be carved out and thus be legally binding (eg, provisions relating to confidentiality or exclusivity), the parties may explicitly refer to such provisions by paragraph number to ensure there is no ambiguity as to their binding effect.

4.11 Restrictive covenants

The buyer may require the seller to outline the terms of any restrictive covenants, such as non-compete provisions or for the non-solicitation of employees. Again, these are typically dealt with in the definitive agreements, as new issues may arise during the course of the buyer's due diligence.

4.12 Costs

A key issue is who will be responsible for costs in the event that the negotiations break down. The parties will need to decide whether they will bear their own costs, or whether one party will bear the other's out-of-pocket expenses. The following language is commonly found in preliminary agreements:

Each Party shall bear its own costs and expenses (including legal expenses and the charges of advisers) incurred in connection with the preparation and negotiation of this preliminary agreement, save for the following costs which shall be borne in equal shares by the Parties….

4.13 Timetable

This can include a longstop date for conditions precedent to be satisfied or, for example, the date when exclusivity obligations expire. Such inclusions of specific dates enforce a timetable for the transaction, but can be amended or extended as required.

5. Conclusion

Preliminary agreements can be an extremely valuable tool: they enshrine the commitment of the parties; provide contractual cover where it is needed; set the ground rules for negotiations; and shine light on any potential 'deal breakers' early on. However, preliminary agreements can be a double-edged sword; parties may find themselves bound by a preliminary agreement, even if it is expressly stated to be 'non-binding' or 'subject to contract'. In some jurisdictions, parties may be surprised to learn that they are under an implied obligation to negotiate in good faith, pursuant to which they may find themselves liable for expectation damages if they walk away from a deal. Depending on the commercial circumstances, the time and money spent in negotiating a preliminary agreement may well outweigh the benefit, and the parties may be better off focusing on the terms of the definitive agreement.

Parties should therefore think carefully before entering into a preliminary agreement, and consider whether it is appropriate to do so having regard to the nature of the transaction, the relationship of the parties and the commercial context in which they find themselves. If they do decide to enter into a preliminary agreement, they should take special care to avoid accidentally contracting by:

- being clear on what their intentions are;
- ensuring that their intentions are clearly drafted into any preliminary agreements; and
- ensuring that any subsequent conduct manifests such intention and language.

Sale structure

Joanna Kay
BW Offshore
Peter Roberts
Cross Keys Energy Limited

This chapter outlines the factors that are key to determining the best transaction structure for the sale and purchase of oil and gas interests. The first part of the chapter reviews the preliminary considerations that will help the parties to select the structure of a particular transaction. The second part compares the two principal sale structures used in the industry: share sales and asset sales. The third part examines the different types of asset sale structures that are common in the oil and gas industry. The fourth and last section considers the essential elements of the sales process, from the initial decision to sell to completion.

1. Preliminary considerations in structuring a transaction

A wide range of factors can affect the structure selection process for a particular transaction. The extent to which any particular factor could influence the decision-making process will also vary from one transaction to another. However, a number of preliminary considerations will help to shape the structuring analysis that is carried out at the outset of a proposed transaction.

1.1 The nature of the interest for sale

The oil and gas industry is extremely diverse. It spans the upstream, midstream and downstream, oilfield services and infrastructure sectors; involves both public (government) and private (company) interests; and includes such varied disciplines as joint venture formation, exploration, project development, production, storage, transportation, processing, commodity trading, financing, intellectual property and compliance. Against this colourful backdrop, it is possible to see how the underlying nature of the interest for sale will affect the structure of a given transaction.

Where a transaction relates to early stage upstream interests, the valuation of the interest and the form that the actual sale and purchase takes will be heavily influenced by the concession obligations that the buyer assumes and the seller transfers to the buyer as a consequence of the transaction. This is one of the reasons why upstream transactions are often based on farmout or earn-in arrangements. Similarly, the underlying joint venture that will regulate the parties' relationship once the transaction has completed will have a material bearing on the transaction documents. It is common to see voting compacts included in upstream sale and purchase agreements (SPAs), as well as in agreements between the seller and buyer, that vary the joint venture position in respect of cost contributions, work obligations, cost recovery entitlements and environmental and decommissioning liabilities.

In the midstream and infrastructure sectors, oil and gas transactions tend to focus more heavily on physical assets such as pipelines and storage. A transaction may be structured as a share sale or an asset sale, but the focus of the due diligence and the protections incorporated in the SPA will be on the assets themselves, whereas joint venture and concession issues could be less prominent.

In the downstream and oilfield services sectors, the focus changes once again. There, the value of the interest will often reside in less tangible assets such as the book of business that has been built up and the intellectual property developed and owned by a target company. These businesses lend themselves more to a share sale structure.

1.2 The rationale for the sale

Just as the nature of the interest being sold varies from one transaction to another, so too do the motivations that inform the seller's decision to sell and the buyer's decision to buy a particular interest.

The primary motivation for any seller will be to realise value from the divestment of its interest in a particular asset or target company. However, a number of other factors may also underlie the seller's decision to sell. These include:

- the desire to reduce costs within its organisation or in connection with that particular asset or target company;
- the desire to mitigate the extent to which it is exposed to any downturn in the performance of the asset or target company, whether that downturn is financial, technical, geological or commercial;
- the desire to manage better the political risk associated with a particular asset or target company – for example, by selling it to a bigger company with greater leverage in the relevant jurisdiction or better local connections;
- as part of a wider strategic review or sector refocus;
- to comply with regulatory requirements;
- as a form of portfolio management to free up cash for the seller to diversify or refocus its business; or
- as a means of bringing in a new set of skills and expertise to enable the asset or target company to develop further.

By selling all or part of its interest in an asset or target company, a seller may be able to realise one or more of these objectives.

A buyer will similarly want to realise value as a result of its acquisition of an interest. That value is unlikely to be realised directly. Instead, the value is generated for the buyer through the upside potential that the asset or target company offers. The acquisition could allow the buyer to establish a presence in a new sector or market that complements its existing portfolio. There may be strategic reasons for the acquisition, such as the ability to acquire transportation rights or to gain access to data that is relevant to the buyer's existing business. Or the acquisition of a new asset or target company may offer the buyer tax savings that can be used to benefit its wider portfolio.

Whatever they are, the underlying motivations of the seller and the buyer will help to shape the structure of a transaction. These motivations will need to be recognised and reconciled within the transaction documentation.

1.3 Regulated companies

Where a transaction involves a public takeover, the structure of the transaction will likely need to comply with certain regulatory requirements. A public takeover is the acquisition of control of a company that is listed on a regulated market.

In the United Kingdom, takeovers are governed by the City Code on Takeovers and Mergers. The code will apply to offers for, and other transactions involving a change in control of, companies with their registered office in (or that are considered to be resident in) the United Kingdom, the Channel Islands or the Isle of Man, if any of their securities are admitted to trading on a regulated market or a multilateral trading facility in the United Kingdom or on any stock exchange in the Channel Islands or the Isle of Man. The code will also apply to all companies whose shares are traded on AIM or ISDX, regardless of whether they have their central management and control overseas. The code does not apply to private companies, unless there has previously been some marketing of their shares to the public.

The code applies to takeover and merger transactions, however they are effected, including by means of a statutory merger or court-approved scheme of arrangement. The code imposes a set of statutory rules on all such transactions creating the form, structure and timetable of the transaction in order to ensure the fair and equitable treatment of shareholders in the target company.

A number of other UK statutory and regulatory provisions will also apply to a transaction where a target company is publicly listed. These include:

- insider dealing provisions under the Criminal Justice Act 1993 and the Financial Services Act 2000;
- market abuse and financial regulations under the Financial Services and the Markets Act 2000;

- shareholder consents under the Listing Rules;
- disclosure and transparency obligations under the Disclosure and Transparency Rules and the Prospectus Rules; and
- merger controls under the Competition Act 1998, the Enterprise Act 2002 and the EU Merger Regulation.

Public takeovers are in the minority of M&A activity in the oil and gas industry and the issues that need to be taken into account in connection with a public takeover will differ from one jurisdiction to another, as they are driven by the legislation specific to a particular jurisdiction. Consequently, the rest of this chapter focuses on structuring private M&A transactions.

2. Share sales and asset sales

The most fundamental decision that the parties will need to make when structuring a transaction is whether to structure it as a share sale or an asset sale.

Under a share sale structure, the interest that is being sold is the shares in the company that owns the asset(s) that the buyer wishes to acquire:

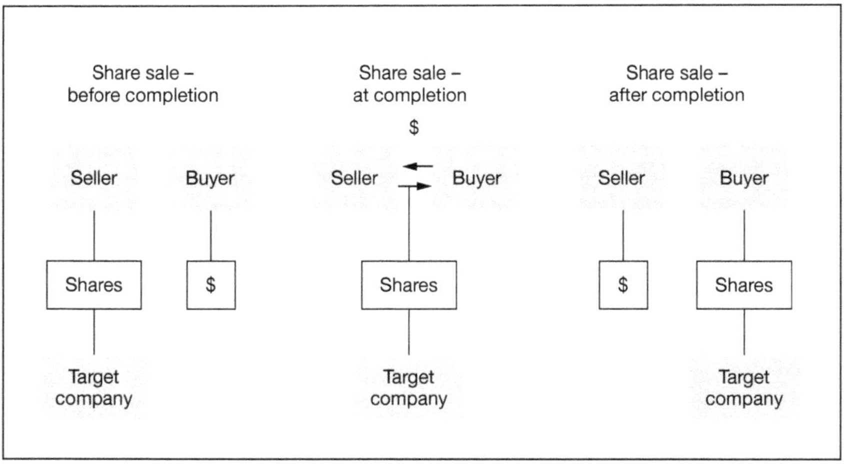

In a share sale, the share purchase agreement effects an indirect transfer of the underlying interest through the sale of the share capital of the target company that holds the relevant interest. The buyer acquires all of the assets, rights and liabilities of the target company, known and unknown, including those arising prior to the acquisition (unless anything is specifically excluded from the sale). The buyer will therefore need to investigate carefully the financial, legal, tax and commercial position of the target company in order to identify and quantify the risks associated with the acquisition of that company.

Under an asset sale structure the interest that is being sold is the asset itself:

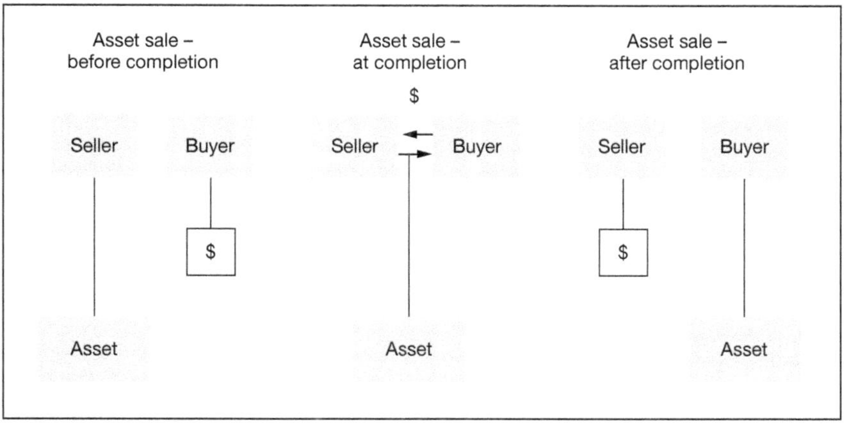

In an asset sale, there is a direct transfer of the relevant interest. The buyer will acquire only an asset (and its corresponding rights and liabilities) and any associated financial or strategic value. The SPA will specify exactly what asset is being sold to the buyer, allowing the buyer to avoid the inadvertent acquisition of other assets (and their corresponding rights and liabilities).

The key factors that will influence the parties' decision as to whether to structure the transaction as a share sale or an asset sale are outlined below.

2.1 Taxation

The tax implications of a transaction will be among the most influential factors in structuring the acquisition or disposal of an interest. Share sales and asset sales have very different tax consequences. As a broad generalisation, the advantages of a share sale will usually be preferable from a seller's tax perspective, whereas the advantages of an asset sale will usually be preferable from a buyer's tax perspective. However, the specific circumstances of the companies and interests involved will be determining. The chapter "Tax aspects of oil and gas mergers and acquisitions" addresses a transaction's tax implications in more detail.

It is also generally assumed that a share transfer is the key to securing accumulated tax losses that sit in the target company and that the buyer could then secure and benefit from. This simple expectation, however, will always need careful verification.

2.2 Complexity

Asset sales are generally perceived to be more complex than share sales. This is because an asset sale requires the buyer to identify each of the assets that it wishes to acquire and each of the liabilities that it is willing to assume (and, correspondingly, any assets or liabilities that it might not wish to acquire). This complexity is a downside that the buyer must balance against the additional flexibility that an asset sale otherwise affords a buyer (eg, because of the ability to select only those assets that it perceives to be of value). Before committing to buy an asset, the buyer will need to assess carefully the contractual arrangements associated with a particular interest to ensure that it acquires all of the rights that it needs to maintain (or enhance) the value of that interest. Furthermore, in an asset sale, there may be a number of different types of assets being transferred (eg, concession interests, trading arrangements, real property and/or intellectual property). Each different type of asset may have a different procedure or registration requirement in order to effect a valid transfer of that asset. This means that the transfer process in an asset sale is also more complex than in a share sale.

In theory, the sales process for a share sale is more straightforward than the sales process for an asset sale. It will involve the transfer of only one asset: the shares in the target company. The transfer of title to those shares from the seller to the buyer will be effected by the simple registration of the buyer as the new owner in the members' registry of the target company. However, in reality, a share sale can be extremely complex. Where a business has grown organically, the assets and services required to operate that business may not all be situated neatly in a single target company ready for sale. A pre-sale reorganisation may therefore be required to clean up an existing subsidiary to ready it for sale or to establish a new special purpose vehicle to package up assets that were formerly sitting in a number of different subsidiaries prior to the sale process. In turn, the buyer may require a post-sale reorganisation. This may be driven by the need to move the target company to a more appropriate place in the group structure of the buyer (since the tax structuring of the original acquisition may have resulted in the target company sitting in a sub-optimal place from an operational perspective). Equally, where the target company was previously a trading company in the seller's group, the buyer may wish to transfer the constituent assets into a known or clean entity and liquidate the target company in order to remove from its books a company that it knows little about. Whether effected pre or post-sale, any reorganisation of the target company will need proper documentation. Intra-group transfer arrangements may be structured as either an asset sale or a share sale; typically, the documents will be much shorter than in a true arm's-length sale. Care will also need to be taken in the structuring of the consideration of any intra-group transfer, to ensure that there is no unintended under-valuation of the transferred interests that could trigger company law issues and either invalidate the transaction or expose the directors to civil or criminal liabilities.

2.3 Third-party consents

Asset sales involve a change in the party that owns the asset. As noted above, where a transaction involves a number of assets, the nature of the assets could be quite diverse and may require the consent of one or more third parties in order to effect the assignment or novation of the assets from the seller to the buyer. This can add time to the sale process and potentially creates an opportunity for those third parties to impose new terms to gain advantage from the change, or even to refuse to effect the transfer.

In a share sale, the interest remains owned by the target company, so there is no direct transfer of the interest. This means that the relationship between the target company and its contractual counterparties in respect of the interest does not change. This considerably reduces the number of third-party consents that may be required to effect a transfer of the target company and therefore reduces the risk of value impairment of the underlying business as a result of the transfer. Consequently, share sales are often simpler to implement than asset sales.

In certain circumstances, however, the requirement to obtain consent may be triggered not only by a change in ownership of the interest itself, but also by a share sale as a result of a change in ownership of the ultimate owner of the interest, through so-called 'change of control' clauses. In the oil and gas industry, the underlying concession that grants title to the upstream interest will often contain such a change of control clause. Thus, host government consent will often be required regardless of whether a sale is structured as an asset sale or a share sale. The other contractual arrangements related to the target company that is being transferred will also need to be analysed carefully to identify any change of control clauses.

2.4 Pre-emption rights

In oil and gas acquisition transactions, joint operating agreements (JOAs) and other joint venture structures commonly include a pre-emption right. Pre-emption rights compel a seller to offer the interests under the JOA or joint venture agreement that it is proposing to sell to the buyer first to its existing co-venturers on the same terms and conditions as those agreed to by the buyer. Only if those existing co-venturers do not wish to exercise their rights to take up the seller's interest can the seller then sell the interests to the buyer. The ostensible purpose of pre-emption rights is to control the entry of a new participant into the joint venture and to limit the ability of an existing participant to build a participating interest stake that gives it complete voting control under the JOA or joint venture agreement.

Typically, pre-emption rights under a JOA or joint venture agreement are triggered only in an asset sale. If a pre-emption right applies, the buyer will need to ensure that any co-venturer's right to pre-empt a transfer under the JOA or joint venture agreement is waived as a condition precedent to the buyer's obligation to acquire the interest.

While less common, pre-emption may also apply on a share sale where a co-venturer's right to pre-empt is triggered by a change of control in the target company. In such a case, the target company is required to offer its co-venturers a right to acquire the interest offered for a monetary amount equivalent to the value ascribed to the interest in the share sale. The valuation method and a mechanism to resolve any valuation disputes will need to be clearly described in the SPA.

3. Types of asset sales

Where the parties have elected to structure a transaction as an asset sale, they will need to make further structuring decisions with regard to what type of asset sale they will enter into. This is particularly the case where the primary asset in question is an upstream interest in a concession, production sharing agreement or other agreement with a host government (generally referred to herein as a 'concession'). The oil and gas industry has developed a number of asset sale structures that are largely unique to the industry. These include farmouts, earn-ins and asset swaps.

3.1 Farmout agreements

A farmout agreement is a particular type of SPA used to sell upstream interests. It is also most commonly used where a seller intends to sell down only part of its interest.

The distinguishing feature of a farmout agreement is that the consideration for the transfer of the interest is commonly linked to the costs incurred in respect of the concession entered into with the host government. The agreed consideration payable by the buyer to the seller could include a number of different components that reflect:

- the recovery of costs already expended on the concession;
- the deflection of costs that will need to be incurred in the future under the concession; and
- a pure profit element generated from the transfer of an interest in the concession.

These different elements can be identified separately in the farmout agreement, but are more often subsumed in the overall value of the consideration that is specified in the farmout agreement.

Under a farmout agreement, the consideration due from the buyer to the seller is not always the payment of a cash sum, as it is under a traditional asset SPA. Instead, the consideration can take the form of either:

- a work obligation – that is, an obligation by the buyer to carry out certain physical works that will benefit the seller and the interest that the buyer is acquiring; or
- a carry – that is, a commitment by the buyer to bear a predefined share of the seller's future costs associated with the concession.

Under a work obligation formulation, the buyer will assume responsibility in the farmout agreement to perform certain works in connection with the concession. Typically, the work obligation will be defined by reference to the underlying minimum work commitments to the host government originally assumed by the seller, as described in the concession. In most international farmout agreements, the buyer will not physically perform the work obligation itself because international oil and gas exploration is often complex and requires specialist technical knowledge (and because the buyer might not be the appointed operator). The works could be subcontracted to a suitably qualified third-party contractor, but the buyer will assume the responsibility for paying the seller's share of the costs of performing those works. Where the seller is the sole concession holder under a particular concession, this could be effected by the seller contracting the buyer to perform the works and the buyer subsequently subcontracting that obligation to the relevant third-party contractor. Where there are a number of concession holders under the relevant concession, the seller and the buyer will need to comply with the provisions set out in the JOA in respect of the subcontracting of works. Typically, the operator appointed under the JOA will enter into the subcontract with the relevant third-party contractor, but the farmout agreement will provide that the buyer will bear the seller's share of the costs incurred under that agreement and the interest transferred (or to be transferred) under the farmout agreement.

Under a carry arrangement, the buyer agrees to pay the seller's share of the costs associated with the performance of certain of the future work commitments under the concession and the JOA. In any such carry arrangement, a number of structural issues between the seller and the buyer must be addressed. These issues relate to:

- specific definition of the costs to be incurred;
- the extent of the carry offered by the buyer to the seller (including a possible cap on the intended carry costs); and
- whether any of the carried costs that are unspent should still accrue to the seller or should remain with the buyer.

The essential issue to consider in respect of any carried costs interest under a farmout agreement is whether all or part of the carried costs paid by the buyer are later repayable (from the proceeds of sale of produced quantities of petroleum) to the buyer by the seller. This will be a matter for negotiation between the seller and the buyer. If the carried costs are recoverable by the buyer, then the carry is popularly described as 'soft'; if the carried costs are not recoverable by the buyer, then the carry is described as 'hard'. A hard carry is akin to a further element of consideration payable by the buyer (which ordinarily would not be refundable by the seller), whereas a soft carry is akin to a form of loan by the buyer to the seller (which ordinarily would be refundable by the seller).

3.2 Earn-in agreements

The conventional approach under most SPAs is for the agreement to provide that the sale interest is transferred from the seller to the buyer at the same time as, or prior to, either the performance of works or the payment of the consideration by the buyer.

Where the consideration payable by the buyer is deferred, such that the seller transfers the interest to the buyer first, the seller will be exposed to the additional risk that the buyer might subsequently fail to perform its obligations in respect of the consideration payable for the interest. This could occur:

- under an asset SPA where the cash consideration is deferred or is contingent on the occurrence of a subsequent event; or
- under a farmout agreement where the consideration is structured as a work obligation or a carry arrangement.

The agreement will therefore typically contain provisions that establish an obligation on the buyer to reassign the interest to the seller in such circumstances. The details of how and when the reassignment of the interest will be effected will need to be clearly set out. Reassignments are often difficult to achieve for a number of reasons. They typically take place when a deal has gone sour and one or more of the parties involved are uncooperative or disincentivised to devote the time and resources needed to unwind the transaction. Furthermore, a reassignment of an interest will typically require further government and other third-party consents, which can prove difficult and time consuming to obtain.

An alternative structuring technique is therefore the 'earn-in'. Under this construction, a buyer is obliged to complete the work obligation or make payment and only then, once the buyer has 'earned' the interest, will the transfer of the relevant interest be effected between the seller and the buyer.

The earn-in structure holds significant appeal for a seller as it mitigates the risk of a buyer's non-performance or unsatisfactory performance. A default by the buyer in respect of its obligations under the SPA will not require any unwinding of the transaction, as the transfer of the interest is conditioned upon the buyer first performing its obligations. Absent proper performance by the buyer, there will be no transfer.

From the buyer's perspective, the earn-in structure carries more risk. The buyer will expect that once it has performed its obligations under the SPA, it will be rewarded by the transfer to it of the agreed interest. It is therefore essential to understand whether the obligations under the SPA have been performed, as a condition precedent to such reward becoming effective. In this context, the distinction under English law between entire and divisible contracts becomes important.

A contract can be described as 'entire' when the complete performance by one party of the entirety of its obligations under the contract is necessary as a condition precedent to the obligations of the other contracting party. The SPA will be an entire contract where the earned interest does not pass from the seller to the buyer until the entirety of the work obligation has been fully completed in accordance with the terms of the SPA. Performance of the contract is therefore strict and the court has no power to apportion the consideration, such that a partial payment and/or a partial transfer of an interest could be ordered.

By contrast, a 'divisible contract' is one that is separable into distinct parts, such that different elements of the overall consideration are attributable to different parts of the contract, and performance of the contract will be measured by reference to individual performance of the individual contract parts as distinct obligations. In a truly divisible contract, the party obliged to make payment will make payment in response to the performance of each divisible part of the overall contract that has been properly rendered, independent of the performance of the other parts of the contract. In the context of the SPA, the buyer could earn a part interest through part performance of the work obligation.

The concept of an entire obligation is rarely recognised by the express terms of the SPA, so careful interpretation of the contract becomes necessary in order to establish the true nature of the obligation. This could lead to some uncertainty of outcome. In the interest of certainty, therefore, a contract that is intended to recite an entire obligation, such as the SPA, should be careful to exclude expressly the possibility that a party might seek to apply the doctrine of substantial performance in order to claim the benefits of a divisible contract.

3.3 Asset swap agreements

An asset swap structure is another alternative to a traditional sale and purchase arrangement. An asset swap involves the exchange of interests between the contracting parties, as mutual consideration.

Where a transaction is structured as an asset swap, there is no clear delineation between the seller and the buyer – each party will act as seller of its respective interest and as buyer of the other's interest. This mutuality of roles means that the asset swap agreement will need to address the giving of reciprocal warranties, representations and indemnities between the parties, and contain an appropriate mechanism for reconciling any claims arising in respect of an interest, possibly including an ability for the parties to net off their respective claims. It may also be that the exchanged interests are not equal in value, in which case additional cash payment may need to be factored into the completion mechanics of the transaction.

Another concern for both parties will be to ensure that completion of the overall transaction occurs simultaneously in respect of all the interests being exchanged. Where the asset swap is documented under one agreement, this can be achieved by reciting, among other things, all third-party consents as conditions to completion. Where the transaction is documented as two separate agreements, this could be achieved by making the completion of the transaction under one agreement conditional upon the completion of the transaction under the other agreement (and vice versa).

4. The sales process

The sales process for an oil and gas transaction follows the same basic sequence as sales of interests in other industries. It consists of a series of different phases of activity, undertaken by either or both of the seller and the buyer, which culminates in the completion of the sale and the transfer of the interest.

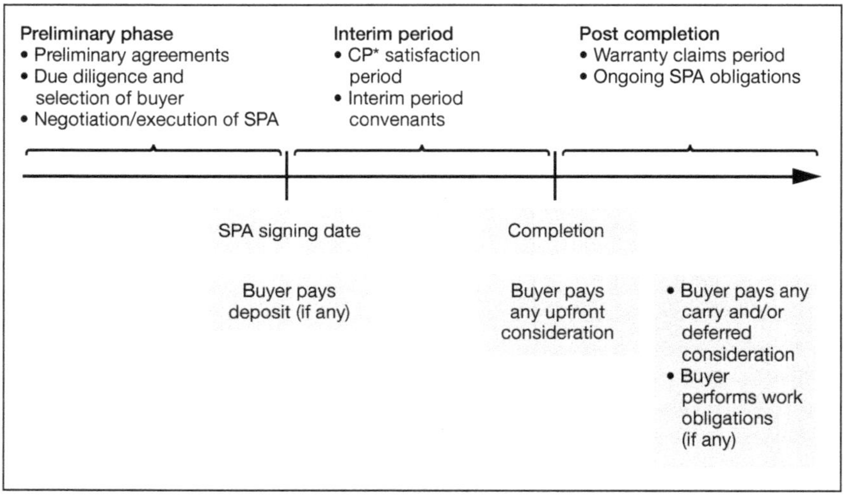

**CP = condition precedent*

The key milestones recorded in the SPA will be the signing date, the effective date and the completion date. The signing date is, as the name suggests, the date on which the SPA is signed by the parties and the obligations on the seller to sell and the buyer to buy the asset(s) or target company become legally effective, subject to any conditions precedent to completion. The effective date is a date nominated by the parties on which economic risk and benefit in the asset or target company being transferred will be deemed to have passed from the seller to the buyer, even though the physical and legal transfer of the asset or target company may occur at a later date (ie, the completion date).

The timing of the effective date will be a matter for negotiation between the parties, but will often be driven by the applicable reporting periods for the particular asset or target company such as the annual work programme and budget or the accounting period of the company. The completion date will occur only once all of the conditions precedent to completion (if there are any) have been satisfied or waived. The completion date is the date on which the asset or target company is legally transferred by the buyer to the seller and the buyer pays the consideration (or commences paying the consideration) to the seller.

4.1 Auction versus private sale

Where a proposed sale of an asset or target company is likely to generate interest from a number of potential buyers, the seller may choose to invite competing offers in an effort to achieve the best possible price and sale terms for that asset or target company. This is typically achieved by marketing the asset or target company through an auction process.

An auction process gives the seller significant control over the sale process. As well as creating competitive tension among prospective buyers, an auction process allows the seller to exert more control over the sale documentation and the sale timetable. From the buyer's perspective, the obverse is true.

However, an auction sale may not always be appropriate. An auction sale requires a more formal and detailed transaction timetable than a private sale, as demonstrated in the table below. This adds time and cost to the transaction for both parties.

The seller may have business or reputational reasons not to want to publicise its planned disposal of the asset or target company to a wide range of prospective buyers. This is particularly relevant where sensitive and confidential information has to be disclosed as part of the sales process. Also, if the planned auction is unsuccessful, the seller's ability to obtain the best price for the asset or target company later could be undermined more than if it had elected to sell the asset or target company by means of a private sale in the first instance. This possibility will need to be taken into account at the outset of the seller's analysis of the preferred route for its intended sales process.

Private sale	Auction sale
Preliminary information shared by the seller with an interested prospective buyer.	Identification of a list of prospective buyers by the seller or its corporate financial adviser and circulation of a 'teaser' (containing abbreviated information about the asset or target company) to those prospective buyers.
Signing of a confidentiality undertaking with the prospective buyer.	Signing of confidentiality undertakings with each of the interested prospective buyers.

continued on next page

Private sale	Auction sale
	Preparation and distribution of a detailed information memorandum that describes the asset or target company for sale by the seller to prospective buyers.
	Submission of indicative offers by a number of prospective buyers.
	Selection by the seller of a shortlist of prospective buyers to receive a process letter explaining the tender process.
The prospective buyer conducts its due diligence of the seller's data room.	Opening of a data room prepared by the seller (or the despatch of a seller-prepared due diligence report to the prospective buyers), often together with draft sale documentation.
The prospective buyer submits its offer. If the seller has previously provided draft sale documentation, the offer could include the buyer's comments to the draft sale documentation. If the seller has not previously provided draft sale documentation, then the buyer could include draft sale documentation with its offer.	Final offers (including comments to draft sale documentation) are received from prospective buyers.
The seller analyses the buyer's offer and the draft sale documentation.	The seller analyses final offers and comments to draft sale documentation submitted by the prospective buyers, ranks the offers and selects a preferred buyer.

continued on next page

Private sale	Auction sale
The seller and the buyer enter into an exclusivity agreement.	The seller and the preferred buyer enter into an exclusivity agreement.
Negotiation of the sale documents.	Negotiation of the sale documents.
Signing of the sale documents.	Signing of the sale documents.
Completion.	Completion.

4.2 Preliminary documentation

The SPA will be the focus for the negotiation and documentation of the sale of the asset or target company. However, the seller and the buyer will need to sign a number of preliminary documents before the negotiation of the SPA can commence. These will include confidentiality undertakings, process letters, offer letters and exclusivity agreements.

During the early stages of a transaction, when the transaction terms have not yet been ascertained, neither party will be keen to enter into contractually binding commitments on anything other than what it perceives to be a necessary protection of its essential commercial and legal interests. The preliminary documents entered into by the parties at the outset of a transaction are therefore generally expressed not to be legally binding on the parties other than in respect of one or two key provisions.

From the seller's perspective, the key concern will be to ensure the confidentiality of any information that it shares with the buyer in respect of the asset or target company to be sold. This is why one of the first documents that will be signed as part of any transaction is a confidentiality (or non-disclosure) agreement.

Under English law, there is a common law obligation of confidentiality. A person that has received information in confidence cannot take unfair advantage of it and must not make use of it to the prejudice of the person that gave the information without obtaining that person's consent. In order to bring a claim for breach of this general principle, the seller will need to demonstrate that the information disclosed was:

- confidential in nature;
- disclosed in circumstances which import an obligation of confidence; and
- used in an unauthorised manner.

However, the scope of the general law of confidentiality can be unclear – particularly regarding the issues of negligent or inadvertent disclosure. This is one of the reasons why most sellers will insist that the prospective buyer enters into a confidentiality agreement before any sensitive or commercially valuable information is disclosed to it. A properly drafted confidentiality agreement will clearly identify the information to be protected and impose a contractual obligation on the buyer not to disclose that information to third parties or to use that information for anything other than the purpose permitted by the seller. The seller will also need to ensure that any confidentiality obligations to which it is subject in respect of the interest are properly reflected in the confidentiality agreement. In the event of a buyer's breach of confidentiality, the seller will have an action for breach of contract without needing to prove the various elements of the common law claim.

One of the buyer's primary concerns could be to ensure that its negotiations with the seller remain exclusive until the transaction is signed. Exclusivity agreements (also known as 'lock-out', 'shut-out' or 'no-shop' agreements) prevent the seller from negotiating with, or soliciting offers from, other prospective buyers for a fixed period of time, allowing the buyer a period of exclusivity in which to negotiate and hopefully complete the proposed transaction.

An exclusivity agreement will be capable of being enforceable under English law only if it is drafted as a restriction on the seller's ability to negotiate with third parties. An agreement that compels the seller to negotiate with the buyer, even if a time limit is imposed on the negotiations, will be unenforceable for lack of certainty.[1] Even where an exclusivity agreement is drafted as a lock-out agreement, the buyer must be careful to ensure that the lock-out period is fixed and certain, and that there is valid consideration given by the buyer for the exclusivity obligations assumed by the seller.

4.3 Due diligence

The due diligence process is the means by which the prospective buyer gathers the information about an asset or target company that it needs to review in order to determine whether it wants to acquire that interest and on what terms. The buyer will review all the commercial, financial, legal and technical information about the asset or target company disclosed by the seller to identify any risks associated with the asset or target company or its sale. The buyer then uses the output from these investigations:

- to value (or verify the value of) the asset or target company; and
- to determine the appropriate transaction structure and what protections it needs to include in the SPA to avoid or mitigate its exposure to those risks.

---

1 *Walford v Miles* [1992] AC 128.

The buyer will also use the due diligence process to confirm that the asset or target company offered for sale offers the full value realisation that the buyer will require to realise future value from the interest. In an asset sale, the buyer will be concerned that the due diligence process properly identifies all assets and contracts necessary for the proper operation of the asset(s) once the sale has been completed. In a share sale, the buyer will be more concerned that the due diligence process identifies any unknown residual liabilities in the target company that the buyer could inherit. In each case, but especially in relation to a target company that has a long trading history, the cost of the due diligence can be disproportionate to the actual value ascribed to the interest. The buyer in this case may attempt to make up for this cost through a combination of indemnities and warranties from the seller to avoid prolonged and expensive due diligence or through an adjustment to, or retention from, the purchase price for the asset or target company to reflect any later-discovered impairment.

The completion of the buyer's due diligence will then lead to the buyer either withdrawing from the process or submitting an offer setting out the terms on which it is willing to acquire the asset or target company. That offer, if accepted by the seller, will then trigger the next stage of the sale process: the negotiation of the SPA.

4.4 Sale and purchase agreement negotiation

The form and content of the agreement that documents a sale will be broadly the same whether it is for an asset sale or a share sale. The SPA will contain provisions addressing the agreement to sell, the consideration payable for the asset or target company, the conditions precedent to completion, the interim period obligations, the completion obligations, the post-completion obligations, representations and warranties, indemnities, limitations on liability and boilerplate provisions. Each of these provisions will be addressed in detail in the following chapters of this book.

An SPA will usually be signed as a simple agreement rather than as a deed. However, a deed may be necessary in certain circumstances. For example, if an SPA includes provisions that are intended to create a guarantee (eg, where the buyer's parent is made a party to the SPA in order to guarantee the buyer's obligations under that agreement), then the execution of the SPA as a deed will remove any argument that the guarantee is invalid for lack of valuable consideration between the seller and the buyer's parent. Equally, if the SPA purports to create a power of attorney in favour of a party (which is common where the agreement contains interest reassignment provisions), then it must be executed as a deed in order to create a valid power of attorney under English law.[2]

2 Section 1(1) of the Powers of Attorney Act 1971, as amended by the Law of Property (Miscellaneous Provisions) Act 1989.

In most instances, the parties will proceed to complete the transaction contemplated under the SPA and the issue of terminating the agreement will not arise. However, where a party seeks to terminate an SPA (eg, because of a later failure to complete the transaction as intended), it should be mindful of the full range of termination rights available to it, both under contract and at law. In *Shell Egypt West Manzala GmbH v Dana Gas Egypt Ltd*,[3] Centurion (which was later bought by Dana) entered into a farmout agreement with Shell in respect of two concessions. Shell paid an initial tranche of cash consideration of $15 million on signature of the farmout agreement. The farmout agreement contained a number of conditions precedent to its effectiveness, as well as a contractual termination right for Shell if the transaction failed to complete within nine months of the signing date (with no right for Shell to recover the initial $15 million), and a right to rescind the agreement in the event of a breach of warranty by Centurion (whereupon Shell would have been entitled to recover the $15 million). In the following months, the relationship between Shell and Centurion deteriorated and disputes arose in respect of a number of alleged breaches by Centurion of the terms of the farmout agreement. Shell exercised its contractual right to terminate the farmout agreement because of the failure by the parties to complete within nine months of signing. The disputes in respect of Centurion's breach of the farmout agreement were referred to arbitration and Shell claimed damages from Centurion for the repudiatory breaches. The arbitral tribunal found that Centurion had committed various repudiatory breaches of the farmout agreement. The arbitral tribunal found, however, that under the farmout agreement and common law, Shell had a number of alternative methods of terminating the agreement. It could have exercised its contractual right to rescind the contract or its common law right to accept Centurion's repudiatory breach and treat that as grounds for terminating the contract, both of which would have resulted in Shell being entitled to receive back its $15 million initial payment. However, Shell elected to issue a notice of termination citing its contractual right to terminate for failure to complete by the agreed longstop date, and this was a termination right that expressly excluded its right to recover the $15 million. The arbitral tribunal therefore determined that Shell was not entitled to recover the initial tranche of consideration. This case demonstrates very clearly the interplay of differing termination rights arising under contract and at law, and the very different consequences that the exercise of one right over another can have.

4.5 Completion and post-completion

'Completion' is the point at which title to and risk in the asset or target

---

3 *Shell Egypt West Manzala GmbH v Dana Gas Egypt Ltd (formerly Centurion Petroleum Corp)* [2010] EWHC 465 (Comm).

company passes to the buyer. The SPA sets out the mechanics for completion and the various obligations and deliverables of the parties.

One of the key legal deliverables at completion is the signing of the documents that transfer legal title to the asset or target company being sold. The transfer documentation required for a share sale is more limited than that for an asset sale. The only transfer document that is usually necessary is the share transfer for the shares in the target company. Under an asset sale, the parties will need to enter into a separate transfer document for each asset being sold, the form of which will be dictated by the nature of the underlying asset.

The SPA will typically contain a number of schedules that set out, among other things, the form of the transfer agreements that will be entered into at completion. It is also not unusual for the schedules to set out the agreed forms of other commercial agreements that will be entered into only at completion, such as a JOA or an agreement on decommissioning liabilities. The SPA will often provide that the signing of such agreements "in substantially the form" set out in the schedules to the SPA is a condition precedent to the completion of the sale. In *Venture North Sea Gas Limited v Nuon Exploration & Production UK Limited*,[4] the parties entered into an SPA to sell a number of interests in UK petroleum production licences to Nuon. Nuon disputed the completion of the transaction and Venture brought a claim for specific performance against Nuon in respect of its obligation to complete. Nuon argued successfully that two JOAs signed in respect of two of the licence interests to be transferred as part of the transaction were not substantially in the form appended to the SPA. The High Court agreed and found that the condition precedent to the effectiveness of the sale had not been satisfied, with the consequences that Nuon was not obliged to complete the purchase of the entire package of licence interests from Venture. The case highlights the importance of ensuring that if any changes are made to completion documents, then they are made with the agreement of both parties. Further, it demonstrates the care that must be taken when multiple assets are sold under one SPA. In the *Venture* case, a more detailed severability clause may have allowed Venture to compel Nuon to complete on the licence interests that were not affected by the issues with the two JOAs.

5. Conclusion

When it comes to the sale and purchase of oil and gas interests, there is no one-size-fits-all solution. Different transaction structures, and different contractual constructions within the selected transaction documents, will be necessary to reflect the precise nuances of the intended transaction between the buyer and the seller.

This chapter remains the same as published in the previous edition.

4 *Venture North Sea Gas Limited v Nuon Exploration & Production UK Limited* [2010] EWHC 204 (Comm).

Consideration in oil and gas sale and purchase agreements

Olivier Chambord
Allison Soilihi
Morgan, Lewis & Bockius UK LLP

1. Introduction

Many of the issues regarding consideration that apply to agreements for the acquisition of assets or companies in various sectors will generally also apply to acquisitions in the oil and gas sector. This chapter is not intended to be a comprehensive study of such issues; rather, it seeks to address the specific issues that arise with respect to consideration in oil and gas share or asset purchase agreements for upstream transactions.

As in other sectors, in a share deal, the buyer purchases some or all of the seller's shares, thus acquiring the partial or total ownership of the targeted oil and gas company. In an asset deal, the buyer acquires only one or several oil and gas assets from the seller.

'Consideration' is what the buyer will pay to the seller in exchange for the company shares or assets being acquired. In oil and gas sale and purchase agreements (SPAs), consideration can take various forms, ranging from a simple cash consideration to an undertaking to carry out work obligations related to oil and gas assets (eg, encountered in farmout agreements – a type of acquisition structure specific to the upstream oil and gas industry).

This chapter only addresses consideration in the most common forms of dispositions in oil and gas SPAs – namely, in share acquisitions, asset acquisitions and farmin/farmout agreements. The chapter also addresses earn-in agreements and asset swaps.

2. Consideration in share deals

The components of the consideration will depend on the agreement of the parties, and the consideration provisions must of course be adapted to reflect the specific requirements of each transaction.

2.1 Consideration and adjustments at completion

A buyer and seller may agree in an SPA on an initial amount of base consideration to be paid at completion of the transaction. This base value can, for instance, be set on a 'net cash/net debt' basis: estimated levels of the working capital of the company and its levels of net debt at completion.

The buyer and seller may also agree to adjust the initial base consideration based on completion accounts that will be produced to establish the actual working capital and actual net debt at completion. The adjustment mechanism will seek to correct discrepancies between the assessments and assumptions that led to the setting of the initial consideration on the one hand, and the reality of the working capital and net debt at completion on the other. In this mechanism, if the working capital or net debt is different from the initial estimates, there will be an adjustment payment made by one party to the other. The working capital adjustment is usually crucial in oil and gas transactions because of the importance of petroleum inventories.

The parties may also wish to include an 'earn-out' component as part of the consideration, whereby the initial consideration paid at completion will be supplemented by one or several deferred payments contingent on the target's business or assets performance during an agreed period following completion of the transaction. For instance, in the oil and gas sector, the payment of an earn-out can typically be contingent on a number of criteria, in combination or not, such as oil and gas prices, geological factors and operational performance of the target's assets.

For instance, earn-out provisions based on oil and gas prices will generally provide that a contingent payment is payable if certain price metrics have been satisfied, based on recognised and published industry benchmarks.

For instance, operational performance earn-outs can be based on different metrics such as increases in levels of production of given deposits, wells or fields; reductions in costs levels from agreed baselines; and performances compared against authorisations for expenditure. Control over operations will need to be carefully considered for this type of earn-out. The buyer will control the business and assets after completion, while the seller's contingent payment under the earn-out provisions will depend on such operations controlled by the buyer. The parties will thus need to strike the right balance in post-completion covenants to provide the seller with reasonable oversight over operations, while providing the buyer with reasonable discretion over operations. The use of expert determination mechanisms can also be helpful to defuse potential disputes on these types of operational earn-outs.

Finally, other types of earn-outs can be based on geological characteristics of assets typically in exploration or appraisal phases. In these cases, contingent payments can depend on a variety of technical factors, such as the amount of hydrocarbons in place or the recoverable hydrocarbon reserves.

2.2 Fixed consideration – the 'locked-box' mechanism

As an alternative to the transaction structure mentioned above, in what has become known as a 'locked-box' transaction, the purchase price will typically be fixed based on the valuation of the target as reflected in a set of accounts prepared at a given 'effective date' prior to completion. These can be the management accounts or another set of accounts prepared specifically for the purposes of the valuation.

In sum, this consideration will usually be based on a historical balance sheet at the 'effective date' and on the working capital, debt and cash at such date. No completion accounts will be required to be produced at or after completion, and the consideration will not be adjusted at or after completion based on any such completion accounts. To avoid any leakage of value between the effective date and the date of completion, the parties will usually agree on a number of 'anti-leakage' provisions in the SPA with respect to this interim period – such as restrictive covenants to avoid increasing debt, incurring capital expenditure or declaring and paying dividends without the prior consent of the buyer. Undertakings and warranties, usually supported by an indemnity to pay an amount equal to any leakage, can also provide protection from leakage of value.

Arguably, locked-box mechanisms are well suited to transactions involving oil and gas businesses, as such mechanisms enable the parties to set value on an effective date that can be de-correlated from the date of completion and avoid the production of completion accounts. In particular, setting value and consideration on an effective date that makes sense from the standpoint of the business being acquired can in some instances be simpler than, and preferable to, the mechanisms of setting value and consideration at the completion date (with the related adjustment mechanisms). For instance, this type of mechanism arguably allows the parties to set the effective date to coincide with key dates of the acquired business – such as the end of a works programme or cash calls – which thus enables the parties to allocate costs and income more easily in relation to the business of the target.

3. Consideration in asset deals

This section addresses the forms of consideration that are specific to asset purchase agreements and farmout agreements. It also considers the types of consideration encountered in transfers of assets where the buyer is either a state or a national hydrocarbons company. Lastly, it covers earn-in agreements and asset swaps.

3.1 Consideration in an oil and gas asset purchase agreement

The consideration clause in an asset purchase agreement may range from a single sentence mentioning the amount that the seller must pay in consideration for the transfer of the assets to more complex price structures where the parties agree additional components to be taken into account when calculating the amount that the seller will actually pay for the assets.

A sample clause of consideration in an asset purchase agreement is as follows:

In consideration of the sale and transfer of the Asset by the Seller to the Purchaser, the Purchaser shall pay to the Seller the sum of [amount in words] Dollars (US$ [amount in figures]) (the "Consideration"), such amount to be paid to the Seller's Account at Completion in accordance with Clause [reference to clause dealing with payment terms and conditions].

The amount of cash to be paid by the buyer (or base price) is provided in fairly simple terms. The parties will usually insert an additional paragraph, or a different clause, in the asset purchase agreement to deal with the payment terms and conditions. In particular, the parties will include the date of payment (usually, at completion) and the means of payment (usually, a transfer in immediately available cleared funds to the seller's designated account).

Where signing and completion occur at different times, the buyer may be required to pay a deposit equal to an agreed portion of the base purchase price to an escrow account. When completion of the transaction takes place, the deposit can then be applied towards the purchase price. If, on the other hand, the SPA is terminated, the deposit can be returned to the buyer or retained by the seller depending on events to be set out in the SPA (eg, in case of breach by the buyer).

A sample clause of payment of a deposit to escrow is provided in the 2020 Association of International Petroleum Negotiators (AIPN) Model Form International Asset Sale and Purchase Agreement in Article 4.3:

ALTERNATIVE #1

4.3 Payment of Deposit to Escrow

4.3.1 On the Signature Date, Buyer shall pay to the Escrow Agent by wire transfer of immediately available funds to the Escrow Account an amount equal to [•] US Dollars (US$ [•]) (the "Deposit").

4.3.2 If Completion does not occur by the Longstop Date:

(a) as a result of breach by Buyer of its obligations set out in Article 3, this Article 4 or Article 5.1, then the Parties shall execute the Escrow Certificate and instruct the Escrow Agent to pay the Deposit (including any interest accrued thereon) to Seller, without prejudice to Seller's other rights and remedies as may be available under this Agreement; or

(b) other than as a result of breach by Buyer of its obligations set out in Article 3, this Article 4 or Article 5.1, then the Parties shall execute the Escrow Certificate and instruct the Escrow Agent to pay the Deposit (including any interest accrued thereon) to Buyer.

4.3.3 If Completion does occur, then the Parties will instruct the Escrow Agent to release the Deposit to Seller in accordance with Article 5.1.2(d).

Another option is proposed in the AIPN model form whereby the deposit is paid not to an escrow account, but to the seller:

ALTERNATIVE #2

4.3 Payment of Deposit to Seller

4.3.1 On the Signature Date, Buyer shall pay to Seller by wire transfer of immediately available funds to Seller's Account an amount equal to [•] US Dollars (US$ [•]) (the "Deposit").

4.3.2 If Completion does not occur by the Longstop Date:

(a) as a result of breach by Buyer of its obligations set out in Article 3, this Article 4 or Article 5.1, then Seller shall retain the Deposit (including any interest accrued thereon); or

(b) other than as a result of breach by Buyer of its obligations set out in Article 3, this Article 4 or Article 5.1, then Seller shall pay an amount equal to the Deposit (including any interest accrued thereon at the Agreed Rate) to Buyer.

The consideration clause may also be supplemented with a contingent component of consideration where payment of a bonus is provided, depending, for instance, on the level of approved reserves in the field, as in the example below:

The Purchaser shall:

(a) pay and be responsible for any and all post-effective date costs;

(b) pay to the Seller an additional amount equal to [amount in words] Dollars (US$ [amount in figures]) for each additional [number of barrels per cubic feet] bcf of approved reserves above [number of barrels per cubic feet] bcf of approved reserves; provided, however, that no bonus payment shall be payable under this clause, unless the amount of approved reserves is equal to or exceeds [number of barrels per cubic feet] bcf of approved reserves.

A separate bonus payment shall be calculated for each deposit in the contract perimeter and more than one bonus payment may be payable by the Purchaser.

Here, an additional amount (or bonus) is to be paid by the buyer if the approved reserves are above a certain threshold set in the asset purchase agreement. The sample clause can be structured to allow for different fields to be treated differently, if required. For instance, the parties may consider setting different volume thresholds to trigger the bonus (or bonuses) depending on the reserves expectations of each field or deposit, as the prospects may be completely different for each field or deposit. In addition, the clause can be structured to provide that the bonus increases depending on the level of the approved reserves.

Another mechanism that may affect the base purchase price is the application of an interest rate to be paid by the buyer. Such an interest rate is meant to take into account the period during which the buyer will have acquired the benefit of the assets, between the effective date on which the transferred assets are valued and the completion date. It is not unusual in oil and gas transfers for a period of time, longer than in other M&A transactions, to elapse between the signing date (or the date on which the assets are valued) and the completion date. This can be explained in particular by the requirement that the governmental authorities of the country in which the transferred assets are located approve the transfer. The parties should ensure that such approval is a condition precedent to the transfer. Depending on the criteria imposed in a given jurisdiction to obtain such approval, completion of the transaction may thus be delayed and the parties may consider providing that interest will apply on the base purchase price in the interim period. The parties should make sure that:

- the interest rate is compatible with the usury rules applicable in the relevant country; or
- they include a fall-back referring to the highest interest rate permitted in said jurisdiction, in order to comply with such rate.

As in the case of share deals, other components may be added or deducted from the base price, and adjustments may be provided to take into account the potential variation of the value of the transferred asset between signing and completion of the transaction.

For example, in the 2020 AIPN Model Form International Asset Sale and Purchase Agreement, the consideration is as follows:

4.1 Consideration

4.1.1 The "Consideration" shall be an amount equal to the sum of:

(a) [the Deposit; plus]

(b) the Completion Payment; plus or minus

(c) the Adjustment Amount.

4.1.2 Buyer will pay the Consideration to Seller in the manner described in this Article 4 and in Article 5.

OPTIONAL PROVISION

4.1.3 The Consideration will be [inclusive][exclusive] of VAT.

The 'completion payment' is defined as an amount in US dollars that can then be adjusted upwards or downwards by an 'adjustment amount' that can include several variables, such as:

- the working capital – the AIPN model form provides for principles to determine the working capital adjustment in Exhibit 8 of the model form, but the working capital can be determined in a simpler way where this is appropriate;
- billings depending on the cash calls paid by the seller during the interim period between signing and completion;
- non-petroleum revenues received by the seller during that same interim period;
- hydrocarbons sales; and
- other expenditures incurred or paid by the seller.

An illustration is set out in Article 4.4 of the AIPN model form as follows:

4.4 *Adjustment Amount*

4.4.1 *The "Adjustment Amount" shall be an amount calculated as follows:*

Adjustment Amount = A plus B minus C minus D plus E [plus / minus F] where:

A = the Working Capital Adjustment, which may be expressed as a positive or negative number;

B = the Billings Adjustment, which may be expressed as a positive or negative number;

C = the NPR Adjustment;

D = the Hydrocarbon Sales Adjustment;

E = the Interim Period Adjustment; and

F = [include any other possible adjustment, e.g. interest to put the parties in the position they would have been had the Consideration been paid on the Effective Date]

4.4.2 *No item taken into account in calculating any element of the Adjustment Amount shall be taken into account in calculating any other element of the Adjustment Amount so as to result in a Party making or receiving payment twice in respect thereof.*

4.5 *Working Capital Adjustment*

The "Working Capital Adjustment", which if positive shall increase the Consideration and if negative shall reduce the Consideration, shall be the amount calculated in respect of each of the categories listed in Exhibit 8 on the Effective Date by reference to the statements provided by the [relevant] Operator and otherwise in accordance with Exhibit 8.

4.6 *Billings Adjustment*

The "Billings Adjustment", which if positive shall increase the Consideration and if negative shall reduce the Consideration, shall be the net sum of all cash calls and invoices paid in respect of the Purchase Interest by Seller during the Interim Period and that are for joint venture billings relating to the period after the Effective Date pursuant to the Documents, less all credits, receipts and reimbursements received by or credited to Seller in respect of the Purchase Interest during the Interim Period in respect of recoveries related to cash calls, billing invoices, claims, demands or statements relating to the period after the Effective Date, pursuant to the Documents.

4.7 *NPR Adjustment*

The "NPR Adjustment", with respect to "non-petroleum revenue", which shall decrease the Consideration, shall be the sum of all income and other receipts received by Seller (other than those dealt with by the Hydrocarbon Sales Adjustment) in respect of the Purchase Interest during the Interim Period, provided that any such income or receipt that relates to any period prior to the Effective Date and that has not been taken into account in the

Working Capital Adjustment shall inure to the benefit of Seller.

4.8 *Hydrocarbon Sales Adjustment*

4.8.1 *The "Hydrocarbon Sales Adjustment", which shall decrease the Consideration, shall be a sum calculated in respect of the sale and/or supply of Hydrocarbons from and in relation to the Purchase Interest during the Interim Period.*

4.8.2 *The Parties agree that no adjustment shall be made at Completion as part of the Hydrocarbon Sales Adjustment in respect of any invoices under or in connection with any contract for the sale or supply of Hydrocarbons where amounts owed under such invoices have not been received by or credited to Seller prior to the Completion Date. Instead, the Parties agree that [promptly following each receipt by or crediting to Seller of any such amounts after Completion, Seller shall pay Buyer an amount equal to such amounts and that pending such payment Seller will hold such amounts in trust for Buyer][amounts under such invoices will be taken into account in the Final Completion Statement].*

4.9 *Interim Period Adjustment*

The "Interim Period Adjustment", which shall increase the Consideration, shall be the sum of all expenditure incurred or paid in respect of the Purchase Interest by Seller during the Interim Period including [demurrage,] brokers' fees, the time written costs of Seller's personnel in respect of the management of the Purchase Interest, and all other costs and expenses incurred or paid by Seller in respect of the Purchase Interest (other than fees of professional advisers engaged in relation to the matters referred to herein), [in each case solely to the extent incurred for or chargeable to the joint account under the JOA (and in each case excluding, for the avoidance of any doubt, any and all internal time-written charges that would not be chargeable to co-venturers as aforesaid)] which are in respect of the Interim Period but excluding any such expenditure forming part of the Billings Adjustment."

The 'adjustment amount' is then determined on the basis of completion statements that the seller provides the buyer with prior to the completion date in the case of the preliminary completion statement and after completion in the case of the final completion statement. The completion statement clause of the AIPN model form is supplemented by a mechanism to resolve disagreements in connection with the statement:

4.10 *Preliminary Completion Statement*

4.10.1 *No later than [[•])] Business Days prior to the Completion Date, Seller shall provide Buyer with a written statement in the format set out in Exhibit 9 of its good faith estimate of the Adjustment Amount based on the information available to Seller at that time (such statement, the "Preliminary Completion Statement," and such estimated Adjustment*

Amount, the "Preliminary Adjustment Amount"), together with supporting information as required by Article 4.13.1.

4.10.2 *If the Preliminary Adjustment Amount is positive, then such amount shall be added to the Completion Payment payable by Buyer to Seller at Completion.*

4.10.3 *If the Preliminary Adjustment Amount is negative, then such amount shall be subtracted from the Completion Payment payable by Buyer to Seller at Completion.*

4.11 *Final Completion Statement*

4.11.1 *Within [[•] ([•])] Business Days after Completion, [Buyer] [Seller] shall prepare and deliver to [Buyer] [Seller] a statement in the format set out in Exhibit 9 of its good faith determination of:*

(a) the Adjustment Amount; and

(b) any difference between the Adjustment Amount as determined by [Buyer] [Seller] in good faith and the Preliminary Adjustment Amount,

(such statement, the "Final Completion Statement"), together with supporting information as required by Article 4.13.2.

4.11.2 *Within [[•]] Business Days of receipt by [Buyer] [Seller] of the Final Completion Statement, [Buyer] [Seller] shall Notify [Buyer] [Seller] whether it agrees with the Final Completion Statement. In the event of any disagreement as to the Final Completion Statement, such Notice (the "Dispute Notice") shall specify in reasonable detail each item in dispute and any adjustments that [Buyer] [Seller] considers should be made to the Final Completion Statement and, accordingly, to [Buyer] [Seller]'s proposed Adjustment Amount.*

4.11.3 *The Parties shall, during the period of [[•]] Business Days commencing on the date of service of the Dispute Notice, seek in good faith to reach agreement on the disputed items in the Final Completion Statement. If, at the end of such [[•]] Business Day period, the disputed items are:*

(a) resolved by the Parties in writing, then the Final Completion Statement and the Adjustment Amount set out in such Final Completion Statement (in each case, as revised as necessary to reflect the Parties' agreement) will be final and binding on the Parties with effect from the date of their agreement; or

(b) not resolved by the Parties in writing, at any time following the expiry of such [[•]] Business Day period, then either Party may, by delivery of Notice to the other Party, require the disputed items to be submitted to a neutral accountant (the "Accounting Referee") for review and final binding resolution. The Accounting Referee shall be a certified public accountant mutually selected by the Parties who is an employee or partner of a recognized independent public accounting firm (or if such Person is unable or unwilling to serve or if the Parties cannot agree, then such Person

selected by the [•] who is an employee or partner of a recognized independent public accounting firm with expertise and experience in oil and gas accounting in the [jurisdiction]) and the Accounting Referee's determination of the Final Completion Statement, and the Adjustment Amount set out in such Final Completion Statement, shall be final and binding on the Parties (except in the case of fraud or manifest error).

Finally, if the adjustment amount anticipated in the preliminary completion statement before completion is greater or lesser than the actual adjustment amount reflected in the final completion statement, the difference will have to be paid by the buyer to the seller, or vice versa, as the case may be:

4.12 Reconciliation Payment

4.12.1 If the Adjustment Amount (as reflected in the Final Completion Statement as agreed by the Parties or determined by the Accounting Referee) is greater than the Preliminary Adjustment Amount, then the difference will be payable by Buyer to Seller.

4.12.2 If the Adjustment Amount (as reflected in the Final Completion Statement as agreed by the Parties or determined by the Accounting Referee) is less than the Preliminary Adjustment Amount, then the difference will be payable by Seller to Buyer.

4.12.3 Any amount payable by Buyer or Seller pursuant to Article 4.12.1 or 4.12.2 will be a "Reconciliation Payment".

4.12.4 Any Reconciliation Payment will:

(a) be paid by wire transfer of immediately available funds to Seller's Account or Buyer's Account (as applicable) within [five (5)] Business Days following the date the Final Completion Statement was either agreed by the Parties or determined by the Accounting Referee [; and

(b) shall include interest at the Agreed Interest Rate from and including the Completion Date through and including the date upon which full and final payment is made under this Article 4.12].

The parties will also need to determine whether the insertion of a tax adjustment is desirable.

3.2 Consideration in a farmout agreement

A farmout is a form of asset acquisition specific to the upstream oil and gas industry. A farmout agreement is "a promise to perform work (or a combination of the performance of work and payment of cash) to earn a participating interest in a host government agreement".[1]

The farmor (ie, the seller) thus transfers an interest to the farmee (ie, the

1 "Purchase and Sales and Participation (Farmout) Agreements", The Core Course on International Oil and Gas Law, Rocky Mountain Mineral Law Foundation, 10–14 March 2014, Istanbul.

buyer); but unlike in traditional SPAs, the consideration in a farmout agreement consists of work to be performed by the farmee or a combination of work to be performed and cash to be paid by the farmee.

Because of the particular nature of the consideration involving the carrying out of work, farmout agreements tend to be encountered before the production phase of upstream assets – that is, during the exploration, appraisal or development phases.

Some of the goals that a farmor seeks to achieve through a farmout agreement may be:

- to share financial costs;
- to benefit from the technical knowledge and skills of the farmee; or
- to reduce and share risks associated with the assets.

For the farmee, the farmout agreement may be an opportunity to access oil and gas fields in a specific country, while reducing the risks and costs associated with the assets, as they will be shared with the farmor.

The first section below addresses consideration in cash and 'drill to earn' clauses in the AIPN 2019 Model International Farmout Agreement; the second section deals with other examples of components that the parties may wish to include in the consideration clause in a farmout agreement.

(a) Consideration in the AIPN 2019 Model International Farmout Agreement

There are several model forms of farmout agreement drafted by various oil and gas organisations. The AIPN 2019 Model International Farmout Agreement, for example, is commonly used as a precedent in the oil and gas industry internationally.

Article 3 of the AIPN model form relating to consideration contemplates that the consideration will be comprised of an optional payment obligation in cash and a work programme. The AIPN committee that prepared the model form recognised that the variations for consideration were virtually limitless. In the event that the parties use a model form – whether from the AIPN or another source – they should adapt the consideration clause to reflect their intent and the specifics of their transaction.

Cash consideration: The model clause proposed in the AIPN model form in respect of optional cash consideration is provided below:

3.1 Payment Obligations

As consideration for the Transfer of the Farmout Interests hereunder, Farmee shall fulfil the following obligations (the "Consideration"):

3.1.1 Payment Obligation(s). Farmee shall pay the following amounts by wire transfer in immediately available funds into a bank account designated in writing by Farmor:

OPTIONAL PROVISIONS — SELECT ALL DESIRED PROVISIONS

OPTION #1 — Reimbursement of Past Cost

(a) pay Farmor [•] USD (US$[•]) [on / within [•] Business Days of the Signature Date] / [on the Completion Date], [as]/[representing] reimbursement of the Costs prior to the Signature Date. [It is understood that this amount shall not be subject to audit under this Agreement or the JOA.] [Drafting Note: The last sentence of Article 3.1.1(a) should be considered/deleted if the audit right set out in Article 3.7 is selected.]

OPTION #2 — Retained Interest, Cash Call Promote

(b) pay [Operator] / [Farmor] [within [•] Business Days of the receipt of a copy of the cash call from Farmor] / [on the Completion Date], the amount pursuant to cash calls under the JOA that are made from the Signature Date until the Completion Date to the credit of Retained Interests up to the amount of [•] USD (US$[•]) [in respect of the Work Obligation to be performed in accordance with Article 3.1.2.]

OPTION #3 — Premium Payment

(c) pay Farmor [•] USD (US$[•]) [on / within [•] Business Days of the Signature Date] / [on the Completion Date] as a premium for the acquisition of the Farmout Interests.]

The cash consideration provided in the AIPN model form thus includes three optional components that can be used individually or in combination.

The first is a share of past costs incurred by the farmor prior to the signature date of the farmout agreement. The parties can agree that the amount to be paid will reflect the participating interest that the farmee acquires under the farmout agreement. The farmee can optionally be granted a right to audit (with an adjustment), before or after completion, the accounts where the past costs were recorded in accordance with the audit right usually provided in the accounting procedure to the applicable joint operating agreement (JOA).[2] For instance, in the AIPN model form of accounting procedure attached to the JOA, this audit right is set out in Article 1.8. The amount may otherwise be fixed and not subject to audit, irrespective of whether these costs represent the farmee's actual share of past costs.

The second optional component is a share of the costs between the signature date and the completion date, as a promote[3] for the farmor's retained interests in the project. The model clause is drafted so that the amount to be paid is capped at an agreed amount, and that payment occurs either when cash calls for these costs are issued by the operator or in one instalment at completion.

---

2 Optional Article 3.7 of the AIPN Model Form Farmout Agreement.

3 Under a promote, sometimes also called a carried interest, the farmee agrees to pay for a portion of the costs accruing to the farmor's retained interest.

The last optional component is a premium payment in an agreed amount to be paid at signing (or within a number of business days therefrom) or at completion. This premium is an *ad hoc* payment which is not intended to cover past costs or project operations in the same way as the amounts contemplated in the first two components above.

Instead of, or in addition to, the cash consideration mentioned above, a drill to earn consideration can be provided. It consists of the undertaking by the farmee to carry out certain work obligations, have them carried out or pay for its share of costs (and optionally for the farmor's share of costs attributable to its retained interest) under the JOA relating to such work obligations, as set out in the consideration clause to earn the agreed participating interest (see Article 3.1.2 of the sample clause below).

Drill to earn clause: The model clause proposed in the 2019 AIPN model form in respect of drill to earn consideration is as follows:

3.1.2 Work Obligations. [In addition to the payment(s) to be made in accordance with Article 3.1.1,] [Farmee shall perform or shall cause to be performed and] / [Farmee shall pay] [•] percent ([•]%) of all Costs under the JOA and the Contract attributable to [the Farmout Interests] / [the Farmout Interests and the Retained Interest] until the following work is completed in the Contact Area ("Work Obligation"):

(a) Subject to Article 3.2.1(a), the acquisition and processing of [[•] kilometres of 2D] [or] [[•] square kilometres of 3D] seismic data in the Contract Area [or both], in accordance with the specifications set forth in Exhibit 9 (the "Seismic Commitment"); and

(b) Subject to Article 3.2.1(b), the drilling, logging, testing, and as applicable, the completion or plugging and abandonment of [an] [•] Exploration Well(s) sufficient to test the Target Zone, or to a depth of [•], whichever is first achieved, in accordance with the specifications set forth in Exhibit 8 (the "Well Commitment").

(c) The Work Obligation shall commence no later than [•] Days after the [Signature] / [Completion] Date.

(d) Farmee's payment obligation under this Article 3.1.2 commences at the Signature Date and all payments shall be made in accordance with Article 2.4.2.

[Drafting Note: Insert any other work to be performed in connection with the Transfer of the Farmout Interests.]

OPTIONAL PROVISION

3.2 Satisfaction

3.2.1 The obligations under Articles 3.1.2(a) and 3.1.2(b), as applicable, shall be deemed satisfied in the following circumstances:

(a) The Work Obligation under Article 3.1.2(a) shall be deemed to be

satisfied if Farmee has spent an aggregate amount of [•] USD (US$[•]) pursuant to Article 3.1.2(a) for the Seismic Commitment. Following such satisfaction, each Party shall pay its respective Participating Interest share of the costs and expenses for the remaining Seismic Commitment.

(b) The Work Obligation under Article 3.1.2(b) shall be deemed to be satisfied if (i) Farmee has spent an aggregate amount of [•] USD (US$[•]) pursuant to Article 3.1.2(b) for the Well Commitment or, (ii) without regard to depth, the Government accepts the Well drilled hereunder as sufficient to satisfy the Well Commitment(s) under the Contract. Following such satisfaction, each Party shall pay its respective Participating Interest share of the costs and expenses for any remaining Well Commitment.

3.2.2 Subject to Article 3.2.1, if Farmee is performing the Work Obligation, then such Work Obligation must be performed in accordance with good international petroleum industry standards [to the reasonable satisfaction of Farmor].

OPTIONAL PROVISION

3.3 Insurmountable Difficulties

If [Farmee / Operator / Farmor] (i) encounters impenetrable substances, basement, or commercial quantities of oil and gas at a lesser depth or (ii) is forced to abandon a well because of difficulties that are insurmountable when employing modern drilling technology in conformity with sound, cost effective practices generally accepted in the international petroleum industry, the Well Commitment under Article 3.1.2(b) will be deemed to be satisfied if [either of the conditions of Article 3.2.1(b) are satisfied, or if] Farmee promptly commences the drilling of another Well.]

The work obligations to be carried out (or paid for) under the drill to earn clause are often a share of the work programme set out in the host government agreement and the related JOA. These obligations can consist of seismic commitments (ie, the acquisition and processing of 2D and/ or 3D seismic data), or of well commitments (eg, drilling, testing, plugging of wells). If the validity period of the licence granted under the host government agreement is divided into several periods (eg, an initial period and one or several renewal periods), the host government agreement may provide different work programmes for each of these periods.

The model form also provides in Article 3.2 the cases in which the work programme set out in Article 3.1.2 is deemed completed, either by way of a minimum expenditure by the farmee or where the government accepts that the well drilled by the farmee under the drill to earn clause is sufficient to satisfy the requirements under the host government contract.

The parties may also wish to address the situation where the farmee encounters technical difficulties when carrying out the work programme set out in Article 3.1.2 relating to wells. In the optional Article 3.3 above, in the event that it is impossible to perform the work obligations because of impenetrable substances, or if it would not be sound and cost effective to do so by reference to the standards generally accepted in the industry, the work programme may be deemed completed if the farmee commences to drill a new well or if either of the conditions set out in Article 3.2.1(b) mentioned above is satisfied.

The fulfilment of the work programme set out in the drill to earn clause does not exempt the farmee from contributing its share of the costs incurred under the host government agreement and the related JOA, after completion of the work programme provided in Article 3.1.2. The farmee will thus have to contribute its share of the related future cash calls. A sample clause is provided in Article 3.6 of the AIPN model form:

3.6 Future Cash Calls

[After completion of the Work Obligations] / [From the Completion Date], and in accordance with Article 6.3.2, Farmee shall pay the Farmout Interests' share of all Costs incurred under the Contract and the JOA.

If the farmee fails to pay any amount or to complete its work obligations in accordance with the farmout agreement, it will be in default. In such case, the farmout agreement can include a reassignment provision whereby, following a cure period, the farmee will have to transfer back the farmout interests to the farmor for a nominal value. An example of such a mechanism is provided below:

If the Farmee fails to make any of its payment obligations as specified in Article [reference to the clause dealing with the farmee's payment obligations] when due in accordance with the provisions of this Agreement and the JOA and does not remedy any such failure within the time periods provided by the JOA, the Farmee shall immediately upon the Farmor's written request, execute and deliver to the Farmor an assignment substantially in the form of Annex [reference to annex setting out a form of the assignment and assumption agreement], mutatis mutandis, reassigning to the Farmor the Farmee's entire Participating Interest.

In the example clause above, the farmout agreement includes a form of the assignment and assumption agreement to be entered into by the parties in the event that the farmee is in breach of its payment obligations and does not cure its default by a certain date. The attachment of such a form agreement will avoid potentially lengthy and difficult negotiations of an assignment agreement at a time when the relationship between the parties may have become tense because of the farmee's default.

The AIPN model form includes additional optional provisions addressing cost recovery and tax deductibility, transfer taxes, accounting and adjustments, information in support of interim costs statements, and transfer costs and fees.

(b) *Other possible components where the farmee is the operator in connection with the drill to earn obligation*

Another illustration of the consideration clause combining cash consideration and completion of an agreed work programme (the drill to earn obligation) is as follows:

1. Work Program

1.1 In consideration for the assignment in accordance with this Agreement, commencing on the completion date, Farmee agrees to:

(a) finance [percentage in words] percent ([percentage in figures]%) of the cost of carrying out the work obligations which are required to be carried out in accordance with the relevant agreed annual work program and budget (as may be amended from time to time) pursuant to the production sharing contract and the joint operating agreement.

(b) provide or procure the provision of drilling units to enable the drilling of one exploration well within the contract area as required in the production sharing contract and the joint operating agreement and as scheduled in accordance with the relevant agreed annual work program and budget.

(c) acting as Farmin Operator, cause the acquisition of a 3-D seismic survey of [number of square kilometers] square kilometers (the "Seismic Survey").

1.2 Farmee shall be the "Farmin Operator" for the Seismic Survey. During the period that Farmee acts as Farmin Operator, [insert name of operator appointed in the joint operating agreement] shall remain as Operator under the joint operating agreement and be responsible for all other rights and obligations. During such periods when Farmee acts as Farmin Operator, Farmee will have the ability to cash call and pay invoices pursuant to the joint operating agreement and will submit all such invoices for services and invoices received and paid by Farmee to [insert name of operator appointed in the joint operating agreement] as Operator for accounting, cost recovery and tax purposes.

2. Future Cash Calls

Subject to Article 1 above, after the completion date, Farmee agrees to pay its participating interest share of costs incurred under the production sharing contract and the joint operating agreement.

3. Payments to Government for Assignment

Any costs, expenses, fees, or duties payable to the Government in connection with the assignment herein shall be borne and paid by [insert Farmor or Farmee].

4. Other Costs

Except as expressly provided in this Agreement, as of the completion date, all costs and expenses including, without limitation, all bonuses due under the terms of the production sharing contract shall be borne by the Parties in accordance with their respective participating interests.

This sample clause combines:

- a cash consideration;
- one aspect of the drill to earn consideration whereby the farmee undertakes to provide materials (eg, drilling units here) to enable the drilling of a well; and
- another aspect of the drill to earn consideration whereby the farmee undertakes to carry out certain works.

A key point of the above sample clause is in Article 1.2, whereby the parties provide that the farmee is to act as the operator[4] for the specific purpose of carrying out its works commitment under the drill to earn consideration. In such case, the usual operator appointed under the applicable JOA related to the participating interest being farmed out will not act as such in connection with the works to be completed by the farmee. The concept of 'farmin operator' will thus be used to distinguish the farmee, acting as the operator to perform a part of the drill to earn work programme (eg, the 'seismic survey' in the above clause), from the usual operator appointed under the JOA. The parties to the farmout agreement will set out which prerogatives are granted (and which are not) to the farmin operator.

The consideration clause should also provide the farmee's obligation to pay its share of the costs incurred after the effective date and may indicate which of the farmee or the farmor bears the various costs and taxes relating to the transfer.

3.3 Consideration in transactions involving a state or a national hydrocarbons company

Where a state or a national hydrocarbons company (or a state entity) is the buyer of the asset being transferred, the form of consideration may have to be adapted.

In some jurisdictions, the national hydrocarbons company or a governmental body or agency is the holder of the hydrocarbons title, authorisation or licence necessary to carry out the works under the host government agreement (eg, concession agreement, production sharing contract).[5] In such jurisdictions, a state entity is thus a stakeholder in every oil and gas project of the country since start-up.

In other jurisdictions, the state (or a governmental body or agency) is not involved in the project other than in its sovereign function, as grantor of the hydrocarbons title, authorisation or licence, and does not hold a participating interest in the project. The applicable hydrocarbons legislation or host government agreement may, however, provide that the state (or the national

---

4 The term 'farmin operator' is used in this example, but the parties may use different terms in different agreements to express the concept of the farmee acting as operator for the specific purpose of carrying out work to be performed by the farmee under the farmin agreement.

5 This is the case, for instance, in Algeria.

hydrocarbons company) has a back-in right, which is an option to acquire a participating interest in the project once it has entered into the production phase. In such case, the acquisition by the state (or the national hydrocarbons company) of a participating interest in the asset will typically be made for no consideration. Such acquisition will not necessarily need to be materialised in an agreement, given that the state's back-in right is often set out in the hydrocarbons legislation and/or host government agreement. In some jurisdictions, an amendment to the existing host government agreement and/or related JOA may be required to include the state (or the national hydrocarbons company) as an owner of a participating interest.

The level of participating interest to which the state is entitled pursuant to the back-in right is usually provided in the hydrocarbons legislation or in the applicable host government agreement. In the event that a state wishes to acquire an additional participating interest in a project, or where the hydrocarbons legislation or the applicable host government agreement does not provide a back-in right, the state will then usually need to purchase a participating interest on terms and conditions to be agreed, including provisions on consideration. One notable difference between state buyers and other types of buyers lies in the type of consideration to which states may be able to agree. The parties may, for instance, be in a situation where the state is unwilling or unable to make a monetary payment for all or part of the purchase price. In such case, the state may provide other forms of consideration, such as a share of its entitlement to production to be allocated to the seller or tax reductions for the seller in an amount equivalent to all or part of the purchase price.

3.4 Consideration in an earn-in agreement

We have seen above how the consideration can be structured in an SPA and in a farmout agreement. 'Earn-in agreements' are a subdivision of farmin (or farmout) agreements. An earn-in mechanism is similar to a farmout in that an interest is transferred in consideration for the performance of the buyer's work obligations. However, in the case of an earn-in, the interest in the asset is transferred only on completion of all the buyer's work obligations. Earn-in agreements are in particular used in cases where it is difficult for the parties to obtain the government consents that would be required to give effect to the transfer of the relevant interest.

The consideration clause can be structured to provide that the buyer has an option to take an interest in the asset by a certain date, in consideration for its commitment to pay a share of the costs relating to the work programme, as for instance in the earn-in agreement entered into between Canadian Overseas Petroleum Limited and BG International Limited in 2011.[6]

6 www.canoverseas.com/wp-content/uploads/nr/02-22-11-final-bg-eia-copl.pdf.

3.5 Consideration in an asset swap

Another type of asset deal is the asset swap. Asset swaps, or asset exchanges, involve the acquisition of an upstream asset in exchange for another, one asset being the consideration for the exchanged asset.

Assets swaps can be a way for companies to diversify their asset portfolio while using no cash at all or a limited amount of cash. This can be of particular interest when crude oil prices are low and companies tend to cut back spending. Indeed, in the event that the assets are of equivalent value, the asset swap occurs without exchanging money. By contrast, in the event that the assets are not of equivalent value, the parties may provide in the SPA:

- the value of each asset;
- that the value of one asset can be netted off against the value of the other asset; and
- which party will make a payment to the other, to settle the balance between the two values.

As with other types of transfer mentioned above in this chapter, the SPA may also contain provisions relating to adjustments to be made on completion, to take into account the potential variation of value between signing and completion of the transaction.

A recent example of an asset swap is the exchange of assets between BASF and Gazprom completed in 2015, where the assets had equivalent value.[7]

4. Conclusion

Each consideration clause must be tailored to the requirements and the specifics of a given transaction. As discussed in this chapter, the parties may wish to include as part of the consideration some factors in addition to the base price, such as adjustments to take into account the potential change between signing and completion of the value of the shares or assets being transferred. In oil and gas transfers, the consideration may take various forms, some of which are very specific to the industry, such as the drill to earn consideration encountered in farmout agreements. As a crucial component of any kind of transfer, whether it is a transfer of shares or a transfer of assets, the consideration clause will undoubtedly be a key factor in the negotiations.

---

7 www.wintershall.com/press-media/press-releases/detail/basf-and-gazprom-complete-asset-swap.html.

Conditions precedent and deferred completions

John C LaMaster
Akin Gump Strauss Hauer & Feld LLP

1. Introduction

1.1 What is a condition precedent?

Black's Law Dictionary defines a 'condition precedent' as "[a]n act or event, other than a lapse of time, that must exist or occur before a duty to perform something promised arises".[1] Similarly, *A Dictionary of Modern Legal Usage* states: "A condition precedent is something that must occur before something else can occur."[2]

In the context of a sale and purchase agreement (SPA) for oil and gas assets or an SPA for shares in a company that owns oil and gas assets, the term 'condition precedent' usually refers to a provision whereby the transactions contemplated by the SPA will take place only upon the occurrence of a specified event or events. For example, in cases where governmental consent is needed for a transfer of upstream oil and gas assets or shares in a company owning upstream oil and gas assets, it is usual and customary for the parties to enter into an SPA containing a condition precedent providing that the sale will not be completed unless and until the governmental consent has been obtained. At the time of entering into the SPA, several provisions of the agreement will be immediately binding on the parties without caveat, such as the conditions precedent, confidentiality, choice of law, dispute resolution, certain pre-completion covenants and 'boilerplate' clauses. The obligations to sell and purchase are binding from the outset (they become effective upon entering into the SPA), but they are conditioned by the condition precedent – that is, the obligation will not become legally operative unless and until the governmental consent has been obtained, thereby satisfying the condition precedent.

A condition precedent is technically different from a condition subsequent. As explained above, a condition precedent is a provision whereby the transactions contemplated by the SPA will take place only upon the occurrence of a specified event or events. A condition subsequent, by contrast, provides

1 *Black's Law Dictionary*, 8th edn, Thomson West, 2014, p312.
2 *A Dictionary of Modern Legal Usage*, 2nd edn, OUP, 1995, p197.

that the relevant agreement may be terminated if a future event takes place or does not take place within a specified period. A condition subsequent therefore brings an agreement to an end. The distinction between a condition precedent and a condition subsequent may sometimes become blurred in the context of an oil and gas SPA. For example, where parts of an SPA come into force and effect at signing, but it is a condition to the obligation to sell and purchase that governmental consent is obtained by a specified longstop date, there will typically be a termination provision if that governmental consent is not obtained by that longstop date. From an optical and practical standpoint, this may (depending on the exact terms of the agreement) be characterised as either a condition precedent or a condition subsequent. This chapter will discuss conditions precedent as described in the preceding paragraph, rather than conditions subsequent.

Under English law, there is no prescribed form of a condition precedent, and the words 'condition precedent' do not have to be used to create a condition precedent. In *Eagle Star Insurance Co Ltd v JN Cresswell*,[3] in the context of a reinsurance case, the Court of Appeal held that "it is not essential that the very words 'condition precedent' be used to achieve the result that reinsurers will not be liable unless a certain event happens. Other words can be used, if they are clear". Despite this precedent, it is best practice to define and describe clearly the conditions precedent in an SPA, and also to separate them from other provisions such as representations, warranties and covenants.

Parties contemplating entering into a sale and purchase transaction have several opportunities to decide whether to proceed. For example, a prospective buyer negotiating a letter of intent may decide that the terms on offer are unacceptable, decline to sign the letter of intent and walk away. Similarly, a buyer that has signed a letter of intent may find issues during due diligence that are not acceptable to it and decline to sign a definitive SPA. Once an SPA has been signed, however, the buyer is obliged to consummate the transactions contemplated by the agreement, subject only to satisfaction of the conditions precedent. Once a sale and purchase has completed, it is unusual and unlikely that the transaction will be rescinded or unwound. Therefore, the conditions precedent to completion can be viewed as the parties' last chance to walk away from the transaction.[4]

1.2 Deferred completion versus simultaneous signing and completion

There are two basic structures of an oil and gas SPA. In the first structure, the parties sign the SPA and complete the transactions contemplated thereby on the

---

3 EWCA Civ 602, [2004] 2 All ER (Comm) 244.

4 Lou R Kling and Eileen T Nugent, *Negotiated Acquisitions of Companies, Subsidiaries and Divisions*, Law Journal Press, 2005, §14.01.

same day, typically without conditions precedent – a simultaneous signing and completion. In the second structure, the parties sign the SPA first, but completion is delayed until a future date – a non-simultaneous signing and completion, sometimes referred to as a 'deferred completion'.[5]

In the oil and gas industry, most sale and purchase transactions are structured as deferred completions. Oftentimes, this is a practical necessity because it is a universal requirement in all oil and gas jurisdictions that an upstream petroleum agreement issued by a host government, such as a production sharing agreement or a concession, cannot be transferred unless and until the government has approved the transfer and the buyer. This requirement for governmental consent is often also required in a share sale and purchase transaction, where the target company is undergoing a change in control. Furthermore, standard joint operating agreements (JOAs) usually require the consent of the co-venturers for an asset transfer, and sometimes for a change in control. Standard JOAs often include pre-emption rights as well. For these reasons and other transaction-specific reasons, the deferred completion structure is more common in oil and gas sale and purchase transactions than the simultaneous signing and completion structure.

Although an SPA for a simultaneous signing and completion is typically simpler than an SPA for a deferred completion, it can sometimes actually take longer to reach the signing of an SPA with a simultaneous signing and completion than the signing of an SPA with a deferred completion. This is because a deferred completion structure allows some issues to be deferred to the interim period between signing and completion; whereas a buyer and a seller will not sign an SPA with a simultaneous signing and completion until absolutely everything is in place for the completion.

In circumstances where a simultaneous signing and completion is even possible, the buyer and the seller may have different views on whether to have a deferred completion or a simultaneous signing and completion. One party may perceive that it can gain a strategic advantage from a particular transaction structure, on the basis that some event may occur before signing that would cause one party, but not the other, to want to avoid the transaction.[6] For example, consider the situation where an SPA is being negotiated in a period of oil price volatility. If prices are falling, a seller may perceive that it would gain an advantage from a deferred completion that may allow it to sign the SPA sooner and thereby obtain a higher price and the protection of a binding agreement. By contrast, in the same market conditions, the buyer may perceive that it would gain an advantage from a simultaneous signing and completion

5 James C Freund, *Anatomy of a Merger: Strategies and Techniques for Negotiating Corporate Acquisitions*, Law Journal Press, 1975, p148.

6 Lou R Kling and Eileen T Nugent, *Negotiated Acquisitions of Companies, Subsidiaries and Divisions*, Law Journal Press, 2005, §1.04[2].

by not being locked into the transaction until the very last minute and thus potentially benefiting from a late renegotiation of the price. Conversely, if prices are rising, a seller may perceive that it would gain an advantage by waiting for a simultaneous signing and completion to see whether a higher purchase price could be obtained; whereas a buyer may want to lock in the seller by means of a deferred completion structure.

1.3 Deferred completion versus simultaneous signing and completion in model form agreements

Model form agreements are often used in the oil and gas industry. This is because, over time, industry participants have realised that they can save time and money during transaction negotiations by using professionally prepared standardised forms, especially where a high percentage of the provisions in those forms are 'boilerplate' that need not vary from transaction to transaction.[7]

The best example of oil and gas industry model form agreements are JOAs. There are several excellent model form JOAs promulgated by professional organisations such as the Association of International Petroleum Negotiators (AIPN),[8] the American Association of Petroleum Landmen,[9] the Rocky Mountain Mineral Law Foundation[10] and Oil & Gas UK.[11] There are also widely used model form agreements for gas sales agreements, unitisation agreements, service contracts, drilling contracts, confidentiality agreements, consultancy agreements and more.

Despite this abundance of model form agreements in the oil and gas industry, there is currently no widely used or widely accepted standard model form SPA. There are generic model form SPAs promulgated by organisations such as the Practising Law Institute[12] and the American Bar Association,[13] but these are not tailored to oil and gas transactions. The closest model form SPAs available in an oil and gas context are two specialised forms: the AIPN 2019 Model International Farmout Agreement and the Oil & Gas UK Model Form SPA for UK continental shelf transactions. This may all change, however, as in 2020 the AIPN issued a new Model Form International Asset Sale and Purchase Agreement (AIPN Model Form ASPA). It remains to be seen how widely used and widely accepted this form becomes; but based on the industry-wide committee that developed the form, it should cater to all interested parties (eg, supermajors, independents).

---

7 A Timothy Martin, "Model Contracts: A Survey of the Global Petroleum Industry", *Journal of Energy & Natural Resources Law*, Vol 22 No3 p281 (August 2004).

8 www.aipn.org.

9 www.landman.org.

10 www.rmmlf.org.

11 www.oilandgasuk.co.uk.

12 www.pli.edu.

13 Model Stock Purchase Agreement with Commentary (American Bar Association 1995); Model Asset Purchase Agreement with Commentary (American Bar Association 2001).

(a) *AIPN Model Form ASPA*

The AIPN Model Form ASPA contemplates a deferred completion, subject to numerous conditions precedent, divided into buyer's conditions precedent and seller's conditions precedent. The only mandatory condition precedent is obtaining the 'approval' (defined as an approval, consent or permission, including a deemed approval) of the relevant host governmental authority. The other conditions precedent are optional, depending on the terms of the relevant transaction, and include, for example:

- a 'bring-down' condition precedent that the other party's [representations and] warranties are true and correct in all material respects as of the completion date;
- a 'bring-down' condition precedent that the other party has performed or complied with all of its covenants and undertakings pursuant to the agreement;
- the seller having obtained a waiver or other evidence in writing of the expiration or non-exercise of any pre-emptive rights;
- if there is an existing JOA, the parties to the JOA and the parties to the asset SPA having executed a novation thereof, or if there is no existing JOA, the seller and the buyer having executed a JOA;
- the operating committee under the JOA having approved the appointment of the buyer as successor operator; and
- the parties having obtained any other required third-party consents for the assignment.

(b) *AIPN 2019 Model International Farmout Agreement*

A farmout agreement is essentially a specialised form of upstream oil and gas asset SPA. The feature that makes farmout agreements unique is that typically the consideration is the undertaking by the farmee (the transferee) to perform certain works that otherwise would have been performed by the farmor (the transferor), such as the drilling of a well. The AIPN 2019 Model International Farmout Agreement contemplates a deferred completion, subject to several conditions precedent, including, for example:

- the parties having obtained 'approval' (defined as an approval, consent or permission, including a deemed approval) of the relevant governmental authority to the assignment contemplated by the farmout agreement;
- the parties having obtained approval of the other parties to the JOA; and
- the parties having obtained any other third-party approvals for the assignment.

(c) *Oil & Gas UK Model Form SPA*

Oil & Gas UK has promulgated a model form SPA for the transfer of interests in a UK petroleum licence by means of an asset sale and purchase. The form is therefore specific to the UK continental shelf. This form also contemplates a deferred completion, subject to several conditions precedent, including, for example:

- simultaneous sale and purchase of the seller's interests in other fields;
- the seller having obtained a waiver in writing of any preferential rights;
- confirmation from other parties to the JOA that they are satisfied with the form of letter of credit to be provided by the purchaser, and that they release the seller from its security; and
- the approval of the Oil & Gas Authority (previously, approval of the secretary of state for trade and industry) to the transactions contemplated by the SPA.

1.4 Consequences of deferred completion

The fact that the deferred completion structure is more common than the simultaneous signing and completion structure in oil and gas sale and purchase transactions has several consequences. Most significantly, an SPA that provides for a deferred completion will be more complicated and contain more provisions than an SPA that provides for a simultaneous signing and completion. An agreement that provides for a simultaneous signing and completion does not need conditions precedent to completion, because the parties are evidencing their satisfaction with any pre-conditions by signing and completing the transaction. Similarly, completion mechanics such as lists of completion actions and completion deliverables can be left out of the SPA, and perhaps be relegated to a non-contractual completion checklist or completion memorandum. A simultaneous signing and completion also eliminates the need to deal with matters that may arise between signing and completion, such as the occurrence of events that may breach warranties or require further disclosure. Lastly, a simultaneous signing and completion eliminates the need to discuss the consequences of a material adverse change (MAC) arising between signing and completion, which can often be a difficult negotiation.

(a) Interim covenants

One of the main differences between an SPA that provides for a deferred completion and an SPA that provides for a simultaneous signing and completion is that the former will typically include certain covenants that govern the interim period between signing and completion. During this interim period, the seller will continue to own and operate the oil and gas assets. The buyer, however, will want assurances and protections that the assets as they existed on the signing date will be substantially the same assets on the completion date – that is, that nothing has occurred during the interim period that would change the commercial agreement between the parties.

There are usually both affirmative and restrictive interim covenants. The affirmative covenants require performance or the taking of certain actions. Examples of affirmative covenants include:

- an obligation on the seller to carry on the business and operations in the ordinary course of business, substantially in the same manner as it has been conducted;
- an obligation to comply with all applicable laws; and
- an obligation to maintain the relevant upstream petroleum agreements, such as production sharing agreements, concessions and JOAs, in full force and effect.

The restrictive covenants prevent or limit certain actions. Examples of restrictive covenants include obligations:

- not to enter into new contracts;
- not to amend or terminate any existing contracts;
- not to sell, transfer or encumber any assets; and
- not to make certain capital expenditures.

The list of interim covenants can be extensive or minimal, depending on the circumstances. As previously mentioned, governmental consent is required for the transfer of oil and gas assets and, most often, of shares in companies that hold oil and gas assets. In certain jurisdictions, such as some countries in Africa, this governmental consent process can take a long time, often many months. In these cases, buyers may rightfully insist on a full set of interim covenants in order to ensure that the value of the target company or target assets is preserved during the interim period. In other cases, the buyer may be satisfied with a less extensive set of interim covenants – for example, when a buyer has strong walk-away rights by means of favourable pro-buyer conditions precedent, the buyer may be willing to accept just a covenant that the seller carry on the business and operations in the ordinary course of business.[14]

(b) Repetition of warranties

Another consequence of the deferred completion structure for an oil and gas SPA is that the parties must decide whether the warranties will be given at signing only or at both signing and completion. This is a matter of negotiation between the parties and is closely related to the condition precedent that states that all of the seller's warranties will be true and correct at completion (this condition precedent is often referred to as a 'bring-down' clause).

An SPA may state that the seller's warranties are true and correct as at the

14 James C Freund, *Anatomy of a Merger: Strategies and Techniques for Negotiating Corporate Acquisitions*, Law Journal Press, 1975, p146.

date of signing of the SPA, or may state that the warranties are true and correct both at the date of signing of the SPA and at completion. An example of the latter is as follows:

The Seller warrants to the Buyer that the statements contained in Schedule [•] are true and correct as of the date of this Agreement and will be true and correct as of the Completion Date.

From a seller's standpoint, it is desirable to consider each warranty separately, in order to determine whether it is appropriate to repeat the warranty in this manner. For example, a seller will typically want to restate only warranties that refer to circumstances that are in the control of the seller. Also, warranties that refer to specific dates, such as circumstances existing "at the date of this Agreement", are not technically repeated as of the date of completion, unless a specific provision is added to state that, for purposes of repetition of the warranties, the phrase "at the date of this Agreement" shall be changed to "at the Completion Date" or equivalent. Similarly, financial statement warranties that refer to the veracity of financial statements "as at the respective dates thereof" are not technically repeated as of the date of completion, as the warranties themselves are limited to the financial statements at a specific point in time.

The examples above can be further complicated in circumstances where the bring-down requires only that the warranties be true and correct "in all material respects" at the completion date. In this case, it is possible that an event that occurs between signing and completion could constitute a breach of warranty, but will not give rise to a walk-away right on the part of the buyer as a result of the failure of a condition precedent because the event did not meet the threshold of materiality.

(c) ***Disclosure during the interim period between signing and completion***

Another complication resulting from a deferred completion is the question of whether the seller has a right or an obligation to update its disclosures in the disclosure letter with respect to events arising between signing and completion if such events would render a warranty inaccurate. Most commonly, the parties do not include these types of provisions, leaving the seller to bear the risk that facts or events may occur between signing and completion that may breach a warranty. If the parties do include this type of provision, the provision will typically obligate the seller to update its disclosure letter based on new facts or events occurring between signing and completion. For example:

Between the date of this Agreement and the Closing Date, each Seller will promptly notify Buyer in writing if such Seller or any Acquired Company becomes aware of any fact or condition that causes or constitutes a Breach of any of Seller's representations and warranties as of the date of this Agreement, or if such Seller or any Acquired Company becomes aware of the occurrence after the date of this

Agreement of any fact or condition that would (except as expressly contemplated by this Agreement) cause or constitute a Breach of any such representation or warranty had such representation or warranty been made as of the time of occurrence or discovery of such fact or condition. Should any such fact or condition require any change in the Disclosure Letter if the Disclosure Letter were dated the date of the occurrence or discovery of any such fact or condition, Sellers will promptly deliver to Buyer a supplement to the Disclosure Letter specifying such change.[15]

The critical issue is: what are the consequences of the update to the disclosure letter? It is possible that the update could affect the buyer's walk-away right under the bring-down condition precedent. The update could also affect the buyer's right to recourse against the seller for breach of warranty. This is a question of which party – buyer or seller – should bear the risk of an event occurring between signing and completion.

If the update does not amend the disclosures in the disclosure letter for purposes of the warranties or the bring-down condition precedent, then – depending on the specific terms of the SPA – the buyer may have recourse against the seller for breach of warranty and/or a walk-away right under the bring-down condition precedent as a result of the disclosure of the event that occurred between signing and completion. This is the most pro-buyer position and the updated disclosure letter is effectively just informational. An example of this type of provision is as follows:

All of Sellers' representations and warranties in this Agreement (considered collectively), and each of these representations and warranties (considered individually), must have been accurate in all material respects as of the date of this Agreement, and must be accurate in all material respects as of the Closing Date as if made on the Closing Date, without giving effect to any supplement to the Disclosure Letter.[16]

If an update of the disclosure letter amends the disclosures in the disclosure letter, with the same effect as if the updated fact or event was disclosed at the time of signing of the SPA, then there will be no breach of warranty and the bring-down condition precedent is not implicated in a way that would give the buyer a walk-away right. In this case, the buyer would bear the full risk that facts or events arising between signing and completion could render a warranty inaccurate. This would be an extremely pro-seller position.

A middle ground position would be for the update of the disclosure letter to cure the breach of warranty for purposes of post-completion recourse against the seller, but not to have effect for purposes of the bring-down condition precedent. In this manner, the buyer may still exercise its right to walk away for

15 Model Stock Purchase Agreement with Commentary (American Bar Association 1995), p150.
16 Model Stock Purchase Agreement with Commentary (American Bar Association 1995), p158.

failure of the bring-down condition precedent; but if it does not do so and proceeds to completion, then it forfeits its right of post-completion recourse against the seller for breach of warranty.

Another middle ground position would be for the update of the disclosure letter to modify the warranties for purposes of the bring-down condition precedent, but not to cure the breach of warranty. In this case, the buyer cannot refuse to proceed to completion, but the buyer will retain a claim for breach of warranty after completion.

The drafting committee for the AIPN Model Form ASPA has recognised the complexities surrounding the consequences of updating the disclosure letter, and has recognised that this would likely be the subject of difficult negotiations. The model form provides simply that the bring-down condition precedent shall not take into account any supplement to the disclosure letter. This is effectively the same as the most pro-buyer position described above, whereby the updated disclosure letter is merely informational and the buyer retains recourse against the seller for breach of warranty and/or a right to walk away.

(d) Interplay among warranties, covenants and conditions precedent

As explained above, the choice of the deferred completion structure will result in the introduction of additional provisions into the SPA, such as interim covenants and conditions precedent to completion. In these circumstances, it is crucial for the parties to understand the interaction between the warranties, interim covenants and conditions precedent, because they are interdependent in many respects.

This interaction is demonstrated by the following example. A buyer of oil and gas assets – whether directly through an asset sale and purchase or indirectly through a share sale and purchase – will typically want to be assured that the assets are in compliance with all environmental laws, or at least that the buyer is aware of all violations of environmental laws. In this case, the buyer will seek a warranty from the seller that, except as disclosed, the assets are in compliance with environmental laws; and the buyer will also want that warranty to be repeated at completion. The buyer will also seek an interim covenant from the seller that between signing and completion, the buyer will continue to operate the assets in compliance with all applicable laws. Lastly, the buyer will also seek conditions precedent that all of the seller's warranties will be true and correct at completion, and that the seller will have complied with all of its interim covenants up to completion. If the buyer is successful in negotiating the inclusion of this warranty, this covenant and these conditions precedent, it will have strong protection against any violations of environmental laws.

Let us assume, then, that an event has occurred prior to signing of the SPA that constitutes a violation of environmental laws, but is discovered only between signing and completion because it was overlooked by the seller during the vendor's due diligence process. Accordingly, the seller did not disclose the violation of environmental law in the disclosure letter. Alternatively, the event could have occurred between signing and completion. In either case, if the buyer has successfully negotiated the inclusion of the above-described warranty, covenant and conditions precedent into the SPA, then – depending on the exact terms of the SPA – it will have several options as a result of the breach of environmental law:

- The buyer could use the failure of the condition precedent to walk away from the transaction.
- The buyer could use the failure of the condition precedent to walk away from the transaction, but also make a claim for damages for breach of warranty or breach of covenant. In this case, the buyer's claim for damages could include that the buyer would not have entered into the SPA had it been aware of the violation of environmental law and, therefore, it would not have incurred various expenses including legal fees in negotiating the transaction.
- The buyer could waive the condition precedent, proceed to completion, but retain a claim against the seller for damages for breach of warranty or breach of covenant. The compensation recoverable for a breach of warranty will depend in part on the governing law of the SPA. Under an SPA governed by English law, recovery can be on a diminution basis, whereby the buyer recovers an amount equal to the difference between the value of the assets or shares subject to the untrue warranty versus the value of the assets or shares had the warranty been true. Alternatively (albeit unusually under English law SPAs), recovery can be on an indemnity basis, whereby the buyer recovers its losses on a pound-for-pound or dollar-for-dollar basis; in this case, the losses could include amounts necessary to remedy the violation of environmental law and pay any associated fines or penalties.
- The buyer may seek to use its right to terminate the SPA as leverage to renegotiate the purchase price or other provisions of the commercial deal. This is a justifiable course of action, as it is the seller that has made the mistake in failing to identify and disclose the violation of environmental law,[17] or in allowing the violation to occur during the interim period. The buyer's position would be that, had it known about the violation of environmental law, it would have factored the financial consequences thereof into its calculation of the purchase price.

17 This assumes that the failure to disclose by the seller was inadvertent. A buyer may have non-contractual recourse under applicable law for an intentional failure to disclose.

The buyer's options in this case will be more limited if it did not succeed in negotiating the inclusion of the above-described warranty, covenant and conditions precedent into the SPA. For example, if the above-described conditions precedent were not included, then – depending on the exact terms of the SPA – the buyer may be forced to complete the transaction, but may have post-completion recourse against the seller for breach of warranty or covenant.

2. Specific conditions precedent

The types of conditions precedent that are included in SPAs for oil and gas assets or in SPAs for shares in a company that owns oil and gas assets depend on the facts and circumstances of each transaction. The following provisions discuss certain conditions precedent that are frequently included.

2.1 All warranties of the other party are true and correct

As mentioned previously, a typical condition precedent is that all of the other party's warranties will be true and correct at completion (ie, a bring-down clause). A bring-down clause can be included as both a buyer's condition precedent and a seller's condition precedent – although in a typical SPA, the seller is giving more warranties and the bring-down condition precedent applies only to it.

An example of a bring-down clause is as follows:

(a) All of Sellers' representations and warranties in this Agreement (considered collectively), and each of these representations and warranties (considered individually), must have been accurate in all material respects as of the date of this Agreement, and must be accurate in all material respects as of the Closing Date as if made on the Closing Date, without giving effect to any supplement to the Disclosure Letter.

(b) Each of Sellers' representations and warranties in Sections [•] must have been accurate in all respects as of the date of this Agreement, and must be accurate in all respects as of the Closing Date as if made on the Closing Date, without giving effect to any supplement to the Disclosure Letter.[18]

(a) Consequences of a bring-down clause

One of the purposes of warranties in an SPA is to give the buyer post-completion recourse against the seller for any inaccuracies in the warranties. A bring-down clause also uses the warranties as a possible basis for a buyer to walk away from a transaction prior to completion. If an event that occurred before signing of an SPA constitutes a breach of a warranty and was not disclosed, or if an event that occurs between signing and completion would otherwise have constituted a breach of a warranty, the buyer may elect not to complete the sale and purchase on the basis of the failure of the bring-down condition precedent.

---

18 Model Stock Purchase Agreement with Commentary (American Bar Association 1995), p158.

(b) *Materiality in a bring-down clause*

Materiality is an important issue in the context of a bring-down clause.

From a seller's perspective, it is important that the bring-down clause not give the buyer a right to walk away for an immaterial breach of a warranty or for breach of an immaterial warranty. This is addressed in Subsection (a) of the sample clause quoted above, by the inclusion of a materiality qualifier that the warranties must be "accurate in all material respects". Notably, this materiality qualifier is absent from Subsection (b) of the sample clause, on the basis that there are some warranties that should be absolute and not subject to materiality. These typically include those warranties relating to ownership of and title to shares and, increasingly, to anti-bribery and corruption and environmental matters.

From a buyer's perspective, even though there may not be one breach of warranty that rises to the materiality threshold, there may be multiple lesser breaches that together rise to the materiality threshold. In this case, the buyer will want to preserve its walk-away right for failure of the bring-down condition precedent. The sample clause quoted above carefully addresses this by referring to both the representations and warranties "(considered collectively)" and to each of the representations and warranties "(considered individually)".

When materiality qualifiers are included in the bring-down condition precedent, the draftsperson needs to be mindful of the possibility of 'double materiality'. This arises where both the individual warranties and the bring-down condition precedent include materiality qualifiers. The combined effect of multiple materiality qualifiers will at a minimum make the level of materiality required to trigger the bring-down condition precedent uncertain, and may also raise the level of materiality required to trigger the bring-down condition precedent to a level higher than that intended by the parties.[19] If the warranties include materiality qualifiers, one way to address this issue in the bring-down condition precedent is to state that, for purposes of the condition precedent, all warranties that contain materiality qualifiers shall be read as if those materiality qualifiers were not included. The following is an example of this type of provision:

For purposes of determining the accuracy of such warranties, all materiality qualifications contained in the warranties shall be disregarded.

The issue of quantification of materiality in the bring-down condition precedent can be addressed in many ways. In most cases, the parties are willing to use the basic phrase "in all material respects". However, in some cases the parties prefer to have more refinement and precision so as to avoid any conflicts

19 Double materiality is discussed in more detail at: James C Freund, *Anatomy of a Merger: Strategies and Techniques for Negotiating Corporate Acquisitions*, Law Journal Press, 1975, p245, Lou R Kling and Eileen T Nugent, *Negotiated Acquisitions of Companies, Subsidiaries and Divisions*, Law Journal Press, 2005, §14.02[3] and Model Stock Purchase Agreement with Commentary (American Bar Association 1995), p159.

as to what is and what is not 'material'. In some cases, this is done by using alternative phrasing such as "in all respects other than *de minimis* inaccuracies", although whether this clarifies the position is debatable. Further clarity can be achieved by specifying a monetary amount that constitutes the materiality threshold for the condition precedent. This can be done, for example, in SPAs that include baskets that specify monetary amounts that limit post-completion recourse against the seller, by quantifying the materiality threshold in the bring-down condition by reference to the monetary amount in the basket.

(c) What point in time does the bring-down refer to?

The sample bring-down condition precedent quoted above states that the seller's warranties must have been accurate "as of the date of this Agreement" and "as of the Closing Date". It is often a point of contention and negotiation whether the bring-down condition precedent should refer to the warranties "as of the date of this Agreement". A seller may argue that for purposes of the bring-down condition precedent, it is irrelevant whether the warranties were accurate on the date of signing of the SPA; it is only important that the warranties are accurate on the completion date. Otherwise, the bring-down condition precedent could give the buyer a walk-away right as a result of a warranty that was breached on the date of signing of the SPA, even though that breach was cured by the completion date. Conversely, a buyer may argue that it expects the seller to stand behind its warranties when they were made on the date of signing of the SPA and also on the completion date, not least in order to ensure that the seller made a full disclosure process prior to the parties signing the SPA. Based on a study by the Business Law Section of the American Bar Association, it appears that the preponderance of buyers (79% in 2014, 83% in 2013 and 82% in 2012) win this argument, and succeed in having the bring-down condition precedent refer to both "the date of this Agreement" and "the Closing Date".[20]

(d) Disclosure letter supplements

The sample bring-down clause quoted above includes the phrase "without giving effect to any supplement to the Disclosure Letter". It is a point for negotiation in an SPA whether the seller is entitled to supplement its disclosure letter between signing and completion. If that right is granted, then the more important point for negotiation is: what are the consequences of a supplement to the disclosure letter? As discussed above, this is a question of which party – buyer or seller – should bear the risk of an event occurring between signing and completion. A buyer will argue forcefully that a supplement to the disclosure

20 *Strategic Buyer/Public Target M&A Deal Points Study (For Transactions Announced in 2014)*, Business Law Section of the American Bar Association (2015), p22.

letter is for information purposes only and does not have the effect of curing any inaccuracy in the seller's warranties for purposes of either the bring-down condition precedent or post-completion recourse for breach of warranty.

2.2 The other party has performed all of its covenants and obligations

A companion piece to the ubiquitous bring-down condition precedent is a condition precedent that the other party has performed all of its covenants and obligations during the interim period between signing and completion. The following is an example:

(a) All of the covenants and obligations that Sellers are required to perform or to comply with pursuant to this Agreement at or prior to the Closing (considered collectively), and each of these covenants and obligations (considered individually), must have been duly performed and complied with in all material respects.

(b) Each document required to be delivered pursuant to Section [•] must have been delivered, and each of the other covenants and obligations in Sections [•] must have been performed and complied with in all respects.[21]

If the individual covenants, the obligations and this condition precedent all contain materiality qualifiers, then the double materiality issue that applies to the bring-down condition precedent can also apply to this condition precedent.[22]

2.3 Transfer restrictions

(a) Government approval

Host governments have a legitimate interest in ensuring that the parties to which they grant upstream petroleum agreements such as production sharing agreements have the reputation and the financial and technical capabilities to conduct petroleum operations in the host country. This legitimate interest also applies to any direct transferee of an upstream petroleum agreement. As a result, it is a uniform requirement that an asset transfer of an upstream petroleum agreement be approved by the host government.[23] This requirement can be set forth in either or both of the upstream petroleum agreement or the applicable regulatory regime.

In an asset sale, a new party becomes the holder of an upstream petroleum agreement. In a share sale, the same legal person remains the holder of the upstream petroleum agreement, but that legal person may have new shareholders and management. In these circumstances, the host government

21 Model Stock Purchase Agreement with Commentary (American Bar Association 1995), p166.
22 See section 2.1(b) above.
23 Claude Duval *et al*, *International Petroleum Exploration and Exploitation Agreements: Legal, Economic and Policy Aspects*, Barrows, 2009, p161.

has a legitimate interest in ensuring that the legal person still has the reputation and the financial and technical capabilities to conduct petroleum operations in the host country. Historically, not all share sales required governmental approval. This led to international oil companies trying to structure their transactions as share sales in order to avoid governmental approval. However, in recognition of the government's legitimate interest, it is increasingly the case that share sales require governmental approval through 'change of control' restrictions at shareholder level. Again, these restrictions can be set forth in either or both of the upstream petroleum agreement and the applicable regulatory regime.

The requirement for governmental approval is addressed in an SPA by a condition precedent. A recent share sale transaction involving upstream assets in Nigeria included a condition precedent regarding governmental approval similar to the following:

The obligations of the Seller to transfer the Shares as contemplated by this Agreement are subject to, and conditional upon, Ministerial Consents having been duly obtained and remaining in full force and effect on the Completion Date.

"Ministerial Consents" means any and all consents required to be obtained from the Minister to permit the sale and purchase of Shares contemplated by this Agreement.

"Minister" means the Minister of Petroleum Resources under the Petroleum Act CAP P10 (Laws of the Federation of Nigeria) or any other person for the time being responsible for carrying out the functions at present carried out by him in relation to the Licence.

Other regulatory approvals may also be required under host country or regional law. For example, competition/anti-monopoly clearances may be required for certain transactions. This can be complicated in the case of cross-border transactions. Thus, for transactions involving a significant impact on trade in Europe, it is necessary to determine whether a transaction requires clearance either by the European Commission and/or by competition authorities in individual EU member states. There are also laws applicable to investments in assets or businesses deemed strategic by host countries which may limit foreign investment in such assets or businesses. An example is the US Committee on Foreign Investment, which is made up of various US governmental agencies and reviews the national security implications of foreign investments in strategic assets or businesses in the United States. These regulatory approvals would also be addressed by conditions precedent in an SPA.

If the obligation to obtain governmental approval is set forth in the upstream petroleum agreement, then it is a contractual obligation on the transferor to obtain the governmental approval. It is typical, however, for an SPA to allocate to the buyer all or at least part of the responsibility to obtain the governmental approval and thereby satisfy the condition precedent. This is because it is primarily the buyer that will need to interact with the relevant governmental authorities in order to prove that it has the requisite reputation and the financial and technical capabilities to acquire the interests.

Requirements for governmental approval can have several consequences for an oil and gas sale and purchase. There is the obvious risk that the approval may not be granted, in which case the condition precedent is not satisfied and the sale and purchase cannot go forward. Additionally, seeking approval from governmental authorities gives those authorities an opportunity to place conditions on the granting of such approval. For example, governmental authorities may seek amendments to the fiscal or other terms of the relevant upstream petroleum agreement in order to reflect changes in industry practices or in the oil and gas market since the date on which that upstream petroleum agreement was initially granted. This latter point is addressed in the AIPN 2019 Model International Farmout Agreement with the following provision:

> *If the Government imposes material conditions for the grant of an Approval, then, upon a Party notifying the other Party of the material conditions to which it objects and stating the reasonably full particulars for its objections, the Parties shall use their reasonable endeavours to remove or amend to their mutual satisfaction those material conditions and, unless the Parties agree, the Approval shall be deemed conclusively not to have been obtained until such material conditions have been so removed or amended.*[24]

In many jurisdictions, the process of obtaining governmental approval can take a long time (eg, more than six months in some jurisdictions in Africa). As discussed above, an SPA with a deferred completion will include various covenants regulating the conduct of the parties during the interim period between signing and completion. When this interim period is prolonged due to a lengthy governmental approval process, the parties will typically want to include broader and more detailed interim covenants, which may have the further consequence of prolonging the negotiation of the SPA.

(b) Third-party consent to transfer

In the same way that governments have a legitimate interest in knowing the capabilities of the parties to their upstream petroleum agreements, the joint venture participants have a legitimate interest in knowing the capabilities of their co-venturers. This is because upstream petroleum operations are by their nature expensive, complicated and long term; and because the joint venture participants are jointly and severally liable to the government for all liabilities and obligations arising from those operations. As a result, it is invariably the case that the JOA among the joint venture participants will contain provisions

24 AIPN 2019 Model International Farmout Agreement, Article 2.3.8, www.aipn.org.

requiring that any transfer of a participating interest be subject to the consent of the other non-transferring joint venture participants.

Different JOAs contain different standards by which the non-transferring joint venture participants can withhold their consent to a proposed transfer. If the non-transferring participants have an absolute consent right, then they may withhold their consent absolutely, in their sole discretion, without the need to provide any reasons or grounds. If the consent is qualified, then the consent of the non-transferring participants may not be unreasonably withheld. And if the consent is conditional, then the participants may withhold their consent only if certain conditions are met (usually, that the proposed transferee lacks adequate financial or technical capabilities). The latter two formulations are the most prevalent in modern JOAs.[25] Regardless of which formulation is used, the consent right will be personal to each non-transferring joint venture participant – that is, consent to the transfer is not subject to a passmark vote under the JOA.

JOAs typically also provide that the transferee must enter into a novation agreement or an accession agreement in which it agrees to perform all obligations and liabilities under the JOA with effect from the date of the transfer. These requirements can be addressed in an SPA as part of the condition precedent regarding third-party consents, as a standalone condition precedent or in a separate covenant regarding deliverables at completion.

There may be other contracts associated with the petroleum operations that require third-party consent, such as drilling contracts and services agreements. In many cases these contracts will have been entered into by the operator on behalf of the joint venture participants, in which case the third-party consent is typically not required – unless the transferor is the operator. This needs to be checked thoroughly during due diligence, however, as some contracts (eg, seismic agreements) may require third-party consent or payment of a licence fee – even for transfers by non-operators.

The AIPN 2019 Model International Farmout Agreement attempts to address all of the foregoing third-party consent issues in the conditions precedent:

The "Conditions Precedent" are as follows:

(a) obtaining the Approval of the Government of [•] [as required under Article [•] of the Contract];

(b) giving notice to [•] under Article [•] of the Contract;

(c) giving notice to the other parties to the JOA under Article [•] of the JOA;

(d) giving such notices as are required under the Specified Instruments and the transactions contemplated by them;

(e) obtaining the Approval of the other parties as required under Article [•] of the JOA;

(f) obtaining the Approvals of other Persons as required under the Specified Instruments;

---

25 Martyn R David, *Upstream Oil and Gas Agreements*, Sweet and Maxwell, 1996, p207.

(g) obtaining the [signature of the other parties to the JOA Novation, conditional upon Completion] or [execution of a JOA];

(h) [•][26]

The buyer should not rely on the bring-down condition precedent discussed above to cover off any requirements for third-party consents. This is because, while there may be a warranty that no third-party consents are required, this warranty will be qualified by the disclosure of any requisite third-party consents in the disclosure letter. Accordingly, the bring-down condition precedent that the warranties are true and correct will still be satisfied even if the third-party consents are not obtained, because the disclosure has qualified the warranty.

(c) Transfer of operatorship

An asset sale may involve a change of operatorship, which typically also requires governmental approval to ensure that the new operator has the requisite reputation and the financial and technical capabilities to be an operator. In a share sale, if the target company is the operator, then there will be no change in the legal identity of the operator. However, the government will nevertheless want to ensure that the operator will still have the requisite reputation and the financial and technical capabilities, even under new ownership. These factors will typically be assessed as part of a 'change of control' review.

Governmental approval to a transfer of operatorship was covered by this condition precedent in a recent farmout transaction in the Middle East:

The validity of the Assignment and the obligations of the Farmee under this Agreement are subject to the satisfaction or waiver of each of the following conditions (collectively called "Conditions Precedent") that: ...

D. The Parties obtain approval by the Government of the transfer of Operatorship to Farmee ...

Governmental consent to the transfer of operatorship may be more forthcoming in some jurisdictions than in others. For example, in situations where it is proposed that operatorship be transferred from one international oil company to another international oil company, the Nigerian government has historically often required that operatorship be instead transferred to the national oil company (the Nigerian Petroleum Development Company Limited). For sale and purchase transactions in Nigeria and jurisdictions with similar policies, a seller will typically want to avoid inclusion of a condition precedent regarding governmental consent to the transfer of operatorship, on the basis that failure of that condition precedent could cause the entire sale and purchase to collapse. In this case, the seller may argue that the SPA should

26 AIPN 2019 Model International Farmout Agreement, Article 2.3.2, www.aipn.org. The bullet point in subsection (h) is for any deal-specific conditions precedent that may be included.

instead include a mutual 'reasonable endeavours' obligation to have the operatorship transferred to the buyer. Conversely, a buyer that considers transfer of operatorship to be a material part of the transaction will argue for inclusion of a condition precedent.

A change of operator also typically requires consent of the non-transferring joint venture participants. In this case, however, the consent right is not personal to the non-transferring joint venture participants; instead, it is typically subject to a passmark vote of the operating committee formed under the JOA. Many JOAs also contain provisions whereby, if there is a change of control of the operator, the other joint venture participants shall vote on whether the operator should be removed and a successor operator be named. This transfer of operatorship under the JOA will also typically be covered by a condition precedent, such as the following example from a UK continental shelf transaction:

The obligations of the Parties under Clauses [•] are conditional on the satisfaction of the Conditions Precedent:

... the co-venturers to the [•] Field JOA having appointed Buyer as successor Operator of the [•] Field ...

(d) Waivers or expiry of pre-emption rights

A 'pre-emption right' is a contractual right under a JOA for each joint venture participant to acquire all, or a proportionate part, of the participating interests of another joint venture participant in priority to a third party. There are two forms of pre-emption right. The first form requires a joint venture participant that intends to transfer its participating interest to offer to its co-venturers the right to acquire that participating interest on the same terms as have been agreed with the prospective third-party buyer. This form of pre-emption is typically dealt with in an SPA by means of a condition precedent. The second form, commonly referred to as a 'right of first negotiation' or a 'right of first refusal', requires a joint venture participant that intends to transfer its participating interest to offer that participating interest to its co-venturers first, prior to making an offer to any third-party buyer. This form of pre-emption does not typically need to be dealt with in an SPA because it will have been dealt with prior to signing of the SPA.

In some host countries, the government or the national oil company has pre-emptive rights. These can be set forth in the relevant regulatory regime, in the upstream petroleum agreement or, where the government or the national oil company is participating as a co-venturer, in the relevant JOA or participation agreement.

Pre-emption most commonly arises in the context of an asset sale rather than in a share sale. However, some JOAs provide for pre-emption in the event of a change of control at shareholder level. For example, this is an optional provision in the 2012 AIPN Model Form JOA.[27] In this case, it is the participating interest that is subject to the pre-emption and must be offered to the co-venturers, rather than the shares that are subject to the share sale.

If pre-emption is applicable, then the parties to an SPA will need to address the pre-emption through the conditions precedent. In a transaction involving the sale of participating interests in a single upstream asset, the exercise of the pre-emption right by an existing joint venture participant would cause the condition precedent to fail. In this case, the condition precedent can be straightforward, as in the Oil & Gas UK Model Form SPA:

The obligations of the Parties under Clause 2.1 are conditional on the satisfaction of the following conditions (the "Conditions Precedent"): ...

... receipt by the Seller of a waiver in writing by the Co-Venturers of their rights pursuant to the provisions of Clause [•] of the Operating Agreement or satisfaction of such provisions without any Co-Venturer attempting to acquire the Asset in accordance with such provisions ...

In a transaction involving participating interests in multiple upstream assets, the buyer and the seller may provide that the overall transaction can proceed even if existing joint venture participants exercise pre-emption rights with respect to one or more upstream assets. These provisions can be more complicated. The following is an example from a transaction in the US Gulf of Mexico, which required both a condition precedent and an accompanying clause.

The obligation of Buyer to close is subject to the satisfaction of the following conditions: ... Seller shall have obtained waivers of all Preferential Rights, or the Preferential Rights shall have lapsed, or if any such Preferential Rights have been exercised, the Sale Price shall have been reduced in accordance with this Agreement.

It is understood by Buyer that certain of the Properties covered hereby are or may be subject to preferential purchase rights, rights of first refusal, or similar rights (herein called "Preferential Rights"). Seller, with Buyer's concurrence, has or will notify all holders of Preferential Rights, and Seller shall promptly notify Buyer if the Preferential Rights are exercised or if the requisite period has elapsed without said rights having been exercised and shall generally keep Buyer informed of material communications between Seller and any holders of Preferential Rights regarding such Preferential Rights. It is specifically understood that the exercise of any Preferential Rights shall not alter the obligations of Seller and Buyer to purchase and sell the remainder of the properties covered hereby, provided that (i) the Sale Price shall not include the price allocated to the Properties where Preferential Rights were exercised, and (ii) Buyer may, at its sole option, terminate this Agreement in the event that Preferential Rights are exercised as to both (x) the

27 AIPN Model International Joint Operating Agreement, Article 12.3.C, www.aipn.org.

Property described on Exhibit A as [•] and (y) the Property described on Exhibit A as [•].

A hybrid of the foregoing approaches may be needed if, for example, there are one or two key assets within the acquisition package that the buyer is unwilling to proceed without. In that case, waivers are needed for those key assets, whereas the acquisition may proceed even if the other assets are pre-empted.

(e) Change in control

If a sale share constitutes a change in control of the corporate entity, then the buyer and the seller may need to include conditions precedent in their SPA to deal with the relevant provisions of the JOA. The 2012 AIPN Model Form JOA[28] sets forth several options for what may be required in the event of a change of control. First, the participant subject to the change of control must obtain any necessary governmental approval and furnish any replacement security required by the government or by the relevant upstream petroleum agreement. Secondly, the participant subject to the change in control must provide evidence which is reasonably satisfactory to the other joint venture participants that after the change in control, it will continue to have the financial and technical capability to satisfy its obligations under the upstream petroleum agreement and the JOA; if it fails to provide such evidence, the other joint venture participants may require the participant to provide security. Lastly, as mentioned above, the change in control may trigger pre-emption rights. If any of these provisions are present in the relevant JOA, the appropriate way to deal with them in the SPA is through conditions precedent.

2.4 No material adverse change between signing and completion

A buyer may seek a condition precedent that there has been no MAC in the upstream petroleum assets or in the target company between signing and completion, in order to protect itself against unpredictable events. Sellers typically resist inclusion of a MAC condition precedent on the basis that risks are an inherent part of the oil and gas industry, and that many MAC risks would be covered by insurance. The seller's argument can be bolstered if the parties have agreed to an 'economic effective date' for the sale and purchase that is on or before the date of signing of the SPA. The issue of whether to include a MAC condition precedent is frequently hotly debated, as it affects the allocation of risk between the buyer and the seller during the interim period between signing and completion.

An alternative way to deal with the same concern is to rely on the combination of:

- the seller's warranty that since the last balance-sheet date, there has not

28 AIPN Model International Joint Operating Agreement, Article 12.3, www.aipn.org.

been any MAC in the business, operations, properties, prospects or condition of the upstream petroleum assets or the target company; and
- the bring-down condition precedent.

Once (or if) an agreement is made to include a MAC condition precedent, an even more hotly debated issue may be how to define what is (and what is not) a MAC. MAC clauses are discussed in more detail in a separate chapter in this book.

2.5 No pending or threatened actions

Another common condition precedent is that there is no legal dispute or action pending or threatened that would prevent consummation of the transactions contemplated by the SPA. Although this condition precedent is commonly included in an SPA, it can take many forms and raise many issues. The following is an example of a buyer's condition precedent:

> *Since the date of this Agreement, there must not have been commenced or Threatened against Buyer, or against any Person affiliated with Buyer, any Proceeding (a) involving any challenge to, or seeking damages or other relief in connection with, any of the Contemplated Transactions, or (b) that may have the effect of preventing, delaying, making illegal, or otherwise interfering with any of the Contemplated Transactions.*
>
> - *"Contemplated Transactions" – all of the transactions contemplated by this Agreement, including: (a) the sale of the Shares by Sellers to Buyer; (b) the execution, delivery and performance of the Promissory Note, the Employment Agreements, the Noncompetition Agreements, the Seller's Releases, and the Escrow Agreement; (c) the performance by Buyer and Sellers of their respective covenants and obligations under this Agreement; and (d) Buyer's acquisition and ownership of the Shares and exercise of control over the Acquired Companies.*
> - *"Proceeding" – any action, arbitration, audit, hearing, investigation, litigation, or suit (whether civil, criminal, administrative, investigative, or informal) commenced, brought, conducted, or heard by or before, or otherwise involving, any Governmental Body or arbitrator.*
> - *"Threatened" – a claim, Proceeding, dispute, action, or other matter will be deemed to have been "Threatened" if any demand or statement has been made (orally or in writing) or any notice has been given (orally or in writing), or if any other event has occurred or any other circumstances exist, that would lead a prudent Person to conclude that such a claim, Proceeding, dispute, action, or other matter is likely to be asserted, commenced, taken, or otherwise pursued in the future.*[29]

29 Model Stock Purchase Agreement with Commentary (American Bar Association 1995), p170.

One of the issues raised by this condition precedent is a question of materiality. The threat of a meritless case with no realistic likelihood of success should not give rise to a walk-away right. It is difficult, however, to assess the merits of a claim, especially for the party that is not the subject of the claim. This is often addressed in the condition precedent by requiring that the claim be material "in the reasonable judgment of the [buyer][seller]" or "in the reasonable opinion of counsel to the [buyer][seller]". Alternatively, the condition precedent may specify that the claim must have a material adverse effect on the defendant or the transactions contemplated by the SPA.

An additional issue that is the subject of negotiation is whether to include 'threatened' claims. This is addressed in the condition precedent cited above by defining the word 'threatened'. Another approach is to include claims threatened by government officials or agencies, which by their nature can be serious, but not include claims threatened by private persons. Based on a study by the Business Law Section of the American Bar Association, in the SPAs that included this condition precedent, only 30% of the SPAs entered into in 2014 included threatened claims by governments, and only 33% of the SPAs entered into in 2014 included threatened claims by non-governmental persons.[30]

2.6 Release of guarantees/provision of replacement guarantees

If the seller or its parent company has given guarantees to the host government or to its co-venturers under the JOA, or to other third parties, there may be a condition precedent requiring that the buyer or its parent company have released the seller or its parent company from its guarantee and have provided a replacement guarantee. Given the logistics and potentially long timeframes involved in releasing a guarantee and providing a replacement guarantee, this is oftentimes dealt with in a post-completion covenant rather than in a condition precedent. An example of this condition precedent is as follows:

> *Seller (or its relevant Affiliates) having been irrevocably released and discharged from all guarantees and other security in relation to the Purchase Interest [as set out in Exhibit [•]][and Buyer (or an Affiliate) having provided all required replacement guarantees and other security;]*[31]

2.7 Execution and delivery of ancillary agreements

Another common condition precedent is the execution and delivery of ancillary documents or agreements. The sale and purchase of assets will typically involve more ancillary agreements than a sale and purchase of shares; and if the transfer of operatorship and/or producing assets is involved, then there could be a large

30 *Strategic Buyer/Public Target M&A Deal Points Study (For Transactions Announced in 2014)*, Business Law Section of the American Bar Association (2015), p38 and p40.

31 AIPN Model Form ASPA, Article 3.2.8.

number of ancillary agreements. If the execution and delivery of ancillary agreements are conditions precedent, it is typical to list such agreements either in the condition precedent or in an annex to the SPA. An example is as follows:

The obligation of the Buyer to consummate the transactions to be performed by it in connection with Completion is subject to the following conditions: ... the relevant parties shall have executed and delivered the agreements in form and substance as set out on Schedules [•] and the same shall be in full force and effect on the Completion Date ...

2.8 Board resolutions and/or officer's certificates

The parties may also include conditions precedent for the delivery of board of directors' resolutions evidencing due authorisation of the transaction and/or the delivery of officer's certificates certifying, for instance, that the warranties are accurate at completion and that all covenants have been complied with. For example:

The obligation of the Buyer to consummate the transactions to be performed by it in connection with Completion is subject to the following conditions: ... the Seller shall have delivered to the Buyer a certificate in form and substance as set forth on Schedule [•], duly signed by an authorized officer of the Seller, to the effect that each of the conditions specified above in Clauses [•] is satisfied in all respects ...

2.9 Legal opinions

Some SPAs require delivery of legal opinions regarding these topics, although this is more common for transactions in the United States than for international transactions. For example:

The obligation of the Buyer to consummate the transactions to be performed by it in connection with Completion is subject to the following conditions: ... the Buyer shall have received from [•], counsel to Seller, an opinion in form and substance as set forth on Schedule [•], addressed to the Buyer, and dated on the Completion Date ...

2.10 Transitional support agreements and employment agreements

Conditions precedent can also be included for delivery of transitional support agreements and employment agreements with key officers or employees. Alternatively, these ancillary documents or agreements can be dealt with in a covenant regarding actions to be taken at completion.

2.11 Reorganisation

In a share sale and purchase, if the target company owns assets or has liabilities that the buyer does not want to acquire or that the seller does not want to sell, the SPA may include, as a condition precedent, a pre-completion reorganisation by the seller to transfer those assets or liabilities from the target company to another member of the seller's group. A buyer will typically request indemnification from any adverse tax or other consequences resulting from this pre-completion reorganisation, and from any liabilities associated with the assets or liabilities that have been transferred out of the target company.

2.12 Non-contravention

The AIPN Model Form ASPA includes a condition precedent that neither the consummation nor the performance of the transactions contemplated by the agreement will contravene, conflict with or violate any laws. Note that it includes an optional provision that would limit the condition precedent to new laws that were not in effect on the signature date:

> *neither the consummation nor the performance of the transactions contemplated by this Agreement will (with or without notice or lapse of time), contravene, conflict with or violate, any Law applicable to Seller or any of its Affiliate [that was not in effect on the Signature Date];*[32]

> Where 'laws' is defined as follows:

> *Laws means all lawful instruments and pronouncements (including laws, decrees, statutes, rules, regulations, ordinances, international agreements, injunctions, orders, judgments, and rulings), and enforcement and other practices, whether or not having the force of law (including extra-statutory concessions, whether or not published) of a Government.*[33]

2.13 Incorporation of local entity or branch

In some jurisdictions, it is a governmental requirement that an international oil company establish a local entity or register a branch office to hold its interest in an upstream petroleum agreement. It is sometimes permissible for this to be formed within a specified timeframe after completion of the acquisition of the upstream petroleum agreement. In this regard, the AIPN Model Form ASPA includes a condition precedent that governmental consent has been granted to form the local entity or register a branch office, but not that such local entity has already been formed or that a branch office has already been registered.

> *the [Government of the country where the Contract is located][Government Oil Company] having granted Buyer written approval to [incorporate local entity / or register a branch] to comply with [refer to requirement];*[34]

2.14 Environmental assessment

The AIPN Model Form ASPA also includes a quite specific condition precedent to apply in circumstances where the buyer and the seller have agreed to prepare

32 AIPN Model Form ASPA, Article 3.2.10 (mirroring Article 3.1.12).
33 AIPN Model Form ASPA, Article 1.1.
34 AIPN Model Form ASPA, Article 3.1.13.

an environmental assessment and baseline study to define pre-effective date environmental liabilities:

> *an environmental assessment and baseline study defining pre-Effective Date Environmental Liabilities having been obtained at [the sole cost of [•][the joint cost of the Parties.]*[35]

3. Conditions precedent that create optionality

SPAs sometimes contain conditions precedent that are within the sole power of one of the parties and therefore transform the SPA into a *de facto* option in favour of that party. For instance, buyers sometimes seek conditions precedent regarding completion of their due diligence or funding of their acquisition financing. Since these circumstances are within the buyer's control, the buyer effectively has discretion as to the satisfaction of the condition precedent, and could arguably manipulate or exploit the failure of the condition precedent in order to walk away from the acquisition. Sellers usually resist these types of conditions precedent because they create an imbalance between the parties and add significant amounts of uncertainty to the transaction, making the transaction less likely to complete.

A condition precedent for the buyer's acquisition financing is typically satisfied by the first drawdown of the financing rather than by the execution by the buyer of definitive financing agreements. If a seller is amenable to this type of condition precedent, the seller ought to request sight of a written commitment letter from the buyer's bank before signing the SPA, at least to get some comfort that the financing will be forthcoming.

An example of a financing condition precedent is as follows:

> *The obligation of the Buyer to consummate the transactions to be performed by it in connection with Completion is subject to the following conditions: ... the Buyer shall have obtained on terms and conditions reasonably satisfactory to it all of the financing it needs in order to pay the Purchase Price, consummate the transactions contemplated by this Agreement and fund the working capital requirements of the Company and its Subsidiaries after Completion ...*

If a buyer seeks a condition precedent that it has completed its due diligence investigation to its satisfaction, or has completed some specific element of its due diligence investigation such as obtaining an environmental site assessment, the seller ought to seek to put a shorter time limit on this condition precedent, requiring that it be satisfied or waived on or before a specific date. The period of time for satisfying or waiving this condition precedent will be shorter than the general longstop date that applies to all of the other conditions precedent. This does not eliminate the optionality in favour of the buyer; but at least it establishes a date by which the optionality will be removed.

---

35 AIPN Model Form ASPA, Article 3.1.15.

If either a buyer or a seller seeks a condition precedent that approval of its board of directors or shareholders must be obtained, then the other party ought to require that the party seeking the condition precedent:

- within a specified timeframe, call a meeting of the relevant board of directors or shareholders for the purpose of approving the transaction;
- recommend the transaction to its board of directors or shareholders; and
- use its best efforts to obtain the approval in a timely manner or within a specified timeframe.[36]

4. Further assurances to satisfy conditions precedent

An SPA will typically include a covenant requiring the party that is responsible for a condition precedent to endeavour to fulfil that condition precedent. Given that the conditions precedent (eg, obtaining governmental approvals) are often outside of the control of the parties, the covenant is typically phrased as a reasonable endeavours obligation rather than an absolute obligation. Occasionally, an SPA may include a different standard, such as a 'commercially reasonable efforts' obligation or a 'best endeavours' obligation. The differences between these qualified obligations will depend on the governing law of the SPA.

The covenant will typically also oblige both parties to use their reasonable endeavours to satisfy the mutual conditions precedent. The parties are also typically obliged to cooperate with each other, and to keep each other updated on the status of satisfaction or failure of any condition precedent.

If completion fails to occur because a condition precedent is not satisfied, a party may have liability to the other party if that first party was responsible for seeking to satisfy that condition precedent and it failed to use its reasonable endeavours to do so, or if it otherwise breached its other obligations in the covenant.

The AIPN 2019 Model International Farmout Agreement attempts to address these issues in the following covenant:

2.3.3 Each Party shall use its [best endeavours] / [reasonable endeavours]:

(a) to satisfy the Conditions Precedent that it is to satisfy at its sole expense; and

(b) to assist another Party to satisfy a Condition Precedent that it is to satisfy (subject to the other Party's request and at the other Party's expense).

2.3.4 The Parties together, but at their own respective expense, shall use their [respective best endeavours] / [respective reasonable endeavours to] satisfy any Conditions Precedent that they are to jointly satisfy.

---

36 James C Freund, *Anatomy of a Merger: Strategies and Techniques for Negotiating Corporate Acquisitions*, Law Journal Press, 1975, p300.

2.3.5 *The Parties shall from time to time discuss and coordinate their respective plans for the satisfaction of the Conditions Precedent, keep each other informed as to progress, and promptly notify each other on becoming aware of any fact or circumstance that is likely to prevent a Condition Precedent being satisfied.*[37]

5. Waivers of conditions precedent

An SPA should be drafted in a manner that makes it clear which party has the benefit of which conditions precedent. This is usually accomplished by segregating the conditions precedent into separate clauses in the SPA, with one clause containing conditions precedent that are for the benefit of the buyer, one containing conditions precedent that are for the benefit of the seller and one containing conditions precedent that are for the mutual benefit of both parties. A condition precedent should be waived only by the party that has the benefit of that condition precedent – that is, by the party whose obligations are conditional upon that condition precedent. Failure to keep the conditions precedent in the right categories could result in a party having the right to walk away as a result of that party's own failure to fulfil a condition precedent.[38]

For example, usually only the buyer may waive the bring-down condition precedent that the seller's warranties will be true and correct at completion. A seller may argue that it should also have the benefit of this condition precedent, on the basis that the buyer may have post-completion recourse against the seller in circumstances where one of the seller's warranties was untrue at completion and the buyer has waived the condition precedent and proceeded to completion.

Some conditions precedent, by their very nature, can be waived only by mutual agreement of the parties, or cannot be waived at all. Examples include obtaining governmental consent to assignment or a change of control, or obtaining regulatory approvals such as competition/anti-monopoly clearances. In jurisdictions where obtaining governmental consent is problematic or can take a long time, the buyer and the seller may agree, after a specified date, to waive a requirement to obtain governmental consent to assignment or a change of control on the basis that the parties will enter into a trust arrangement, whereby the seller will hold the relevant interests in trust for the buyer until the governmental consent is obtained. This is less than ideal from a buyer's standpoint, as the buyer is typically left with only a contractual right against the seller and a beneficial interest in the asset. In most jurisdictions, the parties will simply wait for the relevant governmental consent or regulatory approval.

---

37 AIPN 2019 Model International Farmout Agreement, Articles 2.3.3, 2.3.4 and 2.3.5, www.aipn.org. The 2004 model form has a much less detailed covenant: "Each party shall use [commercially reasonable efforts or its best endeavors] to execute all documents, and do and procure to be done all such acts and things as are reasonably within its power to ensure the Conditions Precedent are satisfied as soon as is reasonably practicable after execution of this Agreement."

38 E Allan Farnsworth, *Farnsworth on Contracts*, 3rd edn, Foundation Press, 2004, §8.7a.

The following is an example waiver clause from a recent UK continental shelf transaction, which makes it clear which conditions precedent are waivable by the seller, which conditions precedent are waivable by the buyer and which conditions precedent are waivable only by mutual agreement. The provision is also interesting in that it expressly reserves the right of the waiving party to make a warranty claim or seek other remedies or recourse in respect of the event or circumstance that is the subject of the waiver:

> *The Conditions Precedent set forth in Clauses [•] may only be waived in writing by the Buyer. The Conditions Precedent set forth in Clauses [•] may only be waived in writing by the Seller. The Conditions Precedent set forth in Clauses [•] may only be waived in writing by mutual agreement of the Buyer and the Seller. Waiver of any of the Conditions Precedent set forth in Clauses [•] shall not prejudice the right of the waiving Party to make a Warranty Claim or seek other remedies or recourse with respect to the event or circumstance that is the subject of the waiver.*

6. Completion

If the conditions precedent are timely satisfied or waived, then the parties will proceed to completion of the sale and purchase. The SPA typically includes closing mechanics, including the timing and place of completion, and a list of actions to be taken and deliverables to be delivered at completion.

7. Longstop date

An SPA will typically include time limits to satisfy or waive the conditions precedent. The deadline is typically referred to as a 'longstop date' or a 'drop dead date'. The purpose of this provision is that the buyer and the seller will not remain bound to the SPA for an unreasonable amount of time, waiting for satisfaction or waiver of conditions precedent that may never occur.

The length of time between the signing and the longstop date is negotiable by the buyer and the seller, and should be determined based on the nature of, and the expected amount of time that it will take to satisfy, the conditions precedent. For example, as noted above, in some jurisdictions it can take a long time to obtain governmental consent to a transfer or change of control. If the interim period between signing and the longstop date is set unrealistically short, then this may give a party that has changed its mind about the sale and purchase during the interim period an opportunity to escape from the transaction.[39]

The SPA will provide either that, on the longstop date, the SPA will automatically terminate, or that either party will have the right to terminate the SPA by written notice to the other party. The latter formulation is usually preferable, in case the parties desire to continue. Of course, the parties can always agree to extend the longstop date.

---

39 Martyn R David, *Upstream Oil and Gas Agreements*, Sweet and Maxwell, 1996, p213.

The following is an example of a longstop date provision that provides for automatic termination on the longstop date:

If all of the Conditions Precedent have not been satisfied or waived before 00:00 hours on [•] ("Long Stop Date"), then this Agreement terminates.

The following is an example of a longstop date provision that provides for termination by either party on or after the longstop date. The provision includes an important caveat: a party cannot terminate the SPA if the failure of the conditions precedent is due to the fault of the party attempting to terminate. So, for example, a party will not be entitled to terminate if it has failed to comply with its covenant in the SPA to use its reasonable endeavours to seek to satisfy the conditions precedent. This is based on the principle that a party should not be able to take advantage of its own wrongdoing:[40]

This Agreement may be terminated only in the following circumstances:

(a) by the Buyer or the Seller, by delivery of written notice to the other, if through no fault of the terminating Party, Completion has not occurred on or before [•] (the "Longstop Date") ...

8. Termination and the consequences of termination

Termination of the SPA is typically without prejudice to the liabilities and obligations of the buyer and the seller that accrued prior to the date of termination. This is in recognition that the parties may have existing liabilities and obligations to each other that should not be extinguished by termination of the agreement. For example, termination of the agreement should not excuse a party that has breached its obligations under the agreement or limit the right of the non-breaching party to seek recourse against the breaching party.

Termination of the SPA does not necessarily mean that the entire SPA ceases to have any force or effect. It is common for the parties to provide that certain provisions of the SPA survive termination. Examples of provisions that often survive termination include:

- confidentiality provisions, including the requirement that the receiving party return confidential information to the disclosing party;
- governing law and dispute resolution provisions, which should survive with respect to the resolution of any ongoing issues, such as liabilities and obligations of the buyer and the seller that accrued prior to the date of termination;
- provisions requiring each party to bear and pay its own expenses in respect of the transactions contemplated by the SPA; and
- definitions and interpretation provisions, to the extent necessary for implementation of the other surviving provisions.

---

40 Peter Roberts, *Petroleum Contracts: English Law and Practice*, OUP, 2013, p305.

The following is an example of a provision setting forth the consequences and effects of termination of an SPA:

If this Agreement is terminated under Section 9.1, all further obligations of the parties under this Agreement will terminate, except that the obligations in Section 11.1 [Expenses] and 11.3 [Confidentiality] will survive; provided, however, that if this Agreement is terminated by a party because of the Breach of the Agreement by the other party or because one or more of the conditions to the terminating party's obligations under this Agreement is not satisfied as a result of the other party's failure to comply with its obligations under this Agreement, the terminating party's right to pursue all legal remedies will survive such termination unimpaired.[41]

This is another example from the AIPN 2019 Model International Farmout Agreement:

If this Agreement is terminated, this Agreement, and any rights conveyed to Farmee under the Assignment of the Contract and the JOA Novation, shall become void and of no further force or effect, except for the provisions of Articles [3.10, 6.3, 8.1, 8.2, 11.2, 11.3, 11.4, 12, 14 and 16] which shall survive the termination. Notwithstanding the foregoing, if any Party is in default or breach at the time this Agreement is terminated, such Party in default or breach shall continue to be liable to the other Party for damages in respect of such default or breach, and the terminating Party shall be entitled to all remedies available at law or in equity, including reasonable attorneys' fees and all other costs and expenses incurred by the terminating Party in relation to the default or breach and the termination.[42]

In the case of a farmout agreement where the assignment was made to the farmee effective as of the signature date of the agreement, the farmee must agree to reassign the farmout interests to the farmor, as per this clause in the AIPN 2019 Model International Farmout Agreement:

After the termination of this Agreement, Farmee shall reassign to Farmor all rights to the Farmout Interests or any assets related to the Farmout Interests (if any) conveyed to Farmee under this Agreement or the other Transaction Documents no later than thirty (30) days after such termination with a special warranty of title, free and clear of any burdens, liens, mortgages, or related encumbrances arising by, through, or under Farmee, and Farmee shall execute such other documents and take such other actions as may be reasonably necessary to reassign the Farmout Interests to Farmor.[43]

In the case of a farmout agreement where a farmee may have performed

41 Model Stock Purchase Agreement with Commentary (American Bar Association 1995), p181.

42 AIPN 2019 Model International Farmout Agreement, Article 11.3.1, www.aipn.org. The referenced articles in square brackets are: 3.10 (Payment Obligations), 6.3 (Indemnity Claims), 8.1 (Tax Treatment of Payments), 8.2 (US Tax Election), 11.2 (Return of Information), 11.3 (Effect of Termination), 11.4 (Reimbursement), 12 (Announcements and Confidentiality), 14 (Governing Law) and 16 (Miscellaneous). Arguably, Article 1 (Definition and Interpretations) should be included in the list, to the extent needed to give effect to the other articles. Also, it is typical to include Article 15 (Dispute Resolution) in the list.

43 AIPN 2019 Model International Farmout Agreement, Article 11.3.2, www.aipn.org.

work obligations during the interim period between the signing and the longstop date, the farmout agreement may include unwinding provisions whereby the farmor is required to reimburse the costs and expenses so incurred by the farmee.[44]

9. Conclusion

SPAs for oil and gas assets or for shares in a company that owns oil and gas assets typically provide for deferred completions which, in the context of the heavily regulated oil and gas industry, is most often necessitated by the requirement to obtain governmental consent. Pre-emption is also commonly dealt with as a condition precedent, and certain other conditions precedent (eg, the bring-down condition precedent) are likely to be included as a matter of standard practice. Further bespoke conditions precedent may be necessary, depending on the facts and circumstances of the transaction. Negotiators and draftspersons should be aware of the myriad legal issues raised by the individual conditions precedent.

44 Geoffrey Picton-Turbervill (ed), *Oil and Gas: A Practical Handbook*, 2nd edn, Globe Law and Business, 2014, p307.

Covenants in upstream acquisitions and divestitures

Kevin Atkins
Matthew Daffurn
Locke Lord LLP

1. Introduction

Upstream sale and purchase transactions are complex. In most instances, they are based not on simultaneous signing and completion, but rather on signing followed by a lengthy period leading to completion. This means that a seller and a buyer can agree on a transaction, enter into a sale and purchase agreement (SPA) and make a public announcement regarding such transaction, if required, but the completion of the transaction (and the transfer of benefits and liabilities) occurs weeks, months or even years afterwards.

As is the case with most other heavily regulated industries and sectors that are reliant on numerous permits and licences, sale and purchase transactions in the upstream sector are frequently subject to regulatory and ministerial approvals, which are required either under the governing laws of the host country where the upstream asset is located or under the terms and conditions of the upstream project documents awarded by the energy ministry of the host country. Such regulatory and ministerial approvals (and other necessary third-party consents and/or the expiry or waivers of any applicable pre-emption rights) are typically structured as conditions precedent under the SPA. Accordingly, it is customary for upstream sale and purchase transactions to require an interim period between signing and completion during which it is the responsibility of the seller and/or the buyer to satisfy these conditions precedent. For the purposes of this chapter, the period between signing and completion will be referred to as 'the interim period'.

There is no hard and fast rule about how long an interim period should last; this will depend very much on how many approvals, consents and other conditions precedent are required, and how quickly regulators tend to respond. For example, in emerging markets interim periods can last for between six months and 18 months, as regulators can be unresponsive. Where the transaction involves an asset sale of a producing oil and gas field with numerous project documents, contracts and joint venture arrangements, the list of required consents and approvals from joint venture partners and service providers and lenders is likely to be longer, thereby necessitating a longer interim period. Buyers and sellers can be held to ransom waiting for regulatory approval, unless the local law or the upstream project documents include provisions of deemed acceptance where the regulator fails to respond within a certain period – although these are uncommon. The existence of an interim period will affect a transaction in other ways; for example, sellers will typically require a degree of financial commitment from the buyer, usually in the form of a deposit (to be refunded in certain limited circumstances to be negotiated), or a corporate guarantee and credit support arrangement designed to ensure that a creditworthy entity with deeper pockets than the buyer will also be responsible for the purchase price at completion.

During the interim period, both the seller and the buyer are contractually committed to proceed to completion. This is obviously in addition to any public market expectations raised by an announcement that the transaction SPA has been signed and a completed deal will follow in due course. The buyer will require adequate protection during the interim period to ensure that what is being purchased is not devalued or otherwise harmed prior to completion. The buyer will want, in particular, some degree of influence and control over operational matters.

There is, however, a balance to be struck between what level of control and influence a buyer may want and what a seller is willing to give. The seller's position will be that until completion occurs, the upstream assets remain the property of the seller and it is unreasonable for the buyer to place an undue fetter on the seller's ability to operate them. The buyer, by contrast, will argue that completion is a formality, especially if the conditions precedent are within the control of the seller and there is a degree of public and shareholder expectation because of a press announcement of the deal. Therefore, the buyer's position will be that:

- the upstream assets are, to all intents and purposes, the property of the buyer during the interim period; and
- the buyer should have a large degree of control and influence over what it is acquiring.

Further factors that will influence the balance of power during the interim period include: the type of acquisition structure being adopted and the length of the interim period; the longer the interim period, the less willing a seller will be to agree to fetters over its own controls and decision making. However, in the authors' recent experience, the proliferation of M&A activity in the North Sea since the first edition of this volume – which has seen the exit of super-majors, the entry of private equity (PE) houses and the expansion by those PE houses of their portfolios – has tilted the balance towards:

- more robust buy-side interim covenants; and
- an increasing number of transactions with shared decommissioning obligations whereby sellers retain a proportion of ongoing decommissioning liabilities.

This move in the market has been prompted, in no small measure, by the PE houses' focus on valuation mechanics (especially following the 2014/15 fall in the oil price) and the necessity of preserving the commercial and operational factors that contributed to those valuations.

2. Transaction structures

Buyers and sellers can elect to implement a number of different transaction structures, each of which will affect the covenant package requested by a buyer.

2.1 Share deal

Perhaps the simplest acquisition structure is a purchase of the shares in the corporate vehicle that holds the upstream asset. Where the upstream asset to be acquired is held in a special purpose vehicle, a corporate sale of the shares in that vehicle is likely to be very attractive to a seller looking for a clean exit. In a share sale, the seller retains no liabilities for the asset being disposed of; although where the seller wishes to retain certain of the assets held by the special purpose vehicle, then some form of asset hive-out or interim reorganisation will be required in order to facilitate the desired sale structure.

The obvious downside to a share purchase from a buyer's perspective is that the buyer will likely require a more robust and detailed due diligence exercise than an asset purchase. Acquiring shares in a special purpose vehicle means that all of the present and historic liabilities of that vehicle are assumed by the buyer (as opposed to a cherry-picking purchase where specific assets are acquired under an asset purchase structure). However, the upside is that the buyer will also assume the benefit of any financial assets of the special purpose vehicle such as historic tax losses.

A potential benefit for both the seller and the buyer is that a share purchase may not require regulatory approval because a change of control in an asset-owning special purpose vehicle is not always caught within the transfer restrictions of applicable hydrocarbon laws and upstream project documents. Share purchases are also less likely to trigger pre-emption rights favouring third parties (especially in the context of a package sale where the special purpose vehicle holds a number of other upstream assets to be sold as part of the same package). This is certainly the case with some of the older joint operating agreements (JOAs), although less likely for JOAs entered into in the past 10 years or so. Thus, the transaction may impose fewer conditions precedent and be more certain to complete, which is a key concern for sellers.

2.2 Asset deal

Buyers and sellers may decide that they prefer an asset level structure where the seller retains the shares in the corporate vehicle holding the upstream asset and only the specific upstream asset itself is transferred to, and acquired by, the buyer.

This may be preferable where the seller wishes to retain financial assets for the benefit of its group or where the corporate vehicle holds a number of upstream assets which are not to be sold. From the buyer's perspective, the due diligence can be more focused and directed only at the assets being acquired, as the buyer will assume neither historic liabilities nor non-asset-related liabilities of the corporate vehicle.

However, unlike a share purchase, an asset purchase will inevitably involve a number of conditions precedent and be subject to regulatory approval and, if applicable, pre-emption rights. This introduces an element of uncertainty to the transaction, as some degree of third-party involvement will be required; this will necessarily affect the transaction timetable and elongate the interim period, which in turn will cause the buyer to request a greater degree of control.

It is not uncommon, though, for asset purchase agreements to include an 'our watch/your watch' indemnity which provides that, as at a certain date, all obligations and liabilities prior to the date are borne by the seller and all obligations and liabilities on and after that date are borne by the buyer. Obviously, where this date is expressed as the completion date, the buyer's need for interim period covenants is somewhat mitigated, as the buyer will already have the benefit of the pre-completion date 'our watch/your watch' indemnity covering this period. Where this date is an economic effective date prior to signing (which, in the authors' experience, can be a common structure), a prudent buyer should request robust interim period covenants as the 'our watch/your watch' indemnity will not apply during the interim period.

2.3 Asset 'farmout' deal

A farmout deal is similar to an asset deal except that, typically:

- only a part of the upstream asset is sold to the buyer (with the seller retaining a portion of that upstream asset); and
- the buyer agrees that, as part of the consideration for that asset transfer, the buyer will perform some sort of work obligation such as a seismic survey and/or drilling commitments.

Consequently, farmout arrangements are more common in the early stages of an upstream project, when work obligations and capex commitments are still required, than in the later production stage of an upstream project, when the assets are generating revenues and projects are cash positive with less exploration risk.

Unlike conventional asset deals, transfers of asset-level interests under farmout transactions do not necessarily occur when the consideration has been fully funded or performed. For example, the buyer will want to be a licensee before undertaking drilling commitments so that, once the necessary regulatory approvals have been granted, completion may occur under the farmout agreement, whereupon:

- the seller will transfer the part of the upstream asset being sold to the buyer with performance of the work obligation by the buyer to follow thereafter; and
- the buyer will transfer the part of the upstream asset acquired back to the seller if the work obligation, or a cash equivalent expense, is not satisfied by a certain date.

2.4 Asset swap deal

An asset swap deal is effectively two asset deals whereby the seller transfers an asset to the buyer and, as consideration, the buyer transfers an asset to the seller. It is therefore the same as an asset deal, except that the consideration is not settled entirely in cash, but rather by way of a reciprocal asset transfer. In the absence of a transaction-specific rationale to the contrary, both parties will look for an equivalent set of interim period covenants to regulate and influence the operations over the other asset during the interim period.

2.5 'Locked-box' valuation

In a locked-box deal, the valuation of the target is pegged to a certain date prior to completion. This date generates an economic effective date for the deal and means that the buyer essentially takes all the benefits and assumes all the liabilities associated with the acquisition target that arise on or after the locked-box date (which is usually determined by reference to recent historical financial statements of the target). The value paid by the buyer is reflective and inclusive of revenues attributable to the target after the locked-box date.

Locked-box deals are often subject to simplified adjustment mechanics as, unlike a completion accounts valuation method, a locked-box deal includes pre-agreed determinations of cash, debt and working capital by reference to the historic financial statements. Locked-box deals are typically adjusted only for leakage and capital contributions. Leakage comprises cash that is extracted from the target after the locked-box date and paid to the seller (because that cash should have belonged to the buyer as it is taken out after the locked-box date), which constitutes a deduction to the purchase price – although the exact scope of what constitutes leakage and what is considered to be permitted leakage (ie, amounts which do not reduce the purchase price) will be vigorously negotiated. Capital contributions are payments by the seller to the target after the locked-box date (because this is cash that should have been funded by the buyer as it is injected after the locked-box date), which constitutes an increase to the purchase price.

Given the historic reference point which operates as an economic effective date for the transaction, interim period covenants are fundamentally important to, for example, PE buyers under a locked-box deal, as buyers will want to exercise as much control and influence from that date as is possible – not only from an operational perspective, but also to preserve the value that the buyer is paying for.

2.6 Completion accounts valuation

In a completion accounts deal, the economic effective date of the deal is set at completion and the buyer will purchase the assets and liabilities of the target with effect from completion. The value paid by the buyer is calculated from completion only and does not include revenues attributable to the target before completion. Accordingly, while interim period covenants will still be very important to a buyer in a completion accounts deal, they are more of an operational control than a value adjustment to the purchase price.

2.7 Relationship with other SPA terms

Aside from providing the buyer with influence and control over the target's operations prior to completion, interim period covenants also affect SPAs in a number of other ways. For example, the influence of PE buyers has led to an increasing number of transactions that include a condition precedent that all covenants have been complied with (typically qualified by a materiality threshold negotiated by the seller). In such transactions, if the seller breaches an interim period covenant and this breach rises to the materiality threshold, then the buyer does not have to proceed to completion (unless it waives that breach).

In addition to the typical operational interim period covenants discussed later in this chapter, SPAs will contain other covenants prior to completion, such as covenants to use 'reasonable' or 'best' endeavours to procure that the conditions precedent for which a party is responsible are satisfied. For example, where shareholder approval is required for the seller or the buyer in order to complete the transaction, the seller or the buyer, as appropriate, will covenant to use reasonable or best endeavours to obtain such shareholder approval. The escalation of the standard of performance to be a 'best endeavours' obligation – which, needless to say, requires more effort and expense than the customary reasonable endeavours standard – will depend on the relative negotiating positions and bargaining strength of the parties.

Since the first edition of this volume, *Astor Management AG v Atalaya Mining plc*[1] has clarified the scope and extent of endeavours clauses (albeit in the context of a mining transaction in Spain). In that case, the defendant argued that a deferred consideration clause in the acquisition agreement was not triggered, as the claimant had not used "all reasonable endeavours". While the court agreed that the deferred consideration was not payable, the court also held that the claimant had not breached the endeavours clause because it had used all reasonable endeavours in the circumstances. The court held that "it

1 [2017] EWHC 425 (Comm).

should almost always be possible to give sensible content to an undertaking to use reasonable endeavours (or 'all reasonable endeavours' or 'best endeavours') to enter into an agreement with a third party". The rationale for the finding was that while it can be difficult to establish whether the required level of endeavours has been met, difficulty in proving a breach of such standard is not a reason to find that there is no obligation at all, as the courts are used to interpreting the meaning and scope of contractual terms and conditions. The case confirms that the English courts will be extremely reluctant to find an 'all reasonable endeavours' clause to be unenforceable for reasons of uncertainty, in circumstances where the object of the clause is to seek to reach an agreement with a third party.

There is also a close relationship between interim period covenants and seller warranties. Most sellers will therefore resist repeating any of the operational warranties at completion where the SPA already includes a robust list of interim period covenants, and will argue that the buyer is already adequately protected. The difference between covenants and warranties, however, is that covenants are narrower than warranties, as a warranty about any particular state of facts can be given, whereas a covenant can be given only to do or not to do something; so, for instance, warranties will cover circumstances where third parties make claims against the target, whereas an equivalent covenant can deal only with whether the seller can respond to such claims. However, in a locked-box deal where the buyer has the economic benefit of the target before completion, it is uncommon for the entire warranty slate to be repeated at completion; rather, only the key title warranties are repeated – thus, the need for a thorough slate of interim period covenants becomes even more imperative.

Additionally, the extent to which a buyer can recover for breaches of covenants may or may not be limited pursuant to the limitations on warranty recovery set forth in the SPA. For example, where the limitations on recoverability apply to all claims under the SPA, as opposed to warranty claims only, recovery for breaches of covenants will also be capped and limited. This, however, is another matter of negotiation.

2.8 Tax covenants, environmental covenants and decommissioning

Certain identified matters relating to the target may also require specific bespoke covenants. These matters are typically tax-related issues and environmental issues. Tax and environmental covenants are sometimes also called tax and environmental indemnities. These are not day-to-day operational controls exercisable by the buyer during the interim period. However, where the financial and tax due diligence and the operational and environmental due diligence identify issues with the target, outside of the customary warranty protections, that the buyer will need to address through specific recourse, tax and environmental covenants will be key provisions in the SPA. For example, where the operational and environmental due diligence identifies a number of missing environmental permits which the target should have maintained, the buyer will undoubtedly require a specific environmental covenant protecting it from liabilities post-completion for the failure by the target to obtain such permits. Alternatively, as is often the case with upstream projects operated under production sharing agreements, cost recovery calculations may be audited for up to six or seven years from when the cost recovery occurred, so buyers will want any tax covenant to cover any historic cost recovery calculations prior to completion.

In this context, and though not necessarily a matter for specific covenant protection, the authors have observed, since the first edition of this volume, an increased focus on the allocation of decommissioning liabilities in North Sea transactions. In the context of the disposal of mature North Sea assets from majors and super-majors to smaller and less well-capitalised investors (which specifically target North Sea opportunities and which may, of course, be better set to extend the lives of those upstream assets and decommission on the basis of longer production profiles), there has been a renewed concentration on whether it is possible to achieve a 'clean break' for sellers in respect of decommissioning liabilities.

In relation to decommissioning security, these North Sea-focused buyers (many of which are experienced management teams backed by PE houses) cannot typically provide customary guarantees or letters of credit, since to do so would erode their balance sheets and reduce their debt capacity. Therefore, parties have increasingly had to develop flexible risk-sharing solutions to address decommissioning risks – for example:

- the seller retaining some proportion of decommissioning liability;
- the seller retransferring decommissioning liability, but providing security on the behalf of the buyer;
- the negotiation of a mechanism that allows for the build-up of revenues from the upstream asset to meet projected decommissioning costs; and/or
- the buyer retransferring the upstream asset to the seller at the point of decommissioning.

This is not to say, however, that the 'clean break' model in respect of decommissioning has been usurped entirely. Obviously, another way of dealing with the types of issues highlighted in the preceding paragraphs (instead of requiring specific covenant protection or a bespoke approach to decommissioning) is to quantify the anticipated expected loss or decommissioning costs as best as possible and factor this into the valuation, thereby reducing the purchase price that is actually paid to the seller.

3. AIPN Model International Farmout Agreement

The provisions set out in this section are taken from the Association of International Petroleum Negotiators (AIPN) Model International Farmout Agreement.[2] If the parties to a transaction do not have a specific set of precedent covenants from which to begin negotiations, the authors contend that the AIPN Model International Farmout Agreement is as good a place to start as any and offers a balanced list of covenants. For the avoidance of doubt, references to the 'farmor' and 'farmee' in the following paragraphs mean the seller and the buyer, respectively.

Each clause is examined in more depth further below, but the AIPN Model International Farmout Agreement is essentially divided into the following main sections:

- a list of positive covenants requiring the seller to do various things;
- a list of negative covenants prohibiting the seller from doing various things;
- a list of things which the seller is permitted to do in any case (effectively, exclusions to the covenants in addition to any carve-outs agreed in the context of individual covenants); and
- a list of mutual covenants on both the seller and the buyer.

In the context of a share transaction where shares in a special purpose vehicle (which holds the upstream assets) are being acquired, the special purpose vehicle itself should give certain covenants, particularly those relating to operational matters affecting the upstream asset. Similarly, the restrictive covenants should apply to the target group of companies, as well as to the special purpose vehicle.

3.1 Positive covenants

From the Signature Date until the Completion Date, and subject to the terms of this Agreement, Farmor shall:

(a) maintain [and operate] the Farmout Interests (i) in a good and workmanlike manner in the ordinary course of business consistent with past practice, and (ii) in accordance with the Contract, [the JOA,][the Specified Instruments], and applicable Laws [, in each case, to the extent required to operate in accordance with the standards set forth in the Contract and the JOA;]/[, in each case, in all material respects;]

(b) maintain its books of account and records relating to the [Farmout Interests / Contract Interest] in the usual, standard and ordinary manner, in accordance with [the usual accounting practices of Farmor / insert accounting standard];

2 The model form cited in this chapter is the 2019 Model International Farmout Agreement set forth at www.aipn.org.

(c) maintain in full force and effect any (i) material license, permit, and other approval from the Government related to the Contract Interest and (ii) bond, letter of credit or other similar credit support instrument maintained by Farmor with the Government or other third party with respect to the Contract Interest;

(d) timely make any and all filings, reports and notices to the Government with respect to the [Farmout Interests / Contract Interest];

(e) maintain insurance coverage on the Contract Interest, and the assets related thereto, [in the amounts and types currently in force / in the amount required by the Contract and applicable Laws];

(f) give prompt written notice to Farmee of any meetings of (i) the operating committee under the JOA, (ii) the operating committee under the Contract and (iii) [•], including copies of the respective meeting agenda and meeting documentation (if any) (in advance of such meetings) and the resulting meeting minutes;

(g) give prompt written notice to Farmee of (i) Farmor's receipt of written notice on any material claim asserting any breach of contract, tort, or violation of Law relating to the Contract, (ii) any investigation, suit, action, or litigation by or before the Government relating to the Contract, (iii) any material spills or other material environmental contamination events occurring with respect to the Contract and (iv) any material damage to or destruction of any of the physical assets comprising the [Farmout Interests / Contract Interest].

Clause (a) is the most fundamental covenant during the interim period and cuts to the heart of the transaction by requiring that the seller maintain and, if it is also the operator, operate the upstream assets being acquired to a certain standard and, most importantly, in accordance with applicable laws. Buyers will insist that this covenant be included and may also require that the covenant refer to good-faith activities and elevate the standard of performance from "good and workmanlike manner" to "good international oilfield practice". Depending on the scope of the definition of 'specified instruments', the seller may limit this by materiality or refer to the specific JOA instead. It would be difficult for any seller to justify not giving this covenant in some form, and any refusal to give such a covenant would no doubt ring alarm bells for the buyer.

Where the compliance with law covenant in limb (ii) of Clause (a) is included, the covenant in Clause (b) is somewhat less material. A seller would typically claim that its content is already covered by Clause (a); although it is arguable, to the contrary, that Clause (a) applies to physical operation of the asset only, whereas Clause (b) goes further than simple physical operation and applies to back-room management of books and records too. However, similarly to Clause (a), a seller's refusal to give this covenant would be difficult to justify, as it is purely a procedural requirement (principally the maintenance of books and records – which presumably the seller is doing in any case).

Clause (c) is another fundamental covenant (although it too is in part potentially covered by limb (ii) of Clause (a), as maintaining permits and credit support would no doubt constitute compliance with specified instruments and laws). A seller could request that limb (c)(ii) also be materiality qualified, consistent with limb (i), although any such credit support arrangements would necessarily be required to be released at completion as the seller would no longer wish to be providing financial support to an asset that it no longer held. Where the due diligence process identifies that any such credit support arrangements are maintained by an affiliate of the seller, the buyer should ensure that the seller confirms that this covenant is applicable to those affiliates too (so that the obligation to maintain such permits and credit support is not somehow diminished or alleviated).

Clause (d) focuses on the relationship between the seller and the host government, and requires that the seller maintain any and all filings required by the host government with respect to the upstream asset. This is a key value driver for any buyer as, in the context of upstream operations, title to any upstream assets is derived from licences with the host government. Accordingly, maintaining a good relationship with the host government is key from the buyer's perspective. A buyer should consider enhancing this covenant by including the words 'properly' or 'accurately', and requiring that such filings be in good faith. A seller will try to argue that this is already covered by limb (ii) of Clause (a), as government filings will be a matter of law. However, given the importance of the relationship with the host government, it is common to see this as a specific further covenant.

With respect to Clause (e), while the seller's insurance policy coverage in respect of the target will terminate upon completion (unless maintained at the target level under a share deal and assumed by the buyer), the buyer will want to know that the target remains suitably insured during the interim period. This is because, pending completion, the buyer will have no way to implement its own insurance at the upstream asset level. The buyer may also want to:

- take an assignment of the benefit of any insurance claims which the seller may have during the interim period; and/or
- include a casualty loss condition precedent in the SPA which enables the buyer to elect not to complete where an insured loss exceeds a negotiated figure.

As with Clauses (b), (c) and (d), the seller could argue that this is also already covered by limb (ii) of Clause (a), as maintaining a minimum level of insurance will in most cases also be a matter of law. The buyer, by contrast, should also require that the assets are either "adequately insured" or "insured to their full replacement value", and that the standard of insurance is to "good international oilfield practice".

Clause (f) provides the informational basis on which the buyer may exercise agreed controls over the seller's actions at meetings of the operating committee in respect of the upstream asset. In the context of a long interim period, controls over the actions of the operating committee represent an important protection for the buyer against value leakage, and the buyer would expect to receive relevant documentation in good time to be able to assess its options ahead of any committee meetings. The inclusion of this covenant, and its scope, are typically determined by the position reached by the parties in respect of the negative covenant discussed in section 3.2(a) below. A strong buyer will seek to extend the covenant to encompass all management committee minutes, operating committee minutes, board minutes and minutes of any similar meeting or proceeding in connection with the company or the asset, as well as any authorisation for expenditure, together with any supporting documentation relating thereto. The seller will, however, expect that such a covenant is qualified by any applicable confidentiality restrictions.

Clause (g) will be extremely important to a buyer from a relationship management standpoint, as it relates to problems and issues that have arisen, which the buyer will have to deal with on and after completion – unless the buyer has the right to elect not to complete (eg, for a failure to satisfy a condition precedent). Some of the matters identified in this Clause (g) may well be outside of the control of the seller (eg, frivolous or vexatious claims by third parties), so the best that a seller can really do in these circumstances is to inform the buyer of the facts so that the buyer can take these things into account in its decision making over the deal. The buyer should seek to enhance this covenant with a 'catch-all' provision requiring the seller to disclose anything material in the context of the target or by reference to some pre-determined amount.

3.2 Negative covenants

From the Signature Date until the Completion Date, and subject to the terms of this Agreement, Farmor shall not (without the prior written consent of Farmee (which consent shall not be unreasonably conditioned, withheld, delayed, or denied):

(a) vote at any meetings held pursuant to the Contract or JOA without prior consulting with the Farmee regarding the respective decision [, after which the Farmor shall vote in accordance with Farmee's instructions];

(b) (i) enter into any contract that, if it had been entered into on or prior to the Signature Date, would have been required to be listed in Exhibit [X] or (ii) materially amend any contract that, if it had been so amended before the Signature Date, would have been required to be listed in Exhibit [X]; except that Farmor shall be allowed to enter into Hydrocarbons purchase and sales, gathering, transportation, and marketing agreements that are entered into in the ordinary course of business and can be terminated without penalty on

ninety (90) Days or less notice; provided, however, that Farmor shall promptly provide Farmee a copy of any such agreement, or any other agreement or material amendment that Farmor enters into in pursuant to this Article [X] or in connection with the activities set forth in Exhibit [X];

(c) transfer, sell, mortgage, pledge, encumber, or dispose of any portion of the Farmout Interests, other than the sale or disposal of Hydrocarbons in the ordinary course of business and sales of equipment that [are no longer necessary in the operation of the [Farmout Interests/Contract Interest] or for which replacement equipment of equal or greater value has been obtained;]/[has a value less than [•] USD (US$[•]);]

(d) other than with respect to the matters described on Exhibit [X], settle any suit or litigation or waive any material claims or rights of material value attributable to the Contract Interest and affecting the period after the Accounting Date;

(e) commit to or commence any operation on the [Farmout Interests/Contract Interest] anticipated to cost [(net to the [Farmout] Interests)] in excess of [•] USD (US$[•]) per operation that was proposed by a third party under an operating agreement with respect to the [Farmout Interests / Contract Interest] without first forwarding the applicable AFE or other notice to Farmee as soon as reasonably practicable following receipt thereof for Farmee's review;

(f) consent to waive any rights of first refusal related to the Farmout Interests;

(g) propose any operations on the Farmout Interests anticipated to cost in excess of [•] USD (US$[•]) per operation;

(h) consent to a change of operator under the JOA;

(i) elect to non-consent or not participate in any operation proposed by a third party under the JOA with respect to the Farmout Interests;

(j) propose or implement any sole-risk operations;

(k) make, change, or revoke any tax election, change an annual accounting period, adopt or change any accounting method, file any amended tax return, enter into any closing agreement, settle or compromise any tax claim or assessment, or consent to any extension or waiver of the limitation period applicable to any claim or assessment, in each case, with respect to taxes affecting the [Contract Interest]; or

(l) commit to do any of the foregoing.

Clause (a) represents a key protection for the buyer in the context of a long interim period. In its most basic formulation, the covenant grants the buyer access to key information about the day-to-day operation of the upstream asset and the opportunity to consult with the seller on matters that may go the value of that asset. A strong buyer will argue that, since it will be taking ownership of the upstream asset (especially where the period of ownership commences with effect from an economic effective date prior to, or on or about, the date of signing), the seller should act on the buyer's instructions in meetings held between the asset owners prior to transfer so as to ensure that no decisions are made that would affect the value attributed to the upstream asset by the buyer (especially as such decisions occur during the buyer's period of economic ownership). Conversely, the seller will be keen to ensure that it is not being 'micro-managed' and forced to engage with the buyer on matters of an immaterial nature, or where to do so would be impractical. A strong seller will typically argue that key elements of this clause are covered elsewhere in the negative covenants (eg, see (f) to (h) below), and restrict this covenant to information and/or consultation only. It is customary for buyer veto rights on voting to apply only to certain specified matters and issues that are of a material nature and/or relate to matters and issues for amounts exceeding a certain threshold.

Clause (b) is a material contract covenant which prohibits the seller from entering into any other contracts material in the context of the target (except for certain 'ordinary course' contracts terminable on 90 days' notice or less). This is a key concern for the buyer, as it will not want the target to be encumbered by further obligations under additional material contracts that it would not have entered into had it been operating the asset. The buyer should also enhance this covenant to refer to no waivers being granted under the existing material contracts (as the buyer will not want to be deemed to have waived a breach by a third party for which the buyer would ordinarily have pursued a claim). The seller, by contrast, will need to be able to enter into and amend contracts that it would otherwise have entered into and amended, and will not want its decision making to be fettered in this respect (especially if completion is highly conditional – as any failure to complete will mean that the target is retained by the seller). At the very least, this covenant should capture licences and production sharing agreements with the host government, JOA and other asset title arrangements. Any resistance from the seller against a covenant applying to these contracts should be a red flag to the buyer.

Clause (c) is as important as Clause (b), as it prohibits the seller from dealing in the target to be acquired and devaluing the asset or creating a third-party interest over the asset, which the buyer must then deal with or otherwise assume the burden created by such third-party interest. In a cash-free/debt-free deal, the buyer will want to take the target unencumbered and be able to do what it wants with it. As with Clause (b), any refusal by the seller to grant a form of this covenant should be a red flag to the buyer, unless either:

- some form of corporate reorganisation is required during the interim period to transfer the targets to the correct special purpose vehicle; or
- a pre-emption right exists in favour of a third party by which the seller is bound.

Clause (d) also represents a key relationship issue that the buyer will need to control as it relates to litigation and claims by third parties. The buyer will normally seek to enhance this covenant and broaden it to restrict any commencement, defence or compromise of claims, and specifically refer to litigation, arbitration and any form of dispute proceeding – whether they are active, pending or threatened. The buyer should also seek to group together series of related claims that in isolation do not rise to the level of materiality, but in the aggregate exceed the materiality level. Additionally, the buyer should agree on a cash value for the materiality level to avoid any potential doubt and minimise any uncertainty as to whether the covenant has been breached. The seller has the option to exclude from this covenant certain claims which it has identified; any such list of exclusions is typically heavily negotiated.

The expenditure covenant in Clause (e) is a key operational control requirement and prohibits the seller from incurring and ramping up significant costs associated with the asset. For example, under a locked-box valuation, these costs would likely be funded either by capital contributions from the seller (which increase the purchase price) or out of cash receivables for the upstream asset (which decreases the working capital being assumed by the buyer at completion). The crux of the buyer's argument here is that the buyer does not want the seller to incur costs that the buyer itself would not have incurred had it been in the seller's position (eg, the buyer may not regard the expenditure as cost effective or may want to direct costs towards a different discovery). The buyer will also want to re-design the covenant, so that instead of requiring notification only, the expenditure is also subject to the buyer's prior approval. However, the seller will resist this and one compromise may be to have two thresholds – beneath the lower threshold, the seller can incur the expenditure; between the lower threshold and the higher threshold, the seller must inform the buyer; and above the higher threshold, the seller must obtain the buyer's consent prior to incurring the expenditure. The same issues arise in the context of the covenant in Clause (g).

The covenant in Clause (f) will not always readily apply, as the target may not have the benefit of any rights of first refusal upon a transfer or sale by any of its co-venturers. However, to the extent that there are any such rights (eg, if another co-venturer seeks to sell its interest in the upstream asset during the interim period which triggers a right of first refusal under the JOA), the buyer will not want the seller to waive such rights without at least some consultation – especially where the buyer is a cash-rich vehicle looking to expand its operations in that particular jurisdiction. The buyer's position will be that it is in the seller's shoes and should have the benefit of any rights to enhance the asset level interest in the joint venture. The seller, however, will not want to be held to ransom by any expression of interest by the buyer to exercise rights of first refusal if there is a high degree of probability that the buyer could be incapable of following through with the acquisition. This would happen, for instance, if the deal between the seller and the buyer terminated because one of the conditions precedent could not be satisfied or a necessary approval could not be obtained; then the buyer would not have stepped into the shoes of the seller in order to exercise the right of first refusal in any case. Accordingly, the seller's liabilities to its co-venture partners should not be prejudiced by any failure of the buyer after the buyer has indicated that the right of first refusal should not be waived. From a buyer's perspective, the language should be enhanced to refer not only to rights of first refusal, but also to pre-emption rights and rights of first offer and other preferential purchase rights.

Clause (h) needs little explanation as it relates directly to the governance and performance of operations of the upstream asset. It would be a big red flag if the seller refused to give this covenant and would suggest some material disharmony between the co-venturers if refused.

Operationally, Clauses (i) and (j) are two sides of the same coin and the buyer will want to know whether the target has potentially ostracised itself from the co-venture group by refusing to participate in an approved operation under the JOA (where backing-in subsequently will be at a substantial premium to the initial cost) or proposed an exclusive operation (where it alone or less than all of the co-venture parties are bearing the sole costs of that exclusive operation). These are increased risk exposures to the buyer and can show clearly the synchronicity and working mechanics of the co-venture group. As with Clause (j), however, Clause (i) should also include an information covenant whereby the seller agrees to notify the buyer if any other co-venture partner proposes its own sole risk programme. To the extent that any such sole risk or non-consent scenarios are expected to arise, they should be fully, fairly and accurately disclosed to the buyer as part of the due diligence phase, so that the buyer can evaluate the risks associated with such operations.

Clause (k) will likely also be covered in the separate tax covenant and deals specifically with taxation liabilities of the target. The buyer will have valued the tax basis of the target and will not want those bases to have changed during the interim period due to an election made by the seller. The buyer should seek to enhance this by also restricting any "entry into or termination or rescission of any agreement with a taxation authority" and, in the context of a share purchase, any "changes to the tax residence of any target company". The seller, by contrast, will likely want to exclude from the covenant anything that is consistent with past practices or that is otherwise required to comply with applicable laws.

3.3 Exclusions to covenants

Notwithstanding anything to the contrary in this Agreement, [Farmor / Operator] may conduct:

(a) emergency operations related to events endangering lives, property, or the

environment; provided Farmor shall notify Farmee of such emergency as soon as reasonably practicable;

(b) operations to avoid any penalty under any order of the Government, provided that Farmor shall provide Farmee with written notice of such operations (including AFEs related thereto) as soon as reasonably practicable following the commencement thereof; or

(c) operations described in the [Disclosure Letter].

As noted above, certain of the specific positive and negative covenants may contain their own individual exclusions that are relevant to the covenant in question. However, it is common for the seller to insist also on general exclusions to the restrictive covenants. For example, the AIPN Model International Farmout Agreement permits sellers to carry out:

- emergency operations where lives, the property or the environment would otherwise be at risk; or
- any operation where not to do so would cause a penalty to be payable under the key upstream asset documents.

The buyer will obviously want to limit the exclusions to the restrictive covenants as much as possible and to permit exclusions to apply only in the most extreme of circumstances. However, the seller will typically request more exclusions, such as the performance of any operations:

- pursuant to an approved work programme and budget disclosed to the buyer;
- under a pre-agreed list of specific documents;
- required by law (although the buyer will argue that this will already be a requirement under the positive covenants – see limb (ii) of Clause (a) in section 3.1 above);
- with the buyer's consent, not to be unreasonably withheld; or
- to carry out any required interim period corporate reorganisation or intra-group arrangement.

3.4 Mutual covenants

From the Signature Date until the Completion Date, and subject to the terms of this Agreement, each of the Parties undertakes to the other Parties:

(a) not to take any action nor fail to take any action prior to the Completion Date that would result in a breach of any of its [Representations and] Warranties under this Agreement;

(b) [•]

As noted previously, the SPA will contain a number of other covenants. Clause (a) is a very buyer-friendly covenant that the seller will typically resist, as it is intended to give effect to the seller warranties throughout the interim period (such that the seller must ensure that those warranties are not breached, regardless of whether they are repeated at completion). The seller may be able to advance some technical arguments in order to change the wording of the warranties clause so as to limit the effect of this covenant (eg, the warranties are given only on the dates expressly set forth in the SPA, so despite the wording of the covenant, there can be a breach of those warranties only on the dates when they are expressed to be repeated, if they are repeated at all); although, as stated above, the seller would typically resist this type of covenant in the first place.

As noted in section 2.7 above, it is also very common for SPAs to deal with each party's obligations to satisfy the conditions precedent and frequently responsibility for each condition precedent will be allocated between the parties. Commonly, the seller and buyer are jointly responsible for regulatory consents from the host government. Buyers may argue that this is technically a seller obligation, as the seller is the incumbent asset-owning party that is subject to the host government's legislation. In reality, the host government will want to assess the incoming buyer's technical and financial capabilities to perform the obligations being assumed as part of the consent process (as, in the authors' experience, a lack of technical and financial capability is the most common ground for refusing government consent), so the regulatory approval is truly a 'joint effort' between the buyer and seller. Obviously, though, any conditions precedent specific to the buyer or the seller (eg, corporate or shareholder or lender approvals, or accuracy of their own representations and warranties) will typically be the sole responsibility of the seller or buyer as appropriate.

4. Draft AIPN Model Form Asset SPA

The Asset Sale and Purchase Agreement Committee (Committee) of the AIPN has recently published an AIPN Model Form International Asset Sale and Purchase Agreement (AIPN SPA). For completeness, the interim covenants of the AIPN SPA are set out below:[3]

Seller obligations

During the Interim Period, Seller shall comply with the following:

(a) Seller shall promptly Notify Buyer and provide details upon the occurrence of: (i) any written notice of default or termination received or given by Seller with respect to the Contract, the JOA, or any of the Documents; (ii) any written notice of any pending or threatened claim, demand, action, suit, inquiry or proceeding related to the Contract, the JOA, or any of the Documents; (iii) any material damage, destruction, or loss to any of the Assets; (iv) any other event or circumstance that has a material impact on operations under the Contract or the JOA; and (v) any event or circumstance that (A) results in, or could

3 The model form cited in this chapter is the 2020 Model Form International Asset Sale and Purchase Agreement set forth at www.aipn.org.

reasonably be expected to result in, a Material Adverse Event or (B) or could reasonably be expected to result in any of Buyer's Conditions Precedent or the Seller's Conditions Precedent not being satisfied by the Longstop Date.

(b) Seller agrees that, unless otherwise approved by Buyer in writing, and to the extent permitted by the Government of [•], the JOA and the Contract it will:

(i) keep Buyer adequately informed of all operations or material operations as are provided by Operator (if Seller is not Operator) conducted pursuant to the Contract [and the JOA];

(ii) keep Buyer fully informed of any changes or proposed changes to the acreage of the Contract Area;

(iii) continue to make available to Buyer, or provide access to Buyer, for its inspection and review all documents and other data, files, records, information, books, accounts, cost recovery filings and the like relating to the Contract Area, as reasonably requested by Buyer;

(iv) [maintain all governmental permits, licenses and approvals affecting operations under the Contract;]

(v) refrain from making or committing to make any expenditure or series of expenditures with regard to any operations within the Contract Area that, in aggregate, exceed [•] US Dollars (US$ [•]) [except to the extent such expenditures are needed to satisfy any minimum work obligations under the Contract];

(vi) [continue to operate the Purchase Interest in a manner consistent with past practices as if the Purchase Interest was not being transferred;]

(vii) [maintain all Data in a secure and accessible fashion;]

(viii) refrain from (A) selling any or all of the Assets, (B) terminating any of the Documents, (C) settling any dispute or litigation to the extent that the settlement amount exceeds [•] US Dollars (US$ [•]) [or (D) voluntarily relinquishing operatorship];

(ix) [refrain from refusing to participate in any Joint Operations under the JOA on the basis of a "non-consent" election;]

(x) [refrain from initiating any Exclusive Operation under the JOA;] and

(xi) consult with Buyer before voting on any decision under [the JOA and] the Contract that is not set out in this Article [(b)].

Mutual Obligations

During the Interim Period Buyer and Seller shall not, and shall procure that their respective Affiliates shall not, take any action or fail to take any action prior to the Completion Date that would result in a breach of any of the Seller [Representations and] Warranties or Buyer [Representations and] Warranties (as applicable to such Party).

Eagle-eyed readers will note that a number of the key themes and, in some cases, identical provisions of the AIPN Model International Farmout Agreement are replicated in the AIPN SPA. This is intentional – the stated aim of the Committee is to take substantial (but not exclusive) guidance from English practice and attempt to harmonise its approach (to the extent possible) with the existing AIPN Model International Farmout Agreement. On this basis, the authors do not propose to consider these covenants in detail, since the arguments for their inclusion and key areas for negotiation are discussed elsewhere in this chapter,[4] but would make the following observations:

- Covenant (a)(i) goes further in scope than its equivalent (see section 3.1(g) above) by including within the seller's notification obligations details of any notice of 'default or termination' under relevant contracts. Such information may not necessarily be covered by the notion of 'breach' in the equivalent covenant of the Model International Farmout Agreement (though a well-advised buyer would typically request this information anyway). The same clause also includes, in (a)(iv) and (v), obligations on the seller to notify the buyer of events or circumstances that could have a material impact on operations under the underlying contracts, that result in or "could reasonably be expected to result in" a material adverse event or "could reasonably be expected to result in" the conditions precedent to the transaction not being satisfied. A strong seller will be wary of the subjective, future-looking nature of these covenants, which introduces a considerable element of ambiguity and uncertainty, and may seek to resist them (though their inclusion in some form is customary). If included, a seller will typically seek to make the determination of whether an event or circumstance is 'notifiable' as objective and certain as possible, by means of clarifying the nature of the tests for 'material adverse event' and 'material', and by arguing for the removal of the forward-facing elements of these covenants.
- Covenants (b)(i) and (ii) are arguably captured by the more general equivalent covenant described in section 3.1(f) above, concerning information relating to meetings of the operating committee – it seeming unlikely that activities relating to operations and changes to acreage would not be discussed in the context of operating committee meetings. Nonetheless, a well-advised buyer would benefit from their inclusion, albeit in some cases qualified by a degree of materiality in relation to (b)(i).

---

4 For completeness: covenants (b)(iii) and (vii) of the AIPN SPA find their counterparts in section 3.1(b) above; covenant (iv) in section 3.1(c) above; covenant (b)(v) in section 3.2(e) above; covenant (b)(viii) in paragraphs 3.2(c)(d)(e) above; covenant (b)(ix) in section 3.2(i) above; covenant (b)(x) in section 3.2(j) above; and covenant (b)(xi) in section 3.2(a) above. The 'mutual' covenants of the AIPN SPA follow closely those in section 3.4 above.

- Although a helpful basis for discussions, covenant (b)(vi) is very narrowly drafted and should not be accepted by a buyer in its current formulation. The authors have highlighted in their comments in relation to section 3.1(a) above that strict controls on the operation of the asset being sold are crucial to maintaining the asset's value during any interim period, and that the standard of operation should refer to an identifiable objective criterion such as "good and workmanlike manner" or "good international oilfield practice". A buyer would be well advised to modify this clause in line those observations.

5. Oil & Gas UK Model Form Sale and Purchase Agreement

The following is taken from the Oil & Gas UK Model Form Agreement for the Sale and Purchase of Assets in the [•] Field:[5]

9.1 Between the date hereof and Completion, the Seller shall (to the extent it is able so to do having regard to the provisions of the Operating Agreement [Unit Agreement]):

(a) continue to carry on its activities in relation to the Asset in the ordinary and usual course so as to protect and maintain the same [in accordance with good oil field practice] and comply with previously agreed decisions of the Operating Committee in relation to the Assets;

(b) consult with the Purchaser with regard to the Asset and co-operate with the Purchaser so as to ensure an efficient handover of the Asset on Completion and use its reasonable endeavours to protect or procure the protection of the Asset for the benefit of the Purchaser;

(c) insofar as reasonably practicable, keep the Purchaser fully informed in a timely manner on any and all matters (not of a routine nature) relating to the Asset; and

(d) not to do or omit to do anything which would result in a breach of any of the Warranties given by it.

9.2 The Seller shall:

(a) not, except with the prior written approval of the Purchaser (such approval not to be unreasonably withheld or delayed) amend or agree to amend any of the Asset Documents in any respect in so far as such amendment or agreement to amend relates to or affects the Asset or waive or agree to waive any of its rights or remedies thereunder or arising therefrom in so far as such rights and remedies relate to or affect the Asset;

(b) if it considers in good faith that a particular matter or proposal is of a nature which may have an adverse effect on the value of the Asset, notify the Purchaser in writing, consult (to the extent reasonably practicable) with the Purchaser in relation to that matter or proposal, take account of any

5 Oil & Gas UK Draft Model Form (reference LEG2520 Final), set forth at www.oilandgasuk.co.uk.

representation which the Purchaser may make and, provided always that such action shall not be prejudicial to any of the Seller's other business interest and the Seller shall not be in breach of any contractual, legal, statutory or regulatory requirement whatsoever by doing so, carry out the wishes of the Purchaser in so far as it is reasonably practicable to do so following such consultation; and

(c) as soon as reasonably practicable provide the Purchaser (to the extent it is contractually and legally permitted to do so) with details of any matter relating to or affecting the Asset on which the Seller is entitled to vote (a "Voting Matter") and, prior to exercising its vote on a Voting Matter, consult (to the extent reasonably practicable) with the Purchaser in relation to the Voting Matter, take account of any representations which the Purchaser may make and provided always that such action shall not be prejudicial to any of the Seller's other business interests and the Seller shall not be in breach of any contractual, legal, statutory or regulatory requirement whatsoever by doing so, exercise its voting rights in a manner which is not inconsistent with the Purchasers' representations.

The interim period covenants in the Oil & Gas UK model form are broadly similar to the covenants in the AIPN Model International Farmout Agreement and the concepts for which protection is sought are the same. For example:

- Clause 9.1(a) is similar to Clause (a) of the positive covenants in the AIPN Model International Farmout Agreement;
- Clause 9.1(c) is similar to Clause (e) of the negative covenants and Clause (g) of the positive covenants in the AIPN Model International Farmout Agreement; and
- Clause 9.1(d) closely follows Clause (a) of the mutual covenants in the AIPN Model International Farmout Agreement.

However, in a number of respects, the Oil & Gas UK model form is substantially more buyer friendly than the AIPN Model International Farmout Agreement, as:

- Clause 9.1(a) elevates the standard to that of 'good oilfield practice'; and
- Clause 9.1(b) requires the seller to ensure an efficient handover of the target to the buyer and to cooperate with the buyer to ensure that this is the case.

Furthermore, Clause 9.1(c) is a more fulsome information-sharing covenant than the requirements of Clauses 9 (f) and (g) of the AIPN Model International Farmout Agreement, in that it is not qualified by materiality or a threshold amount, and applies wholesale to any matters to do with the target assets (other than those matters of a routine nature).

Clause 9.2(a) is reflective of Clauses (b) and (d) of the negative covenants in the AIPN Model International Farmout Agreement (although the waiver in Clause 9.2(a) is not limited by materiality and is therefore again more favourable to the buyer).

Finally, Clauses 9.2(b) and (c) pass, in a more detailed and fulsome manner than as set out in Clause (a) of the negative covenants of the AIPN Model International Farmout Agreement, voting control at the asset level from the seller onto the buyer. Obviously, there are limits to the extent to which the buyer can assume total voting control, but the principle of these clauses is that the seller must vote in accordance with the buyer's instructions (unless that would be prejudicial to the seller's other business interests or cause the seller to be in breach of law or any of the upstream asset documents). These covenants open the door to a significant level of buyer control and any prudent buyer will request some form of voting influence, although sellers will inevitably fight to limit the scope of any such voting covenant.

6. Other typical interim period covenants

Supplementary to the covenant slate in the AIPN Model International Farmout Agreement, the AIPN SPA and the Oil & Gas UK model form, the following are examples of other types of interim period covenants that buyers may request.

6.1 Positive covenants

Adhering to the previously agreed decisions of the target's operating committees:

comply with previously agreed decisions of the operating committees (including with respect to any work programme and budget) in relation to the Assets;

Obviously, to the extent that the seller has exercised any non-consent rights in relation to any such decisions, the seller may seek to exclude those decisions. The seller will need to justify any refusal to include such a covenant or exclusion to such a covenant because non-compliance with operating committee decisions will be a material issue for any buyer.

Allowing a representative of the buyer to attend meetings of the target's operating committees:

allow a representative of the Purchaser, or an Affiliate of the Purchaser, to attend meetings of the operating committee, and any subcommittee that the operating committee may establish, under the Joint Operating;

The buyer may also seek to push for voting rights (as in the Oil & Gas UK model form); but at the very least, the buyer will expect to have observer status at operating committee meetings, so that it can be suitably informed and forewarned about the status of operations.

Paying any and all accounts payable in accordance with their terms:

pay all of its accounts payable, invoices and third party receivables in accordance with their terms;

The buyer will want to ensure that ongoing dealings with third parties (on which the buyer will also be reliant after completion) are also dealt with and handled in the ordinary course (eg, the buyer will not want the seller to interact differently with third parties and jeopardise relationships with third-party suppliers and contractors). The seller will not, however, want this covenant to fetter its right to dispute, in good faith, any amounts in respect of such invoices and receivables. This type of covenant is likely to be even more important where the target being acquired serves as the operator under the JOA of the upstream asset.

Notifying the buyer of any breaches of the upstream asset documents by any of the co-venture partners:

notify the Purchaser of any claim, action, legal proceeding, expert determination reference or arbitration of which written notice has been received by, or which is threatened against, any member of the Seller's Group relating to the Company, the Assets or the Shares;

notify the Purchaser in a timely manner of any facts or circumstances of which it is aware which indicate that there has been a breach by another party of any Upstream Asset Document, any authorisation from any Governmental Authority or any other instrument, document or agreement relating to the Asset.

Although this is similar to the notification covenant described in sections 3.2(a)(i) and (ii) and 4(a) above, the first paragraph above is further reaching and beneficial to the buyer, as it extends beyond the seller to the seller's group. The second paragraph relates to breaches by co-venturers; this will be important from a buyer's perspective, as any such breach could require the buyer post-completion to fund a share of the breaching party's project costs up to the amount of their default. Any such breach could also threaten the sanctity of the upstream asset if, for example, the party in breach is the operator and the other co-venturers cannot step up and fund the operator's share of defaulted costs.

6.2 Negative covenants

Prohibiting the seller from carrying out corporate activities in relation to the special purpose vehicle being acquired in cases of share purchase:

make any adjustments in respect of the share capital of the Company, including issuing any new equity;

acquire or agree to acquire any share, shares or other interest in any company, partnership or other venture;

incur any additional financial indebtedness or prepay or cancel any existing financial indebtedness;

create, allot or issue, or grant an option to subscribe for, any share capital of any Group Company;

repay, redeem or repurchase any share capital of the Company;

make any loan or cancel any loan or other debt (other than in respect of any trade credit in the ordinary course of business) to any person;

enter into any guarantee, indemnity or other agreement to secure any obligation of a third party or create any Encumbrance over any of its material assets or undertaking;

make any change to its accounting practices or policies or amend its constitutional documents;

pass any resolution of its shareholders or any class of shareholders, whether in general meeting or otherwise;

enter into any commitment or take any action with respect to or in contemplation of any liquidation, dissolution or other winding up of any Group Company;

These covenants are typical corporate controls (eg, no share increase or issue, no redemption of capital, no declaration or payment of dividends) that a buyer would expect to see and prohibit corporate actions from being undertaken which directly affect the target being acquired. They are effectively the corporate equivalent of asset-level covenants not to alter the upstream project documents and not declare sole risk operations; they are therefore fundamental to protect the buyer from value erosion of the target. To the extent that a corporate reorganisation is required during the interim period, the seller will likely require an exclusion permitting the seller's group to carry out the necessary corporate actions required for the reorganisation.

Prohibiting the seller from voting in favour of any changes to agreed work programmes and budgets:

vote in favour of changes, revisions or amendments to any approved work programmes or budgets relating to the Asset;

The seller will likely include a *de minimis* exclusion to this covenant, as it will not want to be unduly burdened and prohibited from agreeing to routine and non-material changes to agreed work programmes and budgets.

Prohibiting the seller from agreeing to any other work programmes and budgets:

approve any work programme and budget under the Joint Operating Agreement, or enter into any material expenditure with respect to the Asset;

The buyer will want to control future capital expenditures and not be forced into a costly work programme and budget which it would not otherwise have elected to approve, as this will drastically affect project economics. The longer the interim period, the more likely it is that another work programme and budget vote will be required for a subsequent year; the seller will seek appropriate caveats dealing with this (which will emphasise the importance of satisfying all of the conditions precedent as soon as practicable so that the interim period is shortened). Also, as with Clause (b) of the covenant of the AIPN Model International Farmout Agreement discussed in section 3.2 above, the seller will likely include a *de minimis* exclusion to this covenant.

Prohibiting the seller from amending the terms of any employment contracts with key employees:

make any amendment to the terms and conditions of employment (including remuneration, pension entitlements and other benefits) of any senior employee;

The seller will want to add a materiality qualifier to this covenant so that the restriction does not capture minor *de minimis* amendments of an administrative nature. The seller will also want to narrow the scope of which individuals constitute key employees so that covenant compliance is more manageable.

Prohibiting the seller from dismissing any key employees or engaging any new key employees:

dismiss any senior employee other than for cause or engage or appoint any additional senior employee;

As with the foregoing covenant, the seller will want to narrow the scope of which individuals constitute senior employees and may also include an ordinary course exclusion permitting the buyer to engage new senior employees where required.

Prohibiting the seller from amending any existing or adopting any new employee ancillary benefit programme:

discontinue or amend any benefit arrangements to any material extent or commence to wind them up or terminate them;

The foregoing proposed employee covenants will be a key issue where the buyer expects to be reliant on certain key individuals post-completion and needs their participation and historic knowledge in order to operate the upstream assets. For example, management retention will likely be important where the buyer is entering into a new country by means of the proposed acquisition.

Prohibiting the seller from relinquishing or surrendering any part of the upstream assets:

relinquish or surrender or withdraw from any part of the Asset, or agree or approve or vote in favour of any proposal to do so;

This is a fundamental covenant and is particularly important during the initial exploration phase of an upstream asset when progressing through each exploration stage and into the development phase requires relinquishment of a certain proportion of the upstream asset. Accordingly, any refusal by the seller to give this covenant should be a red flag to a buyer, as the buyer must know the exact acreage that it is acquiring at completion.

Prohibiting the seller from doing or omitting to do anything that could cause any of the upstream asset documents to be terminated or revoked:

do or omit to do anything which could result in the termination, revocation, suspension, modification or non-renewal of any Asset Document, authorisation from any Governmental Authority or any other instrument, document or agreement creating or evidencing the Asset;

This is also another fundamental covenant which cuts to the heart of the transaction; it is a red flag, as any potential termination or revocation of an upstream title document would be catastrophic for the buyer, as there would no longer be any upstream asset to acquire. The seller, however:

- is likely to require that the covenant apply only to acts or omissions which are reasonably likely to cause such termination or revocation; and
- will also narrow the scope of the documents to which this covenant applies (although at the very least the buyer will need this to apply to the upstream title documents).

Prohibiting the seller from commencing any unitisation negotiations:

enter negotiations in respect of the unitisation of any part of the Asset or sign any unitisation agreement relating to any part of the Asset;

This is another key covenant, as unitisation increases the scope of the joint venture group as the target's field will be contiguous with the field of another co-venture group operating a different upstream asset. Unitisation will have a profound effect on reserves figures, as they will be allocated between each separate co-venture group and will affect voting mechanics for operational activities in the unitised area. Accordingly, the seller should have no problem giving such a covenant and the buyer should be fully informed of any unitisation discussions.

Prohibiting the seller from incurring expenditure for any purpose in excess of a pre-agreed maximum figure:

enter into any agreement or incur any expenditure or commitment involving any capital expenditure in excess of US$[•] per item and US$[•] in the aggregate;

As with Clauses (c), (d) and (e) of the negative covenants of the AIPN Model International Farmout Agreement discussed in section 3.2, this is a deal economics issue and the buyer will need to know what financial commitments it is stepping into. The amount agreed will depend on the risk appetite of the buyer and the seller.

Prohibiting the seller from entering into unduly onerous contracts with respect to the target or which are outside the normal course of business of the target:

enter into any contracts which are subject to unduly onerous terms, or which are outside the normal course of business of the Company concerned, or which are not at arms' length, nor terminate any material business relationship (other than expiry in accordance with its terms);

This is a deliberately broad covenant designed to capture any other matters which could be problematic from a buyer's perspective and which are unexpected and out of the ordinary. Sellers are therefore likely to reject this broad covenant and require buyers to identify the specific classes of issue for which they are seeking protection through the other covenants. Sellers will also undoubtedly challenge the ambiguity of the covenant, and argue that referring to issues that cannot be quantified at the time of the transaction is subjective and opens the door for the buyer to shoehorn multiple claims for breach.

There are no hard and fast rules as to which interim period covenants must be provided and this will depend very much on the relative bargaining strength of the parties (although the continued operation of the target in accordance with law and in the ordinary course is clearly a fundamental principle and the most basic of interim period covenants which any buyer should ask for). The need for interim period covenants will also be very much dictated by the transaction structure. For example, where the deal is an asset farmout and the buyer is already a co-venturer in the upstream asset being acquired, the buyer is likely to be already extremely well informed about the asset and will already have a vote at the relevant operating committee level, and may therefore be able to a take a more relaxed approach to interim period covenant protection. However, some combination of the above covenants should be requested by the buyer to protect the target being acquired from losing value in the interim period or from being further encumbered and subjected to other third-party interests. To the extent that the seller is resistant to providing interim covenants, the buyer should insist that more warranties be repeated at completion.

7. Post-completion covenants

While the bulk of protections that a buyer will need relate to the interim period prior to which the buyer owns and has control over the target, a number of other covenants are also typically included in SPAs.

In the context of a share purchase, where the buyer acquires the special purpose vehicle, the seller will want to know that post-completion, the buyer is disassociating itself and the target from the seller's corporate group, as the seller will not want an external unrelated party (the buyer and, post-completion, the target) from holding itself out as part of the seller's group. Accordingly, the buyer will normally provide a covenant to ensure that name changes are made and signage removed within a certain timeframe after completion (this can range from 30 days to 180 days, depending on the complexity of the jurisdiction) – for example:

> *No later than thirty (30) days following the Closing Date the Buyer will, and will cause each Company to, change its name and register such change of name with the registrar of companies in [•], and as soon as reasonably practicable but no later than [•] days following the Closing Date the Buyer will, and will cause each Company to, cease using the word "•" or any variation or derivative thereof (including any logo, trademark or design containing such name or word or derivative or otherwise associated with the Seller or any member of the Seller's Group) in connection with the business of any member of the Buyer's Group, and as soon as reasonably practicable but no later than [•] days following the Closing Date the Buyer will remove any signage or logos or marks referring to any of the above.*

The seller will also want to ensure that it is not prejudiced should the tax authorities conduct an audit of its activities and tax filings post-completion. Accordingly, the seller may require the buyer to covenant that tax and financial records will be maintained by the buyer for a sufficient period of time after completion to satisfy tax legislation and to grant the seller reasonable access to those records in the event that an audit is conducted:

For a period of [•] years after the Closing or, if longer, for the applicable statute of limitations with respect to records and data relating to Tax, the Buyer shall, and shall cause each Company to, preserve and retain the records and data and all other corporate, accounting, legal, auditing and other books and records relating to the Company (including any documents relating to any governmental or non-governmental actions, suits, proceedings or investigations).

As with any other sale and purchase transaction, the seller may try to include customary post-completion restrictive covenants on non-solicitation of employees of the seller's group (a common feature of PE transactions – in which case a full suite of seller protections is customarily proposed – but otherwise relatively uncommon). However, unlike sale and purchase transactions in other sectors, any such post-completion restrictive covenants do not typically include non-solicitation of customers and non-compete clauses, as the very nature of the upstream industry necessitates that sellers and buyers will likely be dealing with the same contractors and offtakers. In any case, the same principles that apply to other restrictive covenants will be applicable. Accordingly, any such covenants will need to be reasonable, proportionate and justifiable to protect the seller's legitimate business interests – consequently, covenants for more than 12 months are, in the authors' experience, uncommon:

Except as permitted pursuant to this Agreement or otherwise agreed to in writing by the Parties, for a period of [•] months from the date of this Agreement no member of the Buyer's Group shall solicit for hire any employee, officer, or representative of any member of the Seller's Group (including any employee of any member of the Seller's Group that is seconded to either Company or works on projects relating to either Company or the Interests).

Additionally, SPAs will include typical covenants to comply with completion obligations, such as entering the buyer into the corporate shareholder books, removing and appointing new directors and officers, and passing the necessary corporate resolutions (especially where the transaction is a share purchase deal and the buyer is acquiring a special purpose corporate vehicle) – for example:

The Buyer will comply with all registration and filing requirements imposed by a Governmental Entity in connection with the matters contemplated by this Clause [•].

In smaller transactions, the handover of books and records during the early exploration phase is frequently dealt with as a completion deliverable. However, where the transaction involves a long-term producing asset, the seller may simply be unable to hand over all the books and records relating to the upstream asset at completion. In this case, the buyer will require a covenant from the seller that those books and records are handed over within a certain period after completion. This period will be subject to negotiation between the parties and depend on how much unbundling is required by the seller to separate the necessary books and records from the other books and records in the seller's group. From the buyer's perspective, though, following completion (unless there is a deferred component to the purchase price), the buyer will have no financial leverage over the seller to incentivise the seller to provide these documents quickly. There is effectively no penalty if the seller breaches this covenant other than a damages claim (for which losses will likely be difficult to quantify). It is therefore in the buyer's best interests to ensure that all of the material books and records are handed over at completion (with the less important ones to follow pursuant to the covenant).

To the extent that the transaction requires a release of liability of any member of the seller's group, the SPA will most likely also include a covenant by the buyer to indemnify the seller post-completion where the seller's group incurs losses as a consequence of the liability not being released by the buyer.

8. Conclusion

Interim period covenants in SPAs are extremely important, and are the only way that a buyer can influence and exercise any element of control over the target assets that it is acquiring before completing the actual acquisition and – crucially from a PE perspective – ensure that the valuation methodology applied to an asset is not undermined during that interim period. Without any interim period covenants, a buyer would essentially be at the behest of the seller and reliant entirely on warranties (many of which may not be repeated at completion, thereby leaving the buyer exposed). Interim period covenants are therefore a fundamentally important component of any transaction with a non-simultaneous signing and completion (although in a seller's initial bid draft in an auction process, it is frequent that either very few or no interim period covenants are included in the draft SPA).

In the opinion of the authors, the recent trend – particularly in a low oil price environment where super-major sellers are looking to exit from non-core assets – is for deal certainty. Therefore, sellers are now more willing than has previously been the case to trade recourse and post-completion liability (including in relation to decommissioning liabilities) for less transaction conditionality, as a certain exit is frequently the main priority for sellers looking to de-risk their asset portfolio. This means that sellers are becoming pragmatic when it comes to buyers' requests for interim period control. Greater deal certainty means a greater chance that completion will occur, and that the buyer will assume the target and the upstream assets; consequently, the buyer will require influence and control over how those assets are to be operated pending completion. This does not mean that sellers write blank cheques and grant buyers whatever interim period covenants they ask for; it does mean, though, that buyers can get a robust slate of controls during the interim period.

In the context of a low oil price, interim period covenants unquestionably take on greater significance as part of any transaction, as the reins are tightened across the sector on project expenditure and capital commitments. Therefore, any incurrence of further costs and expenses and any agreement for extensive further work operations by a seller during the interim period will be key issues for any incoming buyer, and will need to be controlled and influenced to some degree.

As at the date of this second edition, the COVID-19 pandemic is sweeping across the globe. Its impact has put significant pressure on deal certainty and valuations, as buyers foresee doom and gloom and sellers try to capitalise on higher exit prices. This has only placed more emphasis on interim period covenants as transaction counterparties try to ride out the uncertainty created by the pandemic. In particular, the authors have observed buyers seeking more interim period controls to prevent value erosion and requiring more information sharing around potential *force majeure* and frustration claims, which excuse or prohibit the performance of a seller's existing contractual obligations.

Oil and gas warranties

Caroline-Lucy Moran
Akin Gump Strauss Hauer & Feld LLP

1. Introduction

The negotiation of the warranties, above other provisions of a sale and purchase agreement (SPA), plays out as perhaps the best illustration of the allocation of risk between the buyer and the seller. While price and price adjustments will be the central commercial focus in this regard, it is the warranties, indemnities and the associated disclosure letter that best tell the story of the nitty-gritty apportionment of legal liability between parties. Indeed, the negotiation of the warranties is often referred to as the 'battle of risks'.[1]

The discussion in this chapter is relevant to both asset and share transactions in the oil and gas industry. The term 'target' refers to the collective assets or shareholding that is being purchased. The term 'transferred interest' refers more specifically to the legal title (or the participating interest) in the upstream oil and gas asset being acquired, whether directly (in the case of an asset transaction) or indirectly through the purchase of shares.

2. Function of warranties

2.1 Purpose of warranties

The evolution of warranties as a customary feature of an SPA stems from the concept of *caveat emptor* ('let the buyer beware'). By this English law principle, the buyer is something of an underdog in a sale transaction. The buyer is not protected if it transpires that the target is less than expected, other than in the case of specific categories of grievous behaviour by the seller or a breach of express contractual terms. For this reason, buyers have come to demand warranties as binding assurances from the seller: as contractual statements of fact about the circumstances, conditions, status or qualities of the target and matters connected with it.

By giving a warranty, a seller accepts potential liability if it is breached; whereas by refusing to give a warranty, or by caveating or disclosing against it, a seller passes

1 Robert Thompson (ed), *Sinclair on Warranties and Indemnities on Share and Asset Sales*, 9th edn, Sweet and Maxwell, p2.

all or part of that risk to the buyer.[2] While a buyer will usually insist on an extensive set of warranties, which it will justify as market standard, an astute seller will seek to restrict and qualify the warranties and thus reduce its exposure to future liability with respect to a target that it has disposed of. In the negotiation of warranties, the 'devil is in the detail', with lawyers from both sides seeking to alleviate their client's risk through the precise wording of the warranties.

A secondary but more immediate function of warranties is to assist in the flushing out of information about the target. During pre-acquisition due diligence, a buyer will investigate the books, records and agreements of a target, review the disclosure letter and put questions to management to identify risks, liabilities and notable issues, primarily for valuation purposes. A buyer's due diligence findings will influence its negotiation of the purchase price and the SPA terms. It is crucial, from a buyer's perspective, that the risks identified are reflected in the drafting of the SPA. If a buyer has limited capacity to require this (eg, due to a competitive bidding process in which SPA amendments are not permitted), then a due diligence exercise will be of limited value.

2.2 Damages for breach of warranty

When drafting any SPA provision, it is important to keep in mind what rights and liabilities may arise should the parties find themselves in a contentious situation. In practice, the majority of claims relating to warranties are for compensation by way of damages for breach of warranty in contract. Although specific rights are available to the buyer in the case of the seller's grievous behaviour (eg, fraud, undue influence, unconscionable conduct), claims on these grounds are often avoided, as they are difficult to establish at law.

In the case of a warranty statement that is also expressed as a representation, a buyer will also be able to make a claim for misrepresentation in tort and under the Misrepresentation Act 1967, including the remedy of rescission due to misrepresentation. This will depend, however, on the exact wording of the SPA. While it is common to see the seller 'warrant and represent' certain facts and matters, a cautious seller will avoid this language. Recent case law specific to the oil and gas industry has reiterated that without it, English law will not generally construe warranties as amounting to representations.[3] Further, it is common practice for the SPA to contain an express exclusion of liability for misrepresentation, which is seen as beneficial to both parties, on balance, to provide certainty that the transaction cannot be unwound.

---

2 *Ibid*, p1.

3 In *Idemitsu Kosan Ltd v Sumitomo Corporation* [2016] EWHC 1909, Idemitsu (as buyer) alleged several breaches of warranty in relation to issues affecting two oilfields. Idemitsu was time-barred from bringing a claim for breach of warranty and instead sought to bring claims for misrepresentation, thus essentially claiming that the warranties given by Sumitomo under the SPA could be construed as representations. The case failed, and the court held that the wording and structure of the SPA demonstrated that the warranties could not be representations.

Even when a seller gives a representation, the remedy of rescission of a contract (which is to restore the parties as far as possible to their original position) may be of some value to a buyer during an interim period under the SPA, but it is generally an unrealistic solution post-completion – not least because the unwinding of the transaction after this point may be impossible.

Thus, if a warranty is found to be untrue or incorrect, a buyer will commonly seek damages for breach of contract. A full discussion of the assessment of damages is beyond the scope of this chapter, but the summary principles are noted here.

The general rule is that damages should, to the extent that a monetary award is able to, place the claimant in the same position as if the contract had been performed. The award effectively takes the form of a compensation payment to the injured party. In the case of a breach of warranty, a damages award should place the claimant in the same position as if the warranty had been true at the time that it was given. An assessment of damages will take into account all losses incurred by the buyer as a result of the breach, subject to the principles of remoteness, mitigation and causation. There are no rigid rules for the quantification of damages in the case of a breach of contract and each case will turn on its specific facts.

Damages awarded for warranty claims are often described as a method of purchase price adjustment, albeit one that is pursued through a dispute resolution mechanism (and with the accompanying costs, inconvenience and uncertainties). The limitations of liability which may apply to a damages award are set out in a separate chapter.

2.3 Scope of subject matter

Section 4 of this chapter sets out examples of common warranties given by a seller for purposes of an upstream oil and gas transaction. In addition, a seller will provide assurances on topics common to the vast majority of acquisitions, regardless of sector. These include, for example, warranties regarding the due constitution of the seller and target companies, financing and banking, real property, employment, insurance, accounting and the absence of insolvency and disputes. Despite their importance, these issues lack industry specificity and are not exemplified here. Warranties in relation to tax, environmental, decommissioning and anti-bribery matters are discussed in depth in other chapters.

2.4 Warranties versus indemnities

In a chapter on warranties, it is worth acknowledging their distinction from indemnities. As previously discussed, an SPA warranty is a contractual assurance of a target's circumstances on a particular date, and the burden will be on the buyer to prove the breach and the loss in order to recover compensation. An indemnity, by contrast, is a reimbursement obligation, employed in an SPA context in order to shift the risk of an identified matter to the seller (as indemnifying party) so that the buyer (as indemnified party) will recover on a dollar-for-dollar basis in respect of that matter.

An indemnity will work to the advantage of a buyer in several ways. First, a buyer will be able to recover all loss actually suffered, and there is generally no need for the buyer to prove a link between the liability and the value of the target. The nature and quantum of potential loss need not be identifiable in order to be indemnified (and indeed, if the quantum of loss is certain, then it is best dealt with not as an indemnity, but instead by way of an upfront reduction in the purchase price).

Of further advantage to a buyer is that the common law defences and limitations for the assessment of damages (eg, the buyer's duty to mitigate loss) do not definitively apply to an indemnity (which is traditionally seen as a claim in debt).[4] Lastly, by use of an indemnity, the buyer can specifically negotiate, and document in the SPA, that it is 'held harmless' against a wider set of costs and expenses, usually on an after-tax basis, than would be the case if it were recovering under a warranty.

The scope of indemnities under the SPA will be a key point for negotiation, and will be limited to specific matters known by the buyer and entailing risk which it is agreed should be borne by the seller. The very fact of buyer knowledge itself is a justification for the use of an indemnity because, following debate in a couple of high-profile cases,[5] it has become generally accepted that a buyer's awareness of relevant facts and circumstances at the time of entering into an SPA is an arguable defence against a buyer claim for breach of warranty.

It is common in any upstream oil and gas acquisition for a buyer to consider seeking indemnities in relation to, for example, unresolved disputes and certain tax, environmental and decommissioning liabilities. In any SPA, there is likely to be some overlap between the subject matter of the warranties and indemnities; and even with specific indemnity protection, it is not in the buyer's interests to diminish the scope of protection for the same subject matter under the warranties.

Often in the United States, and also on international private equity transactions, a buyer may require the seller to give warranties on an 'indemnity basis'. In an English law context, this approach would see the buyer seeking to

---

4 This approach was called into question by *Total Transport Corp v Arcadia Petroleum Ltd (The Eurus)* [1998] 1 Lloyd's Rep 351, in which it was held that there was no authority for the presumption that an indemnity claim is not subject to the rules of remoteness. Here, the Court of Appeal cited a paragraph in *Halsbury's Laws of England* that the "extent of a person's liability under an indemnity depends on the nature and terms of the contract". If acting for the buyer, it is thus advisable to make expressly clear that the rules relating to remoteness and mitigation are excluded for purposes of the indemnities.

5 See *Eurocopy plc v Teesdale* [1992] BCLC 1067 and *Infiniteland Ltd v Artisan Contracting Ltd* [2005] EWCA Civ 758.

avoid entirely the hurdles to recovery by way of a damages claim for any breach of warranty. The approach, however, is not common in upstream oil and gas transactions and has not found widespread traction in English law SPAs generally, and it is likely to be strongly opposed by a seller.

3. Negotiation of warranties

3.1 Timing of application of warranties

The timing of the application of warranties will depend on the transaction completion structure under the SPA. Where there is simultaneous signing and completion, the warranties will be stated to apply at the date of the SPA. More commonly in the upstream oil and gas industry, there will be an interim period between signing and completion, during which the seller will continue to operate the target business. This period is primarily to accommodate conditions precedent (eg, in relation to regulatory and consent requirements) and may last a significant length of time (sometimes years). This is seen particularly in jurisdictions where political risk is prevalent and where, for example, ministerial approval is a more uncertain process.

A buyer may seek to protect itself with respect to the target's interim business between signing and completion by requiring that the warranties apply at the date of the SPA and are repeated at the date of completion. The rationale for this approach is that a buyer must first rely on the warranties in order to enter into the transaction, but will also need to be protected as far as possible from any changes to, or additional risk incurred by, the target during the interim period, which is outside the buyer's control. A less common approach by a buyer, albeit one that may be encouraged by a transaction lender, is requiring that the warranties be repeated at all times up to and including completion, which will have the effect of accelerating the rights available to a buyer if a warranty becomes inaccurate.

Whether and to what extent the warranties are repeated is a matter for negotiation, and will interplay in part with the scope of other buyer protections under the SPA, such as interim covenants. Where warranties are repeated, the scope of warranties to be repeated is also negotiable. A buyer will ideally seek repetition of all warranties and ultimately will wish to ensure that, at a minimum, certain fundamental warranties are repeated. These will commonly include, for example, warranties in relation to title, tax, environment and anti-bribery and corruption matters. A seller will seek to limit this to a repetition of warranties dealing with matters within its control. The ability of the seller to update its disclosures for events occurring during the interim period is also negotiable. The parties may also agree to specific buyer remedies (eg, an SPA termination right) if a breach of warranty occurs prior to completion.

3.2 Co-participants

Upstream oil and gas projects depend on the grant of a concession, licence, production sharing contract (PSC), risk service agreement or similar instrument (each, in this chapter, a 'licence') issued by a host government ('government'). Given that such projects are often developed by two or more commercial companies, a licence is often held by several entities (each, a 'co-participant'), each having a participating interest and, more often than not, being party to a joint operating agreement (JOA). In the case of a PSC model, the government's state-owned company may be a co-participant, itself having direct contractual rights with respect to joint operations on the licence.

The licence forms the cornerstone of the buyer's contractual and regulatory relationship with the host government and will impose joint and several liability on a future buyer for the acts of co-participants. In conducting due diligence and drafting warranties, the creditworthiness, competence and compliance of non-selling co-participants are therefore relevant considerations. The buyer will want to extend some warranties to cover the activities of non-selling co-participants, and the extent to which a seller will provide this comfort will be negotiated. In the case of warranties where a seller is asked to provide assurances about the conduct of a co-participant, these are typically qualified as being given "so far as the seller is aware".

3.3 Warranty qualifiers

The language described in the preceding paragraph is one example of a number of typical drafting qualifiers to the warranties, which a seller employs to limit their scope. These can be grouped into qualifiers in relation to knowledge, materiality and time. Of greatest importance is the limiting of the warranties by reference to disclosures in the disclosure letter.

(a) Knowledge

It is usual for the seller to seek to caveat certain warranties on a knowledge basis, in order to limit their scope to facts and circumstances of which it is expressly aware. This is seen particularly in the case of warranties regarding facts and circumstances relevant to the target but determined by third parties. These may include, for example, warranties relating to the threat of legal claims, which inevitably exist without seller involvement. A non-operator seller may also wish to caveat warranties regarding operational matters by reference to seller knowledge, on the basis that it is the operator (and not the seller) that is in control of, and has full visibility regarding, operational matters.

Example warranty:

Each Group Company is in compliance with all Environmental Laws. No action, suit, proceeding, hearing, investigation, charge, complaint, demand or notice has been filed or commenced or, so far as the Seller is aware, is threatened against any

Group Company alleging any failure to so comply. So far as the Seller is aware, there are no facts or circumstances that may lead to any breach of or liability under any Environmental Laws or any claim in relation to the Environment.

The wording will vary depending on drafting style, and the above approach is interchangeable with terms such as "to the best of the seller's knowledge". In each case, it is in both parties' interests to expressly specify in the SPA what is meant by the term in question. For the buyer, a knowledge qualifier should be defined to impute a high level of attention and investigation on the seller's part. The seller, by contrast, will wish to be bound to have made only such investigations as it could reasonably be expected to have made, which in the absence of an express statement in the SPA is the standard of awareness that will be taken by the courts to be implied by such a qualifier.[6] Both stances are shown in the example below, which also illustrates the seller-friendly approach of defining seller awareness by reference to a limited group of persons within the seller business.

Example provision:

The phrase "so far as the Seller is aware" shall refer to the actual knowledge of each of [insert] and [insert], [each having made due and careful enquiry] / [as if each such person had made reasonable enquiry of each of the Senior Employees].

Where the drafting refers to named individuals, it is in the seller's interests to limit the list to a small group of senior management, on the basis that those people will be aware of material issues relevant to the business. A buyer, by contrast, should push to also specifically name the personnel responsible for day-to-day operational decisions and who are likely to be the individuals receiving incoming notifications and updates in relation to the topic in question.

In the example above, awareness is limited not only to the actual knowledge of named individuals, but also to those named individuals having made reasonable enquiries. It is in the buyer's interests, if faced with such a seller proposal, to remove this double limiting and push for senior employees to be included in the list of those having actual knowledge. At the very least, the buyer will want to ensure that the combined group of named individuals and defined 'senior employees' are as numerous and relevant a group of individuals as possible.

Rarely, but in cases where the seller has a significant advantage in negotiations (eg, an auction sale) or where the buyer already has detailed knowledge or involvement with the target business (eg, where it is an existing co-participant), the seller may insist that the majority of warranties be qualified by reference to seller knowledge.

---

6 See *William Sindall plc v Cambridgeshire CC* [1994] 1 WLR 1016.

Example provision:

Except for the Absolute Warranties, the Environmental Warranties and the Tax Warranties, all of the Warranties of the Seller shall be deemed to be qualified by the expression "so far as the Seller is aware".

This is not common practice, however, and it is usually justifiable to apply knowledge qualifiers to only a limited number of warranties, on a case-by-case basis, in light of specific shortcomings in the seller's awareness of the facts and circumstances.

(b) Materiality

A seller may also seek to limit certain warranties by reference to materiality, which may or may not be defined. Perhaps the best examples of this form of qualifier are the warranties given in relation to the contractual documents of the target. Given the sheer volume of documentation held by the target business, it is common that an upstream oil and gas SPA uses 'material contract' as a defined term. This is either a specific list of documents (perhaps annexed to the SPA) and/or a list of categories of key documents, including those deemed material by reference to being of value, or involving liability, in excess of a specific monetary amount. The example definition below sets out a typical approach to the use of a monetary threshold concept for purposes of this definition, but note that such a definition will in practice also capture further bespoke, and often lengthy, categories of documents.

Example definition extract:

"Material Contract" means: (x) any agreement (or related group of agreements) for a contract value in excess of United States Dollars [insert] (US$ [•]) per year or by the performance of which any Group Company assumes or incurs a liability, obligation or expense in excess of United States Dollars [insert] (US$ [•]) per year; (y) any agreement for the acquisition, divestment, assignment or transfer of shares or assets with consideration in excess of United States Dollars [insert] (US$ [•]); and (z) [any agreement of strategic importance to any Group Company].

The use of such a defined term, and materiality qualifiers generally, removes matters of a more inconsequential nature from the scope of the warranties and in doing so arguably helps to avoid spurious warranty claims. Importantly for the buyer, the above example includes a catch-all for contracts of strategic importance which may be of low monetary value, but essential to the continued running of the business.

It is also common (as is also seen in limb (d) of the example below) for materiality qualifiers to be left undefined in most contexts. In this case, it would be for the court (or an arbitrator) to determine what is a "material breach or default", a "material omission" or a failure to be "correct and true in all material respects" (being typical examples), given the facts and circumstances of the matter at hand. This approach recognises that certain circumstances are difficult to quantify and also avoids the buyer and seller potentially spending significant time negotiating often arbitrary monetary thresholds.

Example warranty:

(a) The Seller has provided the Buyer complete and accurate copies of all Material Contracts.

(b) Each Material Contract is in full force and effect and is enforceable in accordance with its terms.

(c) No Material Contract has been terminated, suspended, annulled, cancelled, avoided, relinquished, surrendered, forfeited, revoked, rescinded or repudiated, in whole or in part.

(d) No Group Company has committed a material breach or default of a Material Contract, no other party to a Material Contract is in material breach or default of such Material Contract and no event has occurred which has resulted in or which (with the giving of notice and/or the lapse of time and/or relevant determination thereunder or otherwise) is likely to result in a material breach or default thereof.

(e) No new Material Contract is under negotiation (to the extent that a draft contract has been exchanged), and no written demand for any renegotiation has been received. With respect to any such Material Contract that is renewable in the ordinary course, no Group Company intends to not renew any Material Contract at the end of its current term, and no Group Company has received any written notice from another party to any Material Contract that such party does not intend to renew it at the end of its current term.

A seller with the upper hand in negotiations may (rarely) seek to employ a materiality qualifier to the giving of warranties as a whole (eg, by providing that the warranties "shall be true and correct in all material respects"). This should be strongly resisted by a buyer for the purposes of SPA date warranties, because it makes ambiguous the very giving of the warranties and thus undermines the buyer's protection. It may, however, be more palatable for the purposes of warranties to be repeated at completion, given that the buyer will have also had the benefit of interim covenants and information rights to cover issues arising in the preceding interim period.

(c) Time

The warranties in an SPA are generally not time-restricted: there is no backstop date and the warranty is simply given on the date stated (and on any subsequent date of repetition of warranties). This traditional format of warranties means that "there could be a breach however long ago the occurrence of the relevant event".[7] For this reason, a seller may seek to limit the

7 Robert Thompson (ed), *Sinclair on Warranties and Indemnities on Share and Asset Sales*, 9th edn, Sweet and Maxwell, p48.

operation of the warranties to the period of its ownership, thus avoiding liability for facts and circumstances prior to its control. However, as Sinclair notes, this is a flawed approach because one party must take on the historic risk and the argument against doing so is weightier for the buyer.

In practice, the use of time qualifiers in the warranties is thus mostly limited. They may be adopted, however, where warranties are given in relation to recently implemented laws or policies, as is often seen, for example, in certain anti-bribery warranties.

Example warranties:

At no time during the past five (5) years has any Group Company or any Company Representative:

(i) violated applicable Sanctions Laws and Regulations; or

(ii) knowingly engaged in any dealings or transactions with any person, or in any country or territory, that is a Sanctions Target, nor is any Group Company currently engaged in any such activities.

In the two (2) years prior to the date of this Agreement, no member of the Seller Group has received any subpoenas from any United States Governmental Authorities in respect of Sanctions Laws and Regulations or received written notice that it is under investigation by any United States Governmental Authority in respect of Sanctions Laws and Regulations.

The use of any time period qualifier and the length of the time period are matters for negotiation between the parties.

(d) Disclosure

The seller's primary method of qualifying the warranties is by making disclosures against them, typically in a disclosure letter. As well as caveating the seller's assurances, the disclosure letter is central to the purpose of warranties because, as previously mentioned, it is a means for the buyer to obtain upfront information about the target, enabling it best to negotiate the purchase price and/or seek specific indemnities (or indeed walk away) if the target is not as expected. The disclosure letter itself will be negotiated, with the buyer looking both to understand fully and make unambiguous the facts and circumstances of specific disclosures about the target, and to limit the general disclosures that will be included in any standard form.

The seller's first draft general disclosures will be wide-reaching, covering matters with respect to which the buyer has the ability to access information publicly or search for it by an established process (eg, in the United Kingdom, a search of registers filed at Companies House, Her Majesty's Land Registry and Her Majesty's Land Charges Registry).

In each case, the buyer should remove any general disclosure unless it will actually conduct (or at least thinks it is reasonable that it should conduct) the relevant investigation, and should ensure that the timing specified for such investigation in the disclosure letter aligns with the date on which it actually occurs. For example, a seller seeking to disclose generally matters that would be discoverable on an asset site visit on the date of the disclosure letter should be rejected by a buyer if such a visit is nigh impossible (particularly if the asset is remote or offshore). Similarly, the buyer should reject any vague reference to disclosure of matters "in the public domain", which would effectively include any matter discoverable on the Internet.

The buyer will usually need both to mark up the seller's specific disclosures and to make further enquiries as a result of them. Often, the seller's first draft disclosure letter will contain only skeleton details about the facts of a matter disclosed; but it is in both parties' interest to ensure that the disclosure is as clear and complete as possible in order to convey the risk at hand. Most importantly for the buyer, the specific disclosures must ultimately align with the findings of its due diligence process. It is common for a seller to make late disclosures as the signing of a transaction approaches (often, having not sufficiently focused on the details of the warranties until a late stage). Should the disclosure prove material in the buyer's eyes, it will need to stand its ground to negotiate a price reduction or seek appropriate protection in the SPA.

Frequently, particularly on transactions where the seller has the upper hand, the seller may be able to extend the scope of its disclosures beyond those specified in the disclosure letter (which is commonly supplemented by an annexed limited bundle of key documents) to all matters disclosed via information in the data room. This provision may be included in the general disclosures in the disclosure letter or in the SPA itself, perhaps through use of a defined term, as exemplified below.

Example definition:

"Disclosed Information" means: (a) the documents and information made available to the Buyer in the Data Room as at [•]; (b) the Disclosure Letter; and (c) this Agreement.

Whether or not this is acceptable to the buyer will depend on the nature of the data room and the wider context of the transaction. If, for example, the buyer has an existing familiarity with the target and the underlying documentation, this may be a palatable approach If, by contrast, the data room material is vast or the disclosure of documents has been a disorganised process, the buyer should reject this provision. In such cases, it is particularly important that the buyer also reject any provision which states that "brief particulars" in the disclosure letter are sufficient to deem "full disclosure" of a matter, unless the buyer has asked for further details. In general, the buyer should not accept any of the seller's burden to determine what disclosures are required by the warranties.

Whatever the scope of disclosure, it is in the buyer's interest that the SPA contains specific provisions as to the standard of disclosure. It is usual for an

SPA to include a provision that the warranties are qualified only to the extent that they are "fully and fairly" disclosed by the buyer, as exemplified below. These terms will be interpreted in accordance with established common law, a discussion on which is beyond the scope of this chapter.[8]

Example provision:[9]

The Warranties are given subject to matters fully, fairly and specifically disclosed with sufficient details to identify the nature and scope of the matter disclosed in the [Disclosure Letter/Disclosed Information] [but no other information relating to the Target of which the Buyer has knowledge (actual, constructive or imputed) and no investigation by or on behalf of the Buyer shall prejudice any claim made by the Buyer under the Warranties or operate to reduce any amount recoverable, and liability in respect thereof shall not be confined to breaches discovered before Completion].

As previously mentioned, English case law has seen it generally accepted that a buyer's actual awareness of relevant facts and circumstances at the time of entering into an SPA is an arguable defence against a buyer claim for breach of warranty.[10] Nonetheless, in a buyer-friendly SPA (and as exemplified in the square-bracketed portion of the example above), the buyer may attempt to preserve its right to make a claim, even where it has actual knowledge of the issue in hand. The seller should resist this approach, on the basis that it is most likely afforded greater protection under common law. Disclosure letters are discussed in further detail in a separate chapter.

As well as being constrained by the aforementioned disclosures and drafting qualifications to the warranties, a buyer having a warranty claim will also be subject to the limitations on seller liability, which are addressed in a separate chapter.

4. Example warranties[11]

4.1 Use of this section

The remainder of this chapter describes warranty features specific to the upstream oil and gas industry. The warranty examples here and elsewhere in this chapter are included for the purposes of illustrating the issues discussed and are not provided as recommended clauses. Bracketed language in the examples highlights wording which may be subject to negotiation between the parties.

As previously mentioned, these examples relate to upstream oil and gas

---

8 See, for example, *Daniel Reeds Ltd v EM ESS Chemists Ltd* [1995] CLC 1405 and *MAN Nutzfarhrzeuge AG v Freightliner Limited* [2005] EWHC 2347 (Comm).

9 Buyer-friendly example from Practical Law Corporate, practice note, *Disclosure: Acquisitions* by Paul Dolman, Travers Smith.

10 See *Eurocopy plc v Teesdale* [1992] BCLC 1067 and *Infiniteland Ltd v Artisan Contracting Ltd* [2005] EWCA Civ 758.

11 This section contains extracts from the chapter "Due diligence and warranties" in Marc Hammerson and John LaMaster (eds), *Oil and Gas M&A: A Practical Handbook*, Globe Law and Business, 2014.

industry matters; more general warranties given by a seller are not exemplified here. Warranties in relation to tax, environmental, decommissioning and anti-bribery matters are discussed in depth in separate chapters.

The warranty examples used in this section assume a transaction for the asset sale, or farmout, of the transferred interest and related assets. In the case of a transaction where the target is shares of the company holding the transferred interest, as a general rule, references to the seller in the warranties (eg, having title to, or having discharged obligations with regard to, the transferred interest) should be replaced by a reference to the target having such capacity.

4.2 Warranties regarding title

The petroleum rights that a buyer acquires arise to a significant extent from the assumption, assignment or novation of existing contractual rights. In an asset acquisition, the primary contractual right acquired is the participating interest in the licence. In a share acquisition, the licence is held by the target entity and acquired indirectly by the buyer through its purchase of shares in the target.

In either case, the contractual rights to be assumed by the buyer will be set out in the licence together with the JOA and any other key documents between the seller/target and the co-participants (eg, there may be a separate document detailing specific elements of participation, cost sharing or the granting of an option with respect to the licence). For purposes of this chapter, all such documents are included within the defined term 'transferred interest documents'. Although strictly speaking the JOA is not a title document, it is an agreement of vital importance. It allocates the co-participants' assumption of joint and several liability, determines governance procedures for petroleum operations, allocates costs, grants entitlements over lifting of petroleum and (in the event of breach) determines a forfeiture procedure. For these reasons, the JOA is usually given the status of a transferred interest document and thereby made subject to the same warranties as the licence.

It is important that the buyer receives copies of the transferred interest documents at an early stage, with its primary aim being to satisfy itself that the documents demonstrate an unbroken chain of title from the first licensee on the licence to the current seller. A buyer will then require warranties as to the completeness and accuracy of the transferred interest documents, in order to verify its understanding of title issues. These title issues are so fundamental that the relevant warranties are typically excluded from general limitation of liability provisions relating to time, *de minimis* liability thresholds/baskets and financial caps included in favour of the seller. Alternatively, title warranties are made subject to separate limitations which are more generous to the buyer (eg, a financial limit on liability of 100% of the purchase price and a time cap of six years, or the maximum period allowed for claims under the appropriate statute of limitations).

(a) *Particulars and ownership*

Both examples below are typically included in an SPA. The first example uses the defined term 'transferred interest' by cross-reference to schedule 1 of the SPA, which typically sets out key details of the licence, the JOA and the seller's participating interests in both. The seller warrants the accuracy of this summarised information. The second example deals more directly with title, as discussed further below.

Example warranty 1:

The particulars relating to the Transferred Interest set out in schedule 1 are true and accurate in all respects.

Example warranty 2:

The seller is a licensee of the Licence and the sole legal and beneficial owner of the Transferred Interest [free of Encumbrances (other than [Permitted Encumbrances)]] with the right (subject to the satisfaction of the conditions precedent) to sell, transfer and assign the Transferred Interest to the buyer.

In addition to verifying information, the seller warrants that it (in the case of an asset sale) or the target entity (in the case of a share sale) is the legal and beneficial owner of the transferred interest, and that this is held free of encumbrances. This concept is sometimes also expressed (outside the warranty provisions) in the operative clause requiring the seller to sell with "full title guarantee". This term (which, under English law, is taken from the Law of Property (Miscellaneous Provisions) Act 1994) implies that the seller has the right to dispose of its interests, and that the seller will (at its own cost) take all reasonable steps to transfer title. Please see section 4.2(e) below in relation to the references to encumbrances in the example above.

A buyer may also look for a warranty regarding the ownership structure on the licence as a whole.

Example warranty 3:

No person other than the Farmor and the Co-Participants (and, on and after Completion, the Farmee) has any interest in or right in respect of the Transferred Interest Documents whether contingent or otherwise.

(b) *True and complete documentation*

A seller will commonly warrant that it has provided complete and accurate copies of the transferred interest documents. For evidential certainty, copies of the transferred interest documents may be annexed to the SPA or disclosure letter.

Example warranty 1:[12]

The Farmor has provided the Farmee with complete and correct copies of the

12 This is adapted from the Association of International Petroleum Negotiators' (AIPN) Model Form Farmout Agreement (2019) (with some modifications to reflect the subject-matter of this chapter).

Transferred Interest Documents and all amendments thereto. Where the Farmor has provided any translation of a Document, the Farmor has done so as a courtesy to the Farmee and the Farmor makes no, and disclaims any, representation or warranty as to the accuracy of the translation.

Example warranty 2:

True, complete and up to date copies of all Transferred Interest Documents have been provided to the buyer.

Occasionally, a buyer may have a significant advantage in negotiations as to be able to require that the seller warrant the completeness and accuracy of the entire data room. This is unusual, but may arise if, for example, there is urgency around the seller's disposal, or where the volume of due diligence documents has been limited. The buyer may also wish to propose this approach, in the first instance, if the seller's due diligence disclosure has been haphazard and piecemeal, in order to give the buyer comfort that it has seen all that is relevant. If included at all, this warranty will likely be negotiated to include materiality caveats, as below.

Example warranty 3:

The Data Room Documents include all [material] agreements, [material] correspondence and other [material] documents, [material] data and [material] written information in the seller's possession (or in the possession of its Affiliates) relating to the Licence and the seller has not intentionally omitted from the Data Room Documents anything which would [reasonably] likely to render any of the information discussed in them (when read as a whole) [materially] inaccurate.

On the other hand, a seller with the upper hand (eg, in an auction sale process) may seek to include a disclaimer expressly stating that it makes no warranty as to the sufficiency of the data room.

Example disclaimer:

Farmor makes no representations or warranties, express or implied, as to the quality, accuracy, and completeness of the Data Room Documents or the Disclosures.

(c) Entire agreement

As well as being clear that the title documentation disclosed is true and accurate, the buyer will want comfort that the title documentation provided represents the entire suite of agreements pertaining to the creation, existence and validity of the transferred interest, and that there are no other documents containing obligations to the government.

Example warranty 1:

The Transferred Interest Documents and applicable Laws are the only agreements and other documents in force and effect which govern or relate to the creation, existence and validity of the Transferred Interest. The Transferred Interest Documents contain the entirety of the contractual obligations of Farmor to the

Government [and to Co-Participants], and no other understanding or agreement exists between Farmor and the Government [and/or the Co-Participants] in relation to the Assets.

(d) No breaches

A title warranty merely gives a snapshot of ownership issues on a certain date or dates. In addition, a buyer must consider historic and ongoing events which may provide a justification for the government to terminate the licence or for the JOA parties to forfeit a participating interest. Both documents typically include draconian provisions allowing termination or forfeiture for an extended event of default. As a result of the severe consequences of a licence or JOA breach, the SPA typically includes a warranty stating that no such breach exists. Since the buyer may also be jointly and severally liable for an ongoing breach by a non-selling party, this warranty typically extends (subject to a knowledge qualifier) to non-selling co-participants.

Example warranty 1:

The [seller/Target] has not committed any [material] breach of the Transferred Interest Documents [other than historic breaches which have been cured or waived] and the seller has not received any notice of any such [material] breach and the seller is not aware that any of the other current or previous parties to any of the Transferred Interest Documents has committed any such [material] breach.

Example warranty 2:

The Transferred Interest Documents are in full force and effect and no notice of default, termination or breach under any Transferred Interest Document has been received neither by the Farmor nor, to the knowledge of the Farmor, any other party to any Transferred Interest Document.

Example warranty 3:[13]

All payments and obligations due under the Transferred Interest Documents have been paid or performed, and all such agreements are in full force and effect. Neither Farmor, nor to the knowledge of Farmor, any other party is in default under the Contract, the JOA, or the Specified Instruments. No event has occurred or failed to occur which constitutes, or which, with the giving of notice or the passage of time or both, would constitute, a default, violation, or breach under the Contract, the JOA, or the Specified Instruments.

In addition to obtaining a warranty regarding 'no breaches', it is in the buyer's interests to include a catch-all warranty that the seller is not aware of any other matters that may trigger the termination of the licence by the government.

Example warranty 4:

Insofar as the Farmor is aware, no fact or circumstance exists which might

---

13 This is adapted from the Association of International Petroleum Negotiators' (AIPN) Model Form Farmout Agreement (2019) (with some modifications to reflect the subject-matter of this chapter).

invalidate or give rise to a ground for termination, avoidance or repudiation of the Transferred Interest Documents. The Farmor has not received a notice from the Government or any Co-Participant of its intention to terminate, repudiate or disclaim the Documents nor has the Farmor exercised its option to terminate the Transferred Interest Documents by written notice.

Example warranty 5:

Seller has not received notice of any claim, action, suit, audit, demand, inquiry, investigation or proceeding of any Governmental Authority that could reasonably be expected to [materially and] adversely affect its ability to meet and carry out its obligations under this Agreement and/or the Transaction Documents to which it is (or, upon Completion, will be) a party, and to seller's knowledge no such claim, action, suit, audit, demand, inquiry, investigation or proceeding has been threatened.

(e) No encumbrances

As seen in the example in section 4.2(a) (copied below), the title warranty will usually carve out references to encumbrances:

Example warranty 1:

The seller is a licensee of the Licence and the sole legal and beneficial owner of the Transferred Interest [free of Encumbrances [(other than Permitted Encumbrances)]] with the right (subject to the satisfaction of the conditions precedent) to sell, transfer and assign the Transferred Interest Documents to the buyer.

The question of whether a seller holds good title and whether an encumbrance exists over an asset are separate issues. A seller may correctly warrant that it has full legal and beneficial title to an asset which is encumbered in favour of a third party. For this reason, it is common in a final form SPA to have duplicate references to encumbrances in both the warranty covering title issues and in a separate statement of no encumbrances, as exemplified below.

Example warranty 2:

No Encumbrance [(other than a Permitted Encumbrance)] has been created over the Transferred Interest other than those arising under the Transferred Interest Documents and the SPA and the seller is not a party to any agreement to give or create any of the same.

'Encumbrances' is included as a defined term in the SPA, which will list those instruments (eg, charges, mortgages, liens) commonly covered by this term. In an oil and gas context, the definition may be widened to include options, pre-emptive rights, rights of first refusal and royalties over or attaching to the transferred interest. Rights granted under any area of mutual interest agreement will also likely be included in the definition. These types of agreements are common in the petroleum industry and may prohibit a seller from disposing of its interests (or restrict its ability to do so) without first offering such interests to a third party.

Royalties are also a common feature of the petroleum industry. These may be described in different ways: as a non-operating interest, a net profit interest, an overriding royalty interest, a production payment or similar. They provide the royalty owner with a stream of income or petroleum production free and clear of operating and other costs. Often these are created to attach themselves permanently to a participating interest and to burden any future assignee. The term 'encumbrances' is therefore often defined to cover royalties.

'Permitted encumbrances' (which is a definition used to qualify a statement of no encumbrances) typically includes encumbrances created pursuant to the licence, JOA or SPA. For example, if a national oil company has a back-in right (ie, an option to acquire a participating interest from the licensees after a commercial discovery has been made), then this will fall within the definition as a permitted encumbrance created pursuant to the licence. As further discussed below, pre-emptive rights and rights of first refusal are also common features of licences and JOAs. The definition of 'permitted encumbrances' should be wide enough to exclude these provisions from the 'no encumbrances' warranty.

(f) *Transfer restrictions*

Oil and gas sales will always be structured to take account of consent and pre-emption rights in favour of existing parties, as described in detail in the chapter relating to conditions precedent.

Briefly, a licence will nearly always require government consent to any direct or indirect sale, assignment or other transfer of interest in the licence, and often may also grant the government a 'right of first refusal' option to acquire the transferred interest on the same terms and conditions (including price) as negotiated between the commercial parties. Similarly, the JOA nearly always includes one or more of consent rights, pre-emption rights, rights of first refusal and change of control provisions in favour of non-selling JOA parties.

It is usual for the warranties to reference indirectly the requirement that these licence and JOA consents (or waivers of transfer restrictions) have been granted. This is seen in the example at section 4.2(a) (copied below):

Example warranty 1:

The seller is a licensee of the Licence and the sole legal and beneficial owner of the Transferred Interest [free of Encumbrances [(other than Permitted Encumbrances)]] with the right (subject to the satisfaction of the conditions precedent) to sell, transfer and assign the Transferred Interest Documents to the buyer.

The SPA may also include a wider warranty confirming that there are no other transfer restrictions exercisable by a third party.

Example warranty 2:

Save as provided in the Licence and the JOA, with regard to the [seller's/Target's] Relevant Proportion, neither the entry into this Agreement nor the Completion thereof will result in any third party being entitled to exercise any right of pre-emption, right of first refusal or right of approval in respect of the Transferred Interest.

Example warranty 3:

No Person, other than holders of the pre-emptive rights under Article [•] of the JOA, has any call upon, option to purchase, or similar right to obtain production from or attributable to the Transferred Interest or to acquire the Transferred Interest or any portion thereof from seller, other than the rights of buyer pursuant to this Agreement and rights of existing production purchasers to continue taking production pursuant to the terms of existing production sales contracts (including renewals thereof).

4.3 Warranties regarding physical and legal interests

(a) Geological and geophysical information

Warranties in an upstream oil and gas SPA will rarely cover geological and geophysical information. Although a review of technical data will form an important part of a buyer's investigations, interpretation of technical data is inherently subjective; and however carefully such technical data is prepared, relying on it will result in a range of outcomes. Consequently, geological and geophysical information does not lend itself to being covered by warranties. As well as technical uncertainties, the question of whether reserves will be commercially produced (and, if so, in what quantity) will also depend on future oil prices and technological innovations. Such factors, which influence whether a field continues to be economic, are outside the parties' control.

While the seller typically will not give assurances about reserve estimates, a buyer may be able to push for a warranty relating to the seller's provision of the factual information on which a reserve report is based.

Example warranty:

To the knowledge of the seller, the Underlying Factual Information that has been provided by the seller to [the petroleum engineers], to the extent that it was relied upon in the preparation of the Reserve Report, was at the time of delivery true and correct in all respects except for such errors that would not have or could not reasonably be expected to have, materially or in aggregate, a material adverse effect, on the [Business] / [the accuracy of the Reserve Report]. As defined herein, Underlying Factual Information means, with respect to the Assets, all production history data, all data on operating cost history and all data with respect to [insert as relevant]. It is expressly understood that save for the express warranty contained in this section, the seller makes no representations or warranties, express or implied, with respect to the Reserve Report, including without limitation any conclusions, opinions, or judgements that were made by [the petroleum engineers] on the basis of the Underlying Factual Information.

More commonly, however, a seller will aim to include a disclaimer in relation to geological and geophysical data and the buyer will need to rely on its own due diligence.

Example disclaimer:

Farmor makes no representations or warranties, express or implied, as to the quality, accuracy, and completeness of the Reserve Report, and Farmee expressly acknowledges the inherent risk of error in the acquisition, processing, and interpretation of geological and geophysical data.

(b) Relinquishment and withdrawal

A licence provides rights of exploration, development and/or production over a delimited contract area. This is defined by coordinates of longitude and latitude and a statement of the total amount of contract area (eg, expressed as square kilometres), and is most commonly also demarcated on a map attached as a schedule to the licence.

The contract area is, in most licences, subject to an obligation to relinquish to the government a stipulated percentage of the original contract area at specified times. Relinquishment commonly occurs in stages, often after the expiry of certain exploration phases. By the end of a licence term, the relinquishment requirements may have resulted in the contract area reducing to some percentage (often half) of its original size. This compulsory reduction in contract area is intended to accelerate exploration (and ultimately, therefore, production) under the licence.

The licence often also allows voluntary partial relinquishment of the contract area by the licensee, provided that this does not affect the fulfilment of its work obligations. Since the annual licence fee (or rental) is calculated on the basis of the size of the contract area, licensees are incentivised to relinquish areas over which they no longer have any exploration plans. The government may then re-license these rights in future bid rounds.

Since it may be different from that stated on the face of the licence, a buyer must clarify during due diligence what contract area remains. The seller will then typically give a warranty similar to the example below, and the details of any relinquishments will be set out in the disclosure letter.

Example warranty 1:

None of the rights under the Licence have been relinquished, surrendered, forfeited, re-determined or modified, in whole or in part.

Example warranty 2:

Neither the Contract nor any portion of the Contract Area is in the course of being surrendered or relinquished in whole or in part, and neither seller nor, to seller's knowledge, any other party to the Contract has provided written notice of any such surrender or withdrawal.

Many JOAs allow co-participants to withdraw from the joint venture, typically only after all minimum work obligations have been satisfied. It will be important for a buyer to know whether any co-participant has withdrawn or has given notice of its withdrawal, as this could increase the buyer's participating interest and therefore its share of costs of joint operations going forward.

Example warranty 3:

Neither seller nor, to seller's knowledge, any other party to the Contract or the JOA, has given any notice of withdrawal from the Contract or the JOA.

(c) Exclusive operations

Co-participants, as a general principle, conduct exploration and development activities collectively in accordance with their joint venture. The group benefits from an alignment of the parties' commercial objectives and an amicable and consensual decision to proceed with petroleum operations. If consensus between all co-participants is not possible, then the JOA typically allows less than all parties to proceed without the participation of others. These provisions are known as 'sole risk' (if a party proceeds without the majority) or 'non-consent' (if a party opts out of a majority decision). Collectively, they are referred to as 'exclusive operations'.

Despite exclusive operations provisions being common in JOAs, they are rarely used. Exclusive operations are sometimes threatened, but seldom formally invoked. The buyer will therefore have an expectation that the JOA is being administered with all co-participants participating in, and paying for, petroleum operations in accordance with their respective participating interests.

If this is not the case, a buyer will find itself either excluded from a potential opportunity on the licence (where the seller is not participating in a sole risk venture) or paying for a higher proportion of costs than the corresponding transferred interest being acquired (where another co-participant is not participating).

The following example warranty is thus intended to flush out whether any co-participant (including the seller) has exercised the right to exclusive operations.

Example warranty:

No sole risk or non-consent operations have been proposed or carried out by the seller or by any of the other parties to the Licence and the seller is not aware of any proposal to conduct such operations.

(d) Unitisation

If relinquishment and exclusive operations are viewed as a potential diminution of a contract area, unitisation may be considered the opposite. Unitisation enlarges the physical size of the parties' geographic interests in order to take in the full extent of a petroleum reservoir that straddles two or more contract areas.

Most licences and petroleum laws contain regulations regarding unitisation. This is the compulsory joint collaboration and conduct of operations of petroleum reservoirs straddling contract areas held under separate licences. If a discovery is found to extend beyond the boundary of a contract area, arrangements requiring the joint development of a straddling field are usually mandatory and require separate JOA groups to enter into a unitisation and unit operating agreement (UUOA). If a reservoir also straddles an international boundary, then governmental (as well as commercial) agreement is also required.

The UUOA determines the division of equity interests between neighbouring JOA groups. This will be set in accordance with a number of technical factors, including how much of the reservoir falls within each contract area. Each JOA party's interest in the unit development is diluted by a corresponding amount. Therefore, if a seller sells a 20% transferred interest in a licence subject to a UUOA and the JOA group to which the seller belongs has a 25% interest in the unitised block, the transferred interest will represent a 5% equity interest in the unitised block.

The following warranty example intends to establish whether unitisation is relevant.

Example warranty 1:

None of the petroleum reservoirs discovered in the contract area extend beyond the borders of the contract area.

If there is a straddling reservoir, the manner in which unitisation is dealt with in the SPA will depend on the status of the UUOA. If there is an existing UUOA, then that UUOA (and perhaps also operatorship of the unitised block, if currently held by the seller) will be assigned to the buyer and the terms of the UUOA need to be reviewed as part of due diligence. If there is a straddling reservoir but no UUOA is yet in place, execution of such an agreement may be included in the SPA as a condition precedent to the transaction. In either case, the buyer needs to consider the identity and capabilities of the proposed operator of both the licence and any unitised area.

A determination of the appropriate equity split between neighbouring co-participants can be difficult to establish and agree. A better understanding of the boundaries of the reservoir will emerge as production matures. Equity interests between neighbouring licensees are therefore sometimes not permanently fixed and may periodically be re-determined. If a UUOA is in place, then a buyer will want to understand whether a re-determination of the equity interests of the unitised block is contemplated and, if so, when it is next due, what costs are likely to be incurred and whether redetermination is likely to be favourable to the JOA group that the buyer is joining. The below warranty example is used to obtain this information.

Example warranty 2 (where a UUOA exists):

No redetermination is in progress under the UUOA nor [so far as the seller is aware] is there any proposal to carry out any such redetermination [other than in accordance with the UUOA].

(e) Third-party activity or rights

The buyer will want to know whether any third parties have activities in the contract area, and similarly whether there are any easements over the contract area, that could prevent or restrict operations.

Example warranty:

To Seller's Knowledge, there is no third-party activity in the Contract Area, or any easement, condition or circumstance, that would prevent or restrict operations in any portion of the Contract Area.

(f) Plugging and abandonment

Once it is judged that there is insufficient hydrocarbon potential to merit completing a well, or after operations have exhausted production, a well will be retired and undergo a plugging and abandonment process. This usually consists of plugging the wellbore with cement to prevent leakage and environmental damage, among other things. The extent of this process will vary depending on the jurisdiction, ranging from stringent regulatory regimes in, for example, the North Sea and the Gulf of Mexico to a lack of rigorous requirements in many developing hydrocarbon nations. In all cases, the buyer will want comfort in the form of a warranty that such operations have occurred. A more in-depth discussion and further examples of decommissioning warranties are found in a separate chapter.

Example warranty:

Except for those wells that are in use on the date hereof, all wells drilled in the Contract Area have been properly plugged and abandoned in accordance with applicable Laws.

4.4 Warranties regarding financial and technical matters

(a) Participating interest share

It will be central to the buyer's valuation of the target, and the feasibility of the entire transaction, to understand the financial terms of the licence and JOA. In particular, the buyer will need to be clear on the terms of cost sharing and production sharing between the co-participants. In addition to the licence and JOA, there may be separate documentation detailing specific elements of participation, cost sharing or the granting of an option between co-participants, the terms of which will be central to the economics of the target business. The warranty below (together with the entire agreement warranty discussed at section 4.2(c)) aims to ensure that the seller discloses any such arrangements.

Example warranty 1:

Up to and including the Execution Date, the Company has: (a) been paid all amounts due to the Company under the PSC in accordance with its percentage interest set forth therein and the terms and conditions of the PSC and JOA; (b) borne costs and expenses under the PSC in accordance with its percentage interest set forth therein and the terms and conditions of the PSC and JOA; and (c) the Company is not obligated to pay a share of any costs or expenses arising under the PSC or JOA that is disproportionate to its percentage interest under the PSC and JOA.

Should a buyer be aware of any production imbalances (historic or ongoing), it may wish to include a specific warranty to that effect:

Example warranty 2:

Farmor has no obligation to deliver Hydrocarbon production (or cash in lieu thereof) to other owners of the Participating Interests as a result of past sales by Farmor or its predecessors in excess of the share of production to which they were entitled.

An alternative approach to such a warranty is to include an SPA schedule of the summary terms of cost sharing and production sharing between co-participants, with the seller warranting that such schedule is "true and accurate in all [material] respects". This is a less common approach and may not be practical if the terms are complex and not easily summarised.

(b) Payments to the government

Licences (particularly PSCs) often require a range of payments to the host government. These may include a combination of royalties, signature bonuses (payable when the licence is signed), development bonuses (payable when the government grants development consent) and production bonuses (payable when a certain level of production is reached), training fees, community fees (for the purposes of funding local development) and surface rental fees. The licence is typically subject to termination by the government if a payment default lasts for more than a specified number of days, so the buyer will typically require a warranty that all the relevant payments have been made to the government.

Example warranty:

All bonuses, rentals, royalties, production payments and any other payments due and/or payable by the Company to the Government under the Transferred Interest Documents have been timely paid as and when the same have been due and/or payable.

(c) Adequate financial and technical capability

If the seller remains a co-participant on the licence after completion of the transaction (eg, in the case of a sale of part only of a participating interest, or a farmout agreement), then after the transaction the buyer and seller will have an ongoing joint venture relationship governed by the JOA. In this case, both the buyer and the seller will have an interest in ensuring that the other party has the ability, post-acquisition, to finance its share of cash calls and to perform its JOA obligations. If, however, the buyer agrees to carry the future costs of the seller as part of the SPA consideration, concerns about the seller's credit worthiness may be reduced.

Example warranties:

[Seller/Buyer] has sufficient cash, available lines of credit or other sources of immediately available funds to enable it to fulfil all of its obligations under the Transferred Interest Documents and this Agreement.

[Seller/Buyer] has the technical capability, personnel and resources (or access to same) to fulfil its obligations under the Transferred Interest Documents and this Agreement.

4.5 Warranties regarding work performance

(a) Work programme (minimum expenditure and work obligations)

The vast majority of modern licences require co-participants to explore and develop the contract area actively. This concept is set out in licences by way of the minimum work obligations, minimum expenditure obligations or both. A work obligation will specify the minimum amount (and type) of seismic studies that need to be undertaken and the number and depth of drilling operations (in each case, to be performed in accordance with good international petroleum practice). An expenditure obligation, as the name suggests, is a cruder assessment of the monetary amount required to be spent by a licensee during an exploration period.

Governments in developed petroleum jurisdictions may have teams monitoring compliance with these obligations and be willing to terminate the licences of oil companies that are not in compliance with their work obligations. In some cases, licences are drafted to expire automatically if the minimum work obligation has not been completed within the relevant exploration period. As well as requiring a warranty that the obligations have been fulfilled, buyers will want to satisfy themselves during due diligence that the work programme has been (or will be) complied with.

Example warranty:

All accrued obligations and liabilities imposed by the Licence, including all work and expenditure obligations arising from the Licence, have been duly fulfilled and discharged and there is no outstanding work or expenditure obligation to be fulfilled under the Licence.

(b) ***Development plan***

The development plan is the co-participants' proposal to the government regarding how and where a discovery will be exploited which specifies, for example, the drilling programme, the schedule for the completion of wells, and particulars of facilities and installations that are required for the production, storage and transportation of petroleum. It provides details about the cost and timetable, with the date of 'first oil' or gas being of particular concern to the government.

A buyer acquiring a transferred interest post-commercial discovery but pre-production will typically bear its participating share of the expenses set out in the development plan. It will thus need to know whether one is in place and what capital expenditures it envisages. The warranty below intends to clarify the details of any capital expenditure commitments in excess of a specified figure, which will prompt disclosures including regarding any development plan. In reality, this topic will be a key focus of the buyer's questions to management and commercial and technical due diligence from the outset of discussions.

Example warranty:

As of the Execution Date, there are no proposals or commitments to make capital expenditures in excess of [•] U.S. dollars (U.S$ [•]) individually or in the aggregate which are binding on the Co-Participants or the Assets, other than those in the Work Program and Budget.

(c) ***Performance guarantees***

The licence commonly requires that the government have recourse to a performance guarantee in relation to minimum work and expenditure obligations to be performed by the co-participant. This is most usually provided in the form of a letter of credit from an international bank with a minimum credit rating or otherwise in the form of a corporate guarantee provided by the co-participant's parent company. The due diligence process, supported by the warranties, should confirm that such guarantee of the seller's obligations was provided and remains in place, and identify whether it has been called upon by the government.

Example warranty:

The seller has performed its obligations under the Licence article [•], and [up to the Completion Date] the [Bank Guarantee/Parent Company Guarantee] remains in full force and effect and has not been called upon by the Government or otherwise diminished or discharged.

The SPA will also include further provisions regarding performance guarantees to accommodate the transaction at hand. Typically, if post-transaction, the seller will no longer be a co-participant on the licence, there will be a condition precedent for the buyer (or its parent company) to release the seller (or its parent company) from its guarantee and to provide a replacement guarantee. This approach is reflected by the reference to "up to the Completion Date" in the example above.

(d) No force majeure

A *force majeure* event will, if validly asserted, render the affected participant unable to carry out its minimum work and other performance obligations in relation to the licence (other than payment obligations), and will have the effect of suspending such obligations for the duration of the event. Given the likely delays this causes for activity under work programmes and development plans (particularly if the affected party is the operator), the buyer will want to confirm that no such event is in progress.

Example warranty:

There is no Force Majeure *event, condition, or circumstance currently ongoing or present, or reasonably expected, with respect to performance of rights or obligations under the Contract.*

4.6 Warranties regarding operatorship and contracts

(a) *Operatorship*

The operator of a licence is responsible for performing operations on behalf of the consortium of co-participants, while the co-participants (including the operator) are responsible for contributing to the financial commitments and expenses of the joint venture. The licence and JOA contain stringent requirements in relation to the financial and technical capability of the operator and the JOA sets out detailed terms in relation to its role and its liability. The transfer of operatorship under the licence and JOA will typically require the consent of the government and all co-participants. Given this, it is in the buyer's interests to ensure that the existing operator on the licence will remain in place post-transaction, or to understand any envisaged change to the operator.

Example warranty:

The Operator has not given any notice of resignation as operator under the JOA and [to the Knowledge of the Seller] the Operator is not intending to resign, nor [to the Knowledge of the Seller] is the Operator in default of any of the Transferred Interest Documents such as to entitle the other parties to the JOA to remove it as operator. [To the Knowledge of the Seller,] the Operator in its capacity as operator under the JOA, has not entered into any transaction, agreement or arrangement outside the ordinary course of business.

Where the seller is in fact the operator and farming out a part interest only in the licence (thus remaining a co-participant), the knowledge qualifiers in this example would not be necessary.

(b) *Material contracts*

It is standard in any SPA for the seller to give warranties in relation to the contractual arrangements that are material, or strategically important, to the operation of the target. This is no different in the case of an upstream oil and gas transaction. The definition of 'material contract' will be a point for negotiation, with the buyer wishing to include all documents on which the target relies, but the seller wanting to ensure that the definition is not so widely drafted as to impose a disproportionate disclosure burden on it. The parties may agree on a general definition (eg, "any agreement, arrangement, understanding or commitment that the Target is a party to, or bound by, and which is of material importance to the business, profits or assets of the Target"), but it will usually be in the buyer's interest to achieve greater certainty in the scope of the warranties and include such wording only as a catch-all to a wider definition. As previously discussed in section 3.3(b), a buyer-friendly definition is likely to identify certain named contracts, as well as including reference to categories of key documents, including those deemed material by reference to being of value, or involving liability, in excess of a specific monetary amount.

(c) *Related party and multi-licence contracts*

It is not uncommon in the upstream oil and gas industry for an operator to enter into related-party contracts with other companies within, or affiliated with, its corporate group. When entered into between an operator and its affiliate, such a contract may be justified as producing operational efficiencies between the operator and its group company (compared with a similar arrangement with a commercial third-party supplier). However, when the affiliate company requires a profit element for the performance of its services, this may offend against the principle that the operator performs its duties on a 'no loss, no gain' basis. For this reason, JOAs often include procedures that require the operator either to tender service arrangements in accordance with good industry practice or to seek prior operating committee approval for related-party contracts, or a combination of these safeguards, in order to avoid conflicts of interests.

It is in the buyer's interest to understand related-party contracts in two respects. First, if these contracts are to continue after the sale of the transferred interest, they may allow a seller to continue to profit from the project after it has disposed of its interest in the licence, yet the upside to these arrangements (the operational efficiencies between operator and its group company) may no longer be relevant. Secondly, a seller affiliate may have no interest (or the same commercial motivation) in continuing to provide services after the transferred interest has been sold.

A seller warranty in this regard will help a buyer to flush out information in relation to related-party contracts and assist its assessment and negotiation of which are suitable to remain, or be replaced, post-transaction.

Example warranty 1:

The [seller] [operator] is not a party to any [contract] [Material Contract] which has not been entered into on an arm's-length basis.

Example warranty 2:

None of the [seller] [operator], any Affiliate of the [seller] [operator], or any shareholder, director, officer or employee of [seller] [operator] or any Affiliate of the [seller] [operator], is a party to any [contract] [Material Contract] with the Company.

It will also be in the buyer's interest to understand, through due diligence, any multi-party contracts relevant to the licence. Oil companies may enter into multi-licence contracts whereby a contractor provides oilfield services to a group on an international or regional basis. Where a seller disposes of an interest in one contract area (but retains an interest in other contract areas which necessitates keeping the service contract), the buyer needs to consider the likelihood that it can enter into a replacement contract with the same (or similar) service provider on comparable terms. This issue is likely to be more of a concern in developing and remote oil-producing regions. In mature markets, similar replacement services are likely to be readily available. Where there is a possibility that a buyer cannot enter into an alternative contract (or the cost of this will be higher), this may affect the economics of the acquisition.

4.7 Warranties regarding compliance and regulatory matters

(a) Compliance with laws

In most cases, the governing law of the licence will be the law of the host country. As such, the buyer's due diligence process requires not just a legal review of data room documents, but also an analysis of the local legal requirements imposed on the licensee. These will apply to the buyer after its acquisition of the transferred interest. The buyer will appoint local counsel to advise on the petroleum regime (statutory, regulatory or otherwise) and to verify the licensee's compliance with, for example, permits, land use, environmental requirements, labour law requirements, health and safety, and tax matters. These are examples of matters that are likely to be set out in general law (rather than as express terms of the licence). As well as warranting that it has complied with the terms of the licence (as discussed in section 4.2(d)), the seller will warrant that it is in compliance with the wider laws applicable to petroleum operations.

Example warranty 1:

The seller has complied [in all material respects] with all applicable laws, regulations and orders of government agencies in respect of the Licence.

Example warranty 2:

The Farmor is in compliance [in all material respects] with all applicable Laws (including Environmental Laws) of any Governmental authority, and there are no material claims, demands, actions, suits, Governmental inquiries or proceedings pending or, to the Farmor's knowledge, threatened against the Farmor alleging any failure to so comply.

It is in the buyer's interest to require that the seller also give a warranty to confirm that the SPA itself complies with law and meets all regulatory requirements.

Example warranty 3:

All authorisations from, and notices or filings with, any governmental or other authority that are necessary to enable it to execute, deliver and perform its obligations under this Agreement, and each of the Completion Documents to which it is or will be a party, have been obtained or made (as the case may be) and are in full force and effect, and all conditions of each such authorisation have been complied with.

Example warranty 4:

Upon the receipt of the Consents, the signing and delivery of this Agreement and the performance of any of the transactions contemplated by this Agreement will not contravene or constitute a default under any provision contained in any agreement, instrument, law, judgement, order, licence, permit or consent to which the seller is a party or bound.

(b) Permits

It may be in the buyer's interest to seek more extensive warranties regarding the permitting of petroleum operations, particularly if the transaction relates to an asset in a developed petroleum jurisdiction, with an extensive regulatory framework. The examples below will function to ensure that the buyer is made aware of such regulatory requirements, and the seller's compliance in this regard.

Example warranty 1:

All [material] permits, licences, consents, approvals, agreements and certificates required for the carrying out of Petroleum Operations in relation to the Transferred Interest, including under the Transferred Interest Documents, have been obtained and are in effect and have been complied with.

Example warranty 2:

Each Group Company has obtained all permits, licenses, authorizations, consents, exemptions and other approvals required to be obtained from any Governmental Authority by any applicable law which are necessary to operate its business as conducted on the date of this Agreement and as currently proposed to be conducted in the future ("Permits"). All Permits are in full force and effect and have not been challenged by any third party, and no circumstances exist that could reasonably be expected to justify such a challenge. No proceedings regarding a revocation or withdrawal of any Permit have been initiated or threatened, and no circumstances exist that could reasonably be expected to result in a revocation or withdrawal or in any conditions being imposed on any Permit. There are no facts or circumstances that may lead to the revocation, suspension, variation or non-renewal of any Permit. The seller has made available to the Buyer in the Data Room a complete and accurate copy of each permit.

There may be overlap between the warranties regarding permits, the general warranty regarding compliance with law and/or the more specific warranties regarding environmental matters. A seller that is concerned that it is giving different warranties on different terms regarding the same subject matter could consider ring-fencing the environmental warranty – for example, in order to ensure that the only warranty relating to environmental matters is the specific environmental warranty.

Example ring-fencing clause:

The Buyer acknowledges and agrees that the only Warranties given in relation to the Environment, Environmental Laws, Environmental Permits and/or Hazardous Materials or any related claims, liabilities or other matters are set out in Clause [•].

4.8 Warranties regarding local requirements

(a) Locally incorporated company

Several jurisdictions have rules relating to the ownership of companies holding title to oil and gas assets. In some cases, the law requires that a locally incorporated company be the direct owner of the assets, but will not look further up the corporate chain and ultimate ownership can thus vest with a foreign company. Other jurisdictions require that ultimate ownership lie with a domestic company owned in whole or in part by local nationals. Where these rules are in place, a party may be allowed to bid for a licence using a foreign company, but with an obligation to transfer it to a local company after the licence has been awarded.

It is important that the due diligence process identify relevant requirements and ensure that the seller (and its co-participants) have complied with these, and that the buyer (and its acquisition vehicle) will also meet these obligations.

The buyer will derive comfort on this issue from the seller's warranties regarding its compliance with transferred interest documents (which will include the licence's local content obligations) and with applicable law. The warranties below are one example of each, from a range of options exemplified and discussed further in sections 4.2(d) and 4.6(a).

Example warranty 1:

The [seller/Company] has not committed any [material] breach of the Transferred

Interest Documents [other than historical breaches which have been cured or waived] and the seller has not received any notice of any such [material] breach and the seller is not aware that any of the other current or previous parties to any of the Transferred Interest Documents has committed any such [material] breach.

Example warranty 2:

The seller has complied [in all material respects] with all applicable laws, regulations and orders of government agencies in respect of the Licence.

(b) Local content, employment and training

It is common that licences (particularly PSCs) require employment of local nationals and the establishment or sponsorship of higher education, training programmes and community or research projects in order to create opportunity and expertise in the local petroleum industry. Similarly, a licence often requires that operators give preference to local suppliers, producers, manufacturers and service providers. These obligations may be drafted as a statement of general principle or, alternatively, be set out as specific contractual obligations (eg, allowing imported goods only if using a local supplier results in an increase in costs in excess of a certain percentage). Such local employment, training and content requirements may be imposed by both the licence and local law.

The buyer's due diligence should identify:

- licence obligations in this area;
- the extent to which local content arrangements have been put in place;
- the competence and capacity of the domestic oilfield services industry to service the project; and
- the future additional cost of compliance.

In addition to due diligence (which will reveal the counterparties with which the operator has contracted), the buyer derives comfort on this issue from the same seller's warranties as are exemplified in section 4.8(a) above (and further discussed in sections 4.2(d) and 4.7(a)).

(c) Domestic supply obligations

Many licences and petroleum legal regimes in developing countries stipulate a domestic supply obligation requiring a certain percentage of production to be sold to local consumers (often at prices lower than otherwise obtainable on international markets). This type of obligation applies, in particular, to natural gas production. If a domestic supply obligation is included in the licence and if it applies to the type of petroleum development being contemplated, a buyer must consider this obligation in the context of its review of the wider economic terms of the licence. If the project is in production, the buyer should also check that the supply obligation is being fulfilled.

Again, the buyer derives comfort on this issue from the same seller's warranties exemplified in section 4.8(a) above (and further discussed in sections 4.2(d) and 4.7(a)).

4.9 Due diligence considerations regarding economic, political and security risk

(a) *Economic stabilisation*

The buyer should consider during the due diligence process whether it will have the protection of an economic stabilisation provision in the licence. Since a licensee must typically comply with all laws in force from time to time, it is at risk of the government's future change of laws, regulations and tax regime. Economic stabilisation provisions attempt to prevent or limit this political risk. They provide that if there is a change of law that has a material adverse impact on the licensee, the parties will seek to restore and retain the original economics of the licence in order to prevent or limit this impact.

While the protection offered by such economic stabilisation provisions is not a panacea to political risk, the buyer should consider whether this principle is included in the licence. It is not usual for there to be a warranty in this regard.

(b) *Sovereign immunity*

The buyer should also consider, in its assessment of political risk associated with the transaction, whether the licence includes an express waiver of sovereign immunity or whether such a waiver is implied under local law (eg, by virtue of the government engaging, through the licence, in commercial activity). Although the enforceability of such a waiver will in each case need further assessment, and likely require specialist analysis by dispute resolution lawyers, as a starting point it is important for the buyer to establish whether this principle is included in relevant documents.

If the seller is itself a government-owned company, then a similar analysis (and, if applicable, waiver of immunity) should be included in the SPA.

Example warranty:

The seller warrants that this SPA is being executed, and all arrangements hereunder are being performed or delivered as part of a commercial transaction and that it waives sovereign immunity (whether characterised as state immunity, sovereign immunity, act of state or otherwise) that may exist now or in the future.

(c) *Security*

The buyer's due diligence process often identifies security issues in a contract area – for example, local or national conflict, terrorism, militancy, sabotage and theft. These concerns are particularly relevant for onshore operations, although piracy is relevant to offshore activities in certain waters.

These issues may have a tangible impact on petroleum operations – for example, resulting in oil spills and shutting down key infrastructure. Given the potential impact of these issues on the valuation of the transaction and on the conduct of the buyer's future licence obligations, the buyer should seek to understand the political and security context fully, and will often seek input from specialist risk consultants in this regard.

It is typical for the buyer to require that the seller retain, and indemnify it against, all pre-completion liabilities in relation to security matters; and it should also consider what bespoke, risk-specific warranties may be appropriate in this regard.

Disclosure letters

Alexander Msimang
Suzana Vukasinovic
Freddie Wright
Vinson & Elkins RLLP

1. Introduction

A disclosure letter is an important document in any oil and gas sale and purchase transaction. Both parties have an interest in reviewing and negotiating the disclosure letter with care, as it qualifies the warranties, which are typically some of the most heavily negotiated aspects of the sale and purchase agreement (SPA). Given the principle of *caveat emptor* – that the buyer must 'beware' of what it intends to purchase – it will conduct thorough due diligence with a view to negotiating representations, warranties and indemnities in the SPA. As signing brings with it the transfer of legal risk to the buyer, the buyer will want to seek as many protections as possible against any liabilities in the target company or business that exist at signing. The disclosures contained within the disclosure letter provide a buyer with information that qualifies the representations and warranties in the SPA. If the seller warrants in the SPA that there are no problems with the target business, but in fact there are problems which are disclosed in the disclosure letter, then the buyer will have no right to claim compensation from the seller for breach of warranty. Instead, it will have the opportunity:

- to seek alternative protection from the seller in the SPA (eg, by way of an indemnity or condition precedent);
- to try to agree a reduced purchase price reflecting the issues that have been disclosed; or
- to walk away from the transaction entirely if it cannot agree acceptable changes to the deal terms.

This chapter considers the following in turn:

- the purpose of a disclosure letter;
- the disclosure process and timing;
- the form and layout of a typical disclosure letter;
- the importance of the standard of disclosure; and
- some drafting pointers and negotiating tips.

2. Purpose of a disclosure letter

The seller seeks to avoid any breach of the warranties it provides to the buyer in the SPA by making 'disclosures' which describe any events, circumstances or problems with the target business which could be regarded as breaches of the warranties. In effect (whether expressly or by implication), each warranty in the SPA is stated by the seller to be true only to the extent that the disclosure letter does not reveal such warranty to be untrue. So, for example, a seller might give a clear warranty that "the company has no material debt and is not party to any litigation". However, if in fact the company is the debtor under a billion-dollar loan agreement and is the defendant in major court proceedings, and if those matters are revealed in the disclosure letter, then the seller will not be in breach of that warranty as a result of those matters (and the buyer will have no right to be compensated for them). Accordingly, the disclosures limit the scope and application of the warranties and reallocate back to the buyer some of the risks that would otherwise be borne by the seller under the warranties.

Disclosures are statements of facts or events, and should not contain obligations, promises or undertakings of any kind. Disclosures should be detailed enough that the relevant facts are fairly disclosed (see section 5). If a seller makes inadequate or untrue disclosures, those disclosures will not be effective to avoid a breach of warranty, and the buyer may be able to recoup some or even all of the purchase price from the seller by making a warranty claim. The seller should ensure that it meets the standard of disclosure and should provide the buyer with sufficient information to evaluate the issue and to understand its relevance both to the purchase price and to the transaction as a whole.

The buyer, upon reviewing the disclosures, might seek protections against the disclosed risks and liabilities. For example, the buyer might negotiate indemnities to protect itself against the disclosed risk materialising. Alternatively, the buyer might seek price reductions for risks that materially reduce the value of the target business or company (as previously determined by the buyer during its due diligence). In order to protect itself against disclosed matters, the buyer could also amend the SPA to include additional conditions to completion that need to be satisfied. For example, a buyer may include a condition precedent to the effect that the disclosed problem or liability is remedied by the seller or otherwise released before completion, meaning that the buyer is not obliged to complete the purchase if such condition is not satisfied. This allows the buyer to protect itself from, and limit its exposure to, the disclosed matters.

Depending on the drafting and subsequent negotiation of the SPA, the SPA may also include buyer termination rights that will allow the buyer to terminate before completion. A material breach of one of the seller's warranties – particularly if that warranty is a fundamental warranty relating to a key aspect of the assets or business being acquired – may trigger such a right. A similar outcome might be achieved by making it a condition precedent to the buyer's completion obligation that there is no such material warranty breach. If there is a material breach and the condition is not satisfied, the buyer will have no obligation to complete. This has a similar effect to a termination right. If in fact any such termination right or condition precedent is triggered only by breaches of the warranties "as qualified by the disclosure letter", then a comprehensive disclosure letter will reduce the opportunity for the buyer to walk away on the grounds of a material breach of warranty by the seller.

3. Disclosure process and timing issues

The disclosure process is intrinsically linked to the negotiation and acceptance of the warranties. In order to qualify the warranties, the seller typically will not make disclosures against them until the warranties are near-final, so that the seller knows exactly what are the terms of the warranties and exactly which facts and circumstances need to be disclosed to avoid a breach. A disclosure letter is prepared by the seller's legal advisers and addressed to the buyer from the seller. The seller, in assisting in the preparation of the disclosure letter, should ensure that each functional team within its company (eg, the accounts, treasury, commercial, technical and legal teams) reviews the warranties. Each team should be instructed to identify all matters that are inconsistent with, and therefore should be disclosed against, the warranties. The teams should draft disclosures against these warranties where applicable. These disclosures will be included in the disclosure letter following review and amendment by the seller's lawyers. This results in the disclosure letter often being disclosed late in the negotiations, near to the date of signing.

Other factors contribute to the seller making its disclosures at a late stage in the transaction. During the due diligence process, the seller can control the flow of information provided to the buyer through the (nowadays usually virtual) data room. The disclosure letter will contain specific disclosures (see section 4.3) that might prompt the buyer to seek indemnities, conditions or price reductions (also known as 'price chips') or, in the worst case, to walk away. For this reason, the seller will tactically try to leave the disclosures until as late as possible in the process.

Also, the seller will likely seek to refrain from providing the disclosure letter until it is confident that the transaction will proceed such that it is then more comfortable disclosing sensitive information, including information that is subject to confidentiality or legal privilege. The seller will similarly wish to avoid disclosing its most sensitive information to multiple bidders in the early stages of an auction process and will want to make disclosures only to the final successful bidder.

Nevertheless, the buyer should push to receive the disclose letter from the seller as early as possible in the process. As the disclosures may impact upon pricing, the buyer should make it clear to the seller that the price put forward in any indicative offer is subject to the buyer reviewing and being satisfied with the contents of the disclosure letter.

On large, complex transactions, the seller may well make new or amended specific disclosures up until the SPA signing date. The buyer should evaluate these disclosures very carefully with a view to seeking the protections mentioned above. If the seller makes a significant disclosure that fundamentally changes the value of the target company or business, or discloses significant litigation or other problems, the buyer can walk away from the transaction or, at the very least, push back the date for signing the SPA. The buyer may consider communicating to the seller a non-binding long-stop date beyond which it proposes to no longer accept amendments to the disclosure letter. This can be used as a negotiating tactic when agreeing the timetable to the transaction, in order to control the estimated date on which the parties will finalise the disclosure letter. In any event, the buyer should ensure that it has read and contemplated the implications of all disclosures (general and specific) before finalising and signing the SPA.

The disclosure letter will be dated on the date of execution of the SPA. If there is an interim period between signing and completion – for example, to enable the satisfaction of conditions before completion – then it is likely that certain (if not all) warranties will be repeated at completion. In this case there may be two disclosure letters – one being given at the signing date and one at the completion date. This is a matter of negotiation for the parties. A completion date disclosure letter will disclose any new circumstances or events that have occurred between signing and completion which would amount to a breach of warranty (in relation to those warranties repeated on the completion date) if not disclosed. It is in the seller's interests to be able to make further disclosures against the warranties in this way and so avoid any breach of those warranties that are repeated on completion. However, the buyer may wish to negotiate a termination right if post-signing disclosures are made in relation to key warranties. Even if the buyer does not exercise the termination right, the existence of such a right (and the threat of its exercise) may well give the buyer sufficient leverage to renegotiate the price or other terms of the transaction to compensate it for the loss it would otherwise suffer by reason of the newly disclosed events.

4. Form of disclosure letter

The disclosure letter is typically defined as a transaction document in the SPA. English law convention is to draft the disclosure letter as a separate letter. This is also typically done in the United Arab Emirates. However, in the United States and European civil law countries such as Germany and France, the disclosure letter is usually included as a schedule to the SPA.

The disclosure letter typically consists of four parts:

- the interpretative section and scope of disclosure;
- the general disclosures;
- the specific disclosures; and
- the disclosure bundle.

The disclosure bundle, as described in more detail below, is very rarely a physical bundle. It is instead an electronic copy of some or all of the documents in the virtual data room.

The parties will typically negotiate the front end of the letter first, being the interpretative section and scope of disclosure, and the general disclosures. This will include negotiation regarding the interpretation and scope of the disclosure letter. The specific disclosures are referred to in the front end of the disclosure letter, but are typically listed in a schedule to the letter. While the content of the specific disclosures is not often disputed by the buyer, it will seek to amend any wording that it considers unclear or too general.

4.1 Interpretative section and scope of disclosure

(a) Interpretative section

As the disclosure letter will typically carry over the defined terms from the SPA, the below interpretation clause is common:

> *Unless otherwise defined in this letter or unless the context otherwise requires, words and expressions defined in the Agreement shall have the same meanings where used in this letter.*

The seller should be mindful that the definitions in the SPA do not result in any disclosure having an unintended consequence or lead to a possible misinterpretation.

(b) Scope of disclosure

The seller's first draft will typically state that the matters disclosed in the disclosure letter are deemed disclosed against any provision of the SPA, such that no claim can be made under any clause of the SPA for any matters described in the letter. Buyers will negotiate for the disclosure to be against the SPA warranties only.

Ideally (for the buyer), the disclosure letter will make clear that each disclosure amounts to a disclosure against only the specific numbered SPA warranty specified in the letter alongside such disclosure, and that the seller's liability under any of the other warranties is not affected by such disclosure. Conversely, the seller will want to include language to the effect that the disclosures qualify the warranties as a whole. In striking a reasonable balance, it will be more acceptable for a seller to include such language only if there are a large number of disclosures being made. However, it is increasingly common for buyers to accept that all the disclosures qualify the warranties as a whole. In this case the seller should be mindful of the need to ensure that the drafting of the disclosure makes clear to the buyer that it applies to all relevant warranties (and not just the primary warranty to which it relates).[1]

The seller will also state that the disclosures made in the disclosure letter do not constitute an undertaking, representation or warranty in relation to that disclosure or the documents included in the disclosure bundle. As the SPA is the document in which undertakings, representations and warranties are made, this position is generally accepted.

Any references by the seller to documents that are not appended to the disclosure letter, or wording indicating that a reference to part of a disclosed document constitutes reference to the whole document, should be resisted by the buyer. It will be impossible for the buyer to understand and evaluate the impact of a disclosure if a document (or part of a document) is referred to, but not appended to the disclosure letter.

4.2 General disclosures

The general disclosures are broad categories of information that are deemed to be disclosed to the buyer. In contrast to the specific disclosures, which are unique to each transaction, a seller's first draft disclosure letter will likely include a standardised set of general disclosures.

General disclosures are matters deemed to be known by the buyer, which will therefore preclude a claim for breach of warranty regardless of whether the buyer in fact had any knowledge at all of those matters. Consequently, the buyer will seek to narrow the scope of these disclosures significantly. A seller will typically draft the general disclosures to be as broad as possible in the first instance, including both information that the buyer knew and ought to have known as a result of carrying out the searches of public records typical for such a transaction, and information learned from reviewing the contents of the documents and records provided to it during negotiations and that are now deemed disclosed. However, the buyer will want to ensure that it has actual knowledge of all the facts, matters and circumstances disclosed. As a result, the buyer will negotiate only for the most standard of searches to be included as general disclosures.

First draft general disclosures in an oil and gas transaction commonly include:

- the contents of the SPA and each other transaction document, and all transactions referred to in the SPA and such other transaction documents;

---

1 *Daniel Reeds Ltd v EM ESS Chemists Ltd* [1995] CLC 1405.

- all matters contained or referred to in the virtual data room and the disclosure letter, together with the documents and information contained in the appendices to the disclosure letter;
- the contents of the articles of association (as amended) and any other bylaws or equivalent constitutional documents of the company;
- all matters provided for in the accounts; and
- all facts, matters and circumstances that would be revealed by searches of certain public records and registers.

Each of these, alongside additional general disclosures the seller may include, is discussed in more detail below.

(a) *SPA and transaction documents*

The contents of the SPA and any documents defined therein as 'transaction documents' will be deemed disclosed under this general disclosure. Transaction documents will include the disclosure letter and any additional documents entered into between the parties, such as a shareholders' agreement (or deed of adherence to an existing shareholders' agreement) or joint operating agreement (JOA). Both parties should be clear as to which documents are considered disclosed.

It is more contentious for the seller to include language that captures all transactions or documents referred to in the transaction documents. The buyer should resist this or include a reasonableness qualifier, such that only matters that can be reasonably understood from the transactions or documents referred to in the transaction documents are deemed disclosed.

(b) *Data room*

Disclosure of the contents of the data room is a common general disclosure. The seller, in keeping with the broadest possible approach, will try to disclose the entire contents of the data room. While such general disclosure is frequently accepted by the buyer, in a particularly large, technical oil and gas transaction, there could be several thousands of lengthy documents contained in the data room. If these are deemed generally disclosed, then the buyer may be deemed to have knowledge of facts and circumstances it has not reviewed in detail; so in this case (or if there has been a particularly disorganised disclosure process), the buyer may wish to push back against accepting the general disclosure. The buyer may be able to argue that the seller, in disclosing the entirety of the data room, would not meet the standard of 'fair disclosure' (discussed in section 5), as it would be leaving the buyer to infer for itself the significance of the disclosed documents and information.

It is common to include a long-stop date in both the SPA and the disclosure letter beyond which any documents added to the data room will not be caught by the general disclosure. If a virtual data room is being used, the contents of the data room, or such documents within the data room as are agreed to be deemed disclosed, should be burned onto a CD or DVD and each party should retain a copy of the CD or DVD which has been labelled and signed by both parties.

A buyer may seek to include the following warranty language in the SPA to push the seller to consider what it discloses in the disclosure letter and to avoid a 'data dump' situation:

The information contained in the Data Room and, to the best of the Seller's knowledge the Seller's written responses to the questions raised on behalf of the Buyer, are true, complete and accurate in all material respects.

The seller warranting the completeness and accuracy of the contents of the data room deviates from market practice and is likely to be rejected by the seller. The seller should argue that the buyer should concern itself only with whether the disclosures made in the disclosure letter meet the standard of disclosure. If a disclosure does not meet that standard, the buyer will have a claim for breach of warranty whether or not the seller has warranted as to the completeness or accuracy of the information contained in the data room.

(c) ***Constitutional documents***

The seller's draft may include a broad reference to constitutional (or similar) documents such as articles of association. The buyer will want to narrow this reference to specific copies of such documents as are included in the disclosure bundle. Particular attention should be paid to any amendments that may have been made. The buyer should request that the most up-to-date copies be appended to the disclosure letter.

(d) ***Accounts***

While analysis of the target company's accounts, including group or consolidated accounts, forms part of the due diligence process, the buyer should ensure that this disclosure refers only to accounts it has relied on. These would typically be the latest set of audited accounts and any subsequent management accounts. A prudent buyer should insist on deleting a general disclosure of all company accounts and instead should have the accounts specifically disclosed in the disclosure bundle.

If the seller insists on including this general disclosure, the buyer should avoid language such as "all matters referred to in the accounts" and instead opt for matters that are "reasonably apparent" on the face of the accounts. This would include notes and records included in the accounts, but only to the extent that their significance is reasonably apparent.

The buyer should include a look-back date, such that accounts covering any period prior to that date are not deemed disclosed. The buyer should work closely with both its legal advisers and accountants to determine what is a reasonable look-back date in the context of the transaction.

(e) *Registers*

The seller is likely to consider inserting language to the effect that anything that is in the public domain is deemed disclosed. A buyer should push back on this language, as it would have to run extensive and possibly costly searches in order to be confident that there is no publicly accessible source worldwide that contains negative information about the business.

A buyer may wish to restrict registry searches deemed generally disclosed to only those conducted on specific registers, such as Companies House or the Land Registry (or the respective overseas equivalents), depending on the nature of the target business or company and the jurisdiction(s) in which it operates. The seller should be able to widen the ambit of searches the buyer could reasonably carry out, if it communicates to the buyer early in the process which searches will need to be carried out. Buyer's counsel should consider instructing specialist or local counsel to advise on and/or carry out the necessary local searches as appropriate.

Although searches of relevant registers should be covered in due diligence, the buyer may wish to narrow this disclosure by time, through inclusion of a long-stop date. Anything appearing on the register(s) following this date will not be deemed disclosed to the buyer.

(f) *Minute books*

If the company is well established, it could have extensive books with some available only in hard-copy form. The seller should clearly specify which books are publicly available (as these will be deemed generally disclosed). If the books are not publicly available, the seller will need to give a specific disclosure against the corresponding warranty, if the circumstances require.

(g) *Legal, financial and technical vendor due diligence reports*

Any due diligence reports provided by the seller and the matters contained therein will be deemed disclosed either under the general disclosures, under a specific disclosure (where applicable) or as part of the data room documents disclosed. A buyer and its legal, financial and technical advisers should study these reports and review or request any documents referred to therein, as part of a thorough due diligence process.

(h) *Correspondence*

The seller will typically push for the inclusion of a general disclosure of all correspondence passing between the seller and buyer (and their respective advisers). As the buyer may, subject to the wording of the SPA, be deemed by the courts to have the imputed knowledge of its advisers, it would be onerous for its personnel to review every piece of correspondence passing between advisers in order to determine whether it can accept a general disclosure of this nature. A buyer should strongly push back on such a disclosure and ask for specific disclosures of anything material against the relevant warranties (to the extent applicable).

4.3 Specific disclosures

The specific disclosures are disclosures of specifically described and known facts, issues and liabilities within the target business that qualify the warranties. As these are known issues, the buyer will very rarely dispute the substance of a specific disclosure; however, it will mark up the wording of a specific disclosure to ensure that it is clear and unambiguous (and in order to ensure that it meets the standard of 'fair disclosure', as further examined in section 5). The information flushed out through the specific disclosures will prompt the buyer to ask further questions of the seller regarding the matter at hand and potentially to seek indemnities, conditions and/or price chips, as relevant. If the seller does not make the disclosure, however, or the requisite standard of disclosure is not met, the buyer will be able to bring a claim for breach of warranty (assuming that the buyer did not have knowledge of the matter pre-signing through another route). The seller should also consider any additional liability it may incur at common law and under statute.

The seller should be mindful of the offences under both the Financial Services Act 2012 and the Fraud Act 2006. Pursuant to Section 89 of the Financial Services Act 2012, it is a criminal offence to knowingly or recklessly make a false or materially misleading statement or to conceal material facts dishonestly. The seller's solicitors could also be liable to pay compensation to the buyer.[2]

Complete non-disclosure does not equate to misrepresentation; but if silence would render a warranty untrue, then the seller is required to disclose in order to avoid liability for breach of warranty. The seller should always disclose all relevant information.

If there is a legal duty to disclose certain information, or if the seller makes an intentional false representation and intends to gain or cause loss as a result of either, the seller may be found guilty of an offence under the Fraud Act 2006.[3] The maximum penalty for such an offence is imprisonment for a term of 10 years. The seller may also be liable to pay a fine.

Apart from the most fundamental warranties (including title, capacity and authority), the warranties will vary from deal to deal and consequently so will any disclosures against those warranties. As no transaction will contain the

---

2 *Securities and Investments Board v Pantell SA* (No 2) [1992] 3 WLR 896.
3 Sections 1, 2 and 3 Fraud Act 2006.

same set of warranties and corresponding specific disclosures, there is no standardised set of specific disclosures that will appear in a disclosure letter for an oil and gas transaction. The below sets out broad categories of specific disclosure based on the warranties that are typically included in an SPA for an oil and gas transaction. These are organised thematically based on the types of liability being disclosed. The seller should consider disclosing the following.

(a) ***Encumbrances***

If there is a warranty as to no encumbrances over shares or specified assets, the existence of any such encumbrances should be disclosed.

(b) ***Litigation***

This includes any outstanding claims against the target, pertaining to, for example:

- non-payment (or delayed payment) of cash calls due under a JOA;
- refunds claimed from a joint venture account;
- value added tax claims in local tax tribunals;
- excess stamp duty;
- outstanding claims against the target relating to arbitral awards;
- oil export claims by the local government;
- non-payment of fees for crude inspections.
- construction (eg, change orders, liquidated damages);
- employment;
- insurance policies;
- environmental matters (oil spills, clean-up of onshore or offshore chemical contamination);
- disputed licences; and
- dismantling, removal and restoration liabilities.

(c) ***Penalties***

Any late filings with governmental authorities should be disclosed, alongside any associated penalties for late filing.

As the buyer is assuming these risks by proceeding, it will need to evaluate the risks it is assuming as disclosed above. Any encumbrances may hinder its ability to finance the deal with third-party debt finance. The buyer will want to be indemnified against any litigation with a quantifiable value. Any disputed licences may reduce the scope for the target company or business to explore and drill for oil. This could materially reduce the value of the target, prompting the buyer to seek a price chip – especially if the target is engaged in early stage exploration or production, where the right to explore will form a significant portion of the target's value.

4.4 Disclosure bundle

Specific disclosures will cross-refer to the documents included in the disclosure bundle. The disclosure bundle can often be long and should contain all documents referred to in the warranties and specific disclosures. The seller and buyer should each have a copy of the disclosure bundle and the buyer should ensure that it has enough time to review the disclosure bundle thoroughly. The disclosure bundle can be provided in hard copy and initialled, although nowadays it has become increasingly common for CDs or flash drives containing the documents to be provided instead of paper copies.

5. Standard of disclosure

It is in the interests of both parties that the disclosures made are fair. The standard of disclosure required is subject to negotiation between the parties and should be defined in the SPA.

Subject to the definition of 'disclosed' in the SPA, fair disclosure gives the buyer sufficient information to determine, on the face of that information and without having to draw inferences, what is the existing or likely impact of the matter on the business being purchased and the transaction at hand and, accordingly, whether the buyer will need to negotiate any indemnities, conditions or price chips, or walk away from the transaction entirely. The seller will want to ensure that it has met the contractual standard of disclosure and as a result the buyer cannot bring a claim for breach of warranty. The standard of disclosure in the SPA will typically be defined to amount to 'fair' disclosure as described in the case law below. If there is no definition of 'disclosed' in the SPA, the common law position below will apply in any event.

The buyer will want to include as high a standard as possible in the definition of 'disclosed' in the SPA – usually fairly disclosed with "sufficient detail to identify the nature and scope of the matter disclosed" (which is taken from the relevant case law, below). To be fair, the disclosure must be of sufficient detail and must not leave the buyer to infer the significance of the information disclosed if it forms part of a larger body of complex information or documentation:

> *... there must be fair disclosure of facts and circumstances material to the bargain sufficient in detail to identify the nature and scope of the matter disclosed and to enable the purchaser or acquirer of the shares to form a view whether to exercise any of the rights conferred on him by the contract.*[4]

If the disclosures are not precise enough to enable the buyer to identify the matter disclosed as above, the buyer may still have a valid claim for breach of warranty in respect of such disclosure if it cannot draw conclusions as to its significance.[5]

---

4 *Prentice v Scottish Power plc* [1997] SLT 1071.
5 *Levison v Farin* [1978] 2 All ER 1149.

In addition, disclosure by way of omission will not constitute fair disclosure. If, for example, a warranty requires disclosure of all licences that the target requires to carry on its business, these should be listed alongside their renewal or expiry status. Failure to do so would not amount to fair disclosure and, as a result, the buyer could bring a claim for breach of warranty.[6]

The seller should also consider the implications of disclosing a complex body of documents without providing guidance as to which information is relevant:

> *Mere reference to a source of information, which is in itself a complex document, within which the diligent enquirer might find relevant information will not satisfy the requirements of a clause providing for fair disclosure with sufficient details to identify the nature and scope of the matter disclosed.*[7]

If a seller wishes to disclose complex documentation and rely on the buyer deducing for itself the significance of the information to enable it to reasonably understand the implications of the disclosed documents, this should be expressly provided for in the SPA.[8] If this is not provided for, the seller must provide the buyer with sufficient information and context to enable the buyer to understand the implications of the disclosure made. It is with the above case law in mind that both parties should carefully draft and review both the SPA and the disclosure letter.

6. Conclusion

Disclosure letters are an important part of any transaction for the sale and purchase of a company or business, including in the oil and gas sector. Both parties – seller and buyer – must consider the interplay between the wording of the SPA, the standard of disclosure within the SPA and the warranties given by the seller.

The buyer should resist any broad general disclosures given by the seller. If the buyer does accept broad general disclosures, the buyer should ensure that these are limited in scope – for example, by using a long-stop date (such that information published after that date is not deemed disclosed) or a look-back date (such that information created before that date is not deemed disclosed). In a similar vein, any late disclosure of large volumes of documents by the seller should be resisted.

Although the wording of the SPA and disclosure letter will be heavily negotiated in setting the standard of disclosure and scope of disclosures given, the parties should be mindful of the legal principles that operate in the background. Unless a standard of disclosure is specifically contracted for, the

6 *Daniel Reeds Ltd v EM ESS Chemists Ltd* [1995] CLC 1405.
7 *New Hearts Ltd v Cosmopolitan Investments Ltd* [1997] 2 BCLC 249.
8 *MAN Nutzfahrzeuge AG v Freightliner Ltd* [2005] EWHC 2347, affirmed in *MAN Nutzfahrzeuge AG v Freightliner Ltd* [2007] EWCA Civ 910.

common law standard of fair disclosure will apply. The statutory offences of fraud and misrepresentation should be borne in mind, as these will be relevant when the seller makes its disclosures.

Parties often spend vast amounts of time negotiating the warranties, but very little time reviewing and negotiating the disclosure letter, when in fact they need to give proper attention to both, as the latter effectively caveats the former. The language of the disclosures given and information disclosed should be keenly analysed by both parties.

Warranty and indemnity insurance

Matthew Foster
Sophie O'Connor
Norton Rose Fulbright LLP

1. Introduction

The warranties and indemnities in a sale and purchase agreement (SPA) or management warranty deed (MWD) or other transaction document are a key part of the risk allocation between buyer and seller. Warranties are statements of fact about the target company or business and assets being sold. In the first instance, warranties are designed to force disclosure by the seller of any matter or issue that should qualify the warranties concerned and supplement the buyer's due diligence investigations. However, failure to disclose properly against the warranties prior to completion may result in the seller incurring liability for breach of warranty and a claim enabling the buyer to recover the diminution in value of the target company or business and assets it has purchased.

A warranty and indemnity insurance policy (W&I policy) provides insurance cover for financial losses arising from breach of a warranty and (in most jurisdictions) claims under a tax indemnity. Under such a policy, it is typically the insurer, rather than the seller, which bears the financial impact of the losses and compensates the insured accordingly.

The use of W&I policies in global mergers and acquisitions has grown significantly over the last decade as premiums and other commercial terms have become more attractive to insureds. The number of insurers offering such policies has similarly grown, resulting in heightened competition, increasingly competitive commercial terms as between insurers, and increased insurer appetite to offer policies to insureds in a wider range of industries and transaction structures. Many oil and gas transactions are now within insurers' appetites, with policies being offered on commercial terms which are attractive to parties in this sector.

This chapter focuses on a UK-style underwriting process and UK-style buy-side W&I policy. In the United States, policies are known as representations and warranties insurance policies and there are a number of differences in the process and the scope of cover. While we have not considered these in detail, we have sought to flag key areas in which terms may vary below. The distinction between buy-side and sell-side policies is further discussed in section 3 below.

In addition, this chapter does not focus on pricing, limits or other purely commercial terms, and we would recommend that potential insureds contact their insurance brokers to discuss such aspects at the outset of any transaction in which it is proposed that a W&I policy may be used.

2. Use of W&I policies

The use of W&I policies is often a result of certain key deal dynamics:

- Private equity disposals: Traditionally, private equity firms are often unable or unwilling to provide substantive business warranties to buyers, notwithstanding their role as a selling shareholder. The principal reasons are that private equity firms:
  - consider themselves owners rather than day-to-day managers of the target business; and
  - must be able to return sale proceeds quickly to their investors and, as such, are unable to hold proceeds for the duration of warranty periods or to accept proceeds being placed in escrow.
- Individual sellers: Buyers may be concerned about the creditworthiness of individual sellers; in turn, individual sellers may be keen to ensure that their liability is significantly limited (or even limited to nil), and that they may use their sale proceeds freely without the risk of recourse or claw-back.
- Management sellers: If the sellers are part of the management team which will continue to run the business for the buyer following completion, the buyer may be concerned about the consequences of having to take action against the management team to enforce the warranties – in particular, the impact on the buyer's relationship with the management team as a result.
- Strategic positioning for auction sales: Sellers can structure auction transactions which provide for nil recourse to the sellers by offering buyers a customary set of warranties which are pre-underwritten by insurance; and buyers can make an auction bid more attractive to sellers if they offer sellers the possibility of a clean break with very limited or nil liability.
- Insolvency: Insolvency practitioners are unable to give substantive business warranties. While historically rare, synthetic W&I policies entered into directly between buyer and insurer and which contain the substantive warranties – and so do not require the seller to give warranties – are becoming increasingly accepted (see further section 5.3). Market experience of these policies is growing and we expect to see the inception of more policies of this nature in the coming months if the global economic environment continues to become more stressed.

The growth in popularity of W&I policies has been largely driven by private equity firms and the experiences of their counterparties. The increasing acceptance by insurers of nil recourse W&I policies has also driven further growth as, in an M&A market which has broadly been seller friendly for a number of years, sellers have sought to capitalise on the opportunity to agree contractually to limit their liability to buyers under the warranties to a nominal amount of £1 or $1, with buyers bearing the risk of cover under the W&I policy thereafter. Historically, insurers had been concerned by the moral hazard which nil recourse W&I policies present; because, arguably, sellers would not be incentivised to disclose against the warranties properly. However, competition between insurers (as described above) and continued demand from private equity have led to a market where this is now common for relatively straightforward transactions; although it would be more unusual for nil recourse policies to be provided in emerging markets or for the largest or most complex transactions.

Although W&I policies are increasingly being used in M&A transactions, they remain a less common feature of transactions in the oil and gas sector. This is especially true where established oil and gas companies (eg, super majors and majors) are a party to the M&A transaction, principally because such oil and gas companies tend to self-insure their overall risks. However, with a significant number of private equity investments in the oil and gas sector over the past few years and increased experience of W&I among the corporate sector in the industry, the expectation is that W&I policies will continue to establish a more significant foothold in oil and gas transactions.

3. How W&I policies work

W&I policies enable insurers to 'step into the shoes' of sellers by responding to claims brought by the buyer for a breach of warranty or claim under a tax indemnity. However, W&I policies do not generally respond to claims under any specific indemnities in the transaction documents; liability for such known issues will be excluded from cover under the W&I policy. In certain scenarios, these can be insured under specific risks policies, but will attract an additional premium.

W&I policies may be incepted by either the buyer or the seller as the insured. In recent years over 90% of W&I policies have been issued as 'buy-side' W&I policies. Such policies indemnify buyers for losses arising from either breach of warranties or claims under tax indemnities given by sellers in the transaction documents. As such, this enables a buyer to claim directly from the insurer without first having to pursue the seller. 'Sell-side' policies indemnify sellers for losses from claims made by the buyer for breach of warranties and claims under tax indemnities given by sellers in the transaction documents. Such policies rely on the buyer making a valid claim against the seller on the basis of the provisions of the transaction documents. From a buyer perspective, such policies have limited value beyond assisting with seller creditworthiness concerns – more particularly, because they cannot provide the buyer with enhanced protection beyond that for which the seller has accepted liability and do not protect the buyer against the seller's fraud. Accordingly, even in situations where the premium for the policy is to be partly or entirely borne by the seller, policies are typically structured as buy-side policies, with a nil or limited recourse provision for the seller's benefit being included in the transaction documents.

In some cases, and most commonly in an auction process, a policy may begin as a theoretical sell-side policy and then 'flip' from seller to buyer as part of an auction sale process, as described in more detail in section 4.

The remainder of this chapter assumes a 'buy-side' policy unless stated otherwise.

4. The process

Each W&I policy is a bespoke insurance solution tailored to meet the specific needs of a transaction.

When the policy is originated by the buyer, the buyer will appoint a broker, who will seek terms from a number of insurers on the basis of a summary of key information about the transaction and a copy of the draft transaction documents containing the warranties and (if applicable) the tax indemnity. The broker will present those terms, known as non-binding indications (NBIs), to the buyer. The NBIs will set out the insurer's proposed pricing and other commercial terms together with its position on key aspects of cover and areas on which it will be focusing its underwriting review.

The insurer's underwriting review will consider a number of factors when negotiating and finalising a W&I policy for a transaction. Most critically, the insurer will need to understand:

- the rationale for the transaction and the transaction structure;
- the nature of the negotiations between seller and buyer;
- the scope and extent of the due diligence exercise; and
- the thoroughness of the disclosure exercise.

Before commencing its underwriting review, the insurer will require the buyer to enter into an expense agreement for a fixed sum in respect of its underwriting costs; in some cases, this is waived if the policy is incepted and the premium paid.

In the United Kingdom, the duty to make a fair presentation of the risk – as it applies in respect of any insurance policy – will apply to W&I policies. This duty arises under the Insurance Act 2015, which updates and clarifies the common law concept of 'utmost good faith' (similar or equivalent duties exist in certain other jurisdictions). This duty requires that a proposed insured disclose to the insurer all information, facts and circumstances which are, or ought to be, known to the insured and which are material to the risk. An insured's broker will be able to assist the insured with ensuring compliance with this duty, including by identification of relevant materials. In addition, the insurer will usually ask a large number of questions to understand better its key areas of concern considering (among other factors) the sector in which the target company or business and assets operate. Answering such questions openly and transparently is part of complying with this duty.

Once the expense agreement has been signed, the insurer will commence the legal part of the underwriting review, which will focus on the following:

- the due diligence reports and process more generally;
- the SPA and other transaction documents, including the disclosure letter;
- the disclosure process; and
- any other transaction-specific matters.

Insurers may engage external legal counsel to assist with this review. Following the legal review, the insurer and/or legal counsel will formulate views (and legal counsel will typically prepare a report) on the warranties and (if applicable) tax indemnity, including:

- the extent to which such provisions appear negotiated and balanced;
- the due diligence and disclosure exercise; and
- whether it is as one would expect to see for a transaction of the type in question and any material areas of concern or specific risks.

The underwriting review, more generally, enables the insurer to prepare questions for the buyer and its advisers, to be addressed in writing and/or by way of discussion on an 'underwriting call'. On the underwriting call, the insurer will ask the questions or seek clarification on any written responses to further inform its view of the transaction as a whole and understand how the buyer has sought to address or gain comfort with respect to particular issues diligenced/disclosed. These explanations will aid the insurer in determining the level of risk it will assume under the W&I policy – and the extent to which risks may need to be addressed by additional policy wording or by way of specific exclusions or other adjustments to the scope of cover.

Following the underwriting call, the insurer will usually provide a revised draft of the W&I policy which reflects its assessment of risk, to be negotiated and finalised by the insurer and the buyer and its advisers. Typically, at this stage, exclusions and other areas of cover (or lack thereof) will be the focus of the negotiations between the insurer and the buyer.

Where W&I policies originate by seller-led auction, the process is slightly different. Such policies are typically described as a 'sell- to buy-side flip', as it is the seller that initially engages with the insurer. The seller will provide the broker with the auction version(s) of the transaction documents with which to seek insurer NBIs and subsequently appoints an insurer which (following entry into an expense agreement) will commence underwriting on the basis of the sell-side materials, including any vendor due diligence reports. The purpose of this approach is twofold:

- to ensure that all bidders are competing on the same basis, allowing the seller to better compare auction bids (including the liability regime) between bidders; and
- to expedite the process, as the insurer will, subject to the extent of the vendor due diligence, typically expect the successful bidder to have undertaken top-up/supplemental due diligence only, which may be reviewed by the insurer in a shorter time period.

Following its review of the sell-side materials, the insurer will typically provide a process note or other memorandum for bidders setting out its position on the warranties contained in the transaction documents and the areas (including any perceived due diligence gaps) where the insurer would expect bidders to focus their top-up/supplemental diligence in order for the insurer to provide maximum cover. The W&I policy (and broker's responsibilities) then 'flip', with the bidder taking the lead and becoming the broker's client; as such, benefiting from the duties owed by the broker to its client. The bidder will also execute a further expense agreement with the insurer and provide the insurer with copies of the buy-side materials, including any buy-side due diligence reports and mark-up(s) of the transaction documents. Thereafter, the buy-side underwriting continues as described above.

Market practice has developed two variations of the sell-side process, being the 'hard staple' and the 'soft staple'. In the case of the former, the bidder's acceptance of the seller's chosen insurer is considered a requirement of the bid. In the case of the latter, the seller will be unlikely to have chosen an insurer and instead (via its broker) obtained NBIs from interested insurers; notably, it will not be a requirement of any bid that the buyer agrees to obtain a W&I policy from the seller's chosen insurer.

W&I policies are typically underwritten over a period of two or three weeks, but can be underwritten much more quickly. The timeframe will, of course, be driven by the underlying M&A transaction. A sell-side process may allow for an (additional) initial period of underwriting in parallel to the auction timetable. Generally, a longer underwriting period will allow more time for the insurer to understand the transaction, process and specific issues, and request additional information. The more information that can be obtained by the insurer and the further comfort that can be provided to the insurer, the more it may be willing to offer a broader coverage position.

5. The insurance policy

A W&I policy aims to provide back-to-back cover for the seller's liability under the warranties and (if applicable, and subject to the points discussed in section 5.1) tax indemnity. A UK-style W&I policy typically consists of three parts:

- the policy schedules, setting out key information such as the names of the parties, details of the SPA, the policy term, the premium, *de minimis*, retention, key liability limits and broker commission (invariably payable by the insurer);
- the insurer's standard terms and conditions for the policy; and
- a warranty spreadsheet detailing the extent of cover for each warranty.

As noted previously, W&I policies are bespoke policies and are commonly negotiated between the insurer and the insured. Key areas of the policy that an insured will review include:

- the definition of 'loss';
- the exclusions (which are considered in more detail in section 7) and any deemed amendments to the warranty schedule;
- the definitions of 'seller knowledge' and 'buyer knowledge';
- the definition of 'fair disclosure' or equivalent concept, and any deemed disclosures;
- the conditions (to inception);
- the claims and notice provisions;
- subrogation and conduct of claims provisions;
- the no claims declaration (NCD); and
- in the case of a conditional transaction, any bring-down disclosure requirements applicable on completion.

W&I policies are typically subject to a limited number of conditions. Such conditions will likely include:

- the occurrence of completion of the transaction on the terms of the transaction documents;
- the payment of the premium; and
- other practical conditions, such as delivery of final form due diligence reports and a copy of the data room.

In order to achieve back-to-back cover, insureds will want to ensure that definitions and other concepts in the policy mirror those in the transaction documents; this is particularly notable for the definition of 'loss', the 'fair disclosure' standard, seller knowledge and the claims-related provisions. Usually the W&I policy will replicate the transaction documents on such matters, unless the insurer believes that the standards set out in the transaction documents are significantly off-market or the underwriting review reveals material deficiencies in the transaction process – for example, in the disclosure exercise undertaken by the seller (in which case the W&I policy may deem that a different reduced disclosure standard should apply). Certain of these terms may be varied where the insured purchases policy enhancements as discussed in section 5.2.

The exclusions and any deemed variations to the warranties represent the most substantive divergence between the W&I policy and the transaction documents. The W&I policy will include a section clearly headed 'exclusions', in which the exclusions from cover are set out. For further detail on the standard exclusions typically found in UK-style W&I policies, see section 7. Typically, UK and European-style W&I policies include a warranty spreadsheet listing all of the warranties to be given by the seller in the transaction documents, together with a corresponding confirmation or comment as to whether each warranty is covered in full, covered subject to a deemed variation or excluded for the purpose of cover under the W&I policy. The insurer's position with respect to each warranty will reflect its view formed over the course of the underwriting review, including as to the drafting of each warranty, the extent of corresponding diligence (if any) on the subject matter of the warranty in question and, more generally, whether the warranty suite as a whole is reflective of a balanced negotiated position. The amendments deemed by the insurer may (among other amendments) impose a seller knowledge or materiality qualification on all or part of a warranty, or rewrite a warranty which is considered to be too buyer friendly with a more market standard or balanced variation of the same.

Accordingly, one area which is important for the buyer and seller to consider in the context of the transaction documents is how (if at all) to address any gaps in the W&I policy cover and who will bear that liability. This is largely a matter of commercial leverage and bargaining strength, and will often be reflective of the rationale for seeking a W&I policy in the first instance. For example, a seller in a competitive auction process – with a nil recourse liability position under the transaction documents – will likely be well placed to negotiate a position whereby the buyer bears such liability and effectively 'self-insures' for any corresponding loss. In a bilateral context, where the W&I policy contains exclusions driven by the nature of the transaction – for example, a jurisdictional exclusion in an emerging markets transaction – the buyer would appear to be in a stronger bargaining position to negotiate a position whereby the seller bears such liability; for example, by way of a specific indemnity or provisions for a separate warranty regime to apply to 'non-covered' claims for which the buyer retains direct recourse to the seller. In any event, it will be unusual for the seller to accept liability if an exclusion has been imposed by the insurer in relation to a particular topic which the buyer has positively excluded from the scope of its diligence, or in respect of which the buyer's diligence is not adequate for the insurer's purposes.

One provision of the W&I policy of particular interest to the seller is the prohibition on subrogation. In transactions with a buy-side W&I policy, the transaction documents will typically include a warranty or undertaking from the buyer to the seller that the W&I policy contains or will contain a prohibition on the insurer exercising any subrogation rights against (and ability to pursue) the seller, except in the case of fraud by the seller. A buyer ought to ensure that this provision is included in the W&I policy in order to satisfy its corresponding obligation in the transaction documents. Unless the seller will bear responsibility for any liability as a result of gaps in the W&I policy cover (as discussed in the preceding paragraph), this is arguably the only provision that a seller should be interested in and the only reason why a seller may wish to review the W&I policy; although in reality, the seller's comfort should be based on its own limitations of liability, as an insurer can only subrogate to claims that the buyer would have had against the seller in the first place.

Notably, this reflects a key difference between sell-side and buy-side W&I policies. Sell-side W&I policies will not respond to seller fraud and the seller will be obliged to satisfy the corresponding liability directly in favour of the buyer. In contrast, buy-side W&I policies will respond in the event of seller fraud, but the insurer will be entitled to subrogate against the seller in these circumstances. The rationale for this distinction is consistent with common law principles regarding the prohibition on insuring against one's own deliberate default – and a key reason why the majority of W&I policies underwritten are buy-side W&I policies.

The NCD is a statement executed by (or on behalf of) the insured at signing, and (if applicable) repeated at completion, which sets out certain representations from the insured given on its behalf by named members of its deal team stating that the insured has no knowledge of a claim (or, depending on the formulation, of any facts or circumstances likely to give rise to any claim) under the W&I policy.

5.1 Cover for the tax indemnity and tax warranties

UK and European-style W&I policies will usually provide cover for breach of the tax warranties and a claim under the tax indemnity set out in the transaction documents. However, the key difference, for the purposes of the W&I policy, is that disclosures (both general and specific) and the policy *de minimis* apply to the tax covenant. This is a distinction from market practice on uninsured deals, meaning that in this respect the W&I policy offers a buyer less protection than a traditional tax covenant.

There are standard tax exclusions which will apply to most W&I policies for secondary tax liabilities (ie, where the tax is not that of the target, but of a group company), the availability of tax assets, diverted profits tax liabilities and transfer pricing. However, increasingly, it appears that such matters may be capable of being within the scope of cover if the insured has conducted sufficient diligence on these items and demonstrated their impact on their calculation of the value/price.

W&I tax insurance underwriting is a fast-growing specialism whereby if an event is identified, it may be possible for an insurer to agree to cover it either by giving 'affirmative cover' or by offering specific tax insurance policies for an additional premium, which will provide cover. Each of these requires that appropriate legal and tax diligence be undertaken on the relevant issues.

5.2 Common policy enhancements

Insurers now offer a variety of enhancements to their W&I policies which are typically available for an additional premium. These have been developed by insurers to help address the downwards trend in premium rates as the market has become more competitive and also to bridge the gap with US-style policies which usually provide broader cover, but are typically priced higher than UK and European-style policies.

The availability of any particular W&I policy enhancement will be considered by insurers on a deal-by-deal basis, reflecting their view of the risk profile of a particular transaction; and will depend on the particular insurer's underwriting guidelines and risk appetite.

A common enhancement to cover is to provide, in and for the purpose of the W&I policy, for an extension of warranty periods beyond the expiry of those set out in the transaction documents. While typical cover periods in an oil and gas deal might be 12 to 18 months for business warranties and approximately three years for fundamental warranties, at the time of writing insurers are typically willing to cover a period of up to three years for business warranties, a longer period of up to seven years for fundamental warranties and the longer statutory period for tax warranties and the tax indemnity. Insurers may also be willing to dis-apply the *de minimis* for fundamental warranty claims (ie, those relating to title and capacity).

As mentioned above, a number of the common enhancements reflect differences which are common in US-style M&A and corresponding US-style W&I policies, and which have gradually become more common in the United Kingdom and Europe. These include providing for:

- an indemnity measure of damages and therefore a pound-for-pound or dollar-for-dollar recovery of loss;
- repetition of business warranties at completion (in addition to the fundamental warranties); and
- removal of the general disclosure of due diligence reports and the data room.

The general rule in English law is that damages for breach of warranty are calculated by reference to the difference between the value of the shares of the target company as warranted and the true value of the shares.[1] However, in the United States, M&A transaction documents typically provide that loss will be calculated on an indemnity basis, allowing the buyer to recover such loss on a pound-for-pound or dollar-for-dollar basis. In recent years, most insurers in the United Kingdom and Europe have been willing to accept this approach, with the W&I policy defining loss on an indemnity basis for an additional premium. This approach is particularly popular with US private equity buyers which are familiar with this approach in their home market.

Traditionally, as a matter of UK M&A practice, it was unusual to see repetition of warranties on completion (except in the case of the fundamental warranties relating to title and capacity). Increasingly, US-style practice – where the business warranties are more often repeated on completion – has become more common. Insurers appear to be able to accommodate this practice (and charge an additional premium for doing so), provided that there is a requirement on the seller to provide an additional disclosure letter on completion or for the transaction documents (and otherwise the W&I policy itself) to provide for another form of 'bring-down' disclosure mechanism, such as providing the buyer with a confirmation or notice of any post-signing breach(es). The buyer deal team will also be required to give a further NCD on completion confirming that they are not aware of any breach(es) of the warranties subsequent to signing. If a breach is notified to the buyer (or the buyer otherwise becomes aware of such a breach) post-signing but pre-completion, then the buyer will not have a claim for the completion breach under the W&I policy (as it would be a known risk at this stage), but may (if the breach had subsisted at signing) have a claim for the signing breach under the W&I policy.

Although insurers may be willing to remove express general disclosure of due diligence reports or the information in the data room from the W&I policy, insurers may instead seek to address the information gap by including provisions in the NCD (as described above) confirming that the insured (or relevant deal team members) have read and understood the due diligence reports.

Another common enhancement is the 'knowledge scrape' or 'materiality scrape' of the provisions in the W&I policy which contractually deem that any warranties in the transaction documents given on the basis of seller awareness or materiality are given without such qualification, except where expressly required by the insurer for certain limited standard exceptions.

1 Recently reiterated in *Overseas-Chinese Banking Corporation Ltd v ING Bank NV* [2019] EWHC 676 (Comm).

5.3 Synthetic policies

Under a synthetic W&I policy, the warranties and (if applicable) tax indemnity are contained in the W&I policy and not the transaction documents; accordingly, there is no underlying contractual claim in the transaction documents for breach of warranty or (if applicable) under the tax indemnity. A synthetic W&I policy is simply a direct contractual indemnity relationship between the buyer and the insurer (to which the seller is not a party). While the insurer would indemnify the buyer for loss in the same way as in the traditional context, the lack of seller engagement in the disclosure process removes a level of comfort that the insurer might otherwise obtain to supplement the due diligence materials (and also removes comfort for the buyer as regards the seller's good-faith involvement in the transaction).

Synthetic W&I policies have been very rare, for the reason mentioned above regarding seller engagement. However, at the time of writing, this is a current topic of significant discussion in the W&I market as a potentially effective solution when a seller is not only unwilling but also unable to give any warranties – for example, in the case of a sale by insolvency practitioners. Given the global recession arising from the COVID-19 pandemic, many in the W&I market have expressed views that synthetic W&I policies may become more commonplace for distressed M&A transactions.

Synthetic tax deeds are more common and have been seen in many transactions over the last couple of years. They are typically required where sellers are unwilling to give a tax indemnity of any sort (and accordingly not inclined to draft or negotiate the terms of a tax covenant), but the buyer has been given access to information to undertake a thorough tax due diligence process which is sufficient for an insurer to get comfortable enough with the risks for an insurer to provide a standard form tax covenant for the buyer's benefit.

6. Insurance underwriting diligence requirements

As described above, once appointed, an insurer will need to complete its underwriting review before it can issue a binding W&I policy. The insurer (and its legal counsel, if applicable) will review materials including the following:

- the information memorandum or other marketing materials provided to the buyer;
- interim drafts and final versions of the transaction documents (with a focus on the SPA or MWD (if applicable) and disclosure letter), together with any schedules or attachments to such documents;
- all sell-side due diligence reports provided to the buyer (if any), including the scope of the data room (for which the insurer will require access for itself and its advisers);
- all buy-side due diligence reports prepared by the buyer's external

advisers (typically these will include at least legal, tax and financial diligence; but they may also include property, insurance, commercial, environmental, anti-bribery, corruption and sanctions or other specialist advisers' reports);
- if any due diligence has been undertaken in-house by the buyer, any internal reports, memoranda, minutes or similar prepared by the diligence team (and the insurer will seek to understand the qualification of those undertaking such due diligence, and may seek an opportunity to raise questions with the relevant team – particularly if there is no formal written diligence report); and
- the latest audited and (if applicable) management accounts of the target company or relating to the business and assets.

The insurer will state in its NBI if there are increased areas of focus for its underwriting review which it will expect to see the buyer has thoroughly diligence. For a target company or business and assets in the oil and gas sector, particular areas of focus are likely to include:
- title to hydrocarbon deposits;
- licensing and permits;
- contractual arrangements regarding exploration, production, storage, transportation and offtake operations, including joint operating agreements and unit and unitisation operating agreements;
- health and safety;
- environmental;
- decommissioning; and
- anti-bribery, corruption and sanctions (depending on jurisdictions).

In addition, standard areas of focus such as the following will also be important:
- title to shares;
- IT systems and cybersecurity (including security, source code, back-up and adequacy);
- the insurance programme of the target company or relating to the business and assets (and the extent to which this programme will travel on completion);
- general compliance with laws and other regulation (including governance, systems, controls and procedures designed to ensure compliance); and
- employment arrangements.

Ultimately, the scope and substance of the buyer's due diligence exercise will largely determine the scope of cover that the insurer is willing to provide under the W&I policy. This reflects the underlying principle that while insurers will accept the transfer of risk under the W&I policy, this does not absolve buyers of the responsibility to undertake an appropriate due diligence exercise. In the context of an insured transaction, buyers should expect to complete a due diligence exercise to the same standard as would be expected of a prudent uninsured, having applied its judgement to focus or limit the scope of due diligence in such a way that is demonstrably reasonable and based on an understanding and assessment of risk in the context of the transaction.

Accordingly, the quality of due diligence reports cannot be underestimated as a factor in giving insurers comfort about the scope and substance of diligence. While insurers do accept red flag or exceptions-only style reports (if justifiable in the context of the transaction), they will still want to understand the scope of the due diligence exercise on which these were based and, in particular, any explicit or implicit decisions as to materiality or value applied in scoping and/or undertaking the due diligence exercise. It is also important for buyers and their advisers to show that consideration has been given to recommendations made in the due diligence reports and how (if at all) the buyer intends to action any recommendations. Recommendations to 'seek a warranty' or 'rely on seller warranties' are unlikely to provide an insurer with comfort if it appears that the underlying fact or matter has not been fully diligenced.

7. Exclusions

As noted above, the W&I policy will often include standard exclusions relating to:

- issues known to the insured (including any matters that are the subject of specific indemnity protection in the transaction documents);
- asbestos;
- punitive damages;
- forward-looking statements, estimates and projections;
- purchase price adjustment mechanisms;
- pensions underfunding (in the context of defined benefit schemes); and
- unpaid leave entitlements.

Depending on the insurer, the W&I policy may also include exclusions for:

- anti-bribery, corruption and sanctions;
- civil or criminal fines or penalties;
- condition of assets;
- defective property; and
- cyber and environmental liabilities (eg, pollution or contamination).

For oil and gas transactions, it is not untypical for the buyer to consider seeking an additional separate specialist insurance policy for environmental matters, should these be of concern and not covered by the W&I policy. At the time of writing, exclusions for COVID-19 have also been commonly raised by insurers; but as the COVID-19 epidemic has developed, they have increasingly become an area for additional diligence focus rather than an automatic exclusion.

There are also market standard difficulties with transactions in some jurisdictions where there is a lack of confidence in the rule of law or where corruption or political risk is considered to be outside appetite for some or most insurers.

In addition to the above market standard or insurer standard exclusions, there will be some exclusions specific to the industry and further deal-specific exclusions arising from the insurer's underwriting review. In the oil and gas industry, it is common for the following express additional exclusions to apply to most transactions (or at least be subject to heightened underwriting diligence):

- quality, amount or deliverability of reserves, and any hydrocarbon production capacity;
- inaccuracy of predicted/assumed valuation of hydrocarbon assets (if relevant);
- construction defects and development costs (in respect of undeveloped sites);
- geological, geophysical, engineering, economic or other interpretations, forecasts or evaluations;
- state expropriation (depending on the jurisdiction); and
- government subsidy clawbacks and state aid (if relevant).

8. Conclusions

A well-advised or sophisticated buyer or seller should consider whether a W&I policy is appropriate to its M&A transaction, having regard to the principal benefits of reducing tail liabilities and facilitating a clean exit. This is particularly the case for any M&A transaction in the oil and gas industry which, historically, may have been outside appetite for certain insurers. It seems that this is an industry which is well placed to capitalise on competition in the W&I market to obtain competitive terms and realise some or all of the benefits described in this chapter – with a view to taking (at least to some extent) the contentious issue of liability off the deal table. Accordingly, for the reasons stated in this chapter, we would expect that the coming years will likely see an increase in W&I policies being included as part of oil and gas M&A transactions.

Liabilities and indemnities: allocation and limitations on liability, and the use of indemnities

Hussain Kubba
Holly Stebbing
Kimberley Wood
Norton Rose Fulbright LLP

1. Introduction

In the context of a private M&A transaction, the familiar tussle between the buyer and the seller when negotiating the sale and purchase agreement (SPA) is in large part due to the allocation of risk and liability between them, and the method and extent to which such liability will be limited. While the principles that apply to these matters are common across all private M&A transactions, this chapter focuses on upstream oil and gas transactions and considers:

- the principal mechanisms for allocating risk and liability between the buyer and the seller in relation to the sale and purchase of oil and gas interests;
- the key limitations that may apply to such liability (most typically for the benefit of the seller); and
- the nature and typical uses of indemnities as one of the mechanisms for such allocation of risk and liability.

A buyer's concern, faced with the principle of *caveat emptor* ('buyer beware'), is to ensure that upon completion of the contemplated transaction, it has acquired the bargain that it thought it was acquiring at the time it entered into the SPA. A seller, by contrast, will generally seek as clean a break as possible. Where the parties end up in terms of the allocation of risks and liabilities is, as ever, largely a function of the relative bargaining strengths of each party.

Negotiations are often tempered by past or standard industry practice (although this can be a subjective concept in the minds of the two parties and their advisers); and in the oil and gas sector, by the fact that counterparties are often partners in assets in some other part of the world or may in future be partners, which means that the M&A negotiation may be affected by broader industry relationships.

The perfect storm that the oil and gas industry is now facing with reduced commodity prices, the COVID-19 pandemic, increased competition and a move towards more renewable energy sources has ignited renewed focus and scrutiny on the allocation of liabilities in an M&A context by buyers and sellers alike. A large proportion of buyers do not have the balance-sheet strength to take on all liabilities associated with the assets they are purporting to purchase and sellers are consequently having to accept longer-term residual risk and pay-outs – all of which means that we will increasingly see more innovative allocation structures, with the concept of what is 'industry standard' in many cases of little practical value.

This chapter examines the various mechanics for allocating risk and liability between the buyer and the seller. In particular, it looks at the implications of structuring the transaction as a share sale or an asset sale, overall schemes of liability allocation, the giving of warranties, interim period undertakings, material adverse change (MAC) provisions, limitations on liability provisions and indemnities.

2. Allocation of liability

2.1 Share sale versus asset sale

A key preliminary question regarding the allocation of liability in an upstream oil and gas SPA is whether that agreement is for the sale and purchase of the target oil and gas interests directly (an asset SPA) or the sale and purchase of shares in a company that owns oil and gas interests (a share SPA).

A broader examination of the considerations that drive the choice of transaction structure (assets or shares) is beyond the scope of this chapter, although tax, governmental or partner consents and pre-emption rights are often key factors. Relevant to the issue of allocation of liability between the seller and the buyer is the fact that with a share SPA, the starting proposition is that all of the liabilities of the target remain with the company and thus are transferred to the buyer, indirectly, as the new owner of the company. Accordingly, absent express agreement and provisions in the share SPA, all liabilities of the target transfer with it, whether relating directly to the oil and gas interests that it owns, its employees, real property, financing arrangements, any disputes, tax position or otherwise.

The position regarding the share SPA thus contrasts with the position under the asset SPA, where only the specific assets and liabilities that the buyer agrees to acquire are transferred from seller to buyer. In the upstream oil and gas context, the core of what the seller sells and what the buyer buys is the seller's rights and related obligations in and under the matrix of contracts pursuant to which the seller has the right to explore for, develop and produce hydrocarbons, and pursuant to which relevant petroleum operations are conducted. The two key contracts are:

- the relevant arrangement with the host government (whether a licence, concession, production sharing agreement, service agreement or other); and
- assuming that the seller has co-venturers, the joint operating agreement (JOA) governing the relationship between it and its co-venturers.

There may, however, be a myriad of other relevant contracts which the seller has entered into, or which the relevant operator has entered into on its behalf – particularly where the oil and gas interests are in the appraisal, development or production phase of operations. These various contracts are often collectively defined in the asset SPA as the 'interest documents' or similar.

In practice, the positions outlined above on both a share sale and an asset sale are often more nuanced, with sellers and buyers agreeing allocations of specific liabilities that cut across the general allocation in each case. Although it is not uncommon to see transactions involving oil and gas interests structured as company sales, the authors' experience is that there are relatively many more oil and gas transactions structured as asset sales, and the balance of this section looks at liability allocation issues primarily through the lens of an asset SPA (although most of the matters discussed apply in a very similar manner to a share SPA).

2.2 Asset sale general allocation of risk and liability

Absent express agreement and provisions in the asset SPA, all liabilities other than those arising under the transferred interest documents will remain with the seller. In relation to liabilities under the interest documents, the seller and buyer will typically agree that the seller will remain responsible for all liabilities that arose under the interest documents during its period of ownership and the buyer will be liable for all liabilities that will arise under the interest documents during its period of ownership.

The dividing point for the allocation of liabilities is sometimes completion of the sale and purchase, but it is more common for there to be an alternative agreed 'economic date'. The economic date is usually a date prior to the date of signing of the SPA when the parties agree that the transaction will have economic effect – that is, the buyer will, through the relevant provisions of the SPA, bear the economic burden and take the economic benefit of the assets from that date forward. For ease of calculation and due diligence, the economic date is often the same date as the last day of the seller's financial year, where audited accounts are available.

This basic allocation or apportionment of liability for the assets will often be supported by:

- an indemnity from the seller to the buyer for liabilities arising pre-completion or pre-economic date; and
- an indemnity from the buyer to the seller for liabilities arising post-completion or post-economic date.

An important exception to this general scheme of liability allocation is that, in jurisdictions where the seller remains liable for decommissioning or environmental liabilities relating to its oil and gas interests even after it has transferred such interests to the buyer, the buyer may also agree to be responsible for such decommissioning or environmental liabilities, and to indemnify the seller against them. However, with the pool of potential purchasers having smaller balance sheets and acquiring assets towards the end of their field life, sellers are having to agree to retain a portion of decommissioning liabilities, with such retention taking various forms – the details of which are evolving and beyond the scope of this chapter.

The nature and use of these indemnities are dealt with in more detail in section 3 below.

2.3 Warranties

As mentioned, the starting position between the seller and the buyer is 'buyer beware' – that is, the buyer will acquire the relevant oil and gas interests 'as is' and take on all of the liabilities transferred with such interests, whatever they are. The buyer will look to mitigate this risk by carrying out a due diligence investigation which will likely include some combination of technical due diligence on the geological and geophysical data, estimated resources and reserves and, where relevant, production facilities, as well as financial due diligence and legal due diligence. Legal due diligence will primarily focus on confirming the seller's title to the oil and gas interests, confirming that it has, through the various contracts making up the interest documents, all of the rights necessary for the conduct of petroleum operations. Due diligence will also consider whether there are any liabilities associated with those interests that were not known to the buyer at the time it made its offer and which have not been reflected in the price offered by the buyer. In short, the buyer is seeking to confirm that it is getting the deal that it has agreed to pay for.

It is extremely rare for the buyer to rely solely on its due diligence. Instead, the seller will also be required to give it certain warranties in the SPA. Warranties are statements of fact about a state of affairs that exists at the time that the statements are made and that transfer risk from the buyer back to the seller.

As a matter of English law, in the event that a warranty provided in the SPA proves to be untrue or incorrect, the buyer may have a claim following completion of its purchase of the oil and gas interests for breach of contract and for damages for an amount equal to the difference between the value of the interests as they are with the warranty being untrue and the value that they would have had if the warranty had been true. In this way, the warranty claim acts as an adjustment to the price paid by the buyer for the interests, such that the price, as adjusted, reflects the true value of those interests. This should be contrasted with the buyer's right to recover under an indemnity, which is discussed further in section 3.

The seller, in turn, can mitigate the risk of a claim for breach of warranty by making a disclosure. This means that where the seller knows that the warranty as written is not true, it can provide the buyer with information setting out the actual state of affairs regarding the subject matter of the warranty and thus, in effect, render the warranty correct and avoid liability for a breach of warranty. By way of a simple example, if the seller warrants that there are no disputes in existence in relation to the oil and gas interests but, in fact, it is involved in a dispute with a drilling contractor, it renders its warranty true by disclosing details of the dispute with the drilling contractor to the buyer in a disclosure letter. The buyer can thus assess the materiality of this dispute and its impact, if any, on the buyer's economic model and the price that it is willing to pay. Where the buyer considers the matter to be sufficiently material, it may seek a reduction in the purchase price or require the seller to provide it with a specific indemnity in relation to the matter.

This way, the warranties requested by the buyer support the due diligence investigation by eliciting information from the seller on the subject matter of the warranties. Disclosure and other limitations on the seller's liability for warranty claims are discussed further in section 4 below.

The scope of warranties requested and given can depend on numerous variables, but is ultimately a question of the relative bargaining position of the parties. Although buyers and sellers can adopt extreme positions, the scope of warranties on upstream oil and gas deals is rarely a major sticking point between two motivated and pragmatic counterparties. Key areas for warranties relating to oil and gas interests include ones that relate to, for example:

- title to the oil and gas interests, including no encumbrances;
- compliance with the terms/no breach of material contracts;
- compliance with laws;
- litigation, disputes or proceedings relating to the oil and gas interests;
- notices of revocation, withdrawal or sole risk operations;
- environmental and health and safety matters;
- tax matters; and
- anti-bribery and corruption matters.

It is common in an oil and gas asset SPA for the seller to state expressly that it makes no warranty in relation to certain matters, such as:

- amounts, quality or deliverability of reserves;
- geological, geophysical, engineering or economic interpretations, forecasts or evaluations;
- geological formations, drilling prospects or hydrocarbon reserves; and
- the state, condition or fitness for purpose of any of the physical assets.

As noted above, warranties are statements of fact that speak to a state of affairs at the time that they are given. Commonly, warranties are given as at the date that an SPA is entered into. Where there is a significant period between that date and the date on which the buyer actually completes the purchase of the applicable oil and gas interests (eg, because of the time taken to satisfy conditions precedent set out in the SPA), the buyer may want the seller to repeat its warranties at, or immediately prior to, completion, to give it assurance again at that point in time that it is getting what it is paying for. Expectations and practice regarding the repetition of warranties at completion vary. It is often observed that repeating warranties at completion is more prevalent in the United States, and that US counterparties have a greater expectation that warranties will be repeated than counterparties based in, for example, the United Kingdom operating under English law-governed SPAs. A debate about repetition of warranties is often resolved with the agreement of the seller to repeat certain warranties that are regarded as fundamental at completion. Such fundamental warranties would include those relating to title to the oil and gas interests, as well as warranties relating to the capacity and authority of the seller to enter into the SPA, as well as solvency.

2.4 Interim period covenants or undertakings

Where there is a period between signing of an SPA and completion of the transaction (typically because of the need for the satisfaction of conditions precedent such as regulatory approvals or clearances or co-venturer consents), the buyer will be at risk of any changes that materially affect the oil and gas interests during this period. One way to mitigate this risk is, as noted above, to have the seller repeat its warranties at, or immediately prior to, completion. Another mechanism to protect the buyer during this period is to have a series of undertakings from the seller in favour of the buyer designed to preserve the value of the oil and gas interests in this interim period.

Such interim period undertakings normally take the form of a mixture of positive undertakings that the seller shall behave in a certain way and negative undertakings that the seller shall refrain from doing certain things. As with warranties, the length and scope of these undertakings can vary considerably depending on the assets in question (eg, whether the assets are in the exploration phase or in the development and/or production phase), the length of the interim period in question and the relative bargaining position of the two parties. In addition to the natural tension between the buyer's desire for control and the seller's desire to be able to operate its assets as it wishes before completion (in case completion does not occur), some care must be taken to ensure that such undertakings do not give the buyer such a degree of control over the relevant assets that it could be argued that the buyer has, in effect, acquired such assets before any necessary consents from applicable governmental entities or regulators have been obtained, thereby potentially causing the parties to breach applicable antitrust or competition laws.

Typical and relatively uncontroversial interim period undertakings might include that the seller will:

- carry on its business in relation to the oil and gas interests in the ordinary and usual course and in accordance with good oil and gas field practice;
- comply with its obligations under the applicable interest documents in all material respects;
- not, without the buyer's prior approval (not to be unreasonably withheld or delayed), amend or agree to amend any of the interest documents;
- not sell, pledge, transfer or otherwise dispose of or encumber any of the oil and gas interests;
- not voluntarily relinquish all or part of any of the areas comprising the oil and gas interests; and
- to the extent practicable, consult with the buyer in relation to any material decision in respect of the assets taken during this period.

Provisions relating to consultation on decisions, sharing of information, attendance at operating committee meetings and the like are often ones that create the most difficulties, both commercially and from the point of view of the buyer exercising too much control. Agreeing on the right level of buyer input can be difficult when, for example, there are drill or drop decisions to be made or a field development plan to be submitted during the interim period, because the proposed approaches of the seller and the buyer to these matters can differ significantly. The seller does not want to be forced to adopt the buyer's approach in case the transaction does not complete; whereas the buyer does not want the seller to agree to a work programme, budget or other committed expenditure that the buyer will be saddled with if the transaction completes as planned.

2.5 MAC clauses

A material adverse change (MAC) provision, also known as a material adverse effect provision, is another device for passing risk from the buyer to the seller for events that may occur during an interim period and which affect the value of the deal. In short, a MAC provision typically provides the buyer with an express remedy under the SPA prior to completion if an event occurs or circumstance arises that causes a MAC in the oil and gas interests that are the subject of the transaction. The provision may be expressed:

- as a condition to completion that there has been no MAC since the signing of the SPA (so no obligation to complete if the condition is not satisfied);
- a warranty given at completion that there has been no MAC (giving rise to a right to damages post-completion);

- an express right to terminate the transaction upon the occurrence of a MAC event; or
- an express right to a price adjustment.

The key to these sorts of provision is defining what events or circumstances will trigger the MAC provision and, if included, the termination right – that is, determining the appropriate test of how material and adverse the impact must be. As what constitutes a MAC will always depend on the specific drafting construed using the usual principles of contractual interpretation, it is important to pay close attention at the drafting stage to ensure that the balance of risk is acceptable. Provisions vary from those that are undefined, referring only to a MAC or event, to those which seek to develop tightly defined objective criteria which reduce, as far as possible, the scope for argument or litigation about whether the provision is triggered. There has been debate as to whether the current COVID-19 pandemic amounts to a MAC and, for the reasons set out above, that will, of course, depend on the terms of the specific clause. However, in the oil and gas context, it seems unlikely that the fact of a pandemic alone will be sufficient to trigger a MAC. Instead, there will need to be a demonstrable adverse effect on the target business which otherwise meets the criteria in the clause before relief is engaged. Given the unprecedented impact that the dual challenges of COVID-19 and low commodity prices are having on the global economy, it seems inevitable that we will see MAC clauses being invoked over the coming months – whether legitimately or by buyers trying to escape what now look like bad deals – and potentially some helpful judicial consideration of these rarely tested clauses as such claims are challenged in litigation.

However MAC is defined, it is generally the case that a MAC provision will include a list of events or circumstances which will expressly not result in a termination right arising, regardless of how adverse the change or effect resulting from these are. These exclusions limit the ambit of the MAC to the benefit of the seller and promote certainty. Of particular relevance in the oil and gas context, these exclusions will almost always include any changes or events that affect the oil and gas industry as a whole, including any change in market prices for hydrocarbons. Other common exclusions include changes in general political, economic or financial conditions affecting the jurisdictions relevant to the transaction; changes in the state of credit, banking, currency, commodity or capital markets generally; and changes in law.

An example of an undefined MAC provision, which is drafted as a termination right and includes the standard exclusions, is as follows:

- *If, after the date of this Agreement but before the CP [condition precedent] Satisfaction Date, a Material Adverse Event occurs, then the Buyer may by written notice to the Seller, terminate this Agreement with immediate effect and the provisions of clause [**] shall apply.*

- *Material Adverse Event means any change in, or effect on the Seller's Group that is materially adverse to its business, assets, financial position or prospects, taken as a whole; provided, however, that none of the following shall be taken into account for the purposes of determining whether or not a Material Adverse Event has occurred:*
  a) changes or effects generally affecting the international or national economic, market, financial, credit, or political conditions in the [United Kingdom] or worldwide;
  b) changes or effects generally affecting the international or national energy industry;
  c) any change or effect generally affecting the oil or natural gas gathering, transportation or processing industries, or the markets for fuel or other raw materials, feedstock or commodities which are, have been or may be used, gathered, transported, produced or sold in the [United Kingdom];
  d) actions taken of omitted to be taken with the consent of the Buyer;
  e) actions or agreements requirement under or contemplated by this Agreement or referred to in the Schedules;
  f) the announcement, pendency or completion of the transactions contemplated by this Agreement; or
  g) changes that are cured (including by the payment of money before the termination of this Agreement under clause [**]).

For obvious reasons, sellers are reluctant to agree to MAC provisions, even where they include a defined list of excluded events and circumstances. In an oil and gas context, a compromise position may be reached where:

- the MAC is limited to physical damage to facilities which interrupts or delays production for a significant period; and/or
- the resulting damage and delay or loss of production is not covered by insurance or is above an agreed amount.

This allows for a narrower approach, although drafting for it can be challenging and complex.

An example of such a limited MAC provision is as follows:

- *If, prior to forty-eight hours before Completion (but not thereafter), a single event or series of related events which solely and directly causes the physical loss of, damage to, or destruction of Field Facilities such that the extent of the Seller's share of such loss, damage or destruction (before the application of any monies recoverable under a policy or policies of insurance) is estimated in good faith by the Parties (as evidenced by written agreement to that effect between the Parties) to exceed [**]% of the Purchase Price (an "Event") then the Buyer shall be entitled at any time prior to the close of business on the 5th Business Day after the date on which the Parties reach agreement on the estimate* *aforesaid or receive the expert's determination pursuant to clause [**], to give notice to the Seller to terminate this Agreement without either the Seller or the Buyer having any liability to the other. If an Event occurs and the Buyer does not give such a notice, then the Parties shall proceed to Completion on the terms provided in this Agreement as if the Event had not occurred.*

- *If, for any reason, the Parties, acting in good faith, are unable or unwilling to agree the estimates of the Seller's share of such loss, damage or destruction as contemplated in clause [**] within 15 Business Days of a request to do so from either of them, the estimate of the Seller's share of such loss, damage or destruction shall be undertaken by an independent expert appointed by the Parties, or if the Parties are unable to agree on such appointment within 24 hours of the expiry of such period of 15 Business Days, as appointed by the President of the Energy Institute.*

The buyer is, to a large degree, reliant on the seller to provide it with information regarding the occurrence of any such damage. In addition, it may take some time to assess the likely impact of the damage and, where insurance cover is relevant, to deal with insurers. However well drafted the MAC provision, there will usually remain plenty of scope for disagreement on the impact of the damage and whether the associated remedies of the buyer are triggered.

3. Indemnities

3.1 What is an indemnity and what is its purpose?

In a private M&A transaction, the warranties and indemnities are often among the more contentious and heavily negotiated provisions in the SPA. This negotiation process is in essence a battle between the buyer and seller as to where the risk of certain liabilities arising will lie. Buyers – conscious of the principle of *caveat emptor* – want to obtain as much warranty and indemnity protection as possible from the seller; while the seller will resist this, insisting that the buyer should rely on its own due diligence. When dealing with private equity vendors or other financial investors, this becomes particularly acute because such sellers will often have minimal operational knowledge of the company or oil and gas interest that they are purporting to sell, and such knowledge sits primarily within a relatively small management team.

The due diligence process in an M&A transaction is key in ascertaining which issues will be raised from the status of warranties to indemnities. As discussed above, a warranty is a statement of fact or a contractual assurance as to the state or condition of the target company or oil and gas interest on a particular date, breach of which gives rise to a potential claim in damages.

An indemnity, by contrast, is a promise to reimburse the beneficiary, which in an M&A context is more frequently the buyer. in respect of a particular liability should it arise, and is designed to compensate the buyer for losses arising from specific risks or liabilities which are identified during the due diligence process. Examples of circumstances where indemnities are commonly given by the seller in favour of the buyer are losses, liabilities, costs, damages, charges and expenses relating to:

- the period prior to completion or pre-economic date (in an asset sale);
- unresolved disputes or ongoing litigation for which the seller has agreed to retain control and liability;
- certain tax liabilities;
- employee claims arising as a result of completion of the transaction; and
- on a share sale, historic residual liabilities sitting within the company to be acquired, but unconnected to the oil and gas interest or interests which are the target of the transaction.

We should briefly contrast the English law position that we have just outlined, where indemnities are given in respect of specific identified liabilities, with practice in the United States, where sellers commonly provide their buyers with general indemnities for any and all losses arising from a breach of warranty or other covenant in an SPA.

In English law-governed transactions, the parties frequently agree to elevate an identified liability from a warranty to an indemnity because of the wider scope of recovery available to the buyer, and because of the potential uncertainty surrounding the buyer's ability to claim under a warranty where it was aware of the facts or circumstances giving rise to a breach. We will now look at each of these in more detail.

3.2 Scope of recovery

A successful claim for breach of warranty requires the buyer to show that the warranty has been breached and that such breach has reduced the value of the company or oil and gas interest that it acquired. The calculation of damages is therefore by reference to the difference between the actual value of the target company or oil and gas interest and the value had the warranty been true. It is consequently restorative in nature, restoring the buyer to the position that it would have been in had the warranty been true, which in turn requires the buyer to prove loss and results in an adjustment to the purchase price. An example of where a claim for breach of warranty may not be available to the buyer is where the books and records of a target company are found after completion to be in a poor state, in breach of a warranty given by the seller. The reorganisation of such books and records may result in the buyer having to incur costs and expenses, but will not generally give rise to a loss in value of the target itself; as a result, the buyer cannot recover such costs and expenses.

An indemnity claim, by contrast, is a reimbursement obligation which is calculated without reference to the loss of value of the target company or oil and gas interest. Therefore, an indemnity changes the scope of recovery of the buyer. The buyer will be entitled to recover on a 'pound-for-pound' or 'dollar-for-dollar' basis for all losses; and, keeping with our example, if the seller granted an indemnity in favour of the buyer for losses incurred in relation to the reorganisation and updating of the company's books and records, then the buyer would be able to recover its relevant costs and expenses from the seller. An indemnity therefore provides the buyer with a standalone cause of action to recover specific potential losses without having to prove their effect on the valuation of the target company or oil and gas interest itself. For this reason, indemnities are described as producing pound-for-pound or dollar-for-dollar recovery, as opposed to warranties, which are generally inferior in terms of the amount recovered – although they do offer considerably more breadth of coverage of the target company or oil and gas interest to be acquired, its condition and operation.

3.3 Awareness of the buyer

On the issue of awareness, if any particular facts or circumstances resulting in a breach of warranty are known to the buyer at the time that the transaction is entered into, it may mean that any resulting loss is not recoverable by the buyer. Since the Court of Appeal judgment in *Eurocopy plc v Teesdale* [1992] BCLC 1067, it is generally accepted that the buyer's actual knowledge or awareness of the facts and circumstances surrounding the seller's breach of warranty during the period for which the warranty is given is an arguable defence against the buyer's claim for breach of such warranty. Where the buyer chooses to act through an agent, the actual knowledge of the agent – to the extent that such knowledge is within the scope of the agent's engagement – will also be treated as knowledge of the buyer (*Infiniteland Ltd v Artisan Contracting Ltd* [2004] EWHC 955 Ch D). Consequently, if the buyer or one of its advisers discovers a material liability during the due diligence process, there is a risk that the buyer may not succeed in making a claim for breach of warranty; one possible solution (discussed above) is for the seller to grant an indemnity in favour of the buyer to cover any losses associated with the discovered liability that may arise after completion.

3.4 Entitlement to 100% recovery

Does an indemnity entitle the beneficiary to 100% recovery for all losses? The answer to this question depends on its drafting and context. If an indemnity gives rise to a debt claim, then there is authority for the proposition that there is no duty on the part of the beneficiary to mitigate and the rules on remoteness of damage do not apply. In addition, indemnities are not ordinarily subject to time and monetary claim limits in the way that warranties are, unless agreed otherwise in the SPA. However, care must be taken in drafting an indemnity. If a court finds that the claim is one for damages for breach of contract, as opposed to a debt claim, the beneficiary or claimant will be under a duty to mitigate and the rules on remoteness will also apply. It will be a question of fact in each case. Providing as much clarity as possible in the drafting around the amount payable under the indemnity will help to persuade a court that the claim should be treated as one for debt rather than for damages, as well as including express language that the rules on mitigation, remoteness and causation do not apply. But this may not always be possible, especially with more general indemnity clauses. In addition, if the trigger for an indemnity is breach of a warranty or covenant, then it will more likely be treated as a damages claim than if it were triggered by an external event, such as a third-party dispute or an employee claim.

3.5 Indemnity structure and drafting

Indemnity clauses generally follow a similar pattern that includes most, if not all, of the following:

- one party;
- indemnifies;
- another party (as well as potentially its affiliates and their respective directors, officers, employees, agents, contractors and subcontractors (together, the 'indemnified persons');
- against any damage, loss, compensation, award, costs (including reasonable legal costs), expenses, charges, fines, penalties or other outgoings;
- suffered or incurred by an indemnified person;
- in respect of an agreed category of loss or relating to a specified event or series of related events;
- arising before or after an agreed period of time;
- notwithstanding the negligence and/or breach of duty (statutory or otherwise) by the indemnified person; and
- subject to exceptions.

Below is an example of an indemnity from a seller in favour of a buyer in respect of certain environmental liabilities that were discovered during the buyer's due diligence investigation and which contains most of the above elements:

Notwithstanding any other provision of this Agreement, the Seller shall:

a) at its cost and expense perform or satisfy the Seller's Environmental Liabilities; and

b) be responsible for and indemnify and hold the Buyer harmless against all and any Losses however arising (whether arising before, on or after the Completion Date and regardless of whether arising due to the negligence or breach of duty (statutory or otherwise) on the part of the Buyer and/or its Affiliates, and/or the agents, contractors, sub-contractors, employees and officers of the Buyer and/or its Affiliates) in connection with any and all of the Seller's Environmental Liabilities.

Losses means any damage, loss, compensation, award (including any tribunal award), cost (including without limitation [reasonable] legal costs and experts' and consultants' fees), expense, charge, fine, penalty or outgoing suffered or incurred by the indemnified person in respect thereof.

When drafting an indemnity in an agreement governed by English law, the principles of contractual interpretation that have been developed by the courts should also be taken into account. In the event of a dispute between the buyer and the seller regarding the coverage or extent of a particular indemnity, it will fall upon the courts, using such principles, to establish what the parties objectively intended. In looking at the interpretation of an indemnity, the Supreme Court in *Wood v Capital Insurance Services [2017] UKSC 24* held, among other things, that the court's task is to ascertain the objective meaning of the language which the parties have used in their agreement. A court does not solely focus on the words used, but also considers the contract as a whole. Where there are rival meanings, the court may reach a view on which construction is more consistent with business common sense.

Consequently, and in order to avoid future disputes, care should be taken to use clear language in drafting an indemnity to ensure that it covers the loss that is contemplated by the parties, and that such loss is clearly identifiable from the express language used in the SPA.

3.6 Indemnities from the buyer

We have so far looked at indemnities flowing from the seller in favour of the buyer, thereby transferring risk in respect of certain liabilities from the buyer to the seller in the SPA. However, indemnities can also transfer risk the other way. The seller may seek a clean break from liability in certain high-risk areas such as decommissioning and environmental liabilities. As mentioned previously, the risk of residual liability attaching to the seller is limited, especially in the context of a sale of shares, as liabilities generally transfer with the target company. However, there are exceptions. In some petroleum regimes, such as in the United Kingdom, previous asset owners (ie, the seller) can ultimately be held liable for decommissioning costs, notwithstanding their disposal of the underlying asset, if those costs cannot be satisfied by the current licensees/owners. The seller's residual liability in this area can be mitigated by obtaining a counter-indemnity from the buyer, which as a matter of good practice should be supported by a guarantee or other form of security – including the entering into of a decommissioning security agreement. However, if the relevant authorities are seeking decommissioning costs from the seller as a previous owner, then the likelihood is that the buyer in such circumstances is not in a position to fulfil its indemnification obligation under the SPA either, and demand will need to be made under the supporting security arrangements. With the uncertainty and increase in the cost of decommissioning in mature basins such as the UK North Sea, coupled with smaller and less well-capitalised buyers entering the market, sellers' ability to obtain such a clean break is becoming increasingly difficult, with some buyers now demanding that sellers retain an agreed portion of decommissioning liabilities supported by a reciprocal indemnity in favour of the buyer. These negotiations and the resultant indemnities are very much bespoke and as ever, largely dependent upon the relative negotiating positions of the two parties.

4. Limitations on liability

As discussed above, the buyer and the seller will agree on a set of warranties in their SPA. The buyer ideally wants to be able to bring claims against the seller for any breach of warranty without limitation, or perhaps taking into account only such limitations as are imposed by law. The seller, by contrast, nearly always seeks to limit expressly in the SPA the liabilities to which it may be exposed under the warranties that it gives. Such limitations on the seller's liability are often heavily negotiated between the two parties, and a seller in a particularly strong bargaining position will usually seek to have the limitations apply also to any and all claims brought under the SPA, including under any indemnities given. As with other aspects of SPAs relating to oil and gas interests, the provisions relating to limitations of liability are similar to those applying generally in a private M&A context.

Key common limitations in an SPA include time and financial limits on a seller's liability.

4.1 Time limitations

Time limits included in an SPA are typically shorter than the applicable statutory time period limits.

The seller wants as much certainty as possible as to the length of time for which it will remain liable for any claims once the sale and purchase of the oil and gas interests, or the company in a share sale, has completed. Accordingly, it will seek to limit the period following completion during which claims may be brought against it. The buyer, by contrast, ideally wants to be able to claim under the SPA for as long a period as possible. The agreed position in the SPA will largely depend on the bargaining power of the two parties. In most oil and gas SPAs, the timeframe for general warranty claims to be brought against the seller is between six and 24 months, with 12 to 18 months being the normally agreed period of limitation. However, certain warranties relating to, for example, tax may have a longer time limit, due to the longer statutory limitation periods for when claims may be brought by a relevant governmental authority. In SPAs relating to oil and gas interests in the United Kingdom or companies incorporated in the United Kingdom, it is fairly normal practice for the warranties relating to tax to be limited to between six and seven years following completion, to cover the statutory limitation period. Similarly, the buyer may require that certain fundamental warranties in relation to, for example, title and capacity matters be subject to a longer survival period.

The seller may further limit the period during which the buyer can bring a claim – for example, by specifying that a claim that is notified to the seller within the specified time limits (as above) will be deemed withdrawn if the buyer does not issue and serve the seller with proceedings within a certain period following such notification – usually three or six months from the date on which the seller receives notice of a claim from the buyer.

This time limitation prevents the buyer from reserving its right to claim under the warranties indefinitely and gives the seller an increased level of certainty as to its liability for any particular claim. A seller in a particularly strong negotiating position may also wish to include a time period – typically 30 to 60 days – within which the buyer must notify the seller after becoming aware of any circumstances that may lead to a claim, after which the particular claim becomes unenforceable, regardless of whether the overall 12 to 18-month claim period is still available.

An example of a time limitation provision is as follows:

The Seller shall not be liable for:

a) a claim for breach of the Title and Authority Warranties unless the Buyer has given the Seller written notice of that claim by no later than [12 to 24] months after Completion;

b) a claim for breach of the Seller's warranties (other than Title and Authority Warranties) unless the Buyer has given the Seller written notice of that claim by no later than [6 to 12] months after Completion;

c) a tax claim, by no later than [6 to 7] years after Completion; or

d) a claim for any matter other than those set out in paragraphs (a) to (c) above, by no later than [6 to 24] months after Completion, and

in each case, stating in reasonable detail the nature of the claim.

Any claim shall (if it has not been previously satisfied, settled or withdrawn) be deemed to have been waived or withdrawn on the expiry of [6-12] months after the date it was made unless [court/arbitral] proceedings in respect of it have been commenced.

4.2 Complying with contractual notices provisions

In addition to the time limitation provisions that are set out in the SPA, parties should be aware of, and comply with, any contractually agreed notices provisions. The notices provisions will set out:

- how notices (eg, claim notice for breach of warranty) are to be delivered;
- where and to whom they should be addressed; and
- when notices are deemed to have been delivered, depending on how the notice was sent.

This will mean that parties, and more usually the buyer, will need to review the notices provisions to ensure that any notices of claims are effectively deemed delivered in good time before the relevant time limitation is exceeded. The notices provisions may therefore reduce the time limitations further, but usually only by a few days, depending on how the notices are delivered.

4.3 Financial threshold limitations

SPAs will also typically include financial thresholds and limits which cap the seller's liability exposure. In order to prevent small claims which can potentially consume considerable management time with accompanying costs that may exceed the value of the claim itself, the seller will include a *de minimis* or minimum threshold amount over which a claim must be estimated to be worth before notice may be given and liability will attach to the seller. The seller may also add a further layer of financial limitation, by imposing a 'basket' threshold amount which needs to be exceeded before any claims above the *de minimis* threshold may be brought against the seller. The *de minimis* and basket thresholds are often given as percentages of the purchase price, although in some cases the parties prefer to include actual monetary amounts. If the *de minimis* and basket thresholds are given as percentages of the purchase price, there may be some debate between the seller and the buyer as to whether the financial threshold limitation should be calculated based on the base purchase price or the actual cash amount (after any completion adjustments are applied) that the seller receives at completion.

De minimis thresholds in private M&A deals usually range between 0.05% and 0.5% of the base purchase price, with many oil and gas deals having an agreed *de minimis* threshold of approximately 0.1% of the base purchase price. Basket thresholds vary more, depending on the value of the transaction, the parties involved and the comfort level of the seller in respect of the warranties that it has given. Basket thresholds may range between 0.5% and 5% of the base purchase price. In oil and gas SPAs, they can be as high as 10% of the base purchase price, although a basket quantum of 1% of the base purchase price is more typical.

Buyers will also want to be able to make all claims above the *de minimis* amount once the basket quantum threshold has been reached; and sellers will resist this by requiring that the basket be regarded as a deductible, with the seller liable only for claim amounts in excess of the basket quantum. Deductibles are more typical in US transactions; but in oil and gas deals –

especially those governed by English law – the seller is more likely to agree that once the basket is reached, the buyer may bring all claims in excess of the *de minimis* against the seller.

In addition to the minimum and basket thresholds that need to be exceeded before the buyer can make a claim, a well-advised seller will ensure that there is an upper limit, or cap, on the total claims that it may be liable for. As with most aspects of the SPA, the level of the overall cap will depend on the parties' bargaining positions. Warranties in respect of the oil and gas interests or general business, and operational warranties in respect of the company in a share SPA, are usually capped in an English law-governed transaction at around 50% to 75% of the base purchase price. However, recently the authors have seen claims for breaches of business and operational warranties capped at as low as 20% to 30% of the base purchase price. The seller may also consider varied caps for different types of warranty – for example, agreeing to a higher cap – potentially up to the whole of the purchase price that it receives from the buyer – for fundamental warranties such as those relating to title to the oil and gas interests and the capacity and authority of the seller to enter into, and transact pursuant to, the SPA.

An example of a financial limitation provision is as follows:

No liability shall attach to the Seller in respect of a claim unless the:

a) amount of the liability in respect of each individual claim exceeds [0.05% – 0.5%] of the base purchase consideration; and

b) aggregate amount of the liability of the Seller in respect of all claims exceeds [0.5% – 10%] of the base purchase consideration,

in which case the Seller shall be liable for the excess amount.

For the purposes of this clause, if a claim relates to more than one event or circumstance which would separately constitute a claim, that claim shall be treated as a separate claim in respect of each event or circumstance.

Notwithstanding the above, the Seller's maximum aggregate liability: (a) in respect of all claims (other than claims for breach of the Title and Authority Warranties) shall not exceed [20% – 50%] of the base purchase consideration; and (b) in respect of all claims for breach of the Title and Authority Warranties shall not exceed [50% – 100%] of the base purchase consideration.

4.4 General disclaimer regarding reserves

As discussed in section 2 above, an oil and gas SPA typically includes a general disclaimer that the seller makes no warranty regarding amounts, quality or deliverability of reserves, technical, geological, geophysical, engineering or economic reports, interpretations, forecasts or evaluations, levels of production and the state, condition or fitness for purpose of any of the physical assets. An example of this type of provision is as follows:

Notwithstanding any other provision of this Agreement, the Seller makes no representation or warranty as to:

a) the quantity, quality or deliverability of reserves of crude oil, natural gas or other hydrocarbons attributable to the Interests;

b) any geological, geophysical, engineering, economic or other interpretations, forecasts or evaluations;

c) any forecast, estimates, statistics, opinions and prospects (including of expenditures, budgets, costs, revenues and financial projections);

d) any geological formation, drilling prospect or hydrocarbon reserve and the Buyer affirms and acknowledges that it has made its own independent assessment and evaluation of these matters;

e) the physical state, condition or fitness for purpose of any of the physical assets, Facilities and all other installations and structures relating to or employed in connection with the Operations; or

f) the obligations of the Seller under any environmental law or the existence of any decommissioning liabilities of the Seller,

whether implied by statute, common law or otherwise.

4.5 Other limitations on the seller's liability for warranty claims

The SPA will also likely include a variety of other limitations on liability, some of which are considered standard and acceptable to reasonable buyers, and others which may be more bespoke and subject to negotiation between the parties:

- Duty to mitigate: The buyer should take reasonable steps to avoid or mitigate any loss or liability that may give rise to a claim against the seller.
- Disclosure/knowledge: The buyer should not be entitled to make a claim if the facts, matters or circumstances giving rise to the claim were disclosed to the buyer (eg, in the disclosure letter) or were known (or ought to have been known) by the buyer, and potentially its advisers and agents.
- Change of legislation: The seller should not be liable if, after the date of the SPA, there has been a change of law or of accounting or taxation policies.
- Actions of the buyer: The seller's liability pursuant to a claim by the buyer should not be increased as a result of any action by the buyer following completion of the SPA.
- Acts by the seller on the instruction or with the approval of the buyer: The seller's liability pursuant to a claim by the buyer should also not be increased as a result of any acts of the seller taken on the instruction or with the approval of the buyer in the interim period between signing the SPA and completion.
- Insurance coverage or recovery from third parties: The seller should not be liable where the buyer can make a claim under its insurance or from

a third party in respect of the loss or claim, and any claim by the buyer against the seller should be reduced by the amount recovered under any such insurance policy or from a relevant third party.

- No double recovery: The buyer should not recover more than once in respect of the same loss (eg, if the same loss is as a result of a breach of more than one warranty).
- Consequential and other losses: The SPA may also stipulate that the seller shall be liable for direct losses of the buyer only, thereby excluding liability for consequential or other indirect losses. In some jurisdictions, such as England and Wales, loss of profits can be found by the courts to be a direct loss recoverable by a buyer. Consequently, the parties should expressly state whether loss of profits is excluded (which is often the subject of considerable debate between the parties).
- Change of control: In some instances, the seller may also require that in the event of a change of control of the buyer – for example, where it is no longer wholly or majority owned by its ultimate parent (perhaps where a special purpose vehicle entity was the buyer counterparty to the SPA) – the buyer will no longer be able to bring a claim for any breach of warranty against the seller.

5. Final thoughts

The allocation of risk and liabilities in an M&A context, coupled with the granting of indemnities in English law-governed transactions, is one of the more interesting, but also potentially contentious and time-consuming, aspects of negotiation between the buyer and the seller. At a time when the legal spend of exploration and production (E&P) companies is significantly constrained and M&A activity in the upstream sector generally low, it is perhaps an ideal time for all stakeholders to rethink the 'traditional' M&A transaction model. The typical pattern begins with counsel for the seller producing a fairly one-sided initial draft of an SPA which predominately transfers risk onto the buyer, with a laundry list of limitations that effectively thwarts the buyer's ability to make a claim under the agreement. Assuming that the buyer has some negotiating leverage, it will then have to push back some of the transaction risk onto the seller and chip away at the limitations on liability, while trying at the same time to obtain as broad a suite of warranties and indemnities as possible. This battle costs both time and money; in the current environment, all stakeholders should ideally be questioning whether things can be done differently and whether this current model is the best way to transfer ownership of oil and gas interests from one holder to another, whether from a host state's perspective or an E&P company's perspective.

In order for the industry to survive and thrive in view of the many pressures that it now faces – including low oil prices, constrained availability of finance, competing cleaner energies, ageing infrastructure and decommissioning issues – some stakeholders have started to think about how the industry can change its practice. In the United Kingdom, this impetus came from a report published by Sir Ian Wood on 24 February 2014 on maximising recovery from the United Kingdom, in which Wood singled out "overzealous legal and commercial behaviour" as one of the key issues that needs to be addressed in order to maximise recovery from the UK North Sea. The authors suggest that those within the M&A sector can do their part, as a first step, by producing and agreeing to SPAs which are more balanced, where risk and liabilities are fairly apportioned between the buyer and the seller. Beyond this, it would be interesting to see whether there is any appetite for a wider industry standard form SPA as we see in some jurisdictions such as Norway, or with the Association of International Petroleum Negotiators (AIPN) Model Form Farmout Agreement or the AIPN Model Form International Asset Sale and Purchase Agreement, both of which have recently been updated. However, in order for this to work, all stakeholders will need to buy into the benefits and the relevant authorities will need to do their part by rewarding and encouraging the right behaviours. Any form of standardisation needs to be balanced with the fact that sale structurings are becoming increasing complex regardless of deal size, due in part to a move away from the 'standard' allocation of risk and liabilities in an SPA. Notwithstanding this, easing the M&A process from a time and cost perspective, when E&P companies are under ever-increasing pressures, may assist them with their portfolio management, which in turn will help to ensure that oil and gas interests are owned and operated by E&P companies with the right skill set, budget and interest in the asset.

The publisher acknowledges the contribution of Geoff Peters to this chapter in the previous edition.

Environmental provisions in oil and gas transactions

Julie Vaughan
Herbert Smith Freehills LLP

1. Introduction

Environmental provisions have long been a standard feature of oil and gas transactions, given in particular the hazardous nature of hydrocarbons when spilled in the environment. In this respect, offshore production of oil has more potential for environmental harm than gas, but there are risks to safety and the environment inherent in both. Hence, oil and gas production is heavily regulated in most jurisdictions, with the need to comply strictly with environmental permits and to assess and control risks in order to avoid liabilities. Buyers of a company will inherit its accrued liabilities and any that may be yet to arise with regard to past incidents (perhaps a pending prosecution or claim). Buyers of oil and gas assets will not usually inherit liability for past incidents or breaches; but if they take over a non-compliant state of affairs, they will need to take steps to bring it back into compliance to avoid incurring liability in their own right, which may involve expenditure to avoid future regulatory sanctions.

Environmental provisions of the following types are likely to be necessary:

- warranties;
- indemnities – specific or broad;
- conditions relating to permit transfers (on asset sales); and
- interim covenants (between signing and completion).

This chapter examines how these types of provisions apply in the case of environmental matters, including examples of typical drafting; and then goes on to look at the environmental provisions included within the Association of International Petroleum Negotiators (AIPN) Model Farmout Agreement and the Oil and Gas UK Model Sale and Purchase Agreement (SPA).

2. Warranties and indemnities

2.1 Warranties

The [Company] complies and has at all times [in the 2 years] prior to the date of this Agreement complied with Environmental Law.

The [Company] has not received any complaint (whether or not in writing) or a notice alleging a breach of, or a liability under, Environmental Law.

The [Company] is not engaged in any prosecution, litigation, investigation, arbitration, action or other proceedings or settlement under any Environmental Law, or concerning any Environmental Permit or any Hazardous Substance, and so far as the Seller is aware, there are no facts or circumstances which are likely to give rise to any such prosecution, litigation, investigation, arbitration, action, proceedings or settlement by or against the [Company].

The [Company] has obtained and complies, and at all times [in the 2 years] prior to the date of this Agreement has obtained and complied, with each Environmental Permit required to carry on its business.

No action has been taken to vary, revoke or suspend an Environmental Permit obtained by the [Company] and so far as the Seller is aware, no circumstances exist which may give rise to this kind of action.

There is no application currently pending made by the [Company] to vary, transfer or surrender any Environmental Permit.

If problems can be priced with some certainty based on information obtained during due diligence – or, in the case of a company, if adequate provision has been included in the target company's accounts – this may be sufficient. But in order to guard against unexpected liabilities not unearthed through due diligence, buyers of offshore oil interests will usually insist on more general catch-all protection in the form of environmental warranties, such as those above.

These should cover the failure of the seller to disclose past and ongoing non-compliance with regulations, and perhaps also known difficulties for the target business to adapt to forthcoming changes in law, which may involve the need for significant capital upgrades. Buyers will also expect a minimum level of protection in case the seller has failed to disclose that it is missing an environmental permit or is not in full compliance with the conditions of the environmental permits that it holds. They will also be concerned to know that there is no imminent proposal by a regulator to revoke or suspend the target's permits, without which it may need to cease operating. Warranty protection is also usually provided in relation to the existence of regulatory notices and regulatory investigations, and third-party claims arising from environmental impacts caused by the business.

However, limitations on warranty claims are usually such that they offer protection only for a relatively short period, of perhaps 18 months to two years. In the case of offshore operations, this is probably sufficient for environmental issues to come to light; but where transactions involve some onshore assets, such as onshore receiving terminals or processing facilities, problems arising from releases of hazardous substances into the ground may not come to light until long after the ability to claim on the warranties has passed.

Individual environmental claims may also be for amounts which fall below the *de minimis* thresholds agreed for general warranty claims; and it may not be simple or possible for the buyer to establish that a breach of the environmental warranties has led to any reduction in the value of shares that it has purchased, such that unless the contract allows for damages to be assessed on an indemnity basis, it may be difficult to establish a claim.

Given the potential difficulties in bringing a successful claim for environmental warranty breaches, one might wonder what the value of such warranties is. The answer more often lies in unearthing problems that the seller and/or the target can be asked to address prior to completion; or at least in providing the buyer with a good understanding of the priorities to address itself upon assuming ownership.

2.2 Indemnities

(a) Clean break

The Buyer shall indemnify and hold the Seller harmless against all and any costs, expenses, liabilities, obligations, demands, losses, debts, claims and actions (including legal costs on an indemnity basis) however arising (whether arising before, on or after the date of Completion and regardless of whether arising due to the negligence of the Seller and/or its Affiliates or breach of duty (statutory or otherwise) on the part of the Seller and/or its Affiliates, and/or the agents, contractors, sub-contractors, employees and officers of the Seller and/or its Affiliates) in connection with any and all Decommissioning Liabilities and Environmental Liabilities to the extent that such obligations are attributable to and proportionate to the Transfer Interests.

The indemnity given in this Clause [ ] shall not extend to any costs, expenses, liabilities, obligations, demands, losses, debts, claims and actions to the extent only that such costs, expenses, liabilities, obligations, demands, losses, debts, claims and actions (including legal costs on an indemnity basis):

(A) both (i) relate to the period prior to the date of Completion, and (ii) have been fully discharged prior to the date of Completion; or

(B) relate to a breach of a Seller Warranty.

As mentioned above, when buying shares, liability for any pre-completion breaches of environmental permits or regulation, or any actual or potential liability for environmental harm, will continue to rest with the target. Generally speaking, for jurisdictions that maintain the separate legal personality of companies, the seller can expect to have no residual environmental liability. However, where the transaction is an asset sale, the seller of offshore oil and gas assets will generally adopt the position that it wants to have a 'clean break' and divest itself of remaining environmental liability for the sold business. It can achieve this by the buyer providing it with an indemnity of the type above covering a broad scope of environmental matters. This is a market standard position among industry participants, where sellers often wrap environmental liability together with decommissioning liabilities and seek an all-encompassing indemnity for both (as above). It provides a means whereby oil and gas industry buyers and sellers can trade assets back and forth on the understanding that they will not be accumulating residual liability in relation to past ownership.

(b) Pre/post completion indemnity

Increasingly, however, where non-industry participants such as private equity funds are entering the market, their shareholders and owners are generally less willing to provide indemnities – particularly if unlimited in time or amount. Also, as noted above, packages of assets may include some onshore assets, where there is arguably greater potential for latent unknown risks caused by poor past operating practices to materialise in liability for the buyer. This is the case with contamination that may result from undetected slow leaks over time from infrastructure such as buried tanks and pipework, or a past spill that gradually leaches downwards into groundwater or migrates laterally to neighbouring premises, only reaching a sensitive environment some years later; or where the harm is discovered only at a later date. It is therefore difficult to predict where and when an impact might occur; or, if it does occur, how much it might cost to address. Onshore assets may also come with the potential for liability arising not only from the seller's oil and gas operations, but also from the use of the site by others in the past. In particular, a buyer may be unwilling to give the seller an indemnity in relation to contamination that has occurred or been disturbed during the seller's control of the premises.

In that case, far from the buyer providing an indemnity, it may instead seek one from the seller. The following indemnity provision provides an example of 'pre/post-completion' allocation of liability between the buyer and seller:

The Seller must indemnify each Indemnified Person against:

a. each loss, liability and cost which an Indemnified Person suffers or incurs as a result of an Environmental Matter;

b. each loss, liability and cost which an Indemnified Person suffers or incurs as a result of investigating, disputing or settling a claim (whether actual or potential) alleging a loss, liability or cost of the type referred in paragraph (a); and

c. each cost which the Indemnified Person suffers or incurs in enforcing its rights under this paragraph [ ].

"Environmental Matter" means one or more of the following:

(A) an Environmental Condition in relation to which, if a relevant regulatory authority was aware of its existence, the regulatory authority would require remedial works to be carried out;

(B) Environmental Proceedings in relation to:

(1) a breach of Environmental Laws before Completion by the Company or any Subsidiary or in relation to the Premises;

(2) a Hazardous Substance present in, on or under the Premises or any Former Property, on or before Completion or which has migrated (whether before or after Completion) from it;

(3) a Hazardous Substance which has been generated, emitted, released or discharged before Completion by the activities of the Company or any Subsidiary;

(4) a Hazardous Substance on third party land for which the Company or any Subsidiary is responsible or liable by reason of any act or omission before Completion;

(5) waste disposal or similar activity by or on behalf of the Company or any Subsidiary before Completion; or

(6) exposure of a person to a Hazardous Substance before Completion in respect of which the Company or any Subsidiary is responsible or liable; or

(C) a breach of, or liability under, an Environmental Agreement;

"Environmental Condition" means:

(A) the presence of a Hazardous Substance at, in, on, under or about the Premises on or before Completion including migration or release (whether occurring, in either case, before or after Completion) from the Premises;

(B) noise, vibration, radiation, dust, odour nuisance present at or arising from the Premises on or before Completion; or

(C) a breach of Environmental Laws by the Company or any or in relation to the Premises before Completion requiring corrective action;

A pre/post-completion environmental indemnity will also invariably be subject to one or more financial caps on the seller's liability and a limited timeframe – rarely more than 10 years and more commonly five to seven years, possibly covering a declining percentage of the loss over time (a 'sliding scale'). Different expiry dates may apply to different heads of loss, or may even fall outside the five to seven-year expiry date – for example, asbestos claims may only materialise decades after a person was exposed to fibres and thus, depending on when exposure happened, seven years may be inadequate.

The agreement may also include a counter-indemnity from the buyer in favour of the seller, to allow the latter to bring a claim to recover losses that fall on it post-completion and are outside the scope of the indemnity that it is providing to the buyer. Such indemnities can be complex to draft, given the various heads of loss to be covered.

Where environmental indemnities are seeking only to cover a specific issue uncovered by due diligence, they may be fairly succinct and the main objective will be to describe the issue accurately. However, environmental indemnities that are designed to allocate environmental liability as a whole may run to a standalone document in their own right, with a range of definitions prescribing the scope of cover, the usual exclusions from cover and a bespoke set of limitations. They may then selectively incorporate other limitations from the main SPA and include their own procedural provisions for notice of claims and conduct of indemnified third-party claims. The negotiation of such indemnities requires good knowledge of how the parties' liability would ordinarily arise under the applicable law and the extent to which it is possible to reallocate such liability contractually.

One major drawback of indemnities in common law jurisdictions such as England is that the courts will not enforce an indemnity in respect of criminal fines. Given that breach of permit conditions, operation without a necessary permit and non-compliance with many environmental regulations are criminal offences, an indemnity may not always be an acceptable solution. An indemnity can still be given that may be enforceable in relation to associated legal costs or the cost of taking measures to bring the business back into compliance; and for any third-party claims flowing from the same factual circumstances, such as personal injury claims for harm caused by coming into contact with a hazardous substance.

As with indemnities for non-environmental issues, an indemnity will also only be as good as the covenant strength of the person giving it.

3. Conditions precedent and completion deliverables

3.1 Conditions precedent

Offshore oil production facilities will likely require a handful of key environmental permits without which they cannot legally operate, and the operator (ie, the person in overall day-to-day control of operating the asset) may be committing a criminal offence if it operates without one. In addition, there may be a slew of permits for specific aspects of the operations which, although equally necessary for compliance, are viewed as less material to the business.

Where there is doubt as to the seller's ability to transfer any key permits, it may be necessary to include the transfer of those permits as a condition precedent to completion of the sale and purchase. However, it is not normal to include the transfer of less material permits as a condition precedent, since their transfer can usually be obtained after completion without a regulator taking precipitate enforcement action, provided that the regulator has been kept informed. In those circumstances, however, the buyer should ask for evidence to be provided on completion that the relevant transfer applications have been made.

3.2 Completion deliverables

For a share purchase, the permits will likely continue unaffected by the transfer of ownership of the target operator, although there may be a requirement to notify any change in the target's name to the regulator. There is consequently no need to include provisions for the transfer of permits, and any name change notifications can usually be dealt with post-completion within the timeframe allowed by the relevant permit.

However, on an asset purchase, the permits will (if possible) need to be transferred and the relevant statutory regime will prescribe the procedure. In some cases, the statutory regime may not countenance a transfer and the buyer will instead need to apply for a fresh permit. In such case, this should be commenced pre-completion. It will usually be necessary to work through each of the permit types to determine what will be required and when the transfer can be achieved relative to completion.

As such, the completion deliverables may include evidence that the transfer has been approved by the regulator, or that relevant applications have been submitted to the regulator. Where a joint application of buyer and seller is necessary, the purchase agreement will often specify that one party is to coordinate the process, with the other to give all necessary cooperation to sign documents and (in the buyer's case) to provide evidence to the regulator of its suitability to hold the permit and comply with its conditions. The regulator will, for example, be keen to establish that the buyer has in place a robust environmental management system and a suitable number of capable personnel.

Certain permits, such as pipeline authorisations, specify the parties that may use the pipeline for the transport of fuel, as well as the names of owners and the operator. A change in any of these details resulting from the transaction will need to be notified post-completion. Other permits may name an individual in the seller's organisation as the 'responsible person'. If that person is not transferring his or her employment to the buyer, the permit will likely need to be amended or reissued.

Another completion deliverable may be a letter of reliance allowing the buyer (and possibly the buyer's banks) to rely on an environmental consultant's report. This may be either a vendor due diligence report produced for the transaction or a report produced previously in response to environmental concerns. The latter is more usual in relation to onshore assets where there are concerns over soil contamination. Reliance is usually provided for six years from the date of the report and the limit on liability may be negotiable. Although there should be some payment for reliance to be granted in order for it to be contractually binding, this could be nominal. Taking reliance allows the beneficiary to bring a claim in negligence if the consultant can be shown to have been negligent.

4. Further assurance

If any Environmental Permits which the Purchaser requires to operate the Business from Completion have not been transferred, varied, assigned or granted to the Purchaser then pending completion of any transfer or assignment the Purchaser shall:

(A) at its own cost operate the Business in accordance with such Environmental Permit and any of its terms and conditions; and

(B) the Purchaser shall indemnify, defend and hold harmless the Seller from and against any and all actions, claims, proceedings, liabilities, obligations, losses, fines, penalties, damages, costs, expenses and payments incurred or suffered by the Seller as a result of any matter relating to such Environmental Permit pending completion of its variation or its transfer, assignment or grant to the Purchaser and in the event of any non-compliance with such Environmental Permit the Seller may enter the Assets to take any steps considered necessary to ensure compliance with such Environmental Permit.

In order to allow for continued operation in case of a gap between completion of the sale and purchase and transfer of the relevant permit, an environmental further assurance such as the above may be included, along with language obliging the seller to actively pursue the transfer application, but with the benefit of an indemnity from the buyer for liability incurred by the seller as the permit holder in the interim before the transfer is achieved.

5. Interim covenants

Clause [restrictions] shall not operate so as to restrict or prevent the Seller from undertaking, at its sole discretion, any of the following from the date of this Agreement until Completion:

(A) any matter required by any Governmental Authority where failure to comply with such requirement would, or might reasonably be expected to, constitute a breach of any applicable law or regulation then in force or any Environmental Permit conditions; or

(B) any matter undertaken in an emergency or disaster situation (including in relation to Environmental Matters and/or employee or public safety).

Sellers will be keen to ensure that the interim covenants on how the business is managed between the signing of the SPA and completion do not prevent the target business from responding to environmental and safety emergencies or complying with permit requirements and legal requirements. Neither restriction is likely to be in the best interests of the buyer in any case.

Having done its due diligence, the buyer will be equally keen to ensure that the business's permits are not changed in a manner that would impose greater cost or affect the productivity of the assets, for example. This may happen at the initiative of the regulator, which both seller and buyer may resist, but are likely to be powerless to entirely prevent. However, it is reasonable for the buyer to restrict the seller or target from voluntarily applying for the variation or surrender of a permit that is required for the ongoing business, without the buyer consenting to that application.

6. AIPN 2019 Model International Farmout Agreement

As this model agreement involves the transfer of an ownership interest in assets rather than an outright business transfer to a new owner, there is no need in the agreement for provisions on the transfer of permits, unless the farmee is also to take over as the operator of the relevant facility or facilities.

The agreement does, however, include interim covenants and warranties, discussed below.

6.1 Interim covenants

4.2.1 From the Signature Date until the Completion Date, and subject to the terms of this Agreement, Farmor shall:

...maintain in full force and effect any (i) material license, permit, and other approval from the Government related to the Contract Interest and..

give prompt written notice to Farmee of ... (iii) any material spills or other material environmental contamination events occurring with respect to the Contract and (iv) any material damage to or destruction of any of the physical assets comprising the [Farmout Interests / Contract Interest].

4.4 Action without Farmee's Approval

Notwithstanding anything to the contrary in this Agreement, [Farmor / Operator] may conduct:

[•] emergency operations related to events endangering lives, property, or the environment; provided Farmor shall notify Farmee of such emergency as soon as reasonably practicable;

[•] operations to avoid any penalty under any order of the Government, provided that Farmor shall provide Farmee with written notice of such operations (including AFEs related thereto) as soon as reasonably practicable following the commencement thereof; or

[•] operations described in the [Disclosure Letter].

The definition of 'Government' in the model agreement is wide enough to encompass environmental permits issued by a regulatory authority, even where that authority is independent of central government.

The requirement to maintain permits in full force and effect would prevent an application to surrender them, but would not stop the farmor from applying to vary the conditions of the permit, which in practice may have a significant impact. The farmor may arguably be constrained in changing the way the assets are operated if the agreement includes the further optional covenant to maintain the farmout interests in a good and workmanlike manner in the ordinary course of business consistent with past practice. However, it would be less potentially ambiguous to include a specific restriction on applying to vary permits without the buyer's consent.

In some cases, operators do not hold a permit, but either the activities must be notified or registered, or there is a requirement to register reliance on an exemption from the need to hold a permit. It is usual in contracts to define what is meant by 'permits', or to state specifically 'environmental permits', in order to pick up these further variations. A short form that could be used would be:

"Environmental Permit" means a consent, permission, permit, licence, approval or other authorisation issued, or registration or notification made, pursuant to Environmental Laws;

"Environmental Laws" means each applicable law (including statute, secondary legislation, directives, regulations, resolutions, statutory guidance and codes of practice having the force of law, civil, criminal or administrative law, common law, a notice, order, judgment, ruling or other requirement from any governmental, administrative or regulatory agency or body or a court, tribunal or other assembly conducting judicial business) relating to pollution or protection of the environment, or human health and safety.

Since most operations could result in a penalty if badly managed, the second bullet of clause 4.4 above is rather wide and this is not usual in other SPAs. The reference to 'AFEs' is undefined in the model agreement, but this would seem to refer to an authority for expenditure, which is a budget document often used by the oil and gas industry as a cost control measure in order to estimate the cost to the operator and non-operators of drilling a well and obtaining approval. If using the model, this bullet may be further restricted to state that the clause is intended to apply in the event that a penalty has been threatened in respect of alleged non-compliance.

6.2 Warranties

Exhibit 2

Farmor [represents and] warrants to Farmee as follows (the "Farmor [Representations and] Warranties"):

(r) Environmental Matters. Except as disclosed in [•], the Contract Area has been developed, operated, and maintained in compliance with all applicable Environmental Laws [OPTION and all relevant International Standards]. Drafting Note: If this option is selected, definitions for "Environmental Laws" and "International Standards" should be included in the Article 1.1 definitions.

(s) Remedial Obligations. There has been no contamination of, or releases into,

> *groundwater, surface water, or soil resulting from the operation in the Contract Area which require reporting or remediation under applicable Environmental Laws [OPTION or relevant International Standards] (or would require such reporting or remediation, were all facts known to the Government). All hazardous substances and solid, liquid, and gaseous wastes generated from the operation in the Contract Area have been handled and disposed of in accordance with applicable Environmental Laws [OPTION and all relevant International Standards]. Drafting Note: If this option is selected, a definition of "International Standards" should be included in the Article 1.1 definitions.*

With regard to warranty (r) above, although the warranty does not mention permits, it is probably sufficient to include the fact that all necessary permits are in place and have been complied with since operations started. If the definition of 'Environmental Laws' included in Section 6.1 above is included, it will also extend to compliance with health and safety laws.

It does not, however, offer any protection against any pending changes known to the farmor, such as the regulator having given notice that one of the environmental permits is to be varied or that there is an outstanding application by the farmor to vary or surrender a permit.

The first part of warranty (s) – with regard to no contamination having taken place – is clearly more applicable to onshore assets, given the reference to groundwater, surface water and soil; and is a potentially onerous warranty given that leaks may go unnoticed, especially where pipework and tanks are underground. Most warrantors would seek to qualify this warranty by knowledge: "so far as the farmor is aware..."

The warranty is limited to contamination caused by the target's operations, rather than extending to the presence of contamination as a result of former uses of land, which may also give rise to liability for the landowner entity; and the joint operating agreement to be negotiated between the participants is likely to redistribute such liability among the participants according to their interests, should liability materialise. If an alternative allocation is desired in relation to historic contamination, this will need to be addressed.

The second part of warranty (s) – with regard to the handling of hazardous substances and waste streams – is capable of applying onshore and offshore.

Warranty (s) does not address potential liability for environmental damage to the marine environment that has been caused by the operations, where discharge has been done in accordance with permits. So, for example, the farmor may have obtained a permit to discharge chemicals into the sea, but the effect of that chemical discharge over time may impact on protected species that have settled in the vicinity of the platform. Depending on the jurisdiction, compliance with the permit may or may not be a good defence to liability for the harm caused.

Also, the second limb of the warranty does not address some types of environmental impact – for example, disturbance to protected wildlife through noise of a level or frequency that is found to be have a detrimental impact on protected cetaceans such as dolphins, despite noise levels complying with any restrictions imposed by permits.

Another omission from these warranties is the existence of complaints and claims with regard to environmental impacts. The (general) disputes warranty included within the model agreement is very limited and focuses on existing litigation that could adversely affect the farmor's ability to meet and carry out its obligations under the farmout agreement and the other transaction documents. It does not address threatened and pending claims; complaints that have not materialised in a threatened claim as yet; or claims which concern the impacts of the operations on others or the business's prospects after completion of the farmout.

7. Oil and gas UK model SPA

The Oil and Gas UK Model SPA (usually denoting a 'share purchase agreement') is actually an asset sale agreement for the sale of the whole of the seller's participating interest.

It contains a sweeping 'clean break' environmental indemnity in favour of the seller and no environmental warranties. It is therefore an extremely seller-friendly document as far as environmental matters are concerned and any protection with regard to environmental matters would need to be negotiated.

7.1 Indemnity

5.3(b) Without prejudice to the generality of the foregoing, the Purchaser agrees to indemnify, keep indemnified and hold harmless the Seller harmless against any Decommissioning Liabilities and any Environmental Liabilities of whatsoever nature and howsoever arising before or after the Post Economic Date.

"Environmental Liabilities" means all costs, charges, expenses, liabilities and obligations (other than Decommissioning Liabilities) incurred in respect of the Asset in relation to cleaning up, removing debris or any Asset Property from and for reinstating any area of land, foreshore or seabed, wherever situated, whether such costs, charges, expenses, liabilities and obligations are incurred pursuant to any statutory, common law or other obligation and regardless of negligence on the part of the Seller;

In a share purchase, there ought to be little potential, under English law at least, for the seller to retain liabilities of the sort referred to above, unless the seller has at some point operated the asset itself before hiving it down to a subsidiary, perhaps as part of a pre-sale reorganisation.

A shareholder will usually be liable only if it has directly intervened in the operational affairs of its subsidiary such as to assume responsibility. This might be the case, for example, where the directors have routinely turned to the parent organisation for instructions rather than making autonomous decisions on behalf of the subsidiary. The ability of third parties to sue the parent organisation for environmental, social or human rights impacts caused by a subsidiary's actions is a developing area of the law in England and several common law jurisdictions, where cases have been brought against parents in their home courts as a means of seeking redress with regard to an overseas subsidiary's operations.

In agreeing to the indemnity above, the buyer may be assuming a liability to reimburse the seller not just for liability that it incurs under legislation, but also for any contractual obligations that the seller has entered into with a third party for remediation and reinstatement or to fulfil any court orders made against the seller in relation to such matters as a result of a successful third-party claim.

The allocation of all environmental risk to the buyer even if an environmental liability has been caused by the seller's actions (even if acting negligently) pre-completion is at odds with the allocation of risk for other types of liability under the agreement where the seller provides an indemnity to the buyer for 'Pre-economic Date Costs'. Those are defined as "all costs, charges, expenses, liabilities and obligations in respect of the Asset to the extent applicable on an Accrual Basis of Accounting to the period prior to the Economic Date".

There are no other environment-specific provisions.

Decommissioning

Nicholas Antonas
Akin Gump Strauss Hauer & Feld LLP
Marc Hammerson
Stephenson Harwood LLP

1. Introduction

Although commentators note that decommissioning[1] is a factor that should be considered during all phases of the oil and gas lifecycle,[2] the expense associated with this activity is one that, by its nature, arises mainly after the last molecule of production has been extracted. This timing of the decommissioning expense, and the misalignment between the periods in which revenue is generated and expense is incurred, mean that costs must be provisioned while the field remains operational. By setting aside financial provisions, parties protect against the risk of a funding shortfall during decommissioning. Safeguards are included in government legislation and instruments, joint operating agreements (JOAs), security arrangements and sale and purchase agreements (SPAs) pursuant to which petroleum interests are sold.

This chapter focuses on SPAs. Sources of law and resulting commercial practice are briefly summarised. We then discuss the methods by which an SPA[3] apportions liability between the parties.

2. Policy objectives

2.1 Why is decommissioning relevant to the transfer of petroleum interests?

The intersection between oil and gas M&A and decommissioning liability produces competing policy objectives.

In certain respects, it is in the interests of a host government and JOA co-venturers to promote an unrestricted M&A market. It is for the good of common objectives that assets are held by parties enthusiastic about the prospects of ownership.

1 The term 'decommissioning' can be used interchangeably with 'abandonment'. However, in recent years 'abandonment' has fallen out of favour due to negative connotations implying a wilful disregard for clean-up activities.

2 See, for example, Callum Falconer, "Decommissioning and the oil and gas life cycle", in Marc Hammerson and Nicholas Antonas (eds), *Oil and Gas Decommissioning: Law, Policy and Comparative Practice*, 2nd edn, Globe Law and Business, 2016, and Falconer's preface to the same text.

3 In this chapter, 'SPA' is used to refer to any agreement (including a share purchase agreement, asset purchase agreement and farmout agreement) that may be used to transfer petroleum interests.

A seller that fails to obtain consent to an asset transfer or change of control[4] and is therefore prevented from disposing of its petroleum interests is stranded as a reluctant owner. It may become unwilling to spend new money on further exploration and development activity. Lack of additional investment leads to production decline, reduced revenue and dwindling tax receipts for the host government. For non-selling JOA co-venturers, which see value in the field and wish to continue its development, a failed sale may create disunity within the JOA group on future budget and expenditure decisions. An unhappy marriage between frustrated seller and parties exercising an anti-assignment veto is unlikely to produce a harmonious understanding on future funding of a field's development.

Yet – notwithstanding a plethora of anti-assignment provisions variously contained in host government instruments,[5] JOAs and petroleum laws – trading in assets during the life of a field is both commonplace and commercially necessary. In some jurisdictions, host governments and regulators actively promote a dynamic M&A market.

Each stage of a field's development attracts participants with different skills, financial capacity, attitudes to risk and cost of capital. For example, exploration may be conducted by a speculative (in industry jargon, 'wildcat') explorer. If a commercial discovery is made, an exploration company without the financial resources to fund costly drilling commitments may divest part (but not all) of its working interests to pay for the next phase of activity. An explorer gives up some of its future revenue stream in return for a party (often with deeper pockets) carrying the costs of drilling. These carry arrangements require that drilling costs be repaid by the explorer out of – and, importantly, conditional on – future production.

This arrangement is known as a 'farmout' or 'farmin' agreement.[6] The speculative explorer being carried for the costs of drilling is the farmor and the company carrying such costs is the farmee.

If a deep-pocketed farmee carries a wildcat farmor, the host government and JOA co-venturers will welcome the joint venture's improved financial capacity resulting from the transaction and the contractual commitment (expressed as part of the non-cash purchase price for the transfer of working interests) that the farmee's financial resources will be deployed in the field's development. A credit risk analysis of the outcome of the farmout agreement would conclude that it is beneficial for both the host government and other JOA co-venturers. In these circumstances, although host government approval of the transfer of working interest is still required, a withholding of consent on the basis that the

4 Such consents are referred to as 'anti-assignment' provisions. These are a feature of transfer of petroleum interests by way of asset sale (including farmout agreements) and, less commonly, share sales.

5 This chapter is not specific to any jurisdiction. The term 'host government instruments' is intended to cover the full range of government instruments that permit petroleum activities (including exclusive licences and production sharing contracts).

6 The remainder of the chapter refers to this arrangement as a farmout.

farmout worsens the financial strength of the joint venture as a whole is unlikely. We see below that for other types of transactions, the same conclusion cannot be reached.

These development farmouts take place prior to commencement of production. At the other end of the lifecycle, as a producing field approaches middle age or end-of-life production declines, unit costs rise and the economics of investment become marginal. Consequently, the pool of potential buyers typically consists of companies of weaker financial substance than the seller. Replacing a creditworthy seller (eg, an oil major) with a financially weaker buyer (eg, a small independent or start-up) is, in contrast to a development farmout, likely to raise credit risk concerns both for remaining JOA co-venturers and for the host government.

Furthermore, in mid and end-of-life field disposals, the transaction is more likely to be structured as an asset or share sale (whereby seller disposes of its entire interest in the field) than a farmout agreement (whereby both farmor and farmee remain parties to the host government instruments as a joint venture). In the former case, the appropriate credit analysis for the host government involves comparing the strength of the incoming buyer against that of the exiting seller. In the case of a farmout (in which both parties remain liable to the host government on a joint and several basis), the inclusion of an additional party can only improve the host government's credit position against the joint venture as a whole.

The importance of decommissioning liability to these credit analyses depends on the field's stage of development. When an end-of-life field is transferred, potential liability is imminent. There will be a significant focus on an incoming party's ability to meet approaching unfunded decommissioning liabilities. A pre-production farmout, by contrast, may be 20 years or more away from decommissioning and therefore falls at the other end of the risk spectrum.

A conflict therefore arises between competing policy objectives. Although an active trade in petroleum interests is encouraged, in some cases allowing this to take place may increase the credit risk of remaining JOA co-venturers and the host government to unfunded decommissioning liabilities. The closer in time to cessation of production the transfer occurs, the greater the exposure to decommissioning risk. This timing consideration requires an explanation of the role that reserves play in providing security for contractual remedies. As reserves decline, the limitations of forfeiture as a remedy become apparent.

2.2 Forfeiture

There are numerous reasons why non-selling JOA co-venturers or a host government may wish to veto a transfer of petroleum interests by withholding consent to an assignment or change of control. This section discusses considerations relating to decommissioning liability.

Decommissioning occurs at a point when the traditional contractual remedy for breach of contract – namely, forfeiture of a defaulting party's working interest – has no value. This remedy is typically the ultimate recourse against a defaulting party in both JOAs and host government instruments. Forfeiture of the defaulting party's working interest (and the enhanced revenue stream resulting from the additional working interest share acquired by non-defaulting parties) is intended to compensate for breach. Therefore, in order for this remedy to provide adequate compensation, the future additional profit attributable to the forfeited working interest must equal or exceed the loss suffered.

However, in situations where a field has reached cessation of production, there is no remaining value to be attributed to the forfeited interest accruing from future production. At the time when decommissioning activity is performed (ie, after the cessation of production), forfeiture of a defaulting party's working interest therefore has limited value.

This observation about the inadequacy of forfeiture as a remedy is true both at the date of cessation of production (when there will be no further revenue from production) and for a period prior to cessation. The issue arises at any time during which revenue from future production is less than future unfunded decommissioning liability. From this point, the field is in a state of negative equity and the economically rational decision will be to avoid the (greater) decommissioning liability, even if this means forgoing the (lesser) future revenue stream from the field. For obvious reasons, regulations and agreements deter parties from pursuing this course.

All host government instruments provide that where one JOA party defaults, the non-defaulting JOA parties remain jointly and severally liable in relation to the host government for the defaulting party's non-performance. Therefore, without an adequate contractual remedy to ensure that this final phase of a project is performed, default exposes JOA co-venturers to the risk that they will bear the costs of a defaulting party without any meaningful recourse. If there will be sufficient revenue from future production, the forfeiture of a defaulting party's working interest may provide adequate compensation for assuming additional decommissioning liabilities. However, this is not the case if liabilities exceed revenue from future production. In this situation, forfeiture does not provide protection.

In rare examples in which all JOA co-venturers default,[7] a host government is required to assume decommissioning responsibility pursuant to obligations contained in inter-governmental treaties (described below). As previously

7 The Ardmore field in the UK continental shelf provides an example of financial distress for the entire JOA group and the significant effort undertaken by the regulator to find a solution. Although a deal was eventually reached that did not expose the taxpayer to costs of decommissioning, this case is often cited as an example of a government's exposure in situations where all JOA parties are in financial distress.

noted, forfeiture is the contractual remedy provided in both JOAs and host government instruments. The analysis of the inadequacy of forfeiture also applies in relation to host government risk that all JOA co-venturers default on decommissioning obligations.

As a result of this exposure, JOA co-venturers and host governments are reluctant to allow a seller to avoid future liabilities by transferring its working interests to a buyer of weaker financial strength. Anti-assignment provisions provide both contractual and regulatory methods of preventing a seller from escaping future liabilities by sale.

Because of the policy conflict between the benefits of transferring petroleum assets between different owners during the life of a field on the one hand, and an unwillingness of host governments and remaining JOA co-venturers to release a seller from future liability on the other, several techniques have been developed to ensure that decommissioning issues do not create a barrier to M&A. This chapter describes some of these methods.

Section 3 of this chapter provides background information on decommissioning obligations created under law. Duties imposed on governments pursuant to international treaties are passed to commercial parties through domestic law. In turn, commercial agreements entered into between participants allocate among themselves liabilities imposed on them by host governments on a joint and several basis. These are internalised within the joint venture in the JOA and decommissioning security agreement (DSA)[8] and, of particular relevance to this chapter, in SPAs. Section 4 provides a list of issues that influence the importance of decommissioning to SPA negotiations. Section 5 considers methods of allocating liability. Lastly, sections 6 and 7 provide examples of covenants and warranties.

3. What is decommissioning?

In the context of oil and gas, 'decommissioning' refers to the dismantling, removal and disposal of oil and gas infrastructure. Typically (but not necessarily), this occurs after cessation of production. Given the engineering complexity of most oil and gas infrastructure (particularly in a deepwater offshore environment), decommissioning gives rise to costs that are substantial and unpredictable. Their unpredictability covers both amount and timing.

Key tasks of decommissioning include:[9]

- planning and design of the decommissioning works;
- plugging and abandonment of wells (ie, physically isolating reservoirs from the environment);
- cleaning of topsides and pipelines;

8 Sometimes referred to as 'abandonment security agreements'.
9 Falconer, note 2 *supra*, p11.

- isolation of pipelines;
- dismantling and removal of topsides, jackets and subsea equipment and pipelines;
- removal and disposal or recycling; and
- ongoing monitoring.

3.1 Sources of decommissioning law

(a) International law

International treaties are the originating source of most domestic decommissioning law relevant to offshore oil and gas. It is beyond the scope of this chapter to set out international law in detail. However, it is worth noting some key principles.

Broad reach: Key treaties in this area include the Geneva Convention, the United Nations Convention on the Law of the Sea, associated guidelines issued by the International Maritime Organization and the London Convention. Each governs the activities of an expansive list of contracting states and applies to nearly all nations with offshore oil and gas operations. Even if a host government currently has no decommissioning laws in place, due to these international obligations, a country may start to develop a legal regime once its basin is sufficiently mature that fields approach cessation of production. Commercial parties should therefore anticipate future legal developments.

High standards: Many international treaties relevant to this area were drafted at a time when offshore oil and gas exploitation was new and the engineering skills required for deep offshore operations did not exist. Because deepwater exploration had not been contemplated, treaties were entered into when an obligation to remove an offshore asset in its entirety (referred to as the 'entire removal' obligation)[10] was practical and appropriate in the context of then-existing shallow water infrastructure.[11] This entire removal obligation remains a starting assumption of international decommissioning. However, there is a growing recognition that for some of the most challenging deepwater projects, entire removal may not be the most practical, safe or environmentally optimal solution.

Exceptions: Although the entire removal principle remains an appropriate assumption, some regions allow exceptions in limited circumstances. The best-

10 Article 5(5) of the Convention on the Continental Shelf 1958 provides that any "installations which are abandoned or disused must be entirely removed".

11 Shallow water infrastructure, because of its proximity to shore and shipping activity, creates a greater hazard if not removed in its entirety. Because of the shallower water depth, it is also a less challenging exercise.

known example relates to the Northeast Atlantic, where the Convention for the Protection of the Marine Environment of the Northeast Atlantic provides a framework for dealing with decommissioning which allows for limited conditional derogations from the entire removal obligation permitting the leaving in place (in very limited circumstances) of the footings of steel installations weighing more than 10,000 tonnes and gravity-based concrete installations.

The United States is leading the way with what are known as 'rigs-to-reefs' – toppling or partly dismantling existing offshore structures to serve as artificial reefs, thereby keeping the cost and complexity of decommissioning to a minimum.[12] According to the Bureau of Safety and Environmental Enforcement (www.bsee.gov), as of 15 April 2018, there were 532 approved rigs-to-reefs sites in the US continental shelf. However, the majority of jurisdictions have not followed this trend and parties must not therefore assume that offshore infrastructure will be permitted to be left at sea.

Commercial arrangements must be flexible enough to accommodate the fact that an offshore installation may, in future, become subject to derogation from standard international requirements. In this case, the contemplated decommissioning may not be as complicated or expensive as would otherwise have been applicable if entire removal had been required.

(b) Domestic law

Domestic laws will vary between nations, but the regulatory regimes of most advanced oil and gas jurisdictions are likely to include many (although likely not all) of the legal requirements set out below. As a result of risks arising from the timing misalignment between revenue generation and payment of costs, decommissioning is a highly regulated activity. Applicable regulations are imposed by host governments using a variety of sources, including contractual provisions in host government instruments, statutory laws, administrative decisions and guidelines. As a country's oil and gas assets mature and the prospect of decommissioning offshore fields approaches, a host government's focus on this issue increases.

Areas that are likely to be covered by domestic law include:[13]

- a baseline requirement that all equipment be removed unless retention is expressly approved;
- a requirement that JOA co-venturers submit a decommissioning plan[14] around the same time that a field development plan is agreed on and, at

---

12 For more detail on an example rig-to-reef programme, see tpwd.texas.gov/landwater/water/habitats/artificial_reef/rigs-to-reefs.phtml and www.environment.ucla.edu/reportcard/article9389.html.

13 Marc Hammerson and Nicholas Antonas, "Decommissioning", in Peter Roberts (ed), *Oil and Gas Contracts: Principles and Practice* (second edition, Sweet and Maxwell 2019), pp391–393.

14 For example, Section 29 of the UK Petroleum Act 1998.

a minimum, a substantial period before anticipated decommissioning commencement;[15]

- a requirement to publish an approved decommissioning plan which is made public, allowing the market to be aware of future opportunities;[16]
- a requirement that operators have sufficient technical capability to complete decommissioning (which test is reapplied upon any transfer of operatorship as a result, for example, of M&A);
- a requirement that JOA co-venturers (individually and as a group) demonstrate, when tested, that they are sufficiently funded to finance decommissioning;
- a requirement that JOA co-venturers sufficiently provision funds for decommissioning in advance of cessation of production,[17] such funds often being for an amount in excess of a reasonable estimate of the cost;
- minimum technical standards for conduct of decommissioning (which is usually achieved either by specifying the methods and outcome in each individual decommissioning plan or by issuing general regulations setting out minimum technical standards);
- health and safety regulations specific to decommissioning activities (in addition to those required for other ongoing operations);
- joint and several civil liability and criminal offences for failure to conduct decommissioning, including against directors of companies if they are negligent or fail to conduct sufficient diligence when approving business operations;
- recourse against both current and historic JOA co-venturers[18] to cover costs if the host government is required to perform decommissioning due to failure of the commercial parties;
- recourse against affiliated companies of past and current JOA co-venturers, on a joint and several basis;[19]
- a requirement that JOA co-venturers provide a parent company guarantee or bond[20] in favour of the host government with respect to all or certain decommissioning liabilities; and

---

15 For example, Section 5.1 of the Norway Petroleum Activities Act 1996.

16 For example, Resolution 817/2020 (Brazil).

17 For example, Section 571(2) of the Australia Offshore Petroleum and Greenhouse Gas Storage Act 2006 (Cwth) and Minister of Energy and Mineral Resources Regulation 15/2018 (Indonesia).

18 For example, Section 587(2)(a) of the Australia Offshore Petroleum and Greenhouse Gas Storage Act 2006 (Cwth).

19 For example, Section 29(a) of the Danish Subsoil Act.

20 For example, the US Department of the Interior, Bureau of Ocean Energy Management, Notice to Lessees and Operators of Federal Oil and Gas, and Sulfur Leases and Holders of Pipeline Right of Way and Right of Use Easement Grants in the Outer Continental Shelf, NTL 2016-N01 (12 September 2016) replaced NTL 2008-N07 in 2016 and set out circumstances in which the Bureau of Energy Management would require additional financial assurance, particularly where there was only one liable party operating under the lease. However, this notice was rescinded in 2017 and a replacement has yet to be published. The general approach remains for holders and acquirers of oil and gas leases and operating rights holders to maintain a bond in favour of the US government (NTL 2015-N04; Code of Federal Regulations, Section 556.900).

- tax relief or cost recoverability with regard to decommissioning costs and providing for the transfer of tax history to better enable such tax relief.[21]

This list reflects a menu of options that are commonly adopted by a host government seeking to impose obligations on commercial parties.[22]

Whether legal requirements are imposed by statute, regulation or through the host government instruments is an important consideration in any sales process. Host government instruments, being contractual in nature and therefore capable of assignment, provide contractual remedies for the host government that do not survive against a seller after asset assignment or against a parent company after the sale of shares. A host government cannot enforce decommissioning provisions contained in a host government instrument against sellers that have divested their assets, because it is a contractual instrument. For this reason, host governments seek to impose provisions with extra-contractual effect through statute or regulations.

3.2 Contractual sources

Decommissioning obligations, allocation of liability and the requirement for financial provisions are often dealt with by commercial parties in both the JOA and the DSA. It will be a completion deliverable of any asset assignment, and an automatic assumption upon any share purchase, that the buyer directly or indirectly becomes a party to these agreements. Therefore, any potential buyer needs to conduct due diligence in relation to decommissioning arrangements that it assumes as a result of its acquisition.

An agreement between co-venturers to set aside funds for future costs is common and widely considered best practice. Such agreements are voluntary and ensure that sufficient funds are available when the decommissioning expense arises (sometimes up to 20 years in the future). The adverse publicity resulting from failure to meet high standards in this process often motivates JOA parties to self-regulate their behaviour. Such agreements may therefore be entered into even in jurisdictions which do not incentivise parties to set aside provisions.

---

21 For example, since 1 November 2018, Her Majesty's Revenue and Customs in the United Kingdom has permitted a 'transferable tax history' to encourage acquisitions of late-life assets and to extend the life of such assets. The transferable tax history mechanism allows for a portion of the seller's tax payment history relating to the asset to transfer to the buyer, thereby allowing the buyer to set the costs of decommissioning against this transferred tax history.

22 Although commercial parties typically assume decommissioning liability, in some jurisdictions host government instruments provide that ownership of infrastructure passes to the host government at cessation of production or at the expiry of the host government instrument term. These arrangements are usually jurisdictions that first developed an onshore, rather than an offshore, industry – for instance North Africa. These jurisdictions provide rare examples of where decommissioning is a host government risk.

Typically, provisioning arrangements are contained in a separate standalone agreement to the JOA, known as a DSA (see section 2.2 above). They ordinarily provide that financial obligations are posted by way of cash, bond, parent company guarantee or letter of credit to cover the estimated cost of decommissioning (escalated by a risk factor). Typically, all but the most creditworthy parties are required to cash collateralise a bank for providing a letter of credit or guarantee. Therefore, the obligation (whether posted as cash or otherwise) invariably involves an immediate cash commitment. Provisioning ordinarily commences towards the end of field life. For example, in the United Kingdom, the provisioning trigger date is determined as the year in which the estimated remaining revenues of a field (discounted to a net present value) equal the estimated decommissioning costs (escalated by a risk factor).

In developed jurisdictions, DSAs require funds to be held by an independent trustee which holds these funds on behalf of historic licensees, current JOA co-venturers and any company that may potentially be liable as a result of being affiliated to primary obligors. This arrangement has the benefit of making funds remote from bankruptcy of the operator holding moneys. Funds held by a trustee should not be available to general creditors as part of a bankruptcy estate of commercial parties.[23]

By contrast, in less developed jurisdictions, decommissioning funds are held by the JOA party appointed as operator and, in the event of its bankruptcy, disputes may arise as to whether amounts so held are protected from general rules of insolvency law.

DSAs are often used between existing co-venturers to provision for decommissioning liability. These types of DSA are referred to as 'field DSAs'. DSAs can also be used as an M&A tool to apportion decommissioning liability. As we will see below, this can be done through existing field DSAs and also by the entry into of a new bilateral DSA specific to the M&A transaction and entered into between buyer and seller only. This is referred to as a 'sale DSA'.

4. Key SPA considerations

The allocation of liability for future decommissioning obligations is a key consideration when negotiating an SPA.

If a seller disposes of its working interest before cessation of production, it will want liability for future decommissioning to be assumed in full by the buyer. A seller will wish to avoid – or, if not possible to avoid, to protect against – the possibility of unsatisfied liability attaching to itself as a historic owner. If potential liability remains (because the relevant jurisdiction does not release historic owners), a seller will want assurance that at the end of a project's life, sufficient financial provisions will be available to pay for costs. A seller that

23 Although an insolvency analysis will need to be conducted in accordance with applicable laws.

remains liable for future claims may require that funds be held in a trust structure which contemplates itself, as a historic owner, as a class of beneficiary. Ways of achieving these objectives are set out below. In recent years, as mature basins decline and longstanding producers exit basins by transferring to smaller independents, it is increasingly being seen that sellers are unable to achieve a 'clean break' from decommissioning liabilities when selling late-life assets, as buyers are often insufficiently creditworthy to support the decommissioning security or provisioning requirements under the applicable law, and make it a condition of transacting that sellers continue to 'stand behind' these decommissioning liabilities after the date of the transfer.[24]

Prior to negotiating decommissioning-related issues in an SPA, key considerations will determine how much importance should be given to potential liability. They include those set out below.

4.1 Asset profile

Whether the target asset is in the exploration, development or production phase is a key consideration. Given that significant infrastructure must already be in place, producing assets have the greatest decommissioning risk profile. Once a field has commenced production, it is difficult to allocate responsibility to the party that contributed to, or benefited from, different parts of the infrastructure. Consequently, the law does not apportion liability on the basis of period of ownership or benefits received.

In contrast to producing assets, exiting an asset when it has conducted only seismic surveys creates a different risk profile from exiting a producing field with infrastructure in place that has only a few years of remaining life. A seller that has secured revenue from an asset during production is more likely to accept some future responsibility for decommissioning than one that is transferring pre-production assets and will not, as a result, participate in the development of infrastructure or take any benefits of production.

Therefore, for exploration assets, decommissioning liabilities are unlikely to be a negotiated item and a simple indemnity provision (stating that the buyer indemnifies the seller for future liabilities) will provide a typical allocation of risk. However, after development commences, decommissioning liabilities may be one of the most important elements of the deal, second only to purchase price. Targeted SPA provisions and sale DSAs are often used to allocate liability in these situations.

Whether the asset is offshore or onshore and, if offshore, whether it is in

---

24 Notable examples include Shell's disposal to Chrysaor in 2017, in which Shell retained a fixed liability of $1 billion where the decommissioning cost estimate was $3.9 billion (www.shell.com/media/news-and-media-releases/2017/shell-to-sell-package-of-uk-north-sea-assets-to-chrysaor.html); and BP's disposal to Hilcorp Energy in 2019/20, whereby BP retained decommissioning liability for the Trans-Alaska Pipeline System (BP Annual Report 2019, p179).

deep or shallow water are also important considerations. Decommissioning offshore assets is vastly more complex and expensive. The likely cost increases for assets in deeper water.

Lastly, the type of infrastructure in place is important. Floating infrastructure (eg, a floating production storage and offloading facility) is easier to remove than heavy fixed infrastructure (eg, gravity-based concrete structures).

Buyers must therefore conduct technical due diligence to understand the stage of development, age of infrastructure,[25] depth of water and types of assets. If it has been prepared, buyers should also conduct technical due diligence on the decommissioning plan.

4.2 Funding

Co-venturers often self-regulate the provisioning of decommissioning costs by entering into field DSAs. Whether or not a field DSA is in place is important when negotiating the apportionment of decommissioning liability in an SPA. Field DSAs should operate to facilitate M&A by offering a pre-existing and industry-standard framework for dealing with decommissioning costs. A buyer will need to be satisfied that it can estimate, under the terms of the field DSA, when decommissioning provisioning will commence and what amounts will be payable. A seller wants comfort that if it disposes of an asset before financial provisioning has commenced, the remaining and incoming co-venturers (and their successors and assigns) will be able to satisfy the funding obligations of the field DSA. Various ways of dealing with a field DSA in an M&A context are described in section 5.3 below.

4.3 Jurisdiction

Parties will focus more attention on allocating decommissioning liabilities in jurisdictions with stringent regulations. That is not to say that this is not a consideration in all SPAs; but it will be a particular focus of negotiations relating to assets in countries where parties know for certain that at the date of the agreement, they will be responsible for known obligations.

4.4 Full versus partial divestment

Liability is imposed by host governments on co-venturers on a joint and several basis. There is therefore a different risk profile for the seller between a full divestment and a partial divestment (eg, a farmout) where it keeps a working interest. Even where a seller retains a small interest in the field being sold, because of its joint and several liability, it remains exposed to the entire decommissioning liability.

---

25 Modern infrastructure is designed to facilitate future decommissioning.

4.5 Asset versus share sale

Decommissioning liability attaches, in the first instance, to current JOA parties. Therefore, a corporate sale by a parent company of shares in the company holding the working interest represents a cleaner break from decommissioning liability for the seller. In this example, the seller's concern relates only to liability that may be imposed on it as a result of its previous relationship as an affiliate of the target.

There are two qualifications to this general observation about the cleaner nature of a share sale. First, any parent company guarantees given to the host government by the seller group will need to be released and replaced by the buyer group. Where the latter is weaker than the former, there may be reluctance on the part of the host government to agree a release. Alternatively, the host government may make a release conditional on some form of credit enhancement to security arrangements currently in place. Secondly, in some jurisdictions, affiliates may remain liable (even if only theoretically) for liabilities of entities that have been sold from the group. Therefore, even in examples where parent company guarantees have been released, host governments may have claw-back powers against parent companies of historic owners. Although reliance on recourse against a historic owner and its parent company is considered to be a last resort and rarely used power, any use by a host government of this remedy could have significant ramifications for a seller group.

5. Apportioning decommissioning liability in the SPA

5.1 Defining 'decommissioning liability'

The first step in dealing with decommissioning liability in an SPA is to define what is meant by that term. It is typical to see a broad definition used. The Oil and Gas UK Model SPA provides:

> *"Decommissioning Liabilities" means any claims, costs, charges, expenses, liabilities and obligations incurred in abandoning and/or decommissioning any Asset Property (including but not limited to wells an facilities) whether such loss, charges, expenses, liabilities and obligations are incurred pursuant to any statutory, common law or other obligation [and regardless of negligence on the part of the Seller].*[26]

A more detailed example definition is as follows:

> *"Decommissioning Liabilities" means any actual or alleged claims, costs, charges, expenses, liabilities and obligations incurred in, or arising from or in connection with, the decommissioning, removal and making safe all of the Joint Property related to the Licence whether such claims, costs, charges, expenses, liabilities and*

26 Oil and Gas UK Model SPA.

obligations are incurred under or pursuant to the Licence, statute, common law or other obligation and including any residual liability and regardless of whether such claims, costs, charges, expenses, liabilities and obligations arise as a consequence of the Seller's negligence or breach of duty (statutory or otherwise).

It is common to see an express inclusion of liabilities resulting from the seller's negligence in this definition so as to give effect to a complete transfer of liability. This is a negotiated point.

It is important to ensure that the definition of 'joint property' (or 'asset property' or equivalent) and any other descriptions of the assets to which the definition applies are accurate. Cross-referencing the JOA and host government instruments is critical to ensure that the definition covers liabilities that may have accrued under the host government instrument or applicable law. An example definition of 'joint property' is as follows:

"Joint Property" means, at any point in time, all wells, facilities, equipment, materials, information, funds, and property (other than Hydrocarbons) held for use in the operations and activities within the scope of the Licence and the JOA (or whose purpose at the time undertaken was within the scope of the Licence and the JOA) conducted by Operator on behalf of all Parties, including Exploration Operations, Appraisal Operations, Development Operations, Production Operations, and operations and activities for the purposes of Decommissioning.

5.2 Indemnities

Indemnities are a key provision transferring or apportioning decommissioning liability between parties to an SPA.

Sellers want a clean exit from liabilities and obligations. They will therefore provide for the complete transfer of liability to the buyer and will seek an indemnity from the buyer for any residual liability under domestic law. This is equally relevant for an asset sale or share sale, as in many jurisdictions liability can attach to both JOA parties and their affiliated companies (eg, the selling shareholder) on a continuing basis. The reference, below, to both seller and its affiliates is included for this purpose.

An example indemnity is as follows:

Purchaser agrees to indemnify, keep indemnified and hold the Seller [and its affiliates] harmless [on an after tax basis] against any Decommissioning Liabilities and any Environmental Liabilities of whatsoever nature and howsoever arising before or after the Post Economic Date.[27]

The concept of indemnifying the seller against all decommissioning liabilities is a relatively simple one and, consequently, this example is also straightforward. A buyer may seek a carve-out to this indemnity so that it does

27 See for example, Oil and Gas UK Model SPA, clause 5.3(b) (the text in square brackets is a potential supplement proposed by the authors).

not enable the seller to seek reimbursement in respect of decommissioning liabilities paid for by the seller prior to the economic date under the SPA.

An indemnity in relation to decommissioning, like any other indemnity, is only as valuable as the indemnitor's future creditworthiness. Sellers must consider including additional protections if they are concerned about post-completion reliance on the buyer's credit.

The first and most straightforward option is to require the buyer to provide parent company credit support. Subject to satisfaction of the guarantor affiliate's future creditworthiness, this can be a satisfactory approach and often takes the form of a standalone deed of indemnity. When the credit risk is not satisfactory, an alternative option is to require the buyer to procure a yearly renewable letter of credit in favour of the seller and any of seller's affiliates exposed to future liability.[28] This will be issued by a bank with an acceptable credit rating and subject to reissue on an annual basis.

Cessation of production (when the actual cash requirements associated with decommissioning liabilities crystallise) can be several years after signing of the SPA. The creditworthiness of any particular buyer or buyer credit support will change over time. Therefore, sellers frequently require more transparent and reliable access to funds to cover potential liability to which they are exposed. DSAs are the most common method of providing this and are discussed in more detail in section 5.3 below.

For a farmout transaction, whereby parties remain co-venturers, an indemnity of the type above may not significantly alter the allocation of liability set out in the JOA. Parties are most likely to supplement the allocation of liability under the JOA between the farmee and farmor (and any existing joint venturers) in this scenario by way of a DSA (either by the farmee joining the existing field DSA, if there is one, or otherwise creating a sale DSA or a field DSA). The use of DSAs in M&A is discussed in more detail in section 5.3(b) below.

In some circumstances, there may be a discrete identifiable portion of the assets being sold regarding which a buyer is not willing to assume liability for decommissioning. For example, in the sale of a producing field, a buyer may not be willing to assume liability for a disused appraisal well that has previously been plugged and abandoned. In this scenario, the specific well can be carved out of the general indemnity and a new indemnity in favour of the buyer can be added to deal with any liabilities associated with having to decommission that abandoned well (eg, if the host government identifies that the well was improperly plugged and abandoned and requires further decommissioning work).

28 Paula Kidd and Norman Wisely, "Decommissioning in an M&A context", in Marc Hammerson and John LaMaster (eds), *Oil and Gas M&A: A Practical Handbook*, Globe Law and Business, 2018, pp246–247.

5.3 DSAs

Mature basins (eg, the UK continental shelf) are seeing the participation of an increasing number of non-traditional participants (eg, private equity funds, hedge funds and independents), in some cases with lower costs of capital and targeted expertise in end-of-life fields. Regulators of mature basins actively encourage such new entrants. For example, in the United Kingdom, it is formal government policy to encourage the transfer of licence interests to the most cost-efficient commercial parties, as part of a strategy intended to help extend the lives of fields and common-use infrastructure.

However, the increase in non-traditional buyers creates concerns about the creditworthiness of counterparties in M&A transactions. Sellers now take more detailed precautions than simple indemnities to protect them from liability associated with decommissioning infrastructure after they exit an asset. In some jurisdictions, DSAs have become a tool that mitigates risk.

(a) No field DSA in place

For a farmout transaction (where farmor and farmee remain as co-licensees and, therefore, remain partly or fully in control of future joint venture arrangements), it is common to negotiate and attach a draft field DSA to the SPA and include an obligation on the parties to enter into a field DSA in that, or similar, form. Although ideally the field DSA would be entered into at the time of closing, this commonly occurs after closing because negotiating a DSA in parallel with the SPA (and if a new JOA is required, the negotiation of the JOA) could be considered a distraction.[29]

In jurisdictions with no decommissioning laws, the reliance on field DSAs in M&A is less common for a farmout transaction. However, even in those jurisdictions, parties may covenant that they will enter into a field DSA if decommissioning laws are introduced.

An example of this provision is as follows:

[By a certain date] [Prior to the Operator's submission of a Decommissioning Plan] [Immediately upon the introduction of any Decommissioning Laws] the Parties shall negotiate, agree and enter into a Decommissioning Security Agreement.

"Decommissioning Security Agreement" means an agreement in the form attached with any amendments necessary to comply with Decommissioning Law and the principle that the Parties provision financial security to cover the cost of any Decommissioning Liabilities.

For an asset or share sale where the seller is fully divesting its interests, where there is no field DSA in place, it is unlikely that the seller will be in a

29 See Nicholas Ross-McCall, "Decommissioning and the joint operating agreement", in Marc Hammerson and Nicholas Antonas (eds), *Oil and Gas Decommissioning: Law, Policy and Comparative Practice* (2nd edition, Globe Law and Business, 2016) for a summary of the relationship between the negotiation of DSAs and the negotiation of JOAs.

position to force the buyer and the remaining co-venturers to put in place a field DSA as a condition to the transaction. In these circumstances, the seller may require the buyer to enter into a bilateral sale DSA with it under which decommissioning liabilities are (at least partly) funded at the closing of the transaction. It is likely that a buyer will reject this, given:

- the substantial cash outlay involved in provisioning for decommissioning;
- the fact that such provisioning would be in advance of the industry standard timeframe for the commencement of provisioning (ie, when estimated reserves deplete to equal the estimated costs of decommissioning);[30] and
- the resulting duplication of provisioning with future funds that must be posted under any subsequent field DSA with the remaining co-venturers.[31]

Resistance from the buyer can be expected to be greater in the case of transactions dealing with jurisdictions that do not have established decommissioning laws at the time of sale. The best outcome that sellers may be able to achieve in this situation is a covenant that the buyer will enter into a DSA (either a field DSA with the co-venturers or, failing that, a sale DSA with the seller) if decommissioning laws are introduced in that jurisdiction or by the time the remaining co-venturers are required to submit a decommissioning plan to the host government. Some compromises to resolve buyer's concerns at this proposal include:

- discounting the amount of security to be provisioned by the buyer under the sale DSA to reflect the time value of earlier provisioning;
- requiring only a portion of the required buyer funds to be provisioned at closing, with annual additions to the sinking fund over time; and
- the seller offering the buyer some credit support to post the security required under the DSA.[32]

(b) Existing field DSA in place

When fully divesting from an asset with an existing field DSA, a seller will want to recover funds that it has provisioned to date. Sellers will also want to ensure that the field DSA remains fully funded in the future, which requires the buyer to replace the seller's withdrawn financial provisions. This can be achieved by having as closing deliverables:

- the buyer's entry into the field DSA;

30 Kidd and Wisely, note 30 *supra*, pp247–252.
31 *Ibid.*
32 *Ibid*, pp251–256.

- the seller's exit from the field DSA (or, at least, it no longer being a primary participant with funding obligations);
- reimbursement to the seller by the field DSA trustee or the operator (as the case may be) of amounts that it has provisioned or the release of letters of credit or guarantees that it has provided; and
- the buyer's replacement of the seller's existing provision to the field DSA trustee or operator.

It is possible (but not common) that an M&A transaction requires a buyer to enter into a sale DSA in circumstances where there is already a field DSA in place. Such a situation would involve the buyer duplicating provisioning.

In advanced decommissioning jurisdictions (eg, the United Kingdom), this need for a second DSA is resolved through the concept of second-tier participants to field DSAs. A second-tier participant is ordinarily a historic JOA party (ie, a seller) that wants to remain a party to the field DSA so that it can enforce the obligations of remaining JOA parties (ie, first-tier participants) to provision funds under the field DSA, thereby doing away with the need for a separate enforceable agreement to be in place between the seller and the buyer.

This elegant solution for avoiding duplicative DSAs is not perfect. Under the field DSA, buyers are not required to provision funds until the trigger date is reached; whereas under a sale DSA, funds are provisioned immediately. Further, field DSAs ordinarily offset the value of the underlying remaining reserves from the amount that needs to be provisioned.[33] This makes sense from a co-venturer's perspective, because in the event of a default under the DSA, the defaulting party would forfeit its working interests in the field (ie, the right to share production) to non-defaulting parties. From a co-venturer's perspective, each party's share of the asset is readily enforceable security. However, historic JOA parties do not have this advantage. This concern is largely offset by the fact that, as second-tier participants, the historic JOA parties have access to the DSA provisions made by all co-venturers, effectively expanding the amount of security to which they have access.[34]

In addition to second-tier participation (and especially if second-tier participation is not an option), buyers should require a covenant, such as the example below, that the seller will comply with the terms of the field DSA. This is important because although second-tier participation affords the benefits described above, as parties outside the joint venture second tier, participants have limited visibility over anticipated decommissioning costs, timing and funding demands. A covenant may provide that:

Seller agrees that it shall comply in all material respects with the terms of the

33 *Ibid*, pp247–251.
34 *Ibid.*

Decommissioning Security Agreement, including enforcing its provisions relating to the provisioning of financial security against other licensees.

Sellers exiting an asset with a field DSA that does not permit second-tier participation should be mindful when relying on the buyer's entry to the field DSA that subsequent M&A could result in the asset being held by a sole licensee. Depending on the risk appetite of the subsequent exiting licensees and any sole licensee that remains, it is possible that parties will elect to wind down the field DSA in order to release cash. Second-tier participation addresses this issue by allowing historic licensees to continue to enforce terms of a field DSA, preventing this scenario. Without second-tier participation, the following provision is recommended:

If the Purchaser becomes the sole licensee it shall promptly enter into a Decommissioning Security Agreement with the Seller and will use its best endeavours to procure that the host government also enters the Decommissioning Security Agreement, or if that is not achievable the Purchaser shall use its best endeavours to enter into a separate Decommissioning Security Agreement with the host government.

Arrangements are simpler for a share sale with an existing field DSA, as the licensee entities (and hence the field DSA parties) do not change. Depending on the negotiated commercial terms, security provisioned by the licensee entity to date may be retained in place and simply reflected as part of the value attributed to the purchase price for the target licensee entity. If a parent of the target licensee entity (eg, the seller itself) provided security, then this security will need to be replaced under similar provisions to those set out above.

6. Covenants

Host government consent is almost always required for the sale of an interest in an oil and gas asset (and often for a share sale). If the sale is from a creditworthy seller to a less creditworthy buyer, the host government may require that sufficient security to cover decommissioning costs be put in place, either through a DSA or potentially even directly to the host government, before it will provide consent to the transfer. SPAs can therefore require that the buyer provide security demanded by the host government, or enter into any agreement required by the host government (including a field DSA), with respect to decommissioning liability. It is possible for a host government to require that it become a party to the field DSA so that it can monitor it directly. The following provision can address this:

Buyer shall provide and/or procure the provision of any guarantee or security, or shall enter into any Decommissioning Security Agreement, required by the host government in order to fulfil the conditions precedent.

In many jurisdictions, the host government requires a guarantee from licensees and will not release a seller's guarantee until it has been replaced by the buyer. Sellers should thus require a provision such as the following:

Buyer shall provide and/or procure the provision of any guarantee or security required by the host government in order to fulfil the conditions precedent and will support Seller to procure that the host government release any guarantee or security provided by the Seller to the host government with respect to Decommissioning Liability.

The following covenant can be used if, as in the United Kingdom, the host government issues notices on licensees with respect to decommissioning liability that make the recipient primarily liable to conduct decommissioning:

Buyer shall support Seller to procure that the host government withdraw any notice issued to Seller with respect to Decommissioning Liability.

Similarly, if the host jurisdiction has a mechanism for formally releasing exiting co-venturers from decommissioning liability, a seller should require that the SPA deal with that process, such as by way of the following provision:

Buyer shall use its reasonable endeavours to support any application by the Seller for the release of the Seller from its [insert description of local law decommissioning obligations and liabilities].

The following are additional common decommissioning covenants in SPAs:

Buyer shall comply with all applicable laws with respect to decommissioning and Decommissioning Liabilities.

Buyer will not make a material change to its obligations in respect of Decommissioning Liabilities, including the provision of security and the entry into a Decommissioning Security Agreement, unless required by the host government.

7. Warranties

Although decommissioning obligations are a future concern (traditional oil and gas M&A does not involve the sale of assets currently in decommissioning),[35] there are still a number of warranties that can provide a buyer with protection.

It is common to see decommissioning warranties combined with environmental warranties. This is not best practice, as these two topics are distinct.

The following is an example of a buyer-friendly warranty:

Seller has at all times complied with all applicable Decommissioning Laws.

Whereas the following approach is seller-friendly:

Seller makes no representations, warranties or undertakings in respect of Decommissioning Liabilities.

A buyer may also want to flush out the status of the underlying obligations and documentation relating to decommissioning under the licence. Some warranties that may be proposed by the buyer include the following:

---

35 Although some decommissioning contractors are looking to take over oil and gas assets that have reached end of life for a lump-sum decommissioning payment on the basis that they will be able to decommission the asset more cost efficiently than traditional oil and gas companies.

So far as the Seller is aware there is no current obligation to make payments on account of future Decommissioning Liabilities with respect to the Licence.

No Decommissioning Security Agreement has been entered into with respect to the Licence.

So far as the Seller is aware the Decommissioning Security Agreement is the only agreement relating to the provision of financial security with respect to Decommissioning Liabilities.

All information provided by the Seller with respect to Decommissioning Liabilities was, at the time it was supplied, complete, true and accurate in all material respects.

The plugging or abandonment of disused wells is an obligation that may be applicable while a field is still producing or under development. This type of ongoing (rather than end-of-life) decommissioning obligation is more appropriately borne by the seller, which should remain liable if it has not performed its obligations (eg, if the disused wells were not properly plugged and abandoned and further work is required).[36] A buyer may therefore seek a provision as follows:

All wells that have been drilled in the Licence area that are not producing hydrocarbons have been plugged and abandoned or suspended in accordance with good oilfield practice and with the terms of the Licence and applicable regulations.

The Association of International Petroleum Negotiators' 2020 model form Asset Sale and Purchase Agreement includes the following seller warranty that a buyer may wish to include in a SPA:

Except for those wells that are in use on the Signature Date, all wells drilled in the Contract Area have been properly plugged and abandoned in accordance with applicable Laws and relevant International Standards.[37]

8. Conclusion

The apportionment of decommissioning liabilities in an SPA is a key topic to be negotiated and the authors expect this issue to increase in prominence in the future.

Many important oil and gas basins are now approaching depletion and, as a result, decommissioning has become more regulated. Host governments are reaching the point where they may be required to comply with international treaty obligations to remove disused infrastructure. They therefore want to be able to anticipate problems with a commercial party's performance of these obligations before the taxpayer is left responsible for the cost, without recourse

At the same time, specialised companies with end-of-life and

36 See Marc Hammerson and Caroline-Lucy Moran, "Due diligence and warranties", in Marc Hammerson and John LaMaster (eds), *Oil and Gas M&A: A Practical Handbook*, Globe Law and Business, 2018.

37 Association of International Petroleum Negotiators 2020 Model Form International Asset Sale and Purchase Agreement, Exhibit 12, paragraph 1.23.

decommissioning expertise are entering the M&A market. Their business models are based on the belief that (compared to traditional participants) they can create value by extending field lives and reducing decommissioning costs. Given the current low oil price environment, oil majors welcome the opportunity offered by these new entrants to transfer liability. Existing owners are therefore becoming increasingly creative in structuring solutions that facilitate M&A without decommissioning becoming a barrier.

Parties have been utilising combinations of techniques set out in this chapter. In addition, in the future it may become common to see sellers offering to retain some decommissioning liability or leave security in place to sweeten the deal. Sellers may also consider providing credit support (eg, backing letters of credit) to buyers for periods of time until sufficient funds are provisioned. Entry into sale DSAs or new field DSAs at signing of the SPA may become the norm, rather than softer obligations to enter into DSAs in the future.

These options, and the other provisions set out in this chapter, will be used by parties to facilitate M&A in spite of issues produced by decommissioning.

The authors would like to thank Aaron Jenman for his research assistance in the preparation of this chapter.

Competition law provisions in sale and purchase agreements

Peter Crowther
Lisa Hatfield
Winston & Strawn LLP

1. Introduction[1]

Given the global scope of competition law and substantial liability for failure to comply with applicable competition laws, all corporate transactions should be considered from a competition law perspective. This chapter focuses on the two main ways in which competition law influences an oil and gas sale and purchase agreement (SPA) through:

- the application of merger control laws (and implications for conditions precedent); and
- the protection sought by way of warranties and indemnities in respect of competition law infringements.

The application of competition laws, including merger control rules, to any given transaction (regardless of its structure) could have a material impact on the timing and implementation of the transaction. Competition laws can also result in the parties having to divest parts of their business or assets.

Competition law is particularly important in oil and gas transactions because competing oil and gas companies often act together to share costs, risks and expertise, which can have an anti-competitive effect on market conditions. Individual country (domestic) or regional (eg, EU) competition laws may therefore dictate the nature of any contractual provisions that may be required in a transactional document entered into by a company operating in the sector.

At the time of writing (June 2020), the United Kingdom was in the Brexit transition period (during which EU law continued to apply to the United Kingdom as if it were still an EU member state) and any post-transition period deal had not been agreed upon. The below is intended as a general guide to

1 For the purposes of this chapter, we have considered the application of EU and UK competition laws. Transacting parties should be aware that other competition laws exist and should seek advice from appropriate counsel about the application of such competition laws to the relevant transaction. It might also be necessary to include additional provisions in the transactional documents to deal with such competition law issues.

potential considerations that will need to be taken into account after the end of the transition period. The precedents have been drafted in a way that allows for adaptation to take account of different outcomes and these should be adapted in accordance with the prevailing legal landscape at the time and the jurisdictions relevant to the particular transaction.

2. Conditions precedent

Where a transaction exceeds the merger control thresholds of one or more jurisdictions, the transacting parties are typically prohibited from closing the transaction without first obtaining a clearance decision from the relevant competition authority.

In the case of transactions meeting the thresholds under the EU Merger Regulation (139/2004),[2] the transaction will need to be notified to the European Commission. Otherwise, within the European Union, the parties may have to notify one or more domestic competition authorities. It should be emphasised, however, that there are more than 100 merger control jurisdictions worldwide, most of which have a mandatory notification process that is not based on any substantive competition test (eg, an analysis of whether the parties have any competitive overlaps). Rather, the process works by way of an assessment of the parties' revenues or assets, or respective market shares.

Such notification will, in most jurisdictions, take the form of a formal merger control filing. Where filings are required, the parties will usually need to consider whether to include provisions (usually in the form of condition precedents) that stipulate that competition approval is required before the transaction is closed. The parties will also want to establish the process and timing for submitting the filing, and allocate among themselves any risks associated with obtaining such competition approval.

It is therefore prudent for the parties to the SPA to determine from the outset:

- any jurisdictions where a pre-notification filing to the relevant competition authority is mandatory;
- any jurisdictions where, although not mandatory, it may be prudent to submit a pre-notification filing;
- whether closing must be suspended pending approval from any relevant competition authority;
- whether, in circumstances where obtaining approval from the relevant competition authority does not legally suspend closing, the parties would, in any event, prefer to wait until clearance is obtained; and
- the chances that the transaction may be subject to an extended review

2 Council Regulation (EC) 139/2004 of 20 January 2004 on the control of concentrations between undertakings.

by any competition authority. Where such risk exits, the buyer may wish to seek the option to walk away from the transaction in the event of such extended review.

Given that successful completion of a transaction may depend on obtaining competition approval, competition-related conditions precedent serve an important function in protecting the parties' respective positions in the event that the transaction is unable to close as originally contemplated (ie, the acquisition may be able to close so long as certain businesses/assets do not form part of the acquisition/merged entity), or in the event that the transaction is unable to close at all.

Accordingly, conditions precedent should essentially:

- address the circumstances in which the transaction might not legally be completed until the necessary approvals have been obtained; and
- provide for what happens in the event that the competition authority decides to instigate a protracted investigation into the transaction (often known as a Phase 2 investigation) or requires the parties to divest any part of their businesses.

Depending on the particular facts of the transaction and their relative bargaining strengths, the parties may agree to abandon the transaction in the event that the second situation highlighted above occurs. Alternatively, the transaction may still proceed despite such a protracted investigation, whereby the parties agree that if necessary, they will divest certain assets in order to secure the relevant approval. The parties will want to ensure that any divesture package is clearly defined and ultimately does not negate the commercial rationale for the merger/acquisition.

2.1 Example conditions precedent

Set out below is an example of standard wording that could be used as a starting point for a condition precedent for a merger or acquisition. This example contemplates a scenario where a pre-notification filing is required under the EU Merger Regulation, and also separately under the domestic competition regime of additional jurisdictions.

Example 1:

1. Conditions Precedent

1.1 The sale and purchase of the Shares is conditional on:

1.1.1 a decision from the European Commission under:

(a) Article 6(1) (a) of the Merger Regulation; or

(b) Article 6(1)(b) of the Merger Regulation; or

(c) Article 6(2), of the Merger Regulation; or

(d) Article 8(1), of the Merger Regulation; or

(e) Article 8(2) of the Merger Regulation; or

(f) the European Commission not adopting a decision within the specified time limits such that the European Commission is deemed to have cleared the transaction; and

This clause will be applicable where the transaction meets the relevant jurisdictional thresholds under the EU Merger Regulation. Note that this language does not permit the buyer to walk away from the transaction in the event of a decision by the European Commission to launch a detailed Phase 2 investigation. In general terms, the European Commission will commence a Phase 2 investigation where it has serious competition law concerns about the notified transaction.

1.1.2 the national competition authorities of [jurisdictions]:

(a) taking a decision that the sale of the Shares to the Purchaser does not fall within the scope of the relevant competition laws; or

This sub-clause will be of relevance only where the parties have agreed to notify the relevant authority as a precaution. It will often be the case that, instead of granting approval, the authority will merely confirm that the transaction does not fall within the scope of the relevant competition law, and that it is therefore not within its remit to consider.

(b) taking a decision that allows the sale of the Shares to the Purchaser under the relevant competition laws; or

This is where the authority has provided approval (or equivalent) for the transaction to close.

(c) not taking a decision within the time limits set by the relevant competition laws and as a result the sale of the Shares to the Purchaser is deemed to have been allowed.

This sub-clause applies where any statutory period for review has lapsed without the competition authority providing approval; as a result, the transaction has 'deemed consent' under the relevant competition laws.

1.2 The Purchaser must use its best efforts to procure that the Conditions set out in Clause 1.1 are satisfied as soon as possible and furthermore, the Purchaser must:

1.2.1 make all necessary filings to obtain the required approval(s) in a form or forms reasonably acceptable to the Seller as soon as permitted under the relevant competition laws and in any event before [date], and use its best efforts to obtain the approval of the relevant authorities referred to in sub-clauses 1.1.1 and 1.1.2 (the "Competition Authorities"); and

The parties should take care not to provide an arbitrary period for filings. Careful consideration must be given to any statutory period within which a competition authority must receive a filing (as well as the practice of relevant authorities in deciding when to 'accept' notifications as complete for the purposes of a notification), along with the period within which the authority is obligated to make a decision, and any other commercial sensitivities.

1.2.2 accept all conditions or obligations imposed by the relevant Competition Authority in its decision and offer to restructure the activities of the Group or its own business to satisfy the conditions or obligations imposed by each such Competition Authority.

As explained above, the parties may wish to set out expressly in further detail how any restructuring of activities might be conducted to ensure that any divestment required by a competition authority is reasonable and does not undermine the commercial rationale for the transaction. The purchaser might want to carve out specific parts of the business that are of particular value, by stating that, for example:

for the avoidance of doubt, any request, requirement or imposition by/of the Competition Authority on the Purchaser to restructure its business or the activities of the Group, shall not include the divestment, in whole or in part of [name of subsidiary] and/or any of its business divisions ("Company X").

The purchaser may then wish to set out what would happen in the event that the relevant competition authority required it to dispose of Company X in order to obtain its approval of the transaction (ie, the purchaser would have a right to terminate).

1.3 For the purposes of the Conditions, the Purchaser and the Seller must:

1.3.1 promptly notify each other of any material communication (whether written or oral) from any Competition Authority;

1.3.2 give each other reasonable notice of all meetings and telephone calls with any Competition Authority and give reasonable opportunity to participate in them (except to the extent that a Competition Authority expressly requests that either Party should not be present at the meeting or part or parts of the meeting); and

1.3.3 provide each other with drafts of all written communications intended to be sent to any Competition Authority, give each other a reasonable opportunity to comment on them, not send such communications without the prior approval of the other (such approval not to be unreasonably withheld or delayed) and provide each other with final copies of all such communications (except that in relation to all disclosure under this sub-clause, business secrets and other confidential material may be redacted so long as each Party acts reasonably in identifying such materials for redaction).

The party that is not responsible for submitting the pre-notification filing may want to reserve its right to comment on the content of any filing or any communications with the competition authority, especially when it involves the dissemination/discussion of commercially sensitive information with respect to the parties and the transaction. The notifying party will usually also want some assurances that the other party will cooperate and provide any information requested by the competition authority (with respect to worldwide or domestic turnover figures, etc) to enable it to secure the necessary approvals and meet its obligation(s) under the condition precedent.

1.4 The Purchaser must use its [best reasonable[3]] efforts to procure that the Conditions are satisfied on or before [date falling [xx] months from signing] or such later date as is agreed in writing between the Parties after the date of this Agreement (the "Long Stop Date").

1.5 By the Long Stop Date, if the Conditions have not been satisfied or if any Competition Authority has taken action or given an indication that any Condition will not be satisfied, the Seller may serve notice on the Purchaser terminating this Agreement and in that event:

1.5.1 except for this sub-clause, clauses [(Interpretation), (Confidentiality), (Assignment), (Third Party Rights), (Waiver and Variation), (Severability), (Entire Agreement), (Remedies), (Counterparts), (Notices), (Governing Law and Jurisdiction), (insert further provisions)], all of the other provisions of this Agreement shall lapse and cease to have effect; but

1.5.2 neither the lapsing of those provisions nor their ceasing to have effect shall affect any accrued rights or liabilities of any Party in respect of damages for non-performance of any obligation under this Agreement falling due for performance prior to such lapse and cessation.

The parties should consider their respective rights of termination in the event that they do not obtain approval from the relevant competition authorities, and how any termination rights might affect any 'hell or high water' provision(s) within the document. For example, the purchaser may have committed to divest certain assets in order to obtain the approval of the relevant competition authority. As such, this clause may be subject to a lengthy commercial negotiation of how to allocate any competition/antitrust risk between the parties.

Below is example wording that could be used in a competition-related condition precedent where the parties envisage that the merger/acquisition might be reviewed as part of an in-depth investigation (ie, where the process for obtaining approval may be more protracted).

Example 2:

2. Conditions Precedent

2.1 Completion is conditional on:

2.1.1 Both Parties agreeing, considering or being satisfied (whether or not as a result of receiving confirmation to this effect from the relevant Competition Authority), that:

(a) the Transaction does not constitute a concentration having a Community

3 The standard of best/reasonable/best reasonable efforts will be subject to negotiation between the transacting parties.

dimension within the meaning of Council Regulation (EC) No 139/2004 (as supplemented and amended from time to time),

(b) the Transaction constitutes such a concentration, but the European Commission has decided not to oppose the concentration and declared it to be compatible with the internal market; or

(c) the Transaction does not constitute a relevant merger situation within the meaning of Part 3 of the Enterprise Act 2002 (as supplemented and amended from time to time); or

The above provisions are an alternative means of setting out reference to the articles of the EU Merger Regulation noted in Clause 1.1.1 of Example 1 above and the relevant condition under UK competition law.

2.1.2 the Parties receiving [written] confirmation from the relevant Competition Authority that the Transaction will not be referred to an In-Depth Investigation;

The parties should consider whether it is appropriate to require written approval from the relevant competition authority, or whether informal approval will be satisfactory. Informal approval might be satisfactory where the relevant competition authority makes it clear, albeit informally, that the transaction will not be referred to an in-depth investigation (see definition further below) because it does not consider the transaction to involve serious competition law concerns.

2.1.3 the Parties receiving [written] confirmation from the Competition Authority that the Transaction will not be referred to an In-Depth Investigation, on the condition that the Parties provide the Competition Authority with undertakings acceptable to them pursuant to Part 3 of the Enterprise Act 2002 and/or Article 8(1) of the EC Merger Regulation, such undertakings being to the satisfaction of any Party required to provide such undertakings;

It is important to note that, for the purposes of this example clause, the definition of 'competition authority' refers to the UK Competition and Markets Authority (and/or its successor, or any equivalent) and the European Commission. In the event that approval must be sought from the competition authority of any additional jurisdiction, this clause and any defined terms referenced should be amended accordingly.

2.2 For the purposes of clause 2.1, an "In-Depth Investigation" shall mean:

2.2.1 a reference to a Phase II investigation made by the UK Competition and Markets Authority to its chair for the constitution of a group under Schedule 4 to the Enterprise and Regulatory Reform Act 2013;

2.2.2 a decision of the European Commission to conduct a second phase assessment pursuant to Article 6(1)(c) of the EC Merger Regulation;

2.2.3 [description of any equivalent assessment/investigation undertaken by a competition/regulatory authority of a relevant jurisdiction.]

As noted at Clause 2.1.3 above, any potential in-depth investigation by another jurisdiction's competition authority should be noted here.

The parties must consider a number of factors when negotiating merger control-related competition precedents in order to ensure that their intentions are accurately reflected.

2.2 Drafting considerations

(a) Purchaser

- Is a pre-notification filing required in a particular jurisdiction?
- Are there any jurisdictions which operate only a voluntary basis notification regime in which clearances should be sought?
- Does the triggered merger regime legally prevent completion?
- Does the jurisdiction have a specified period for notification after signing?
- Where the purchaser has not had time to conduct a thorough jurisdictional analysis of the relevant thresholds and legitimacy of the relevant competition authorities, should the conditions precedent be drafted widely in scope?
- With respect to filing obligations, which party will be responsible for preparing and submitting the filing, and:
  - where the seller is the notifying party, will the purchaser have the opportunity to comment on the filing prior to submission?
  - where the purchaser is the notifying party, is there a duty on the seller to cooperate (reasonably)?
- How long will it take the competition authority to make its (initial) decision (ie, where there is a set statutory period within which it must provide a response)?
- How might any risks posed by competition/antitrust laws affect the transaction?
- How will any competition/antitrust risks be allocated between the purchaser and the seller?
- At what stage will the purchase no longer be commercially viable and when should the transaction be abandoned (ie, if approval is not obtained within a specified time period, or in the event of an in-depth investigation)?
- Where the relevant competition authority is willing to provide approval that is conditional on the purchaser providing undertakings (ie, to divest of certain assets):
  - does the purchaser agree to comply with such conditions (subject to such divestments being reasonable)?
  - what method/calculation should be adopted in order to determine the level of divestiture that is considered reasonable in order to secure approval?

- What are the consequences of the parties being unable to meet the condition precedent, and in that event:
  - what are the purchaser's termination rights?
  - will a break-up fee be required?

(b) Seller

- With respect to filing obligations, which party will be responsible for submitting the filing?
- Where the purchaser is the notifying party, will the seller have the opportunity to comment on the filing prior to submission?
- Where the seller is the notifying party, is there a duty on the purchaser to cooperate (reasonably)?
- How might any risks posed by competition/antitrust laws affect the transaction?
- How will any competition/antitrust risks be allocated between the seller and the purchaser?
- At what stage will the sale no longer be commercially viable and when should the transaction be abandoned (ie, if approval is not obtained within a specified timeframe, or in the event of an in-depth investigation)?
- What are the possible consequences of the parties being unable to meet the condition precedent, and in that event:
  - what are the seller's termination rights? and
  - will a break-up fee be required?

3. Warranties

3.1 Due diligence and resulting warranties

At the outset of a transaction, particularly in respect of a share acquisition, the purchaser will typically undertake an extensive due diligence exercise to determine potential liabilities of the target. Competition law infringement (through anti-competitive arrangements or agreements entered into between the target and third parties) is a vital area for due diligence, given the potentially substantial liability that it entails, including joint and several liability for the conduct of all other parties to an infringement in which the target participated. The identification of any such liability may render the transaction no longer commercially viable; or, in the event of a much less severe liability, increase the bargaining power of the purchaser and result in a reduction in the purchase price of the target/asset. As such, identifying the relevant risks under competition law can result in the avoidance of substantial financial penalties.

The identification of competition law infringements also serves an important function for the purchaser when determining any legal recourse that it will have against, or financial compensation that it will be entitled to receive from, the seller in the event of a breach of warranty. For example, following completion, a discovery by the purchaser that a competition authority is investigating a previous acquisition by the target may result in the target being forced (by the competition authority) to divest of the acquired business/asset in whole or in part. Where the business/asset being the subject of divestment is of commercial value, the purchaser will want to have financial recourse against the seller.

When trying to identify potential competition law-related liabilities as part of any due diligence review, a purchaser should pay close attention to any agreement entered into by the target. This includes provisions relating to:

- joint development;
- joint purchasing; and/or
- joint supply (especially when it is to/from another competitor).

The purchaser should also pay close attention to any arrangements that:

- restrict supply or market shares;
- have the effect of fixing prices;
- involve the exchange of commercially/competitively sensitive information with actual or potential competitors; and/or
- impose exclusivity or non-compete restrictions.

Any provision creating any of the above outcomes, whether directly or indirectly, may infringe competition laws and, in some cases, render the relevant contract unenforceable. One undesirable result might be the invalidation of a valuable customer contract (see the section on restrictive covenants below). The existence of any of the above provisions may also result in a fine imposed by a competition authority or, in some instances, even in criminal liability.[4]

In the oil and gas industry, bid rigging for oil and natural gas leases has in recent years come under scrutiny from competition authorities. A thorough due diligence review will therefore be of particular importance; for that reason, the parties should engage competition counsel to conduct a careful review in order to identify any potential issues.

Even the apparently smallest restrictive provision in an agreement with a supplier, distributor or licensor can have significant legal consequences. Any information – however important or inconsequential it may seem – might need to be investigated during the due diligence review. In particular, the purchaser should request information on all decisions, judgments and correspondence between the seller/target and any competition authority, government body,

4 Article 102 of the Treaty on the Functioning of the European Union.

agency, court or third party finding or alleging that there has been an actual or suspected competition law infringement. These questions, and the answers supplied by the seller/warrantor, will then form the basis of any warranties that the seller/warrantor is requested to provide in the SPA.

From a purchaser's perspective, the warranties should not only encompass all actual or threatened investigations, proceedings and breaches of competition law; they should also seek to reveal whether the seller/target has provided any undertakings to any regulatory authority that may adversely affect the way the target manages or conducts its business. The purchaser should also try to ensure that there is no limitation period on this warranty as, invariably, competition infringement investigations can be both protracted and retrospective.

From a seller's perspective, the warranties should be limited in scope in order to reduce the purchaser's right to recourse so far as possible. With regard to competition laws, the seller should limit its warranties to specific jurisdictions, such as where the target's business is conducted, in order to limit its exposure to any anti-competitive conduct that was not reasonably foreseeable prior to completion. The seller should also limit the warranties to conduct that is material, to avoid potential breaches of warranty for any minor infractions (ie, those which would not have a material adverse effect on the target's business). The seller should also seek to carve out from the warranties any anti-competitive conduct of which it could not have been reasonably aware.

3.2 Example warranties

The example warranties set out below are drafted to contemplate the position solely from an EU and UK law perspective. In the event that the target conducts its business outside the scope of the EU and UK legislation, the parties will need to consider the competition law of any other applicable jurisdictions.

In addition, while these examples serve as a useful guide for a seller or purchaser, it is important that they pay close attention to the facts of the transaction and any responses received following the due diligence review before they determine the scope and necessity of certain warranties.

Example 3 (purchaser-friendly warranty):

3. Competition and anti-trust

3.1 The Seller warrants that no Group Company:

3.1.1 practice or conduct which amounts to an infringement of applicable legislation relating to restrictive or other anti-competitive agreements or practices, dominant or monopoly market positions (whether held individually or collectively) ("Competition Legislation");

3.1.2 is the subject of any investigation, inquiry or proceedings (actual or threatened) by any relevant government body, agency or authority in connection with any actual or alleged infringement of Competition Legislation; and/or

3.1. has received any correspondence from a government body, agency, authority and/or third party alleging that there has been an actual or suspected competition law infringement.

This warranty provides a simplified way of addressing any non-specific competition concerns that a purchaser may have. The lack of specificity is favourable to the purchaser, as Clauses 3.1.1 and 3.1.2 do not expressly limit the seller's warranty to infringements under certain legislation or within certain jurisdictions.

Example 4 (seller-friendly warranty):

4. Competition, Regulation and Compliance

4.1 So far as the Seller is aware:

4.1.1 No Target Company has ever been engaged in or threatened with legal proceedings for any breach of Competition Law, or taken steps to compromise any such action or threatened action.

In contrast to Example 3, this warranty is limited to those infringements of which the seller is aware, and specifically under EU and UK competition laws (see the definition of 'competition law' at Clause 4.1.4). If the target conducts business in any other jurisdiction, this clause should be adapted accordingly.

4.1.2 No Target Company is engaged in any agreement, arrangement, practice or conduct which amounts to an infringement of Competition Law in [the EU/UK/other jurisdiction(s)] and none of their respective directors, officers or employees is or has been engaged in any activity which would be an offence or infringement under any such Competition Law.

This warranty captures any anti-competitive conduct that might not have come to the attention of a competition authority or third party, as set out in Clauses 4.1.1 and 4.1.3. Although it addresses anti-competitive conduct of officers and employees of the target (which is purchaser-friendly), it is drafted to limit the scope of the seller's liability to those jurisdictions expressly identified as those where the target conducts its business (which, for the purposes of this example, are the European Union and the United Kingdom).

4.1.3 Neither it nor any Target Company is the addressee of any existing or, pending decisions, judgments, orders or rulings of any relevant government body, agency, authority or court responsible for enforcing the Competition Law of [the EU/UK/other jurisdiction(s)], nor have they given any undertakings or commitments to such bodies which affect the conduct of any Target Company's business.

This warranty addresses any threatened action by a competition authority that may not be considered to be legal/court proceedings (see Clause 4.1). This provision also compels the seller to disclose any undertakings that it or any target may have provided to a competition authority which may affect the manner in which the target conducts its business.

4.1.4 For the purposes of this Clause [4], "Competition Law" shall mean [EU or UK Competition Law] / [the Competition Act 1998, the Enterprise Act 2002,

Article 101 of the Treaty on the Functioning of the European Union, Article 102 of the Treaty of the Functioning of the European Union, or EC Regulation 139/2004] which governs the conduct of companies or individuals in relation to restrictive or other anti-competitive agreements or practices (including, but not limited to, cartels, pricing, resale pricing, market sharing, bid rigging, terms of trading, purchase or supply and joint ventures), dominant or monopoly market positions (whether held individually or collectively) and the control of acquisitions or mergers.

This definition provides added comfort to the seller by specifically setting out the applicable competition legislation.

Below is an example of a provision that you might expect to see where the purchaser's due diligence review has uncovered material actual or threatened litigation or an investigation.

Example 5:

5. No legal proceedings or regulatory investigations

5.1 The Seller has disclosed to the Purchaser in writing prior to the date of execution of this Agreement all material litigation, arbitration, administrative proceedings or investigations of, before or by any court, arbitral body, agency, governmental/ regulatory body, to the best of its knowledge, being current, pending or threatened against it.

As noted above, this clause provides an example of where the due diligence review has uncovered material actual or threatened legal proceedings, or similar. From the perspective of the seller, the inclusion of this Clause 5.1 provides it with protection against any future claim made by the purchaser that it was unaware of certain proceedings affecting the value or purchase price of the target, further to which the purchaser suffered a loss. Any material proceedings identified during the due diligence process will usually be formally documented in the disclosure letter.

5.2 No litigation, arbitration or administrative proceedings or investigations are current, pending or, to the best of the Seller's knowledge, threatened against the Target Company [or any of its Subsidiaries and Affiliates], in each case which has or would reasonably be expected to have a Material Adverse Effect;

A definition of 'subsidiary' and/or 'affiliate' will need to be included in the definitions and interpretation clauses where relevant. With respect to proceedings having a 'materially adverse effect', this qualifier is negotiable and, if used, the parties will agree on a test for 'materiality' tailored to the target's business, operations, assets and liabilities.

While contractual or other infringements may at times be relatively easy to detect, competition law infringements can often, by their nature, take unusual forms or be conducted surreptitiously to ensure that they remain undetected. Arrangements in relation to price fixing or agreements to exclude another competitor from a particular market may take place during an oral conversation and, as such, are not documented in a manner that would allow for easy detection during a due diligence review. The purchaser should therefore require an express warranty to be included with respect to any actual or potential competition law infringements (as shown at Example 3 above). Standard 'no litigation' warranties will often solely relate to court proceedings and will not cover the actions taken by governmental or regulatory bodies, including competition authorities.

To ensure that the transactional documents accurately reflect all perceived or potential risks, the parties should consider all relevant factors in detail.

3.3 Drafting considerations

(a) Purchaser

- Are all foreseeable and contemplated competition law infringements covered under the warranties in order to compel the seller to reveal all actual or potential competition infringements?
- Where necessary, do the warranties cover sector-specific infringements (eg, conduct of a telecommunications company in contravention of the Communications Act 2003)?
- Do the warranties address any undertaking(s) that the seller/target may have provided to a competition authority/regulatory body which may affect the commerciality of the target's business?
- Where the seller is attempting to limit the scope of its warranty, is the purchaser able to ensure that the existing liabilities will not be transferred with the target company's business? To the extent that this is not possible (ie, if the purchaser is unable to contract out of certain liabilities), the purchaser should consider what impact the liabilities will have on the price of the business.
- Is the seller negotiating a limitation period for any competition warranties that it has provided?

(b) Seller

- Can the scope of the warranties provided be limited in order to reduce the purchaser's right to recourse so far as possible, such as:
  - warranting only to the extent that the seller is 'reasonably aware' of such conduct;
  - limiting the warranty to those specific jurisdictions in which the target's business operates;
  - stating that any alleged or actual infringement will be deemed as such only under the specific legislation of the jurisdiction(s) concerned;
  - providing a limitation period in respect of any warranty; and

- limiting the warranty only to such conduct which would have a materially adverse effect on the target company's business?
- Do any of the competition warranties provided reflect conduct already disclosed to the purchaser in the disclosure letter?

By having regard to the above considerations, the contracting parties will be able to ensure that the warranties are drafted so as to strengthen their respective positions in relation to any risks associated with any actual or suspected competition law infringements.

4. Covenants

4.1 Overview of covenants

On the whole, the inclusion of a covenant in an agreement can prove an effective method of compelling a counterparty to take certain action, or of preventing a counterparty from taking certain action. Any covenant which has the effect of restricting effective competition may need to be assessed to ensure that it is compliant with the relevant competition laws.

It is, however, crucial that although the buyer will typically want to include covenants to ensure that the value of business does not change between signing and closing, such provisions should not allow for the integration of the target business or for the buyer to interfere otherwise with the operation of the target business: the target business must be free to carry on its business on a standalone basis until clearance has been received from the relevant competition authorities. Any such interference by the buyer with the target business is likely to be seen as 'jumping the gun' by competition authorities and could result in the imposition of large financial penalties.

In the context of an acquisition, covenants will be of relevance in two particular instances:

- In the SPA: As part of the transactional arrangements, the seller might agree to include restrictive covenants in the SPA, which prevent it from soliciting the target's employees and/or competing with the target's business following completion.

  With respect to a merger/acquisition that meets the thresholds for review by the EU or a domestic competition authority, such restrictive provisions will usually form part of that authority's review and will not need to be addressed through a separate review process.
- In commercial contracts between the target and third parties: The use of restrictive covenants is prevalent within a multitude of contracts used in the oil and gas sector. Non-compete clauses, in particular, can sometimes be found in supply agreements or site leases. Any material agreements between a target and a third party which includes a covenant or

restriction should therefore be reviewed carefully as part of the due diligence process.

The following examples illustrate the circumstances in which restrictive covenants are utilised in the oil and gas sector:

- Gas SPA: Where the supplier agrees not to supply a competitor of the purchaser.
- Long-term supply agreement: Where the purchaser is committed to obtaining a certain volume of gas from the supplier for a prolonged period at the expense of obtaining gas at a lower price from a competitor of the supplier.
- Site lease deed: Where the leasing company agrees to lease a site for its energy facility from the leaseholder company on the condition that:
  - the leaseholder company agrees not to allow the leasing company's competitors to lease any other part of the (remaining) land;
  - the leaseholder company agrees not to allow companies carrying out the same or similar business activities as the leasing company from leasing any other part of the land; or
  - the leaseholder company agrees not to allow any remaining land not forming part of the site to be used for a specific purpose.

4.2 Enforceability of restrictive covenants

(a) Under UK law

A restrictive covenant will be enforceable where:

- the provision is reasonable;
- the provision is necessary to protect a legitimate business interest; and
- the provision will survive only for a duration that is absolutely necessary to protect that contracting party's business legitimate interest(s).

Any provision falling outside of these conditions will be considered a restraint of trade and rendered unenforceable.

What is considered 'reasonable', a 'legitimate business interest' and of a suitable duration will often be a matter for the national courts. Parties should therefore have regard to existing case law and use this as a guide in determining whether the courts would, on the facts, be likely to enforce the restrictive covenant in question.

Ultimately, the restrictive covenant should not be wide enough so as to impose a restraint that falls outside the scope of the activities or territories in contemplation under the agreement or be of a duration that is likely to be deemed arbitrary.

(b) *Under EU law*

EU competition law draws a distinction between restrictive agreements and competitive restrictions when assessing whether the parties have engaged in conduct "which may affect trade between Member States and which have as their object or effect the prevention, restriction or distortion of competition within the internal market".[5]

In particular, the existence of a restrictive agreement will not, as a matter of course, have a restrictive effect. In some instances, a restriction on the conduct of a party may, in fact, increase competitive market conditions. Licence agreements are one such example of how a party could not reasonably be expected to pay for a licence/invest in a business where it does not have the benefit of exclusivity or the adequate protections to safeguard its investment.

Similarly, restrictive covenants will be considered, in the context of a merger or acquisition, to have a beneficial effect on competition where they are "necessary to the transfer of the undertaking concerned" and their duration and scope is "strictly limited to that purpose".[6] More generally, such competitive restrictions within agreements, also commonly referred to as 'ancillary restraints', will be considered to be enforceable where they are "directly related and necessary for the implementation of a main operation".[7] Therefore, as a matter of EU law, the parties should consider whether a restriction is objectively necessary and whether it is proportionate in order to determine the likely enforceability of the provision. Once again, the parties should have regard to relevant EU case law when determining whether a restrictive covenant is necessary to effect the sale and protect the purchaser's legitimate commercial interest.

Below are examples of restrictive covenants that most typically arise within the context of a merger or acquisition, being non-compete provisions and non-solicitation provisions.

A basic non-compete clause is shown below. This will not be suitable for target companies with varied business activities across multiple jurisdictions (as explained later in further detail).

4.3 Example covenants

Example 7:

7. Covenants

7.1 The Seller shall not directly or indirectly (through any owner, partner, investor, consultant, agent, employee, joint venture partner or other third party), conduct any or all of the Restricted Activities within the Territory during the Restricted Period.

---

5 Article 101(1) of the Treaty on the Functioning of the European Union.
6 *Remia BV v Commission*, Case 42/84 [1985].
7 *M6 v Commission*, Case T-112/99 [2001].

7.2 In this Clause [7], the following definitions shall apply:

7.2.1 "Restricted Activities" shall mean [e.g. description of the Target Company's business].

This provision can also be adapted to cover non-solicitation by including, under the definition of 'restricted activities', "the solicitation or encouragement of any customer of the Target Company in order to, or with the effect of, adversely affecting the relationship between the Target Company and/or Purchaser and that customer". Care should be taken, however, to ensure that the restricted period is appropriate for all activities encompassed under 'restricted activities'. See also drafting notes at Clause 7.2.3 below.

Additionally, while the purchaser will want to ensure that this definition is drafted as widely as possible, to protect the commercial value of the business by (in the case of the above example) preventing the seller from setting up a competing business, the purchaser must carefully consider the legal implications of this. In the event that the definition of 'restricted activities' is wider in scope than the actual activities of the target as contemplated under the agreement, the restriction will likely be rendered unenforceable.

7.2.2 "Territory" shall mean [specific territory in which the Target Company's business operates];

Similarly, it is prudent to set out clearly only those jurisdictions in which the target currently operates. Arguably, any attempt by a seller to start the same or a similar business as the target in a country in which the target does not operate or conduct business will not result in those parties becoming direct competitors and will therefore be considered unreasonable.

7.2.3 "Restricted Period" shall mean for a period of [x] [months/years] commencing on the [Closing Date] / [Effective Date].

Where the definition of 'restricted activities' encompasses a range of activities undertaken by the target, the parties may find it useful to provide separate periods in respect of each type of activity (see Example 8). This is so that, as explained in further detail below, where the agreement contains a severability clause and any period specified in respect of a particular activity is deemed unenforceable, the periods specified in respect of the other business activities will remain in force.

Given the commercial value of a restrictive covenant, it is important that the purchaser insist that the agreement contains a severability clause. This will ensure that the remaining provisions within the clause (and within the entire agreement) remain legally enforceable in the event that any provision relating to a business activity, duration period and so on is deemed unenforceable (see Example 8). As noted above, a cautious approach would be for the parties to consider the reasonable duration for each restricted activity and to specify this accordingly in order to provide maximum protection to the purchaser.

Below is a more detailed example whereby the parties have sought to ensure the severability of each of the restricted activities. This clause contains specific non-compete and non-solicitation provisions.

Example 8:

8. Undertakings

8.1 The Seller undertakes that, except with the prior consent in writing of the Purchaser it will not directly or indirectly for a period of [x] years from the [Completion Date]:

8.1.1 carry on or be employed, engaged, concerned or interested within [jurisdiction(s)] in a Restricted Business, but this clause will not prevent the Seller from:

(a) holding up to [x%] per cent of any class of securities of a company which are quoted or traded on a recognised investment exchange (within the meaning of Part XVIII Financial Service and Markets Act 2000 (UK)) or a public securities market regulated by a recognised investment exchange; or

This sub-clause provides a useful carve-out in circumstances where it would not be reasonable to prevent the seller from making a reasonable business investment.

(b) carrying on and (in a manner which does not compete with the Target Company's business as carried on at the Completion Date) developing any business carried on by the Seller that was carried on immediately before the Completion Date; or

8.1.2 in relation to a Restricted Business solicit, canvass or approach or otherwise seek the custom of any person who, at any time during the 12 months immediately before Completion, was a [substantial customer]/[Material Customer] or [supplier] / [Material Supplier] of the [Target Company] / [Company Group]; or

8.1.3 solicit or entice away or endeavour to solicit or entice away from the [Target Company] / [Company Group] or offer to employ or conclude any contract for services with any senior employee at or following the Completion Date (but for the avoidance of doubt, this shall not prevent the Seller from advertising generally for staff and employing anyone who responds to such an advertisement).

8.2 The Seller undertakes that it will not at any time after the Completion Date use as a trade or business name or mark or carry on business under a title including the word "[Target Company name/Target Company business name]".

As noted above, it is useful to set out the clause in a manner which ensures that each of the provisions is separately enforceable in the event that one of them is deemed ineffective (see Clauses 8.3 and 8.4).

8.3 Each of the undertakings in Clauses 8.1 and 8.2 are separate undertakings and independent of each other.

8.4 Whilst the Parties consider that those undertakings are fair and reasonable in all the circumstances, if any of them is found to be unenforceable, but would be valid and enforceable if any part of the wording were deleted or if the period or area of application were reduced, that undertaking shall apply with the minimum modification necessary to make it valid and enforceable.

Although Clause 8.3 allows for the severability of each of the provisions under Clause 8, Clause 8.4 helpfully provides a method by which the parties might circumvent any issues of enforceability arising from the use of ambiguous language or ineffectual terms.

The decision as to whether to use a clause modelled on Example 7 or a clause modelled on Example 8 will somewhat depend on the size of the transaction and, in particular, the number of business activities being carried out by the target company/target company group. In any event, when considering the inclusion of a restrictive covenant (whether it be a non-solicitation clause, non-compete clause and so on), it may be helpful to have regard to the drafting considerations set out below.

4.4 Drafting considerations

(a) Purchaser

- Which legitimate business activities might need to be protected? Ensure that the description of such activities is closely aligned to the description of the target's business contained in the transaction documents.
- Which employees/agents are of significant value to the target? Consider whether a non-solicitation restriction should be required only in respect of the target's key/senior employees.
- Which customers have the most significant commercial value? Should the restriction operate only in relation to those customers that, if solicited by the seller (acting as a competitor), would have a materially adverse effect on the target's business?
- Where are the territories in which the target operates its business? Consider any jurisdictions where a third party (ie, agent) acts on the target's behalf.
- What could conceivably be a reasonable duration for the restrictions imposed in respect of each of the relevant activities, based on what is both necessary and reasonable? This will require a review of relevant case law to obtain an indication as to what the courts may consider to be reasonable.
- Must the duration of the restrictions in respect of each restricted activity be expressly set out, together with a severability clause, in order to allow a restrictive provision (which is deemed to be unenforceable) to be severed from the contract, while ensuring the validity of the remaining restrictive provisions?

With regard to conducting a due diligence review of commercial agreements which contain restrictions or have the effect of restricting competition, the purchaser should also take into account any regulations specifically governing the type of contract which the target has entered into with a third party. In particular, the following EU provisions are too complex to be addressed in any meaningful detail within this chapter, but should be borne in mind by the purchaser, the seller and their respective legal representatives:

- the EU guidelines on vertical/horizontal restrictions; and
- any EU block exemptions.

At the time of writing, unless agreement is reached to the contrary on any post-Brexit transition period deal, the EU block exemption regulations will be preserved in UK law after the transition period ends as 'retained exemptions' and will remain in force until their expiry.

(b) Seller

- Where are the territories in which the target operates its business? Ensure that the restriction(s) imposed cover only what is strictly necessary to protect the purchaser's legitimate business interests.
- What could conceivably be a reasonable duration for the restrictions imposed in respect of each of the relevant activities, based on what is both necessary and reasonable? This will require a review of relevant case law to obtain an indication as to what the courts may consider to be reasonable.

As noted in the section on warranties above, restrictive covenants should form part of any due diligence review of a target's commercial contracts. In particular, when reviewing customer contracts of a high commercial value, it will be necessary to check the enforceability of any restrictive covenants that might render them unenforceable and lower the commercial value of the target.

5. Conclusion

While each of the example provisions provided above should help in deciding what may need to be included in an SPA to satisfy any competition law concerns, it should be noted that conditions precedent, warranties and covenants by no means comprise an exhaustive list of such provisions. When drafting and reviewing the SPA, it will be important to consider the agreement in its entirety to ensure not only that it includes provisions that adequately protect the parties against competition/antitrust risks, but also that none of the provisions have unintended anti-competitive effects.

The publisher acknowledges the contribution of Jade-Alexandra Fearns to this chapter in the previous edition.

Anti-corruption

Paige Berges
Amanda Raad
Sean Seelinger
Ropes & Gray (London)

1. Introduction

The oil and gas industry presents elevated bribery and corruption risk for a number of reasons. First, commodities such as oil and gas can be incredibly lucrative, presenting opportunities for corrupt activity related to securing access or commercialising those commodities. Secondly, there is significant government interaction at each stage of the oil and gas exploration and production process, from granting drilling rights to contracting with state-owned oil companies, as well as building permitting, licensing, tax and trade. Each of these touchpoints provides opportunity for bribes to government officials to be offered or requested in order to obtain rights or required approvals. In some countries, national oil companies or regulators have more extensive operational involvement and approval rights, providing further opportunities for improper benefits to be requested, or for service and supply contracts to be directed to connected parties.

Additionally, a substantial portion of the world's oil and gas reserves are located in countries perceived to be at higher risk of bribery and corruption, namely Africa, Latin America and the Middle East. Half of the top 20 oil producing countries rank in the lowest 50% of the world on Transparency International's Corruption Perception Index 2019 (CPI) – for example, Russia (137 out of 180), Nigeria (146), Iran (146) and Iraq (162).[1] Regulators and enforcement agencies expect companies to take into account enhanced inherent corruption risk in a jurisdiction to determine the adequacy of anti-corruption controls such as due diligence and contractual protections. However, the CPI measures only the perception of corruption and there are other inherent risks to consider, as described further throughout this chapter. China – which ranks 80th out of 180 countries on the CPI – has been the location of misconduct for 67 US Foreign Corrupt Practices Act (FCPA)-related enforcement actions as of mid-2020; while Russia has seen 18 despite its less favourable CPI

1 Corruption Perceptions Index (2019 World Map), Transparency Int'l, (2019 World Map), www.transparency.org/en/cpi/2019/results/bra; see also Venezuela (173), Kazakhstan (113), Algeria (106), Brazil (106) and Mexico (130).

score.[2] The United Arab Emirates – which ranks a high 21st out of 180 on the CPI (the United States is 23rd) – has instead been identified by Transparency International as an intermediary destination for money laundering, including helping corrupt actors from other countries to disguise their criminal proceeds.[3]

The oil and gas industry has the most US FCPA enforcement actions of any other sector (88 since the FCPA was enacted in 1977), while healthcare and industrial goods have seen 64 and 58 enforcement actions, respectively.[4] Although anti-corruption enforcement in the United Kingdom is relatively nascent, there have been a number of UK cases related to oil and gas companies – in particular, concerning the award of rights and contracts.[5] The oil and gas industry has similarly been the subject of enforcement in Europe and local jurisdictions. Companies can incur liability as a result of the behaviour of their employees, agents, intermediaries and other third parties. Companies can also inherit liability for acquired entities – a concept known as 'successor liability'. Given these inherent risks, enforcement authorities expect organisations to take significant measures to comply with applicable anti-bribery and anti-corruption regimes, including the US FCPA, the UK Bribery Act 2010 (UKBA) and applicable local laws.

This chapter provides an overview of:

- the main international and select local anti-bribery and corruption laws;
- key areas of inherent bribery and corruption risk;
- how corruption risks apply in the oil and gas industry; and
- the main steps companies should take to mitigate bribery and corruption risk in oil and gas.

2. Overview of relevant anti-corruption legislation

The most well-known and enforced anti-corruption legislation globally is the US FCPA, enacted in 1977. It has a broad geographical scope: nearly 500 combined corporate and individual enforcement actions have been brought

2 Brazil has been the location of misconduct in 23 actions, Venezuela 14, Nigeria 23, Mexico 22, Saudi Arabia 16, Iraq 24, India 21, Indonesia 22 and Kazakhstan 13. Stanford Law School, Foreign Corrupt Practices Act Clearinghouse, "Location of Misconduct Alleged in FCPA-Related Enforcement Actions (by Country)", http://fcpa.stanford.edu/statistics-analytics.html?tab=8.

3 Dominic Dudley, "Dubai Has Become a 'Money Laundering Paradise' Says Anti-Corruption Group", Forbes (29 January 2019), www.forbes.com/sites/dominicdudley/2019/01/29/dubai-has-become-a-money-laundering-paradise-says-anti-corruption-group/#370f8cfe315e.

4 Industry Classifications of FCPA Matters, Stanford Law School, Foreign Corrupt Practices Act Clearinghouse http://fcpa.stanford.edu/statistics-analytics.html?tab=9.

5 See, for example, United Kingdom, Serious Fraud Office, Case Information, *Afren PLC* (18 October 2019), www.sfo.gov.uk/cases/afren-plc/; United Kingdom, Serious Fraud Office, Case Updates, *FH Bertling Sentenced for $20m Angolan Bribery Scheme* (3 June 2019), www.sfo.gov.uk/2019/06/03/fh-bertling-sentenced-for-20m-angolan-bribery-scheme/; United Kingdom, Serious Fraud Office, News Releases, *Osman Shahenshah & Shahid Ullah Sentenced to 30 Years for Afren Fraud & Money Laundering* (29 October 2018), www.sfo.gov.uk/2018/10/29/osman-shahenshah-shahid-ullah-sentenced-to-30-years-for-afren-fraud-money-laundering/; United Kingdom, Serious Fraud Office, News Releases, *SFO Recovers £4.4m from Corrupt Diplomats in "Chad Oil" Share Deal* (22 March 2018), www.sfo.gov.uk/2018/03/22/sfo-recovers-4-4m-from-corrupt-diplomats-in-chad-oil-share-deal/.

under the act, involving conduct in approximately 130 countries.[6] The UKBA – enacted in 2010 to better implement in UK law the requirements of the Organisation for Economic Co-operation and Development's (OECD) Anti-Bribery Convention[7] – has been in force for only 10 years, but has already become influential in advancing global best practice in anti-bribery and corruption compliance. Companies operating globally, even if incorporated outside of either the United States or the United Kingdom, should be aware of the requirements of both. Not only do both statutes have broad jurisdictional and extraterritorial application, but many other countries have followed and continue to follow suit in implementing their own similar anti-bribery and corruption legislation.

2.1 Foreign Corrupt Practices Act

The FCPA contains both criminal and civil offences. The US Securities and Exchange Commission (SEC) enforces the civil offences (ie, the accounting provisions, discussed further below), while the US Department of Justice (DOJ) enforces the criminal offences.

The criminal bribery offence prohibits companies, agents and individual employees from directly or indirectly making, offering, promising or authorising improper payments or 'anything of value' to foreign officials for the purpose of influencing officials' decisions in order to obtain or retain business.[8] The term 'foreign official' is interpreted broadly to include essentially anyone working on behalf of a state-owned or controlled entity. In addition to appointed and elected officials, this includes state-owned companies and their employees. In the oil and gas industry, this can include employees of a national oil company. Other institutions or agencies over which the government has some control can also be deemed 'foreign officials' under the FCPA.[9]

'Anything of value' is broadly interpreted, going beyond pecuniary gain such as cash or cash equivalents, and can apply to benefits provided to family members of the foreign official. For example, it can include the hiring of foreign officials' relatives, gifts, travel and entertainment expenses, charitable or

6 See Stanford Law School, *supra* note 4; *Heat Maps of Related Enforcement Actions: By Geography*, Stanford Law School, Foreign Corrupt Practices Act Clearinghouse, http://fcpa.stanford.edu/ geography.html.

7 The OECD is an intergovernmental economic organisation that has 37 members: Australia, Austria, Belgium, Canada, Chile, Colombia, the Czech Republic, Denmark, Estonia, Finland, France, Germany, Greece, Hungary, Iceland, Ireland, Israel, Italy, Japan, Korea, Latvia, Lithuania, Luxembourg, Mexico, Netherlands, New Zealand, Norway, Poland, Portugal, the Slovak Republic, Slovenia, Spain, Sweden, Switzerland, Turkey, the United Kingdom and the United States (www.oecd.org/about/). Officially known as the Convention on Combating Bribery of Foreign Public Officials in International Business Transactions, the OECD Anti-Bribery Convention establishes "legally binding standards to criminalize bribery of foreign public officials in international business transactions", focusing on the supply side of the bribery transaction (www.oecd.org/corruption/oecdantibriberyconvention.htm). There are 44 signatories to the convention, including all OECD member countries and an additional seven non-OECD countries.

8 15 USC § 78dd-1, § 78dd-2.

political contributions, and providing discounts or other benefits such as facilities and equipment.

To be guilty of 'indirect' bribery – that is, through a third party – the person must 'know' that all or a portion of the benefit will be offered to a foreign official. A person's state of mind is 'knowing' if the person: (1) is aware that such person is "engaging in such conduct, that such circumstance exists, or that such result is substantially certain to occur;" or (2) has a "firm belief that such circumstance exists or that such result is substantially certain to happen".[10] Actual knowledge does not have to be proven – knowledge can be established if it is shown a person is aware of "a high probability of the existence of such circumstance, unless the person actually believes that such circumstance does not exist".[11] Indeed, US enforcement authorities have prosecuted cases of wilful blindness or conscious avoidance under the FCPA. This can occur where an actor has reason to believe or suspect impropriety based on a high probability of corruption, but fails to conduct appropriate due diligence or intentionally shields itself from learning information that it believes can constitute knowledge later and form the basis of a prosecution.[12] In the case of criminal liability for books and records and internal controls violations, the FCPA Resource Guide makes it clear that in order to constitute a criminal violation, knowing and wilful failures to maintain accurate books and records or implement adequate systems of internal accounting controls are required.[13]

The FCPA's anti-bribery provisions apply to all US persons, issuers of US securities and conduct in the United States, including foreign companies and non-US citizens who "cause, directly or through agents, an act in furtherance of such a corrupt payment to take place within the territory of the United States".[14]

---

9 The FCPA deems a 'foreign official' to be "any officer or employee of a foreign government or any department, agency, or instrumentality thereof, or of a public international organization, or any person acting in an official capacity for or on behalf of any such government or department, agency, or instrumentality, or for or on behalf of any such public international organization" (15 USC § 78dd-1(f)(1)(A)). The Eleventh Circuit established a fact-specific framework for evaluating whether an employee of a foreign state-owned entity is a 'foreign official' under the FCPA, requiring an assessment of the degree of control the state has over the entity and whether the relevant employee was acting pursuant to his or her state function with respect to the underlying bribery. The court set out the definition of 'instrumentality' as an "entity controlled by the government of a foreign country that performs a function the controlling government treats as its own" (*United States v Esquenazi*, 752 F 3d 912, 925 (11th Cir 2014)). The court additionally provided a non-exhaustive list of factors that guides the meaning of 'control', including:

- the foreign government's formal designation of the entity;
- the extent to which the government funds the entity if it fails; and
- the government's ability to hire and fire the entity's principals (*id.* at 925–27.

And the DOJ's Resource Guide to the US Foreign Corrupt Practices Act echoes the Eleventh Circuit, adopting this definition, noting that the term is broad and that the determination requires a fact-specific inquiry as illustrated by the Eleventh Circuit. See US DOJ, Crim Div and US SEC, Enf't Div, *A Resource Guide to the U.S. Foreign Corrupt Practices Act*, at 20 (July 2020), www.justice.gov/criminal-fraud/file/1292051/download.

10 American Bar Association, *Is "Conscious Avoidance" Sufficient to Establish Knowledge Under the FCPA?*, (28 February 2012), www.americanbar.org/groups/business_law/publications/blt/2012/02/01_friedman/.

11 *Ibid*; see FCPA Resource Guide, *supra* note 9, at 23.

12 See *"Conscious Avoidance," supra* note 10.

13 See FCPA Resource Guide, *supra* note 9, at 45.

The FCPA has jurisdiction over both domestic and international conduct of US persons, which includes US citizens, US nationals, US residents and US-based companies. The FCPA similarly applies to companies (including non-US companies) with securities listed on a US exchange that have periodic SEC reporting obligations (ie, issuers), as well as to their agents, employees, officers, directors and shareholders when they act on the company's behalf, regardless of whether the conduct is domestic or international. It also applies to the conduct of foreign persons while present in the United States. US prosecutors have increasingly sought to expand the scope of the FCPA's extraterritorial application, and there have been several deferred prosecution agreements involving non-US persons on the basis that they 'aided and abetted' a US domestic concern. For example, in 2012, Japan's Marubeni Corporation agreed to pay $54.6 million to settle conspiracy and aiding and abetting charges for its role as an agent in a scheme to bribe Nigerian government officials to obtain engineering, procurement and construction contracts,[15] even though it took no actions within the United States.[16] However, in *United States v Hoskins*, the Second Circuit limited this expanded scope of accomplice liability, holding that foreign nationals could not be held liable under the FCPA as accomplices – specifically, as aiders and abetters – if they did not otherwise fit the categories of persons subject to the FCPA's jurisdiction.[17] This caveat is noteworthy because if the foreign national is considered an agent of the relevant US company, he or she will still be liable under the FCPA.[18]

The FCPA contains a narrow exception for facilitation payments (sometimes called 'grease' payments): payments to secure non-discretionary routine government actions – that is, to expedite the performance of a routine governmental action by a foreign official to which the payer is legally entitled, such as processing papers. The application of the exception depends on the purpose of the payment, not its value, but is very narrow. As set out in guidance issued by the DOJ on interpretation of the FCPA, facilitation payments may still violate other laws, including in the relevant foreign country. Significantly, the UKBA expressly prohibits facilitation payments. Most other anti-corruption laws either explicitly prohibit facilitation payments or are silent. Where laws are silent, it should be presumed these payments are prohibited under broad definitions of 'bribery' and 'corrupt payments'.

---

14 US DOJ: Justice News, "Foreign Corrupt Practices Act: An Overview" (3 February 2017), www.justice.gov/criminal-fraud/foreign-corrupt-practices-act.x

15 US DOJ: Justice News, "Marubeni Corporation Resolves Foreign Corrupt Practices Act Investigation and Agrees to Pay a $54.6 Million Criminal Penalty", (17 January 2012), www.justice.gov/opa/pr/marubeni-corporation-resolves-foreign-corrupt-practices-act-investigation-and-agrees-pay-546.

16 *Id.*

17 902 F 3d 69 (2d Cir 2018).

18 Significantly, the FCPA Resource Guide, updated in July 2020, asserts that the DOJ's position in this respect remains "unsettled", and that "[u]nlike the FCPA anti-bribery provisions, the accounting provisions apply to 'any person,' and thus are not subject to the reasoning in the Second Circuit's decision in *United States v Hoskins* limiting conspiracy and aiding and abetting liability under the FCPA anti-bribery provisions". See FCPA Resource Guide, *supra* note 9, at 46.

The FCPA's civil provisions apply to companies with US-listed securities – known as 'covered' companies. These provisions – also known as the 'books and records' and accounting provisions – require that covered companies:

- make and keep books and records that accurately and fairly reflect the transactions of the corporation;[19] and
- devise and maintain an adequate system of internal accounting controls.[20]

These requirements mean that foreign-owned companies that are listed in the United States can be subject to SEC enforcement for violating the accounting and record-keeping provisions.

The FCPA does not specify a statute of limitations for violations, but the five-year limitation period set forth in the general statute for federal criminal offences[21] applies to the substantive criminal violations.[22] And for violations of the accounting provisions – specifically, 'securities fraud offences' – there is a six-year statute of limitations.[23] However, in cases involving alleged conspiracy to violate the FCPA, this period can be extended as long as the government proves an act in furtherance of the conspiracy occurred during the limitations period.[24] Significantly, the statute of limitations can be extended at least two ways:

- via a voluntary tolling agreement for companies or individuals cooperating with the DOJ; and
- via a court order sought by the government to suspend the statute of limitations up to three years to obtain evidence from foreign countries.[25]

In civil enforcement actions, there is a five-year period running from when the claim first accrued.[26] As with criminal enforcement, the statute of limitations can be extended via a voluntary tolling agreement and, in the case of individuals who are not US residents, the statute is tolled for any period when the defendants are not "found within the United States in order that proper service may be made thereon".[27]

The penalties for violating the FCPA are significant. The criminal penalties for each anti-bribery violation include fines per violation up to $2 million for

---

19 15 USC § 78m(b)(2)(A).
20 15 USC § 78m(b)(2)(B).
21 18 USC § 3282.
22 US DOJ, Crim Div and US SEC, Enf't Div, *A Resource Guide to the U.S. Foreign Corrupt Practices Act*, at 34 (14 November 2012), www.sec.gov/spotlight/fcpa/fcpa-resource-guide.pdf ('FCPA Resource Guide'). See FCPA Resource Guide, *supra* note 9, at 36.
23 *Ibid* at 36, pursuant to 18 USC § 3301.
24 *Ibid* at 34–35, 37, pursuant to 18 USC § 371.
25 *Ibid* at 35, pursuant to 18 USC § 3292.
26 *Ibid* pursuant to 28 USC § 2462.
27 *Ibid.*

corporations (and up to $250,000 for individuals as well as imprisonment for up to five years). For each accounting and record-keeping violation, fines for corporations are capped at $25 million per violation (and up to $5 million and imprisonment of up to 20 years per violation for individuals). Notwithstanding these limits, under the Alternative Fines Act, courts may impose significantly higher fines than those enumerated in the FCPA, including up to twice the benefit the defendant received in making the corrupt payment.[28] Criminal penalties are calculated using the US Sentencing Guidelines. The civil penalties for each anti-bribery violation for both corporations and individuals go up to $21,410 per violation; while for accounting and record-keeping violations, the SEC can penalise individuals between $9,639 and $192,768 and corporations between $96,384 and $963,837, or based on the "gross amount of pecuniary gain". The FCPA also permits disgorgement of profits to avoid unjust enrichment.

The DOJ has issued materials to help companies understand the FCPA and expectations for compliance, most significantly the FCPA Resource Guide.[29] The FCPA Resource Guide was first published in November 2012 and was not updated again until July 2020. The guide sets out FCPA-related enforcement actions, discussions of various areas of the law and recent case law.

(a) FCPA enforcement actions

The below cases illustrate corruption in the oil and gas industry and the significant potential penalties from FCPA enforcement.

In 2009, a federal jury decided *US v Kozeny (Bourke)* – a seminal case establishing the potential for individual FCPA prosecution in the context of a minority investment and the potential consequences for ignoring 'red flags' (potential indicators) of bribery and corruption. US-based investor Frederic Bourke invested in a business run by Czech national Viktor Kozeny in connection with the privatisation of Azerbaijan's state oil company. Kozeny allegedly obtained the rights by paying $11 million in bribes to Azeri officials. Although Bourke's investment totalled around 2% of the total amount raised for the project, he was sentenced to a year and a day in prison and ordered to pay a $1 million criminal fine.[30] Kozeny was found to be an 'agent' of Bourke's and Bourke was deemed to have known of (or was at least wilfully blind to) Kozeny's misconduct. The court found that Bourke was aware of a high probability that Kozeny was paying bribes based on significant information in the media regarding Kozeny's reputation.[31]

---

28 18 USC § 3571(d).

29 See FCPA Resource Guide, *supra* note 9.

30 *United States v Kozeny*, 667 F 3d 122, 128-29 (2d Cir 2011); Judgment, *United States v Bourke*, 1:05cr00518-02(SAS) (12 November 2009), www.justice.gov/sites/default/files/criminal-fraud/legacy/2012/06/01/11-12-09bourke-judgment.pdf.

31 *Kozeny*, 667 F 3d at 134.

In September 2018, the DOJ and SEC announced coordinated resolutions with Brazilian state-owned oil giant Petroleo Brasileiro SA (Petrobras) – considered one of the largest FCPA settlements in history – in connection with numerous schemes to bribe Brazilian public officials. The investigation revealed that more than $2 billion was siphoned from the company in bribes and secret payments.[32] Prosecutors alleged that Petrobras officials colluded with a cartel of companies to overcharge the oil company for construction and service work, sharing the money with political figures.[33] Petrobras entered into settlements with US and Brazilian authorities, agreeing to pay a combined total of $853.2 million in penalties, in addition to disgorgement and pre-judgment interest of over $933 million to the SEC.[34] Several individuals were implicated and convicted in the corruption scheme as well, including the CEO of Petrobras, Aldemir Bendine, who was sentenced in Brazil in May 2020 to six years and eight months in prison for 'passive'[35] corruption.[36]

US authorities have increasingly sought to charge individuals in addition to companies. The DOJ publicly announced charges against 34 individuals in 2019 – more than in any other year.[37] This follows an upward trend in the number of prosecutions by the DOJ of wrongdoings by individuals – there was a total of 17 indictments and guilty pleas to FCPA charges in 2016,[38] 24 indictments and 18 guilty pleas in 2017,[39] 31 indictments and 18 guilty pleas in 2018,[40] and 34 indictments and 26 guilty pleas in 2019.[41] Since 2015, a significant number of individual prosecutions have arisen in connection with Venezuela state oil company Petróleos de Venezuela, SA (PDVSA), in which individuals were alleged

32 Jonathan Watts, "Operation Car Wash: Is this the Biggest Corruption Scandal in History?", *The Guardian* (1 June 2017), www.theguardian.com/world/2017/jun/01/brazil-operation-car-wash-is-this-the-biggest-corruption-scandal-in-history.

33 David Segal, "Petrobras Oil Scandal Leaves Brazilians Lamenting a Lost Dream", *New York Times* (7 August 2015), www.nytimes.com/2015/08/09/business/international/effects-of-petrobras-scandal-leave-brazilians-lamenting-a-lost-dream.html.

34 US DOJ: Justice News, "Petróleo Brasileiro SA – Petrobras Agrees to Pay More Than $850 Million for FCPA Violations" (27 September 2018), www.justice.gov/opa/pr/petr-leo-brasileiro-sa-petrobras-agrees-pay-more-850-million-fcpa-violations.

35 Passive bribery – as opposed to active bribery – means accepting or requesting an advantage. Notably, it is an offence under the UKBA but not the FCPA, which only criminalises the offer or payment of a bribe.

36 He had been previously sentenced to 11 years in prison for corruption and money laundering in May 2018, which was overturned in August 2019. José Vianna and Ederson Hising, *Lava Jato: Aldemir Bendine, ex-presidente da Petrobras, é condenado por corrupção*, G1 (11 May 2020), https://g1.globo.com/pr/parana/noticia/2020/05/11/lava-jato-aldemir-bendine-ex-presidente-da-petrobras-e-condenado-por-corrupcao.ghtml.

37 US DOJ: Justice News, "Assistant Attorney General Brian A. Benczkowski Delivers Remarks at the American Conference Institute's 36th International Conference on the Foreign Corrupt Practices Act" (4 December 2019), www.justice.gov/opa/speech/assistant-attorney-general-brian-benczkowski-delivers-remarks-american-conference.

38 US DOJ, Crim Div, *Fraud Section Year in Review*, at 4 (2016), www.justice.gov/criminal-fraud/page/file/929741/download.

39 US DOJ, Crim Div, *Fraud Section Year in Review*, at 5 (2017), www.justice.gov/criminal-fraud/file/1026996/download.

40 US DOJ, Crim Div, *Fraud Section Year in Review*, at 5 (2018), www.justice.gov/criminal-fraud/file/1123566/download.

41 US DOJ, Crim Div, *Fraud Section Year in Review*, at 4-5 (2019), www.justice.gov/criminal-fraud/file/1245236/download.

to have engaged in a currency exchange scheme designed to embezzle around $600 million from PDVSA, made corrupt payments to secure and retain energy and logistics contracts, and attempted to launder a portion of the proceeds of that scheme.[42] As of January 2020, the DOJ announced charges against 25 individuals in connection with the PDVSA bribery case, 19 of whom have pleaded guilty.[43] The US Department of Treasury has also implemented sanctions against PDVSA in part as a result of the pervasive corruption within the entity.[44]

DOJ also charged a number of individuals in 2018 in connection with its investigation of Empresa Pública de Hidrocarburos del Ecuador (PetroEcuador), Ecuador's state-owned oil company. By January 2020, 13 individuals had pleaded guilty, including former PetroEcuador officials who are alleged to have received and concealed bribe payments, in addition to individuals who paid the bribes to obtain lucrative oil services contracts from PetroEcuador. The charges also included financial advisers and other intermediaries alleged to have facilitated laundering the proceeds through the use of US and offshore companies and bank accounts.[45]

And in October 2019, the former CEO and chief operations officer of a Monaco-based intermediary company – both UK nationals – pleaded guilty in connection with an FCPA enforcement action involving corrupt payments of millions of dollars to officials in Algeria, Angola, Azerbaijan, the Democratic Republic of Congo, Iran, Iraq, Kazakhstan, Libya and Syria between 1999 and 2016 in order to secure oil and gas contracts. The company's former business development director also pleaded guilty for his role in paying bribes in Libya.[46]

More recently, in April 2020, the SEC announced that Eni SpA agreed to pay $24.5 million in connection with an improper payment scheme in Algeria by Eni's 43% minority-owned and controlled subsidiary at the time, Saipem SpA, between 2007 and 2010. The SEC's order indicates that Saipem entered into four sham contracts, paying an intermediary €198 million, to help it win at least seven contracts from Algeria's state-owned oil company. The intermediary directed a portion of the money to Algerian government officials or their designees.[47]

42 US DOJ: Justice News, "Two Members of Billion-Dollar Venezuelan Money Laundering Scheme Arrested" (25 July 2018), www.justice.gov/usao-sdfl/pr/two-members-billion-dollar-venezuelan-money-laundering-scheme-arrested.

43 US DOJ: Justice News, "Florida Businessman Sentenced to 48 Months in Prison for Role in Venezuela Bribery Scheme" (8 January 2020), www.justice.gov/opa/pr/florida-businessman-sentenced-48-months-prison-role-venezuela-bribery-scheme.

44 US Department of the Treasury, "Treasury Sanctions Venezuela's State-Owned Oil Company Petroleos de Venezuela, SA" (28 January 2019), https://home.treasury.gov/news/press-releases/sm594.

45 US DOJ: Justice News, "Miami-Based Businessman Pleads Guilty to FCPA and Money Laundering Violations in Scheme Involving PetroEcuador Officials" (23 January 2020), www.justice.gov/opa/pr/miami-based-businessman-pleads-guilty-fcpa-and-money-laundering-violations-scheme-involving.

46 US DOJ: Justice News, "Oil Executives Plead Guilty for Roles in Bribery Scheme Involving Foreign Officials" (30 October 2019), www.justice.gov/opa/pr/oil-executives-plead-guilty-roles-bribery-scheme-involving-foreign-officials.

47 US SEC, "SEC Charges Eni S.p.A. with FCPA Violations" (17 April 2020), www.sec.gov/enforce/34-88679-s.

Another recent example of an FCPA enforcement action in the oil and gas space involves South Korea-based Samsung Heavy Industries Company Ltd, which agreed to pay $75 million in global penalties to resolve investigations into corruption. According to the DOJ, the company paid millions of dollars to a Brazilian intermediary, knowing part of the funds would serve as bribe payments to high-level executives at Petrobras in exchange for a lucrative shipbuilding contract.[48]

2.2 UK Bribery Act

The UKBA criminalises both active bribery (offering, promising or giving an advantage) and passive bribery (requesting, agreeing to or accepting an advantage). It prohibits bribery of domestic and foreign public officials as well as bribery in the private sector (notably, the FCPA does not criminalise commercial bribery). Like the FCPA, the UKBA applies broadly to UK citizens, residents and organisations incorporated in the United Kingdom (wherever the conduct occurs), as well as to individuals and entities conducting business in the United Kingdom. Unlike the FCPA, the UKBA does not require a corrupt or illegal intent in order to constitute a violation of the prohibition on bribes to public officials;[49] it requires only an intent to influence a foreign official in his or her official capacity.[50] The UK Serious Fraud Office (SFO) has primary responsibility for prosecutions.

Uniquely, the UKBA introduces a separate offence for companies which fail to prevent bribes by employees and 'associated persons'. 'Associated persons' are defined in the UKBA to include employees, agents and subsidiaries and anyone who "performs services on behalf of" the company. Whether a person will be considered an associated person depends on "all the relevant circumstances".[51] Companies will be strictly liable unless they can show that they have "adequate policies and procedures" in place to prevent bribery.

The UKBA, unlike the FCPA, criminalises facilitation payments under the broad definition of 'bribery'.

The UK Ministry of Justice has issued guidance on the UKBA, in which it sets

---

48 US DOJ: Justice News, "Samsung Heavy Industries Company Ltd Agrees to Pay $75 Million in Global Penalties to Resolve Foreign Bribery Case" (22 November 2019), www.justice.gov/ opa/pr/samsung-heavy-industries-company-ltd-agrees-pay-75-million-global-penalties-resolve-foreign.

49 According to the UKBA, the term 'foreign public officials' includes:

> *officials, whether elected or appointed, who hold a legislative, administrative or judicial position of any kind of a country or territory outside the UK. It also includes any person who performs public functions in any branch of the national, local or municipal government of such a country or territory or who exercises a public function for any public agency or public enterprise of such a country or territory, such as professionals working for public health agencies and officers exercising public functions in state-owned enterprises. Foreign public officials can also be an official or agent of a public international organisation, such as the UN or the World Bank.*

Ministry of Justice, The Bribery Act 2010 Guidance, at 11 (March 2011), www.justice.gov.uk/downloads/legislation/bribery-act-2010-guidance.pdf.

50 *Ibid.*

51 *Ibid* at 16.

out six guiding principles for anti-bribery and corruption compliance.[52] These principles are:

- proportionate procedures (proportionate to the risks an organisation faces and the nature, scale and complexity of its activities);
- top-level commitment (from senior management to foster a culture of compliance);
- risk assessment (whereby organisations assess the nature and extent of exposure to bribery risks);
- due diligence (proportionate to inherent risks faced);
- communication (to employees of the importance of compliance, including training); and
- monitoring and review (to test effectiveness and adequacy of controls).

This has been followed by additional 'internal' guidance from the SFO in January 2020 on evaluating the effectiveness of an organisation's compliance programme.[53]

As with the FCPA, the penalties for violations of the UKBA can be significant, although so far they have not reached the staggering sums paid by violators of the FCPA. Individuals can face up to 10 years' imprisonment and unlimited fines based on the seriousness of the offence; while corporations can face unlimited fines, a mandate to implement an anti-bribery programme, confiscation of financial gains and, with respect to directors, dismissal and a potential 15-year ban on holding a director position.[54] Notably, the UKBA does not have a statute of limitations.

2.3 Local anti-bribery and corruption laws

Countries around the world have passed new laws or strengthened existing laws that prohibit bribery and corruption. The United Nations Convention Against Corruption (UNCAC) is legally binding and requires signatories to implement policies and procedures aimed at preventing corruption in both public and private sectors, to adopt laws criminalising corruption and to take measures to enforce anti-corruption laws, including through prosecutions, asset recovery and international cooperation (eg, technical assistance and information exchange).[55] There is a peer review process, the Implementation Review Mechanism, intended

52 *Ibid.*

53 SFO, *SFO Operational Handbook: Evaluating a Compliance Programme*, (January 2020), www.sfo.gov.uk/download/evaluating-a-compliance-programme/?wpdmdl=25403.

54 Bribery Act 2010, c 23 (Eng), www.legislation.gov.uk/ukpga/2010/23/contents; see Ministry of Justice guidance, *supra* note 49, at 8; Company Directors Disqualification Act 1986, c 46 (Eng), www.legislation.gov.uk/ukpga/1986/46/contents.

55 UNCAC has broader applicability than the OECD Anti-Bribery Convention (which influenced the UK Bribery Act), as the OECD Convention applies only to the 37 OECD countries (plus Argentina, Brazil, Bulgaria, Costa Rica, Peru, Russia and South Africa); *see* www.oecd.org/corruption-integrity/explore/oecd-standards/anti-bribery-convention/. Therefore, UNCAC is the standard against which many global anti-corruption laws are measured.

to assist signatory countries to implement the convention. Country reports are available on the UN Office on Drugs and Crime (UNODC) website.[56]

According to a 2017 UNODC study on the state of implementation of UNCAC, most countries globally – including across the developing world – have implemented their own anti-corruption laws.[57] Moreover, as in the Petrobras example, foreign enforcement authorities have begun to participate with their US and UK counterparts to enforce bribery and corruption breaches.

For example, Nigeria – home to Africa's largest oil industry[58] – implemented the Corrupt Practices and Other Related Offences Act, 2000, which criminalises active and passive bribery of public officials.[59] It is also a crime under the act for individuals or companies to pay or attempt to pay a bribe to a public official. Private bribery is also penalised.[60] Nigeria has increased enforcement in the past year, investigating and prosecuting a range of matters, including illegal dealing in oil products, with 115 such cases brought.[61] To assist in detecting bribery of public officials, officials are expected to declare their assets upon assumption of office and before they begin to perform their duties, as well as at the end of their term, with similar requirements placed on their spouses and minor children.[62]

In Nigeria, the government regulates and participates in the petroleum industry through the Nigerian National Petroleum Corporation (NNPC). As revealed by local and international enforcement cases, there is a particular corruption risk in Nigeria in bidding and licensing processes, and with local public officials who have various levels of approval authority. There are also risks in the accurate reporting of oil sales. In mid-2019, NNPC's group managing director announced plans to tackle corruption in the industry using automation to measure downstream activities.[63] This follows another control initiative, Operation White, meant to account for every 'white' petroleum product.[64] The NNPC has been subject to controversy in recent years; for example, a 2014 audit revealed that NNPC "failed to pay" about $16 billion in revenue owed to the state's treasury.[65]

---

56 United Nations Office on Drugs and Crime, UN Convention Against Corruption (2004), www.unodc.org/unodc/en/corruption/tools_and_publications/UN-convention-against-corruption.html.

57 United Nations Office on Drugs and Crime, *State of Implementation of the UN Convention Against Corruption* (2d ed 2017), www.unodc.org/documents/treaties/UNCAC/COSP/session7/V.17-04679_E-book.pdf.

58 Nshira Turkson, "The Nigerian Oil Company's Missing Billions", *The Atlantic* (18 March 2016), www.theatlantic.com/international/archive/2016/03/nigeria-oil-corruption-buhari/473850/.

59 Laws of the Federation of Nigeria, Corrupt Practices and Other Related Offences Act, 2000 Act No 5 (2000), https://publicofficialsfinancialdisclosure.worldbank.org/sites/fdl/files/assets/law-library-files/Nigeria_Corrupt%20Practices%20Act_2000_en.pdf.

60 *Ibid.*

61 Corruption Cases Summary, TransparentcIT, https://corruptioncases.ng.

62 United Nations Office on Drugs and Crime, *Nigeria's Implementation of Chapter 11 of the United Nations Convention Against Corruption (UNCAC)*, www.unodc.org/documents/treaties/UNCAC/WorkingGroups/workinggroup4/2012-August-27-29/Responses_NVs_2012/20120827_Nigeria_English.pdf.

63 Damilare Famuyiwa, "There is Corruption in NNPC – New Boss Admits", Nairametrics (10 July 2019), https://nairametrics.com/2019/07/10/how-new-nnpc-boss-plans-to-approach-corruption/.

64 "NNPC to Automate Downstream Facilities", ThisDay (21 November 2019), www.thisdaylive.com/index.php/2019/11/21/nnpc-to-automate-downstream-facilities/.

65 See Famuyiwa, *supra* note 63; *see also* Turkson, *supra* note 58.

The DOJ and SFO have investigated several oil and gas companies as a result of alleged bribery and corruption in Nigeria.[66] One notable example was the Nigerian Bonny Island enforcement actions, which involved four joint venture partners – US-based KBR/Halliburton, Italy-based Snamprogetti Netherlands, BV (Italian oil giant ENI SpA's wholly owned subsidiary), France-based Technip and Japan-based JGC – which had jointly formed and operated a joint venture known as TSKJ. The companies were awarded four engineering, procurement and construction contracts to build facilities in which NNPC would be the largest single shareholder, owning 49% of the company. Although the partners held minority interests, they were considered direct participants in the bribery scheme to make payments to Nigerian officials, through sham third-party contracts, to secure construction contracts for liquefied natural gas trains in Nigeria. Between 2009 and 2011, US regulators settled with each of the four entities for between $218 million and $579 million each to resolve FCPA charges.[67]

3. Key areas of inherent corruption risk

Inherent risks are factors that make it more likely that an outcome will occur, in the absence of any controls. Regulators and enforcement authorities expect that companies will take into account inherent risks to determine the level of control to apply to mitigate risks. This section explores the characteristics of the oil and gas sector that create and contribute to the heightened risk of corruption

66 Royal Dutch Shell PLC and Italy's state-owned oil company, Eni SpA, were alleged to have paid $1.3 billion in 2011 to Nigerian officials for the rights to a valuable offshore oil field, which was allegedly funnelled to a company used for bribes to more than 100 recipients, allegedly including former Nigerian President Goodluck Jonathan, Nigerian politicians and Eni executives. The company used for the bribes was controlled by former Nigerian oil minister Dan Etete, who was convicted of money laundering in an unrelated case in France in 2007. A series of international investigations were launched, including in Nigeria. Emilio Parodi, "Eni, Shell knew of 'sharks' in Nigeria graft case: judge", Reuters (17 December 2018), www.reuters.com/article/us-shell-eni-nigeria-trial-idUSKBN1OG0YQ; Sarah Kent and Eric Sylvers, "Inside the Bribery Scandal Sweeping Through the Oil Industry", *Wall Street Journal* (13 February 2018), www.wsj.com/articles/inside-the-bribery-scandal-thats-sweeping-through-the-oil-industry-1518543648. On 22 May 2020, an English court dismissed a $1.1 billion suit filed in 2018 by the Nigerian government against Royal Dutch Shell and Eni, but criminal proceedings remain underway in a Milan court. "UK court throws out Nigerian oil corruption case against Shell, Eni", Reuters (22 May 2020), www.reuters.com/article/us-eni-shell-nigeria-court/uk-court-throws-out-nigerian-oil-corruption-case-against-shell-eni-idUSKBN22Y1Q8. And before that, in October 2019, the DOJ closed its investigation into Royal Dutch Shell and Eni over the $1.3 billion deal. Dylan Tokar, "Shell Discloses End of U.S Bribery Probe Into Nigerian Oil Deal", *Wall Street Journal* (4 October 2019), www.wsj.com/articles/shell-discloses-end-of-u-s-bribery-probe-into-nigerian-oil-deal-11570209374.

67 US DOJ: Justice News, "JGC Corporation Resolves Foreign Corrupt Practices Act Investigation and Agrees to Pay a $218.8 Million Criminal Penalty" (6 April 2011), www.justice.gov/opa/pr/jgc-corporation-resolves-foreign-corrupt-practices-act-investigation-and-agrees-pay-2188; US DOJ: Justice News, "Snamprogetti Netherlands B.V. Resolves Foreign Corrupt Practices Act Investigation and Agrees to Pay $240 Million Criminal Penalty" (7 July 2010), www.justice.gov/ opa/pr/snamprogetti-netherlands-bv-resolves-foreign-corrupt-practices-act-investigation-and-agrees; US DOJ: Justice News, "Technip S.A. Resolves Foreign Corrupt Practices Act Investigation and Agrees to Pay $240 Million Criminal Penalty" (28 June 2010), www.justice.gov/opa/pr/technip-sa-resolves-foreign-corrupt-practices-act-investigation-and-agrees-pay-240-million; US DOJ: Justice News, "Kellogg Brown & Root LLC Pleads Guilty to Foreign Bribery Charges and Agrees to Pay $402 Million Criminal Fine" (11 Febuary 2009), www.justice.gov/opa/pr/kellogg-brown-root-llc-pleads-guilty-foreign-bribery-charges-and-agrees-pay-402-million.

and offers insights into how such situations might arise during the course of business activity.

There are many challenges to ensuring compliance in the oil and gas sector, including a potentially extensive and international supply chain, involvement of third parties, local customs, geopolitical issues, state involvement, offset obligations and a myriad of other bribery and corruption risks. Conducting pre-acquisition or third-party diligence may be complicated by poor record keeping or lack of publicly available information. Additionally, the assets or rights granted by the government may have been obtained by corruption. This concern is particularly relevant in regions where oil and gas assets are partially or entirely state owned (such assets are particularly prevalent outside of the United States and make up most or all of oil and gas assets in many emerging markets) and/or managed, and where oil regulators and other contracted – sometimes by directive – third parties are involved, which may all be arms of the same government entity.

Bribery and corruption risks can therefore arise in a broad variety of contexts, and – as described further below – it is imperative for a company to conduct periodic risk assessments and ongoing monitoring to identify the risk areas most pertinent to its business activities. This section is intended to provide an overview of some of the most common areas of corruption risk for companies operating in the oil and gas sector.

3.1 Third-party agents, consultants and other intermediaries

Risks posed by third parties – such as agents, consultants and other intermediaries working for or on a company's behalf – are the single largest area of potential bribery and corruption risk exposure. According to the OECD's most recent report on the involvement of third-party intermediaries in bribery cases, third parties were involved in three-quarters of the 427 foreign bribery cases concluded between 2014 and the entry into force of the OECD Anti-Bribery Convention in 1999.[68] In 41% of those cases, the relevant intermediaries were local agents, such as sales and marketing agents, brokers and distributors.[69] In 35% of those cases, the intermediaries were corporate vehicles such as subsidiary companies, local consulting firms, companies located in offshore financial centres or tax havens, or companies established under the beneficial ownership of a public official who received the bribes.[70] Moreover, as of late 2019, approximately 90% of all FCPA enforcement actions involved bribery

---

68 OECD, *OECD Foreign Bribery Report: An Analysis of the Crime of Bribery of Foreign Public Officials*, at 8 (2014), http://dx.doi.org/10.1787/9789264226616-en. Although the OECD publishes data on global bribery trends annually, the 2014 report contains the most recent comprehensive data on involvement of third parties in bribery cases.

69 *Ibid.*

70 *Ibid.*

schemes that involved third parties.[71] Further risk may arise in this regard where a given country has certain local content requirements, and funds intended to train local labour or develop local industries in order to satisfy local content requirements may in fact be used for other improper means.

Both the FCPA and UKBA expressly prohibit bribes or corrupt payments made through third parties or intermediaries. The FCPA expressly states that a corporate or individual may be held directly liable for bribes paid by a third party where the relevant corporate or individual knew that all or part of those payments would be directly or indirectly used to bribe a foreign official. In that context, 'knowledge' includes both "conscious disregard" and "deliberate ignorance".[72] Similarly, the UKBA expressly prohibits bribes made through third parties. Moreover, the UKBA makes a company liable for failing to prevent bribery committed by its 'associated persons', a term which includes those performing services for or on behalf of the company. Notably, the failure to prevent an offence does not require that the relevant corporate have had any knowledge of the relevant misconduct.

Third-party bribery risks arise in a broad variety of contexts, including as a consequence of the activities and conduct of local agents, freight forwarders and customer agents, and business consultants, as well as co-investors and joint venture partners (which may, in the oil and gas industry, be state-owned enterprises). To address third-party corruption risks, and as discussed in further detail in section 4 of this chapter, it is imperative that companies implement appropriate procedures – as described further below – to mitigate third-party risks. Such measures should include, in particular:

- robust due diligence of all third parties;
- ongoing monitoring and risk assessment; and
- adoption of appropriate contractual protections.

This section provides an overview of the key areas of third-party corruption risk in the oil and gas sector.

(a) Agents, consultants and other intermediaries

Third-party intermediaries can serve as conduits for improper payments by paying improper benefits (whether cash or in kind) to influential government officials or other commercial partners on behalf of a company (whether knowingly or unknowingly). Government enforcement actions have often focused on agreements between oil companies and technical experts who never rendered any legitimate service and were engaged for the sole purpose of

71 Stanford Law School, Foreign Corrupt Practices Act Clearinghouse, "Third Party Intermediaries", http://fcpa.stanford.edu/chart-intermediary.html.

72 See FCPA Resource Guide, *supra* note 9, at 23.

channelling funds indirectly to public officials in exchange for business. In many of these instances, the firms or individuals hired by oil companies were wholly unqualified to provide the services.

Companies should have procedures to investigate whether third parties are connected to, or otherwise owned or controlled by, government officials (eg, through direct ownership, ownership by a family member or close associate and so on). Such connections may increase the risk that the third parties may be misused to channel funds to government officials. Local companies and consulting agencies may have complex ownership structures or may be linked to a larger holding company whose beneficial ownership is unknown. Such structures can be a means to disguise government interests. Companies should also evaluate whether third parties lack a demonstrable track record or readily apparent expertise relating to the role or project for which they will be engaged. Companies therefore must take the necessary steps – such as conducting due diligence and carrying out politically exposed person (PEP) and reputational assessments – to better understand a potential third-party business partner and its operations.

(b) Joint ventures and consortiums

Companies in the oil and gas industry often operate through joint ventures or consortiums with other companies, foreign governments or state-owned entities. Such business structures present risks, as there may be considerable overlap between public and private functions. For example, joint venture agreements between oil companies and state-owned entities often allow the government to appoint senior-level directors to the joint venture's executive body and management teams, who in turn participate in high-level decision making on behalf of the entity. The involvement of public officials in such roles increases the level of risk associated with the commercial partnership. The grant of benefits to government officials, including board seats or a share of ownership, can be considered a relevant benefit under applicable anti-corruption laws.

Relevant company personnel and legal advisers should therefore carefully review all transaction documents forming any such private-public joint ventures to ensure that relevant protections are in place, that any benefits to government officials are justified and well understood, and that the company can exercise sufficient control over operations (eg, by allowing veto powers and requiring company approval of government-appointed directors).

3.2 Government interaction

Significant exposure to governmental authorities and government officials tends to raise an organisation's corruption risk profile. Not only does increased government interaction provide additional opportunities for corruption; but many countries – most notably, the United States – also apply harsher penalties for public sector corruption. Government exposure may arise in a variety of contexts, including when a company:

- depends heavily on local or central government licences, inspections, permits or other authorisations;
- derives substantial revenue from government customers;
- participates in public tenders; or
- frequently conducts contractual negotiations with public sector counterparties.

Cross-border trade and transportation of goods or services can also pose significant bribery risks, as border crossings provide an opportunity for customs officials to solicit improper payments. With respect to routine payments such as customs, companies must remember that although facilitation payments (ie, small payments made to expedite an existing official duty, such as customs clearance) are permitted by the FCPA, they are prohibited in almost all circumstances by most other anti-corruption laws, including the UKBA. As a matter of best practice, therefore, many companies elect to prohibit facilitation payments entirely.

When assessing a company's exposure to government entities and officials, it is also important to bear in mind that the scope of a 'foreign official' or 'government official' can, in most jurisdictions, be extremely broad. Under the FCPA, for example, a 'foreign official' includes: "[A]ny officer or employee of a foreign government or any department, agency, or instrumentality thereof, or of a public international organization, or any person acting in an official capacity for or on behalf of any such government or department, agency, or instrumentality, or for or on behalf of any such public international organization."

Although there is no definitive guidance on what constitutes an 'instrumentality' of a foreign government, the term has been broadly interpreted to include SOEs. The UKBA's definition of 'foreign public official' is similarly broad, extending to any individual who "exercises a public function". As such, a wide range of individuals may be considered to be within scope of relevant anti-bribery laws targeting government officials, including – with particular reference to the oil and gas industry – employees of state-owned or state-controlled entities such as national oil and gas companies and, of course, officials and employees of state energy ministries. Further key corruption risks specific to the oil and gas sector are set forth below.

(a) Bid and tender processes

Negotiating high-value licences, concessions, permits and other similar agreements that grant rights for companies to explore for and produce oil and gas presents a key corruption risk. In fact, the OECD Working Group on Bribery noted that more than half of foreign bribery cases involved the payment of a bribe for the specific purpose of obtaining a public procurement contract.[73] Such risk relates in large part to the significant number of organisations and entities in the extractives sector that are state owned or controlled.

In light of the above, purchasers of oil and gas assets, or of shares in a company that owns oil and gas assets, should exercise caution when participating in bidding and tender processes, particularly because such activities may involve non-transparent negotiations and contracts, as well as inadequate legislative and regulatory frameworks governing the public bidding, concessions and licensing processes. In recent years, irregularities stemming from public procurement-related wrongdoing have resulted in anti-corruption inquiries, enforcement actions and/or settlements involving the oil and gas industry. One notable example of this trend is French oil and gas company Total SA's 2013 resolution with the US DOJ and SEC. As part of its settlement with the US authorities, Total admitted to making approximately $60 million in bribe payments in order to induce an Iranian official who served as the chairman of a state-owned engineering company to secure a lucrative contract with Iran's national oil company.[74]

(b) *Government interactions during oil and gas extraction process*

Another primary corruption risk that companies operating in extractive industries face is the significant role that government actors and state-owned entities play in the oil and gas extraction process. Government involvement occurs at all stages of the process:

- awarding rights to drill;
- overseeing operations and approving certain activities;
- granting regulatory licences and conducting inspections; and
- frequently partnering with national oil companies in the operations themselves.

This comes as no surprise, given oil's status as a critical source of energy and revenue for numerous countries across the globe. Extensive dealings with government officials and state-owned entities enhance risk, due to the increased likelihood that officials will seek improper payments and benefits in exchange for regulatory approvals or otherwise abuse their official authority in order to threaten a company's business. Because these types of interactions occur at

73 See OECD *Foreign Bribery Report*, *supra* note 68.

74 US DOJ press release, "French Oil and Gas Company, Total S.A., Charged in the United States and France in Connection with an International Bribery Scheme" (29 May 2013), www.justice.gov/opa/pr/french-oil-and-gas-company-total-sa-charged-united-states-and-france-connection-international.

numerous stages of a typical oil and gas project, companies operating in the sector should take note of specific risks that arise during the course of such activity, including when in direct contact with state entities and when engaging in public procurement activity, among others.

(c) *Regulatory oversight*

The oil and gas sector is subject to significant regulation: oil and gas companies typically require a number of licences, permits and other authorisations to carry out their operations. Furthermore, as heavy industrial operators, where the risk of leak poses significant environmental and human risk, health, safety and environmental inspections are a frequent occurrence for most operations.

Navigating a foreign country's administrative and regulatory landscape can be time consuming and often requires local expertise, contacts and a sufficient amount of resources in order to ensure compliance with local and foreign legislation. For example, oil companies must secure and maintain various types of health and environmental safety certifications that involve frequent interaction with local inspectors and regulatory authorities in order to ensure that all operations and equipment comply with legislative requirements. At each stage, there is a risk that public officials may demand bribes in order to issue the necessary licence or certificate; or that an employee (or third party acting on the company's behalf) may be tempted to make a facilitation payment to speed up the process.

Occasionally, government officials are required to travel to inspect remote sites and may make other requests such as payment of improper or disproportionate expenses. Companies must be aware of these risks and take measures to mitigate the likelihood of wrongdoing (eg, drafting clear policies and procedures prohibiting bribery and governing expenses for high-risk interactions, and providing training, including enhanced training for employees who work directly with government officials).

(d) *Procurement risks*

Oil and gas operations rely on large-scale infrastructure projects, including drilling and fracturing technology, to carry out essential activity. This can be a challenge, as many companies operate in remote and difficult-to-reach locations that lack the resources and expertise that complex extraction efforts demand. Limited availability of local service providers and skilled labour often compels oil companies to hire local providers through single-source procurement procedures, rather than opening a competitive tender process.

While single-source procedures allow for flexibility as an exception to competitive tendering requirements, employees of oil and gas companies often use such mechanisms to fast track certain items and services without conducting sufficient due diligence or vetting vendors. In addition to assessing a vendor's qualifications, one must carefully identify the service provider's beneficial owners and connections to public officials and PEPs. As a result, expedited processes and vetting procedures that lack the proper levels of rigour and oversight create the potential for conflicts of interest, kickback schemes and other types of improper payment arrangements. Companies subject to UK jurisdiction should take particular note, because – unlike the FCPA – the UKBA criminalises private, commercial bribery, including situations in which a private person offers, promises or gives a financial or other advantage to another private person or entity (including through a third party).

In addition to the risks described above, large-scale infrastructure projects may easily permit parties to submit overpriced and inflated contracts or inaccurate cost estimates relating to the procurement of drilling equipment and the construction of oil platforms. In September 2017, the US DOJ and SEC alleged that senior executives at Brazil's state-owned energy company, Petrobras, inflated the cost of infrastructure projects by deliberately overpaying its largest contractors in order to pay kickbacks to Brazilian politicians.

(e) Payment risks

Oil and gas companies are frequently required to make payments to government agencies for licences, revenue sharing and other purposes. Companies should be on the alert for unusual and suspicious payment requests that may result in the misappropriation of a legitimate payment in the context of an oil concession renewal or even a simple payment to a local third-party service provider. For example, a government official may request the transfer of funds to an account that appears to belong to a governmental entity or agency (eg, similar name or acronym), but whose beneficial owner is actually the government official or a connected individual in his or her personal capacity. The DOJ recently issued an advisory opinion, concluding that it would not take any enforcement action where a company intended to pay a fee to a government-owned entity, but there was no indication that the funds would be diverted to any individual, and the company was paying for specific, legitimate services from the entity.[75] The opinion follows on from guidance in the FCPA Resource Guide cautioning that, while the FCPA prohibits corrupt payments to foreign officials and not to foreign governments, "companies contemplating contributions or donations to foreign governments should take steps to ensure that no monies are used for corrupt purposes, such as the personal benefit of individual foreign officials".[76]

Oil companies should endeavour to obtain documentation to verify the

75 FCPA Opinion Procedure Release 20-01 (14 August 2020), www.justice.gov/criminal-fraud/file/1304941/download.

76 FCPA Resource Guide, *supra* note 9, at 19.

ownership and legitimacy of any bank account into which they transfer funds, and document all efforts to vet payment information and reasons for payment. When vetting information, relevant accounting personnel should determine whether the owners of a bank account (and any entities associated with the account) are PEPs or influential individuals who present higher risk. Lastly, oil and gas company employees should escalate any suspicious or unusual payment requests made by government officials to designated company personnel (eg, company compliance officer, financial director, country operations director).

(f) Cross-border transportation of goods

The transportation of oil itself, as well as of drilling equipment in and out of oil fields, also carries significant corruption risk. Exposure for companies often occurs at 'checkpoints' in governmental processes and procedures, such as customs clearance processes, port fees and usage, and other situations that require government approval or discretionary decision making by public officials. For example, local freight forwarders and logistics providers may know customs officials personally and offer to navigate complex local legislation and contacts to facilitate the import and export of goods and items. Companies should exercise extra caution when hiring such service providers and regularly monitor the relationship over time, as the actions of such third parties could incur liability for the company.

Additionally, the customs clearance process often entails a significant amount of paperwork involving different customs codes, tariff rates and other fees such as storage and similar administrative charges whose justification may be difficult to decipher at first glance. Local employees of oil companies may be tempted to take advantage of these confusing documents to disguise kickbacks, improper payments or inflated fees, which they then funnel back to public officials in the form of bribes. Lastly, port authority officials in foreign countries sometimes demand additional port fees at a moment's notice, threatening to bar the entry or exit of any equipment and oil until the additional fees are paid. Avoiding these risks requires oil and gas companies to act proactively by implementing clear policies and practical guidance on how employees and company representatives should react in such situations to minimise exposure across operations.

3.3 Gifts, meals and corporate hospitality

Although there will in many cases be a legitimate business purpose for offering or providing gifts, meals and corporate hospitality (G&E) to third parties, the provision of such benefits can serve as a means for channelling improper payments where they are not reasonable, proportionate and *bona fide* business expenses. The FCPA and UKBA, as well as many other anti-corruption laws, do not prohibit G&E absolutely. However, when offered or given with the intention to influence a third party – particularly when offered to government officials or any other individuals with the power to make decisions that could influence the company's business – G&E can constitute a significant bribery risk.

While some countries have laws regarding G&E limits with respect to public officials, generally, there are no specified rules for determining the appropriateness of G&E. Small, token gifts of a nominal value may be acceptable, provided that they are not given with the intention to influence a third party. Improper G&E can go undetected, however, because it may at first appear legitimate. For example, offering a paid trip to a government official to inspect company equipment may be reasonable, particularly when required under local regulations; but not when the same company also provides airfare for the inspecting official's family members. Lavish and extravagant hospitality and gifts are also clear indications of improper advantages. In May 2015, the SEC found that global resources company BHP Billiton had violated the FCPA by failing to devise and maintain sufficient internal controls over its global hospitality programme, which enabled its employees to provide all-expenses-paid trips to government officials and their spouses to attend the 2008 Olympic Games in Beijing, China.[77]

Many local communities, however, have deep-rooted traditions and expectations relating to gifts and hospitality. What is a modest payment in a company's home jurisdiction could be a larger and more significant amount in a foreign country (eg, hiring a public official's family member for a part-time internship).[78] Furthermore, neither the FCPA nor most anti-corruption laws contain a minimum threshold amount for corrupt gifts or payments, which leaves room for interpretation regarding the subjective value of an advantage offered to a public official, as well as the context in which the act occurred.[79]

To mitigate such risks, companies should adopt anti-bribery procedures setting out thresholds for acceptable gifts, meals and corporate hospitality, together with robust approval requirements. In the context of an oil and gas transaction, robust pre-transaction due diligence should include consideration of a counterparty's gifts, meals and corporate hospitality controls, together with identification and analysis of any historical issues arising from this area of risk.

3.4 Corporate social responsibility, charitable donations and political contributions

Many companies, including in particular those that operate in developing markets, are increasingly developing charitable and corporate social

77 US SEC press release, "SEC Charges BHP Billiton with Violating FCPA at Olympic Games" (20 May 2015), www.sec.gov/news/pressrelease/2015-93.html.

78 See FCPA Resource Guide, *supra* note 9, at 16.

79 *Ibid.*

responsibility (CSR) programmes as a means of contributing to the welfare of the local communities in which they operate. CSR activities are often required under the terms of production sharing agreements and similar arrangements. While such activities and contractual requirements have laudable aims and honest intentions, there is also a risk that funds intended for CSR or charitable purposes may be corruptly misappropriated and not used for their intended purpose.

Political donations similarly are an area of significant corruption risk. Given their substantial reliance on government licences, permits and authorisations, companies operating in the oil and gas sector should have strict controls to review requests for political donations and provide employees with guidance on personal political donations. As discussed further in section 5 of this chapter, pre-transaction due diligence should assess the presence and adequacy of such controls, and historical risk should be managed through the inclusion of suitably drafted representations and warranties addressing the relevant counterparty's historical conduct.

3.5 Impacts of corruption risks

(a) Financial and reputational risks

Companies accused of corruption often suffer significant financial and reputational harm. Such companies typically must commit significant resources to investigate and remediate the root cause of the corruption and cooperate with and/or defend against government enforcement actions. These efforts require large teams of individuals – both inside and outside the company – and an immense amount of time and cost. The investigations may also involve one or more foreign jurisdictions, adding to both time and expense.

Enforcement actions may also result in the debarment or suspension of a company from being able to participate in public procurement or obtain government contracts. Companies may also find that their potential and existing business partners are reluctant to enter into or continue commercial relationships for fear of a repeat incident. Other impacts can be more subtle, but still significant. For example, research has shown that employee morale suffers where a company has been involved in significant misconduct, and that employees become more likely to engage in wrongdoing if even only one co-worker has a history of misconduct.[80]

80 Stephen Dimmock and William C Gerken, "Research: How One Bad Employee Can Corrupt a Whole Team", *Harvard Business Review* (5 March 2018), https://hbr.org/2018/03/research-how-one-bad-employee-can-corrupt-a-whole-team.

(b) Legal risks

Successor liability: Purchasers of oil and gas assets can become liable for corruption-related issues when assuming the liabilities of a predecessor or target company. This principle – known as successor liability – may apply where a purchaser acquires an asset or merges with another company with pre-existing criminal liabilities. While asset deals minimise successor liability risks in some contexts, because of the nature of oil and gas exploration and production rights, a bribe paid to secure rights may taint future revenue and profits earned under those drilling rights, even if they are bought and sold in subsequent years.

To mitigate against the risk of successor liability, adequate due diligence is critical to detect red flags or potential indicators of misconduct. Where red flags are detected, the company should follow up. To the extent that misconduct is detected, the company should seek to ensure that it ceases such misconduct either prior to investment or as soon as reasonably possible post-investment. In addition to conducting robust due diligence to identify and remediate pre-acquisition misconduct, companies may need to consider disclosing to relevant government authorities misconduct by the acquisition target that occurred prior to an acquisition or merger in order to mitigate their own liability post-acquisition.

Government authorities – such as the US DOJ and SEC, as well as the UK SFO – will often reduce penalties for companies that voluntarily disclose and remediate conduct discovered during the acquisition process and have rewarded such behaviour by declining to commence enforcement actions.[81] On the other hand, enforcement authorities will be more likely to take action against successor companies that concealed prior issues of corruption, or that directly participated in ongoing violations or otherwise failed to stop wrongdoing post-acquisition. In *SEC v El Paso Corp* the SEC alleged that Texas-based El Paso Corporation's predecessor in interest, Coastal Corporation, indirectly paid nearly $5.5 million in illegal surcharges to Iraq in connection with its purchases of crude oil from third parties under the United Nations Oil for Food Programme. The SEC filed FCPA charges against El Paso as a successor company for continuing the kickback scheme that Coastal Corporation had initiated prior to the acquisition.[82]

Proceeds of corruption: Corruption is a 'predicate offence' to money laundering under the laws of most countries globally, including the United States and the United Kingdom.[83] This means that dealing with the proceeds of

---

81 See FCPA Resource Guide, *supra* note 9, at 30.

82 Complaint, *SEC v El Paso Corp*, No 07-cv-899 (SDNY 7 February 2007), ECF No. 1.

83 Financial Action Task Force (FATF), *Mutual Evaluation Report on the United States*, ¶ 38 (December 2016), www.fatf-gafi.org/media/fatf/documents/reports/mer4/MER-United-States-2016.pdf; Financial Action Task Force (FATF), *Mutual Evaluation Report on the United Kingdom*, ¶ 44 (December 2018), www.fatf-gafi.org/media/fatf/documents/reports/mer4/MER-United-Kingdom-2018.pdf.

corruption could subject a company to liability under applicable money-laundering laws, or lead to the seizure and confiscation of assets obtained as a result of corruption. Direct proceeds of corruption include funds received as a result of a bribe. Anti-money laundering legislation often allows law enforcement authorities to confiscate any ill-gotten proceeds that have been intermingled with property acquired from legitimate sources (up to the assessed value of the intermingled proceeds), as well as income or other benefits derived from such proceeds of crime.[84] This further supports companies' need to conduct robust due diligence to determine whether any aspect of a business may have been acquired through corruption – such as the licence to operate or lucrative supply contracts.

4. Mitigating corruption risks that arise in the oil and gas context

There are a number of ways that companies can mitigate risks in their business. According to both FCPA and UKBA guidance, the hallmarks of an effective compliance programme include:

- a commitment from senior and middle management;
- well-designed compliance policies and procedures;
- oversight for the compliance programme by employees with sufficient seniority, experience and resources;
- risk assessments assessing the nature and extent of exposure to bribery risk;
- regular employee training;
- incentives and disciplinary measures; and
- third-party due diligence, and monitoring and review.[85]

There are a number of ways in which companies can mitigate risks in their business. This section summarises the key factors affecting transactional protections to mitigate corruption risks in the oil and gas context. These include:

- ensuring that companies have adequate policies and procedures to govern employee conduct;
- conducting risk assessments and pre-investment due diligence to evaluate inherent risks and red flags; and
- incorporating contractual protections into transaction documents, in line with risks identified during due diligence.

---

84 UK Proceeds of Crime Act of 2002 c 29, www.legislation.gov.uk/ukpga/2002/29/contents; US Money Laundering Control Act of 1986, 18 USC § 1956, www.congress.gov/bill/99th-congress/house-bill/5077; US Bank Secrecy Act of 1970, 31 USC§ 5311, www.occ.treas.gov/topics/supervision-and-examination/bsa/index-bsa.html; FATF, *Financial Action Task Force Recommendations 2012* (as amended June 2019), Recommendation 3, www.fatf-gafi.org/publications/fatfrecommendations/documents/fatf-recommendations.html.

85 See FCPA Resource Guide, *supra* note 9; *see also* Ministry of Justice guidance, *supra* note 49.

4.1 Policies and procedures

Companies operating in the oil and gas sector must ensure that they have adequate policies and procedures to address the risk of employees and other associated persons engaging in corrupt activity on behalf of the company.[86]

While individual policies and procedures will necessarily vary and be tailored to each company's specific risk profile, FCPA and UKBA guidance suggests that compliance programmes should include a clearly articulated policy broadly prohibiting corruption and setting out conduct expectations.[87] Depending on where the target is located, local regulations may also require the implementation of an anti-corruption compliance programme.[88] Key points for a compliance programme and related policies to address include responsibilities for oversight, conflicts of interest, facilitation payments, reporting or whistleblowing, anti-retaliation and consequences of failure to comply. Oil and gas companies should also provide guidance, either as part of their anti-corruption policy or as a standalone document, regarding acquisition and third-party risk management, travel, gifts and entertainment, charitable and political donations, events and sponsorships, and the submission and approval process for these expenses.

They should also train their employees – particularly in sales, procurement, finance, management and similar positions – on the application of written policies and procedures, and refresh that training periodically. Another integral aspect of a compliance programme is monitoring, which may include periodic audits or check-ins – both internally and of third parties – to assess whether compliance policies and procedures are implemented as designed. Companies should similarly evaluate the compliance programmes of target companies, and potentially third parties such as agents, when assessing risks and mitigants (discussed further below).

4.2 Pre-diligence risk assessment

One of the primary means to mitigate risk in the oil and gas context is to conduct adequate due diligence prior to the transaction to identify inherent risk factors, and any historical or ongoing issues that may pose potential liability to the target or the buyer. Companies should leverage information collected during commercial due diligence, in addition to publicly available information such as news media, blogs and the target's website, to identify risks and red flags.

---

86 *Ibid.*

87 *Ibid.*

88 See, for example, the Transparency, Anticorruption and Economic Modernisation Act n° 2016-1691 (9 December 2016), www.cjoint.com/doc/16_12/FLknuHuFltM_loisapin2.pdf.

(a) Inherent risk factors

As discussed in further detail above, key inherent factors to consider during a pre-acquisition due diligence include:

- whether the target is located or operates in emerging markets, which can indicate enhanced inherent risk of corruption;
- whether the target has significant government touchpoints; and
- whether the target places significant reliance on third parties such as agents, consultants and other intermediaries for conduct of its business.[89]

Where an investment is located helps to inform the types of corruption risks that are typical in that country. It is also advisable to evaluate which government officials within the country have the power to influence decisions relating to the transaction, such as the award of contracts, permits or licences; and be alert to indications that such government officials may be involved in the transaction, such as through ownership of a joint venture partner or key contractor. The target may also need to remove or recuse employees who may be considered government officials, depending on local 'cooling-off' restrictions.[90] An investor may ask the target to confirm in representations and warranties that there are no government officials employed by the target, or to disclose any such government connections. Other relevant protections include:

- representations that the target maintains accurate books and records;
- covenants regarding policies and procedures governing government interactions; and
- indemnities regarding government enforcement actions.

Investors should be alert to any indication that the original award of rights or assets was obtained by corruption. If there are high inherent risks or concerns that there may have been historical corruption, the transaction documents should address the risk and consider extending the lookback period for the representations and warranties to the asset's origin.[91]

In the case of third parties, the target should evaluate the role(s) that any third parties play and whether they have powers to act on behalf of and bind the target, which typically enhances risk. If the third party makes payments on behalf of the target, the target should confirm that the third party is subject to either internal controls or the target's own controls to prevent improper

---

89 Although sanctions considerations are not within the scope of this chapter, parties should also be cognisant of the impact of trade and economic sanctions on operations in the oil and gas sector, which is frequently is the target for both list-based and sectoral sanctions imposed by the United States, European Union and others.

90 See, for example, 18 USC § 207, www.oge.gov/Web/oge.nsf/Resources/18+USC+%C2%A7+207:++Restrictions+on+former+officers,+employees,+and+elected+officials+of+the+executive+and+legislative+branches

91 The FCPA has a five-year statute of limitations for the criminal provisions and a six-year statute of limitations for the accounting provisions. The UKBA does not have a statute of limitations.

payments. In the event that the target cannot reconcile payments made by a third party, the target may need to consider contract termination. The buyer can mitigate third-party red flags by including representations and warranties regarding third-party payments, covenants regarding third-party due diligence and/or veto rights over third-party agreements.

4.3 Risk-based anti-corruption due diligence

The purpose of pre-transaction due diligence is to determine the nature and extent of mitigating measures that will be required to proceed, including documentary protections. While the pre-transaction risk assessment provides a baseline of the initial inherent risks and red flags which require further examination, due diligence is an evolving process that may uncover further issues that require the initial risk assessment to be updated and further due diligence and mitigation measures to be applied. Typical due diligence steps will include database searches and source intelligence, document and information requests, and third-party due diligence.

(a) Public database searches and source intelligence

Public records and reputational searches can provide market intelligence on the target, any subsidiaries or affiliates within the transaction scope, and key personnel. For transactions involving assets, source intelligence can help to confirm an asset's origin and ownership.

A third-party vendor may also conduct transaction testing or asset tracing. Transaction testing or a forensic audit can confirm whether internal controls are effective in enforcing policies and preventing fraud. If the target is unwilling or unable to provide the amount of access required to conduct such testing, transaction testing may be incorporated into transaction documents as a condition precedent to closing or a post-closing covenant to be completed within a set time period.

(b) Document and information requests

Requests sent to the target generally seek to understand the nature and extent of the target's government interactions and use of third parties, historical issues and compliance programme. These requests may take the form of written questions, document requests and/or management interviews. The scope of such requests should be based on the results of the initial public research and due diligence information provided by the target.

The target's compliance programme is relevant to assessing the internal controls that are in place to manage the target's risk profile. Consider the following questions when evaluating the target's compliance programme:

- Does target management demonstrate a commitment to compliance and provide a 'tone from the top'?

- Has the target conducted a risk assessment to tailor policies and procedures to specific applicable corruption risks?
- Does the programme have sufficient staffing and funding relative to the target's risk level and size? If the programme lacks internal personnel, does it have the resources to engage assistance such as outside counsel, accountants or consultants?
- Does the target provide training for employees, including additional training for employees in higher-risk roles?
- Does the programme track and monitor gifts, travel and entertainment expenses?
- Does the target manage third-party risk effectively?
- Are there pending or ongoing investigations, either internal or governmental, that will require additional resources in the future, or that will pose financial or reputational risk?
- How were known or alleged historical issues addressed and remediated?[92]

(c) *Third-party due diligence*

Due diligence may also extend to key third parties and require the company to assess the third party's internal controls. Examples of key third parties include exclusive distributors in high-risk geographies, consultants and lobbyists, joint venture partners, major suppliers and downstream purchasers.

All third-party agreements should be in writing and contain representations regarding the third party's anti-corruption compliance, accurate books and records, and the target's audit rights. Where commercially feasible, third-party agreements – particularly joint venture agreements – should contain representations that the third party will institute and maintain sufficient compliance policies and procedures.

Consider the following questions when evaluating the target's third-party relationships:

- Do distributors in high-risk geographies take any steps to prevent sales to restricted parties or geographies subject to sanctions?

---

92 Purchasers should assess:
- the credibility and timing of any allegations;
- the results of any investigations;
- the sufficiency of remediation conducted or disciplinary action taken by the target to date; and
- the likelihood of enforcement and successor liability.

If there is any likelihood of enforcement or successor liability, the transaction documents should clearly define who will bear the costs of the target's internal investigation, defence against enforcement and any penalties or damages. Additionally, if due diligence uncovers significant concerns, the company must determine:
- whether it is commercially reasonable for the target to address and remediate the issues prior to closing;
- whether the company is willing to accept the risk of potential successor liability and the cost of remediation; and
- how the transaction documents can address these points.

- Do consultants and lobbyists who are interacting with foreign governments on the target's behalf adhere to policies regarding gifts, entertainment and political and charitable contributions?
- Did the company conduct anti-bribery and corruption diligence its joint venture partners? Does the company conduct and renew restricted party screening of its suppliers and purchasers?
- If any of these parties is subcontracting the company's business, are the subcontractors held to the same compliance standards?

4.4 Transaction documents

The inclusion of robust representations, warranties and undertakings in transaction documents is a core component of mitigating risk. It is particularly important in relation to transactions in the oil and gas sector, however, given the inherent corruption risks posed by operations in extractive industries. When implemented in conjunction with robust pre-transaction due diligence, appropriately drafted representations and warranties can provide a buyer with comfort in relation to the target's historical conduct and approach to anti-corruption compliance. Likewise, effective use of forward-looking covenants can effectively mitigate forward-looking risk, both by compelling a counterparty to take certain steps to remediate identified historical risks or deficiencies in its compliance programme and by establishing a framework for future anti-corruption compliance. Such provisions should, where possible and subject to commercial considerations, be underpinned by a suitably broad indemnity that appropriately covers historical and ongoing liabilities.

Ultimately, the precise nature, scope and extent of anti-corruption compliance provisions will depend on the buyer's assessment of the target's inherent risks and any red flags identified during pre-transaction due diligence. Below is an overview of the various types of provisions that parties typically seek to include to address corruption risks in oil and gas transactions.

(a) Lookback periods

Representations and warranties in oil and gas deals may require longer lookback periods than other provisions in the agreement because of the relevance of the origin and ownership of assets, particularly if those assets were obtained as a result of a government award or tender. Where agreements include representations and warranties that the seller's historical conduct was in compliance with the FCPA, the UKBA and any other applicable anti-corruption laws, those provisions should typically cover a period of at least five years (the statute of limitations for offences under the FCPA). But depending on the asset's inherent risk profile, the relevant time period for those representations may need to reach back to the asset's origins. In that regard, it is important to note that the UKBA, among other anti-corruption laws, does not have a statute of limitations.

(b) *Representations and warranties*

Transaction documents typically should include representations and warranties addressing the following risk areas:

- compliance with applicable anti-corruption laws by the target, its affiliates (ie, subsidiaries and other group companies, as well as joint venture partners) and other related parties (ie, officers, directors, employees and third-party intermediaries such as agents, consultants and distributors). The representations should be drafted with reference to a suitably broad definition of 'applicable anti-corruption laws', which should encompass all laws potentially applicable to the target's business, as well as that of its affiliates and other related parties;
- confirmation that the target has no knowledge of pending or threatened government investigations or allegations of suspected corruption-related misconduct;
- confirmation that the target, its affiliates and related third parties have not historically:
  - conducted any internal investigation; or
  - made a disclosure (whether voluntary or involuntarily) regarding corruption-related misconduct;
- confirmation that the target and its affiliates have maintained accurate books and records in line with appropriate financial reporting standards or generally accepted accounting principles;
- confirmation that, save as otherwise disclosed in the transaction documents, none of the target's officers, directors or shareholders with a shareholding of at least 25% in the target or its affiliates is, or was previously, a government official; and
- confirmation that the target and its affiliates have and maintain effective anti-corruption policies, procedures, systems and controls (if the target is unable to give this representation, the transaction documents should ideally contain a covenant requiring it to implement an anti-corruption compliance programme – see below).

(c) *Covenants*

Depending on the risks posed by the target and the degree of control that the buyer will have post-closing, it may be appropriate to include in the transaction documents a range of forward-looking covenants. Such provisions may include the following:

- A covenant may be included requiring the target, its affiliates and related parties (when acting for or on the target's behalf) to conduct the target's business ethically and in compliance with all applicable anti-corruption laws.
- If the buyer is unable to complete certain due diligence steps prior to

closing, whether due to commercial or time constraints, the parties should consider including a covenant requiring supplemental due diligence or transaction testing to be completed in a timely manner after closing.

- Remediation steps may be required to close any gaps identified in the target's compliance programme during pre-closing due diligence or to integrate the acquired asset into an existing compliance programme.
- To the extent that an issue was discovered during due diligence and the parties were unable to resolve it prior to closing, the parties may elect to include provisions for investigation and closure or disclosure to relevant governmental authorities following closing. In such circumstances, the buyer should look to ensure that relevant indemnification provisions (discussed further below) entitle it to recover any costs or losses arising from the relevant pre-closing misconduct.
- Provision may be made for risk assessments or audits to be conducted on an ongoing, periodic basis after closing to identify compliance areas that may require additional attention or remediation, and to require ongoing monitoring and audit of anti-corruption risks to proactively address new issues. In non-control scenarios, a buyer may require the target to periodically provide a compliance certification and/or complete a compliance due diligence questionnaire as part of its ongoing monitoring efforts.
- Particularly in non-control scenarios, a covenant may be included requiring the target to notify the buyer of any material changes to the target's (or its affiliates' and/or related parties') compliance with applicable anti-corruption laws, including details of any investigation or proceedings instigated by a governmental authority and any material allegations of suspected misconduct. Any such clause should provide the buyer with an appropriate degree of access to relevant books and records, as well as the target's employees. It should also make clear who will be responsible for the costs of such inquiries.
- Other covenants may include veto rights on key decisions (eg, material contracts or transactions, the payment of dividends or alteration of the business plan), and the right to appoint or approve board members (or observers) or executives charged with certain key control functions.

(d) Risk allocation and indemnification

In many SPAs, anti-corruption provisions may fall within the scope of the agreement's general provisions addressing indemnification and limitation of liability. If so, the buyer should verify this and ensure that the general indemnification/liability clauses are drafted to appropriately address identified historical risks. However, parties will often include specific indemnity provisions addressing anti-corruption issues, particularly where pre-closing due diligence has identified significant corruption-related concerns that might result in liability for the buyer. In these circumstances, transaction documents in both control and non-control deals should include specific provisions regarding any historical issues that were identified during the due diligence process to resolve indemnification, exemption and limitation of liability issues *ex ante*. Any indemnification caps should ideally be sufficient to cover the costs of a corruption investigation, related outside counsel costs and remediation measures. Where such historical issues are identified, the buyer may also need to request and review relevant insurance coverage (and exclusions) during due diligence.

Tax aspects of oil and gas mergers and acquisitions

Paul White
Druces LLP

1. Introduction

The primary purposes of the tax provisions in an M&A transaction are to allocate liability and benefits in respect of expected taxes and reliefs, and to share the risk of unexpected tax charges between the seller and purchaser. Where the sale of an oil and gas business is concerned, the basis of taxation and the availability of tax benefits may be significantly different from other businesses, but the overarching objective of the tax provisions remains the same.

As discussed further below, the tax risks for a purchaser of shares are significantly greater than for a purchaser of assets or of a business as a going concern. Accordingly, the tax elements of a share deal – from initial due diligence through drafting and negotiation to completion – are likely to be greater and more time consuming than for an asset transaction.

When drafting and negotiating tax warranties and indemnities, the purchaser's tax counsel must contemplate all probable and possible tax scenarios by reference to the target's current and past tax status; whereas the seller's tax counsel will be expected to advise on the tax consequences of the disposal and to ensure that the documentation supports the intended treatment. Consequently, tax counsel for both parties will want to know more about the target, and the seller's group, than may seem necessary to the non-tax specialist.

2. Seller taxation

Early-stage oil and gas companies are characterised by high levels of long-term pre-trading investment and uncertain future viability. They are also likely to be subject to non-standard tax rules; in the United Kingdom, these include the ring-fence trade rules, supplementary charge and, in some cases, petroleum revenue tax and the onshore allowance regime. As a result, the tax profile of an oil and gas company may differ significantly from, say, a manufacturing business; this needs to be taken into account when documenting and negotiating M&A transactions.

The first consideration when planning the disposal of a UK oil and gas company is whether it has started to trade, because the company's tax position is likely to change significantly on the day that trading begins. Her Majesty's Revenue and Customs' (HMRC) view is that oil exploration by itself does not constitute a trade, and that a petroliferous trade does not begin until the decision is made to proceed with commercial development of a discovery that will lead to production. Usually, this will be no earlier than the date that the Department of Business, Energy and Industrial Strategy gives its approval for commercial development.

The pre-trading or exploration stage generally comprises the period between the licence being granted and the decision being made to develop the field. Most expenditure incurred in the exploration stage will be for the evaluation of the licence area and the drilling of exploration and appraisal wells. Accordingly, the majority of pre-trading expenditure will be capital in nature and any relief for tax purposes will be under the capital allowance regime. In the majority of cases, the only significant revenue expense before trading begins will be annual licence fees.

Although most pre-trading expenditure is likely to qualify for tax relief in one form or another, the benefits are delayed until the trade commences. Deductible revenue costs incurred in the seven years before a trade begins are treated as incurred on the day that the trade commences. Relief for capital expenditure is similarly delayed until trading starts.

So a pre-trading oil and gas target is likely to be in the unusual tax position of having a current liability to corporation tax on its interest income, but with the prospect of a high level of losses, comprising capital allowances and deductible expenses, immediately upon starting to trade.

Whether or not the trade has started will be relevant to the first question to be addressed on the disposal of any corporate business: should the company sell the business as a going concern or should the parent sell the company that carries on the business? In the latter case, this may be as simple as selling the existing subsidiary's shares; or, more likely, may include an element of pre-sale restructuring. Inevitably, these options have different tax consequences for the parties and, consequentially, carry different tax risks for the purchaser.

Outside the oil and gas industry, the received tax view is that the seller will usually prefer to sell the shares in a company and the purchaser will prefer to avoid exposure to the company's history by acquiring assets, unless the target has tax reliefs – for instance, carried-forward losses – that the purchaser wants to preserve for future use.

While the same is generally true in the UK oil and gas industry, the analysis is affected by particular aspects of the UK tax code. A potential significant difference for oil and gas companies is that the disposal of assets is a ring-fence transaction, whereas the disposal of shares is not. In addition, HMRC has recently indicated that on a sale of a company carrying on a ring-fenced trade, it would be "unusual for HMRC to take the view that there has been a major change in the nature or conduct of the trade"[1] which might otherwise prevent the use of pre-acquisition losses.

3. Pre-sale reorganisation

Oftentimes, a degree of pre-sale reorganisation will precede a share sale. As a minimum, assets that the selling group wants to retain may be transferred out of the target before it is sold, and other assets may be transferred in; or assets may be transferred from one or more group companies to a newly incorporated target. It is usually crucial to the economics of the disposal that the pre-sale reorganisation can be achieved without any increased tax liability for the group, so the restructuring steps should be carried out with one eye on the criteria for relief and the other on the anti-avoidance rules.

Even in a jurisdiction such as the United Kingdom, where some level of group taxation and group tax relief is available, it is unwise to assume tax neutrality for intra-group transfers undertaken in anticipation of the group relationship being broken upon the target's sale. Where negotiations for the sale have all but concluded before the intra-group transfer is made – perhaps because the selling group does not want to be faced with unwinding the transfers if the Department of Business, Energy and Industrial Strategy does not agree to the change of control – there may be a point at which the seller's group is broken, and tax neutrality lost, before the hive-down to the target is completed.

Although the primary concern will be corporate income taxation, the criteria for group relief from transfer taxes such as stamp duties and value added tax (VAT) are likely to be different and require separate consideration.

Until fairly recently, the possibility of a corporation tax de-grouping charge arising on the sale of a subsidiary was a major issue in the negotiation of share purchase agreements because the charge arose in the target on sale. Consequently, the purchaser would expect contractual recourse against the seller for the de-grouping charge that arose in the acquired target. But now any such charge generally arises in the seller by way of a notional increase in the sale proceeds; and even then, there should be no additional taxation if the disposal qualifies for the substantial shareholding exemption. Despite this, the purchaser may look to amend the standard tax warranties or, if there is one, tax covenant so that it expressly addresses unexpected tax consequences of the pre-sale reorganisation.

The substantial shareholding exemption was introduced as part of a legislative package to enhance the reputation of the UK tax regime as business friendly, by exempting from UK corporation tax the gain realised by corporate

1 *HMRC Oil Taxation Manual* 21069.

owners on the disposal of a UK or non-UK trading subsidiary. In 2014, access to the relief was extended significantly to make it especially favourable for early-stage oil and gas companies; and in Summer 2016, HMRC consulted on further relaxations to the criteria for the substantial shareholding exemption.

4. Substantial shareholding exemption

The substantial shareholding exemption is the capital gain element of the UK participation exemption that exempts from the charge to corporation tax the gain realised by a company on the sale of shares where the exemption qualifying criteria are met. The main requirements were significantly relaxed with effect from 1 April 2017 and are now broadly that:

- the selling company owns a substantial shareholding in the target for a continuous 12-month period beginning not more than six years before the day on which the target is sold; and
- the target is a trading company or a holding company of a trading group or trading sub-group from the start of that 12-month period.

Originally, the target also had to continue to be a trading company, or the holding company of a trading group or trading sub-group, immediately after the sale; but for disposals made on or after 1 April 2017, that further requirement applies only if either the seller and purchaser are connected or group trading assets have been transferred to the target in preparation for the sale (see below).

A 'substantial shareholding' means, for these purposes, a holding of at least 10% of the issued ordinary shares capital of the target which, in addition, entitles the selling company to at least 10% of the target's profits and, on a winding up, its assets.

At first sight, the trading requirements would appear to prevent pre-trading sales and pre-sale reorganisations qualifying for the substantial shareholding exemption, but the standard tests have been modified to benefit the oil and gas industry.

Since 2011, the substantial shareholding exemption may be available on the sale of a hive-down company (Newco) where:

- the transferred assets were owned and used by another group company for its trade;
- when Newco is sold, the assets are being used for the purposes of its trade; and
- the selling company has a substantial shareholding in Newco immediately before the sale.

If these criteria are satisfied, then when applying the tests for the substantial shareholding exemption, the selling company's period of ownership is extended by any time in the final 12-month period in which the transferor group company held the assets.

In addition, following HMRC's consultation on ways to support the UK oil and gas industry, the substantial shareholding exemption was extended to early-stage oil and gas companies by a new statutory interpretation of the word 'trade'. With effect from 1 April 2014, 'trade' – in relation to both the requirement for use by another group company and the target's use of the assets at the time of sale – is deemed to include oil and gas exploration and appraisal activity.

The effect of this is that the sale of the whole or part of a substantial shareholding in an exploration stage company that has not yet started to trade may nevertheless qualify for the substantial shareholding exemption because periods of exploration and appraisal are treated as qualifying periods of trading for the purposes of the exemption.

5. Reinvestment, or 'rollover', relief

In the case of an asset or business sale, the selling group may be able to shelter some or all of any chargeable gain realised on the disposal with losses, or to defer the charge to tax by claiming rollover relief. However, the net chargeable gains in any period from the sale of oilfield interests or other assets used in relation to the field are generally ring-fenced from other losses, with a more restricted regime of shelter than applies outside the oil and gas arena.

Rollover relief generally allows a trading company to reinvest the whole or part of the proceeds from the sale of specified classes of assets in other qualifying assets, with the effect that the taxation of any gain on the disposal is held over until the disposal of the replacement assets or any further rollover assets.

The general rollover rules are extensively amended in their application to the disposal of interests in UK continental shelf oilfields and business assets used in connection with oilfields in relation to ring-fence corporation tax and the supplementary charge. Specific provisions provide that in some cases where rollover relief would otherwise be available, the selling company may instead claim 'reinvestment relief' which exempts the gain from tax.

Relief may be claimed where proceeds of an interest in an oilfield are reinvested by the selling company or a group company in assets for the ring-fenced trade from one year before to three years after the disposal. Furthermore, the incurring of exploration, appraisal and development expenditure in the course of a ring-fenced trade can also qualify to be treated as the acquisition of oil assets for the purposes of the rollover rules.

The package of measures that extended the substantial shareholding exemption to pre-trading oil and gas companies in 2014 similarly extended the availability of rollover relief to companies that are carrying on oil and gas exploration and appraisal in the United Kingdom or an area of the UK continental shelf, but that have not yet commenced a ring-fenced trade. Consequently, pre-trading exploration companies now have the opportunity to claim reinvestment relief when making a disposal and acquisition in the course of UK (including continental shelf) oil and gas exploration and appraisal activities.

6. Transferable tax history

On cessation of production, the costs of decommissioning are likely to produce allowable tax losses which are fully relievable only if carried back against prior period profits. Historically, the risk that a purchaser of late-life assets would find its ability to utilise decommissioning relief limited by reference to its post-acquisition profits added to the complexity of late-life assets deals and made company purchases more likely.

However, for licence transfers since 1 November 2018, the buyer and seller may jointly elect for an element of the seller's tax history to be transferred to the purchaser. The consequence for the purchaser is that pre-acquisition profits of the seller are available as 'transferable tax history' to provide relief for the excess decommissioning costs of the purchaser.

7. Non-UK seller

Generally, a company that has been incorporated outside the United Kingdom is subject to UK corporation tax on its worldwide profits, including capital gains, only if it has become tax resident in the United Kingdom by virtue of being centrally managed and controlled from the United Kingdom. If the company is non-UK resident, but earns the income or uses the assets in the course of a trade carried on by a permanent establishment in that country, the profits of the UK business calculated on an arm's-length basis may be charged to corporation tax, depending on the effect of any applicable double tax treaty. A taxable permanent establishment usually consists of a branch, office or dependent agent that carries on the non-resident's trade on the mainland or in UK territorial waters. In addition, since April 2019, a non-UK resident may be charged tax on chargeable gains arising on certain direct and indirect disposals of UK land.

So, it is generally safe to assume that if a foreign company neither has a UK branch nor trades through a tied agent, it is not subject to UK tax on its non-UK land related capital assets; but that assumption should not be made where oil and gas companies are involved.

In relation to profits from activities and rights connected with the exploration or exploitation of the natural resources of the seabed and subsoil, the United Kingdom's taxing jurisdiction extends to its continental shelf. Profits that arise from such activities and/or rights are treated as profits arising in the

United Kingdom. Similarly, gains accruing on the disposal of exploration or exploitation rights in relation to the UK continental shelf are treated as gains accruing on the disposal of assets situated in the United Kingdom. Companies that are taxable under these provisions must file annual corporation tax returns and pay tax at the main rate of corporation tax and not the higher ring-fence rate.

More surprisingly, gains accruing on unquoted shares that derive the whole or greater part of their value from such oil and gas assets are similarly deemed to accrue on the disposal of assets situated in the United Kingdom. These deeming provisions raise the prospect that what appears to be a foreign gain on, say, the disposal by a non-UK company of a subsidiary that operates in the North Sea would be a gain under the UK corporation taxes legislation.

Under the general UK tax regime, such a gain would not be taxable because the selling company would be outside the UK tax net on the disposal; but the chargeable gains tax regime is specifically extended to impose a liability in such circumstances.

Governments rarely seek to tax capital gains that arise to overseas companies without a business presence in their jurisdiction, partly because of the difficulty of tax collection. When they do so, collection is most easily achieved by way of a withholding obligation, but that works only if the payer is in the taxing jurisdiction. Alternatively, a secondary liability may be imposed on another party within the taxing jurisdiction, which is what the United Kingdom has done where the tax relates to a UK continental shelf licence.

The legislation includes provisions to overcome the information and collection difficulties that may arise through the extension of the charge to non-residents that may have no physical presence in the United Kingdom. HMRC will seek such information from an exploration or production licensee about transactions connected with its licence areas (eg, payments to contractors and their subcontractors) that may give rise to tax liabilities. Unpaid tax assessed on a non-resident under those provisions may be recovered from the relevant licensee. If any tax payable by the non-resident is not paid within 30 days of the due date, a tax inspector may require the licence holder to pay the tax within a further 30 days.

Where the oil business disposal is structured as a share sale, the purchaser may be protected from this type of secondary liability by general tax indemnities, but a standard asset or business purchase agreement would be unlikely to afford the purchaser a similar level of protection. Accordingly, it will be necessarily to include specific indemnification and perhaps to consider an escrow deposit where there are credit concerns about the selling group.

Where a non-UK party is involved in a taxable UK transaction, it is important to consider whether the applicable double taxation treaty limits the application of the UK rules. In relation to oil and gas mergers and acquisitions, a particular point will be whether the treaty meaning of 'United Kingdom' is the same as the United Kingdom's extended statutory definition for oil and gas companies.

Many UK treaties will preserve the United Kingdom's right to tax the income and gains of its permanent establishments, but it is important always to check the actual terms. UK treaties may be divided into three broad categories. First, some treaties apply a restricted definition of the 'United Kingdom' that excludes the continental shelf. Secondly, some use an extended definition that includes the continental shelf, but do not have an offshore activities article that deems certain offshore activities to be carried on through a UK permanent establishment. Thirdly, some are similar to the second category, but have an offshore activities article.

8. Purchaser taxation

By buying all, or the majority of, the shares in a company, the purchaser becomes exposed to the current and future tax consequences of the company's past acts and omissions. Almost always, the purchaser will seek protection against unexpected tax charges that arise as a consequence of pre-acquisition events through a combination of contractual tax warranties and indemnity covenants. The purchaser of an oil and gas company is no different, although, as explained below, there may be circumstances in which the seller resists giving a tax covenant.

In addition, where the availability of certain tax assets has been taken into account in the valuation of the target, the seller may be liable to the purchaser by way of an adjustment to the calculation of the purchase price, instead of the indemnities, if it transpires that those tax assets were not available. While this is conceptually straightforward, it can be challenging to find a form of words that satisfies both parties. The seller will not want to be liable if any act of the purchaser resulted in the shortfall or for any failure by the target to use the losses; whereas the purchaser, having paid for the losses, will want a refund to the extent that they are not available to use as expected.

9. Asset purchase agreement

The tax provisions in an asset purchase agreement are typically significantly simpler, and shorter, than those in a share purchase agreement. There is less warranty/indemnity protection for the purchaser, because assets do not generally carry historic tax risk. The purchaser should consider, however, whether an indemnity for secondary tax liabilities is appropriate, as discussed under section 7 above.

Both parties will want to be sure that they enjoy complementary tax treatments for the sale and purchase of the assets, so while there may be debate about the figures, the drafting is unlikely to prove contentious.

Arguably the most important tax drafting in an asset purchase agreement is the allocation of the consideration between:

- the various assets which, unless challenged by HMRC, determines the disposal proceeds to be brought into account by the seller; and
- any potentially taxable gains, and the purchaser's expenditure which it expects to qualify for capital allowances.

The petroleum revenue tax regime includes lengthy provisions in relation to the transfer of the ownership of determined fields and interests in fields. The rules' general intention is to allow the purchaser to take over the same position in relation to petroleum revenue tax as the seller held before the transfer. HMRC guidance says that the purchaser "inherits the field history of" the seller, but warns that it "does not necessarily follow that the tax paid by [the parties] will be the same as would have been the case had there been no transfer".[2]

Typical asset purchase agreement drafting will require the parties to give the necessary notice to HMRC within the statutory time period and not to opt out of the regime. The drafting of the statutory rules has been subject to some criticism and one of the benefits of a share purchase for an oil and gas business is that the statutory apportionment rules for petroleum revenue tax are not brought into play.

However, as time has gone by, the significance of these provisions has reduced. Petroleum revenue tax is charged only on profits from taxable fields that were approved before 16 March 1993; and in its 2014 Autumn Statement, the UK government published the conclusions of Her Majesty's Treasury review of the oil and gas fiscal regime in *Driving Investment: A Plan to Reform the Oil and Gas Fiscal Regime*. The review concluded that the government should consider reducing the rate of petroleum revenue tax, when fiscal conditions allow, both:

- to level the playing field between investment opportunities in areas that are subject to the tax and opportunities in other fields; and
- to ensure that key assets attract the right level of investment.

A reduction in the rate of petroleum revenue tax from 50% to 35% was announced in the Budget 2015, and the Budget 2016 reduced the rate to 0% for chargeable periods ending after 31 December 2015.

Asset purchase agreement drafting for VAT typically follows a similar approach of ensuring that seller and purchaser adopt matched filing positions. The disposal of a licence within the 12-mile limit is generally viewed as a supply relating to land. But in most cases, the parties will expect the sale to qualify as the transfer of a business, or part of a business, as a going concern, and therefore as a supply of neither goods nor services for VAT purposes. If a purchase is not

2 *HMRC Oil Taxation Manual* 18020.

a transfer as a going concern and the supply is within the United Kingdom, the purchaser must pay chargeable VAT in addition to the purchase price and fund it until it has reclaimed it in the normal course of business.

The VAT provisions on transfers as going concerns tend to be lengthy, but not contentious, because they do little more than:

- set out the criteria for the availability of treatment as such transfers;
- record that the parties believe that the transaction is a transfer as a going concern; and
- explain what is to happen if HMRC disagrees.

10. Share purchase agreement

The tax consequences and risks of selling, or buying, a business by means of the transfer of ownership of shares in the company that owns the business are generally significantly more complicated than those arising in a business sale. Accordingly, the tax provisions in a share purchase agreement are typically more extensive than in an asset purchase agreement, although UK model share purchase agreements for oil and gas companies sometimes include shorter tax provisions that one might expect to see in agreements for similar-sized businesses outside the oil and gas sector.

In particular, in an exploration stage sale, the seller may resist giving the purchaser the protection of a tax indemnity, or tax covenant, of the type usually seen in UK corporate acquisitions. This is discussed further below, but broadly the seller's argument is that the type of covenant used for the sale of a typical trading company is unnecessary verbiage for a pre-trading target. Even if a purchaser accepts this position, consideration should be given to whether there are parts of a typical tax covenant that should be included in the share purchase agreement, even if the indemnity element is missing.

An English law share purchase agreement typically includes three types of tax provision. The tax warranties and tax covenant are chiefly concerned with protecting the purchaser's investment, while the general commercial tax provisions broadly allocate transaction taxes between the parties.

10.1 Tax warranties

Typically, warranties under share purchase agreements are set out in a schedule to the main agreement and include a set of tax warranties that are 'given' by the seller at the time that the agreement is executed, and that the purchaser will want to have repeated at completion. The primary purpose of the tax warranties is to elicit information about the tax history and current tax status of the target company.

A non-UK transaction will include perhaps 20 or so tax warranties that address the tax position of the target in general terms, including warranties that the target:

- has duly and punctually paid all tax that it has become liable to pay;

- has properly withheld tax and accounted for it in accordance with applicable law;
- has within any applicable time limits made all returns and registrations, provided all information, maintained all records and given all notices and invoices in relation to tax as are required, and that all such returns, registrations, information, records, notices and invoices were and remain true, complete and accurate in all respects;
- is not, and is not expected to be, involved in any dispute in relation to tax and has not been the subject of a tax authority investigation other than under routine tax audit procedures;
- has duly submitted all claims, disclaimers, elections and applications that have been assumed to have been made for the purposes of the accounts or any tax return;
- has not benefited from any special arrangement in relation to its tax affairs;
- has not required any consent, direction or clearance from any tax authority for any act;
- is not contracted to make any payment outside its ordinary course of business and has not incurred any payment obligation to make any payment, other than any capital expenditure reflected in the accounts, which will not be wholly tax deductible;
- has not been involved in any scheme or arrangement, the main purpose, or one of the main purposes, of which was to avoid, reduce or defer tax;
- is not, and has never been, a member of a group for any tax purpose;
- has at all times been resident in, and only in, the territory in which it was incorporated and has never had a taxable permanent establishment in any other territory;
- has never claimed relief from tax under a double tax treaty; and
- has not, since the last accounting date, entered into any transaction that was not entered into in the ordinary course of business, and has never entered into any transaction in circumstances such that the consideration might be adjusted by any tax authority, whether as the result of the transfer pricing regulations or otherwise.

A UK transaction may have more than twice as many tax warranties, with the additional warranties referring to specific provisions of the UK tax code, although it is questionable whether that specificity adds significantly to a full set of general tax warranties. The tax warranties should be as wide in their application as possible. The intention is to oblige the seller to disclose any matters that conflict with the warranted statements, which enables the purchaser to reconsider the terms, including pricing, of the transaction and potentially protects the seller from liability for the disclosed events.

The purchaser's counsel may also propose additional transaction-specific warranties where either the due diligence process has revealed unusual circumstances relating to the target's tax history or the target is subject to a non-standard tax regime. In an oil and gas share purchase agreement, warranties may be added in relation to the target's ring-fence trade, its petroleum revenue tax status, its history of acquisition and disposal of capital assets, rollover relief and so on.

Because North Sea oil and gas companies are subject to ring-fence corporation tax, the supplementary charge and, potentially, petroleum revenue tax, it might be thought that these charges would require significant changes to standard M&A tax clauses; but that is not necessarily true. This is because standard tax protections for the purchaser are usually drafted in terms that will include all taxes. By way of example, while it would be common to add these taxes into the definition of 'taxes', it should not be necessary, provided that the list of taxes is merely illustrative. Similarly, the main tax warranties relate to compliance matters that are not specific to any one tax, and should be capable of applying in an international context where there may not be certainty about what foreign taxes are relevant.

Warranties are expressed to be 'given' by the seller because they are, in effect, promises about what has or has not happened in the history of the target and about its tax status as of the date that the warranties are given. If a warranty proves to have been untrue when given, the purchaser may be entitled to claim damages for breach of contract. The measure of damages should be calculated to compensate the purchaser for the diminution in value of its investment. In theory, the same analysis applies to the tax warranties; but in practice, damages may seldom be appropriate compensation for unexpected tax liabilities in the target, and the seller's liability for tax of the target should not cut off at completion, which are some of the reasons why the UK market has developed to include a tax covenant.

10.2 Tax covenant

The limited effectiveness of warranty protection in relation to post-completion tax liability and the inadequacy of damages to compensate for unexpected tax are usually addressed in UK-authored share purchase agreements by the inclusion of a tax covenant. It is frequently referred to as a 'tax indemnity' because the seller is obliged to compensate for indemnified tax on a dollar-for-dollar basis, but is actually documented as a 'covenant to pay'. This is because the receipt of an indemnity payment by a UK target would likely be taxable in its hands. This might not matter if the corresponding tax payment were deductible for corporation tax purposes; but because that is generally not the case, the target would not be made whole on an after-tax basis unless the payment were to be grossed up by the seller.

In order to avoid this tax inefficiency, the seller usually promises, or covenants, to pay a dollar-for-dollar compensatory amount to the purchaser, instead of the target, by way of adjustment to the share purchase price, under a tax covenant or tax deed. The tax covenant may be either a standalone document or a schedule to the share purchase agreement. The latter may be preferred where the seller is unfamiliar with UK M&A documentation; although the fact that increasingly often, the seller's counsel drafts the share purchase agreement, while the purchaser's counsel drafts the tax covenant, can result in the covenant being a separate document. If the tax covenant takes the form of a separate document, it will usually be executed as a deed. This avoids technical concerns as to whether the purchaser has given consideration for the covenants and extends the limitation period to 12 years, twice as long as for a simple contract.

Another key difference between a claim under the tax warranties and a claim under the tax covenant is that the English common law mitigation requirement that applies in relation to damages does not apply to an indemnity or covenant to pay. With this in mind, the seller may seek a contractual undertaking from the purchaser to procure that the target acts to mitigate any tax charge that may give rise to a claim under the covenant.

The core of the tax covenant is a short and very broad indemnity for tax arising in the target, after – as well as before – completion, in relation to pre-completion income or gains or as the result of pre-completion events, and to protect tax reliefs which have been taken into account in the pricing. That broad covenant is followed by, usually, much lengthier limitations on its operation and the purchaser's right to bring a claim.

The document will also typically include tax-related housekeeping provisions – for example:

- a claims notification clause that requires the claimant promptly to notify the seller after the claim is identified, together with details of the circumstances giving rise to the claim and an estimate of the amount due;
- a payment clause that specifies the due date for settlement of tax claims by reference to the date on which the indemnified tax is due or would have been saved where the non-availability of benefits is involved. As with the warranties, this clause may be adapted to reflect the tax payment dates for a ring-fence trade, but it is generally advisable to allow the general wording to pick up all possible payment obligations;
- a clause that records which party is responsible for the tax returns for the pre and immediately post-completion period, and the rights of the other party to participate in the preparation of those returns. Where there is a material period between exchange and completion, the seller may be subject to contractual limitations on what it may do and not do during that period, which may extend to tax matters;

- a conduct of tax disputes clause that generally gives the seller certain rights to direct, or even lead, the conduct of negotiations with the tax authority in relation to alleged liabilities for which the seller may be contractually liable to the purchaser; and
- a tax savings and refund provision that applies if the purchaser receives compensation for a tax liability from the seller and subsequently receives a related tax benefit such as a refund or credit against tax, or enjoys a pre-completion tax benefit that was not taken into account in the transaction pricing. The clause broadly requires an adjusting payment to be made by the purchaser so as to ensure that it does not retain a cash windfall.

Lastly, the seller may look to include a 'reverse indemnity' under which the purchaser agrees to indemnify the seller for certain secondary tax liabilities that may potentially be claimed against the seller's group as a consequence of the purchaser's conduct of the target after completion.

10.3 Limitations on seller's liability

The fact that the seller may be liable to compensate the purchaser for certain tax liabilities of the target both under the tax warranties and the tax covenant may suggest that the seller potentially has a double exposure. But often, the opposite is true in practice, because the interaction of various documented limitations may leave the purchaser with less protection against tax than it expected.

In theory, the limitations and procedural provisions in the tax covenant should apply to tax claims under both the covenant and for breach of the tax warranties. But where seller's counsel drafts the share purchase agreement and purchaser's counsel drafts the tax covenant, it can be a challenge to mesh potentially overlapping provisions to avoid them contradicting each other and thus the purchaser's protections being undermined. The share purchase agreement's general limitations are unlikely to distinguish between tax and non-tax claims, so the purchaser's counsel will be faced with having to modify them to prevent the purchaser's tax covenant protection being undermined. That process needs to cover several different aspects.

First, there are straightforward drafting distinctions that can usually be dealt with between the tax lawyers, the most obvious of which is that the cut-off period for all tax claims, whether under the warranties or the tax covenant, should be longer than that for non-tax claims. In the United Kingdom, the cut-off period is typically the seventh anniversary of completion.

Secondly, there are distinctions to be negotiated between the principals. The best example is that from the purchaser's perspective, the tax covenant claim, which is on a dollar-for-dollar basis, should arguably not be subject to the same financial hurdle and cap that apply to general warranty claims.

Thirdly, the 'house-keeping' provisions of the tax covenant – for instance, the claim notification and conduct of disputes provisions – need to apply to all tax claims, and tax should be excluded from the corresponding general provisions.

Lastly, some of the basic definitions in share purchase agreements may need to be revised; a typical example is the apparently simple term 'claim'. If the definition does not distinguish between tax and non-tax claims under the warranties and tax covenant, the term potentially limits the purchaser's protections without obviously appearing to do so. The agreement's limitations may say that a claim cannot be made in relation to any disclosed matter, or that the purchaser must take reasonable steps to mitigate the circumstances giving rise to any claim, neither of which a purchaser would expect to apply to tax matters.

In very broad terms, the overall intention of the tax covenant is that when the indemnity is read subject to the limitations, the seller should be liable to the purchaser only for unexpected taxation in the target and the non-availability of expected tax benefits, as the result of the target's pre-completion activities or the acts of the seller's group.

To achieve this, there may be two or three pages of limitations, but most will fall in one of several groups. The seller should not be liable for tax arising from:

- matters already taken into account in the calculation of the acquisition price. Usually, this roughly equates to the matters reflected in the target's accounts. From the purchaser's perspective, this should be narrower than matters disclosed, unless a disclosed matter has already resulted in a price adjustment;
- the voluntary acts of the target, as managed by the purchaser, after completion;
- the result of a change in law or HMRC practice after completion; or
- the ordinary course of the target's business between the date of the accounts and completion of the sale.

Because the tax covenant has been developed to protect the purchaser against historic tax charges and past acts, seller's counsel may argue that, in the case of an exploration stage sale, a covenant adds unneeded complexity. Broadly, they would argue, if the target has not even begun to trade, it cannot have historic tax exposure; and the current position could be adequately addressed in the tax warranties.

A purchaser that accepts this should consider whether the share purchase agreement needs to be amended to bring the consequences of a tax warranty breach closer to what would have been the case had there been a tax covenant – so, for example, whether the purchaser's claim should be dollar-for-dollar instead of the usual measure of damages, and whether any of the covenant housekeeping provisions need to be included.

This type of wholesale amendment can often prove more time consuming and therefore expensive than including a standard tax covenant and, where there is a tight timetable, can lead to documentation errors. The seller's argument is not that the purchaser should have any less protection, but only that a tax covenant is unnecessary for an early stage target. This, however, overlooks the reasons for the covenant and what it does in addition to the indemnity section. The purchaser might argue that the seller is not prejudiced by the inclusion of a tax covenant and transaction costs are likely to be increased by tinkering with the usual suite of transaction documents.

10.4 General tax provisions

The third category of share purchase agreement tax provisions comprises the general transaction tax clauses of the type found in most sophisticated commercial agreements. These provisions allocate the liability for certain expected, and unexpected, transaction charges between the parties.

The sale transaction itself may give rise to tax liabilities, the most obvious being stamp or registration taxes on the transfer of shares and, potentially, VAT on the consideration for the sale.

In foreign transactions, tax advice – and perhaps a formal opinion – should be sought from local counsel on the quantum of transaction taxes and which party is primarily liable under the relevant law. Although the parties may agree that all or part of the economic burden falls on a different party, most likely the party that pays the relevant tax will be the party that insisted on the transaction step that carries a tax charge that would otherwise fall on the other party.

This category typically includes provisions relating to the following issues:

- VAT: Given that the United Kingdom does not impose VAT on share transfers, the typical share purchase agreement clause seldom aims to do more than ensure that the party receiving a taxable supply pays the VAT in addition to the agreed consideration, and the supplier delivers an appropriate invoice.
- Stamp duties and registration taxes: The tax warranties usually address stamp duties chargeable on transactions undertaken by the target prior to completion, while this clause addresses duties on the transaction documents and share transfers. Usually, but not always, the purchaser will pay all these charges.
- Withholding taxes: The term 'withholding tax' refers to any tax that is collected by the payer deducting, or withholding, an amount on account of tax from any payment and then accounting for the amount withheld to the tax authority.

A taxable receipt is likely to be taxable in the country of source; but if that jurisdiction is uncertain about its ability to collect tax from the recipient, it may instead impose a payment obligation on the local payer. The payer will be required to deduct an amount of tax from the payment, effectively collecting the tax for the government on account of the payee's liability.

In commercial transactions, withholding taxes of this type are most common in relation to income streams paid cross-border; but they are not unheard of where capital is paid by instalments or even in relation to one-off capital payments.

In wholly UK transactions, the gross-up clause is often omitted, but its inclusion should always be considered where cross-border or periodic payments are concerned. Even when all parties are confident that no withholding tax applies to payments under a transaction, a typical tax lawyer will want to include a gross-up clause in case there is a change of law.

The basic mechanism of a gross-up clause is that, where a withholding is required, the amount due is increased by such amount as will, after all withholdings, leave the payee with the amount that it expected to receive. This may result in the payee enjoying a windfall if, for example, the withheld tax is reclaimed under a double tax treaty, so the payer should look to include a repayment obligation on the payee where a related tax credit is utilised.

11. International dimension

For the most part, this chapter is written from a UK perspective, highlighting aspects of the United Kingdom's oil and gas tax code that affect the tax structuring and the drafting of tax provisions that would otherwise typically apply in a UK business acquisition. However, it is appropriate to end with a warning about using the mores of the UK market in a non-UK context.

Although successive UK governments have tinkered with oil and gas taxation on almost an annual basis, the overall taxation of a UK oil and gas business is fairly certain; the published *HMRC Oil Taxation Manual* provides extensive guidance on how the rules are operated by the tax authority in practice; and the UK tax courts are generally not swayed by the political environment. As a result, the risks attached to M&A transactions in the UK oil and gas market are generally quantifiable. The same is not true of all jurisdictions where oil and gas transactions are common.

An important case on the operation of tax indemnities is the Court of Appeal decision in *Heritage Oil and Gas Ltd v Tullow Uganda Ltd* [2014] EWCA Civ 1048. For present purposes, the most significant aspect of the case is not the interpretation of the tax indemnity, but the manner in which the underlying tax liability arose.

The Ugandan government assessed the seller to tax of $434 million, which the seller disputed. As a result of the dispute, the government imposed conditions on its consent to the share purchase agreement – namely, that the seller pay all taxes accruing from the transaction as assessed by the Ugandan tax authority. The government was not satisfied by the manner in which the seller provided security for the assessed tax and notified the parties that "accordingly ... the transfer is of no effect". Next, the tax authority began to pursue the purchaser for the tax allegedly owed by the seller.

The Ugandan tax code empowered the tax authority to require a person "in possession of an asset including money" belonging to a non-resident "to pay tax on behalf of the non-resident" and permitted it to designate the purchaser as the seller's statutory agent. The UK court heard that the purchaser had been under immense commercial pressure to pay the disputed tax. It had paid a $1.45 billion purchase price, but – because the Ugandan government would not recognise the transfer – it had nothing to show for it. In addition to withholding consent to the transfer, the Ugandan government was refusing to grant certain petroleum production licences. Eventually, the purchaser paid the tax and claimed reimbursement from the seller.

Among other things, these facts demonstrate that when negotiating and documenting a non-UK acquisition, the principals and their advisers need to bear in mind the local environment. It may be that a typical UK oil and gas precedent that has been developed for use in the relatively benign UK climate for oil and gas may not be the best place to start for either party. In particular, the so-called 'housekeeping' provisions may warrant more consideration than is usual to ensure that in the event of a tax authority challenge, the parties have agreed on, and clearly documented, appropriate contractual rights to manage the appeals process.

Material adverse change clauses

John C LaMaster
Akin Gump Strauss Hauer & Feld LLP

1. Introduction

In any acquisition of upstream oil and gas assets or companies that own upstream oil and gas assets, there will typically be a period of time between signing of the sale and purchase agreement (SPA) and completion of the sale and purchase.[1] This is because it is a nearly universal requirement that the host government in the country where the upstream oil and gas assets are located have the right to approve the buyer.[2] In any transaction with deferred completion of this type, there is a risk that the target assets or target company may somehow deteriorate between signing and completion. This risk is often dealt with by means of a material adverse change (MAC) clause.

A MAC clause is a provision in an SPA that allows the buyer to terminate the transaction during the interim period between signing and completion if certain events occur that have a substantially adverse effect on the target assets or company. A MAC clause is therefore a means of allocating risk between a seller and a buyer.

As is discussed in this chapter, a MAC clause can take several forms, including:

- a standalone MAC termination clause;
- a condition precedent; or
- a warranty combined with a 'bring-down' condition precedent.

Whatever the form, a MAC clause typically gives the buyer an opportunity to terminate the SPA prior to completion if a MAC has occurred. At a minimum where a MAC has occurred in a sale and purchase where the SPA includes a MAC clause, the buyer will have leverage to renegotiate more favourable commercial terms by threatening to terminate the SPA via the MAC clause.[3]

1 This chapter is a modified and updated version of a chapter by the same author entitled "Dealing with material adverse changes in upstream acquisitions and divestitures", which appeared in *Oil and Gas M&A: A Practical Handbook*, 2nd edn, Globe Law and Business, 2018.

2 Claude Duval *et al* (2009), *International Petroleum Exploration and Exploitation Agreements: Legal, Economic and Policy Aspects*, 2nd edn, Barrows, 2009, at 161; Lou R Kling and Eileen T Nugent, "Negotiated Acquisitions of Companies, Subsidiaries and Divisions", *Law Journal Press* 2005, §2.08[3].

3 Bryan Monson, "The Modern MAC: Allocating Deal Risk in the Post-IBP v. Tyson World", 88 *California Law Review* 769 at 803 (2015).

A MAC clause has three seemingly simple elements:

- There must be a change;
- The change must be adverse; and
- The adverse change must be material.

These three elements, however, are typically heavily negotiated by the parties to the SPA. There is also some limited case law interpreting elements of a MAC clause. As a result, MAC clauses have evolved over recent years from relatively simple boilerplate provisions into increasingly sophisticated and complicated provisions, often including exceptions and even exceptions to exceptions.[4]

This chapter examines how MAC clauses are interpreted and some of the issues that arise from those interpretations. It goes on to discuss some practical drafting techniques for MAC clauses in SPAs. Lastly, it considers MAC clauses in light of the unique circumstances of the COVID-19 pandemic, which is ongoing at the time of writing.

2. Interpreting MAC clauses

2.1 Lack of case law

There are few cases interpreting MAC clauses. There appear to be several reasons for this. First, many oil and gas SPAs provide for dispute resolution by arbitration rather than through the courts, which means that the resulting decision – absent appeal to the courts – will remain confidential. Secondly, disputes regarding MAC clauses are very fact specific and depend in large part on the contractual language of the MAC clause. This makes it difficult for buyers and sellers to rely on precedent to predict the outcome of the dispute. Rather than incurring substantial expense and time in litigating an unpredictable dispute, it is more likely that parties will try to negotiate an acceptable resolution.[5] Thirdly, the few cases that do exist – especially in the United States[6] – tend to be quite pro-seller, which may have a chilling effect on buyers seeking to enforce MAC clauses by litigation. Fourthly, if a buyer attempts to terminate an SPA based on a MAC clause, but without proper grounds, this may constitute a repudiatory breach that could result in significant liability for the buyer. Because of the inevitable uncertainty and risk associated with MAC clauses, they tend to be invoked as a last resort.

There is a difference in practice between the United States and England

4 Robert T Miller, "Canceling the Deal: Two Models of Material Adverse Change Clauses in Business Combination Agreements", 31 *Cardozo Law Review* 99 at 105 (2009); Andrew C Elken, "Rethinking the Material Adverse Change Clause in Merger and Acquisition Agreements: Should the United States Consider the British Model?", 82 *Southern California Law Review*, 291 at 307 (2009).

5 "A Change for the Worse", *The National Law Review*, www.natlawreview.com/article/change-worse-material-adverse-effect-upstream-acquisitions.

6 See, for example, *IBP, Inc v Tyson Foods, Inc*, 789 A 2d 14 (Del Ch 2001).

regarding MAC clauses. These clauses have been common in SPAs in US sales and purchases for many years, but it is only recently that the practice has transferred into private English sales and purchases. Partly as a result, there is more US case law than English case law regarding MAC clauses. Despite the overall dearth of case law, some generalities can be drawn with respect to interpreting MAC clauses under both US and English law.

2.2 Generalities in interpreting MAC clauses

(a) MAC clauses will be narrowly construed

Both the US[7] and English[8] courts have stated that MAC clauses should be narrowly construed. There are several policy reasons underlying this interpretation. First, public policy favours enforcement of signed deals, especially where the contracting parties are sophisticated entities represented by legal counsel. Secondly, courts are aware that buyers may use MAC clauses as a means to walk away from deals when they get cold feet or otherwise change their minds about the benefits of the transaction.[9] Thirdly, courts want to maximise economic efficiency by preventing the adverse economic effects that inevitably befall the target of a failed acquisition.[10] Fourthly, a seller-friendly interpretation theoretically reduces transaction costs by avoiding the need to draft detailed MAC clauses with multiple exceptions and 'carve-outs' to protect the seller.[11] This last policy reason seems questionable, however, as in practice buyers and sellers often spend more time negotiating the carve-outs than the description of the MAC itself.[12]

(b) MAC clauses must be read in the context of the entire agreement

Courts in both the United States[13] and England[14] will consider and interpret MAC clauses in the context of the entire agreement. For example, in *Ipsos SA v Dentsu Aegis Network Ltd*,[15] the buyer claimed that a downward revision of an economic forecast constituted a MAC. The English court considered this in the context of the entire agreement and concluded that considering the revised forecast as a MAC would in substance give the buyer a warranty regarding the

7 See, for example, *IBP, Inc v Tyson Foods, Inc*, 789 A 2d 14 (Del Ch 2001).

8 See, for example, *Grupo Hotelero Urvasco SA v Carey Value Added SL* ([2013] EWHC 1039 (Comm)).

9 Bryan Monson, "The Modern MAC: Allocating Deal Risk in the Post-IBP v. Tyson World", 88 *California Law Review* 769 at 781 (2015), citing *IBP, Inc v Tyson Foods, Inc*, 789 A 2d 14 (Del Ch 2001) as a case involving buyer's remorse.

10 Adam B Chertok, "Rethinking the U.S. Approach to Material Adverse Change Clauses in Merger Agreements", 19 *U Miami Int'l and Comp Law Review* 99 (2011) at 137.

11 Bryan Monson, "The Modern MAC: Allocating Deal Risk in the Post-IBP v. Tyson World", 88 *California Law Review* 769 at 800 (2015), citing *IBP, Inc v Tyson Foods, Inc*, 789 A 2d 14 (Del Ch 2001).

12 See sections 3.2 and 3.6.

13 See, for example, *Hexion Specialty Chemicals, Inc v Huntsman Corp*, 965 A 2d 715 (Del Ch 2008).

14 See, for example, *Ipsos SA v Dentsu Aegis Network Ltd* ([2015] EWHC 1171 (Comm)).

15 [2013] EWHC 1039 (Comm).

forecasts, which would be inconsistent with the express exclusion of warranties in the agreement. Similarly, in *Hexion Specialty Chemicals, Inc v Huntsman Corp*,[16] a Delaware court rejected a buyer's claim that decreased earnings projections constituted a MAC on the basis that such a conclusion would fall foul of the merger agreement's express disclaimer of representations or warranties regarding projections, forecasts or other estimates.

(c) The MAC event must be significant

Both the US[17] and English[18] courts have stated that the event triggering the MAC must be 'substantial' or 'significant'. The rationale, in the context of an SPA, is that in a transaction between a sophisticated seller and a sophisticated buyer, the parties will not have intended for the MAC clause to have set such a low standard for the buyer's termination right that the SPA would become, in effect, an option agreement in favour of the buyer. The requirement of materiality seems self-evident, but in practice it can become one of a buyer's greatest challenges in seeking to enforce a MAC clause.[19]

(d) The MAC event must not have been previously known

Both the US[20] and English[21] courts have held that a party cannot trigger a MAC clause on the basis of facts or circumstances of which it was aware at the time it entered into the SPA. There appear to be two rationales for this requirement. First is the idea that, if the parties were concerned about existing known facts or circumstances, they would have dealt with them in a specific clause in the agreement, such as a warranty or an indemnity. If they failed to do so, it can be assumed that they agreed to enter into the agreement despite those facts or circumstances. Secondly, known events or circumstances do not constitute a 'change'. A MAC clause, therefore, must be intended to deal with unforeseen or unforeseeable events.

(e) The MAC event must be durationally significant

Both the US[22] and English[23] courts have held that the MAC must generally be durationally significant – that is, not an event that is temporary or has only

---

16 965 A 2d 715 (Del Ch 2008).
17 See, for example, *IBP, Inc v Tyson Foods, Inc*, 789 A 2d 14 (Del Ch 2001).
18 See, for example, *Grupo Hotelero Urvasco SA v Carey Value Added SL* ([2013] EWHC 1039 (Comm)).
19 Rafal Zakrzewski, "Material Adverse Change and Material Adverse Effect Provisions: Construction and Application", 5 *Law & Fin Mkt Rev* 344 at 348 (2011); Bryan Monson, "The Modern MAC: Allocating Deal Risk in the Post-IBP v. Tyson World", 88 *California Law Review* 769 at 797 (2015).
20 See, for example, *IBP, Inc v Tyson Foods, Inc*, 789 A 2d 14 (Del Ch 2001), where Tyson was deemed to have knowledge of the cyclical nature of the beef industry.
21 See, for example, *Grupo Hotelero Urvasco SA v Carey Value Added SL* ([2013] EWHC 1039 (Comm)).
22 See, for example, *IBP, Inc v Tyson Foods, Inc*, 789 A 2d 14 (Del Ch 2001); *Hexion Speciality Chemicals, Inc v Huntsman Corp*, 965 A 2d 715 (Del Ch 2008); *Akorn, Inc, v Fresenius Kabi AG*, CA 2018-0300-JTL (Del Ch 1 October 2018).
23 See, for example, *Grupo Hotelero Urvasco SA v Carey Value Added SL* ([2013] EWHC 1039 (Comm)).

short-term consequences. For example, in *IBP, Inc v Tyson Foods, Inc*, Tyson tried to invoke a MAC clause on the basis that, among other things, IBP had restated its earnings during the interim period between signing and closing. The court held that: "A short-term hiccup in earnings should not suffice; rather the Material Adverse Effect should be material when viewed from the longer-term perspective of a reasonable acquiror."[24] This was recently reiterated in the Delaware case *Akorn, Inc, v Fresenius Kabi AG*, where the court stated: "The important consideration... is whether there has been an adverse change in the target's business that is consequential to the company's long-term earnings power over a commercially reasonable period, which one would expect to be measured in years rather than months."[25]

(f) *The party seeking to invoke the MAC clause has the burden of proof*

Absent clear language to the contrary in the SPA,[26] in both the United States[27] and England,[28] the party seeking to invoke the MAC clause has the burden of proving that a MAC has occurred. For example, in *IBP, Inc v Tyson Foods, Inc*, the court held that the buyer which was attempting to invoke a MAC to terminate the transaction had the burden of proving that the MAC had occurred.[29] Similarly, in *Grupo Hotelero Urvasco SA v Carey Value Added SL*,[30] the court held that a lender which was seeking to cease lending under a finance document on the basis that the borrower had suffered a MAC had the burden of proving that the MAC had occurred.

3. Drafting MAC clauses

The generalities discussed above regarding how MAC clauses will be interpreted inform draftspersons about how MAC clauses ought to be drafted, whether representing a buyer or a seller. The following are some specific drafting points relevant to MAC clauses.

3.1 The form of a MAC clause

As explained above, the fundamental purpose of a MAC clause in an SPA is to give the buyer a termination right if, during the interim period between signing and completion, certain events occur that have a substantially adverse effect on the target assets or the target company. This purpose can be achieved by drafting a MAC clause as:

---

24 *IBP, Inc v Tyson Foods, Inc*, 789 A 2d 14, at 68 (Del Ch 2001).
25 *Akorn, Inc, v Fresenius Kabi AG*, CA 2018-0300-JTL (Del Ch 1 October 2018).
26 Bryan Monson, "The Modern MAC: Allocating Deal Risk in the Post-IBP v Tyson World", 88 *California Law Review* 769 at 798 (2015); Kenneth A Adams, "A Legal Usage Analysis of 'Material Adverse Change Provisions", 10 *Fordham Journal of Corporate & Financial Law* 9 at 47 (2004).
27 See, for example, *IBP, Inc v Tyson Foods, Inc*, 789 A 2d 14, at 68 (Del Ch 2001).
28 See, for example, *Grupo Hotelero Urvasco SA v Carey Value Added SL* ([2013] EWHC 1039 (Comm)).
29 *IBP, Inc v Tyson Foods, Inc*, 789 A 2d 14, at 68 (Del Ch 2001).
30

- a standalone MAC termination clause;
- a condition precedent; or
- a representation and warranty (or, more commonly in an English law SPA, just a warranty) that is repeated at completion.

(a) *Standalone MAC termination clause*

A MAC clause can be drafted as a standalone termination clause. The Association of International Petroleum Negotiators (AIPN) recently issued a new Model Form International Asset Sale and Purchase Agreement (AIPN Model Form ASPA). The AIPN drafted the MAC clause as a detailed standalone termination clause. The clause is included as an 'optional provision' and includes some other optional elements. Clause 3.5 reads as follows:

3.5 [Material Adverse Event

3.5.1 Notwithstanding any other provision hereof, if at any time prior to Completion, Buyer considers that a Material Adverse Event has occurred, it shall promptly Notify Seller including sufficient detail as to the nature of the alleged Material Adverse Event (the "MAE Notice").

3.5.2 Within [five (5)] Business Days following receipt of the MAE Notice Seller shall Notify Buyer either that:

(a) it agrees that a Material Adverse Event has occurred; or

(b) it disagrees that the event alleged to be a Material Adverse Event in fact amounts to a Material Adverse Event.

3.5.3 If, pursuant to Article 3.5.2(a), Seller agrees that a Material Adverse Event has occurred, and either:

(a) despite the Parties using their [best][reasonable] endeavors to remedy the Material Adverse Event, such Material Adverse Event has not been remedied within [ninety (90)] Days following the date of Seller's response to the MAE Notice in accordance with Article 3.5.2 (the "MAE Time Limit"); or

(b) the Parties determine that such Material Adverse Event is not capable of being remedied within the MAE Time Limit,

Buyer may terminate this Agreement immediately without penalty by delivery of Notice to Seller.

3.5.4 If (a) pursuant to Article 3.5.2(b), Seller Notifies Buyer that it disagrees that a Material Adverse Event has occurred, or (b) the Parties disagree that the Material Adverse Event is capable of being remedied within MAE Time Limit and if either Party Notifies the other Party of the same (a Notice given under sub-clause (a) or (b) of this Section 3.5.4 being a "MAE Dispute Notice"):

(i) then Seller and Buyer shall, within [five (5)] Business Days after the date of the MAE Dispute Notice, meet and use their good faith, [best][reasonable] endeavors to resolve the dispute; and

(ii) if Seller and Buyer fail to resolve the dispute within [fifteen (15)] Business Days of the date of the MAE Dispute Notice, then either Party may [refer the

dispute to an Expert in accordance with Article 12, and such Expert shall determine][issue a Notice of Dispute in order to resolve] whether or not, as applicable, (A) the alleged event does in fact amount to a Material Adverse Event, or (B) the Material Adverse Event is capable of being remedied within the MAE Time Limit.

3.5.5 To allow the Parties time to remedy a Material Adverse Event, if a MAE Notice is issued by Buyer in accordance with Article 3.5.1, the Longstop Date shall be extended until a date that is [•] days after the first to occur of (a) the last day of the MAE Time Limit, or (b) if the Material Adverse Event is remedied prior to the last day of the MAE Time Limit or the Parties determine [(or the Expert determines)][or it is resolved pursuant to Article 14] either that such Material Adverse Event is not capable of being remedied before the last day of the MAE Time Limit, the date of such remedy or determination; provided, however, that if the first to occur of the dates determined pursuant to Article 3.5.5(a) or (b) falls prior to the original Longstop Date, then such Longstop Date will not be amended.

3.5.6 If, after the procedure set out in Article 3.5.4 (and Article 12, as applicable) has taken place, the Parties determine [(or the Expert determines)][or it is resolved pursuant to Article 14] that a Material Adverse Event has taken place and is not capable of being remedied within the MAE Time Limit, Buyer may terminate this Agreement immediately without penalty by delivery of Notice to Seller.

3.5.7 The procedure set out in Articles 3.5.4 – 3.5.6 (inclusive) (and Article 12, as applicable) shall only apply if a MAE Dispute Notice has been served. If Buyer serves an MAE Notice and no MAE Dispute Notice is subsequently served then Buyer shall have the right to terminate in accordance with Article 3.5.3.]

For the purposes of the AIPN Model Form ASPA, the term 'material adverse event' is defined as follows, and includes some optional elements such as exceptions:

[Material Adverse Event means any change, effect, event, result, occurrence, condition or fact (for the purposes of this definition, each, an "event") (whether foreseeable or not and whether covered by insurance or not) occurring during the Interim Period that has had or would be reasonably likely to have, individually or in the aggregate with any other event or events, a material and adverse effect on the ownership, development, operation or financial condition of the Purchase Interest, taken individually or as a whole, as operated as of the Signature Date OPTIONAL: [or the ability of the Party claiming such Material Adverse Event to consummate the transactions contemplated by this Agreement];

provided, however, that Material Adverse Event shall not include such material adverse events resulting from:

OPTIONAL PROVISIONS, CHOOSE ONE OR MORE APPLICABLE PROVISIONS

(a) entering into this Agreement or the announcement of the transactions contemplated by this Agreement;

(b) changes in general market, economic, financial or political conditions (including changes in commodity prices (including Hydrocarbons), fuel supply or transportation markets, interest rates, financing costs or currency exchange rates);

(c) changes in conditions or developments generally applicable to the international or national oil and gas industry, including changes in oil gas or condensate prices;

(d) acts of God, including hurricanes, storms or other naturally occurring events;

(e) civil unrest, any outbreak of disease or hostilities, terrorist activities, sabotage, vandalism, or war (declared or undeclared) or any similar disorder;

(f) matters that are cured or no longer exist by the earlier of the Closing Date and the termination of this Agreement;

(g) changes in Laws (including taxes) [except where the changes have a disproportionate adverse effect on the Purchase Interest];

(h) any reclassification or recalculation of reserves in the ordinary course of business;

(i) any actions or inactions taken by the Party claiming such Material Adverse Event;

(j) natural declines in well performance;

(k) changes in the prospective resource or actual reserve potential of the [area of interest or the host country in general] that results from any oil and gas operations, where such operations shall include drilling, seismic acquisition, processing, or interpretation of geoscientific or other technical data;

(l) industry-wide or host country-wide strikes, work stoppages, slowdowns or similar acts of labor unrest; or

(m) imposition by the United Nations or another relevant Government of any sanction, retribution, or other penalty.]

(b) Condition precedent

A MAC clause can be drafted as a standalone condition precedent to completion stating that there has been no MAC in the target assets or the target company between the date of signature of the SPA and the completion date. If the condition precedent is not satisfied by a specified longstop date, then the buyer will have the right to terminate the SPA for failure to satisfy the condition precedent. A simple standalone condition precedent could be formulated as follows:

The obligation of the Buyer to consummate the transactions to be performed by it in connection with the Completion is subject to satisfaction of the following conditions:...

([•]) there having been no Material Adverse Change during the interim period between the Signature Date and the Completion Date that is persisting at the Completion Date.

(c) *MAC warranty repeated at completion*

MAC provisions can be incorporated into warranties in one of two ways. First, an SPA can include a specific warranty from the seller that the target assets or the target company has not suffered a MAC between a specified date and completion. A simple example of a specific warranty of this type would be:

Since [date], no events or circumstances have occurred that constitute, individually or in the aggregate, a Material Adverse Change to [the Assets] [the Target Company].

Another example is as follows:

Since the date of the Balance Sheet, there has not been any material adverse change in the business, operations, properties, prospects, assets, or condition of any Acquired Company, and no event has occurred or circumstances exist that may result in such a material adverse change.[31]

Secondly, a MAC provision can be used as a qualifier to a seller's warranties so as to indicate the absence of any events or circumstances leading to a MAC. For example, the seller could warrant that there is no litigation other than litigation that would not reasonably be expected to result in a MAC.

In order for a MAC provision that is formulated as a seller's warranty to serve the intended purpose of giving the buyer a termination right if the warranty is not true, the warranty must be repeated at completion by means of a bring-down condition precedent. A bring-down condition precedent is a condition precedent that all of the seller's warranties are true and correct at completion. An example of a bring-down condition precedent is as follows:

All of the Sellers' representations and warranties in this Agreement (considered collectively), and each of these representations and warranties (considered individually), must have been accurate in all material respects as of the date of this Agreement, and must be accurate in all material respects as of the Closing Date as if made on the Closing Date, without giving effect to any supplement to the Disclosure Letter.[32]

Representations and warranties can be repeated without use of a bring-down condition precedent. For example, the lead-in to the representations and warranties could state:

The Seller represents and warrants to the Buyer that each of the following representations and warranties is true and accurate as at the Signature Date and as at the Completion Date (taking into account any Disclosure).

The primary difference between this formulation and a bring-down condition precedent is that under this formulation, the buyer will not have a

31 Model Stock Purchase Agreement with Commentary (American Bar Association 1995), p81.

32 Model Stock Purchase Agreement with Commentary (American Bar Association 1995), p158. With respect to the inclusion of the phrase "in all material respects" in the bring-down condition precedent, see the discussion of the 'double materiality' issue in section 2.1(b) of the separate chapter in this book entitled "Conditions precedent and deferred completions".

right to walk away for failure of the condition precedent. The buyer is therefore forced to complete the acquisition and then claim for damages for breach of representation and warranty, which is unlikely to be a suitable remedy when the breach involves a MAC.

(d) *Considering the differences between these structures*

There are several important differences between structuring a MAC clause as a standalone MAC termination clause, a standalone condition precedent or a warranty coupled with a bring-down condition precedent.

First, the buyer's remedies may be different under each structure. If a standalone MAC termination clause is triggered or if a condition precedent is not satisfied by the specified longstop date, the buyer will have the right to terminate the SPA and walk away from the transaction. Conversely, if a warranty is untrue, the buyer will have the right to terminate the SPA and walk away from the transaction on the basis of the bring-down condition precedent; but the buyer may also have a cause of action for damages for breach of warranty.[33] For example, if a natural disaster such as a hurricane, flood or earthquake damages the target assets, the seller may face unintended liability for something that was outside of its control. This possibility for the buyer to 'walk and sue' is the main reason why sellers typically prefer that MAC clauses be structured as a standalone MAC termination clause or as a standalone condition precedent rather than as a warranty coupled with a bring-down condition precedent.[34]

Secondly, a standalone MAC termination clause may allow termination of the SPA earlier than either a standalone condition precedent or a warranty coupled with a bring-down condition precedent. A standalone condition precedent or a warranty coupled with a bring-down condition precedent will typically allow termination only on a specified longstop date. The timeframe from signing the SPA to the longstop date can be long, especially in jurisdictions where it can take many months to obtain governmental consent. Conversely, the standalone MAC termination clause can provide for termination once the parties have determined that the MAC has occurred. The MAC termination clause quoted above from the AIPN Model Form ASPA contains a more elaborate structure, including notices between the buyer and seller and a possible cure period, but nonetheless provides for possible termination prior to the longstop date. But the AIPN clause also allows for an extension of the longstop date in certain circumstances.

Thirdly, the different structures may cater for a MAC occurring over different

33 Kenneth A Adams, "A Legal Usage Analysis of 'Material Adverse Change' Provisions", 10 *Fordham Journal of Corporate & Financial Law* 9 at 12 (2004); Model Stock Purchase Agreement with Commentary (American Bar Association 1995), p165.

34 Model Stock Purchase Agreement with Commentary (American Bar Association 1995), p165.

periods of time. Typically, a standalone MAC termination clause and a standalone condition precedent cover only the period between the signature date of the SPA and completion. Conversely, a warranty regarding the absence of a MAC can be drafted to cover any period. For example, it is not uncommon for a warranty to state that there has been no MAC since the date of the most recent audited accounts of the target, which will typically be prior to the signature date of the SPA. This difference can have consequences. For example, assume that the target's business has improved between the date of its most recent audited accounts and the signature date of the SPA, but has deteriorated since the signature date of the SPA. If the MAC clause is structured as a standalone MAC termination clause or a standalone condition precedent that applies to the period between the signature date of the SPA and completion, then the determination of whether there has been a MAC will focus only on the deterioration in the business since the signature date of the SPA. Alternatively, if the MAC clause is structured as a warranty coupled with a bring-down condition precedent, then the determination of whether there has been a MAC will have to take into account the net effect of the improvement in the business between the date of the most recent audited accounts and the signature date of the SPA, and the deterioration in the business between the signature date and completion.[35]

Fourthly, a standalone MAC termination clause can be structured to include dispute resolution mechanisms that are specific to the MAC. The MAC termination clause quoted above from the AIPN Model Form ASPA includes mechanisms for the parties to meet to try to resolve any disagreement and ultimately for referral to an expert.

3.2 Vague or specific MAC clause

When contemplating a MAC clause, draftspersons must consider whether to draft the description of what constitutes a MAC (as opposed to carve-outs of what does not constitute a MAC) in general terms or with specificity. Traditionally, descriptions of what constitutes a MAC have been written in general terms – some would say vaguely or ambiguously. From a seller's standpoint, generality may be viewed as preferable, because it makes it more likely that the transaction will close or, if there is a dispute, that a court will not find a MAC. Given the pro-seller interpretations applied to MAC clauses by both US and English courts, as discussed above, this would seem to be a reasonable viewpoint. But traditionally, buyers also seem to prefer more general descriptions of what constitutes a MAC. This may be because buyers think they can use the resulting ambiguity to their advantage in arguing with the seller

35 Model Stock Purchase Agreement with Commentary (American Bar Association 1995), p164.

that a MAC has occurred and that the deal should be either renegotiated or terminated.[36]

The risks of deliberately general, vague or ambiguous descriptions of what constitutes a MAC is that the parties may have conflicting interpretations, which can lead to disputes and even to arbitration or litigation. It seems, however, that traditionally, both sellers and buyers are willing to trade this risk for the savings realised upfront in lower transaction (drafting and negotiating) costs.[37]

The alternative approach is for the buyer to negotiate specific examples by way of inclusions or 'carve-ins' to the description of what constitutes a MAC, in order to ensure that those specific risks are catered for. This would seem to be an advisable approach, considering the reluctance of both the US and the English courts to find that a MAC has occurred. The downside to this approach is that a court may not consider a specific event or circumstance to constitute a MAC if it does not resemble the specific examples. This downside could possibly be addressed by making the specific examples illustrative rather than exhaustive – for example, by using an 'including without limitation' proviso to the carve-ins. However, the concept of adding specific examples also goes against the idea that a MAC clause is intended to cover unforeseen and unforeseeable events or circumstances. As a result, if there are specific risks known to the parties, these are usually addressed in other clauses, such as warranties, covenants or indemnities.[38] For example, the specific risks could be covered by a warranty that those risks have not and will not manifest themselves which, combined with a bring-down condition precedent, would give the buyer a termination right.

The MAC termination clause quoted above from the AIPN Model Form ASPA includes a fairly detailed definition of 'material adverse event', but the list of possible exceptions is much longer and more detailed.

3.3 Defining 'material'

The concept of what is or is not 'material' is inherently imprecise and somewhat abstract, like the concept of what is or is not 'reasonable'. When deciding what is or is not material, courts tend to use a fact-specific, case-by-case analysis.[39] The resulting decisions do not provide much guidance to sellers and buyers as to what events or circumstances may constitute a MAC.

Parties to an SPA could attempt to define the concept of 'materiality', either

---

36 Adam B Chertok, "Rethinking the U.S. Approach to Material Adverse Change Clauses in Merger Agreements", 19 *U Miami Int'l and Comp Law Review* 99 (2011) at 109.

37 Adam B Chertok, "Rethinking the U.S. Approach to Material Adverse Change Clauses in Merger Agreements", 19 *U Miami Int'l and Comp Law Review* 99 (2011) at 111.

38 Kenneth A Adams, "A Legal Usage Analysis of 'Material Adverse Change' Provisions", 10 *Fordham Journal of Corporate & Financial Law* 9 at 43 (2004); Bryan Monson, "The Modern MAC: Allocating Deal Risk in the Post-IBP v Tyson World", 88 *California Law Review* 769 at 800 (2015).

39 Adam B Chertok, "Rethinking the US Approach to Material Adverse Change Clauses in Merger Agreements", 19 *U Miami Int'l and Comp Law Review* 99 (2011) at 121.

objectively or subjectively. An objective definition of 'material' could be based, for example, on a quantitative benchmark. For example, the value of the target assets could be deemed to be materially affected if their value were reduced by a specified dollar or pound sterling amount, or by a specified percentage of the purchase price. Similarly, the value of the target could be deemed to be materially affected if it suffered a specified decline in earnings before interest, taxes, depreciation and amortisation. An example of a quantitative benchmark used to define 'material' was in *Great Lakes Chem Corp v Pharmacia Corp*, where the SPA defined a 'MAC' as "a negative effect or negative change on the operations, results of operations or condition (financial or otherwise) in an amount equal to $6,500,000 or more".[40]

Alternatively, the parties to an SPA could set a subjective standard. An example of a somewhat subjective standard would be the phrase: "in the reasonable opinion of the buyer there has been a Material Adverse Change." This approach would typically be resisted by a seller, as it appears to give wide discretion to a buyer (subject to the requirement that the buyer's opinion must be 'reasonable'). Further, it layers the vague concept of 'reasonableness' over the already vague concept of 'materiality'.

There are several difficulties in trying to define 'material'. As discussed above with respect to the inclusion of specific examples in the description of what constitutes a MAC, the downside of including a specific quantitative benchmark is that not every adverse event or circumstance may meet the same quantitative benchmark, and a court may not consider a specific event or circumstance to constitute a MAC if it does not meet that same benchmark. Further, not all events or circumstances may be easily measured against a quantitative benchmark (eg, a newly filed lawsuit whose outcome is uncertain). Also, a 'one size fits all' quantitative benchmark seemingly goes against the idea that a MAC clause is intended to cover unforeseen and unforeseeable events or circumstances. Lastly, introducing a quantitative benchmark to negotiations of an SPA will add time and cost to the negotiation process. Given these difficulties, it is perhaps unsurprising that most SPAs for oil and gas transactions do not attempt to define 'material'.

3.4 Forward-looking MAC clauses

It is often a subject of debate between sellers and buyers whether a MAC clause should be concerned only with events or circumstances that have already occurred, thereby causing a MAC, or whether a MAC clause should also be forward looking. Forward-looking elements can be included in a MAC clause in various ways. For example, the MAC clause could refer to the 'prospects' of the target. Alternatively, the MAC clause could refer to events or circumstances that

---

40 *Great Lakes Chem Corp v Pharmacia Corp*, 788 A 2d 544, 557 (Del Ch 2001).

"would be reasonably likely to have a material adverse effect" on the target assets or the target company.

From a buyer's perspective, a forward-looking element is important, as the buyer is purchasing the target assets or target company for its future business opportunities. But from a seller's perspective, the inclusion of a forward-looking element can be troublesome, because it involves determining the probable future consequences of an event of circumstance, rather than determining just the actual consequences that have already occurred. This predictive element can be especially worrying where the seller has given a MAC clause in the form of a warranty, as that structure potentially opens up the seller to damages for future losses, even where the relevant event or circumstance has not yet actually caused a material adverse change.[41]

The MAC termination clause quoted above from the AIPN Model Form ASPA includes a forward-looking element, referring to an event "that has had or would be reasonably likely to have, individually or in the aggregate with any other event or events, a material and adverse effect..."

3.5 Not requiring a 'change'

It is debatable whether 'material adverse change' or 'material adverse effect' is the better formulation in an SPA. Arguably, "a change is easier to note than an effect is to measure".[42] Some SPAs use just one of the two terms, others use both terms and some use the terms interchangeably.

In either case, it is clear that some sort of 'change' is required. The *Concise Oxford English Dictionary*[43] defines 'change' as to "make or become different" or "the action of changing"; and defines 'effect' as "a change which is a result or consequence of an action or other cause". So, in the context of an SPA, if an event or circumstance has a 'material adverse change' or a 'material adverse effect' on the target assets or the target company, this means that it has changed some aspect of the target assets or the target company.[44]

The MAC termination clause quoted above from the AIPN Model Form ASPA neatly sidesteps this issue by defining a 'material adverse event' to include "any change, effect, event, result, occurrence, condition or fact".

Of course, the parties to an SPA are free to draft the MAC clause so that it does not require a 'change'. For example, the MAC clause could include the "continuation of any events or circumstances". This formulation is more commonly seen in finance

41 Lou R Kling and Eileen T Nugent, "Negotiated Acquisitions of Companies, Subsidiaries and Divisions", *Law Journal Press* 2005, §11.04[9]; Rafal Zakrzewski, "Material Adverse Change and Material Adverse Effect Provisions: Construction and Application", 5 *Law & Fin Mkt Rev* 344 at 347 (2011).

42 "A Change for the Worse: Material Adverse Effect in Upstream Acquisitions", *The National Law Review*, www.natlawreview.com/article/change-worse-mateiral-adverse-effect-upstream-acquisitions.

43 *Concise Oxford English Dictionary* (12th ed 2011).

44 See also Kenneth A Adams, "A Legal Usage Analysis of 'Material Adverse Change' Provisions", 10 *Fordham Journal of Corporate & Financial Law* 9 at 43 (2004).

documents than in SPAs. An example is in the Loan Market Association Mandate Letter – Joint Arrangers – Underwritten,[45] which provides:

> *The obligations of each Mandated Lead Arranger, each Bookrunner and each Underwriter under the Mandate Documents are subject to the absence, in its opinion, of any event(s) or circumstance(s) (including any material adverse change or the continuation of any circumstance(s)) which, in its opinion, has (have) adversely affected or could adversely affect:...*

3.6 Exceptions or carve-outs to MAC clauses

It is commonplace for the parties to an SPA to exclude certain exceptions or carve-outs from the definition of 'MAC', regardless of the form of the MAC clause. The purpose of the carve-outs is to remove certain risks from the definition and thereby shift those risks from the seller back to the buyer. The carve-outs are therefore seller-friendly provisions.

The carve-outs tend to fall into several generic categories. Below are descriptions of the various categories, together with some examples that sometimes appear in SPAs for upstream oil and gas transactions. Note that some of the examples could fit into one or more of the general categories.

(a) Systemic risks

Perhaps the most usual and customary carve-outs are systemic or macro-economic risks that are deemed to be beyond the control of the seller. These carve-outs are almost universally included in MAC clauses, regardless of industry sector. Examples of these types of carve-outs include:

- changes in conditions in the global economy generally or in global capital, credit or financial markets generally;
- changes in interest rates, financing costs or currency exchange rates; and
- changes in accounting standards or practices (eg, generally accepted accounting principles).

(b) Industry risks

In an SPA for an upstream oil and gas transaction, it is also usual and customary to carve out certain risks that are specific to the oil and gas industry. Examples of these types of carve-outs include:

- changes in oil and gas commodity prices (including forecasted and future prices);
- any general economic trend affecting any aspect of the exploration, development, extraction, transportation, purchase, refining or sale of oil or gas (or any by-product of oil or gas);

---

45 Rafal Zakrzewski, "Material Adverse Change and Material Adverse Effect Provisions: Construction and Application", 5 *Law & Fin Mkt Rev* 344 at 345 (2011).

- any reclassification or recalculation of reserves in the ordinary course of business;
- natural declines in well performance;
- changes in the prospective resource or actual reserve potential of the area of interest or the host country in general that result from any oil and gas operations, where such operations include, but are not limited to, drilling, seismic acquisition, processing and/or interpretation of geoscientific or other technical data; and
- a casualty loss, property loss, accident or other incident affecting the target assets or the target company that is covered by insurance (except for usual and customary deductibles); and
- industry-wide strikes, work stoppages, slowdowns or similar acts of labour unrest.

(c) Force majeure *risks*

Force majeure events are by definition beyond the control of the seller. Examples include:

- natural disasters such as hurricanes, floods or earthquakes; and
- war (whether or not declared), outbreak of disease, acts of terrorism, vandalism, sabotage or civil unrest, or any worsening of any such circumstances existing on the date of signing the SPA.

(d) Political risks

Political risks are government-based risks, such as changes in law, governmental decisions, changes in governments themselves or even governmental instability. These risks are therefore different from the types of market, financial or physical risks described above. Political risks are often an issue for the oil and gas industry, which is active in many developing countries around the world, where political risks are typically perceived to be higher than in developed countries. Examples of political risks that may be included in carve-outs to the definition of 'MAC' in an SPA for an upstream oil and gas transaction include:

- changes in applicable law (including rules, regulations, codes, judgments, orders, decrees or rulings, or interpretations of any of the foregoing);
- changes in applicable taxes;
- country-wide strikes, work stoppages, slowdowns or similar acts of labour unrest;
- the imposition by the United Nations or another relevant government of any sanction, retribution or other penalty;
- a change of government; and
- any action required by law.

(e) *Transaction-specific risks known to the parties*

The sale and purchase may present certain transaction-specific risks that are known to the parties. Depending on whether the buyer has factored these risks into its purchase price, the buyer may agree to include these as carve-outs. Some examples include the following:

- the effect of the negotiation, execution, announcement or pendency of the SPA or the transactions contemplated by the SPA on the target's relationships – contractual or otherwise – with its customers, suppliers, vendors, lenders, joint venture partners or employees;
- any deterioration in the business, assets, prospects or financial condition of the target assets or the target company resulting from circumstances or conditions existing on the date of signing of the SPA that were generally known publicly as of the date of signing of the SPA;
- loss of employees;
- compliance by the seller or the target with the terms of the SPA;
- announcement of the transaction or the change of control of the target as a result of the transaction;
- any failure to meet analysts' or internal earnings estimates;
- actions taken by the seller or the target with the express written consent of the buyer; and
- any matter disclosed by the seller in the disclosure letter.

Transaction-specific risks may also affect the drafting and negotiation of some of the risks described above. For example, if the transaction is taking place in a jurisdiction that is particularly susceptible to terrorism or civil unrest, the parties may want to provide additional wording around the 'terrorism' carve-out in the *force majeure* risks mentioned above.

(f) *Carve-outs to carve-outs*

Some of these carve-outs can be further qualified by a statement that the carve-outs do not apply if the target assets or the target company is disproportionately affected thereby, in which case the relevant event, occurrence, circumstance, development, change or fact can be a MAC rather than an exception to a MAC. These carve-outs to the carve-outs bring the described event or circumstance back into the definition of 'MAC' and thereby shift the risk from the buyer back to the seller. The following is a typical example:

> *changes in applicable law (including rules, regulations, codes, judgments, orders, decrees or rulings, or interpretations of any of the foregoing), except where the changes have a disproportionate adverse effect on the [Assets] [Target Company].*

4. Risk issues

If a buyer invokes a MAC clause and attempts to terminate an SPA without proper grounds, it will be at risk of possibly significant liability. This may be a repudiatory breach by the buyer if the buyer is subsequently found not to have been entitled to assert the MAC and terminate the SPA. The seller may elect to accept the repudiation, terminate the SPA and sue for damages, leading to potentially substantial liability for the buyer.

5. The COVID-19 pandemic

5.1 Does the COVID-19 pandemic constitute a MAC?

In late 2019, the COVID-19 virus began to spread around the world, affecting numerous lives and businesses. On 11 March 2020, the World Health Organization declared COVID-19 a pandemic. As of the time of writing, there remains a huge amount of uncertainty regarding the duration of the pandemic and its long-term human and economic consequences. As things currently stand, the pandemic appears to have sent the worldwide economy into (at least) a recession. In the oil industry, the pandemic has greatly reduced demand for oil, and this – combined with conflicts between Russia and Saudi Arabia – has caused the price of oil to collapse.

Doubtless, there were many SPAs that had been signed, but not completed during the pandemic. If any of these SPAs included MAC clauses, the existence of the pandemic may entitle the buyers to terminate the transactions. The pandemic may result in future litigation and arbitration that could affect the drafting and interpretation of MAC clauses for many years.

Whether MAC contractual relief is available will depend on several factors, including the following:

- the precise wording of the MAC clause, including in particular its carve-outs and exceptions;
- whether the facts of the pandemic (including its duration) meet the criteria for relief under the MAC clause; and
- whether the buyer has complied with all relevant procedures (if any) specified in the SPA for invoking the MAC clause (eg, sending proper and timely notices).

The precise wording of the MAC clause will be critical in determining whether the pandemic and its consequences constitute a MAC. Of particular importance will be the list of carve-outs or exclusions from the definition of 'material adverse change' (if any), as those often include systemic or macroeconomic risks that are deemed to be beyond the control of the seller. Specific pandemic or disease carve-outs are common; but whether these carve-outs are ultimately included will be a question of risk allocation, pricing and bargaining power.

In considering the MAC termination clause quoted above from the AIPN

Model Form ASPA, the definition of 'material adverse event' refers to events:

> *whether foreseeable or not and whether covered by insurance or not) occurring during the Interim Period that has had or would be reasonably likely to have, individually or in the aggregate with any other event or events, a material and adverse effect on the ownership, development, operation or financial condition of the Purchase Interest, taken individually or as a whole, as operated as of the Signature Date.*

It will be a question of fact whether the pandemic has had or is reasonably likely to have a material adverse effect on the ownership, development or operation of financial condition of the relevant assets. Of particular importance in this regard will be the duration of the pandemic, given the case law referred to in section 2.2(e) above, which requires that the MAC be "durationally significant".[46]

Assuming that the pandemic meets the threshold in the definition of 'material adverse event', we must then consider the listed carve-outs. In this regard, what the definition of 'material adverse event' gives, the carve-outs appear to take away. There are at least three possibly applicable carve-outs. Subparagraph (b) carves out "changes in general market, economic, financial or political conditions",[47] which would appear to capture the economic fallout of the pandemic. Subparagraph (d) carves out "acts of God, including hurricanes, storms or other naturally occurring events", which could apply assuming that the pandemic was not an act of man rather than God. More specifically, subparagraph (e) carves out "any outbreak of disease". Therefore, in an SPA using the precise and full wording of the AIPN Model Form ASPA, the occurrence of the COVID-19 pandemic would appear to have been carved out and as a result not constitute a MAC.

In interpreting other MAC clauses, buyers will have to continually evaluate the development of the COVID-19 pandemic and its impacts on the relevant target assets or company. The existence of the COVID-19 pandemic may also entitle parties to invoke other contractual provisions, such as *force majeure* (although these are rarely included in SPAs, other than in the specialised forms of SPA known as farmout agreements). Outside of the express terms of an SPA, relief may be available by operation of law, such as the common law doctrine of frustration.

Lastly, buyers will need to properly and timely follow any procedures included in the SPA for invoking the MAC clause. In the MAC termination clause quoted above from the AIPN Model Form ASPA, the buyer would have to

46 *Grupo Hotelero Urvasco SA v Carey Value Added SL*, [2013] EWHC 1039 (Comm).

47 An ongoing case in the Delaware Chancery Court poses the question (among others) of whether a pandemic could be included in a generic carve-out for general economic conditions, social and political unrest and similar in a case where a seller had failed to negotiate or obtain a specific pandemic carve-out. *Juweel Investors Ltd V Carlyle Roundtrip LP*, Case 2020-0338, in the Court of Chancery of the State of Delaware.

promptly provide notice to the seller, in accordance with the SPA's notice provision, including sufficient detail as to the nature of the material adverse event. The AIPN Model Form ASPA then requires a response notice from the seller and further procedures to attempt to resolve any disputes.

5.2 What should contractual counterparties do now?

Faced with an uncertain future caused by the COVID-19 pandemic, there are several practical steps for contractual parties to consider:

- Keep a detailed written record of the impacts (both direct and indirect) that COVID-19 is having on the target business, assets or company. These types of contemporary records can be valuable in any later disputes. These records can also be useful when preparing the type of detailed MAC notice contemplated by the MAC termination clause quoted above from the AIPN Model Form ASPA.
- Review relevant contractual clauses as the COVID-19 pandemic evolves, and continually assess contractual rights and obligations against the ever-changing factual situation. As noted above, the consequences of invoking a MAC clause wrongly can be significant, including repudiatory breach and potentially substantial damages.
- Consider opening a dialogue with contractual counterparties as to how best to manage a contract during the impact of the pandemic.
- As a seller, consider how to mitigate the consequences of the pandemic on the target business, assets or company, now and in the future. Keep a detailed written record of all such mitigation efforts. As noted above, these types of contemporary records can be valuable in any later disputes.

As a buyer, consider raising specific due diligence enquiries in relation to the seller's handling of the impact of the pandemic. This may include, for example, enquiries regarding measures taken to mitigate financial loss, to handle continued supplies of goods and services, and to manage workplace health and safety in compliance with local requirements.

- As noted above, ensure prompt and full compliance with all contractual procedures, including notice requirements. Be proactive in responding to any notices.
- For contractual counterparties negotiating SPAs in the time of the COVID-19 pandemic, consider more explicit language regarding disease and pandemics, to ensure that the MAC clause is clear as to whether the pandemic and its consequences can constitute a MAC. Although, as noted above in section 2.2(d), both US and English courts have held in certain circumstances that a party cannot invoke a MAC clause on the basis of facts or circumstances that it was aware of at the time it entered

the SPA, it may still be possible to draft specific wording to address the possibility that the consequences (including the duration) of the pandemic are not known now and may not be known for some time. In this regard, consider the discussion above in section 3.5 regarding not requiring a 'change' and the 'continuation of any events or circumstances.'

6. Conclusion

MAC clauses are important provisions for the allocation of certain risks between sellers and buyers. It is therefore no surprise that MAC clauses can be some of the most controversial and heavily negotiated provisions in an SPA for upstream oil and gas assets or companies. It looks likely that the COVID-19 pandemic will further shape the landscape for the drafting and interpretation of MAC clauses in the years to come.

Private equity considerations

Simon Tysoe
Latham & Watkins LLP

1. Private equity involvement in the oil and gas industry

A notable feature of the oil and gas M&A market in recent years has been the increasing involvement of private equity in the oil and gas sector and the impact that this has had on sale processes. This interest is not a new development occurring only in the last few years, but the culmination of years of growing interest in the sector. Specialist oil and gas-focused private equity funds started coming into existence during the 1980s, primarily in the United States, focusing on a mixture of upstream, midstream and oil field services targets. Interest was by no means universal, as many private equity funds were wary of taking on the reservoir risk (ie, the risk of hydrocarbons being present or, if present, being non-recoverable or recoverable at lower rates than make economic sense) inherent in acquiring upstream assets, and also of the large capex exposure of projects; and this coloured their view of the sector. However, the number of specialist funds increased slowly during the intervening years. In the early to mid-2000s, a number of the larger global private equity houses began to develop their own special energy funds seeking to deploy capital into the sector, often avoiding reservoir risk (at least directly) by investing in midstream or oil field services assets, but nevertheless actively engaged in the sector. By 2014, there were a wide range of private equity investors interested and active in the sector, ranging in size from multibillion-pound funds managed by some of the largest private equity houses in the world to small multimillion-pound funds which were typically little more than private offices for wealthy families.

A step change in the scale of private equity investment into the sector came in the aftermath of the 2014 oil price collapse, whereby private equity saw that the downturn represented a great opportunity for investment at a time when oil prices and corporate valuations were low, so as to take advantage of a future uptick in the market. At the same time, the development of fracking techniques in the production of shale gas and tight oil, especially in North America, had effectively removed reservoir risk in relation to those projects, greatly widening the pool of potential investors. Investors poured capital into the oil and gas market: it is estimated that private equity invested over $64 billion into the oil and gas industry from 2015 to 2016.[1] The primary target for this investment, representing over two-thirds of the capital deployed, has been the United States, spread across shale gas and tight oil plays, with the remainder placed into conventional assets. Outside of the United States, the primary destination for investment was Europe, where it has been estimated that roughly $13 billion was invested over the same period. Much of this investment went into the UK and Norwegian North Sea and, from a very low base, private equity-backed companies now control upwards of 10% of the total North Sea oil and gas production.

It is now the case that no oil and gas sales process can ignore private equity, and either the funds directly or their portfolio companies participate in a large proportion of the M&A activity in the sector. As such, M&A processes for oil and gas sellers are now often designed to accommodate and in some cases target private equity investors. Further, although the majority of private equity activity to date has been buy-side investment, such investments will always require an exit, so sales by private equity funds will likely be an increasing feature of the market in the coming years. Therefore, an awareness of the drivers for private equity investments, and indeed the drivers for subsequent exits from such investments, is important for any participant in the market. This chapter seeks to explain some of the differences that private equity investors are likely to insist on in sale and purchase documentation compared to other strategic investors. The chapter concentrates on the differences as they apply to upstream oil and gas transactions, an approach that is common across this book. However, some of the techniques and preferences mentioned will equally apply to midstream, downstream and oilfield services subsectors. At this stage, there is a much clearer picture of what the private equity 'markets' look like on the buy side than on the sell side. However, a number of points can be made regarding the private equity approach to the sell-side scenario, based on the author's experience.

2. Key drivers for private equity investment

For anyone negotiating opposite a private equity-backed company in a buy-out transaction for the first time, it is important to remember that there may be a number of different constituents on the other side of the table, whether you can see them or not. First, there is the portfolio company itself, typically established and led by the management team, members of which will be well versed in the oil and gas industry. Most will have spent many years in oil and gas companies and will be well aware of the techniques and issues discussed elsewhere in this book. Secondly, there is the private equity fund itself, which is responsible for

1 Wood Mackenzie, cited by Simon Flowers in "Private Equity assesses its options for exiting oil and gas", *Forbes*, November 2019

providing the portfolio company with the majority of the capital for the acquisition – either entirely on its own or with other funds joining with it on a co-investment basis. This lead fund itself may be led by people who are highly knowledgeable in the oil and gas sector, or it may be a generalist fund. Thirdly, there are usually the lenders which are providing debt to the portfolio company through arrangements put in place by the funds. The latter two constituents have particular requirements that are likely to influence the shape of the sale and purchase documentation.

2.1 Particular requirements of the fund

Private equity funds possess a number of features that drive, and to some extent constrain, the decisions that they make in connection with investments and the position that they take on sale and purchase documentation. The first of these is the nature of the fund itself. A typical private equity fund is a closed-ended, limited partnership consisting of limited partners (LPs) representing a wide range of investors, from public or corporate pension funds to insurance companies, high-net-worth individuals, family offices, endowments, sovereign wealth funds and so on. These LPs typically own around 99% of the shares in a fund and have limited liability. The LPs are advised by a general partner (GP), which is responsible for managing the fund and executing acquisitions and disposals on the fund's behalf, and has full liability for the fund's activities. While the GP typically has a small percentage ownership in the fund, generally 1%, the main focus for it will be the management fees which the GP charges the LPs for managing the assets owned by the fund. The GP acts as a fiduciary for the LPs and as such has a degree of duty towards the LPs to safeguard their money. This means that private equity general partners are traditionally reluctant to take on risky investments and it was this that informed their historic view of reservoir risk. Furthermore, the GP will be very wary of any risk of certain liabilities (eg, environmental liability and decommissioning costs) which might pierce the corporate veil and 'infect' the other corporate entities in their fund structure. As well as concern for investors in oil and gas-focused funds, GPs may well manage a range of funds, including funds that are focused on energy and those that are not. If the GP is exposed to liabilities such as environmental liabilities which could potentially pierce the corporate veil, then the management of not only an energy-focused fund (where the investors might arguably be said to have been cognisant of the risks that attend energy investment) but also other, non-energy-focused funds and investors might be impacted by these liabilities.

The twin problems of environmental risk and reservoir risk traditionally caused many private equity firms investing in the energy space to avoid investment in the upstream and instead invest in less risky areas, such as oilfield services and midstream energy infrastructure. However, the need to invest in higher-return option investments over time has led to increasing focus on investment in the upstream and the attendant risks that brings with it. As they have moved further towards investing in the upstream, this has meant that private equity firms have looked to manage their risk in this regard through thorough due diligence, transaction structuring and the inclusion of certain provisions within the terms of the acquisition documentation, which are addressed later in this chapter.

As noted, the typical fund is closed-ended – that is, it is not a permanent structure, but rather designed to be wound-up after a limited lifespan, usually 10 years plus a possible period of extensions, by which point investments entered into by the fund will have been liquidated and returns made to the investors. Further individual investments will have a finite period during which the private equity fund will typically expect to demonstrate returns before exiting the investment, the time from the initial investment to the exit being the 'hold period' for that investment. Hold periods vary from fund to fund, but typically in general private equity are between three and six years. However, given the slightly longer investment periods of the energy industry, hold periods and overall fund duration in the energy sector tend to be a little longer, at between five and seven years and 10 years respectively.

This feature of private equity has a number of important consequences. First, there is an impetus to make investments as soon as possible in the fund's life, to give the greatest opportunity to turn them around in the time available. Secondly, there is profound concern to avoid long-term commitments (contingent or actual), especially any which might extend past the projected life of the fund and therefore impede its liquidation and the return of capital to the investors. Thirdly, and crucially, private equity investment activity has foremost in its mind the need to successfully carry out an exit within the intended hold period. Due diligence is carried out with this in mind, with turnaround plans being prepared even before the investment is made to address issues identified. The prospect of unidentified issues coming to light and changing the investment thesis is unappealing. For many funds, therefore, the warranty and disclosure exercise is particularly key, as is recourse if the warranted position proves not to be true.

While funds have liquidity, they are not typically highly capitalised. When funds are raised, they do not – unlike companies raising equity capital and issuing fully paid-up shares – typically receive the proceeds of their fundraising directly. Funding will be contractually committed by investors subject only to limited excuse and cancellation rights; however, it is only as and when investments are identified by the GP that the LPs are approached and their funds are drawn down. Although the LPs will typically have little discretion as to whether to fund up to their committed amount (being already contractually bound), they will require clarity as to the amount required for an investment and GPs will be sensitive to making draw-down requests more than once in respect of an investment without good reason.

Even outside of the particular risks attendant with upstream investments, private equity firms are subject to stringent internal regulatory and compliance regimes, and have a particular focus on anti-bribery and corruption due diligence, as well as the regular 'know your customer' due diligence that we would expect from a financial institution. Most large private equity funds are subject to anti-corruption laws and will be obliged (or otherwise will seek) to comply in particular with the US Foreign Practices Act 1997 and the UK Bribery Act 2010. Each of these statutes has broad scope and has the ability to make companies responsible for the activities of their employees and agents. The energy industry has a particular focus on this, given that many investments are carried out in non-Organisation for Economic Co-operation and Development countries where corrupt activities present a greater risk because they are not subject to the same legislative prohibitions and active enforcement. A private equity investor acquiring a target company or assets will therefore need to satisfy itself that the historic activities, training guidance and procedures of the target are adequate; and to do so, it will consider reasonably extensive due diligence on partners or contractors to confirm that their companies comply with such laws. In addition, where a target was not previously subject to the legislation itself, the private equity fund will need to ensure that, post-acquisition, the company puts in place procedures adequate to ensure compliance going forward.

2.2 Requirements of the lenders

Almost all private equity buy-side transactions include a degree of leverage in the form of debt financing and those that do not put debt financing in place in the initial acquisition will almost certainly be looking to put debt in place soon thereafter. This debt finance enhances the potential returns on the equity investment and historically the majority of this finance has been provided by major commercial and investment banks. In recent years, numerous other sources of financing – such as specialist investment funds and hedge funds, insurers, pension funds, high-yield bond investors and, in the energy space, commodity traders – have augmented the ranks of potential lenders. Discussion of the private equity financing structures is outside the scope of this chapter, but it is worth noting that any private equity fund looking to execute a buy-side transaction will inevitably have to keep in mind the requirements of its lender group, which may vary depending on the lenders involved. Some of these requirements will flow through into the sale and purchase documentation in the form of warranties and covenants. These will include provisions for putting a security package in place as well as certain conditions precedent which the lenders will include as conditions to the drawdown of funds under the loan facility. For many sellers facing private equity, these requirements will be novel, since the financing arrangements of many large oil and gas companies are put in place at the corporate level and rarely directly impinge on individual assets.

3. Impacts on sale and purchase agreements

3.1 Structure – share sale versus asset sale

For private equity investors looking to acquire an energy business, there will be two or more competing considerations. The first is liability. Briefly, a share sale means that the historic liabilities of the company will come across in the transaction; whereas an asset sale enables the buyer to acquire the assets of the business without taking on the historic liabilities for their operation. It is therefore a cleaner way to do the acquisition and, consequently, one would expect that a private equity house would be attracted to it. However, an asset sale can also be much more complex, which – given that a private equity fund has relatively limited internal resources – may in and of itself be enough to dissuade a fund from pursuing that route. In addition, asset deals almost invariably require a larger number of third-party consents and may well open up the transaction to the exercise of third-party pre-emption rights and possibly government consent which, in the context of a share sale, would not apply. Practice is slightly different in the United States, where private equity firms traditionally push much more strongly for asset deals in the context of upstream transactions. In the midstream, it is acknowledged that these can often be more challenging and it is less common that private equity firms would be able to insist on an asset deal.

The two conflicting considerations may be reconciled by a two-step transaction in which assets are 'hived in' to a new, clean company which the private equity fund then acquires. This has the potential for reconciling the issues, as the private equity fund acquires a clean company without historic operational liability; and at the same time, the restructuring of the assets in order to effect the 'hive-in' can be done by the selling entity, possibly as an intragroup transaction – potentially therefore avoiding some of the worst disadvantages of an asset sale. From a tax point of view, this structure might also allow the buyer to re-base the value of the assets, which a share purchase alone might not allow, as well as potentially preserving the tax efficient nature of the share sale for the seller.

Private equity acting on the sell side will almost certainly prefer to structure the sale as a share sale, so as to maximise the chance of disposing of liabilities associated with the business and also to take advantage of the more tax-efficient regime on offer to share sales in many jurisdictions.

3.2 Consideration

Many private equity investments into the oil and gas industry have been carried out during periods of downturn within the industry. It is, of course, a feature of private equity investment that investments are sought when valuations are at their lowest and pools of liquidity are not necessarily open to the seller. This tends to mean that there is a degree of gap between the valuations that buyer and seller would have, particularly in circumstances where the future oil price is unpredictable. Private equity is very keen, therefore, to seek inventive ways to bridge this gap. One limitation that a private equity investor suffers is that, unlike a listed entity, it cannot offer the seller listed securities which would help bridge the gap, but instead will often look to be very inventive in the terms of deferred or contingent consideration that it may offer to bridge pricing gaps. Given the structure of private equity funds, as mentioned before, the general partner is unlikely to wish to go back to its LPs to get extra funding for the contingent consideration. Similarly, the LPs are unlikely to put the general partner into funds for the payment of contingent consideration if it remains contingent and certain not to crystallise for a number of years. Therefore, in most cases, contingent consideration mechanisms provided by private equity funds tend to be based on cash-flow generations by the target itself.

Although some form of deferred and contingent consideration may be agreed in the sale and purchase documentation linking to, for instance, certain milestones or oil price metrics, a true earn-out mechanism based on, for instance, profitability or earnings is generally resisted by private equity buyers. It is considered to be very much the business of the private equity fund to improve the functioning and performance of the target and therefore participation of the seller in this tends to be resisted. In addition, private equity buyers tend to be resistant to the sorts of restrictions, controls and audit rights that a traditional earn-out arrangement would entail. Any deferred consideration will need to be reviewed closely by tax specialists to ensure that the amounts received under any deferred arrangement are considered to be capital rather than income, as this would be tax inefficient.

The simplest of these, commonly seen in 2016 and 2017, was the consideration payment triggered upon the oil price reaching certain prescribed prices in the future. Typically, payments were then to be made based on profits and cash flow achieved by the underlying asset being acquired. The last part is crucial, since reliable measurement of the performance of the assets once under the control of the buyer is important and there is always an underlying concern in any earn-out arrangement that the buyer will under-report the performance. Notably, when considering such a mechanism, the contingent payment obligation is likely to be on the purchasing company, but the producing assets on which the payment is calculated may likely reside in a subsidiary lower in the structure. Therefore, in order to avoid the need to source funds for payment of the contingent consideration from the LPs, the buyer will want to pay the calculated amount only once sufficient cash has been distributed up to it by the asset holding subsidiary – a process which may in turn be regulated by the restrictions imposed by the fund's lenders. Ensuring that this does not provide the buyer with a broad discretion to reduce or delay payment is a key concern for the seller.

Other triggers for contingent consideration – such as milestone production targets or the achievement of a final investment decision in relation to a certain project – are still common within the industry, but may require a drawdown of funds from the private equity fund if the consideration exceeds the cash flows of the company. For this reason, they are likely to be the exception rather than the norm for private equity fund buyers, although the larger funds typically have more flexibility in this regard.

On the sell side, private equity is more reluctant to accept contingent consideration, since it is keen to achieve certainty in respect of consideration and, particularly as the fund nears the end of its term, cannot accept terms that would defer payment until after the end of the fund's life. Funds which are early in their lifecycle may have more flexibility in this regard.

3.3 Equity commitment letter

The payment of the consideration itself is also the focus of the quintessential private equity instrument: the equity commitment letter. The equity commitment letter originated as a means of assuring a buyer portfolio company and its management that the private equity fund would in fact pay the consideration, or at least the equity percentage of the consideration, on completion of the deal. Since the portfolio company itself, at the point of committing to its initial acquisition, was unlikely to have sufficient funds to pay the consideration when it fell due, the directors would be in breach of their fiduciary duties to the company to permit the company to enter into the agreement unless they had a back-to-back obligation from the fund. The provision of an equity commitment letter from the fund ensured that the portfolio company directors had the necessary assurance to enter into the sale and purchase agreement (SPA). Over time, this feature of the private equity market and the use of special purpose acquisition vehicles led sellers to commonly require not only to see the terms of the equity commitment letter (so that they themselves had assurance that the portfolio company buyer would have the relevant required funds at completion), but also to require some degree of reliance on the letter by having the letter addressed to the seller or having the benefit of some form of step-in rights. This means that if that the portfolio company cannot or refuses to draw down the funds, then the seller can itself step in and draw down the funds in order to effect completion or potentially claim damages against the fund. A private equity buyer with the upper hand will still often push back hard on addressing the equity letter to the seller or providing step-in rights, and this is often a hard-fought point in negotiations. If the buyer concedes a more seller-friendly letter, then in negotiating the equity commitment letter, both the seller and the portfolio company have a degree of alignment as against the fund. Conditionality of the commitment will be key. Funds will often seek to make the commitment conditional upon debt financing reaching closing and successfully being drawn down, but that leaves both the portfolio company and the seller in an uncertain position, so they will resist this conditionality. Further, unless the buyer has succeeded in negotiating a debt financing condition in the SPA – which is indeed a rare event – the portfolio company and the seller will both be keen to see that the commitment extends to payment of the whole of the purchase price and not just the equity element, which for structural reasons is difficult for the buyer (the debt element being outside its control). Finally, in order to cover scenarios where closing fails to happen because of a contractual breach by the portfolio company, the seller will want to see that the commitment letter covers not only payment of the consideration, but also the payment of damages incurred by the portfolio company for its breach.

The equity commitment letter therefore seeks to fulfil the same functions that a parent company guarantee offered by the credit-worthy strategic parent in respect of its thinly capitalised subsidiary would. However, the equity commitment letter is typically capped and is drafted so that the obligations of the fund are not open ended.

3.4 Completion adjustments

The two principal forms of price adjustment in sale and purchase agreements, as discussed elsewhere in this book, are completion accounts and the locked-box mechanism. Most oil and gas transactions have traditionally had some form of accounts-based adjustment included in them. For instance, in an upstream transaction, there is typically some form of working capital adjustment either at completion or potentially at an earlier effective date, seeking to adjust for material working capital matters such as overlift and underlift. The adjustments under completion accounts can sometimes be quite significant and there may well be disputes which arise over the amount of any adjustments which, if not resolved in a certain period, will be referred to an independent expert chartered accountant for determination. This can result in prolonged deferment of receipt of consideration. Even where there are no disputes as to the calculation, there can be dynamics that are hard to handle. In downstream transactions, especially the sale of refineries, much of the value of the transaction is frequently tied up in the crude oil and refined product stock held by the refinery, and this therefore forms a very material part of the overall consideration. Typically, this stock is valued as at the date of completion and swings in the oil price between signing and closing, plus the cyclical nature of stock holding, mean that there can be large variations in purchase price to be paid at completion. Any post-closing clawback of consideration poses difficulties for funds which are obliged to return capital to investors as quickly as possible, so private equity sellers display a very marked preference for using a locked-box mechanism when they are selling companies. The locked-box mechanism offers a high degree of certainty, since – provided that the 'leakage' and 'permitted leakage' definitions are properly negotiated – reduction to the purchase price due to leakage should happen only due to circumstances in the seller's control.

Although the concerns of private equity funds are mainly in respect of their position of the sell side, and stem from the desire for certainty and the reluctance to accept post-completion liability, even on the buy side, private equity buyers are often reluctant to accept completion accounts because of the practical difficulties for the private equity fund of drawing down further funding at short notice from their LPs, co-investors and lenders. In order to mitigate these potential issues, if they do accept completion accounts, then funds will often be concerned to ensure that the degree of swing is minimised – for instance, by using a target working capital work construct and ensuring that, in any event, as much work as possible is done to agree what the accounts will look like ahead of signing. Since it is impossible to eliminate all possible movement while at the same time keeping the usefulness of the mechanism itself, buyers will be keen to see that adequate information on the changes to the working capital position of the target between signing and completion are regularly passed to the buyer in a timely manner, so that there are no surprising increases in the purchase price come completion.

3.5 Interim covenants

Almost all energy transactions involve a split signing and completion process. This is normally mandated by the need to obtain government approval which is required in order to close the transaction. This might take the form of regulatory consent under the terms of a hydrocarbons licence in an upstream transaction or antitrust approval in a downstream transaction. Satisfaction of these conditions precedent may take some time and it is not unusual to expect that there will be a period of up to one year between signing and completion of a transaction. During the period between signing and completion (the interim period), private equity buyers, like any buyer, will normally insist on there being a suite of restrictions and indeed positive obligations on the seller. The interim covenants insisted on will normally fall into two categories.

(a) General covenants

The first category of interim covenants is aimed at delivering information on and control over the company and the business going forward. These are in nature the same as, although may often be more detailed than, those insisted upon by strategic buyers. A typical private equity buyer will include extensive obligations on the seller to share information during the interim period, including operational information. In the upstream context, this may well involve the sharing of information of operating committee meetings and an insistence that buyer representatives attend such meetings. With a view to ensuring that the position of the company at closing is not materially different from that at signing, a private equity buyer may well insist that the seller not agree to any increases in budget or authorisations for expenditure over a certain low threshold. It is also usual to include a positive obligation on the seller to ensure that the business is continued on the ordinary course and in compliance with relevant laws and the terms of any hydrocarbons licences. Notification by the seller in the event of any material event, including the commencement of any litigation or the discovery of any environmental issue, will also be expected.

One area of the interim covenants in which private equity buyers might seek unusually detailed provisions is insurance. Since the fund and its portfolio company will not have significant reserves of capital to fix problems and funding of the company will to a large extent rely on cash flow, private equity buyers will be keen to ensure that the SPA includes a positive obligation to keep insurances in place and maintain payment of insurance premia. This clause typically will deal also with the use of insurance proceeds in event of a claim. This can be a contentious area for sellers, since they will wish to protect their group insurance policies from claims arising in the period between signing and completion, arguing that risk should pass at signing save to the extent that there are specific warranties, interim protections or termination events. An example of a typical clause is set out below:

1. *From the date of this Agreement until the Completion Date, the Seller shall ensure that all policies of insurance relating to the business or assets of the Group in force as of the date of this Agreement (the "Current Insurance Policies") are kept in force in accordance with past practices. In the event that the Sellers shall become aware of any fact, event or circumstance arising after the date of this Agreement and prior to the Completion Date in respect of which a claim may be made under the Current Insurance Policies, the Seller shall (a) notify the Purchaser (b) cause the Target Company to file a claim in respect of such event or circumstance and (c) have such claim paid to the Target Company prior to the Completion Date, in each case in accordance with its customary past practices.*
2. *In the event that such a claim is not paid prior to the Completion Date, the Sellers shall use all reasonable endeavours to:*

   2.1 pursue payment in respect of such a claim on behalf of the relevant Operating Company;

2.2 keep the Purchaser informed as to all relevant developments with respect to such claim;

2.3 ensure that the relevant Operating Company shall receive any payment made in respect of any such claim, when and to the extent such claim shall be paid by the insurers.

3. *At any time after the Closing Date and subject to the Seller's consent (such consent not to be unreasonably withheld, delayed or conditioned) the Purchaser may elect to take sole conduct of any such claim and the Seller shall give and shall procure that the relevant members of the Seller's Group give the Purchaser all assistance as it may reasonably require to enable it to pursue payment in respect of such claim under the Current Insurance Policies.*

(b) Financing covenants

The second category of interim covenants comprises those that flow from how a private equity acquisition is being financed. Certain negative covenants will be put in place to prevent the target from taking actions that would jeopardise the financing because, if they occurred, they would breach covenants in the debt facility agreement or trigger an event of default under the facility either immediately or immediately upon the target joining the borrower group at closing. Some typical covenants in a facility agreement which might need to be flowed down into the SPA include:

- disposing of or creating security over assets;
- taking on indebtedness or entering into guarantees;
- amending or terminating material contracts;
- granting credit or making distributions; and
- entering into hedging arrangements.

With reference to the last covenant mentioned above, given the variations in oil prices, the putting in place of hedging arrangements can also be a key part of the acquisition process from the private equity buyer's point of view, and so control over the replacement of existing hedging arrangements and cooperation in putting in place new hedging arrangements to take effect on completion are important elements to include. To that extent, the obligations would be no different from those you would expect any buyer to put in place, although the private equity buyer necessarily has less flexibility to compromise on these provisions than a buyer that is not reliant on debt financing.

It is also likely that the private equity buyer will require not only assurance in the form of negative covenants that the target will not put itself in a position to jeopardise the financing, but also positive covenants that the target will cooperate with the financing in order to achieve financial close and drawdown of the acquisition funds. A basic and buyer-friendly version of this type of provision is set out below:

Subject to the terms of this Agreement, the Seller shall give the Purchaser all reasonable assistance as is customary for a seller and target company to give in international acquisition financings and as may be requested in writing by the Purchaser in order to assist the Purchaser to secure the Financing including assisting in the creation of security and pledging of collateral and the putting in place of price hedging arrangements in respect of the hydrocarbon production of the Target Group. Without prejudice to the foregoing, the Sellers shall, as soon as reasonably practicable and in any event within two (2) Business Days of the request, (a) provide the Purchaser such financial information in respect of the Target Group and (b) undertake such actions or deeds, in each case as may from time to time be required under or reasonably requested by the Purchaser in connection with the Financing.

The obligations under this Clause shall not require the Sellers to incur any costs at their own expense and, on written request, the Purchaser shall pay the Sellers' reasonable third party out of pocket expenses incurred in complying with their obligations under this Clause.

Sellers may well be reluctant to enter into such open-ended obligations, especially where they are not used to the requirements of acquisition financing themselves, and may seek to negotiate more granular obligations. Where the acquisition is being financed by the issuance of securities, such as high-yield bonds (which is a typical structure used by private equity portfolio companies), the terms of the cooperation provisions may well be very detailed, since the buyer will require a good deal of financial data and financial cooperation between signing and closing in preparing offering memoranda and the like. In such cases, interim obligations on the seller may extend to:

- preparing audited accounts (especially where recent audited accounts of the target are not available);
- cooperating with obtaining ratings for the debt financing;
- co-operating with the marketing endeavours for any part of the debt financing;
- providing, and using reasonable endeavours to cause third parties to provide, such financial statements and financial information as to satisfy securities regulations;
- participating in a reasonable number of presentations, management meetings, bank meetings, road shows, presentations to prospective lenders, investors and rating agencies, conference calls, due diligence sessions and other similar meetings, and preparing of auditors' comfort letters; and
- assisting efforts to effect the pledging of collateral at the closing date in connection with the debt financing.

Given the degree of involvement in the buyer's financing and the possibility of liability to third parties being incurred, the seller will most likely seek broad indemnification from the buyer in respect of any liability relating to its assistance, especially any liability under relevant securities laws. Typically, a buyer will accept such indemnification provided that the scope of it is not so broad as to negate the point of the provision in the first place and with a carve-out for the wilful default of the seller.

(c) ***Separation issues***

Given that many oil and gas transactions involve the carving out of a target business from a larger entity, a range of other items may need to be addressed in the interim period in order to ensure that the target group is ready to operate as a standalone entity. Separation issues arise in all transactions; but it should be remembered that the issues in private equity transactions are particularly acute, since instead of the target being assimilated into a larger group with existing support functions such as insurance, IT and payroll, these may well be being established for the first time during the interim period or being sourced from third parties. Assistance with, for instance, putting in place energy package insurance into a group which has typically self-insured will be important. Further, a robust process, to be carried out pre-closing, for identifying services provided by the seller group and either replacing those with third-party vendors or agreeing transitional service arrangements with the seller is a key part of most transactions.

The same rules as regards gun jumping apply to private equity transactions as to any other, and therefore a buyer must carefully review the terms of any interim covenants so as to ensure that the degree of restriction and information that it has in place does not infringe antitrust rules and risk enforcement action by a regulator.

3.6 Interim period termination rights

(a) ***Pre-emption rights***

Typically, an upstream sale and purchase agreement (asset or share) regarding multiple assets will provide that if pre-emption is exercised by a third party, then those individual assets drop out from the deal and a price adjustment is put in place to reflect that, to the extent necessary. For a financed acquisition, the removal of certain assets through pre-emption may be more problematic. If the financing is predicated on there being a certain amount of production in place at closing, then pre-emption of the 'crown jewels' may well jeopardise the transaction, and this scenario is likely to be set out in the terms of the finance agreement as an event that would allow the lender to cease funding. As a result, it is not unusual for a private equity buyer to insist on a termination right should certain assets be pre-empted.

(b) Material adverse change

The existence of an interim period also creates a risk for the buyer that the target may suffer some material decline in its performance during that period notwithstanding the interim period covenants. Buyers may seek to include termination rights to guard against this through a material adverse change (MAC) clause. MAC clauses have been discussed elsewhere in this book, but it is worth considering them from the point of view of the private equity buyer.

The private equity buyer is typically dependent on the lenders providing financing for the transaction at close. Over time, the private equity funds have worked with providers of acquisition finance to reduce the conditions to drawdown in their facilities to practically none, so that the private equity buyer can be assured that at signing, it has 'certain funds' as regards its debt component. In the broader private equity market, where such 'certain funds' acquisition financing is available to be put in place, the risk for the private equity company is slim. As a result, in most European transactions outside of the energy sector, MAC clauses are not a large feature of SPAs. However, particularly in the context of upstream financing, many of the acquisition finance packages available contain conditions to drawdown, including liquidity tests or events of default, such that they fall short of what private equity would typically view as 'certain funds'. Many of these requirements may be covered off through interim covenants in the SPA (as discussed above) with relatively little seller push-back. However, some may not be able to be treated this way, and the key issues frequently wrestled with include expropriation or nationalisation of assets, physical loss and damage where insurance is insufficient to cover repair, or illegality of certain obligations under the finance documents, such as the repatriation of funds. This creates a potential mismatch which could lead to a situation where the private equity company is required to close the transaction even though the lenders are not required to provide funding under their documentation. To close this gap, it is often the case that a limited MAC clause is insisted upon by the private equity buyers in the energy space. This is typically not a broad MAC clause focusing on any downturn in the performance of the target, but more a specific clause looking at certain individual events which would jeopardise financing. In other words, a private equity buyer will seek to 'back-to-back' the limited situations in which the lenders can refuse to fund and turn those into termination rights under the SPA. As such, the provisions typically focus on events that would mean that the target is no longer able to generate revenue and therefore no longer able to service its debt. They may also target certain changes in law that, for instance, jeopardise the investment or the repatriation of cash, such as the imposition of sanctions. Two examples of such definition of a MAC are set out below.

"Material Adverse Change Event" , means an event occurring between the date hereof and Completion, including the exercise of any pre-emption rights, which causes the Target to cease to own or be deprived of or any of the rights attaching to any of the Key Assets or which results in any damage to or destruction of any Key Asset:

(a) which causes or is reasonably anticipated to cause the cessation of production of hydrocarbons from such Key Asset for a period of more than three months or the reduction of in the daily aggregate production of hydrocarbons from the Key Assets to below [X] barrels per day for a period of at least six consecutive months; or

(b) in respect of which the Seller's aggregate direct costs (excluding costs associated with loss of production, loss of profits, loss of revenue, loss of goodwill, loss of opportunity, loss of business or any indirect or consequential losses) in restoring production from such Key Asset would exceed thirty percent (30%) of the Consideration (prior to any adjustments thereto), having disregarded any amount which is or may be recoverable by the Seller from its insurers.

"Material Adverse Change Event" means a change to any applicable Laws or of its interpretation or application, that:

(a) is not and was not caused by a wilful act or wilful omission by the Purchaser;

(b) occurs after the date of this Agreement;

(c) applies to any of (i) the Purchaser or the Group or (ii) the transactions contemplated under or connected with this Agreement; and

(d) causes or will cause:

(i) a material adverse impact on the financial condition of the Purchaser or the Group as at the date of this Agreement or the value of the business or the assets of the Group, taken as a whole, of thirty percent (30%) or more of the Consideration; or

(ii) any Relevant Contract to become invalid, unenforceable or ineffective; or

(iii) a restriction on the ability of the Target Company to grant or effect security over or in respect of any Relevant Contract, asset or material Property, including without limitation, the ability to validate, perfect, enforce, subordinate, secure or grant encumbrances over any such Relevant Contract, asset or material Property or to sell, assign or transfer any of them to a third party;

3.7 Warranties

A private equity buyer will typically require a fuller suite of warranties than many trade buyers, the reasons for which are often quite closely linked to the preoccupations of private equity funds that we have mentioned above. In particular, they are concerned to ensure that they have a full picture of those liabilities that could potentially infect the fund more broadly – most notably around environmental issues, decommissioning obligations and bribery and corruption issues. In addition to the warranties that are insisted on by the private equity house for its own reasons, it is likely that the lenders will include certain warranties in the financing agreement that will need to be replicated or mirrored as best they can be in the underlying SPA. Lenders will be particularly concerned that the target business has complied with applicable laws, and especially that it is not in breach of applicable environmental laws. Further, they will look to pick up litigation and regulatory action. Therefore, the private equity buyer's ability to accept a strong seller-friendly position is to some extent dictated by its ability to negotiate a satisfactory outcome with banks.

(a) *Financial statements*

Given the importance of an accurate valuation of the assets, both the fund and its lenders will also be concerned that the target accounts (balance-sheet, profit and loss and cash-flow statements) are true and accurate, and that there has been no MAC since the date of the last set of financial statements. In situations where audited accounts are not available, or in a carve-out situation, where the carve-out process means that the last set of audited accounts is no longer reliable in respect of the target, this can cause problems, since the buyer will often nonetheless want the accounts warranted to the standard typically give in respect of audited accounts. Sellers will potentially feel exposed and unable to give the warranty. Difficulties can also arise when trying to reconcile local generally accepted accounting principles with International Financial Reporting Standards, for instance. For both parties, therefore, engaging in financial due diligence at an early stage is crucial.

(b) *Disclosure*

One particular provision that can cause some difficulty in negotiation is the lenders' frequent insistence on a warranty that all information disclosed to the lenders by the borrowers, including information relating to the target, is true and accurate in all material respects. This warranty in itself will need to be replicated in the SPA, not in the form of a 'full disclosure' warranty that the seller has disclosed everything of material relevance to the target, but rather that the information which it has disclosed in the data room or otherwise is materially accurate. This warranty can be difficult for the seller to give, particularly when it has relied on information given by third parties such as operators; and therefore, it is often important to specify in the warranty contained in the SPA exactly which materials have been produced and shared with the lenders and are the subject of the warranty in the facility agreements.

> *True, complete and accurate copies of each Material Contract have been included in the Data Room and are in full force and effect and the Company is not in material breach or default of any Material Contract and, so far as the Seller is aware, no other party to any Material Contract is in material breach or default of any of them.*

(c) *Insurance*

As noted above, private equity buyers will have a particular interest in the insurance of the target and this will include the scope of warranties required by the buyer regarding this subject. A set of insurance warranties might look like the following.

(a) Each member of the target Group has material insurances in respect of its business and assets in place in accordance with the good practice of international oil companies operating in [region of assets] ("Material Insurances"). The policies in respect of all such Material Insurances are on terms standard in all material respects to those accepted by international oil companies operating in [region of assets].

(b) Details or copies of the Material Insurances and any claims made or being considered in respect of them have been disclosed and are true, accurate and not misleading.

(c) The Material Insurances are in full force and effect, with all premia paid, and neither the Sellers, nor any member of the target Group, have done or omitted to do anything the doing or omission of which would make such insurances void or voidable.

(d) *Separation issues*

Many private equity buyers seeking to acquire assets from large oil and gas companies are concerned by the carve-out nature of the transaction and are particularly interested to cover off whether there will be separation issues that come to light as the business leaves the parent entity. This is typically addressed through warranties in relation to separation issues asking for disclosure of all relevant intergroup arrangements and also potentially a sufficiency of assets warranty confirming that the assets of the target company owned by it on completion of the transaction are sufficient to carry on the business of the company as carried out in the previous 12 months – for example:

The Company will immediately following Closing have in its possession and control and good title to, and all appropriate authorisations, consents, licences, exemptions and filings to use, the assets (including relevant management systems, operating procedures and operations manuals) used in, and/or for the benefit of, or necessary to conduct the business of the Company in relation to the Interests in the manner conducted during the twelve (12) months prior to the date of this Agreement.

(e) *Environmental warranties*

In terms of environmental liability, private equity buyers tend to ask for more specific warranties than other buyers in the same industry might. As well as comfort that the target has been operating in material compliance with environmental laws, as noted previously, the buyer may well ask for confirmation that all material environmental licences and authorisations are in place and have not been revoked or suspended by the regulatory authority, and that there are and have been no environmental claims. Both the buyers and their lenders typically require a longer 'look-back' as regards environmental claims and enforcement action, usually four years or more. An example suite of provisions might look like this:

(a) *The Company has all material Environmental permits and/or licences in relation to the Interests to lawfully operate the Interests and, in the four years prior to the date of this Agreement, has not received written notice that it is in material default under any such permits and/or licences.*

(b) *The Company has complied in all material respects with its obligations under Environmental Law in so far as they relate to operations carried out in connection with any of the Operated Interests and has been in such material compliance for a period of four years prior to the date of this Agreement and any breaches of Environmental Law by the Company have been disclosed.*

(c) *No material release, migration, leakage, spillage, discharge, entry, deposit or emission of any Hazardous Material has occurred as a result of or in connection with operations carried out in connection with any of the Interests at any time within the period of four years prior to the date of this Agreement.*

(d) *There are no threatened or ongoing claims for breaches of Environmental Law in the four years prior to the date of this Agreement and so far as Seller is aware, there are no facts which are likely to give rise to any such claim.*

(e) *So far as the Seller is aware, no expenditure greater than USD$[5,000,000] is required in the 12 months after the date of this Agreement to ensure material compliance with Environmental Law for operations carried out in connection with any of the Interests.*

Further, where environmental reports have been disclosed, it is likely that these will be subject to accuracy and completeness warranties. It is also not unusual (although usually resisted) to see buyers request a targeted 'full disclosure' warranty as regards all environmental reports in the possession of the target and seller group.

In addition to information disclosure, private equity buyers are very keen to make sure that clean-up obligations have been carried out correctly to the extent they have been incurred, and that adequate provisions have been made by the target in respect of any environmental liability or decommissioning obligations that might affect the target. Where a local regime requires the establishment of funds for the decommissioning of oil and gas assets, the buyer will be keen to ensure that adequate provision has been made and, where required, that deposits have been made into the escrow funds or other funding and security mechanisms as required under local law or under contract. The scrutiny of such decommissioning security has intensified over time – and rightly so. Since decommissioning is a joint and several obligation, not only is the compliance of the target key, but so is the performance of other parties to the interest. The examples below are not unusual in terms of a buyer's position in a mark-up.

Example 1:

So far as the Seller is aware, all abandoned Wells which may at any time have been operate by or on behalf of the Company have been plugged and abandoned, pipelines removed as required and sites made safe in accordance with Good and Prudent Oilfield Practice and the terms of the relevant Licence, Environmental Permit and Environmental Law.

Example 2:

All decommissioning programmes required at any time by the Company under Environmental Law have been approved by the applicable Government Entity and have been prepared and are supported by suitable and adequate financial security, in accordance with Environmental Law and Good and Prudent Oilfield Practice.

Example 3:

Any decommissioning security which should have been provided by the Company or by any third party under any decommissioning security agreement relating to any of the Interests has been provided in accordance with such decommissioning security agreement and is in full force and effect and all decommissioning security instruments to which the Company is party, or to which any other member of the Seller Group is party to in respect of the Interests, have been disclosed.

The difficulty in warranty Example 2 below is the use of "suitable and adequate financial security" – a term which requires a degree of judgement and inevitably a degree of subjectivity. It is much more likely that a seller will accept a warranty such as Example 3, which requires the reporting of fact and the disclosure of what is in place; it is then for the buyer to determine what is suitable and adequate.

Environmental and decommissioning matters, including warranties, are discussed in detail in separate chapters.

(f) ***Anti-bribery and corruption***

Anti-bribery and corruption warranties in a private equity SPA tend to be more fulsome than would typically be offered by a seller. This partly stems from the concern of the private equity group that it might be simultaneously subject to Foreign Corrupt Practices Act and Bribery Act obligations, and therefore will seek to cover requirements of both sets of legislation in the warranties in relation to the target groups. In many respects, private equity buyers are no different from other oil and gas sector buyers, in that both are highly focused on anti-bribery and corruption matters. One additional focus is politically exposed persons – given that private equity is also a financial institution, it has anti-money laundering obligations, which are increased where government officials are involved. Therefore, even though no impropriety is to be inferred, the buyer may well include warranties such as the following:

Save as disclosed:

(a) no officer, director or employee of the Group is a Government Official or Politically Exposed Person.

(b) no Government Official or Government Entity owns, whether directly or indirectly, legally or beneficially any interest, in any member of the Group.

Where:

"Government Entity" means (i) any Governmental Authority; (ii) any public international organization; (iii) any company, business, enterprise, agency or undertaking whether incorporated or unincorporated owned, in whole or in part, or controlled by any government, entity, organization, or other person described in the foregoing clauses (i), (ii) or (iii) of this definition; or (iv) any established political party;

"Government Official" means any official or employee of any Government Entity (at any level), any person acting in an official capacity for a government regardless of rank or position, any official or employee of a company wholly or partially controlled by a government (for example, a state-owned oil company), a political party and any official of a political party, any candidate for political office or any officer or employee of a public international organisation, such as the United Nations or the World Bank or any immediate family member (meaning a spouse, dependent child or household member) of any of the foregoing;

"Politically Exposed Person" means (i) means a Politically Exposed Person (PEP) as defined by the Financial Action Task Force (FATF) or Groupe d'action Financière sur le Blanchiment de Capitaux (GAFI); or (ii) any company, business, enterprise or other entity owned, in whole or in part, or controlled by any Government Official;

In addition, buyers will insist on sanctions warranties to ensure that the target group is not subject to any sanctions and has not been involved in the violation of sanctions laws. Anti-bribery and corruption matters, including warranties, are discussed in detail in a separate chapter.

(g) *Repetition of warranties*

As for the repetition of warranties at completion, the market position that title warranties and other fundamental warranties are repeated at closing, but that broader business warranties are not generally repeated, also holds true when dealing with a private equity buyer. However, it is often the case that the private equity buyer's list of preferred title and fundamental warranties will be longer than a seller is typically used to seeing. This is because certain warranties will be informed by the financing warranties – that is, the buyer will wish to reflect those warranties which would, if incorrect under the facility agreement, permit the lenders to refuse to fund. This often means that, in the context of a share sale, the buyer will insist that (as well as the title and fundamental warranties) the warranties as to the good standing of petroleum licences, encumbrances over the targets assets, sanctions and anti-bribery and corruption matters are also repeated.

3.8 Broader allocation of liability

In relation to the allocation of environmental and decommissioning liabilities and broader pre and post-effective date liabilities, there is no significant difference between private equity buyers and sellers and the normal market. However, a fundamental difference with respect to risk allocation is likely to lie not necessarily in the documentation and the provisions of the SPA itself, but rather in the terms of any credit support that goes around it. Private equity buyers will be particularly keen to ensure that liability in respect of any indemnification (eg, in relation to environmental and decommissioning liability) is kept to a minimum and that it is, as far as possible, kept as an obligation of the portfolio company. To the extent that it is accepted that any liability is extended to the fund, a private equity buyer will want to ensure that it is well defined and ideally limited by reference to a cap. A full parent company guarantee from the fund will never be possible to obtain, so credit support tends to be structured in such a way that it can be provided by the portfolio company and the cash flows from that entity itself, all vented perhaps by letters of bank and letters of credit.

Taking liability for decommissioning as an example, private equity buyers of upstream assets will typically, if not happily, accept the customary position that they will indemnify the seller in respect of all environmental and decommissioning liabilities attaching to the assets of the target being acquired. However, this will be subject to two caveats. The first is that the environmental warranties and claims under them will be respected notwithstanding the indemnity; the second is that adequate due diligence (and disclosure to facilitate this) has been carried out. For midstream and downstream assets, where the contractual allocation of environmental liability in sale and purchase documentation is less clear cut in favour of the seller than in the upstream, private equity buyers will push as hard as they can to obtain clean-up indemnification from the buyer; but whether this is achieved is really just a function of the commercial position of the buyer in each particular transaction.

As mentioned above, the private equity buyer will seek to keep decommissioning liability to a minimum and with limited exposure for the fund. Indeed, in the case of decommissioning liability, a guarantee from the fund will not necessarily be suitable for the sort of long-life liabilities that decommissioning entails, since the fund itself may well be wound up years before decommissioning of a particular asset takes place. Instead, many private equity-backed buyers of assets have entered into complex decommissioning arrangements with the sellers which often allocate decommissioning liability and credit support for it in a more complex way.

Many of the deals in the North Sea seen in the last five years have involved arrangements through which, although on the face of the documentation the buyer accepts full liability for the underlying decommissioning obligations of the target, in fact the funding of decommissioning security in respect of the assets is split between buyer and seller going forward, such that the seller remains liable for providing a certain portion of the credit support. The reason behind this is that in many upstream scenarios, the cost of decommissioning of equipment is provisioned for by the operating parties by means of parent companies guarantees or other forms of security, including letters of credit or cash deposits, to ensure that at the time of decommissioning, there are sufficient funds in place to pay for the works necessary. In the North Sea, this is carried out through field-wide decommissioning security agreements that establish trust funds into which the participants place their security as and when required by the operator, according to a certain formula in relation to the estimated cost of decommissioning versus the estimated value of reserves left in the field. Large corporations may in most cases satisfy their obligations to put security in place by providing corporate guarantees. Smaller companies without a credit rating may not, and will need to provide either letters of credit or cash deposits in order to satisfy their obligations. This is obviously more expensive and has been a major cost and impediment to doing deals in the North Sea for many years.

Despite their readily accessed cash, private equity-backed entities are typically in the same position as a small company in this regard, because although they are essentially part of the same group as a large private equity firm, the private equity funds themselves will not be in a position to give corporate-style guarantees. The reason for this, as touched upon above, is that the fund is required to return funds to the investors at the end of its life and cannot therefore be encumbered with contingent liabilities of such a long-life nature as decommissioning obligations. In 2015 and 2016, as private equity-backed entities sought to do large deals in the North Sea, the search for a more equitable solution to decommissioning began in earnest. Sellers took a number of different approaches to this; but all shared a similar approach by which, in order to get the deal done, a portion of liability for the provisioning of decommissioning security in respect of the assets beings sold to the private equity-backed entities was retained by the seller.

The issues are not unique to private equity and have been grappled with for the past 20 years as the super-majors sold off assets to smaller entities, but the influx of private equity has made the matter more acute. This is only one part of the equation, of course. Allocating and reducing liability for decommissioning obligations to the seller only gets you half of the way, since many jurisdictions have extensive decommissioning legislation enabling the government to pursue former asset owners and members of their group. Private equity buyers will spend a good deal of time analysing the way in which this legislation may seek to infect the private equity group and the funds, with specific liability provisioning and structuring around the issue. Many private equity funds that specialise in investment into upstream projects have sophisticated structuring within their fund structure so as to decrease the likelihood of the ultimate limited partnership funds and the general partner becoming liable. This is usually done by ensuring that there is enough dilution of control and ownership throughout the fund such that tests for majority ownership or majority control typically used by decommissioning legislation to identify members of the same group are not necessarily triggered by the structure. However, there is a realisation within most private equity firms that this structuring, while potentially of use now, is not necessarily the final word on the subject, since legislation is regularly updated and liability may be found and attached to the fund in the future.

3.9 Recourse and limitation of liability

(a) Sell side

As usual, the limitation of liability of the seller is a matter of commercial positioning and when acting on the sell side, private equity sellers are as keen to limit their liability under the sale and purchase agreement as the next seller. Traditionally, in the general market, private equity sellers have sought to limit the warranties they give on the sale of a company solely to warranties as to the ownership of the shares being sold, their lack of any encumbrance and the seller's capacity to sell them. Warranties in respect of the company itself and the business it carries are normally given by the management team only and as a result had relatively little in the way of financial substance behind them in the event of a claim for breach of warranty arising, unless warranty and indemnity insurance could be arranged. In the general private equity market, such insurance is readily available and is increasingly hardwired into sales processes through the use of stapled policies. As the insurance market has developed, the scope of coverage has increased and the degree of risk that the seller needs to take (measured by the amount of liability it will take before the policy takes over) has reduced, so that the seller has minimal, indeed sometimes nominal, exposure, while at the same time the buyer enjoys an acceptable degree of coverage.

While this has been a standard position in many European private equity transactions, it has not so far become a position which private equity has been able to consistently hold on the sell side in the oil and gas business. The reason for this is in part that warranty and indemnity insurance is at the moment relatively limited for oil and gas transactions in the upstream, although it has certainly been used very successfully in certain sub-sectors such as fuels, marketing and storage. This can lead to gaps in coverage of general warranty and indemnity policies, especially regarding certain environmental and tax matters, which can make the policy less attractive to a buyer. Further, the European oil and gas M&A market is more heavily informed by practice in the United States than European practice in other industry sectors, and it is notable that the insistence by private equity sellers on giving title warranties only and the expectation that only management will be giving wider warranties has not been a feature of the private equity market in the United States. Therefore, private equity sellers tend to largely conform to the broader market as regards financial limitation, with a high cap on title claims and a lower cap on other claims such a business warranties. However, the depth of market experience on private equity that exists in the oil and gas sector outside of the United States is relatively shallow, since many investments were made in 2015 onwards and are only just getting to the end of their hold periods. Whether the market responds to this, and in particular whether the warranty and indemnity insurance market responds to it so as to enable a clean exit for these investments, will be an interesting question.

(b) Buy side

In terms of the acceptance of caps, thresholds and baskets, it is similarly not really possible to identify a typical buy-side private equity position that differs from any other buyer. The only observable theme is private equity's concern to ensure meaningful financial recourse in respect of claims for breach. Whereas some buyers are content to have warranties which are in effect rendered 'information only' because of caps or the credit of the seller, private equity buyers, conscious of their fiduciary duties to investors, will be keen to ensure meaningful recourse. Aside from negotiation of deal terms, this concern will often manifest itself in a more detailed analysis of seller credit position of the seller, and the seeking of credit support (eg, robust sell-side parent company guarantees) or monetary retentions and attendant escrow arrangements. It also led many private equity buyers to actively consider putting in place warranty and indemnity insurance to the extent adequate coverage is available in the market for the relevant deal.

4. Conclusion and future trends

The nature of private equity funds themselves and the involvement of third-party leaders in most of the deals that they do clearly have an impact on the sale and purchase documentation which parties on the other side of the table should note. Currently, the market, especially outside of the United States, is seeing these mainly on the buy side. As investments in the sector mature and come towards the end of their hold period, we will see more sell-side activity, perhaps including the development of a deeper secondary market between private equity-backed buyers and sellers, as we have seen in other sectors. This will likely stimulate the further development of liability allocation tools such as warranty and indemnity insurance. The cyclical nature of the oil and gas business also has an impact. The period 2014–15 created opportunities which, according to the timetables of many closed-ended funds, are due to be realised through exits in the next few years. The oil price crash of 2020 has reminded everyone of the cyclical nature of the industry and difficulties of exiting during a downturn. This drives longer hold periods and a refocusing on investment theses to de-emphasise the exit as being the key driver of return by maximising dividend returns during the hold period. Longer term, we are seeing a move away from closed-ended funds and a move towards open-end, permanent capital vehicles. These structures offer greater flexibility as to the timing of the eventual sale of investments and therefore can wait out market downturns better. Just as the lessons of the financial crisis of 2008 increased the use of open-ended funds in debt funds, it is possible that the volatility in the oil and gas sector over the last six years will have the same impact here.

The author would like to thank his partners Nick Dhesi, Samuel Newhouse and Stephen Szalkowski for their assistance with this chapter.

Governing law and jurisdiction clauses

Richard Ellison
Solicitor
David Waldron
Morgan, Lewis & Bockius UK LLP

1. Introduction

The importance of effective governing law and jurisdiction clauses is often overlooked. They may be disregarded as they appear towards the end of the operative provisions of sale and purchase agreements (and of this book!), and are surrounded by boilerplate clauses which are rarely the subject of extensive negotiation. It is also the case that, on occasion, in the positive atmosphere that may surround the nearing of the conclusion of a major agreement, the parties (which may well be on very good terms at the time that the agreement is being negotiated) lose sight of the fact that disputes can and do arise, and must be adequately provided for. It is a dangerous, and dangerously frequent, assumption that the governing law and dispute resolution provisions that were appropriate to one contract can be endlessly copied and pasted into subsequent contracts without regard for the specific circumstances that apply to each one.

This chapter aims to explain the reasons why governing law and jurisdiction clauses are particularly important, and to provide guidance as to how they can be most effectively drafted. Where appropriate, we look at the specific application of governing law and jurisdiction clauses in relation to oil and gas sale and purchase agreements, but much of the material which follows can be applied to international contracts more generally. We also briefly examine investment treaty arbitration as used as an alternative, or in addition, to contractually agreed dispute resolution methods.

We have generally adopted a commercial approach to the issues covered without entering into detailed academic discussion, although of necessity some of the topics below require a level of theoretical knowledge in order to set out effectively the potential advantages and pitfalls involved. We have taken a moderately Anglo-centric approach, while (we hope) taking into account the international nature of the oil and gas sector as far as possible.

The example clauses in this chapter are illustrative only. They should be treated with great caution and never be presumed to be suitable without further specific advice. A clause should always be drafted having regard to all the relevant context.

2. The importance of effective governing law and jurisdiction clauses

2.1 Enforcement

An agreement can prove to be unreliable, for practical purposes, or unenforceable without adequate or balanced jurisdiction provisions. To maximise its effectiveness, an agreement should be enforceable in as many jurisdictions in which the adverse party has assets as possible.

By way of example, a contract for the purchase of assets of, or shares in, a state-owned enterprise in Country X (where the judiciary is not advanced and/or independent of the state) may provide for the exclusive jurisdiction of the courts of that country. Assuming that a dispute arose after the date of completion, the purchaser would in principle be entitled to claim against the seller only before the courts of Country X. As well as the more general risk of 'home court advantage', in this case the courts of Country X may also be unlikely to make an award against the state-owned enterprise, particularly if the purchaser is from a jurisdiction which is not currently on friendly terms with the government of Country X.

A further consideration, as noted above, is the place where an award or judgment is likely to need to be enforced should the claim be successful. Again, as a practical example, let us assume that a sale and purchase agreement was concluded between a large English-headquartered international oil exporter (as purchaser) and a small company headquartered in Country Y (as seller), where the latter's only assets were in Country Y, and the sale and purchase agreement provided for the exclusive jurisdiction of the English courts. Were a dispute to arise with claims and counterclaims on both sides, the seller (if it were to win) would have little difficulty enforcing any court judgment against the assets of the purchaser in England. Should the purchaser win, however, it would need to attempt to enforce a judgment of the English courts in Country Y, which might at best be a difficult and lengthy procedure, and at worst a practical impossibility. Not only would this mean that any successful claim by the purchaser could prove devoid of any practical benefit, but it could also create a situation where there was little or no incentive for the seller to make any genuine attempt to settle a dispute because it would be confident that it would either win and be able to enforce, or lose and have little or no risk of any judgment being enforceable against it.

2.2 Certainty, cost and time

Disputes relating to high-value contracts are by no means always resolved by formal court or arbitration proceedings. In practice, the parties to a dispute are frequently able to reach a mutually acceptable settlement. This is much more easily achieved if the governing law and jurisdiction provisions of the underlying agreement(s) are effectively drafted and as certain as possible:

settlement relies in large part on each side being able to take a dispassionate view of its chances of success both on the merits of its case and at the enforcement stage. An accurate assessment of the chances of success is made simpler by having a clear view of the law which would apply to the dispute and the forum in which it would be heard.

However, not all disputes settle; and, of those that do, many settle at a relatively late stage. The process of reaching a hearing on any given dispute can be lengthy and costly at the best of times, and that is only exacerbated where there is a dispute not only in relation to the underlying merits, but also regarding:

- the correct jurisdiction in which it should be heard; and/or
- the correct law(s) to apply.

There can also be a real risk of parallel proceedings where, for example, an arbitration clause is not clearly drafted and one side believes it has the right to commence court proceedings, whereas the other side thinks that arbitration is the only permissible mechanism. Where parallel proceedings arise, costs escalate and there can also be further problems – both at the time when those two distinct authorities assert their jurisdiction over the dispute, and later at the enforcement stage in the case of conflicting awards/judgments.

2.3 Equality of arms

It is not at all uncommon for one party to be significantly better resourced than the other. Where the governing law and jurisdiction provisions of an agreement are either unclear or unbalanced, the better-resourced party can often use that to its advantage, using delaying tactics and manoeuvres to increase costs such that the less affluent party can be forced to surrender valid claims or to settle on unfavourable terms. This is not to suggest that a better-resourced party should deliberately insert ambiguous provisions, since (for the reasons set out above) this can lead to wasted costs regardless. However, particularly when representing the financially weaker of two parties, it is crucial that the dispute resolution provisions be clearly drafted and effective, and not favour the interests of the party with deeper pockets.

2.4 Governing law

We will address governing law provisions in more detail below, but it is worth underlining the fact that in the absence of any effective governing law clause, a contract may be governed by the law of a jurisdiction which was not that which the parties intended. Consequently, the contract may be interpreted in ways that one or both parties would not have anticipated.

2.5 Elements of particular relevance to oil and gas sale and purchase agreements

Oil and gas sale and purchase agreements are typically international in scope, with parties from different jurisdictions and often assets in one or more further jurisdictions. This makes it all the more important that the governing law and jurisdiction provisions be appropriate to the transaction in question; frequently, this will involve obtaining local law advice in a variety of jurisdictions.

Further, oil and gas sale and purchase agreements often involve, either directly or indirectly, state-owned enterprises and/or state-owned assets. We have previously noted the importance of avoiding home court advantage in such situations, but it can also have an impact in other ways. In some cases, states or state-owned entities can be immune either from legal action altogether or from the enforcement of judgments. A complete discussion of this issue is beyond the scope of this chapter, and it is very much dependent on international law and on the jurisdiction(s) in which proceedings are launched and/or enforcement sought. However, in simplified terms and as a matter of English law only, states are immune from suit other than where any of the following applies:

- The relevant state has submitted to the jurisdiction of the courts of any part of the United Kingdom, such as by commencing or taking material steps in court proceedings;
- The proceedings relate to a commercial transaction entered into by the relevant state – that is, not an exercise of the state's sovereign authority;
- The proceedings relate to a contractual obligation on the state that is to be performed wholly or partly in the United Kingdom; or
- The state has agreed in writing to submit the dispute to arbitration (which is typically in the form of an arbitration clause in the relevant agreement).

There are further general limits on the ability of the English courts to hear disputes involving the exercise by states of their sovereign authority, in addition to those set out above.

In relation to enforcement, the English courts will, in general terms, not enforce a judgment against the property of a state other than:

- where the state has given written consent to enforcement, such as by a waiver in a contract of its sovereign immunity from enforcement; or
- over property that is primarily intended for commercial use.

There are also further restrictions on the enforcement of foreign court judgments against state property.

The effect of the restrictions described above is that, when contracting with states or state-owned enterprises, it is important to consider the jurisdiction where proceedings are to be launched and where enforcement is likely to be sought. A waiver of sovereign immunity is likely to be desirable, but local law advice may well be necessary to determine the extent to which this will be effective.

3. Governing law

3.1 General considerations

The term 'governing law' is used to refer to the law which applies to the substantive content of an agreement, rather than that which will govern the procedural elements of any dispute (these are often, but by no means always, the same).

The first and most important consideration is that all contracts should contain an express choice of governing law. There are mechanisms by which a choice of law can be inferred in the absence of an express provision, but these can lead to complex questions of conflict of laws and are likely to depend on the jurisdiction in which proceedings are brought. An example of a governing law clause is set out in section 3.4 below.

English law has traditionally been highly favoured in the international oil and gas context because of its stability and predictability and also, in part, its ability to take into account commercial rather than strictly legal aspects of disputes. Of course, this is not to say that the laws of other jurisdictions can never be appropriate – not least because in some cases, a party will insist on a particular law applying. It is crucial to involve local counsel from an early stage of negotiations where necessary, and it is unwise to assume (for example) that closely related legal systems (eg, those of England and those of various commonwealth jurisdictions) will necessarily produce the same results when applied to any given agreement.

We noted above the importance of including an express governing law clause. We should add for the sake of completeness that, although such clauses will generally be upheld by national courts, there may be exceptions. In the European Union (including, at the time of writing, the United Kingdom), those exceptions are limited in scope, and unlikely to apply to oil and gas sale and purchase agreements. For the purposes of other jurisdictions, it is always advisable to obtain local law advice. Generally speaking, most developed jurisdictions will recognise an express choice of law clause, provided that:

- the chosen law has some relationship with the parties or the transaction;
- the choice was not made deliberately to avoid a mandatory provision of a national law; and
- there are no public policy reasons for disregarding it.

A final point to consider is whether it is advisable to have the courts of one jurisdiction ruling on a contract which is governed by the law of a second jurisdiction. Although the English courts are comfortable with this situation, that is not always the case with the courts of other jurisdictions.

3.2 Hybrid clauses

Agreements occasionally provide for certain elements of a contract to be governed by one law and others by a different law. Other agreements provide for one or more national laws to apply in addition to concepts such as 'generally accepted industry practice' or 'generally accepted principles of international law'. Unless there is an overriding need for such additions, they are unlikely to be desirable.

Having different parts of a contract governed by different laws may be problematic in that it invites ancillary disputes about which aspects of the contract are in dispute and therefore which law, or laws, apply. It can also lead to the need for proceedings to be considered under two separate legal systems, which can be unwieldy and incur additional costs.

Adding references to 'generally accepted principles' of whatever type is also potentially problematic. Most notably, it introduces a significant level of uncertainty: the parties, by the time there is a dispute, may not be prepared to agree on what is or is not generally accepted, each adopting whichever approach is most beneficial to it. This can also cause problems where there is a conflict between, for example, standard industry practice and national law provisions (although this can be lessened by stating that one or the other will generally apply – most often national law; this statement can cause problems in itself, as there can be disputes about whether national law is or is not silent on a particular point). References to codified non-legal rules (eg, International Financial Reporting Standards) should be less problematic where they are used only in relation to a clearly defined, limited element of an agreement.

3.3 Exclusive/non-exclusive jurisdiction clauses

National court jurisdiction clauses can be either exclusive (in which case only the courts of the stated country are entitled to hear a dispute) or non-exclusive (in which the courts of the stated country will always have jurisdiction if seised, but other courts can also take jurisdiction if a dispute is submitted to them).

Exclusive jurisdiction clauses, where they operate in favour of the jurisdiction whose law governs the substantive contract, eliminate much of the uncertainty that can arise where the courts of a given jurisdiction are called upon to interpret the law of a jurisdiction with which they are unfamiliar. They also generally ensure that there is not a 'race to the courts' whereby both parties to a dispute attempt to be the first to launch proceedings in a jurisdiction which they feel is more favourable to them. They do not, however, entirely eliminate the possibility that the courts of a country other than that chosen could take jurisdiction on the basis, for example, of national public policy.

Non-exclusive jurisdiction clauses have the obvious advantage of permitting a party to decide at the time that a dispute arises which courts would be preferable to hear the dispute. However, they can lead to parallel and satellite proceedings, and all the cost and delay that these can entail.

3.4 Drafting effective governing law clauses

Governing law clauses should, above all, be simple and unambiguous. A workable, standalone English governing law provision (although note the drafting tips later in this chapter in relation to arbitration clauses) might be:

This agreement and any dispute or claim (including non-contractual disputes or claims) arising out of or in connection with it or its subject matter, formation or existence shall be governed by and construed in accordance with the laws of England.

This sample clause provides for a wide class of disputes to be governed by English law (notably by including non-contractual claims, which would in principle cover claims in tort). In very general terms, the inclusion of non-contractual claims in the scope of a governing law provision will typically be enforceable as a matter of English law, although there can be exceptions. It is advisable to include language to this effect, since failure to do so can lead to the law of other jurisdictions applying to certain classes of dispute, with unpredictable results.

4. Arbitration or litigation?

4.1 Background

The two principal methods of final dispute resolution are arbitration and court litigation; negotiation and mediation are generally a precursor to these, and are dealt with further below. A further alternative is expert determination, which is also briefly examined below.

Where parties have agreed not to use international arbitration, but instead refer matters to litigation, a short, simple jurisdiction clause will often suffice. As noted above, there will need to be a consideration of, and an agreement regarding, exclusive (the courts of one jurisdiction) or non-exclusive jurisdiction (which would entitle the parties to use the courts of one jurisdiction, but potentially also the courts in other jurisdictions as an alternative). A basic example might be:

The parties irrevocably submit to the [exclusive/non-exclusive] jurisdiction of the courts of England and Wales in respect of any dispute which arises out of or in connection with this agreement, its performance, formation or validity.

Arbitration as a dispute resolution mechanism has been steadily growing in popularity in recent years, and continues to do so. Arbitration was traditionally advertised as being quicker and cheaper than litigation, although it is doubtful whether that remains the case (if indeed it was ever true). It does, however, have various other significant advantages over litigation and some potential drawbacks, which we will examine in turn.

Before doing so, it is worth setting out some of the main features of typical international arbitration proceedings for the benefit of the lay reader, most of which will be developed in more detail later in this chapter. International arbitration consists of a private tribunal, usually formed of either one or three arbitrators appointed jointly by the parties to a dispute to adjudicate and make a final ruling. In most cases the tribunal will apply the law of a particular jurisdiction; but the parties are free, within certain parameters generally set by the arbitration law of the legal place ('seat') of the arbitration, to decide on the law and rules to be applied.

The parties to most types of contract in most jurisdictions (employment contracts are a common exception) can opt to submit any contractual dispute to arbitration by including an arbitration clause in the contract itself; where there is already a dispute, the parties may, by agreement, submit that dispute to arbitration rather than to litigation. Arbitration exists for the most part outside the court system, but national courts can in certain circumstances be called upon to act either in support of the arbitration or in ancillary proceedings; some national courts are more supportive of arbitration than others.

4.2 International arbitration: potential advantages

(a) Confidentiality

A key consideration for many parties when choosing international arbitration is that the proceedings, up to and including the hearing itself, will generally be confidential unless the parties agree otherwise. From a commercial perspective, this is attractive primarily because information which could confer a business advantage on the parties' competitors can be kept confidential, as can the existence of a dispute (which may be valuable from a reputational standpoint). Court proceedings and documents, by contrast, are usually public, although this is not the case in all jurisdictions.

(b) Enforcement

The Convention on the Recognition and Enforcement of Foreign Arbitral Awards (the New York Convention), which entered into force in 1959 and has some 163 signatories at the time of writing, provides for the international enforcement of arbitral awards on the same basis as domestic arbitration awards. This has been a significant factor in the growth of international arbitration, since enforcement of national court judgments in the absence of any bilateral or multilateral enforcement treaty can prove difficult or impossible.

Despite the existence of the New York Convention, it should not be assumed that any arbitral award will automatically be enforceable worldwide.

First, a number of states with significant hydrocarbon deposits are not currently signatories to the New York Convention, including Chad, Iraq, Libya, Turkmenistan and Yemen (guidance is given later in this chapter as to how best to procure a decision which is enforceable in non-convention countries.)

Secondly, although the New York Convention applies in theory in any signatory state, its application is inconsistent. In order to enforce an arbitration award, it is necessary to convert it to the status of a national court judgment, and the willingness of national courts to do so can vary.

Thirdly, there are a limited number of bases on which, under the rules of the New York Convention, local courts can refuse to enforce a foreign arbitral award – notably:

- where the relevant arbitration agreement is not valid under local law;
- where the parties were not given notice of proceedings;
- where the award relates to a subject not covered by the arbitration agreement; and
- where it would be contrary to public policy to recognise or enforce the award.

The latter is the most common and contentious ground for refusal to enforce, and it is advisable to seek local law advice on this point for the jurisdictions where enforcement is likely to be sought.

(c) ***Location***

The parties to an arbitration are free to decide jointly on the place of the arbitration. This covers both the physical location of the hearings and the legal seat that determines the procedural law which will apply to the conduct of the arbitration, the latter being an important strategic and legal decision.

(d) ***Consensual procedure***

The parties to an arbitration are also in principle free (with some exceptions) to decide jointly on the procedure which will govern the conduct of an arbitration. This is a significant departure from national court proceedings, which are typically highly prescriptive in nature and can, as a result, in certain circumstances lead to cost savings where (for example) the parties agree that an abridged procedure is appropriate to the dispute in question.

Arbitrations are often governed by the rules of one of the major arbitration bodies (as discussed further below), but these can be varied by agreement between the parties, either by including provisions to that effect in the relevant contract or subsequently by consent. Once an arbitral tribunal is appointed, the parties will in principle be bound by its decisions; but tribunals will also typically give effect to any jointly agreed directions of the parties.

(e) ***Nomination of arbitrator(s)***

In contrast to national court proceedings, where a judge or judges will be appointed without reference to the parties, it is open to the parties to an arbitration to agree on the procedure by which the member(s) of an arbitral tribunal are to be appointed.

Arbitrators are often lawyers, but that is not compulsory. Arbitration agreements often prescribe the qualifications and/or experience that an arbitrator must have; care should be taken to avoid uncertain qualification requirements or overly prescriptive requirements that would reduce the pool of candidates to an unrealistically low level.

The method of appointment of the arbitrator(s) can again be set out either in the underlying agreement or subsequently by agreement between the parties.

4.3 International arbitration: potential disadvantages

(a) ***Costs***

Comparative costs in litigation and arbitration will very much depend both on the nature of a particular case and on the jurisdiction in which litigation is contemplated. In particular, court fees vary hugely between jurisdictions; some require the payment of a certain percentage of the amount claimed. Despite recent increases, English court fees remain at the lower end of the spectrum.

In arbitration, fees will generally be payable both to the institution (if any) which oversees the arbitral process and to the arbitrators themselves. By way of comparison, arbitrators' fees will almost always be more expensive than English court fees, although they can vary significantly.

However, the costs of the document production (or disclosure/discovery) process in arbitration are generally much lower than in analogous court proceedings in the main common law jurisdictions; in our experience, this remains the case at the time of writing, despite ongoing attempts by the English courts to limit the costs of document production. An imbalance in spending power between the parties to a dispute can be harder for an arbitral tribunal than a court to remedy, due to the comparatively limited compulsive powers of an arbitral tribunal and the comparative lack of prescriptive procedural rules which apply in arbitration.

Lastly, arbitral tribunals are often less willing than, for example, the English courts to award legal and other ancillary costs in full on the basis of the 'loser pays' principle; 60% to 70% costs awards to the successful party are more typical. This consideration will not, of course, apply when the alternative to arbitration is the court system of a jurisdiction in which the 'loser pays' principle does not apply.

(b) *Joinder and consolidation*

We will examine this topic in more depth below. For present purposes, it is sufficient to note that, despite recent attempts to address this by the major arbitral institutions, national courts generally have – in practice – greater powers than arbitral tribunals both to join third parties to existing proceedings and to order the consolidation of parallel proceedings.

(c) *Interim remedies*

Interim remedies such as injunctive relief are available in litigation due to the compulsive powers of national courts. Although the English courts have powers to award interim remedies in support of arbitration, these can for the most part be excluded by agreement between the parties to a dispute, either in the underlying arbitration agreement or subsequently.

Although there has been an increasing trend in the rules of the major arbitral institutions towards allowing arbitral tribunals to make interim awards in certain circumstances, these are typically slower, limited in scope and more difficult to enforce than orders of a national court. For example, failure to comply with a worldwide freezing order of the English courts may have criminal consequences under English law, and such an order is thus likely to be complied with by any individual or corporate entity which has links to or is likely to travel to the United Kingdom or any jurisdiction which is friendly to the United Kingdom.

By comparison, not only is a worldwide freezing order unavailable from an arbitral tribunal as a matter of English law, but those limited interim remedies which a tribunal may be able to order (eg, an order for the conservation of evidence) will ultimately rely on enforcement via national courts. As a result, an arbitration agreement in a contract can on occasion prove an impediment to successful enforcement of a party's rights where, for example, it can be demonstrated that the arbitration agreement precludes recourse to interim remedies in national courts by permitting the parties to obtain interim relief only from a duly appointed arbitral tribunal.

(d) *Default and summary judgment*

Summary judgment (whereby claims or defences that are substantially without merit can be dismissed) is not typically available in arbitration. Neither is default judgment (whereby a claim against a party that does not participate in proceedings is awarded by default), which can mean that a claimant is required to go through all the usual stages of an arbitration even where its claim is effectively unopposed.

(e) *Confidentiality (continued)*

We noted above that confidentiality is frequently a determinative factor in opting for arbitration rather than litigation. However, there are occasions when the reverse is the case: that is, the commercial benefit to publicising the fact or nature of a dispute is sufficient to outweigh any considerations in favour of maintaining its confidentiality.

It is not necessarily possible to predict when it will be preferable to make a dispute public (and there can be potential routes to achieve this through court proceedings ancillary to arbitration in certain circumstances). However, it is worth bearing in mind that, having opted for arbitration, it can be either difficult or impossible to use publicity to put pressure on an adverse party to reach a settlement of a dispute.

4.4 Comparing different arbitral institutions

(a) Background

An increasing number of institutions worldwide administer arbitrations. However, only a relatively small number of these are generally considered to be appropriate for complex oil and gas disputes.

As a preliminary point, it is worth noting that, while all the major arbitration institutions have their headquarters in a particular city, there is no reason in principle why they cannot administer arbitrations in different jurisdictions. There can, however, be some logistical advantages to appointing an institution to administer an arbitration in its home venue (time zone considerations in particular can play a part in this regard).

The following paragraphs are not intended to be an exhaustive exploration of the institutions which would be best placed to administer a dispute under any given oil and gas sale and purchase agreement. Rather, they give a high-level overview of the key features of four institutions, in order to provide general guidance. Of course, each contract (and each dispute) is distinct, and one should consider which institution is most appropriate in any particular case.

It also bears repeating that the parties can vary the rules of the institutions, either expressly in the relevant agreement or by agreement once a dispute has arisen.

(b) ICC

The International Chamber of Commerce (ICC) is based in Paris and is one of the oldest and best-regarded arbitral institutions. Its rules are, in general terms, relatively detailed, and ICC arbitration contains several distinctive features, most notably the following:

- Arbitral awards are scrutinised by the ICC Court, in theory enhancing correctness and enforceability, but also adding additional costs to the arbitral process;
- There is a requirement to agree to 'terms of reference' at the start of an arbitration, which involves cost and potential delay;

- Arbitrators' fees are calculated by reference to the value of the claim(s) (and counterclaim(s)) in dispute;
- The ICC rules, surprisingly, do not provide that the proceedings are confidential by default; so if confidentiality is desirable, it will be necessary to vary expressly the provisions of the ICC rules (preferably in the underlying arbitration agreement) or to apply to the ICC Court or the arbitral tribunal for proceedings to be confidential;
- The most recent ICC rules (in force as of 1 March 2017) provide for the potential appointment of an emergency arbitrator, although only in certain relatively restricted circumstances; and
- The time limit for issuing an award is six months from the date of signature of the terms of reference, although this is frequently extended (often significantly) in practice.

The ICC's recommended arbitration clauses at the time of writing, together with those of the London Court of International Arbitration (LCIA) and the Singapore International Arbitration Centre (SIAC), are set out in section 4.7.

(c) *LCIA*

The LCIA has become increasingly popular in recent years. Its rules were revised in 2014 to take into account recent developments in international arbitration (most notably to permit consolidation of related arbitrations).

Key features of LCIA arbitration include the following:

- It is confidential, unless confidentiality is waived by joint agreement of the parties;
- It provides for the appointment of an 'emergency arbitrator' with powers to award a variety of interim remedies if a party can demonstrate that urgent relief is required before a tribunal could be constituted, and also (where there is exceptional urgency) for the expedited appointment of a full tribunal;
- Arbitrators' fees are charged at an hourly rate, subject to a cap (at the time of writing) of £450, which may in particular lead to a lower overall cost than with those institutions charging on an *ad valorem* basis; and
- There is no time limit for issuing awards.

(d) *SIAC*

SIAC has made significant progress in establishing itself as a regional arbitration centre. It published new rules which came into force on 1 August 2016. Key features include:

- fees set by reference to the value of the amount in dispute;
- a mechanism whereby claims or defences entirely lacking in merit may be struck out;

- streamlined provisions for joinder and consolidation; and
- provisions for both expedited proceedings and the appointment of an emergency arbitrator.

(e) Ad hoc *arbitration*

An alternative to having an arbitration administered by one of the bodies above is to agree to an *ad hoc* arbitration – that is, one in which the parties themselves determine the procedures to be followed. This can sometimes prove cheaper than institutional arbitration, since it avoids the fees payable to the administering institution, and is more flexible since the parties (subject to the mandatory laws of the seat) are free to choose the applicable procedures.

However, it often relies in large part on the cooperation of the parties once a dispute has arisen, which is in many cases the time at which the parties are least inclined to cooperate. It can also take a considerable amount of time (and thus expense) to negotiate the applicable procedures and, accordingly, should be approached with caution. Further, the seat of the arbitration may have a significant effect on the interpretation and implementation of the *ad hoc* agreement.

The United Nations Commission on International Trade Law (UNCITRAL) has developed a set of rules for use in *ad hoc* arbitration and has published further guidance information on this topic. The UNCITRAL model clause (at the time of writing) is as follows:

Any dispute, controversy or claim arising out of or relating to this contract, or the breach, termination or invalidity thereof, shall be settled by arbitration in accordance with the UNCITRAL Arbitration Rules as at present in force.

4.5 Choosing the seat of an arbitration

The legal 'seat' of an arbitration is the jurisdiction whose court has a supervisory role over the arbitration, and may be called upon to support that process. It may also determine the procedural rules that will apply to the arbitral proceedings (in addition to the applicable rules of any arbitral institution). The seat is typically also the jurisdiction of the country in which hearings physically take place, although this does not necessarily have to be the case.

A complete discussion of the benefits and disadvantages of any particular seat is beyond the scope of this chapter, but generally speaking, it is important to choose a seat that:

- has an advanced arbitration culture and laws;
- does not excessively prohibit some classes of dispute from arbitration; and
- is (or will be perceived to be) neutral with regard to the parties.

Obtaining local law advice on the characteristics of a particular seat is often advisable. Simple logistics may also play a role: for example, if the parties and their advisers are not Swiss, why would the cost of a multi-week arbitration in Geneva be desirable?

Popular seats are London, Paris, Geneva, Singapore, Hong Kong and New York; Dubai has also risen to prominence recently, and Mauritius is taking steps to establish itself as a seat of choice for Africa-related disputes.

4.6 Drafting effective arbitration clauses

As noted previously, arbitration clauses should not be adopted on a 'one size fits all' basis; a clause which works for one contract may well not be appropriate for another and local law advice is often necessary. However, the following features should be borne in mind:

- The seat should always be specified, and (where different) so should the physical place of the arbitration;
- The language of the arbitration should be specified;
- The number of arbitrators should be specified;
- A method of appointment of arbitrators and the qualifications that they should have is often helpful; institutional rules often provide for a method of appointment, but the parties may wish to vary the relevant provisions; and
- The rules governing the arbitration should be specified (or if the arbitration is to be on an *ad hoc* basis, detailed procedural rules should be set out).

The major arbitral bodies have suggested arbitration clauses, which are generally a good starting point. They are typically short; lengthier and more detailed clauses may be appropriate, depending on the situation.

4.7 Institutional standard/model clauses

(a) ICC

The ICC model clause is extremely brief:

All disputes arising out of or in connection with the present contract shall be finally settled under the Rules of Arbitration of the International Chamber of Commerce by one or more arbitrators appointed in accordance with the said Rules.

We would recommend expanding it to include, at least, the requirements set out in section 4.6.

(b) LCIA

Any dispute arising out of or in connection with this contract, including any question regarding its existence, validity or termination, shall be referred to and finally resolved by arbitration under the LCIA Rules, which Rules are deemed to be incorporated by reference into this clause.

The number of arbitrators shall be [one/three].
The seat, or legal place, of arbitration shall be [City and/or Country].
The language to be used in the arbitral proceedings shall be [ ].
The governing law of the contract shall be the substantive law of [ ].

(c) SIAC

Any dispute arising out of or in connection with this contract, including any question regarding its existence, validity or termination, shall be referred to and finally resolved by arbitration administered by the Singapore International Arbitration Centre ("SIAC") in accordance with the Arbitration Rules of the Singapore International Arbitration Centre ("SIAC Rules") for the time being in force, which rules are deemed to be incorporated by reference in this clause.
*The seat of the arbitration shall be [Singapore].**

*The Tribunal shall consist of ________________ **arbitrator(s).*

The language of the arbitration shall be ________________.
**Parties should specify the seat of arbitration of their choice. If the parties wish to select an alternative seat to Singapore, please replace "[Singapore]" with the city and country of choice (eg, "[City, Country]").*
***State an odd number. Either state one, or state three.*

4.8 Issues specific to arbitration clauses

(a) 'Escalation' or 'multi-tiered' arbitration clauses

'Escalation' clauses, also known as 'multi-tiered' arbitration clauses, are clauses which specify that one or more preliminary stages must be entered into by the parties to an agreement before they are permitted to commence formal arbitral proceedings.

The precise content of escalation clauses varies significantly, but most typically they include:

- an obligation on the parties to engage in a period of negotiation; and/or
- a more formal mediation procedure (which is often required when the first option has not succeeded in resolving the underlying dispute).

They can read like this (note, however, that this is not a recommended clause – quite the opposite!):

a. Any dispute shall be settled amicably.
b. Prior to any arbitration the dispute shall be referred to the CEOs who shall have three months to resolve it.
c. If not resolved then it shall be referred to a panel of three members of the board who shall have up to three months to resolve the dispute or difference.

d. Thereafter the parties may submit to arbitration in accordance with Clause [X].

Escalation clauses are often seen as desirable because the parties wish to avoid formal proceedings where possible, in the interest of maintaining a working business relationship. The intent is that following the steps set out in escalation clauses will encourage both parties to work amicably towards resolving their differences, and thereby avoid the cost and antagonism that may result from court or arbitral proceedings.

Preliminary discussions or mediation can also provide the parties with time to assess the strength of their respective cases and their available options, and to calculate the most cost-effective route of proceeding. Where a party is clearly at fault, it may also give an opportunity to rectify the issue and possibly prevent early termination of a contract.

A major drawback to escalation clauses is the uncertainty that they can create in the dispute resolution process. As we have noted above, uncertainty is a significant barrier to effective dispute resolution. Particularly as regards arbitration, it can lead to lengthy and costly jurisdiction challenges (which are particularly problematic where one party has significantly greater financial resources), and can also create difficulties with challenges to awards and/or to their enforceability.

Looking specifically at the above example, disputes could arise over what 'amicably' or 'resolved' (used twice) means and, therefore, whether the right to arbitrate has crystallised.

By way of further example, as a matter of English law, the position has until recently been that, given (and despite) the fact that an agreement to agree is not enforceable, the more readily ascertainable the parties' obligations under a mandatory negotiation procedure, the more likely it is to be upheld (and, on this basis, mandatory mediation has typically been upheld). The waters were further muddied by a 2014 English court judgment that a clause requiring the parties to engage in 'friendly discussions' was enforceable;[1] and then by subsequent judgments[2] that have cast some doubt on the question of whether that judgment remains good law. This all serves as a further illustration of the pitfalls of using mandatory negotiation provisions.

In terms of practical tips, the parties to a contract should first consider whether an escalation clause is necessary. If either party does not wish to enter into good-faith negotiations at the time of a dispute, little will be gained by attempting to force it to do so. Conversely, if both parties wish to negotiate when a dispute arises, they are always free to do so; and, for as long as both parties feel that these negotiations are worthwhile, they are unlikely to

1 *Emirates Trading Agency LLC v Prime Mineral Exports Private Limited* [2014] EWHC 2104 (Comm).

2 *Emirates Trading Agency LLC v Sociedade de Fomento Industrial Private Ltd* [2015] EWHC 1452 (Comm); *DS-Rendite-Fonds NR 1066 VLCC Titan Glory GmbH v Titan Maritime SA* [2015] EWHC 2488 (Comm)

commence formal proceedings (which calls into question the need for an escalation clause).

If the parties to an arbitration agreement feel that, for whatever reason, an escalation clause is desirable, the simplest way to ensure that this clause is enforceable is by using a supervised mediation procedure.

Almost all the major arbitral institutions offer supervised mediation procedures with detailed rules, and a clause providing for mediation under the auspices of one of these bodies (depending on the law of the seat and of the contract) is much more likely to be upheld than one providing for simple negotiation. Another reason to consider mediation rather than negotiation is that a neutral mediator, with experience in resolving commercial disputes, will oversee the mediation process; in our experience, even the most apparently intractable disputes can be resolved to the satisfaction of both parties under the supervision of a skilled mediator. Be aware, however, that an unsuccessful mediation can add further cost, delay and wasted management time to a dispute.

If compulsory negotiation (despite the legal uncertainty that this creates) is nevertheless the desired option, the parties should ensure that they set out as clearly as possible the steps that are to be taken as part of this process. Most notably, the agreement should specify:

- the individuals (by reference to their job title, rather than by name) who are to be involved;
- the timeframe for negotiations; and
- the consequences of an impossibility to commence the negotiation process for any reason.

A stipulation that a third party is to be involved in negotiations may also assist in persuading a court or arbitral tribunal that a mandatory negotiation provision is enforceable. The parties should nevertheless be aware of the real risk of challenges to the jurisdiction of a tribunal, and subsequently to the enforceability of an arbitral award, that results from mandatory negotiation provisions.

As a final, more technical point, provisions should be included alongside escalation clauses to ensure that mediation or negotiation does not cause a limitation period to expire, thereby preventing a party from making a substantive claim on the merits of a dispute. For example:

Where time is of the essence due to the operation of any relevant limitation period, the provisions of clauses [xx] shall not apply.

or

The provisions of this Clause [xx] shall be waived in the event that their application would prevent any Party from obtaining a final arbitral award or judgment regarding a dispute due to the operation of any relevant limitation period.

(b) *'Asymmetric' arbitration clauses*

Once fashionable, 'asymmetric' or 'unilateral' arbitration clauses are clauses that permit one party to choose between either court jurisdiction or arbitration, while the other is limited to one of those two options. The advantage for the party with the benefit of the option is that, at the time that a dispute arises, it can decide which possibility is preferable in all the circumstances.

However, asymmetric arbitration clauses are of dubious enforceability in certain jurisdictions, and in others they are entirely unenforceable – such that a party will be held to have submitted solely to either court jurisdiction or arbitration. This can also cause problems when enforcing an arbitration judgment made in a jurisdiction that recognises asymmetric arbitration clauses in a different jurisdiction that does not.

Consideration should be given to whether enforcement is likely to be sought over assets situated in a jurisdiction that does not recognise asymmetric arbitration clauses. Conversely, when an asymmetric arbitration clause is proposed, it is important to assess whether it is likely to be enforceable in the jurisdiction(s) in which assets are held.

(c) *Joinder and consolidation*

Disputes arising from multi-party and multi-contractual relationships frequently give rise to difficult issues in international arbitration. Most commonly, these occur when one or both parties to an arbitration wish either to join a third party to the proceedings (joinder) or to consolidate parallel arbitral proceedings (consolidation) so as to avoid conflicting awards and the expense of multiple proceedings.

The arbitration community is aware of the increasing demand for joinder and consolidation, and is taking steps to ensure that these are possible. However, parties should be aware of the difficulties involved, and it remains the case that joinder and consolidation are more likely to be consistently successful in national courts than in arbitration proceedings. It should also be noted that an arbitration agreement providing for joinder and/or consolidation may still require the cooperation of the parties to a dispute at the time that the dispute occurs, which may be the time that such cooperation is least likely to be forthcoming. Various problems can arise in relation to both joinder and consolidation, many of which stem from the fact that party consent is the cornerstone of the arbitral process. It is the parties' express agreement to arbitration that empowers the tribunal and waives the parties' right to invoke the jurisdiction of national courts; joining an unwilling non-signatory to the proceedings or consolidating proceedings without the consent of the parties is in direct contradiction to the consensual nature of arbitration. Although in certain cases consent can be deemed to be implied (eg, by conduct or in a group company context), the default rule is nevertheless that the consent of each party must be unambiguously demonstrable if any resulting award is to be safely enforceable (notably, to satisfy the requirement for 'agreement' in the New York Convention).

The right of the parties to participate in the selection of the tribunal is also fundamental. Therefore, particular problems arise when an attempt is made to join a party to existing proceedings where a tribunal has already been constituted. A request for joinder prior to the nomination of the tribunal will generally have a greater chance of success.

The 2014 LCIA Rules and the 2017 ICC Rules give the supervising authority the right to nominate the tribunal in the absence of agreement between the parties, which can be particularly relevant in the context of consolidated proceedings or proceedings which may potentially be consolidated. Delegating responsibility for nominating arbitrators to the institution potentially allows the appointment of the arbitrators to proceed regardless of further claims and interventions, although it may sometimes result in the appointment of arbitrators that are unsuitable. A further means of achieving an equitable nomination process is to provide in the arbitration agreement that each 'side' (made up of one or more parties) may choose one arbitrator, with the institution acting only if agreement cannot be reached.

Consolidation and joinder under the 2014 LCIA Rules can be achieved in a number of ways:

- If a third party is to join the arbitration, the third party and the applicant must consent either in the arbitration agreement or following the commencement of the arbitration.
- The tribunal may order consolidation if agreed by the parties in writing and approved by the LCIA Court.
- Where there are multiple arbitrations under the same, or compatible, arbitration agreement(s) and only one tribunal has so far been appointed or both tribunals are the same, approval by the LCIA Court is still required.
- Consolidation may be ordered by the LCIA Court, after giving parties the opportunity to state their views, if the arbitrations are under the same arbitration agreement between the same parties, and no tribunal has yet been appointed.

Under the 2017 ICC Rules, arbitrations can be consolidated if:

- the parties agree;
- all claims are under the same arbitration agreement; or
- the claims are under different arbitration agreements (where the ICC Court considers those arbitration agreements to be compatible), but are still between the same parties and under the same legal relationship.

Without institutional rules to provide for the consolidation of concurrent proceedings, a significant obstacle to such consolidation is the general inability of arbitral tribunals to bind other tribunals. This means that a decision of one tribunal to order consolidation may well not be binding on a second (or third) tribunal. Even if the matters in dispute are the same (eg, if all contracts are identical in content or were negotiated in the same factual context), each arbitral tribunal can in principle issue its own independent decision.

Although achieving joinder and consolidation cannot at present be guaranteed, the chances of success can be maximised by:

- choosing arbitral rules which expressly permit joinder and consolidation;
- signing a separate standalone 'umbrella' dispute resolution clause;
- incorporating a global arbitration agreement by reference into each contract;
- including a materially identical arbitration clause in each contract, providing for joinder and consolidation, in multi-contract transactions; and/or
- each side to the arbitration agreeing to the joint nomination of the arbitrator(s) (and a mechanism for appointing in default of agreement).

(d) Law governing the arbitration clause

As discussed above, the law governing the contract and the law governing the arbitral procedure are conceptually distinct. However, there are occasions on which a third factor becomes relevant: the law governing the arbitration clause itself.

Where arbitration is chosen, it is crucial that arbitration clauses be valid and enforceable. The validity of an arbitration clause is generally determined by the law applicable to that arbitration clause, and it is important to be aware that the governing law of a contract will not necessarily be the law applicable to an arbitration clause – in particular, where the seat of the arbitration is not the jurisdiction whose laws govern the substantive contract. This is of more than simply theoretical interest, since it can lead to a situation where the arbitration clause is held to be invalid under the law of a jurisdiction which was never intended to determine its validity.

The simplest means of ensuring certainty as to which law will govern an arbitration clause is generally to include in the governing law clause a provision that the governing law is applicable both to the contract and to the arbitration clause itself. If it is the intention that the governing law of the arbitration clause be different from that of the underlying contract, this should be stated expressly. Examples of such provisions might include the following:

The governing law of this arbitration agreement shall be the law of England.

*This agreement (*including the arbitration agreement*) and any dispute or claim* *(including non-contractual disputes or claims) arising out of or in connection with it or its subject matter, formation or existence shall be governed by and construed in accordance with the laws of England.* [emphasis added]

4.9 Expert determination

Expert determination is a contractual mechanism by which the parties agree to submit certain classes of dispute (particularly disputes that are technical in nature, such as accounting disputes) for adjudication by an expert.

If expert determination is required, care should be taken to stipulate the method of appointment (with appointment by a specified body in the event that the parties are unable to agree) and the means of agreeing to the expert's terms of reference. Care must also be taken in their use; an expert provision should be drafted to fit the contract being negotiated. Attempts to use clauses 'off the shelf' by simple incorporation in a detailed agreement may lead to gaps in drafting, clashes with the main arbitration clause and jurisdiction problems.

The LCIA has proffered a long and detailed clause for expert determination. It is too lengthy to reproduce in this chapter, but may be found online.

The ICC has a short clause cross-referring to its rules:

In the event of any dispute arising out of or in connection with [clause X of the present contract] the parties agree to submit the dispute to ad hoc expert proceedings. The expert shall be appointed by the ICC International Centre for ADR in accordance with the Rules for the Appointment of Experts and Neutrals of the International Chamber of Commerce.

As a matter of English law, an expert's decision is binding on the parties (so that there would be a claim for breach of contract were a party not to abide by it). However, it is not enforceable via the English courts in the same way as an arbitration award and the English courts do not have the same supervisory powers over experts as they do over arbitration proceedings, which can lead to difficulties where, for example, a party refuses to engage in the appointment process.

5. Jurisdictions not within the New York Convention

We have previously mentioned that a number of jurisdictions that have significant hydrocarbon deposits are not parties to the New York Convention and that, as a result, difficulties can arise in obtaining arbitration awards that are enforceable against parties based in those jurisdictions. The following gives a brief, non-exhaustive list of suggestions for overcoming those difficulties; it is worth underlining again here that ensuring reliable enforcement, although sometimes overlooked, is key to effective dispute resolution provisions. It is also worth noting that – in contrast to the International Centre for the Settlement of Investment Disputes (ICSID) Convention, discussed below – it remains the case that the number of New York Convention signatories continues to increase, so care should be taken to ensure the current status of any given jurisdiction.

Notwithstanding the suggestions below, there will be some cases in which it can be impossible to be certain that effective enforcement will be achievable. As a result, there may be a commercial balance to be struck in such situations between the desirability of concluding an agreement and the risk that any breach by a counterparty will be incapable of remedy.

5.1 Reciprocal enforcement treaties

Countries often have treaties providing for the reciprocal enforcement of court judgments. These arise most frequently in the context of countries with strong historical links or with analogous legal systems (eg, the English courts will normally recognise the judgments of most Commonwealth countries and vice versa).

Home court advantage can thus be avoided by choosing a more neutral national court jurisdiction whose judgments will nevertheless be enforceable in the parties' 'home' jurisdictions. However, it is also important to be certain that the treaty in question is itself upheld in practice.

5.2 International assets

If a contracting party has international assets in a jurisdiction that will uphold the enforceability of arbitration awards, that fact may in part mitigate any concerns about enforcement in the party's home jurisdiction.

Most notably, sovereign states may have international assets over which (subject to sovereign immunity issues) enforcement can be sought; a common example is aircraft belonging to a state-owned airline.

5.3 Investment treaty claims and contractual ICSID arbitration

Bilateral and multilateral investment treaties permit qualifying investors holding a qualifying investment to commence arbitral proceedings against a host state for breach of the investment protection standards set out in the relevant treaty. These typically consist primarily of protection against:

- expropriation;
- unfair treatment;
- treatment less favourable that that accorded to a domestic national; and
- treatment less favourable than that accorded to an investor of the most favoured nation.

Investment treaty arbitration can take a variety of forms and investment treaty claims can in certain circumstances be brought in addition to contractual claims. Most notably for present purposes, where a host state is a party to a contract, the parties can agree that any dispute is to be submitted to ICSID arbitration. To be able to do so, it is important to identify at an early stage which investment treaties could permit a claim, and to structure the relevant investment through entities which would be able to use those treaties.

ICSID is an arm of the World Bank; some 154 countries have ratified the ICSID Convention and can thus be subject to ICSID arbitration. ICSID awards can be relatively simple to enforce against developed jurisdictions because of the authority of the World Bank and its ability to impose sanctions on members that do not enforce ICSID arbitration awards, up to and including expulsion from the World Bank itself.

5.4 Regional enforcement agreements

A small number of regional agreements provide for reciprocal enforcement of arbitration awards; one example is the *Organisation pour l'Harmonisation en Afrique du Droit des Affaires*, which applies across a number of West and Central African states, although it is currently of uncertain effectiveness.

6. Brexit

The effect of the withdrawal agreement between the United Kingdom and the European Union is that, until 31 December 2020 (subject to any extension which may be agreed), there will be no material change in the cross-border recognition arrangements between the United Kingdom and the European Union in relation to both governing law clauses and recognition of court judgments (recognition of arbitration agreements and arbitral awards is not governed by EU law). While both sides have expressed a desire to maintain a regime analogous to that which is currently in place, the ultimate outcome will of course depend on the result of the ongoing broader negotiations. Should no agreement on cross-border recognition be reached, it may be the case that where international parties are likely to seek enforcement against a UK party within the European Union, or vice versa, arbitration rather than domestic court jurisdiction will be preferable.

7. Notices

Frequently, contracts include a notice clause whereby formal written notices (up to and including notices of the commencement of litigation or arbitration proceedings) must be sent in a particular way, failing which the notice itself may be invalid.

One of the practical issues arising from these clauses is that they may be out of date by the time they are needed – for example, "Notice to be sent to Mr X [the then CEO] by email to mrxceo@[company name].com" or "Notice to be sent by fax to [phone number]" where, by the time a notice needs to be served, Mr X has left or changed his email (without forwarding) or there is no longer an active fax number. Additionally, the COVID-19 pandemic has made it even clearer that such clauses should be robust; for example, lockdown measures preventing hand delivery could be an issue.

Consideration should be given to fall-back provisions; as an alternative, for example (perhaps in addition to named persons):

- notices being by reference to the job title of a recipient in the relevant company (eg, the then CEO, general counsel, general director); or
- notice to the company's main email address (or its email address for enquiries) as advertised on its website at the time of delivery of the notice, with hard-copy delivery (via courier, post, hand) to follow if and when possible.

8. Concluding remarks

We hope that this chapter makes it clear that governing law and jurisdiction clauses should not be regarded as a topic of purely academic interest, or as an afterthought when negotiating sale and purchase (or, indeed, any) agreements in the oil and gas sector. Rather, these clauses go to the heart of how those contracts will be interpreted and whether and how they will be enforceable. Although obtaining specialist advice on the content of governing law and jurisdiction clauses necessarily involves some initial costs, in the long term those costs will be minimal compared to the savings that result – both in preventing disputes from arising and in resolving those disputes that do arise as quickly, effectively and efficiently as possible.

Oil and gas boilerplate provisions

John C LaMaster
Akin Gump Strauss Hauer & Feld LLP

1. Introduction

It is appropriate that the last chapter of this book deals with boilerplate provisions in oil and gas sale and purchase agreements (SPAs), because boilerplate provisions are customarily included at the end of SPAs.

The term 'boilerplate' originated in the United States in the 19th century in the context of newspaper production. National news services would send national news typeset on metal drums to local newspapers. The local newspapers would use the metal drums to incorporate sections of the national news, without editing such sections, into their newspapers alongside their more bespoke local news. The metal drums were called boilerplate, and the term 'boilerplate' then came to refer also to the standard national copy that was incorporated into the local newspapers.[1]

Today, boilerplate contractual provisions are generally standardised provisions that are often included in a variety of commercial agreements, not just SPAs. The provisions are typically mostly legalistic (eg, governing law, dispute resolution, notices), but can often include important commercial terms (eg, whether the parties are entitled to *force majeure* relief or whether they can assign their rights under the contract).

When preparing an SPA or other commercial agreement, lawyers may tend to use the boilerplate provisions from their most recent successful transaction. This tendency, however, should be resisted, as most commercial agreements will require at least some minor changes to standard boilerplate provisions. In the context of an oil and gas SPA, some boilerplate provisions will remain standardised, whereas other provisions will need to be tailored due to the unique nature of transactions in the oil and gas industry.

This chapter will discuss only those boilerplate provisions that typically require customised treatment in an oil and gas SPA. Accordingly, the following types of boilerplate provision will not be discussed (although, depending on the facts of the relevant transaction, even these boilerplate provisions may require customisation)

1 M Anderson and V Warner, *A-Z Guide to Boilerplate and Commercial Clauses*, 3rd edn, Bloomsbury Professional, 2012, p9.

- amendment;
- confidentiality;
- costs and expenses;
- interpretation;
- language;
- notices;
- priority of agreement;
- public announcements;
- severability;
- termination and survival;
- time is of the essence; and
- waivers and releases.

2. Specific boilerplate provisions in oil and gas SPAs

2.1 Definitions

A definitions clause is intended to set forth the meaning of certain terms used in the SPA. In an oil and gas SPA, the underlying assets that are the subject of the transaction (whether a share sale or an asset sale) are typically host government upstream agreements such as concessions, production sharing agreements or service agreements (each, a 'contract'). If the seller is not the sole non-governmental party to the contract, then most likely there will also be a joint operating agreement (JOA) in place governing the relationship among the non-governmental parties. In order to ensure consistency in interpretation across documents, the definitions clause in an oil and gas SPA should take into consideration the definitions contained in the contract and the JOA, as well as the applicable laws and regulations of the host country.

It is common to incorporate by reference into an oil and gas SPA terms that are already defined in the contract and/or the JOA. For example, the Association of International Petroleum Negotiators (AIPN) 2019 Model International Farmout Agreement includes the following provision:

Unless otherwise defined in this Agreement:

1.1.1 a word or expression defined or used in the Contract has the same meaning when used in this Agreement; and

1.1.2 subject to Article 1.1.1, a word or expression defined or used in the JOA has the same meaning when used in this Agreement.[2]

2.2 *Force majeure*

SPAs typically do not include *force majeure* clauses. This is because buyers and sellers of assets or shares do not usually expect the sale and purchase transaction

2 Article 1.2 of the AIPN 2019 Model International Farmout Agreement.

to be subject to suspension as a result of a *force majeure* event. This is equally the case with respect to SPAs for the sale and purchase of oil and gas assets or shares in companies that own oil and gas assets. There is, however, one exception.

It is not uncommon to include a *force majeure* clause in a farmout agreement. A 'farmout agreement' is a specialised form of upstream oil and gas asset SPA. The feature that makes farmout agreements unique is that the consideration is usually the undertaking by the farmee (the buyer) to perform certain operations that otherwise would have been performed by the farmor (the seller), such as the acquisition of seismic data or the drilling of a well. If these operations must be performed within a specified period of time (eg, during a work commitment phase under a production sharing agreement), then it will be usual and customary to include a *force majeure* clause in the farmout agreement in order to give the farmee some relief in case its operations are interrupted by a *force majeure* event.

Farmout agreements can be structured so that the participating interest being assigned is not assigned unless and until the operations that serve as the consideration have been performed. Alternatively, the participating interest can be assigned upfront, with the operations that serve as the consideration being performed after completion of the assignment. Under the latter structure, which is more common, the inclusion of a *force majeure* clause will not have the effect of delaying completion of the assignment.

If a *force majeure* clause is included in a farmout agreement, it is usually important that the definition of the term '*force majeure*' correspond to the definition in the relevant underlying host government upstream agreement (eg, a production sharing agreement) and possibly to the definition in the relevant JOA. If this is not the case and, for example, the definition of '*force majeure*' in the farmout agreement is broader than the definition of the same term in the host government upstream agreement or the JOA, then, upon the occurrence of an event, the farmee may be excused from performance under the farmout agreement, but the farmor and its joint venture participants may not be excused from performance under the host government upstream agreement or the JOA.[3]

The following *force majeure* provision is taken from the AIPN 2019 Model International Farmout Agreement. Note that the last line defines *force majeure* by reference to the host government upstream agreement.

> *9.1.1 If as a result of* Force majeure, *any Party is rendered unable, wholly or in part, to carry out its obligations under this Agreement, other than the obligation to pay any amounts due, then the obligations of the Party giving notice in accordance with Article 9.1.2, so far as and to the extent that the obligations are affected by such* Force majeure, *shall be suspended during the continuance of any inability*

3 Claude Duval *et al*, *International Petroleum Exploration and Exploitation Agreements: Legal, Economic and Policy Aspects*, 2nd edn, Barrows, 2009, p323.

so caused and for such reasonable period thereafter as may be necessary for the Party to put itself in the same position that it occupied prior to the Force majeure, *but for no longer period.*

9.1.2 The Party claiming Force majeure *shall notify the other Parties of the* Force majeure *within a reasonable time after the occurrence of the facts relied on and shall keep all Parties informed of all significant developments. Such notice shall give reasonably full particulars of the* Force majeure *and also estimate the period of time that the Party will probably require to remedy the* Force majeure.

9.1.3 The affected Party shall use all reasonable diligence to remove or overcome the Force majeure *situation as quickly as possible in a commercially reasonable manner but shall not be obligated to settle any labour dispute except on terms acceptable to it. All such disputes shall be handled within the sole discretion of the affected Party.*

9.1.4 For the purposes of this Agreement, "Force majeure" *shall have the same meaning as is set out in the Contract.*[4]

An alternative way to deal with similar adverse events is by means of a material adverse change (MAC) clause. A buyer may seek a condition precedent that there has been no MAC affecting the assets or the target company between signing and completion in order to protect itself against unpredictable events, including some adverse events that could have qualified as *force majeure* events had the agreement included a *force majeure* clause. Sellers typically resist the inclusion of a MAC condition precedent on several grounds, including that it shifts certain risks from the buyer to the seller during the interim period between signing and completion. If an event occurs between signing and completion that meets the definition of a MAC, then the condition precedent will not be satisfied and the buyer will not have to proceed with the transaction, unless:

- it waives the condition precedent; or
- the underlying MAC ceases to exist before the occurrence of any longstop date that would have terminated the SPA.

An example of a buyer-friendly MAC condition precedent, which includes events that would usually be included in the definition of *force majeure*, is as follows:

The obligations of the Buyer under Clause [•] are conditional on the satisfaction of the following conditions (the "Buyer's Conditions Precedent"): ...

there shall not have occurred an event, occurrence, circumstance, development, change or fact that either alone or in combination with other events, occurrences, circumstances, developments, changes or facts has, or is reasonably expected to have or to result in, an effect that is materially adverse to the business, assets, prospects or financial condition of the target company, the upstream petroleum

4 Article 9.1 of the AIPN 2019 Model International Farmout Agreement.

agreements or the participating interests in the upstream petroleum agreements, taken as a whole.

MAC clauses are discussed in more detail in a separate chapter in this book.

2.3 Sovereign immunity

The issue of sovereign immunity arises when a party, such as an international oil company, enters into an SPA or another agreement with a host government or its national oil company. In this case, the host government or national oil company may be able to claim sovereign immunity from suits and from execution of judgments on its assets. This defence will most likely bar any action in contract or in tort, regardless of whether it is brought in a court or in arbitration. There are some ways that a host government or national oil company can impliedly waive sovereign immunity, but the best way for a counterparty to overcome this defence is to require that an express waiver of sovereign immunity be included in the boilerplate provisions of the SPA.[5]

A comprehensive waiver of sovereign immunity should include waiver of the following elements:

service of process; pre-award interim relief; the jurisdiction of the chosen forum to hear the dispute; the jurisdiction of appropriate courts to enforce any obligation to arbitrate; the jurisdiction of any court to enforce an award or judgment; and post-award execution or attachment of assets.[6]

A thorough example of a waiver of sovereign immunity is included in the AIPN's 2012 Model International JOA, although the same clause would be appropriate for an SPA:

Any Party that now or later has a right to claim sovereign immunity for itself or any of its assets hereby waives any such immunity to the fullest extent permitted by the laws of any applicable jurisdiction. This waiver includes immunity from:

A. *any expert determination, mediation, or arbitration proceeding commenced under this Agreement;*

B. *any judicial, administrative or other proceedings to aid the expert determination, mediation, or arbitration commenced under this Agreement; and*

C. *any effort to confirm, enforce, or execute any decision, settlement, award, judgment, service of process, execution order or attachment (including pre-judgment attachment) that results from an expert determination, mediation, arbitration or any judicial or administrative proceedings commenced under this Agreement.*

For the purposes of this waiver only, each Party acknowledges that its rights and obligations under this Agreement are of a commercial and not a governmental nature.[7]

---

5 Claude Duval *et al*, *International Petroleum Exploration and Exploitation Agreements: Legal, Economic and Policy Aspects*, 2nd edn, Barrows, 2009, p355.

6 *Id* at 356.

7 Article 18.4 of the AIPN 2012 Model International Joint Operating Agreement.

2.4 Relationship of the parties/no partnership

Participants in an upstream oil and gas exploration, development and production project typically enter into a JOA. Depending on the terms of the JOA and the facts and circumstances of the project, the alliance between the participants may be interpreted under applicable law as a mining or other partnership, a joint venture, an association, a trust or a principal-agent relationship.

Certain of these relationships, such as a partnership or a principal-agent relationship, typically create fiduciary duties among the parties, which include a high standard of care, good faith and trust.[8] There may also be unintended tax and accounting consequences if the alliance is treated as a partnership.

For these reasons and others, the participants under a JOA will usually include a boilerplate provision in the JOA that the alliance shall not create, or be deemed to create, a mining or other partnership, a joint venture, an association, a trust or a principal-agent relationship.[9] Such a clause may not be conclusive, however, because it is the substance of the relationship among the participants (which depends on the terms of the JOA and the facts and circumstances of the project), rather than a clause in the JOA, that will determine the nature of the relationship between the parties.[10] But the standard practice is to include such a provision in the JOA.

As explained above, a farmout agreement is a specialised form of upstream oil and gas asset SPA, in which the consideration is typically the undertaking by the farmee (the buyer) to perform certain operations that otherwise would have been performed by the farmor (the seller), such as the acquisition of seismic data or the drilling of a well. The farmout agreement thereby has a role in establishing a collaborative relationship between the parties beyond the completion of the acquisition of the relevant participating interest. Therefore, it is also standard practice to include a boilerplate provision in a farmout agreement that the agreement does not create an association, trust, partnership, joint venture or principal-agent relationship.

In an oil and gas SPA or farmout agreement where there is more than one seller or farmor, or more than one buyer or farmee, the question arises as to whether an undertaking given by them is joint, several or joint and several. Where parties have joint liability, the liability is shared. In an action against those joint obligors, all of the obligors must be joined to the action to enforce performance of the joint liability. Where parties have several liability, each party's liability is separate and distinct from each other party's liability. In an

---

8 P Roberts, *Joint Operating Agreements: A Practical Guide*, Globe Law and Business, 2010, p281.

9 See Article 14.1 of the AIPN 2012 Model International Joint Operating Agreement.

10 M Anderson and V Warner, *A-Z Guide to Boilerplate and Commercial Clauses*, 3rd edn, Bloomsbury Professional, 2012, p28; P Roberts, *Joint Operating Agreements: A Practical Guide*, Globe Law and Business, 2010, p253.

action against several obligors, the obligation can be enforced against each obligor separately. Where parties have joint and several liability, all such parties are promising together and each such party is promising on its own. In an action against joint and several obligors, the entire obligation can be enforced against any one obligor, as well as against all obligors together.

In the context of an oil and gas SPA or farmout agreement where there is more than one seller or farmor, or more than one buyer or farmee, each party will want to be liable only for its proportionate percentage share of each undertaking – that is, the parties desire several liability, rather than joint or joint and several liability.

Each of the foregoing points is addressed in the AIPN 2019 Model International Farmout Agreement:

> *Except as specified, the duties, obligations, and liabilities of the Parties under or relating to this Agreement are several and not joint or collective, and nothing contained in this Agreement shall be construed as creating an association, trust, partnership, joint venture, or principal–agent relationship.*[11]

One issue that is not addressed in the foregoing provision is the question of whether, in cases where there is more than one seller or farmor, those sellers or farmors owe a duty of good faith to each other. A similar question would arise among multiple buyers or farmees. In most civil law jurisdictions, parties to a commercial agreement generally owe a duty of good faith to each other. Although this duty of good faith is not generally recognised under English law, it may be worth considering supplementing the foregoing provision to eliminate any duty of good faith.[12]

2.5 Assignment/successors and assigns

Upstream oil and gas operations are by their nature long term, complicated and expensive. Furthermore, it is typical that all of the participants under a host country upstream agreement (eg, a production sharing agreement) are jointly and severally liable to the host government. As a result, the participants have a strong interest in ensuring that their co-participants have adequate financial resources and technical capabilities to meet their respective obligations. This is one of the main reasons why JOAs typically include provisions prohibiting assignments by participants without the consent of the other participants.[13]

A farmor/seller under a farmout agreement or an asset SPA also has a strong interest in ensuring that its buyer has adequate financial resources and technical capabilities to meet its obligations. This will be the case whether or not the

---

11 Article 16.19 of the AIPN 2019 Model International Farmout Agreement.

12 R Fowler, P Roberts and E Pereira, *The AIPN Joint Operating Agreement: A Practical Guide*, Globe Law and Business, 2019, p410.

13 Marc Hammerson and John LaMaster (eds), *Oil and Gas M&A: A Practical Handbook*, Globe Law and Business, 2014, p76.

farmor/seller retains an interest in the asset after completion of the transfer. If the farmor/seller retains an interest in the host country upstream agreement and JOA, then the farmor/seller and the farmee/buyer will become jointly and severally liable as co-participants under the host country upstream agreement and JOA after the transfer is completed. If the farmor/seller does not retain an interest in the asset after the transfer is completed, the farmor/seller will still want to ensure that its farmee/buyer has the requisite financial resources and technical capabilities in order to obtain the host government's and JOA parties' consent to the transfer, and also to minimise the risk of the farmor/seller retaining any secondary liability (eg, in relation to environmental and decommissioning matters). For these reasons, the parties to a farmout agreement or SPA will typically want to include a provision whereby a party may not assign its interest under the farmout agreement or SPA without the consent of the other party.

An exception sometimes arises where the proposed assignment is to an affiliate of a party to the SPA. In these cases, consent of the non-assigning party may not be required. The parties may want to include some restrictions in the SPA around this, however, such as requiring that the assignor remain jointly and severally liable with its affiliate assignee. Furthermore, the parties may want to provide for a 'clawback' mechanism whereby, if the affiliate assignee leaves the assignor's group and is no longer an affiliate of the assignor, the affiliate assignee must reassign the assigned interests to the assignor.

Another exception may arise where the interests in a host country upstream agreement must be held by a company incorporated in the host country, as is the case in Nigeria. In this case, the buyer may enter into the SPA before forming the local company and the parties may agree that, prior to completion, the buyer may assign its participating interests to its local company affiliate once it is formed.

Once it is determined that consent to assignment will be required, the next issue is what type of consent will be required. In some cases, the SPA may provide that the non-assigning party can withhold its consent only if certain conditions are met – for example, that the proposed assignee lacks adequate financial or technical capabilities, or is in a category of persons or entities defined in the SPA as 'prohibited assignees' (eg, assignees from a country that is subject to governmental sanctions). The SPA may alternatively provide that the non-assigning party's consent may not be unreasonably withheld, or may not be unreasonably withheld or delayed. Lastly, the SPA may give the non-assigning party an absolute consent right, meaning that the non-assigning party can withhold its consent, in its sole discretion, for any reason or for no reason.

In the case of a farmout agreement, the agreement may preclude any assignment whatsoever by the farmee until the farmee has completed the operations that it has committed to perform as consideration for the farmout.

The following example is from the UK Oil & Gas Model Form SPA:

No Party shall have the right to assign, transfer or otherwise dispose of its rights and/or obligations under this Agreement without the consent of the other Party, which consent shall not be unreasonably withheld.[14]

A more comprehensive example is as follows:

No Party may assign either this Agreement or any of its rights, interests or obligations hereunder without the prior written approval of the other Party, such approval not to be unreasonably withheld or delayed; provided, however, that the Buyer may assign any or all of its rights, interests or obligations hereunder to its Affiliate, provided that: (i) the Buyer agrees in an instrument reasonably satisfactory to the Seller to remain liable for its Affiliate's performance of its obligations; and (ii) in the event that the assignee is intended to undergo a Change of Control whereby the Affiliate will no longer be an Affiliate of the Buyer, then prior to the Change of Control all of the assigned rights, interests or obligations must be assigned back to the Buyer or to an Affiliate of the Buyer.

A companion clause to the assignment clause is a clause stating that the SPA will be binding on and inure to the benefit of the parties' successors and assigns. An important drafting tip is to ensure that the successors and assigns clause does not conflict with the assignment clause; this is typically done by limiting the clause to "successors and permitted assigns".

... this Agreement will apply to, be binding in all respects upon, and inure to the benefit of the successors and permitted assigns of the parties.[15]

2.6 Joint preparation/independent advice

There is much debate regarding which party – buyer or seller – should prepare the first draft of an oil and gas SPA. In an auction process, the seller typically prepares the first draft SPA and asks the buyer to provide its comments on the draft together with its bid. In other cases, it is said that it makes sense for the buyer to prepare the first draft, on the basis that most of the provisions of an SPA are for its benefit (eg, the seller's warranties).[16] In practice, however, most lawyers want to draft the SPA or at least portions thereof on behalf of their clients, whether buyers or sellers, because the drafting process allows lawyers to make choices regarding wording that is most beneficial to their client.

The *contra proferentem*[17] common law rule of contractual construction states that where an agreement or a clause in an agreement is ambiguous, the words should be construed against the party that proffers them or puts them forward – the proferens. In the context of an SPA, the proferens could be the party that

14 Article 10 of the UK Oil & Gas Model Form Agreement for the Sale and Purchase of Assets in Relation to the [•] Field.

15 Model Stock Purchase Agreement with Commentary (American Bar Association, 1995), p225.

16 James C Freund, *Anatomy of a Merger: Strategies and Techniques for Negotiating Corporate Acquisitions*, Law Journal Press, 1975, p27.

17 Latin for 'against the offeror'. *Black's Law Dictionary*, 8th edn, Thomson West, 2004, p352.

drafted the ambiguous clause, or the party that seeks to rely on the clause. There is authority[18] that the *contra proferentem* rule does not apply to wording that has been jointly drafted by the parties, on the basis that you cannot hold the wording against a party if that party did not draft the wording.

Accordingly, the *contra proferentem* rule is typically addressed in an SPA with wording that provides that the SPA shall be construed as if it were drafted jointly by the parties. A simple example is as follows:

No consideration shall be given to the fact or presumption that one Party has a greater or lesser hand in drafting this Contract.[19]

A more detailed example is as follows:

The Parties have participated jointly in the negotiation and drafting of this Agreement. In the event an ambiguity or question of intent or interpretation arises, this Agreement shall be construed as if drafted jointly by the Parties and no presumption or burden of proof shall arise favoring or disfavoring any Party by virtue of the authorship of any of the provisions of this Agreement.

A related issue is that parties do not want an SPA or provisions thereof interpreted against them on the basis that the counterparty did not have independent financial and legal advice. This is typically addressed by a boilerplate provision such as the following example from the AIPN 2019 Model International Farmout Agreement:

Each Party affirms that it has received independent financial and legal advice relating to this Agreement and the valuation of the Farmout Interests and this Agreement, the instruments to be executed under it, and to the transactions contemplated by it.[20]

2.7 Entire agreement

In the context of an SPA, the entire agreement clause typically has three objectives. First, it makes it clear that the full contractual agreement of the parties is contained within the four corners of the SPA, thereby superseding prior oral or written agreements. This ensures that there cannot be any conflicts between the terms of the SPA and any prior oral or written agreements. Secondly, it eliminates pre-contractual statements between the parties that could constitute representations or other contractual commitments even after the SPA is signed. Thirdly, the entire agreement clause will eliminate certain implied terms, such as implied warranties.[21]

Each of these three objectives is relevant to an oil and gas SPA. In particular, it is usual and customary in oil and gas acquisitions and divestitures for the

---

18 *Levinson v Farin* [1978] 2 All ER 1149; *Kleinwort Benson Ltd v Malaysia Mining Corpn Berhad* [1988] 1 WLR 799.

19 Article 22.10 of the AIPN 2002 International Model Well Services Contract.

20 Article 16.15 of the AIPN 2019 Model International Farmout Agreement.

21 P Roberts, *Petroleum Contracts: English Law and Practice*, OUP, 2013, p411.

buyer and the seller to enter into preliminary agreements, such as a confidentiality agreement, or a letter of intent, heads of terms or memorandum of understanding. These preliminary agreements are usually superseded in the SPA by means of the 'entire agreement' clause. However, if the SPA does not include a confidentiality provision, the parties may desire that the preliminary confidentiality agreement remain in force and effect, at least until completion of the transactions contemplated by the SPA; in this case, a carve-out from the entire agreement clause will be necessary so that the entire agreement clause will not supersede the preliminary confidentiality agreement, at least until completion of the sale and purchase contemplated by the SPA.

A good example of an entire agreement clause that achieves each of the three objectives described above is in the AIPN 2019 Model International Agreement:

16.16.1 This Agreement constitutes or expressly refers to the entire agreement of the Parties concerning the subject matter. Any prior, collateral, or other promise, understanding, agreement, or arrangement, whether written or oral, express or implied, is of no force or effect.

16.16.2 Each Party confirms that, in making this Agreement, it is not relying on any statement, warranty, or representation given or made by or on behalf of another Party and not expressed in this Agreement, and that it shall have no rights or remedies otherwise than under this Agreement.[22]

One pitfall in drafting entire agreement clauses arises where the parties have entered into multiple agreements together with the SPA or on completion of the transactions contemplated by the SPA. In this case, in order to avoid confusion, the entire agreement clause should either refer specifically to these other agreements or include general wording such as "except as otherwise contemplated by this Agreement".

An example of an entire agreement clause that expressly supersedes a preliminary agreement and also refers to other agreements contemplated by the SPA is as follows:

This Agreement supersedes all prior agreements between the parties with respect to its subject matter (including the Letter of Intent between Buyer and Seller dated [•]) and constitutes (along with the documents referred to in this Agreement) a complete and exclusive statement of the terms of the agreement between the parties with respect to its subject matter.[23]

It is common for entire agreement clauses also to include wording that does not exclude liability for fraud, such as: "Nothing in this Agreement shall exclude liability for fraud." The reasoning is that the entire agreement clause would be overbroad and therefore unenforceable if it attempted to shield a party from its

22 Article 16.16 of the AIPN 2019 Model International Farmout Agreement.
23 Model Stock Purchase Agreement with Commentary (American Bar Association, 1995), p222.

liability for fraud. Recent case law, however, has confirmed that this additional wording is not strictly necessary, although it remains common practice.[24]

2.8 Third-party beneficiaries

The common law doctrine of privity of contract provides that contractual rights are binding on, and enforceable only by, the parties to a contract. This means, among other things, that the parties to a contract may sue each other to enforce the contract, but that third parties (ie, anyone that is not a party to the contract) may not do so. The Contracts (Rights of Third Parties) Act 1999 modified the doctrine of privity of contract with respect to English law-governed contracts, by providing in general that a third party may enforce a term of a contract if the contract expressly states that it can do so, or if that term of the contract purports to give some benefit to the third party. The Contracts (Rights of Third Parties) Act 1999 therefore gives greater rights to third parties than they had under previous English common law.[25]

Since the passage of the Contracts (Rights of Third Parties) Act 1999, it has become standard practice to include boilerplate wording preventing third parties from enforcing terms of the contract. For example:

A Third Party may not enforce a provision of this Agreement, whether under the Contracts (Rights of Third Parties) Act 1999, or otherwise.

It is not uncommon for an oil and gas SPA to include indemnities or other provisions that are intended to be enforceable by third-party beneficiaries, such as indemnities for environmental and decommissioning liabilities. For example, if the SPA includes an indemnity and the indemnified parties are "the Buyer, its Affiliates and their respective directors, officers and employees", then presumably those affiliates, directors, officers and employees ought to be able to enforce that indemnity directly against the indemnifying party. In this case, the relevant boilerplate clause ought to carve out the indemnity. Furthermore, once the third-party beneficiaries have rights to enforce the indemnity, the boilerplate clause ought to deal with related issues – namely, that:

- the parties to the SPA can amend the SPA (including the relevant indemnity) without consent of the third-party beneficiaries; and
- the third-party beneficiaries cannot transfer their beneficial rights.

For example:

16.8.1 Except as specified, a Third Party may not enforce a provision of this Agreement, whether under the English Contracts (Rights of Third Parties) Act 1999, or otherwise.

24 M Anderson and V Warner, *A-Z Guide to Boilerplate and Commercial Clauses*, 3rd edn, Bloomsbury Publishing, 2012, p277.

25 *Id* at 204.

16.8.2 If a provision is enforceable by a Third Party:

(a) the Parties may rescind or amend that provision or any other provision (including the right of that Third Party to enforce that provision) without the Third Party's approval; and

(b) that Third Party may not Transfer or Encumber that right.[26]

2.9 Counterparts

Before electronic communications, SPAs were typically signed by both parties at a signing ceremony. If the parties could not get together in the same location, then the SPA was physically circulated between the parties, with each party signing the originals and the SPA becoming effective once both parties had signed.

Technology has changed the customary practice, and nowadays agreements are usually signed and exchanged either by fax or by email with the SPA attached, usually in a PDF. These 'virtual' signings are often a practical necessity in the international oil and gas industry, where many transactions are between parties in different countries, making it more difficult and costly to arrange a signing ceremony.

These types of arrangements are facilitated by counterparts clauses in SPAs. The traditional counterparts clauses still contemplated original (wet ink) signatures being exchanged between the parties:

This Agreement may be executed in one or more counterparts, each of which will be deemed to be an original copy of this Agreement and all of which, when taken together, will be deemed to constitute one and the same agreement.[27]

If the parties intend for electronic signatures to be treated as original signatures, then they should expressly provide for this in the SPA:

This Agreement may be executed in counterparts or duplicates, each of which when executed and delivered shall be deemed a duplicate original, but all of which, together, shall constitute one and the same contractual document. In the event that any signature is delivered by facsimile or by e-mail delivery of a portable document format (.pdf) data file, such signature shall create a valid and binding agreement of the Party executing such signature page with the same force and effect as if such facsimile or portable document format (.pdf) signature page were an original thereof.

There have been cases under English law regarding the effectiveness of virtual signings where documents and/or signature pages are transmitted either by fax or by email.[28] A joint working party of the Law Society Company Law

---

26 Article 16.8 of the AIPN 2019 Model International Farmout Agreement. If the only clause that gives rise to third-party rights is a specific indemnity, then the phrase "Except as specified..." could be modified to cross-refer to that specific indemnity.

27 Model Stock Purchase Agreement with Commentary (American Bar Association, 1995), p232.

28 *R (on the application of Mercury Tax Group) v HMRC* [2008] EWHC 2721; *J Pereira Fernandes SA v Mehta* [2016] 1 WLR 1543; *Mr Stavros Neocleous v Ms Christine Rees* [2019] EWHC 2462 (Ch) (holding that an automatic email signature was a valid signature).

Committee and the City of London Law Society Company Law and Financial Law Committees has published guidance entitled "Note on Execution of Documents At A Virtual Signing or Closing".[29] Most recently, the Law Commission has issued a report (2019) on the validity of electronic signatures, and the Law Society has issued a note (2019) on signing and exchanging documents.

In summary, different rules apply to documents to be executed as deeds and to real estate contracts than apply to guarantees and simple contracts. This guidance should be consulted prior to any virtual signing or completion. Subject to such guidance, the parties can agree either that the entire agreement must be transmitted by fax or as an attachment to an email, or that only the signature page must be transmitted:

Transmission of [an executed counterpart of this Agreement (but for the avoidance of doubt not just the signature page)] [the executed signature page of this Agreement] by facsimile or by e-mail delivery of a portable document format (.pdf) shall take effect as delivery of an executed counterpart of this Agreement.

References in counterparts provisions to transmission by fax are becoming less relevant, as that technology is phasing out.

The counterparts provision will doubtless need to be updated again once e-signatures become more commonplace in business-to-business agreements.

Finally, in SPAs specifying a governing law other than English law, the relevant governing law should be checked with respect to its requirements regarding counterparts execution, and especially with respect to the validity of counterparts execution by fax or PDF.

3. Conclusion

Boilerplate provisions are sometimes considered to be boring parts of an SPA, because they are standardised and typically require less thought or effort by the parties or their lawyers than the more exciting commercial terms of the SPA. We have seen in this chapter, however, that some boilerplate provisions in oil and gas SPAs need to be customised because of the unique nature of transactions in that industry.

---

29 May 2009 (with minor amendments in February 2010).

About the authors

Afzaal Abidi
Trainee solicitor, Vinson & Elkins RLLP
aabidi@velaw.com

Afzaal Abidi is a trainee in the London office of Vinson & Elkins, currently seated in the energy transactions and projects group. He has advisory and transactional experience in project development and finance, mergers and acquisitions, and engineering, procurement and construction contracts, primarily in the energy sector.

Nicholas Antonas
Counsel, Akin Gump Strauss Hauer & Feld LLP
nantonas@akingump.com

Nicholas Antonas is a counsel with Akin Gump Strauss Hauer & Feld LLP, based in London. He advises international energy companies, private equity and hedge funds, bondholders and lenders, primarily in relation to energy-related cross-border mergers and acquisitions, project developments and restructurings. Nicholas has extensive experience advising on decommissioning matters, and has presented and co-edited a text on the subject.

Kevin Atkins
Partner, Locke Lord LLP
kevin.atkins@lockelord.com

Kevin Atkins is a partner in the corporate department at Locke Lord LLP in London. His practice focuses on the energy sector, and he has more than 15 years' experience advising on international cross-border upstream oil and gas mergers and acquisitions, joint venture arrangements, equity capital markets work and debt financings for energy companies and energy and infrastructure projects. He has worked on a number of high-profile upstream transactions across Africa. He is very familiar with the issues facing equity investors and project lenders and host governments in the context of corporate transactions, and the needs of energy companies developing oil and gas projects during the M&A process. He is also a regular contributor to oil and gas texts.

Paige Berges
Counsel, Ropes & Gray (London)
paige.berges@ropesgray.com

Paige Berges is counsel in Ropes and Gray's anti-corruption and international risk practice group. She is a US and UK-qualified lawyer with broad cross-border experience conducting internal investigations, enforcement and defence as well as in-house experience in private equity and investment banking. She focuses on advising clients on pre-investment due diligence and post-investment monitoring to ensure compliance with economic sanctions, anti-money laundering/counter-terrorist financing and anti-corruption regulations. In addition to US, UK and pan-European practice, Paige brings significant experience helping clients build compliance programmes across sub-Saharan Africa, Southeast Asia and the Middle East and North Africa.

Olivier Chambord
Partner, Morgan, Lewis & Bockius UK LLP
olivier.chambord@morganlewis.com

Olivier Chambord represents a variety of international clients in project development, mergers, acquisitions and disposals in Europe and Africa. In particular, he focuses on acquisitions and dispositions of oil and gas and mining assets. Olivier also assists clients on the development of oil and gas and mining assets and infrastructure, including by advising on intergovernmental and host government agreements, production sharing and joint operating agreements, concessions, transportation agreements, supply and sale agreements. Olivier is listed in a number of legal guides, including the *International Who's Who of Oil and Gas* and *The Legal 500*.

Peter Crowther
Partner, Winston & Strawn LLP
pcrowther@winston.com

Peter Crowther is the managing partner of Winston's London and Brussels offices and is widely recognised as a leading competition and trade lawyer. A significant part of his practice involves advising companies on a wide range of cartel and merger proceedings and associated litigation.

He has extensive experience advising on trade/sanctions laws, EU merger control, state aid, free movement and general EU competition and regulatory compliance. A substantial part of Peter's practice involves defending multinational companies in a wide range of national and international proceedings, often simultaneously across a number of jurisdictions.

Peter has a long track record of advising household-name companies across a significant number of sectors, including broadcasting, pharmaceuticals, commodity products, petrochemicals and telecommunications. He also devises and implements compliance programmes covering areas such as competition, trade/sanctions, bribery, and corruption.

Peter is a former law lecturer and the former holder of a Jean Monnet professorship in European law.

Matthew Daffurn
Partner, Locke Lord LLP
matthew.daffurn@lockelord.com

Matthew Daffurn is a partner in the London office of Locke Lord LLP. He has significant experience acting for corporations, lenders, sponsors, governments, multilateral agencies and insurers in relation to the development, financing, acquisition and disposal of energy and infrastructure assets in Africa and other emerging markets. Matthew has advised on a number of high-profile transactions across all areas of the oil and gas value chain. In addition to advising buyers and sellers of oil and gas assets and issuers and investors alike on capital raising transactions, he has particular expertise in addressing the issues presented by lending on the basis of oil and gas collateral.

Richard Ellison
Solicitor
richard.p.m.ellison@gmail.com

Richard Ellison has worked for Magic Circle and prominent US firms in the City of London for over 11 years. He has a degree in English law and a *maîtrise* in French law and specialises in international arbitration, while also frequently advising on English High Court and cross-border litigation.

He has advised on high-value disputes before all the major international arbitration organisations, with an emphasis on the energy sector. His cases are almost always international in nature, with a particular focus on the Commonwealth of Independent States countries, West Africa and the Far East, often working alongside local counsel in relevant jurisdictions. He has also regularly worked on disputes involving bilateral investment treaties, in particular in relation to the extractive industries.

He frequently advises on how best to achieve the effective enforceability of oil and gas transactions, and his clients have included both national oil and gas companies and a range of privately owned enterprises.

Matthew Foster
Partner, Norton Rose Fulbright LLP
matthew.foster@nortonrosefulbright.com

Matt Foster is a corporate partner in the financial institutions group of Norton Rose Fulbright LLP's London office. He focuses on the banking and insurance sectors, and advises clients on the full variety of corporate transactions, including mergers and acquisitions, takeovers, joint ventures and general corporate, commercial and regulatory matters. Since 2017, Matt has been recognised by *The Legal 500* as a "Next Generation Lawyer" in its Insurance: Corporate & Regulatory section. Matt has been advising both insurers and insureds on warranty and indemnity insurance matters for nearly 10 years and is a regular commentator on the market.

Marc Hammerson
Partner, Stephenson Harwood LLP
marc.hammerson@shlegal.com

Marc Hammerson is a partner and head of oil and gas at Stephenson Harwood LLP. He is an international energy lawyer with 25 years' private practice and in-house experience working on mergers and acquisitions and projects in over 75 countries. His clients include private equity, oil majors, independents, national oil companies and governments. Marc currently works from the firm's London office, but during his career he has also been based in Dubai, Houston, Singapore and Tokyo.

Recent editions of *Chambers Global* refer to him as "an excellent lawyer" and "extremely effective and able to find solutions to complex problems and very technically sound". *Chambers UK* ranks Marc in Energy & Natural Resources: Oil & Gas – UK-wide and states that he has "extensive experience in M&A, joint ventures and corporate restructurings in the energy sector. Sources report: 'He is fantastically commercial. He is highly effective and has all the tricks of the trade in difficult negotiations'".

Lisa Hatfield
Associate, Winston & Strawn LLP
lhatfield@winston.com

Lisa Hatfield is an associate in the London office of Winston & Strawn. She advises clients across a wide range of sectors on EU and UK antitrust/competition law matters, including dawn raids and cartel investigations, merger proceedings, state aid and compliance issues. She also advises on various regulatory matters.

Joanna Kay
Senior legal counsel, BW Offshore

Joanna Kay is a senior commercial and corporate lawyer with over 10 years of experience working in emerging markets in the energy and natural resources sector. She has led on a range of complex and demanding international transactions across Africa, South America, Europe and the Middle East, in both in-house and private practice environments. Her particular expertise includes upstream and midstream oil, gas and liquefied natural gas transactions, oil and gas M&A, joint ventures, commercial and contract law and dispute resolution. She is a committee member of the UK Energy Lawyers Group and has contributed to a number of leading oil and gas market publications.

Hussain Kubba
Partner, Norton Rose Fulbright LLP
hussain.kubba@nortonrosefulbright.com

Hussain Kubba is an energy M&A and corporate partner based in London. His practice focuses on advising international oil and gas companies and national oil companies on corporate and commercial matters, including asset and corporate acquisitions and disposals, farmins/outs, host government contracts, joint venture arrangements, decommissioning matters and operator and commercial contracts in the oil and gas industry.

Hussain has advised on transactions in the United Kingdom, Europe, Africa, Central and South Asia, the Middle East, South and Latin America, and has also been on secondments to major oil companies in the United Kingdom, including in Aberdeen.

He also holds a mechanical engineering and management undergraduate degree from McMaster University (Canada), and was a professional engineer for seven years in Ontario prior to qualifying as a lawyer in England and Wales.

Hussain is a member of the Association of International Petroleum Negotiators (AIPN) and a committee member of the UK Energy Lawyers Group.

John C LaMaster
Partner, Akin Gump Strauss Hauer & Feld LLP
jlamaster@akingump.com

John C LaMaster has more than 30 years of experience in virtually all areas of the oil and gas industry – including upstream, midstream and downstream – throughout Europe, Africa, Russia and the former Soviet Union, the Middle East and the United States. John is highly rated by various publications, including being one of only six lawyers rated Band 1 in Energy & Natural Resources: Oil & Gas in the 2020 edition of *Chambers & Partners*. He is a frequent author on oil and gas subjects, including co-editing *Oil and Gas M&A – A Practical Handbook, Second Edition* (2018) and *Oil & Gas in Africa – A Legal and Commercial Analysis of the Upstream Industry* (2015), and contributing chapters to both of those books and several others. He holds a BA in economics and business administration from Vanderbilt University and a JD with honours from the Paul M Herbert Law Centre at Louisiana State University.

Caroline-Lucy Moran
Counsel, Akin Gump Strauss Hauer & Feld LLP
cmoran@akingump.com

Caroline-Lucy Moran practises in the cross-border transactions department of Akin Gump Strauss Hauer & Feld LLP in London. She specialises in international M&A, joint ventures, project development and equity capital markets transactions, with a particular focus on upstream and downstream oil and gas and power sectors.

Caroline-Lucy has worked on transactions throughout Europe, Asia, the Middle East and West, East and sub-Saharan Africa. She has significant private equity experience, having recently been seconded to the London office of The Carlyle Group for over a year. As a trainee, she completed a secondment to ExxonMobil.

Caroline-Lucy has been identified as an "Associate to Watch" in the 2020 edition and prior editions of *Chambers & Partners UK* and won the "Rising Star: Corporate" award at the *Euromoney/IFLR* Women in Business Law Awards 2016. She graduated from the University of Oxford in 2006 and was admitted as a solicitor of the senior courts of England and Wales in 2010.

Alexander Msimang
Managing partner, Vinson & Elkins RLLP
amsimang@velaw.com

Alex Msimang has two decades of experience advising clients on the full range of energy-related projects and transactions. He focuses the majority of his work on global energy M&A – principally in the oil and gas sector – with the balance made up of project development and regulatory advisory work.

Alex advises clients across the globe. In the United Kingdom, he helps them navigate the highly sophisticated and regulated energy market and brings that experience to bear on projects across Africa, the Middle East, Latin America and Europe.

Alex serves as the managing partner of the London office, where he has helped lead the firm to continuous recognition in *Chambers & Partners UK* for Oil & Gas. In 2020, *Chambers* recognised Alex for his individual efforts as an "eminent figure in oil and gas". He has previously been recognised by the same publication as "one of the world's best lawyers" for oil and gas matters.

Sophie O'Connor
Partner, Norton Rose Fulbright LLP
sophie.o'connor@nortonrosefulbright.com

Sophie O'Connor is a corporate partner in the financial institutions group of Norton Rose Fulbright LLP's London office. She is an experienced private equity practitioner with over a decade of experience advising sponsors, portfolio companies and management teams on the range of mainstream private equity transactions. Sophie also advises other investors seeking to deploy private capital, including investment banks, asset managers and major corporates. In addition, she applies her extensive deal experience to advise on warranty and indemnity insurance policies – typically, in relation to large-scale multi-jurisdictional transactions.

J Scott Porter
Vice president, new business development,
Shell Exploration & Production
Vice president, planning and board of directors,
Association of International Petroleum
Negotiators
scott.s.porter@shell.com

J Scott Porter has over 30 years' experience negotiating a wide range of transactions in the energy sector. He began his career in corporate banking in both New York and Houston, where he focused on project financing and acquisition financing in gas storage, cogeneration, pipelines and oil and gas. In 1996 he moved to Enron International to lead business development efforts in Latin America, including building gas and power positions in both Argentina and Brazil. Mr Porter joined Royal Dutch Shell in 2002 and has lived in London, The Hague and Singapore. His experience during this period included working on a variety of both upstream and downstream projects including divestments in Africa, joint venture restructurings in the former Soviet Union, and various acquisitions and divestments in Europe and Southeast Asia.

In May 2019 Mr Porter was appointed vice president commercial/new business development, North America & Brazil for Shell's upstream and integrated gas businesses. He graduated from Duke University and attended business school at the Thunderbird Graduate School of International Business in Phoenix.

Amanda Raad
Partner, Ropes & Gray (London)
amanda.raad@ropesgray.com

Amanda Raad, a US lawyer also admitted as a solicitor in England & Wales, serves as co-chair of Ropes & Gray's award-winning global anti-corruption and international risk practice, as well as London's white collar and enforcement practice. Amanda has substantial experience negotiating with regulators on behalf of companies and individuals concerning cross-border matters involving corruption, money laundering and other forms of financial fraud. These matters are often subject to scrutiny by foreign regulators, given their multi-jurisdictional nature. Amanda also proactively works with clients across industries and geographies to identify and mitigate risk. Amanda has worked with numerous oil and gas and energy clients to conduct global anti-corruption compliance reviews and risk assessments, and develop and update compliance policies and procedures. Amanda contributes to GIR's *The Practitioner's Guide to Global Investigations*, serves as a director for Lawyers Without Borders and is consistently listed in *Chambers UK* and *UK Legal 500*.

Peter Roberts
Principal, Cross Keys Energy Limited
petro@crosskeysenergy.com

Peter Roberts advises governments and companies on domestic and international oil and gas transactions, including country entry, joint ventures, M&A, liquefied natural gas project developments and commodity sales contracts. A former chairman of the International Bar Association's Oil and Gas Law Committee, Peter has authored seven leading industry textbooks (published variously by Globe Law and Business, the Oxford University Press, the Qatar University Press and Sweet & Maxwell); is the editor of the AIPN's *Journal of World Energy Law and Business*; and is a visiting professor of law at *Universidad Austral*, Buenos Aires. He was previously the general counsel for a UK energy company and has worked for several leading law firms in London, Hong Kong and Singapore.

Sean Seelinger
Counsel, Ropes & Gray (London)
sean.seelinger@ropesgray.com

Sean Seelinger is a US-trained lawyer based in London and a member of the firm's litigation and enforcement practice group. Sean's practice focuses on government-initiated and internal investigations of cross-border anti-corruption, anti-money laundering and trade compliance matters, as well as advising private equity firms regarding compliance and Committee on Foreign Investment in the United States risk associated with cross-border transactions. He also regularly advises multinational corporations on corruption, money laundering and sanctions issues associated with prospective business agreements, and assists companies implement best-practice compliance programmes. Sean frequently assists newly acquired non-US portfolio companies of US private equity firms review their business dealings and internal procedures to ensure compliance with applicable Office of Foreign Assets Control sanctions. While previously based in the New York office, Sean was seconded to the Global Compliance Group of a Fortune 100 multinational oil and gas company. During his secondment, Sean led several internal investigations and assisted with the restructuring of the company's anti-corruption and anti-boycott compliance programme.

Allison Soilihi
Associate, Morgan, Lewis & Bockius UK LLP
allison.soilihi@morganlewis.com

Allison Soilihi represents companies in the extractive industries sector, with a geographical focus on emerging markets. She advises on issues involving acquisitions and dispositions, project development and commercial aspects relating to oil and gas and mining assets. Allison drafts and negotiates agreements encompassing production sharing, joint operations and the transportation and supply of extracted resources. She also counsels on host government agreements, joint ventures and more generally on mergers and acquisitions and general corporate matters relating to extractive companies.

Holly Stebbing
Partner, Norton Rose Fulbright LLP
holly.stebbing@nortonrosefulbright.com

Holly Stebbing is a dispute resolution lawyer based in London. Her practice focuses on disputes in the energy, renewables and natural resources sectors, both domestic (including UK continental shelf) and international. She has a wide range of experience, including litigation in the High Court and appellate courts, institutional and *ad hoc* commercial arbitration, and all forms of alternative dispute resolution, including expert determination.

Holly advises international and national energy and mining companies, oilfield services providers, utility companies, petrochemical companies and financial institutions on high-value, cross-border and complex disputes relating to M&A, including breach of warranty claims, construction matters, joint venture arrangements and all forms of industry contract, including licences and concession agreements, service contracts, decommissioning arrangements, third-party access to infrastructure, sale and purchase agreements – including long-term gas supply agreements and power purchase agreements – and transportation and processing agreements.

Christopher Strong
Partner, Vinson & Elkins RLLP
cstrong@velaw.com

Chris Strong is an accomplished member of the London energy transactions and projects practice, who represents corporate clients around the world on transactions in the energy and natural resources space.

Chris advises oil companies, banks, private equity funds and government entities on the acquisition and disposition of assets, and on project development transactions relating to upstream oil and gas, power plants, petrochemical facilities, refineries, pipelines, liquefied natural gas, and mining and metals.

In addition, Chris counsels on highly technical commercial agreements that are unique to the energy sector, such as gas sale agreements and power purchase agreements.

Chris is active in the AIPN, where he was the co-chair of a drafting committee to develop the AIPN's Model Form Asset Purchase Agreement.

Simon Tysoe
Partner, Latham & Watkins LLP
simon.tysoe@lw.com

Simon Tysoe is a partner in the London office of Latham & Watkins and co-chair of the firm's global oil and gas practice. He specialises in mergers and acquisitions, private equity, joint ventures, project development, restructurings and general corporate matters, exclusively in the energy sector, primarily focussing on oil and gas. Although based in London, Simon advises a range of national oil companies, majors, independents and private equity funds on transactions in Europe, Africa, Asia, the Middle East and Latin America.

Julie Vaughan
Senior associate, Herbert Smith Freehills LLP
julie.vaughan@hsf.com

Julie Vaughan is an environmental lawyer based in London, whose work includes large energy and infrastructure projects, real estate transactions, corporate M&A, some litigation (including the *Lungowe* case on UK parent company liability) and regulatory compliance advice. In the oil and gas space, she has worked on transactions involving all parts of the hydrocarbons value chain, from decommissioning of upstream platforms to gathering pipelines, onshore receiving terminals, cross-country fuel delivery pipelines, refineries, oil storage terminals, trade in hydrocarbon products, contaminated land issues and chemicals compliance for hydrocarbon products. She also has experience working in-house with an oil major and over the last few years has advised the frontrunner in the UK shale gas industry on environmental permitting and liability. She has a master's degree in international and EU environmental and natural resources law from University College London, and is named in the legal directories as a star associate.

Suzana Vukasinovic
Associate, Vinson & Elkins RLLP
svukasinovic@velaw.com

Suzana Vukasinovic is an associate in the firm's London M&A and capital markets practice. She has experience advising clients on M&A, disposals, joint ventures, corporate restructurings and general corporate and commercial matters.

David Waldron
Partner, Morgan, Lewis & Bockius UK LLP
david.waldron@morganlewis.com

David Waldron is a partner in the litigation practice group of Morgan, Lewis & Bockius in London. He holds a BSc and a master's degree. He has specialised in dispute resolution for over 20 years. He is a solicitor advocate and accredited mediator. In addition, he is authorised to conduct proceedings at the Dubai International Financial Centre courts.

David has litigated and arbitrated many disputes in the oil, gas and energy industry, involving matters such as gas supply agreements, pipeline agreements, refinery fires, fraud, seismic provisions and carbon allowances.

David's international arbitration work includes matters before the International Centre for Dispute Resolution, the International Chamber of Commerce and the London Court of International Arbitration.

Paul White
Partner, Druces LLP
p.white@druces.com

Paul White is a tax partner at Druces LLP. He has over 25 years' experience with UK and US law firms in the City of London. He has advised on the tax aspects of power and energy projects throughout the world, as well as broader UK and international corporate and finance tax matters.

Kimberley Wood
Independent director and energy lawyer, Norton Rose Fulbright LLP
kimberley.wood@nortonrosefulbright.com

Kimberley Wood is an energy lawyer with 20 years' experience, specialising in M&A. Most recently, she was head of oil and gas for Europe and Middle East at Norton Rose Fulbright LLP and remains a senior consultant for the firm. Throughout her career, she has advised a wide range of companies in the sector, from small independents to super-majors. Kimberley was a partner at Vinson & Elkins LLP from February 2011 to April 2015, and was previously at Dewey & LeBoeuf LLP. She is included in *Who's Who Legal Energy 2020* and as an expert in *Women in Business Law 2020*.

Kimberley is also an independent director and sits of the board of various exploration and production companies, including Energean plc and Gulf Keystone Petroleum, both of which are listed on the London Stock Exchange (LSE). She is also an independent director of Africa Oil Corp, which is listed on TSX (Canada) and Nasdaq OMX (Stockholm), and Valeura Energy Inc, which is LSE and TSX (Canada) listed.

Freddie Wright
Associate, Vinson & Elkins RLLP
fwright@velaw.com

Freddie Wright is an associate in the M&A and capital markets team at Vinson & Elkins RLLP. He has assisted on a range of transactions for private equity funds and state-owned entities across Europe and the Middle East.

Index

absolute consent rights 82
accounting procedures, audit rights in 56
accounts
  completion 46, 47, 104
  payable, payment of 121
accrued liabilities, inheritance of 217
accuracy of documentation, warranties on 144–145
acquisitions in oil and gas industry
  contractual rights 143
  motivations for 26
  by national oil companies 62
action pending or threatened condition precedent 87–88
active bribery 284
***ad hoc* arbitration** 388
adjustment payments 46
advice, independent, boilerplate provision on 410
affiliates
  consent for assignment of interests to 407
  covenants on 109
  liabilities of 243
  warranties on 158
affirmative covenants 71
Africa, reciprocal enforcement agreements in 398
agreements
  ancillary 88–89
  asset purchase 102, 316–318
  asset swap 35–36, 63, 103
  exclusivity 40
  preliminary 411
  regional 388
  share purchase 28, 316
  supply 267
  see also **DSAs; farmout agreements; host government agreements; JOAs; SPAs; UUOAs**
AIPN (Association of International Petroleum Negotiators)
  Asset Sale and Purchase Agreement Committee(Committee) (draft, 2020)
    interim covenants in 116
  Model Form ASPA 69, 74, 90, 337–338, 340, 345
    environmental assessment 90–91
  Model Form Farmout Agreement (2019)
    conditions precedent in 68, 81, 82, 92–93
  Model Form Farmout Agreement (draft, 2015)
    entire agreement clause 411
    force majeure clause in 402, 403
    independent advice provision in 410
    relationship between parties provision 406
  Model Form International Asset Sale and Purchase Agreement (2020) 50
  Model Form International Farmout Agreement (draft, 2019)
    interim covenants in 107–116
  Model Form JOA (2012)
    conditions precedent in 85
    sovereign immunity waiver in 405
  Model International Farmout Agreement (2019)
    consideration clauses in 55–59
all reasonable endeavours clause 104–105
ancillary agreements, execution and delivery of 88–89
anti-assignment provisions 232
anti-corruption and bribery 275–276
  legislations 276–277
    UK Bribery Act 2010 (UKBA) 276, 277
    US Foreign Corrupt Practices Act (FCPA) 275–276, 277–284
  local laws 285–287
  private equity firms 353, 368–369
approval by governmental authorities *see* **governments**, consent requirements of
arbitral awards
  of costs 384
  enforcement of 382–383, 396–398
arbitral institutions 386–388
arbitration
  international 382–393
  investment treaty arbitration 375, 397–398
  versus litigation 381–382
  location 383
  provisions 10 (*see* **arbitration clauses**)
arbitration clauses 376, 389, 389–393
  governing law of 395–396
arbitrators
  emergency 387
  fees of 387, 388
  nomination of 384, 394
Ardmore field (UK) 234 (footnote 7)
assessments
  of damages 133
  environmental 90–91
  pre-diligence risk assessment 300–302
  reputational 290
  of risk 306
asset purchase
  agreements 102, 316–318
    consideration clauses in
      asset sales 47–54
      sample provisions 47–48
  and permit transfers 223
Asset Sale and Purchase Agreement Committee (draft, 2020) 251
  interim covenants in 116

asset sales
complexity of 29–30
consideration in 47–62
government consent requirements for 50, 83, 232, 249
liability allocation in 197–198
decommissioning liabilities 243
pre-emption rights in 31, 84
taxation of 29, 316–317
third-party consent requirements 30–31
transaction structures of 26, 28–29, 102
transfer documentation for 43
types of 32–36
asset swap agreements 35–36, 103
consideration in 63
assets
description of
in preliminary agreements 20
in SPA 244
international, and enforcement of arbitral awards 397
joint operating agreements 21
late-life 241
profile of, and decommissioning liabilities 241–242
sale, private equity investments 354
tracing 302
upstream, interim covenants on relinquishing or surrendering of 124
value of 26, 40
waivers needed for 86
assignments of interests, consent requirement provisions for 407–409
associated persons, under UKBA 284, 289
Association of International Petroleum Negotiators
2020 model 251
Association of International Petroleum Negotiators (AIPN) 9, 332
clause 336
Model Form Farmout Agreement 215, 217
and environmental matters 226
and interim covenants 225–226
and remedial obligations 226
warranties 227–228
Model Form International Asset Sale and Purchase Agreement 215
Astor Management AG v Atalaya Mining plc 104
asymmetric arbitration clauses 393
auctions 37–39
audit rights 56
audits 306
authority for expenditure (AFEs), in interim covenants 226
awareness *see* **knowledge**

back-in rights, of national oil companies 62
balance of power, in interim periods 100
banks, letters of commitment by 91
Barbudev v Eurocom Cable Management Bulgaria Eood 14 (footnote 1)
BASF, asset swap with Gazprom 63
basket thresholds 211
benefits
of conditions precedent, separation of 93–94
of share sales 101
bespoke conditions precedent 97
bespoke covenants 105
best endeavours obligations 104
BHP Billiton 296
bid and tender processes, corruption risks 291–292
binding commitments, preliminary agreements 12, 13, 14–19, 21, 23, 24
board of directors, consent of, as condition precedent 92
boilerplate provisions 375, 401
on assignment of interests consent 407–409
counterpart clauses 412–413
entire agreement clauses 410–411
force majeure clauses 402–405
on independent advice 410
on joint preparation of SPA 409–410
on relationship between parties 405
on sovereign immunity waiver 405
on third-party rights 412–413
bonus payments, component of consideration 49
books and records, post-completion handover of 127
breaches
compensation for 75, 132–133
of contracts 40
of covenants 92, 104–105
of JOAs, warranties on non-existence of 146
of licenses, warranties on non-existence of 144
and walk-away rights 76
of warranties 72
claims by buyers 134, 142, 199, 205, 206, 320
caps for 212
materiality thresholds for 77, 138–139, 211, 265
time limits for 209–210, 212
Brexit 253, 398
bribery risk 275
see also **corruption risks**
bring-down clauses 76–79
bring-down condition precedent, in MAC clause 335
budgets, of work programmes, interim covenants on 123
burden of proof, MAC clause-invoking party 331
Bureau of Energy Management 238 (footnote 20)
Bureau of Safety and Environmental Enforcement 237
businesses *see* **companies**
buyers 27
of assets 30, 35, 61
claims by
for breach of warranties 134, 142, 199, 205, 206, 320
caps for 212
and knowledge 134, 142, 199, 206
materiality thresholds 77, 138–139, 211, 265
time limits for 209–210, 212
for misrepresentation 132
under tax covenants 321, 322
competition law concerns of 260–261, 262, 267, 272–273
consideration due (*see* **consideration**)
control of
and interim covenants 100, 128, 200

voting control 121
creditworthiness of 45, 233, 247
exclusivity provision 22–23
guarantees by, host government demands for 249
indemnities from 208–209, 244–245, 321
knowledge of 41, 121, 121–122, 134, 142, 199, 206
of late-life assets 314
liabilities of 195, 197
non-traditional 246
notification requirements for 321
obligations of 34, 40, 80–81
payment of a deposit to escrow 48
protection of
from tax liabilities 315, 322
through warranties 131, 139, 142
remedies of 336
representatives of 121
risk evaluation by 175
risk exposure of 28, 114, 123, 195, 204, 309
states acting as 62
taxation of 311, 316
termination rights, and disclosure letters 166–167, 168
walk-away rights of 66, 71, 72, 73, 77
buy-side warranty and indemnity insurance policy 181–182, 184, 187

capital contributions, by sellers 103
capital expenditure commitments, warranties on 156
capital gains, taxation of 314–315
caps, for warranty claims 212
carry arrangements 33
cash
consideration in 55–57
leakages of 103
cash-free/debt-free deals 112
catch-all provisions 110
***caveat emptor* principle (buyer beware)** 131, 195, 198
Centurion (Company) 42
certainty
in contract interpretation 35
in governing law/jurisdiction provisions 380–381, 395
seeking of 128, 391
change of control clauses 31, 86
charitable donations, corruption risks 296–297
choice
of arbitration proceedings 383, 388
of governing law 379
of jurisdiction/seat of arbitration 379, 388–389, 397
of place of arbitration 383
City Code on Takeovers and Mergers (UK) 13, 27
civil law jurisdiction, position of preliminary agreements in 17–19
claims
by buyers
for breach of warranties 74, 134, 142, 199, 205, 206, 320
caps for 212
and knowledge 134, 142, 199, 206
materiality thresholds 77, 138–139, 211, 265
time limits for 209–210, 212
for misrepresentation 132
under tax covenants 321, 322
in environmental provisions
indemnities 222
negligence 223
warranties 218–219
by third parties, in interim periods 113
Clarke, Lord 16
clean break environmental indemnity, in Oil and Gas UK Model SPA 228
clean break for sellers, in indemnities 219–220
clean break model 106
Coastal Corporation 298
commercial agreements, linked to SPAs 43
commitment letters 91, 356–357
companies
locally incorporated, host government rules 161–162, 408
specialised in decommissioning 251–252
see also **state-owned companies**
compensation
for breach of warranties 75, 132–133, 199, 205, 320
for indemnity changes 206
competition clearance
as condition precedent 80, 254–261
EU rules on 80, 254
warranties on 261–267
competition law 28, 254
and covenants on competition restrictions 267–273
of EU 255–256, 258, 269, 272
infringements of, uncovering of 265
complaints and claims, omission from warranties 228
complete non-disclosure, and misrepresentation 174
completeness of documentation, warranties on 144–145
completion
accounts 46, 47, 104
adjustments 357–358
dates 36
condition precedent waivers on 93
disclosure letter 167
division of liabilities on 197
simultaneous with signing dates 67, 70, 135
time from signing dates to 49
warranty repetition on 71–72, 78, 135, 200
deferred 66–68, 97, 99, 135, 200
deliverables, in environmental provisions 222–223
obligations of 127
of transactions 42–43
of work obligations 59
complexity, of transactions 29–30
compliance
with laws
due diligence reviews, competition 261–262, 265, 272
of interim covenants 267–269
of warranties/representations on 159–160
with previously agreed decisions 121
concessions
agreement 61
and change of control clauses 31
sale of 32

concurrent proceedings 377
consolidation of 385, 394–395
conditional consent rights 82
conditions precedent 65–66, 74, 97, 166, 167
in drafting MAC clause 334
in environmental provisions 222
failure of 74, 75
materiality thresholds in 71–72, 77–78, 88
model forms/sample provisions on 68, 76–79, 80, 82, 85, 86–87, 87–88, 88, 93–95, 114
optionality created by 91–92
in SPA 21
types of 76
bring down clauses 76–79
change in control 86
competition clearance 254–261
government consent requirements 65–66, 67, 71, 79–81, 93, 97
MAC clauses 86–87, 334, 404
no pending or threatened actions 87–88
pre-emption rights 84–86, 97
third-party consent requirements 81–83
transfer of operatorship 83–84
transfer restrictions 79–86
warranties true and correct on completion 76
waivers/satisfaction of 93–95, 99, 104
conditions subsequent 65
confidentiality
agreements 40, 411
in arbitration proceedings 382, 385–386, 387
and disclosure letters 167
and preliminary agreements 22
conflicts of interest 294
conscious avoidance, under FCPA 278
consent
in arbitration proceedings 393
of board of directors, as condition precedent 92
of co-venturers 67, 81–83, 84
of governments
for asset transfers 50, 83–84, 232, 249–250
as condition precedent 65, 67, 79–81, 93, 97
for share sales 50, 79
time needed for 99
interests 407–409
of shareholders, as condition precedent 92
of third parties 30–31, 81–83
absolute consent right 82
conditional consent right 82
qualified consent right 82
consideration 45, 63
in asset sales 47–62
in asset swaps 63
components of 45
deferred 34
in earn-in agreements 34, 62
in farmout agreements 32, 54–61, 69, 403
mutual 35
in share sales 45–47
consolidation of proceedings, in arbitration 385, 394–395
contamination handling, and warranties 227
contemplated transactions 87
context of entire agreement, MAC clause interpretation of 329
contingent components, of consideration 49
contingent payments 46
details of, in preliminary agreement 20
contra proferentem **rule** 409–410
contract areas
relinquishments of 150–151
third-party activity/rights in 153
unitisation of 125, 151–153
contract interest 107–108
contracts
breach of 40
employment, interim period prohibition on changes in 123
enforcement of, by third parties 412–413
entering into, interim covenants on 125
entire agreement 34–35, 410–412
governing law of 395
material 112, 138, 158
multi-party 158–159
price
assumptions 20
details in preliminary agreements 20
related-party 158–159
rescission of 132
with third parties, restrictive covenants in 267–268
for upstream oil and gas transactions 196
contractual notices provisions, complying with 210–211
contractual rights, acquisition of 143
control
changes of, clauses on 31, 86
in interim periods 41, 100, 200
of mergers, laws on 27, 254, 255–256, 258
Convention for the Protection of the Marine Environment of the Northeast Atlantic (OSPAR Convention) 237
Convention on the Continental Shelf (1958) 236 (footnote 10)
Convention on the Recognition and Enforcement of Foreign Arbitral Awards (New York Convention, 1959) 382–383
jurisdictions not party to 396–398
co-participants in PSCs, non-selling, warranties for 136, 146, 151
corporate actions, prohibition of, interim covenants on 122
corporate social responsibility, corruption risks 296–297
corruption, criminalisation of 285–286
corruption, inherent risks 287–288
charitable donations 296–297
corporate social responsibility 296–297
gifts, meals and corporate hospitality (G&E) 295–296
government interaction 290–295
mitigation of 301–302
political donations 297
third parties 288–290
Corruption Perception Index 275–276
corruption risks 275
financial and reputational risks 297
legal risks
proceeds of corruption 298–299
successor liability 298
mitigation of 299
inherent risk factors 301–302
policies and procedures 300
pre-diligence risk assessment 300–302
risk-based anti-corruption due diligence 302–304

transaction documents 304–307
private equity firms 353
costs
of arbitration/litigation 284
bearers, in preliminary agreements 23
of decommissioning 231, 242
of due diligence process 41
of exploration/drilling 60, 310
incurred in interim periods 113
of preliminary agreements 13–14, 24
see also **consideration**
counter-indemnity, in environmental provisions 221
counterpart clauses 413–414
covenants
on decommissioning liabilities 249–250
indemnities for non-environmental issues 222
interim covenants, private equity investments 358
financing covenants 360–362
general covenants 358–360
separation issues 362
interim period 70–71, 74, 102, 104, 105, 126, 128, 200–201
on competition restrictions 267–273
performance of 79
sample provisions 107–126
and warranties 104–105, 115, 135
post-completion 126–128, 320–322
precedent 92, 104
tax 105, 114, 127, 318, 320–324
in transaction documents 305–306
co-venturers
consent of 67, 81–83, 84
decommissioning liabilities of 234, 242
pre-emption rights of 31, 84–86
sole-risk programmes by 114
coverage period, and MAC occurrence 336–337
covered companies, under FCPA 280
COVID-19 pandemic 129, 398
exclusions in warranty and indemnity insurance policy 193
and MAC clause 344–346
applicable carve-outs 345
contractual counterparties, practical steps for 346–347
durationally significant event 345
invoking other contractual provisions 345
SPA's notice provision, use of 346
credit support arrangements 109
creditworthiness, of buyers 233, 245, 247
cross-border trade and transportation, and corruption risks 291, 295
customs clearance process, corruption risks 295

damages *see* **compensation**
data rooms, warranties on completeness and accuracy of 145
dates
for commencing financial provisions for decommissioning 240
completion 36
condition precedent waivers/satisfaction on 94
warranty repetition on 71–72, 78, 135, 200
for division of liabilities 197
effective 36
value and consideration set at 47, 103, 104
for settlement of tax claims 321
signing 36
time to completion from 49
warranties on accuracy of SPA on 78
simultaneous, for signing and completion 67, 135
***de minimis* thresholds** 211
deal breakers, identifying with preliminary agreements 12, 19, 24
debt claims, indemnities giving rise to 206–207
debt financing 353–354
decommissioning 235
companies specialised in 251–252
costs 231, 242
legal requirements 236–239, 246
liabilities 106, 198, 208–209, 233, 240–243, 252
clean break from 241
covenants on 249–250
in DSAs 246–247
and forfeiture as remedy 233–235
indemnities on 244–245
in SPAs 235, 243–245, 250–251
warranties on 250–251
security 106, 208
deeds
for site leases 268–269
SPAs as 41
default judgments 385
defaulting
of buyers 34
of co-venturers 122
of decommissioning obligations 234, 248
of farmees 59
of license payments 154
of material contracts 138
defendants, in pending or threatened action condition precedent 88
deferred completion 66–68, 97, 99
consequences of 70–76
model forms on 69–70
and warranty application 135, 200
deferred consideration 34
definitions
of claims 323
of competition authority 259
of decommissioning liability 243–244
of disclosed information 141
of DSA 246
of encumbrances 147
of *force majeure* 403
of joint property 244
of jurisdiction 269
of material adverse change 86–87
of material contracts 138, 158
of restricted activities 269
of restricted period 270
of seller knowledge 136–138
definitions clause 402
definitive agreements, and preliminary agreements 21
de-grouping charges, in sale of subsidiaries 311
development plans, warranties on 156
diminution basis for compensation recovery 75
disclaimers, on reserves 212–213
disclosure bundle 169, 176
disclosure letters 78–79, 140, 142, 165, 177–178
amendments to 167

and buyer termination rights 166–167, 168
content of 166
disclosed risks and liabilities, protection against 166
disclosure bundle 169
disclosure process and timing issues 167–168
form of 168–176
front end of 169
general disclosures 170–171
accounts 172–173
constitutional documents 172
correspondence 173–174
data room 171–172
due diligence reports 173
minute books 173
registers 173
SPA and transaction documents 171
interpretative section 169
purpose of 166–167
references, avoidance of 170
scope of disclosure 169–170
specific disclosures 174–175
disclosure bundle 169, 176
encumbrances 175
litigation 175
penalties 175
updates of 72–74
and warranties 165, 166, 167, 169
disclosures
'bring-down' disclosure mechanism 189
full and fair 142, 176
negligent/inadvertent 40
private equity investments 365
reinstatement of correctness of warranties by 199
requirements for sellers 72–73, 74
standard of 176–177
updating between signing and completion 72–74
and warranties 140–141
dispute resolution
by arbitration 328
mechanisms, in MAC termination clause 337
provisions 375, 377, 395 (*see also* **arbitration clauses; governing law provisions**)
disputes
on farmout agreements 42
methods for resolution of 381–382 (*see also* **arbitration; litigation; mediation**)
settlement of 376
on SPAs 376, 378
on taxes 322
third parties joining 384–395, 385
divestments
competition authorities requirements for 257
partial, and decommissioning liabilities 242
divisible contracts 35
document and information requests 302–303
documentation
ancillary, delivery and execution of 88
of asset swap arrangements 35–36
of material contracts 138
post-completion handover of 127
preliminary 39–40
of reorganisations 30
of tax covenants 320
transferred interest/title 43, 124, 143, 144, 197
domestic courts
interim remediation by 385
international arbitral awards conversion by 383
joinders by 385
domestic laws
on competition 28, 255
on decommissioning obligations 237–239
and state interests in oil and gas industry 61
domestic supply obligations, warranties on 162–163
double materiality 77, 79
double taxation treaties 315
downstream transactions, SPAs for 26
drill to earn consideration 57, 57–59
DSAs (decommissioning security agreements) 235, 239–240, 246–247, 252
field 241–242, 246–247
due diligence investigations 40–41
competition compliance reviews in 261–262, 265, 272–273
condition precedent on completion of 91
during COVID-19 pandemic 346–347
disclosure of 167, 189
in environmental provisions 218, 221–222
pre-acquisition misconduct 298
pre-transaction due diligence 297, 300, 302, 304
risk-based anti-corruption due diligence 302–304
risks identified in 132
tax due diligence process information, access to 190
technical 242
third-party due diligence 303–304
and warranties 145, 163
durationally significant event, MAC clause interpretation of 330–331
duty of good faith
implied into preliminary agreements 13
preliminary agreements 17–18, 21, 24

Eagle Star Insurance Co Ltd v JN Cresswell 66
earn-in agreements 26, 34–35, 62
earn-out components, of consideration 46
economic dates *see* **effective dates**
economic stabilisation provisions, warranties on 163
education, compulsory support for, warranties on 162
effective dates 36
division of liabilities on 197
value and consideration set at 47, 103, 104
El Paso Corporation 298
employees
hiring and firing of, interim covenants on 123
local, compulsory hiring of, warranties on 162
employment contracts 89
prohibition on changes in, interim covenants on 123
Empresa Pública de Hidrocarburos del Ecuador (PetroEcuador) 283
encumbrances
disclosure of 175
warranties on non-existence of 147–148
enforcement
of arbitral awards 382–383, 396–398
of asymmetric arbitration clauses 393
companies 378
of contract terms, by third parties 412–413

of interim remedies 385
of restrictive covenants 268–272
of SPAs 375
English courts, international commercial, disputes handling by 385, 396
English law 9
caveat emptor principle in 131
on competition 27
confidentiality obligation in 40
contract law 409–410, 412
conditions precedent 66
entire contract concept in 34–35
on termination rights 42
on virtual signings 413
convention for disclosure letters 168
expert decisions in 396
indemnities in 205, 208
MAC clauses, interpretation in 328–329
negotiations 391
oil and gas industry application of 378
on property ownership 144
warranties in 132, 198
Eni SpA 283, 287 (footnote 66)
entire agreement clause 410–412
entire agreement warranty 145–146
entire contracts 34–35, 410–412
environmental condition, meaning of 221
environmental impacts, and warranties 227–228
environmental laws
meaning of 226
protections against violations of 74
environmental liabilities/risks 198
meaning of 228
in share purchase 228–229
environmental matters
meaning of 220–221
warranties in AIPN Model Farmout Agreement 226
environmental permits 105, 218, 220–221
in completion deliverables 222–223
definition of 226
environmental provisions 217–229
AIPN 2019 Model International Farmout Agreement 225–228
and completion deliverables 223
conditions precedent in 222
further assurance in 224
and indemnities 219–222
interim covenants 224–225
oil and gas UK model SPA 228–229
permit transfers in 217, 222–223
and warranties 217–219
environmental risk 351–352
environmental warranties, private equity investments 366–367
equality of arms, in dispute resolution 377
equity commitment letter 356–357
escalation clauses 390–392
Etete, Dan 287 (footnote 66)
Eurocopy plc v Teesdale 206
European civil law countries, convention for disclosure letters 168
European Union
competition clearances in 80
competition law
Merger Regulation (139/2004) 254, 255–256, 259
on restrictive covenants 269, 273
exceptions
from decommissioning obligations 236–237
to recognition/enforcement of arbitral awards 383
to upholding governing law clauses 379
exceptions or carve-outs to MAC clauses 341–343
carve-outs to carve-outs 343
force majeure risks 342
industry risks 341–342
political risks 342
systemic risks 341
transaction-specific risks known to parties 343
exclusions
in interim covenants 114–115
in SPAs
for liability for misrepresentation 132
MAC clauses 202
warranties 133, 199, 212–213
exclusive jurisdiction clauses 380–381
exclusive operations provisions, warranties on 151
exclusivity agreements 40
exclusivity provision, in preliminary agreements 22–23
expenditure covenants 113, 125
expense agreement 182–183
expert determination 396
expertise, in local petroleum industry, local rules on enhancement of 162
exploration 33, 232
decommissioning liabilities in 241
deepwater 23
taxation of 310, 313
express clause, describing non-binding nature of documents 15

facilitation payments, under FCPA 279
fact specific disputes, regarding MAC clauses 328
false representation, penalty for 174
farmout agreements 25, 32–33, 102–103, 232, 406
boilerplate provisions in
on consent for assignment of interests 407–409
force majeure clauses 403
on relationship between parties 406
consideration in 32, 54–61, 403
decommissioning liabilities in 245, 246
disputes on 42
unwinding conditions in 97
see also **Model Form Farmout Agreement (AIPN)**
FCPA *see* **United States Foreign Corrupt Practices Act (FCPA)**
fiduciary duties 406
field DSAs 242, 246–247, 247–249
filing, of transactions with competition authorities 256–257, 260, 261
financial and reputational harm, due to corruption 297
financial losses, warranty and indemnity insurance policy (W&I policy) 179
Financial Services Act 2012 174
financial statements, private equity investments 365
financial thresholds *see* **materiality thresholds**

financial warranties 71, 153–155
financing
availability of 91
covenants, private equity investments 360–362
of decommissioning, provisions for 231, 235, 240, 242
first refusal rights, waivers of 113
fixed consideration 46–47
fixed infrastructure, decommissioning of 242
floating infrastructure, decommissioning of 242
force majeure **clauses** 157, 402–405
force majeure **events** 342
force majeure **risks**, carve-outs to MAC clauses 342
foreign investments, security implications of 80
foreign officials
under FCPA 277, 291
under UKBA 284
forensic audit 302
forfeiture as remedy, and decommissioning liabilities 233–235
formal written notices 398
forward-looking elements, in MAC clause 339–340
fracking techniques 349
Fraud Act 2006 174
full title guarantees 144
further assurance, in environmental provisions 224

Gazprom, asset swap with BASF 63
general covenants, private equity investments 358–360
general partner (GP), private equity funds 351, 352, 353
geological and geophysical information
excluded from warranties 21, 149, 199
general disclaimer on 212
gifts, meals and corporate hospitality (G&E), corruption risks 295–296
governing law provisions 375, 377, 379–381, 395–396, 398
government, defined in modal agreement 225
government interactions, corruption risks 290–291
bid and tender processes 291–292
cross-border transportation of goods 295
oil and gas extraction process, interactions during 292–293
payment risks 294–295
procurement risks 293–294
regulatory oversight 293
governments
consent requirements of
for asset transfers 50, 83–84, 232, 249–250
as condition precedent 65, 67, 71, 79–81, 93, 97
incorporation of local entity/branch 93
for share sales 50, 79
time needed for 99
credit risk concerns of 233
and decommissioning liabilities 235, 237–239, 249–250
good relationships with 109
interests of 61, 232 (footnote 5), 234–235
legal requirements of
on competition 255
on decommissioning 237–239
on local incorporation of companies 161–162, 408
warranties on compliance with 159
payments to, warranties on 154
pre-emption rights of 84–86
releases approved by 243
as stakeholders in oil and gas projects 61
threatened claims by 88
gross-up clauses 325
guarantees
from buyers, host government demands for 249
on performance, warranties on 156–157
release of 88

hard carry arrangement 33
hazardous substances and waste streams handling, and warranties 227
hedging arrangements 360
Heritage Oil and Gas Ltd v Tullow Uganda Ltd 325
Hilcorp Energy 241 (footnote 24)
historical issues assessment 303 (footnote 92)
host government agreements 59, 61, 62, 197
host governments *see* **governments**
hybrid governing law clauses 380

ICC (International Chamber of Commerce) 386–387, 389, 394, 396
ICSID (International Centre for the Settlement of Investment Disputes) 397–398
Idemitsu Kosan Ltd v Sumitomo Corporation 132 (footnote 3)
immunity, of states/state-owned companies 163, 378
waivers of 163, 378, 405
Implementation Review Mechanism 285–286
improper payments 291, 294, 295
incorporated companies, locally, host government rules on 161–162, 408
indemnification
private equity investments 362
in transition documents 306–307
indemnities 195, 197, 204–205, 204–209, 244–245, 315, 320, 321
claims for changes of 134 (footnote 4), 206
clean break environmental indemnity 228
and disclosure letters 165
in environmental provisions
clean break 219–220
counter-indemnity 221
environmental condition, meaning of 221
environmental matter, meaning of 220–221
law jurisdictions 222
pre/post completion indemnity 220–222
residual environmental liability, accumulation of 219–220
scope of cover 222
timeframe 221
in preliminary agreements 22
third party enforcement of 412
and warranties 133–135, 205
see also **warranty and indemnity insurance policy (W&I policy)**
independent advice, boilerplate provision on 410
individual sellers, warranty and indemnity insurance policy 180

industry risks, carve-outs to MAC clauses 341–342
information
for buyers
and due diligence process 40, 132
interim covenants on 121
warranties on 140–141
on licensees, and taxation 315
see also **knowledge**
infrastructure
removal/decommissioning of 236 (footnote 11), 242
transactions 26
inherent risk factors 301–302
insolvency, warranty and indemnity insurance policy 180
insurance 109
private equity firms 359
underwriting diligence requirements 190–192
see also **warranty and indemnity insurance policy (W&I policy)**
Insurance Act 2015 182
interest rates 49, 50
interests
assignment/re-assignment of 34, 59
consent requirement provisions for 407–409
exchange of 35
forfeiture of 233–235
of host governments 62, 232 (footnote 5)
and decommissioning liabilities 234–235
ownership of 144
sale of 25–28 (*see also* **asset sales; share sales**)
consideration for (*see* **consideration**)
VAT rules on 317
of third parties, interim period prohibition on creation of 112
interim covenants
in environmental provisions 217, 224–225, 225–226
private equity investments 358
financing covenants 360–362
general covenants 358–360
separation issues 362
interim periods
conditions precedent 97
between signing and completion 50, 81, 99, 100
covenants for 70–71, 74–76, 102, 104, 105, 126, 128, 200–201
on competition restrictions 267–273
performance of 79
sample provisions 107–126
and warranties 104–105, 115, 135
disclosure requirements of sellers in 72–74
mutual obligations 117–119
seller obligations 116–117
termination rights, private equity investments
material adverse change 363–364
pre-emption rights 362
interim remediation 385, 387
international arbitration 382–390
International Chamber of Commerce *see* **ICC**
international law, on decommissioning 236–237
interpretation
of contracts 35
of technical data 149
intra-group transfers 30, 311
investigations
by buyers of shares 28
see also **due diligence investigations**
investment treaty arbitration 375, 397–398

Jirehouse Capital v Beller 16
JOAs (joint operating agreements) 26, 110, 144, 197, 402, 405
in assets sale 21
breaches of, warranties on non-existence of 146
corruption risks 290
co-venturers consent requirements in 67, 81–83, 84
drill to earn consideration 57
exclusive operations provisions in 151
liability and risk allocation in, for decommissioning 239, 245
linked to SPAs 43
model forms of 68, 86, 405
pre-emption rights in 31, 85
refusal by sellers to participate in operations of 114
and subcontracting of works 33
transfer restrictions in, warranties on 148–149
joinders, in international arbitration 385, 394–395
joint preparation of SPA provisions 409–410
joint property 244
joint ventures *see* **JOAs**
Jonathan, Goodluck 287 (footnote 66)
judgments
enforcement of 378
summary and default 385
jurisdiction clauses 375, 377, 380, 399
exclusive jurisdiction 380–381
jurisdictions
choice of 379, 380, 397
and competition clearance 254
and decommissioning liabilities 242, 246
and dispute resolution 376
governing law clauses acceptance by 379
not party to New York Convention 396–398
and public takeovers 28

key terms, and preliminary agreements 12
kickback schemes 294, 298
knowledge
of buyers, and claims for breach of warranties 134, 142, 199, 206
of sellers, warranties/representations on 136–138
drafting 137
see also **information**
knowledge scrape, warranty and indemnity insurance policy 189
Kozeny, Viktor 281

late filings with governmental authorities, disclosure of 175
late-life assets, buyer of 314
laws
compliance with, warranties/representations on 159–160
on decommissioning 236–239, 246
see also **competition law; English law; environmental laws; governing law provisions**
LCIA (London Court of International Arbitration) 387, 389–390, 394, 396
leakages, of cash 103

legal privilege, and disclosure letters 167
legal relations, intention, and preliminary
  agreements 14–16, 19
legal risks, due to corruption
  proceeds of corruption 298–299
  successor liability 298
legitimate interests, of governments 79
letter of intent, parties' conduct 16
letter of reliance, in completion deliverables 223
liabilities
  allocation of 195, 196, 196–204, 214–215
  bearers of 186
  of buyers 195, 197
  for competition law infringements 261–262
  for decommissioning 198, 208, 233, 240–243,
    252
    clean break from 241
    covenants on 249–250
    in decommissioning security agreements 208
    in DSAs 235, 239–241, 246–249, 252
    and forfeiture as remedy 233–235
    in SPAs 235, 243–245, 250–251
  disclosed 166
  environmental 198, 228
    in share purchase 228–229
  indemnities on 134 (footnote 4), 197, 205,
    244–245, 315
  limitations, in preliminary agreements 22
  limitations on 209–214, 322–324
  post-completion 128, 195, 197, 240, 252
  private equity investments 354
    broader allocation 370–372
    recourse and limitation 372–373
  secondary, for taxes 315
  of sellers 128, 132, 195, 197, 208, 210, 240,
    252
  successor liability 276
  warranties on 198–200, 250–251
licensees
  information on, and taxation 315
  sole 249
licenses
  acquisition of 143
  breaches of, warranties on non-existence of
    146
  concession 136
  economic stabilisation provisions in,
    warranties on 163
  in host government agreements 59
  obligations of 162–163
  in PSCs 136
  relinquishments of contract areas in 150–151
  risk service agreement 136
  sovereign immunity waivers in, warranties on
    163
  transfer restrictions of, warranties on 148–149
  unitisation in, warranties on 151–153
  work obligations in 155
  see also **permits**
lifecycles, in oil and gas industry 233
limitations
  on liabilities 209–214, 322–324
  on time (*see* **time, limits**)
  on warranties 263
limited partners (LPs), private equity funds 351,
  352–353, 355
litigation
  versus arbitration 381–382
  costs of 384
  disclosure of 175
  on tax issues 325–326
  by third parties, in interim periods 113
location, of arbitration 383
locked-box deals 46–47, 103–104
  private equity firms 357, 358
lock-out agreements 40
London Court of International Arbitration *see*
  LCIA
longstop date, in MAC termination clause 336
longstop dates, for conditions precedent
  satisfaction/waiver 94–95
lookback periods 304

management sellers, warranty and indemnity
  insurance policy 180
markets
  completion 67
  regulated 27
material, definition of 338–339
material adverse change (MAC) clause 86–87,
  201–204, 327
  as alternative to *force majeure* clauses 404–405
  as condition precedent 86–87, 404
  contractual relief 344
  and COVID-19 pandemic 202, 344–347
  drafting of 331–343
  elements of 328
  interpretation of
    be read in the context of the entire
      agreement 329–330
    burden of proof 331
    case law, lack of 328
    MAC event must be durationally significant
      330–331
    MAC event must be significant 330
    MAC event must not have been previously
      known 330
    narrowly construed 329
    in US and English law 328–329
  private equity investments 363–364
  risk allocation, provisions for 327, 347
  risk issues in 343–344
  termination clause 336
material adverse change (MAC) clause, drafting
  of
  change requirement 340–341
  clause form 331–337
    condition precedent 334
    and MAC warranty 335–336
    standalone MAC termination clause
      332–334
    structures, differences between 336–337
  exceptions or carve-outs to MAC clauses
    341–343
    carve-outs to carve-outs 343
    force majeure risks 342
    industry risks 341–342
    political risks 342
    systemic risks 341
    transaction-specific risks 343
  forward-looking elements in 339–340
  generality and specificity in 337–338
    risks of generality 338
    specificity using carve-ins 338
  material, definition of 338–339
material adverse effect 345

material adverse event 333, 345
material contracts 138
covenants on 112
warranties on 158
material omission 138
materiality scrape, warranty and indemnity insurance policy 189
materiality thresholds
in conditions precedent 72, 77–78, 88
in interim covenants 113
in warranties 77, 138–139, 211, 265
mediation 391–392
mergers and acquisition
laws on control of 27, 254, 255–256, 259
warranty and indemnity insurance policy (W&I policy) in 179, 181, 193
micro-management 112
midstream transactions, SPAs for 26
misrepresentation, claims for 132
Model Arbitration Rules (UNCITRAL) 388
model form agreements, in oil and gas industry 68, 215
Model Form Farmout Agreement (AIPN, 2019)
conditions precedent in 81, 82, 92–93
Model Form Farmout Agreement (AIPN, draft 2015)
entire agreement clause in 411
force majeure clause in 403
independent advice provision in 410
relationship between parties provision 407
Model Form International Asset Sale and Purchase Agreement 9
Model Form International Asset Sale and Purchase Agreement (2020) 50
Model Form International Asset Sale and Purchase Agreement (AIPN Model Form ASPA) 332
Model Form International Farmout Agreement (AIPN, draft 2019)
interim covenants in 107–116
Model Form JOA (AIPN, 2012)
conditions precedent in 86
sovereign immunity waiver in 405
Model Form SPA (Oil & Gas UK)
boilerplate provisions in 407–408
conditions precedent in 69–70, 85
interim covenants in 114–119, 119–121
Model Form SPA
clean break environmental indemnity in 228
environmental liabilities
meaning of 228
in share purchase 228–229
and indemnity in 228–229
Pre-economic Date Costs 229
Model International Farmout Agreement (AIPN, 2019) 92, 96
conditions precedent in 69
consideration clauses in 55–59
optional payment obligation 55–57
monetary amounts, for materiality threshold 78
money laundering, and corruption 298–299
moral commitment, through preliminary agreements 12
multi-party contracts, warranties on 158–159
multi-tiered clauses 390–393
mutual consideration 35
mutual covenants 115–116
mutual reasonable endeavours obligations 84
narrowly construed, MAC clause interpretation of 329
national oil companies *see* **state-owned companies**
negative covenants 110–114, 122–126
negotiations
and disclosure process 167
of indemnities 204
mandatory, in dispute resolution 391, 392
and preliminary agreements 12
on risk and liability allocation 195, 208
for SPAs 41–42
with third parties, restrictions on 40
unitisation, interim covenants on 125
of warranties 132, 135–142
New York Convention *see* **Convention on the Recognition and Enforcement of Foreign Arbitral Awards**
Newco 312
Nigeria 286–287
Corrupt Practices and Other Related Offences Act 286
governmental consent requirements in 80, 83
local company requirement in 408
Nigerian National Petroleum Corporation (NNPC) 286, 287
Nigerian Bonny Island enforcement actions 287
no breaches warranties 146–147
no claims declaration (NCD) 187, 189
no encumbrances warranties 147–148
no litigation warranties 265
no material adverse change *see* **MAC clauses**
nomination
of arbitrators 384, 394
of experts 396
non-binding indications (NBIs) 182, 184, 191
non-compete clauses 267, 270–272
non-compete provisions, in preliminary agreements 23
non-compliance *see* **compliance**
non-control scenarios, covenants in 306
non-disclosure *see* **confidentiality**
non-exclusive jurisdiction clauses 380–381
non-residents, taxation of 314–315
non-simultaneous signing and completion *see* **deferred completion**
non-solicitation
clauses 270, 271–272
of employees, in preliminary agreements 23
Northeast Atlantic, decommissioning obligations in 237
notices 398
notices provisions, complying with 210–211
notification requirements
for buyers 321
for competition clearance 254, 260, 261
for sellers, interim covenants on 109, 112, 122
Nuon (Company) 43

obligations
of best endeavours 104
of buyers 34, 40, 80–81
of competition law 254, 257–258, 260, 261
of completion 127, 167
of confidentiality 40
of contracts 34–35
of decommissioning 234–235, 236–240, 248

of licences 162–163
to preliminary agreements 18
of reasonable endeavours 92
of reimbursement, for indemnity changes 206
see also **work obligations**
obligors 406–407
OECD 292
OECD Anti-Bribery Convention (1999) 277, 288
OHADA ***(Organisation pour l'Harmonisation en Afrique du Droit des Affaires)*** 398
Oil & Gas UK 9
Model Form SPA 217
boilerplate provisions in 407–408
clean break environmental indemnity in 228
conditions precedent in 69–70, 85
environmental liabilities
meaning of 228
in share purchase 228–229
and indemnity in 228–229
interim covenants in 114–119, 119–121
Pre-economic Date Costs 229
oil and gas extraction process, government interactions during, corruption risks 292–293
oil and gas industry 25, 196
and competition law 253
English law application in 378
exploration activities 33, 232
lifecycle in 233
model form agreements in 68, 215
risks in, and MAC condition precedent 86
royalties in 148
sales process in 35–43
in United Kingdom 215
taxation of 309–310, 312–316, 317, 325, 326
Oil Taxation Manual (HMRC) 325
oilfield services transactions 26
operating committee 110
operatorship
rights, description in preliminary agreements 20
transfer of, governmental consent for 83–84
warranties on 157
optionality, conditions precedent's creation of 91–92
our watch/your watch indemnity 102
out-of-pocket expenses 23
ownership
of companies, host government rules on 161, 408
historic 243
of transferred interest 144

parallel proceedings 377
consolidation of 385, 393
parties
advisers of, use of preliminary agreements 12–13
conduct of, and preliminary agreements 15–17
details, in preliminary agreements 20
flexibility, impact of preliminary agreements on 13
passive bribery 282 (footnote 35), 284
past costs 56
payments
of accounts payable 123
adjustment 46
bonus 49
of earn-out 46
to host governments, warranties on 154
of interest 50
risks 294–295
penalties
disclosure of 175
for UKBA violations 285, 298
for US FCPA violations 280–281
performance guarantees, warranties on 156–157
performance of businesses, consideration based on 46
performance of contracts 34–35
interim covenants 79
work obligations, impossibility of 59
permits
environmental 106
transfers, conditions relating to 217, 222–223
variations, in interim covenants 224–225, 225–226
and warranties 227
warranties on 160–161
see also **licenses**
permitted encumbrances 148
Petroleo Brasileiro SA (Petrobras) 282, 286, 294
Petróleos de Venezuela, SA (PDVSA) 282–283
petroleum revenue taxes 317
pipeline authorisations, permit transfers in 223
plugging and abandonment process 153
policies and procedures, for mitigating corruption risks 300
political donations, corruption risks 297
political risks
carve-outs to MAC clauses 342
warranties on 163
politically exposed person (PEP) 290
port fees, corruption risks 295
positive covenants 107–110, 121–122
post-closing liability, limitations 22
post-completion covenants 46, 126–128
on taxation 128, 320–322
post-completion liabilities 128, 195, 197, 240, 252
pre-diligence risk assessment 300–302
Pre-economic Date Costs 229
pre-effective date environmental liabilities 91
pre-emption rights 31–32
as condition precedent 84–86, 97
private equity investments 362
preliminary agreements 24, 411
advantages 12–13
avoiding accidental contracting 19, 24
binding commitments 23
clear drafting 15
conditions 21
confidentiality provisions in 22
costs bearer 23
decision making to enter 24
definition of 11
and definitive agreements 21
disadvantages 13–14
under England and Wales laws 14
exclusivity provision 22–23
form of 19–23
indemnities in 22
and legal relations intention 14–16, 19
liability limitations in 22
necessity of 11–14
non-binding conditions 15

and parties' conduct 15–17
parties' details 20
position in non-UK jurisdictions 17–19
price details 20
restrictive covenants 23
risks 11
timetable in 23
transaction description 20
in US
legislation 18–19
Types I and II 18
use of 11
vague and ambiguous drafting, impact of 15
warranties in 22
pre-transaction due diligence 297, 300, 302, 304
previously agreed decisions, compliance with 121
prices
adjustment 357
and deferred or simultaneous completion 67
details, in preliminary agreements 20
of purchases
de minimis and basket thresholds based on 211
fixed 46
private equity disposals, warranty and indemnity insurance policy 180
private equity (PE) houses 100–101
private equity investments
buy side 350, 353, 358, 373
closed-ended funds 351, 352
conditionality of commitment 357
fund requirements 351–353
future trends 373–374
'hive-in' effect 354
lenders requirements 353–354
lenders to portfolio company 351
locked-box mechanism 357, 358
M&A activity 350
in oil and gas industry 349–350
portfolio company 350, 356–357
private equity fund 350–351
sell side 350, 354, 356, 358, 372–373
private equity investments, SPAs
completion adjustments 357–358
considerations 355–356
equity commitment letter 356–357
interim covenants 358
financing covenants 360–362
general covenants 358–360
separation issues 362
interim period termination rights
material adverse change 363–364
pre-emption rights 362
liability
broader allocation of 370–372
recourse and limitation of 372–373
pricing gaps 355
share sale versus asset sale 354
warranties 364–365
anti-bribery and corruption 368–369
disclosure 365
environmental warranties 366–367
financial statements 365
insurance 366
repetition of 369–370
separation issues 366
private equity vendors 204
private sales, versus auction sales 37–39
proceedings 87
avoidance of 391
of international arbitration
choice of 383, 388
confidentiality of 382, 385, 387
consolidation of 384, 393
proceeds of corruption 298–299
procurement risks 293–294
production 232
and decommissioning liabilities 233–235, 241
production sharing contract 61
property, joint 244
pro-seller nature, cases in US 328
PSCs (production sharing contracts), non selling co-participants in, warranties for 136, 146, 151
public announcement, and preliminary agreements 13
public policy exceptions, for recognition/enforcement of arbitral awards 383
public procurement-related wrongdoing 292
public records and reputational searches 302
public takeovers, legislation on 27
purchase agreement, and permit transfers 223
purchasers *see* **buyers**

qualified consent rights 82
quantification
of damages 133
of materiality 77–78
quantitative benchmark, in MAC clause 339

reasonable endeavours obligations 92
re-assignments, of interests 34, 59
reciprocal enforcement treaties 397
recourse, against historic owners/parent companies 243
recovery *see* **compensation**
regional agreements, for reciprocal enforcement of arbitration awards 398
registration taxes 324
regulatory approval 116
regulatory oversight, corruption risks 293
regulatory process, and preliminary agreements 13
reimbursement obligations, for indemnity changes 206
reinvestments, and rollover relief 313–314
related-party contracts, warranties on 158–159
releases, government approval for 243
relinquishments, warranties on 150–151
remedial obligations, in AIPN Model Farmout Agreement 226
remediation
forfeiture as, for decommissioning defaults 233–235
interim 385, 387
reorganisations 30, 89–90
and taxation 311–312
repetition of warranties 71–72, 78, 135, 200
replacement guarantee provisions 88
representations
in transaction documents 305
warranties as 132
representatives, of buyers, attendance of meetings by 121
repudiatory breach, as liability for buyer 328, 344

reputational assessments 290
rescission of contracts 132
reserves
bribery and corruption in countries of 275
and decommissioning risks 233
general disclaimer on 212–213
reservoir risk 351–352
residual environmental liability 219–220
responsibilities
for tax returns 321
see also **liabilities**
restorative compensation 205
restrictions
on competition, covenants on 267–173
on negotiations with third parties 40
on time (*see* **time, limits**)
on transfers
as condition precedent 79–86
warranties on 148–149
restrictive covenants 71, 107, 267–273
retained exemptions 273
'rigs-to-reefs' projects 237
risks
allocation of 192–204, 195, 214–215
in transaction documents 306–307
anti-corruption due diligence based on
document and information requests
302–303
public records and reputational searches 302
third-party due diligence 303–304
assessments 306
buyers' exposure to 28, 114, 123, 195, 204, 309
of decommissioning 233, 239 (footnote 22)
disclosed 166
of dispute, minimisation by using preliminary
agreements 15
due diligence identification of 132
of earn-in arrangements 34
environmental 198
fair presentation 182
of joint ventures, decommissioning liabilities
234
political 163
precedent 86
warranties on 131–132, 163
rollover relief 313–314
Royal Dutch Shell PLC 287 (footnote 66)
royalties, in oil and gas industry 148
RTS v Muller 16

Saipem SpA 283
sales
of concessions 32
of interests (*see also* **asset sales; share sales**)
consideration for 32
nature of 25–26
rationale for 26–27
process 35–43
see also **Asset Sale and Purchase Agreement Committee (draft, 2020)**
Samsung Heavy Industries Company Ltd 284
seat of arbitration, choice of 380–381
SEC v El Paso Corp 298
second-tier participation, in field DSAs 248–249
security
foreign investment implications for 81
warranties on issues of 163–164
sellers 26
of assets
advantages of auctions for 37
in asset swap arrangements 35, 103
deal certainty preferred by 128
competition law concerns of 261, 262–263,
266–267, 273
contingent payments under the earn-out
provisions 46
disclosures by
completion 72–74
requirements for 72–74
warranty correctness reinstated by 199
individual sellers 180
and interim periods/interim covenants 70–71,
74, 100, 109, 112, 114, 122, 124
knowledge/awareness of, warranties on
136–138
liabilities of 195, 197
environmental 198
post-completion 128, 209, 240, 252
in SPAs 132, 210
management sellers 180
negotiations with third parties restrictions for
40
ownership of transferred interests by 144
risk exposure of 195
taxation of 309–311, 314–315
sell-side warranty and indemnity insurance policy 181–182, 184, 187
hard staple 184
soft staple 184
sensitive information, disclosure of 167
separation issues, private equity investments
362, 366
settlement of disputes 376
severability clauses 43, 271–272
shallow water infrastructure, removal of 236
(footnote 11)
share purchase, and permit transfers 223
share sales 30, 102
agreements 28, 318
consideration in 45–47
definitive agreements 21
due diligence process in 41
government consent requirements for 50, 79
interim covenants for 108
liability allocation in 196–197
decommissioning liabilities 243
pre-emption rights in 31–32, 84
price provisions in agreements 20
private equity investments 354
taxation of 29, 309, 315, 316, 318
third-party consent requirements for 30–31
transaction structures of 26, 28–29, 101
transfer documentation for 43
shareholders
consent of, as condition precedent 92
substantial, tax exemptions for 312–313
Shell Egypt West Manzala GmbH v Dana Gas Egypt Ltd 42
SIAC (Singapore International Arbitration Centre) 387–388, 390
signing breach, under warranty and indemnity
insurance policy 189
signing of SPAs 412–413
and completion 66–67, 70, 99, 135
consequences of 67
dates for 36

time to completion from 50
warranties on accuracy of SPA on 78
simultaneous signing and completion of SPAs 66–67, 70
and application of warranties 135
Singapore International Arbitration Centre *see* SIAC
single-source procurement procedures 293–294
site lease deeds 267–268
soft carry arrangement 33
sole licensees 249
sole-risk programmes, by co-venturers 114
source intelligence 302
sovereign immunity 163, 378
waivers of 163, 378–379, 405
SPAs (sale and purchase agreements) 9, 26, 69, 69–70, 116, 327
allocation of 197, 214, 215
arbitration clauses in 388, 389–393, 395–396
sample provisions 388, 389–391, 393, 395
for asset sales 29, 196–197
boilerplate clauses in 375, 401–414
sample provisions 404–405, 409, 411, 412–413
completion of 36, 42–43, 94
deferred 66–67, 68–76
conditions precedent in 65–66, 69–70, 74, 76–94, 114, 254–261, 404
sample provisions 76–79, 80, 82, 84, 85, 87–88, 88, 92, 94, 114, 255–260
consideration clauses in 45, 63
asset swaps 63
earn-in agreements 34
farmout agreements 54–61
sample provisions 55–59
share sales 45–47
covenants/interim covenants in 104–116, 126–128, 128–129, 267, 318, 320–324
sample provisions 107–116, 270–273
decommissioning liabilities 235, 243–245, 250–251
sample provisions 243–244, 249, 250
definition of disclosed in 176
documents linked to
commercial agreements 43
preliminary documents 39–40
drafting of 214, 409
enforcement of 375
as entire contracts 34–35, 410–412
general disclaimers on reserves in 212–213
indemnities in 134, 207–209, 315
sample provisions 207–208, 244–245
interpretation clause 169
jurisdiction/governing law provisions in 375, 378, 379–381, 395–396, 399
sample provisions 381, 395
legal opinions required for 89
limitations on 209–214
MAC clauses, sample provisions 86–87, 201–204, 404–405
negotiations 41–42
preliminary agreements 11
signing of 36, 412–413
and completion 66–67, 66–68, 70, 99
consequences of 67
tax provisions in 106, 116, 126–127, 210, 309, 316–325
termination of 42, 75, 95—97, 202
clearance 258
and conditions subsequent 66
on longstop date 95
walk-away rights 66, 72, 75, 76
warranties in 132, 133, 133–164, 199, 318–320
sample provisions 136–164, 210, 212–213, 250–251, 263–266
stamp duties 324
standalone MAC termination clause, in drafting MAC clause 332–334
state-owned companies
consideration in transactions involving 61–62
disputes involving 376, 378
international assets of 397
pre-emption rights of 84
see also **sovereign immunity**
stock sales *see* **share sales**
strategic positioning for auction sales, warranty and indemnity insurance policy 180, 182
'subject to contract' 16–17, 18, 24
subrogation, prohibition on 187
subsidiaries, sale of, and de-grouping charges 311
substantial or significant event, MAC clause interpretation of 330
substantial performance doctrine 35
substantial shareholders exemptions 312–313
substantial shareholding 312
successor liability 276
and corruption risks 298
successors and assigns clauses 409
summary judgments 385
supervised mediation procedures 392
supply agreements 267
supply obligations, domestic, warranties on 162–163
synthetic policies, warranty and indemnity insurance policy 190
synthetic warranty and indemnity insurance policies 190
systemic risks, carve-outs to MAC clauses 341

tax indemnities 190
claims under 181
insurance cover for 187–188
tax provisions 309, 316–318
covenants 105, 114, 126–127, 318, 320–324
general provisions 324–325
warranties 210, 318–320
tax returns, responsibilities for 321
tax savings, refund provisions for 322
tax warranties, insurance cover for 187–188
taxation
and pre-sale reorganisations 311–312
rollover relief 313–314
of sellers 309–311, 314–315
substantial shareholders exemptions 312–313
and transaction structure 29, 309, 310, 316
Teachers Insurance & Annuity Assoc v Tribune Co 18 (footnote 9)
technical capabilities, warranties on 154–155
technical data
excluded from warranties 149, 199, 212
general disclaimer on 212
technical difficulties, and work obligations consideration 58
technical due diligence investigations 242
termination of SPAs 42, 47, 95–97, 202, 336
and conditions subsequent 66

and disclosure letters 166–167
for failure to obtain competition clearance 258
on longstop date 95
walk-away rights 66, 72, 75, 76
third parties
activity/rights, in contract areas 153
consent requirements of 30–31, 81–83
contracts with, restrictive covenants in 267–268
enforcement of contract terms by 412–413
interim period of 112
litigation and claims by
in interim periods 113
joining arbitration proceedings 385, 393–394
negotiations with, restrictions on 40
transfer restrictions exercisable by 148–149
third-party consent to transfer
absolute consent right 82
conditional consent right 82
qualified consent right 82
third-party corruption risks 288–290, 301–302
agents, consultants and other intermediaries 289–290
joint ventures and consortiums 290
third-party due diligence 303–304
threatened actions 87
thresholds
for costs incurred in interim periods 113
see also **materiality thresholds**
time
limits
authorities 256
for issuing arbitration awards 387, 392
for restricted activities 271
for tax claims 322
for warranties/representations 139–14, 209–210, 210
needed for obtaining governmental approvals 99
precedent 95, 99
for preliminary agreements 19, 24
requirements for work obligations 59
between signing date and closing date 49, 81
timeframe, in environmental provisions
in indemnities 221
in letter of reliance 223
title
documentation 145
documents 124, 143
warranties 143–149
Total SA 292
Total Transport Corp v Arcadia Petroleum Ltd 134 (footnote 4)
training programmes, compulsory support for, warranties on 162
transaction documents
covenants 305–306
lookback periods 304
representations and warranties 305
risk allocation and indemnification 306–307
transaction structures 25–28, 43
asset sales 26, 29, 101
complexity of 29–30
and interim covenants 126
and liability allocation 196
decommissioning liabilities 242, 246
and product life cycle 233
share sales 26, 28–29, 101
and taxation 29, 309, 310, 316
transaction testing 302
transactions
competition clearance for
as condition precedent 254–261
EU rules on 80, 254
warranties on 261–267
contemplated 87
description of, in preliminary agreements 20
disclosure letters and negotiations 167
documents, and warranty and indemnity insurance policy 186–187
duty to good faith 17–18
necessity of preliminary agreements 12
timetable, in preliminary agreements 23
unwinding of 133
see also **downstream transactions; upstream transactions**
transaction-specific risks known to the parties, carve-outs to MAC clauses 343
Trans-Alaska Pipeline System 241 (footnote 24)
transfer restrictions
as condition precedent 79–86
warranties on 148–149
transferable tax history 239 (footnote 21), 314
transfer/transferred interest documentation 43, 113, 143, 145, 197
transitional support agreements 89
Transparency International, Corruption Perception Index 275–276
'true and correct/complete' warranties 76, 144–145
trust arrangements 93
TSKJ (joint venture) 287

Uganda, taxation in 326
UKBA *see* **United Kingdom Bribery Act 2010 (UKBA)**
UNCITRAL (United Nations Commission on International Trade Law), rules on *ad hoc* arbitration proceedings 388
unforeseen or unforeseeable events, MAC clause interpretation of 330
unilateral arbitration clauses 393
United Arab Emirates, convention for disclosure letters 168
United Kingdom
competition law in 27, 259
oil and gas industry in
taxation of 309–311, 312–316, 317, 325, 326
Serious Fraud Office (SFO) 284, 285, 298
United Kingdom Bribery Act 2010 (UKBA) 276, 284–285, 294, 304
associated persons 284, 289
bribery involving third parties 289
effective compliance programme 299
facilitation payments under 279, 284
foreign officials 284
foreign public officials 284 (footnote 49), 291
gifts, meals and corporate hospitality (G&E) under 295–296
guidance on 284–285
jurisdiction and applicability 284
private equity firms under 353
statute of limitations, absence of 285
violation of 284
violations of
penalties for 285, 298

United Nations Commission on International Trade Law *see* UNCITRAL
United Nations Convention Against Corruption (UNCAC) 285, 286
United Nations Office on Drugs and Crime (UNODC) 286
United Nations Oil for Food Programme 298
United States
convention for disclosure letters 168
decommissioning policies in 237
Department of Justice (DOJ) 277, 282, 283, 287, 294, 298
MAC clauses, interpretation in 328–329
private equity firms, share sale versus asset sale 354
Securities and Exchange Commission (SEC) 277, 282, 283, 287, 294, 296, 298
security clearances for foreign investments in 80
warranty and indemnity insurance policy (W&I policy) in 179
United States Foreign Corrupt Practices Act (FCPA) 275–276, 277–284, 287, 294, 304
'anything of value' 277–278
bribery involving third parties 288–289
covered companies 280
effective compliance programme 299
enforcement actions 281–284
facilitation payments, exception for 279
foreign officials 277, 278 (footnote 9), 291
gifts, meals and corporate hospitality (G&E) under 295–296
indirect bribery 278
jurisdiction and applicability 278–280
private equity firms under 353
prosecutions 282–283
Resource Guide 278, 279 (footnote 18), 281
statute of limitations for violations 280
violation of
penalties for 280–281
United States v Hoskins 279
unitisation
interim covenants on 125
warranties on 151–153
updates, of disclosure letters 72–74
upstream assets, of sellers, interim covenants on 124
upstream transactions 79, 99
US v Kozeny (Bourke) 281–284
'utmost good faith' 182–183
UUOAs (unification and unit operating agreements) 152–153

Vacold LLC v Cerami 18 (footnote 9)
value
of assets 26, 40
buyer's realisation of 27
of consideration set at effective date 47, 103, 104
erosion of, buyer's protections against 123
VAT provisions 318, 324
Venture North Sea Gas Limited v Nuon Exploration & Production UK Limited 43
violations
of environmental laws, protections against 74
of United Kingdom Bribery Act 2010 (UKBA) 284
penalties for 285, 298
of United States Foreign Corrupt Practices Act (FCPA) 280–281
penalties for 280–281
statute of limitations for 280
see also **breaches**
virtual signings 413
voluntary partial relinquishments 150
voluntary tolling agreement 280
voting compacts, in upstream SPAs 26
voting control, of buyers 121

waivers
of condition precedent 93–94
of first refusal rights 113
of sovereign immunity 163, 378–379, 405
walk-away rights 66, 72, 75, 76
warranties 131–164, 133, 179, 198–200
breaches of 72, 166, 176, 181, claims by buyers
claims by buyers 134, 142, 199, 205, 320
caps for 212
and knowledge 134, 136–137, 142, 199, 206
materiality thresholds for 77, 138–139, 211, 265
time limits for 139–140, 209–210, 210
damages for 75, 132–133
and walk-away rights 76
and co-participants 136
disclosure 140–142, 174–175
disclosure letters 165, 166, 167, 169
in environmental provisions 217–219
due diligence, information obtained during 218
environmental permits, compliance of 218
environmental warranty breaches, successful claim for 219
warranty claims, limitations on 218–219
warranty protection, from environmental impacts 218
and indemnities 133–135, 205
and interim period covenants 104–105, 115–116, 135
negotiation of 132, 135–142
in preliminary agreements 22
private equity investments 364–365
anti-bribery and corruption 368–369
disclosure 365
environmental warranties 366–367
financial statements 365
insurance 366
repetition of 369–370
separation issues 366
purpose of 131–132
repetition of 71–72, 78, 135, 189, 200
sample provisions 136–164, 210, 250–251, 263–266
timing of application of 135
in transaction documents 305
true and correct at completion 76, 144
types of 143–149
competition 261–267
compliance and regulatory 159–161
decommissioning 250–251
exclusive operations 151
financial and technical 153–155
geological and geophysical information 149–150
local requirements 161–163

material contracts 158
no breaches 146–147
no encumbrances 147–148
operatorship 157
participating interests 153–154
physical and legal interests 149–153
related party contracts 158–159
relinquishment 150–151
tax 210, 318–320
title 143–149
transfer restrictions 148–149
unitisation 151–153
work performance 155
see also **warranty and indemnity insurance policy (W&I policy)**
warranty and indemnity insurance policy (W&I policy) 179–180
areas of focus 191
back-to-back cover 185
buy-side policies 181–182, 184, 187
conditions 185
duty to make a fair risk presentation 182
exclusions 186, 192–193
growth of 181
individual sellers 180
insolvency 180
insurance cover 185–190
common enhancement to 188–189
synthetic policies 190
for tax indemnity and tax warranties 187–188
insurance underwriting diligence requirements 190–192
insurer's underwriting review 182–183
key review areas 185
knowledge scrape 189
management sellers 180
materiality scrape 189
mechanism of 181–182
nil recourse policies 181
private equity disposals 180, 181
private equity investments 366
process of 182–184
prohibition on subrogation 187
sell- to buy-side flip 183–184
sell-side policies 181–182, 184, 187
strategic positioning for auction sales 180, 182
timeframe for underwriting 184
and transaction documents 186–187
UK-style 185
underwriting call 183
use of 180–181
wells, disused
decommissioning liability for 245
plugging/abandonment of 251
wilful blindness, under FCPA 278
withdrawal
from contract 150–151
from transactions 66
withholding taxes 324
Wood v Capital Insurance Services 208
work obligations
as consideration 32, 34–35, 55, 57, 60, 61
in licenses 155
work programmes
interim covenants on 123
warranties on 155
working capital adjustments 46
working interests, forfeiture of, and decommissioning liabilities 233–235
written notices 398

About Globe Law and Business

Globe Law and Business was established in 2005, and from the very beginning, we set out to create law books which are sufficiently high level to be of real use to the experienced professional, yet still accessible and easy to navigate. Most of our authors are drawn from Magic Circle and other top commercial firms, both in the UK and internationally.

Our titles are carefully produced, with the utmost attention paid to editorial, design and production processes. We hope this results in high-quality books which are easy to read, and a pleasure to own. All our new books are also available as ebooks, which are compatible with most desktop, laptop and tablet devices.

We have recently expanded our portfolio to include a new range of journals and Special Reports, available both digitally and in hard copy format, and produced to the same high standards as our books.

We'd very much like to hear from you with your thoughts and ideas for improving what we offer. Please do feel free to email me at sian@globelawandbusiness.com with your views.

Sian O'Neill
Managing director
Globe Law and Business

www.globelawandbusiness.com

www.ingramcontent.com/pod-product-compliance
Ingram Content Group UK Ltd.
Pitfield, Milton Keynes, MK11 3LW, UK
UKHW062251150926
8656IPUK00007B/46

9 781787 42398